P9-DTS-010

Theoretical and Experimental Bases of the Behaviour Therapies

Theoretical and Experimental Bases of the Behaviour Therapies

Edited by

M. Philip Feldman
and
Anne Broadhurst

The Department of Psychology,
University of Birmingham

JOHN WILEY & SONS

London · New York · Sydney · Toronto

Library of Congress Cataloging in Publication Data:
Main entry under title:

Theoretical and experimental bases of the behaviour
    therapies.

    Includes indexes.
    1. Behaviour therapy.   I. Feldman, M. P.
II. Broadhurst, Anne. [DNLM: 1. Behaviour therapy.
WM420 T396]
RC489.B4T5   616.8'914   75–20000

ISBN 0 471 25705 2

Photosetting by Thomson Press (India) Limited, New Delhi and
printed in Great Britain by The Pitman Press Ltd., Bath, Avon.

To
P. L. BROADHURST
who, though not himself a clinical psychologist, has fostered the development of clinical psychology in our region

CONTRIBUTORS

MORRIE BAUM — *Alberta Alcoholism and Drug Abuse Commission, Edmonton, Canada*

DEREK E. BLACKMAN — *Department of Psychology, University of Birmingham, England.*

ANNE BROADHURST — *Department of Psychology, University of Birmingham, England.*

RAYMOND COCHRANE — *Department of Psychology, University of Birmingham, England.*

IAN M. EVANS — *Department of Psychology, University of Hawaii, U.S.A.*

H. J. EYSENCK — *Department of Psychology, Institute of Psychiatry, London, England.*

M. PHILIP FELDMAN — *Department of Psychology, University of Birmingham, England.*

JEFFREY A. GRAY — *Department of Experimental Psychology, University of Oxford, England.*

JAMES HOGG — *Hester Adrian Research Centre, University of Manchester, England.*

BARBARA J. LANYON — *Tufts University School of Medicine, Boston, U.S.A.*

RICHARD I. LANYON — *Department of Psychology, Arizona State University, Tempe, U.S.A.*

S. J. RACHMAN   *Department of Psychology, Institute of Psychiatry, London, England.*

MICHAEL P. SOBOL   *Department of Psychology, University of Guelph, Canada.*

GLYN V. THOMAS   *Department of Psychology, University of Stirling, Scotland.*

P. H. VENABLES   *Department of Psychology, University of York, England.*

PREFACE

When the need for this kind of book was first envisaged some eight years ago, there was not then the flood of literature on the behaviour therapies that we have seen in recent years. Still less was there any single volume displaying the theoretical background of the behaviour therapies; this appeared as a very serious breach urgently needing to be filled because, in common with others working in the clinical field, we became dismayed by the growing separation of behaviour therapy from general experimental psychology. This apparent distance between clinical practice and theory was particularly disturbing since those who pioneered the application of the behavioural approach to psychological problems were explicitly concerned with building and maintaining bridges.

In the interim, as this volume gestated, we have had several valuable contributions to the building of bridges between theory and practice in clinical psychology. Notable among these is Kanfer and Phillips' *Learning Foundations of Behavior Therapy*. However, we see a need for extension and maintenance of existing bridges and above all for more bridges. The foundations of behaviour therapy are no longer solely in the psychology of learning, which is only one section of the current volume, and the behaviour therapies must finally be recognized for the plurality that they are.

Hence the editors see their role as taking up and extending the job of bridge-building so that the methods and findings of general experimental psychology, particularly the rapid developments of the past few years, will continue to be available to clinical psychologists and thus to the population at large. We planned a wide coverage of specialized areas of immediate or developing clinical relevance. The contributions are divided, as laid out in the Table of Contents, into the three major relevant areas of experimental psychology—biological psychology, the psychology of learning, and cognitive and social psychology—all of which have both current and future relevance to clinical work. We have added also an important section on theoretical, methodological and ethical issues in the behaviour therapies. The weight given to the cognitive and social area reflects the growing relevance of this area of research. Behaviour modifiers have tended to leave problems of interpersonal behaviour and 'internal' functioning to psychotherapy, but it is possible to discern the beginnings of a behavioural approach to such problems. We intend that this book will accelerate this development. The psychology of learning has often been the major experimental source for the behaviour therapy movement and it will continue to play an important part, the more so if behaviour therapists are brought up-to-date with current developments. The least obviously relevant of the broad areas represented is biological psychology. Yet this apparent lack of relevance is no more than a reflection of the divorce between the biological and environmental sources of behaviour—another of the unsatisfactory trends in contemporary psychology. Behaviour, after all, has a biological substrate as well as being influenced by environmental events. Recognition of this is beginning in the behaviour therapies; hence the recent emphasis on the instrumental control of such physiological responses as heart rate and brain electrophysiology. Just as there are individual variations in learning experiences so there are innate differences between persons in their biological make-up, differences which will interact in important ways with environmental events to determine the development and form of psychological problems as well as requiring individually adapted treatment approaches.

The absence of a section on developmental psychology requires comment. After much consideration and consultation, the editors concluded that there was insufficient experimental and theoretical material, which was peculiar to developmental psychology over and above the areas of psychology already represented and which was relevant to behaviour therapy, to warrant a separate section. However, much material relevant to the problems of the young intellectually handicapped patient is presented in the chapter by James Hogg.

To summarize, this book is intended to take stock of the present situation in the behaviour therapies, to rebuild and to add to the existing bridges between the clinician and his psychological background, theoretical and experimental, and to look forward to the ways in which experimental psychology may be expected to contribute to the health and development of the behaviour therapies in the next ten years. We intend it to be useful to practising clinical psychologists, both those in training and the more experienced. It will obviously interest most those of a behavioural orientation from any discipline, but is not intended solely for them. Then again, in our experience doctors and psychiatrists in training today are eager for information such as we have been able to provide. In addition, we see our readership as including research workers in experimental psychology and advanced psychology undergraduates, particularly those hoping to specialize in clinical psychology.

In the preparation of this book many people have assisted us and our contributors. Peter Evans, A. W. MacRae, Professor Peter Mittler, Dr. Robert Remington and Dr. J. Stewart were most valued discussants and readers of draft chapters. The following permitted reference in Chapter 1 to their unpublished data and we are duly grateful to them: N. McNaughten, D. T. D. James, P. Kelly, R. F. Drewett, A. Drewnowski and J. Stewart. Our especial thanks are due to S. R. Jenkins and his colleagues of the Barnes Library for assistance with the editorial bibliographic work. We are grateful also to the

Medical Research Council and the Smith, Kline and French Foundation for their support of the experimental work referred to in Chapter 1. Our particular thanks are due to Professor P. L. Broadhurst, Head of the Department of Psychology, University of Birmingham, who has encouraged this work and the development of training and research in clinical psychology in its proper habitat.

University of Birmingham, M. PHILIP FELDMAN
March, 1975 ANNE BROADHURST

CONTENTS

SECTION I

Biological Psychology

1

THE BEHAVIOURAL INHIBITION SYSTEM: A POSSIBLE SUBSTRATE FOR ANXIETY

Jeffrey A. Gray

It has long been known that an individual's personality is related both to the likelihood that he will display a behavioural disorder and to the nature of the disorder actually displayed. In particular, the combinations of extreme neuroticism and extreme introversion on the Eysenck personality scales (Eysenck and Eysenck, 1969), or the equivalent high scores on Cattell's (1966) or Spence and Spence's (1966) anxiety scales, are associated with the development of what Eysenck has termed 'dysthymic' disorders, i.e. phobias, obsessive–compulsive neurosis, anxiety state and reactive depression (Eysenck, 1957, 1960). Rather less certainly, the combination of extreme extraversion with extreme neuroticism appears to be associated with criminal, delinquent and antisocial behaviour (Burgess, 1972; Eysenck, 1970; Passingham, 1972; Shapland and Rushton, 1975). This chapter is concerned with the psychological and physiological processes which may underlie the susceptibility to develop dysthymic disorders. It will not be directly concerned with the modification of dysthymic behaviours, but it seems likely that knowledge of these psychological and physiological processes would hold important implications for therapy and prophylaxis in this field.

However, it is not established knowledge which this chapter offers—it is a theory. This theory is grounded principally in observations of animal behaviour and of the effects of alterations in brain function on animal behaviour. I have tried to justify elsewhere this particular kind of application of animal data to human behaviour (Gray, 1973), so the reader is asked to forego any further justification here. Rather, my present purpose is to spell out in fuller detail than hitherto that part of the overall theory (Gray, 1973) which refers to the 'behavioural inhibition system'. It is activity in this psychophysiological system which, I believe, underlies individual differences in the susceptibility to dysthymic neurosis.

It will be convenient to contrast this theory with the much better known

4

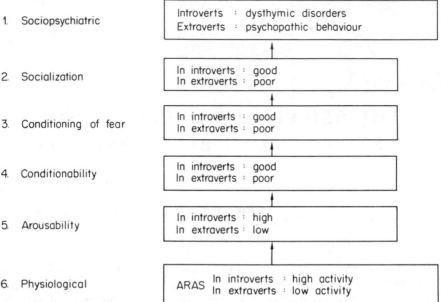

Level

1. Sociopsychiatric

        Introverts : dysthymic disorders
        Extraverts : psychopathic behaviour

2. Socialization

        In introverts : good
        In extraverts : poor

3. Conditioning of fear

        In introverts : good
        In extraverts : poor

4. Conditionability

        In introverts : good
        In extraverts : poor

5. Arousability

        In introverts : high
        In extraverts : low

6. Physiological

        ARAS In introverts : high activity
              In extraverts : low activity

FIGURE 1.1 Structure of Eysenck's theory of introversion–extraversion. Arrows indicate direction of causation. (From Gray, 1970a, p. 251, Figure 2 by permission of Pergamon Press Ltd.).

Level

1. Sociopsychiatric

        Introverts : dysthymic disorders
        Extraverts : psychopathic behaviour

2. Socialization

        In introverts : good
        In extraverts : poor

3. Conditioning of fear

        In introverts : good
        In extraverts : poor

4. Susceptibility to
    punishment

        In introverts : high
        In extraverts : low

5. Arousability

        In introverts : high
        In extraverts : low

6. Physiological

        Feedback loop comprising   In introverts :
        ARAS, frontal cortex,   high activity
        septal area and hippocampus   In extraverts :
                                        low activity

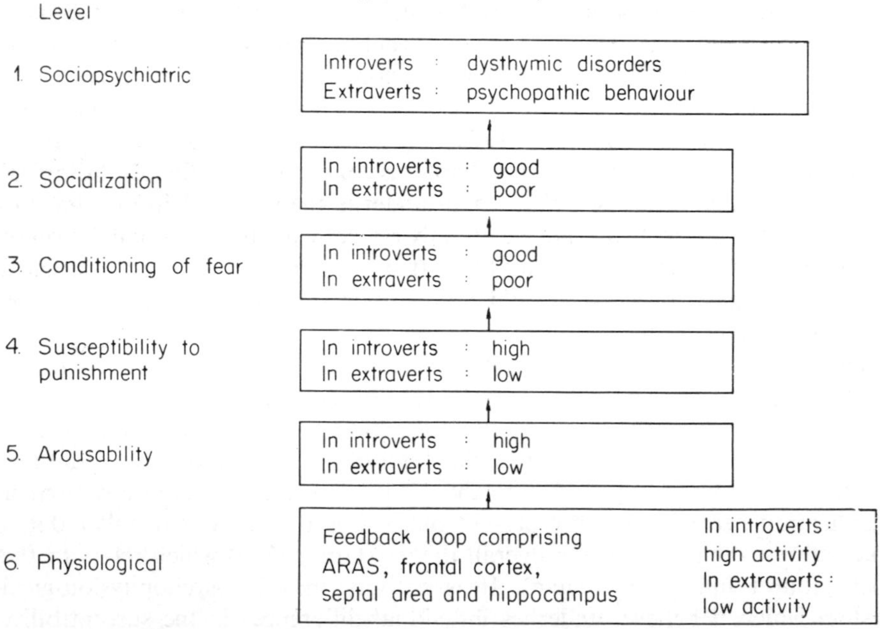

FIGURE 1.2 Modification of Eysenck's theory (Figure 1.1) proposed by Gray, 1970a, p. 262, Figure 6. By permission of Pergamon Press Ltd.

theory proposed by Eysenck (1957, 1967), of which it is, indeed, a natural descendant (Gray, 1970a). I have therefore set out the two theories in schematic fashion in Figures 1.1 and 1.2. But this device is for expository purposes only; it is not intended to evaluate fully the comparative merits of the two theories (although relevant recent findings will be discussed as appropriate). There are, in any case, insufficient data to make such an exercise yet worthwhile. At present it can be said that both theories are well able to encompass some data and that both face serious difficulties posed by others. However, Eysenck's theory of the psychophysiological bases of neuroticism and introversion has been for so long the only serious contender in this field that a second theory intended to explain the same essential facts may serve a useful heuristic purpose, even if it too has obvious deficiencies. At any rate, it is in this spirit that the alternative theory is outlined here.

ROTATION OF AXES

The first point at which the two theories differ concerns the location of the axes in the two-dimensional space required to describe the individual differences in personality which are associated with the development of dysthymic disorders or antisocial conduct (Eysenck and Eysenck, 1969). These axes have been derived from factor-analytic studies of responses to questionnaires and rating scales. The methods of factor analysis allow one to determine objectively the minimum number of independent dimensions which are required for a description of individual differences in such responses (or in any measurements, psychological or otherwise). There is very considerable agreement in the literature that two such dimensions are required to deal with individual differences in personality of the kind associated with dysthymic disorders and anti-social conduct (Eysenck and Eysenck, 1969; Pawlik, 1973). However, the methods of factor analysis cannot provide an objective solution to the problem of where to locate these dimensions or axes in the two-dimensional space they define. This is as arbitrary a decision (unless considerations other than the factor-analytic ones are introduced) as the choice between referring locations in real space to a line running from north to south or to one running from north-west to south-east. The different choices made by Eysenck and myself are set out in Figure 1.3.

Actually, the differences between the two theories concerning the location of axes are not quite so stark as Figure 1.3 makes out. As pointed out above, factor-analytic or other statistical criteria cannot decide this issue. It must therefore be decided by psychological or theoretical criteria. These criteria can be found at two levels. They can be concerned with the origins of the causal influences at work in the production of the relevant individual differences or they can be concerned with the effects of these individual differences.

It is at the first of these two levels—the *causal* one—that the two theories are clearly different. According to Eysenck, there are two physiologically-based dimensions of individual differences in psychological processes which

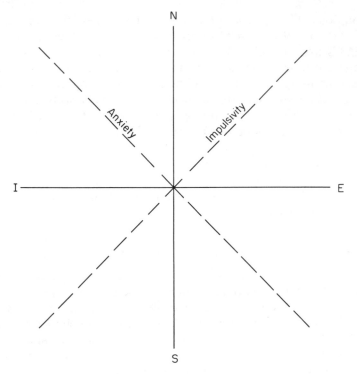

FIGURE 1.3 Eysenck's two-dimensional space of neuroticism (N)–stability (S) and introversion (I)–extraversion (E) and Gray's (1970a) proposed rotation of axes to lie along 'anxiety' and 'impulsivity'.

underlie the patterns of individual differences observed in the actual test situations used to describe personality (questionnaires, rating scales, behaviour in the laboratory, etc.). These two causal dimensions run along his neuroticism and introversion–extraversion axes (Figure 1.3), and he has produced a detailed theory (Eysenck, 1967) of the nature of the physiological and psychological processes which these two dimensions reflect. My own alternative theory locates the causal influences along the axes labelled 'anxiety' and 'impulsivity' in figure 1.3; and it holds that they consist in rather different physiological and psychological processes to the Eysenckian ones. This paper will be concerned principally to spell out the nature of the physiological and psychological processes attributed to the putative causal dimension of 'anxiety'.

With regard to the *effects* of the two underlying dimensions, however, the differences between the two theories are much less clear-cut. This is because both theories would need to explain the behavioural syndromes displayed, not only by those individuals who are located at one or other pole of either dimension but also by those individuals who are located in the intervening quadrants. Thus Eysenck must explain not only the characteristics of the extreme introvert and the extreme neurotic but also the characteristics of the dysthymic, who is, for him, the consequence of an interaction between his two fundamental causal processes. For my part, I must explain not only the characteristics of the dysthymic (who is, for me, a pure case of an extreme value along the anxiety dimension) but also those of the extreme introvert and the extreme neurotic, who are the consequences of interactions between anxiety and impulsivity. Thus the simple cases for the one theory become interactive ones for the other and vice versa. As it happens, our present concern is with dysthymia, so we shall need to consider two dimensions to set out the Eysenckian scheme and only one (anxiety) to set out my alternative. But this, of course, does not mean that the alternative theory is simpler across the board; the tables would be turned if, for example, we were considering the nature of extreme introversion.

EYSENCK'S THEORY

With these preliminaries out of the way, let us turn to a detailed consideration of Eysenck's (1957, 1967) theory, proceeding from top to bottom of Figure 1.1, i.e. from (a) the effects which (in the dysthymic quadrant) Eysenck's dimensions of neuroticism and introversion are required to explain to (b) the causal influences which produce these dimensions themselves. We start with the introversion–extraversion axis.

According to Eysenck, the difference between the introverted neurotic (i.e. the dysthymic) and the extraverted neurotic (the criminal or psychopath?) is that the former has been oversocialized and the latter undersocialized. The dysthymic has developed a cluster of conditioned fear or guilt reactions which are easily triggered by the relevant conditioned stimuli or by stimuli which are on a suitable gradient of stimulus generalization originating at these conditioned stimuli. It is these conditioned fear or guilt reactions which constitute the phobias, anxiety states and obsessive–compulsive rituals which such patients present. In contrast to the dysthymic, the psychopath has failed to develop, or has developed only to an insufficient degree, the conditioned fear or guilt reactions which prevent the average citizen from taking his gratification as and where he finds it. Hence the stealing, lying, sexual delinquency, careless driving or unrestrained aggressive behaviour with which the archetypal psychopath plagues society.

The next question we must ask, as we proceed down the Eysenckian causal chain, is: 'Why do introverts become oversocialized and extraverts undersocialized?'. It is clear from the foregoing that Eysenck treats the process of socialization as essentially a matter of classical conditioning. The formation of the conscience is, in his view, the establishment of a number of conditioned aversive reflexes. These may be described as conditioned fear reactions or conditioned guilt reactions. The former arise when the aversive unconditioned stimulus, or 'punishment', is delivered before the child has completed whatever forbidden act he is being punished for; the latter arise when it is delivered after completion of the forbidden act. At its simplest, Tommy may be slapped when he is reaching for the chocolate (leading to a conditioned fear of chocolate-approaching behaviour) or when he turns a chocolate-covered face to mother (leading to a conditioned guilt feeling consequent upon chocolate ingestion). But what does it matter if Tommy is introverted or extraverted? Eysenck's answer is that introverts in general are *more conditionable* than extraverts: they form *any* conditioned reflexes more easily.

This difference in conditionability is, in turn, related by Eysenck to a still more fundamental psychological process, the 'inhibition–excitation balance'. This is a Janus-like concept: we can either think of the introvert as having a more intense 'excitatory process' (in essentially the same sense as that originally used by Pavlov, see Gray, 1964a) or, as I would prefer to put it, as being more highly 'arousable' (Gray, 1964b); or we can think of the extravert as being more likely to develop inhibitory processes. The more intense excitatory process of the introvert is thought by Eysenck to facilitate conditioning and the greater inhibitory process in the extravert is thought to hamper it. Either way, the introvert ends up more easily conditioned than the extravert. The ramifications of Eysenck's concept of the excitation–inhibition balance are, of course, very much more extensive than this, and they have been explored in a large number of important experiments (see, for example, Eysenck, 1957, 1967) which are not our concern here. We shall return later, however, for a second look at the concept itself.

We come finally to the physiological level in Eysenck's theory. This is represented by the 'ascending reticular activating system', or ARAS (Magoun, 1963). All levels of this system, from the bulb to the thalamus, appear to receive inputs from all the main sensory tracts. However, the function discharged by this stimulation is, apparently, not to convey precise information about the quality of the sensory input (this is done by other mechanisms) but to vary the general level of alertness and excitement. In particular, the cerebral cortex, in which the most precise analyses of environmental information are carried out, requires a constant input from the ARAS if it is to perform its functions efficiently. The level of functioning of the cortex, indeed, appears to be regulated quite precisely by the amount of such input from the ARAS, in a manner which is reflected in the pattern of electrical activity recorded in the EEG. It is a postulate common to quite a number of theories (Gray, 1964b) that this physiological system underlies variation in the psychological process of 'level of arousal', and Eysenck's theory conforms to this pattern. It holds that the introvert is tipped towards the excitation end of the excitation–inhibition balance (or, more simply, that the introvert is more highly arousable) because, relative to the extravert, he experiences, for any given set of environmental circumstances, a higher bombardment of the cerebral cortex by impulses coming from the ARAS.

So far, we have been considering the role of introversion in the production of dysthymia, given that the person is neurotic. What of the role of neuroticism, given that the person is an introvert?

Eysenck conceives of high neuroticism as a tendency towards strong emotions which are easily aroused. Its importance in the genesis of dysthymic disorders is that it acts to increase the effective intensity of the unconditioned punishments which, as we have seen, are given a central role by Eysenck in the process of socialization. Thus it is an individual who is both neurotic and introverted who forms strong and well-conditioned fear and guilt reactions. This way of looking at the role of neuroticism stays within the framework of classical conditioning used above to describe the role of introversion. But one may also consider the matter in an instrumental learning framework. (Eysenck, in fact, does not distinguish between classical and instrumental conditioning—in strong contrast to the alternative theory which will be advanced below—so that the two frameworks are for him equivalent.) Within the instrumental framework, one may regard conditionability (i.e. introversion) as the ease with which a Hullian habit strength ($_sH_R$) is established and emotionality (i.e. neuroticism) as a source of drive which adds to the total magnitude of Hullian general drive (D). Thus introversion and neuroticism are seen by Eysenck as interacting multiplicatively in the same way that Hull (1943) multiplies $_sH_R$ by D to produce total reaction potential $_sE_R$. It is when values along both dimensions are high that the potential for manifesting extreme conditioned fear and guilt reactions is high; and it is these reactions which, as we know already, constitute the dysthymic neuroses.

Just as the arousability which is the fundamental psychological process underlying introversion is given by Eysenck a physiological substrate in the activities of the ARAS, so Eysenck also gives the emotionality which is the fundamental psychological process underlying neuroticism its own physiological substrate. This he finds in the autonomic nervous system and, more recently, in the central brain structures, especially in the limbic system and hypothalamus (Gellhorn and Loofbourrow, 1963), which control the autonomic nervous system. In particular, he postulates that the highly neurotic individual is one who has easily aroused, strong and labile responses in the autonomic nervous system (e.g. increased heart rate, sweating, vascular changes, etc.) to unconditioned punishments; and therefore, after conditioning, also to stimuli associated with such punishments. It is this autonomic disturbance which, in Eysenck's view, constitutes the unconditioned emotional response to punishment, as well as the conditioned fear and guilt reactions which are built up on the basis of this unconditioned emotional response. Thus a child which experiences strong autonomic upsets when punished (a neurotic) and has these upsets easily conditioned (an introvert) has a strong probability of reaching adulthood with a load of conditioned fear and guilt reactions ready to be further elicited by appropriate stimuli. If he then encounters these stimuli, a dysthymic neurosis is the result.

EYSENCK'S THEORY MODIFIED

This, then, in broad outline is Eysenck's theory of introversion and neuroticism and their joint causation of dysthymia. My modification of it (Gray, 1970a) occurs at two main points: the postulate that introverts have greater condition-ability than extraverts and the proposed location of the physiological substrate for introversion–extraversion in the ARAS.

With regard to the conditionability postulate, the experimental evidence summarized by Gray (1970a) permits the following conclusions:

(1) Introverts are better than extraverts at eyeblink conditioning under some conditions but not all.

(2) The conditions which favour introvert superiority in such experiments are relatively underarousing ones and the conditions which favour extraverts are relatively overarousing ones. These conditions may themselves be deduced from the hypothesis that introverts are more highly arousable than extraverts (Eysenck and Levey, 1972; Levey, 1967).

(3) The superior conditioning of the introvert appears especially in experiments which involve a degree of threat.

The most important of these conclusions for Eysenck's overall theory is the first. As is clear from Figure 1.1, the conditionability postulate is a critical link in this theory. If introverts are only *sometimes* more conditionable than extraverts, and if introverts are nonetheless to reach adulthood with a greater degree of socialization than extraverts, then the conditions encountered during the childhood socialization process must be of the kind which typically favour conditioning in the introvert rather than the extravert. There is no warrant for such a major new assumption. It therefore seems that the conditionability postulate cannot bear the theoretical weight which is put on it.

In place of the conditionability postulate, I have proposed that we substitute a 'fearfulness' postulate (Figure 1.2). This postulate, which is set out schematic-ally in Figure 1.4, holds that the greater the degree of anxiety (in the trait sense, i.e. the diagonal in Figure 1.3 running from stable extraversion to neurotic introversion), the greater is the sensitivity or reactivity to signals of punishment. (The notion of 'signals of punishment' is one which will be amplified later.)

As far as the nature of dysthymia is concerned, we may ignore the other diagonal of Figure 1.3, i.e. the one labelled 'impulsivity' and running from Eysenck's stable introvert quadrant to the neurotic extravert one. However, a brief look at it is required to see how the present theory deals with Eysenck's introversion–extraversion and neuroticism dimensions themselves. According to this theory, the impulsivity dimension reflects increasing sensitivity to signals of reward. Consequently, as can be seen in Figure 1.4, introversion reflects increasing sensitivity to signals of punishment relative to the individual's sensitivity to signals of reward. Neuroticism, on the other hand, reflects increasing sensitivity to *both* signals of punishment *and* signals of reward. This latter step can be regarded as a change in the technical translation of Eysenck's original intuition that neuroticism is a dimension of emotionality, while retaining that intuition itself. Effectively, what has been done is to replace Hull's notion of general drive (D), which is used by both Eysenck and the Spences (Spence and Spence, 1966) to deal with individual differences in

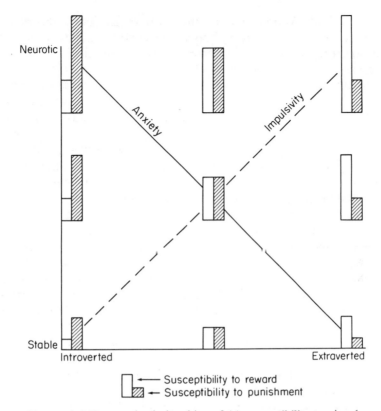

Neurotic

Stable

Introverted   Extraverted

⊢— Susceptibility to reward
⊬— Susceptibility to punishment

FIGURE 1.4 Proposed relationships of (a) susceptibility to signals
of reward and susceptibility to signals of punishment to (b) the
dimensions of introversion–extraversion and neuroticism. The
dimensions of anxiety and impulsivity (diagonals) represent the
steepest rate of increase in susceptibility to signals of punishment
and reward, respectively. (From Gray, 1970a, p. 263, Figure 7.
By permission of Pergamon Press Ltd.).

emotional reactivity, by the notion of incentive. The latter can be both positive
(symbolized by K in the Hull–Spence system: Spence, 1956) and negative
(treated variously as 'fear' and 'frustration' by neo-Hullian learning theorists:
e.g. Amsel, 1958; Mowrer, 1960). This shift in emphasis from drive to incentive
is in line with a similar shift which has been going on in the basic theory of
learning—a shift which has been motivated by a large number of considerations,
both empirical and theoretical (Gray, 1975).

   Let us now leave impulsivity on one side and return to a further consideration
of the dimension of anxiety. For simplicity's sake, we may treat the present
theory of anxiety as a revision of Eysenck's theory of introversion–extraversion,
while not forgetting that it is actually, as explained earlier, a theory of a rotaion
of introversion–extraversion by 45° (Figure 1.3). In this revision, then, the
postulate of conditionability is replaced by the postulate of fearfulness. This

step can be made without altering that part of Eysenck's theory which is pictured in Figure 1.1 as lying above the conditionability postulate. The greater socialization of the introverted neurotic can still be attributed to a relative ease in the establishment of the conditioned fear reactions which make up the conscience; but this now arises, not because the introverted neurotic is generally good at conditioning, but because he is generally sensitive to conditioned stimuli which have been paired with punishment. This view may be supported by the same evidence which Eysenck uses to support the conditionability postulate, because this evidence derives exclusively from conditioning situations which have used aversive unconditioned stimuli. Furthermore, the evidence that introvert conditioning is favoured when the experimental situation contains an element of threat (Gray, 1970a) supports the new theory in preference to the original Eysenckian one. We need make no special assumptions concerning the conditions typically encountered during the process of socialization, other than the plausible one that they often contain threats of punishment. In any case, the part played in the new theory by social-ization and the formation of conditioned fear or guilt reactions during child-hood is less critical than it is in Eysenck's theory. For, on the present view, many and perhaps most of the symptoms which constitute a dysthymic neurosis are due to the continuing role played by a high level of fearfulness in adulthood.

Let us now turn to the task of specifying more fully what is meant by the notion that an individual high on the dimension of anxiety (whom I shall henceforth call a 'dysthymic') is one who is highly sensitive to signals of punish-ment. This specification will take the form of describing a system which, it is proposed, carries out a certain kind of behavioural function and consists of a certain set of interacting physiological structures. It should be noted that this system—the 'behavioural inhibition system'—is derived in the first instance from studies of animal behaviour. Its application to problems in the field of human personality has come later. Thus, on the assumption that the animal data correctly indicate the existence of such a system and on the further assump-tion that there are indeed individual differences in the functioning of this system in Man it might nonetheless be quite erroneous to pick out the anxiety dimension as the one which reflects these individual differences. There are many other choices one could make, both at the highest-order factor-analytic level at which Eysenck's theory is located and at the level of primary or second-order factors favoured by Cattell (1965). For example, the factor called 'threctia' by Cattell would be a plausible candidate for such a role. I hope, therefore, that a description of the behavioural inhibition system will be of value to workers in the field of human psychopathology whether or not it is correct to relate it to the proposed personality dimension of anxiety.

THE BEHAVIOURAL INHIBITION SYSTEM: PSYCHOLOGICAL

The evidence for the existence of a behavioural inhibition system is of two essential kinds: psychological (i.e. derived from purely behavioural experiments) and psychophysiological (derived from experiments on the behavioural effects of a variety of pharmacological, endocrinological and neurological treatments). I have recently discussed the psychological evidence as part of a general review of two-process learning theory (Gray, 1975). Thus, if no further reference is given below, it may be assumed that the relevant data are summarized there (see especially the final chapter). Let us start, then, with the description of the behavioural inhibition system as it emerges from the behavioural evidence.

This description may profitably be viewed as a series of variations on a theme first clearly enunciated by Eysenck (1957) in his distinction between 'cortical inhibition' and 'behavioural inhibition'. In Eysenck's view, as we have seen, the extravert has more powerful inhibitory processes at work somewhere in his nervous system. But this high level of central inhibition does not give rise to inhibited *behaviour*—on the contrary, it gives rise to impulsive behaviour which it is difficult to inhibit. More formally, Eysenck sees a highly aroused cerebral cortex as necessary for the restraint of immediate behavioural responses when such restraint is required by environmental contingencies. The introvert, in his system, is therefore an individual who combines high central levels of arousal with inhibited behaviour. And it is precisely this combination which is central to my view of the behavioural inhibition system. The difference between the theory advanced here and Eysenck's own views concerns the details in which this fundamental intuition is clothed. These details must be examined at four points: the stimuli which activate the behavioural inhibition system, the conceptual structure of the system, the physiological substrate in which this structure is thought to be instantiated, and the behavioural responses produced by the behavioural inhibition system.

Let us start with what the behavioural inhibition system does and the stimuli which activate it. What it does, of course, is to inhibit ongoing behaviour. This inhibition may affect different kinds of behaviour, and it has received different names in different contexts. The first adequate description was given by Pavlov under the name of 'external inhibition'—the inhibition of a classically conditioned response by a novel stimulus. The same kind of effect can be observed if the behaviour studied is not a classical conditioned reflex but an unconditioned response or a complex pattern of innate behaviour such as eating or drinking. Instrumental responses such as lever-pressing for a food reward can equally well be inhibited by novel stimuli. However, the kind of behavioural inhibition which has most often been studied in the case of instrumental behaviour has involved other kinds of stimulus. Those most investigated have been punishing stimuli and stimuli associated with the omission of anticipated reward ('frustrative non-reward'). The names most typically used in these two cases are 'conditioned suppression' or 'passive avoidance', and 'extinction'.

A punishing stimulus is, by definition, one which, if made contingent upon the emission of a response, causes that response to diminish in probability. On the assumption that this reduction in probability is produced by an inhibitory system actively suppressing the response (an assumption which is explored and defended in some detail by Gray, 1975), it cannot be the punishing stimulus itself which activates such a system, because, of course, the behavioural inhibition system has to be activated in advance of presentation of the punishing stimulus or it could not effectively suppress the punished response. For this reason, it has to be assumed that, in a punishment or passive avoidance experiment, the stimuli which activate the behavioural inhibition system are stimuli which have previously been paired (probably according to a classical conditioning paradigm) with the unconditioned punishing stimulus. I shall call such stimuli 'Pun-CS'.

Turning to the case of frustrative non-reward, there is good evidence that the reduction in the probability of a response when a reward (by which it has usually been followed in the past) is discontinued is also due to an active inhibitory process. There is also an accumulation of evidence that this inhibitory process is the same as the one which produces response suppression in a punishment experiment (Gray, 1971). And, as in the case of punishment, the response suppression observed in a typical experiment on the extinction of an appetitive instrumental response cannot be due to the frustrative non-reward itself, for this follows the response which is eventually suppressed. The behavioural inhibition system must, then, be activated by stimuli which have been paired with frustrative non-reward, or '$\overline{\text{Rew}}$-CS'.

So far, then, we have distinguished three kinds of stimuli which activate the behavioural inhibition system: novelty, Pun-CS and $\overline{\text{Rew}}$-CS. Two other kinds may be added to the list, but more tentatively. They are high-intensity stimuli and dominance or aggressive signals arising in the course of social interaction.

High-intensity stimuli were studied by Pavlov, who showed that, when used as conditioned stimuli in a classical conditioning experiment, they sometimes give rise to an unexpectedly small conditioned response. This phenomenon he attributed to the operation of 'transmarginal' or 'protective' inhibition (Gray, 1964a), which, furthermore, he linked in later writings with external inhibition (Gray, 1975). In an earlier discussion of transmarginal inhibition (Gray, 1964b) I suggested that this phenomenon could be the outcome of activity in a reticulo-cortico-reticular feedback loop of the kind described by Hugelin and Bonvallet (1957). The basic structure of this feedback loop, as we shall see (Figure 1.5), closely resembles the behavioural inhibition system as proposed here. Furthermore, the phenomenon of transmarginal inhibition is known to occur more readily in individuals with a 'weak nervous system' (Gray, 1964a) and there is some evidence, albeit equivocal, that such individuals are introverted (Eysenck and Levey, 1972; Gray, 1967b; Mangan, 1972; Zhorov and Yermolayeva-Tomina, 1972). At any rate, it is at least worth bearing in mind the possibility that the behavioural inhibition system is also activated by intense stimuli, i.e. that the phenomenon of transmarginal inhibition is a further outcome of the operation of this system.

The importance of the possible link between transmarginal inhibition and the behavioural inhibition system lies in the light such a link might throw on the basic psychophysiological processes involved in the dimension of anxiety. The importance of stimuli of social interaction, in contrast, lies in the role they may play in the actual causation of dysthymic neuroses. Some of the most important and most crippling of these syndromes, e.g. agoraphobia and social phobia (Marks, 1969), appear to be above all responses to such stimuli. It would therefore be parsimonious if one could account for the occurrence of these syndromes in predisposed individuals (*ex hypothesi*, those with a behavioural inhibition system which is activated relatively easily or strongly) simply by saying that stimuli arising in the course of dominance interactions are among the kinds of stimulus which activate this system. Recently, evidence that this might be the case has been provided by experiments on the behavioural effects of lesions to the septal area in the rat. As we shall see, the medial septal area plays a crucial role in the behavioural inhibition system proposed here. It is therefore of some significance that lesions to this area cause rats to reduce their 'personal space': that is to say, the lesioned animal actively seeks out a companion, stays closer to it and is less daunted by aggressive behaviour on the part of the companion (Jonason and Enloe, 1971; Poplawsky and Johnson, 1973).

Three kinds of stimuli—novelty, Pun-CS and $\overline{\text{Rew}}$-CS—rather definitely, and two more—intense stimuli and stimuli of social interaction—more tentatively, activate the behavioural inhibition system. That is to say, they cause an inhibition of ongoing behaviour, be this innate, classically conditioned or instrumentally conditioned behaviour. However, this is not all they do; they also give rise to an increase in the level of arousal, thus completing the Eysenckian picture of high central arousal combined with behavioural inhibition. The evidence for this claim comes from a diversity of sources which we can do no more than indicate here. They include experiments on the orienting reflex (Gray, 1964b; Sokolov, 1963), on transmarginal inhibition (Gray, 1964a, 1964b), on the summation of drives in the Hullian sense (Gray, 1971) and on the arousing properties of frustrative non-reward and stimuli associated with frustrative non-reward (Amsel, 1958, 1962; Gray, 1971). The ways in which this increase in arousal has been measured have been various; and, indeed, merely to describe exactly what is meant by an increase in the level of arousal would take us far afield (see for discussions of this concept Corcoran, 1972; Eysenck, 1967; Gray, 1964b). At its simplest, however, what is meant is this: if, in spite of the operation of the behavioural inhibition system, some behaviour actually occurs (whether this behaviour is itself involved in the production of the stimuli which have activated the behavioural inhibition system or whether it is an act which occurs when the dominant behaviour is first suppressed by the behavioural inhibition system), this behaviour will occur with greater intensity than it would display in the absence of activity in the behavioural inhibition system. This increased behavioural intensity is due to a rise in the level of arousal.

A mathematical model which produces this joint outcome of behavioural inhibition and increased level of arousal has been described by Gray and Smith (1969). Although this model was intended originally to apply to the results of experiments on conflict behaviour, partial reinforcement and discrimination learning in rats and pigeons placed in runways or Skinner boxes, it is in principle capable of much wider application. At any rate, it is the Gray and Smith model which forms the conceptual core of the behavioural inhibition system. The reader who wishes to pursue this matter in more detail must refer either to the original paper or to Gray (1975), in which it is given a less mathematical, more discursive treatment.

In understanding a phenomenon it is, of course, necessary to consider what it is different from as well as what it is like. Nowhere is this strategy more important than in the case of anything termed 'inhibition', for this word has been used, with innumerable modifying adjectives, to refer to a huge diversity of different phenomena. Furthermore, Eysenck makes considerable use of a number of kinds of inhibition—'cortical', 'reactive', etc.—and these are typically thought by him to be greater in the extravert. So it is rather important to set out clearly what 'behavioural inhibition', as it is used here, is not.

To begin with, it has nothing to do with 'reactive inhibition', whether used by Hull or Eysenck. Indeed, there is no reason to suppose that any real psychological process corresponds to the term 'reactive inhibition' (Gray, 1972a), which we would do well to drop altogether from the psychological vocabulary. Nor is it the same thing as 'habituation of the orienting reflex' (Sokolov, 1963), though it may be its obverse—i.e. it is possible that an individual who has a strong tendency to react to novel stimuli with external inhibition may habituate this tendency only slowly.

More importantly, it is quite different from Pavlov's 'internal inhibition', which undoubtedly does refer to a real psychological process (Gray, 1975). It is not difficult to show where the distinction between behavioural inhibition and internal inhibition lies. Consider an experiment in which a stimulus, S_1, is a signal that a response will be followed by an electric shock and a second stimulus, S_2, is a signal that the response will not be followed by a shock. The response, we may assume, declines in probability in the presence of S_1; S_1 is then an instance of a Pun-CS, and the decline in the probability of the response is an instance of behavioural inhibition. But S_2 has been paired with the *absence* of the unconditioned stimulus (UCS), shock, which follows S_1; S_2 is therefore in a position to become a Pavlovian internal inhibitory stimulus, i.e. a stimulus which, as the result of being paired with the absence of a UCS, acquires the capacity to inhibit the conditioned reflex elicited by stimuli which have been paired with that same UCS. Furthermore, there are many experiments (Rescorla and Solomon, 1967; Gray, 1975) which demonstrate that S_2 in an experiment of this kind does indeed acquire such internal inhibitory capacities. What is more, among these capacities is that of *reversing* the behavioural inhibition produced by S_1. It is hardly possible, therefore, to hold to the view that internal inhibition and behavioural inhibition are the same process. This view has nonetheless been proposed by Kimble (1969), and in a context which is of particular relevance to the present argument, since he attributes what he calls 'internal inhibition' to the same brain structures to which I attribute behavioural inhibition. Eysenck, too, frequently treats the internal inhibition which airses from the non-reinforcement of a classical conditioned stimulus as equivalent to the behavioural inhibition which arises from the non-reward of an instrumental response; or, rather, he simply ignores the distinction between classical and instrumental conditioning—a distinction which, in my own view (Gray, 1975), is an essential one.

The distinction between internal inhibition and behavioural inhibition comes out in a particularly interesting manner in the case of what might be called the 'side-effects' of frustrative non-reward. A number of such side-effects have been described in the Skinner box, including two which are of particular relevance in the present context, since it has been possible to reproduce them in Man and to establish correlations between their magnitudes and neurotic introversion (Nicholson and Gray, 1972). These are 'behavioural contrast' and 'peak shift'. Both arise in a multiple-component successive discrimination. The animal (most commonly a pigeon) is rewarded on an intermittent schedule (typically variable interval) for responding in the presence of one stimulus (the discriminative stimulus, or S^D) but never rewarded in the presence of a second stimulus, the S^Δ. In the simple case in which the S^Δ is the absence of the S^D, the phenomenon of behavioural contrast is observed: as the pigeon learns the discrimination and comes to peck at the response key less frequently in the presence of S^Δ, his response rate rises above the pre-discrimination baseline in the presence of S^D. In the more complex case in which the S^Δ is another stimulus which stands at a different point from S^D on some stimulus continuum (e.g. orientation of line), peak shift is observed during generalization testing: the peak of the resulting generalization gradient is not at the angle of orientation represented by the S^D (as it would be in the absence of such 'intradimensional' discrimination training), but rather an angle which is further removed from S^Δ than is the S^D itself. Now these two phenomena may both be regarded as consequences of activity in the behavioural inhibition system and have been explicitly treated in this way (Gray and Smith, 1969), though there are a number of alternative hypotheses in the literature (Rachlin, 1973; Reynolds, 1961; Terrace, 1972). It is therefore of some importance that Terrace (1972) has shown that, if the discrimination is learnt without errors (i.e. with the pigeon never making a response in the presence of S^Δ), neither behavioural contrast nor peak shift occurs. Thus it is necessary, if these phenomena are to be observed, that the pigeon make a response which is not followed by reward; the mere correlation between S^Δ and the absence of reward is insufficient. Or, to put the same point differently, behavioural contrast and peak shift result from the operation of the behavioural inhibition system, and not from internal inhibition.

A further indication that the behavioural inhibition to which instrumental non-reward gives rise has different properties from the internal inhibition caused by the absence of the UCS in a classical conditioning paradigm is provided by the literature on partial reinforcement. It is well known that a random schedule of partial reinforcement of an instrumental response gives rise to a much greater resistance to extinction than is observed after continuous reinforcement (Lewis, 1960). Less well known is the fact that this 'partial reinforcement extinction effect' does not occur in classical conditioning (Gray, 1975). Indeed, the more common outcome of such an experiment, as already reported by Pavlov, is that resistance to extinction is less after partial classical reinforcement than after continuous reinforcement. Furthermore, performance at the end of acquisition is often superior in an instrumental partial reinforcement group as compared to continuously reinforced controls; but again the opposite is the case in classical conditioning. This difference between instrumental non-reward and classical internal inhibition is, again, of particular relevance to the present argument, since the effects of instrumental partial reinforcement are blocked by sodium amytal and, as we shall see, sensitivity to this drug is almost the touchstone of the behavioural inhibition system.

A final distinction which must be drawn concerns punishment and frustrative non-reward, on the one hand, and stimuli which signal these events, on the other. Since I have argued this point at length elsewhere (Gray, 1972b), I will here be brief. There is evidence, both behavioural and psychophysiological, that painful stimuli of the kind which experimental animals are typically taught to avoid (e.g. electric shock) and also the unconditioned event of frustrative non-reward excite different behavioural tendencies and involve a different neural substrate from those which relate to signals of punishment and signals of non-reward. In particular, the unconditioned events provoke fight or flight rather than the freezing or slow withdrawal typically elicited by Pun-CS and $\overline{\text{Rew}}$-CS.

We have considered what the behavioural inhibition system is and what it is not. It remains to consider what it feels like. To what subjective state in Man (if any) might activity in the behavioural inhibition system relate?

The title of this paper gives away the answer to this question: viz. the emotional state which is sometimes labelled 'anxiety'. I have discussed elsewhere the general question of how the emotions are to be treated within experimental psychology (Gray, 1971, 1972b). In common with a number of other writers (e.g. Millenson, 1967; Mowrer, 1960), I regard the emotions as states of the 'conceptual nervous system' which are elicited by instrumentally reinforcing stimuli (rewards, punishments, frustrative non-reward and 'relieving non-punishment') or by originally neutral stimuli which have been paired in a classical conditioning process with such instrumental reinforcers. Thus activity in the behavioural inhibition system (triggered as it is by Pun-Cs and $\overline{\text{Rew}}$-CS) qualifies as such an emotional state. The only question is, which emotion? The work of learning theorists, who were originally responsible for developing most of the ideas I have been using, suggests two strong candidates: 'fear', which is the term used by Mowrer (1960) and Miller (1959) to describe the state set up in an animal exposed to a Pun-CS, and 'frustration' (more exactly, anticipatory frustration), which is the term used by Spence (1956) and Amsel

(1958) to describe the state set up in an animal by $\overline{\text{Rew}}$-CS. On the view that these two states are in any case identical (Gray, 1967a; Wagner, 1966), we might use either label. Ordinary language offers an alternative to 'frustration', namely 'disappointment', which appears more apt for many of the situations typically used in experiments with rats; and 'anxiety' is typically used in a clinical setting for 'fear' (though, as far as I can judge, it means no more than 'fear', unless it be 'fear of unknown origin and which I cannot explain'). This plethora of names for what (if the theory presented here is correct) is a single state need neither alarm nor surprise us. Schachter's (Schachter and Singer, 1962) well-known experiments on the naming of one's own emotional state make it clear that the labels used depend both on the state one is in and on what the subject thinks put him into that state. Since there are many different kinds of stimuli (novel, Pun-CS, $\overline{\text{Rew}}$-CS, intense stimuli and stimuli of social interaction) which appear to activate the behavioural inhibition system, it is not surprising that English is able systematically to use a number of different words (including many more than I have yet mentioned) to label the state which is produced when it is active.

THE BEHAVIOURAL INHIBITION SYSTEM: PHYSIOLOGICAL

We turn now to a consideration of the behavioural inhibition system as it emerges from psychophysiological experiments. If the previous section could be regarded as a meditation on the theme of 'arousal and inhibition', this section is a meditation on the drug sodium amytal. What does it do and where and how does it do it?

The importance of this theme lies in the evidence (Eysenck, 1967) that alcohol and the barbiturates (of which amytal is one drug with three names, the others being 'amylobarbitone' and 'amobarbital') have an extraverting effect on behaviour. It follows that, if one had an adequate description of the psychological effects of these drugs, one would have a clue as to the psychological processes which differentiate introverts from extraverts; and if one knew how these drugs affected the activity of the brain, one would have an equally good clue as to the physiological substrate of these processes. It would therefore seem worth devoting a considerable effort to an understanding of the action of amytal and alcohol.

In fact there is now a considerable literature on the effects of these drugs (especially amytal) on the behaviour of rats (Gray, 1967a, 1971; Ison and Pennes, 1969; Miller, 1959, 1964; Wagner, 1966). This literature may be summarized fairly simply (with only a few loose ends left lying around) as follows: neither drug affects learning to obtain rewards nor learning to escape from or actively avoid punishments; they do, however, impair learning to suppress responses followed by punishment or by frustrative non-reward and they also block a number of side-effects of exposure to Pun-CS and $\overline{\text{Rew}}$-CS; finally, where active and passive avoidance are in conflict with each other, as in the shuttlebox, they suppress the passive avoidance tendency and thus indirectly facilitate active avoidance. In addition, there is evidence that in the rat amytal impairs the detection of novel stimuli (McGonigle, McFarland and Collier, 1967) and that in man it facilitates habituation to novel stimuli (Lader and Wing, 1966). Thus the behavioural effects of three of the five classes of stimuli which activate the behavioural inhibition system—Pun-CS, Rew-CS and novelty—are attenuated by these drugs. With regard to a fourth class— stimuli of social interaction—I am happy to rely on anecdotal reports and personal observation for the conclusion that in Man the behaviourally inhibitory effects of large gatherings of my conspecifics are reduced by alcohol.

These conclusions regarding the behavioural effects of the barbiturates and alcohol, then, suggest (in conformity with the conclusions we reached in the previous section) that the psychological process which differentiates (neurotic) introverts from (stable) extraverts is sensitivity or reactivity to Pun-CS, Rew-CS, novelty and threatening stimuli of social interaction. Our next question is: where in the brain, and by what neuropharmacological action, do these drugs produce these magical effects? It is to this question that much of my own experimental research has been directed over the last six years.

The starting point for this research is the perception that much of the behavioural syndrome which is produced by injections of sodium amytal or alcohol can also be produced by lesions to a number of parts of the brain (Gray, 1970b: see Figure 1.5). The most important of these are the septal area (McCleary, 1966) and the hippocampus (Douglas, 1967; Kimble, 1969). (The orbital frontal cortex also appears to form part of the same system, though we shall not be considering it in the present paper.) From this perception it is but a short step to the hypothesis that the drugs in some way impair the functioning of these parts of the brain, thus producing a temporary and incomplete lesion which is sufficient to affect behaviour in a similar way to a permanent and complete one. But in what way does this impairment occur? Our hypothesis is next helped along by the knowledge (Stumpf, 1965) that one of the areas concerned—the septal area, or, rather, the medial septal nucleus located in the heart of the septal area—controls certain specific features of the electrical activity of the other—the hippocampus.

These features are the presence, and the frequency when it is present, of the hippocampal theta rhythm. This is a regular high-voltage slow wave which lies in the frequency band 4–7 Hz in rabbits, cats and dogs, but in the frequency band 6–10 Hz in rodents, including the rat (in which my own studies have been conducted). It is well established that the medial septal nucleus contains the pacemaker cells for this rhythm: these cells fire in bursts which are synchronized with the hippocampal theta rhythm, and if they are temporarily or permanently lesioned the theta rhythm disappears with them (Stumpf, 1965). It is possible, furthermore, by delivering short pulses via implanted electrodes to the medial septal area at frequencies within the theta range, artificially to drive the theta rhythm in the hippocampus, a technique which we have adapted for use (under the shorthand title of 'theta-driving') in the free-moving rat (Gray and Ball, 1970); or, by delivering a train of high-frequency pulses

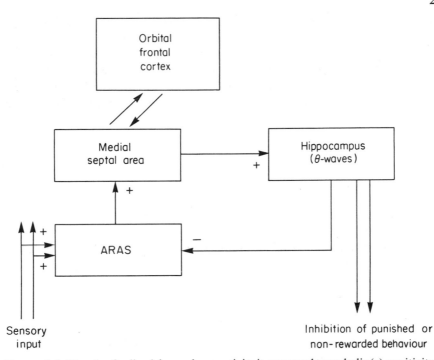

FIGURE 1.5 Negative feedback loop whose activity is presumed to underlie (a) sensitivity to signals of punishment and non-reward and thus also (b) individual differences in 'anxiety' (Figure 1.3) (From Nebylitsyn and Gray, *Biological Bases of Individual Behaviour*, 1972. Academic Press, London, with permission).

(about 100 Hz) to the medial septal area, artificially to block the hippocampal theta rhythm.

We thus have the hypothesis that (a) the hippocampal theta rhythm is functionally involved in the production of behavioural inhibition (which would offer a parsimonious account for the fact that lesions both to the hippocampus and to the septal area impair behavioural inhibition) and (b) amytal and alcohol impair behavioural inhibition by impairing in some way the hippocampal theta rhythm (which would account for the similarity between the behavioural effects of these drugs and those of lesions to the septal area and hippocampus). This hypothesis in turn was sharpened up after we had done some simple experiments in which we recorded from the hippocampus in the free-moving rat exposed to reward and non-reward for running down an alley (Gray and Ball, 1970). We observed that there were predictable relations between the frequency of the theta rhythm and the rat's behaviour. When the rat was engaging in such 'fixed action patterns' as eating, drinking, grooming, etc., the theta rhythm was rather irregular and tended to be about 6–7 Hz. When the animal was traversing the runway (often at a rather high speed) towards a well-learned goal, the theta rhythm was of very high amplitude and frequency (typically, 9–10 Hz). When the rat was either exploring a novel environment or exposed to frustrative non-reward, the theta rhythm was of an intermediate frequency which averaged exactly 7.7 Hz. Thus the final hypothesis (Gray, 1970b) is that the operation of the behavioural inhibition system involves a hippocampal theta rhythm in an intermediate frequency band centred on 7.7 Hz and that amytal and alcohol impair the functioning of the theta rhythm in this frequency band. (This is by no means the only hypothesis about the functional significance of the hippocampal theta rhythm; indeed, there are at least eight or nine others—too many, certainly, to review here—most of which are a good deal more popular than this one. Currently the most favoured is probably Vanderwolf's, 1971.)

The experiments we have conducted to test our hypothesis have been of several kinds, all revolving round septal control of the theta rhythm. The behavioural end points we have used have been simple resistance to extinction after rewarded training on an alley-running response. As background to the rationale of these experiments, I should first remind the reader of the effects produced by sodium amytal in comparable circumstances. If this drug is injected during the extinction phase of the experiment, after the animal has been trained on continuous reinforcement (CR), extinction is retarded (an attenuation of the behavioural effects of $\overline{\text{Rew}}$-CS). If, in a slightly different experiment, the drug is administered, during the acquisition phase only, to two groups of rats, one on CR, the other on random 50 per cent partial rein-forcement (PR), the partial reinforcement extinction effect (PREE) is abolished (Gray, 1969, 1972b) or at least attenuated (Gray and Dudderidge, 1971; Ison and Pennes, 1969), and this change is due to the fact that the drugged PR group closely resembles the placebo CR controls—i.e. once more the behavi-oural effects of $\overline{\text{Rew}}$-CS are attenuated.

Now, if the behavioural effects of $\overline{\text{Rew}}$-CS are mediated in part by a 7.7 Hz hippocampal theta rhythm controlled by the pacemaker cells located in the medial septal nucleus, the following predictions can be made:

(1) Septal driving of a 7.7 Hz theta rhythm during extinction after CR will facilitate extinction. This prediction was verified by Gray (1972c).
(2) Septal driving of a 7.7 Hz theta rhythm on a random 50 per cent schedule during CR acquisition will mimic the PREE, i.e. it will increase subsequent resistance to extinction. This prediction was verified by Gray (1972c). More recently, Glazer (1974) has verified a similar prediction: he showed that training rats by instrumental procedures to produce 7.7 Hz theta to obtain reward increased the resistance to extinction of a subsequently learned lever-pressing response, a phenomenon which mimics the general-ized PREE described by Ross (1964).
(3) Septal blocking (by high-frequency stimulation) of the naturally occurring theta response to non-reward on a random 50 per cent PR schedule will reduce resistance to extinction. This prediction was verified by Gray, Araujo-Silva and Quintão (1972).
(4) Lesions to the medial septal area will reduce the PREE both by increasing resistance to extinction in a CR group and by decreasing resistance to

extinction in a PR group. This prediction was verified by Gray, Quintão and Araujo-Silva (1972) and by Henke (1974), though in the latter experiment lesions were of the total septal area.

THE PHARMACOLOGY OF THE THETA-DRIVING CURVE

Another line of investigation which we have been pursuing concerns the effects of a number of drugs and hormones on the 'theta-driving curve'. This is the curve obtained by plotting in the free-moving rat the threshold current applied to electrodes in the medial septal area able to drive the hippocampal theta rhythm as a function of the frequency of the stimulating current. This line of investigation was started by Gray and Ball (1970), whose results for our touchstone drug, sodium amytal, are presented in Figure 1.6. There are two features to note about this figure. The first is that the drug, which was administered with exactly the dose, timing and route of injection known to be effective in the behavioural experiments, has a quite selective effect on the threshold at 7.7 Hz (which is raised), while the thresholds at frequencies above and below this value are unaffected. The second is that the curve obtained from the undrugged rat has a minimum or 'dip' at this same frequency—7.7 Hz. When this result was first obtained, our attention was mainly caught by the effect of the drug, for this was exactly in agreement with the hypothesis that sodium amytal has its effects on behaviour by virtue of an impairment in the normal functioning of the hippocampal theta rhythm only in that frequency band which is associated with frustrative non-reward, viz. at about 7.7 Hz. The fact that the theta-driving curve in the undrugged animal has a dip at this same frequency did not at the time seem to be of any particular interest.

In following up the rather remarkable effect of amytal on the theta-driving curve, the natural first step was to investigate other drugs which also impair behavioural inhibition. Only if these, too, selectively raise the threshold at 7.7 Hz would it be reasonable to conclude that such a change is a necessary condition for a drug to exert this kind of behavioural effect. A key test drug in this context is undoubtedly ethanol (alcohol, in the everyday sense of the word). The behavioural similarities between alcohol and amytal were long ago pointed out by Miller (1959, 1964). Figure 1.7 shows that the effect of ethanol on the theta-driving curve closely resembles that of amytal. It also shows the effects of two other common drugs: cannabis, or rather one of its active principles, Δ^9-tetrahydrocannabinol (THC), and 'Librium' (chlordiazepoxide). Both drugs act on the theta-driving curve in much the same way as amytal. Chlordiazepoxide, of course, is well known to counteract fear in both rats and men (Garattini, Mussini and Randall, 1973). As for THC, when Drewnowski and I obtained the results shown in Figure 1.7 for this drug, we did not yet know much about its behavioural effects. Its effect on the theta-driving curve made a clear prediction possible: it ought to act like amytal. To test this, we examined the effects of THC on the PREE, which it duly abolished (Figure 1.8; Drewnowski and Gray, 1975). Thus it is a reasonable conclusion

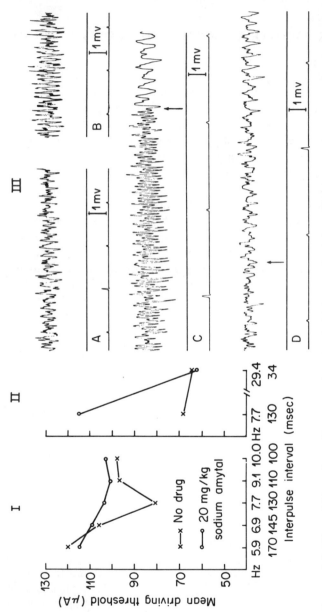

FIGURE 1.6 Effect of 20 mg/kg sodium amytal on threshold for septal driving of hippocampal theta rhythm as a function of driving frequency (i.e. on 'theta-driving curve') in two groups (I and II) of five rats. (III) Examples of driven hippocampal response. Bottom channel: time in sec. A: Driving current 5.9 Hz, 175 μA. B: 10 Hz, 150 μA. C: 29.4 Hz, 150 μA (arrow marks termination of stimulation). D: 7.7 Hz, 60 μA (arrow marks start of stimulation). From Gray and Ball, *Science*, **168**, 1246–1248, Figure 1. Copyright 1970 by the American Association for the Advancement of Science.).

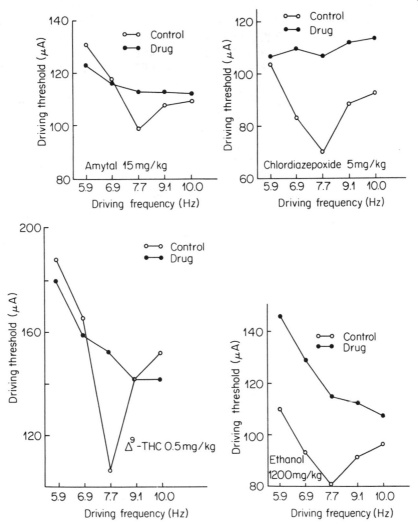

FIGURE 1.7 Effects of four drugs which impair behavioural inhibition on the theta-driving curve.

that drugs which raise the threshold for septal theta-driving selectively at 7.7 Hz also antagonize the behavioural effects of signals of punishment and frustrative non-reward. (It should be added in parenthesis that we have data on a large variety of drugs which do not have this effect on the theta-driving curve; it is not simply a non-specific indicator that a psychopharmacologist has been at work.)

Now in the course of these experiments, we decided to look at the female sex hormones. My colleague, Robert Drewett, implanted some female rats with our standard septal-stimulating and hippocampal-recording electrodes. To our surprise, the curves obtained from these animals had no dip at 7.7 Hz.

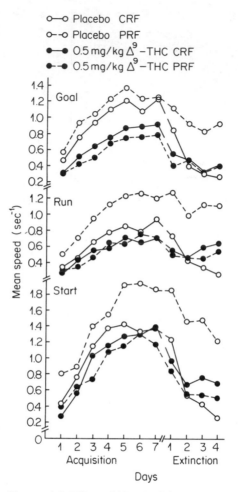

○—○ Placebo CRF
○--○ Placebo PRF
●—● 0.5 mg/kg Δ^9–THC CRF
●--● 0.5 mg/kg Δ^9–THC PRF

FIGURE 1.8 Effect of Δ^9-THC injected during acquisition on the partial reinforcement extinction effect in three sections of straight alley. During extinction all rats were given placebo. CRF: continuous reinforcement. PRF: partial reinforcement. (From Drewnowski and Gray, 1975.)

All our previous rats had had such a dip, but all had been males. This was our first indication that the shape of the *undrugged* theta-driving curve might itself be of importance: that the 7.7 Hz dip, in other words, is of sufficient physiological significance for the brain to control it rather carefully. It took us some time to discover how this control gave rise to the sex difference we had observed. Our results (Drewett, Gray, James and Dudderidge, in preparation) are set out in Figures 1.9 and 1.10. They demonstrate that the female sex hormones can be absolved of all responsibility; it is a matter for the male

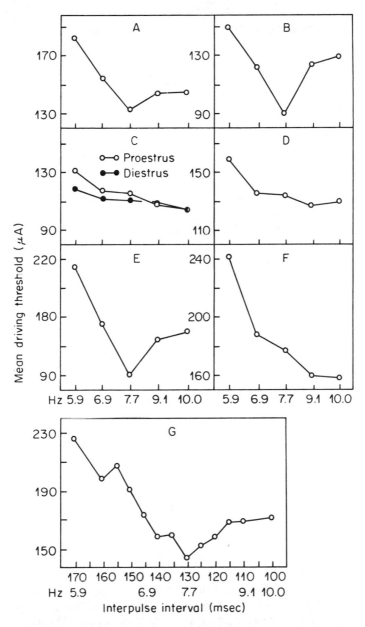

FIGURE 1.9 Thresholds for septal driving of hippocampal theta rhythm as a function of stimulation frequency. A: mean of five Wistar male rats. B: single male rat. C: mean of four females during proestrus and diestrus. D: mean of six ovariectomized females. E: mean of three male rats tested at 49, 59 and 69 days after castration, respectively. F: mean of same three male rats as in E, tested at 70, 79 and 72 days after castration, respectively. G: results from single intact male tested with 5 msec increments of interpulse interval (abscissa).

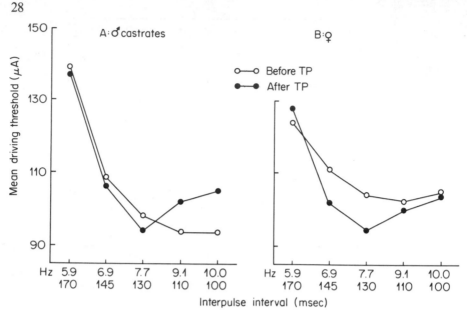

FIGURE 1.10 Effect of daily injection of testosterone propionate (TP) on theta-driving curve in castrated male rats (A) and ovariectomized female rats (B).

sex hormone, testosterone, alone. The castrated male rat loses his 7.7 Hz dip (though it takes from 7 to 11 weeks after castration for this change to take place), but injections of testosterone propionate (as little as 250 µg for two consecutive days) restore the dip. Furthermore, testosterone injections can also produce a 7.7 Hz dip in the female at doses which are little, if at all, higher than those required in the castrated male. From these results we would predict that testosterone increases behavioural inhibition. However, there is no evidence supporting this proposition, and our own attempts to obtain such evidence (unpublished data) have so far failed.

The fact that testosterone has such a powerful effect on the theta-driving curve led us to ask how else the brain might control the shape of this curve. In particular, what synaptic transmitters are involved? An answer to this question might also tell us more about the action on the theta-driving curve of sodium amytal. With what transmitter substances does this drug interfere in order to produce its characteristic effect on the curve? According to the pharmacological literature, the actions of the barbiturates are quite non-specific, so no help was forthcoming from that direction. Possibly we could find an answer for ourselves by mimicking the amytal effect with drugs which are known to have more specific effects on synaptic transmitters.

On the assumption that we are dealing with a behavioural inhibition system, there are two neural transmitters one might expect to be involved in determining the shape of the theta-driving curve. These are acetylcholine and 5-hydroxy-tryptamine or serotonin, both of which have been implicated in the control of behavioural inhibition in psychopharmacological studies (Carlton, 1963;

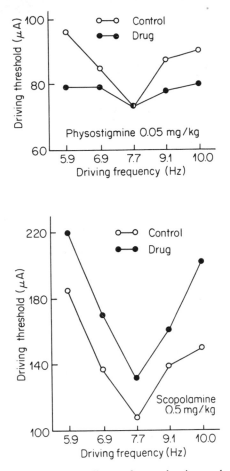

FIGURE 1.11 Effects of scopolamine and physostigmine on the theta-driving curve.

Dominic, 1973; Warburton, 1972; Weissman, 1973). We therefore investigated the effects of cholinergic and anticholinergic, and serotonergic and antiserotonergic, drugs on the theta-driving curve. As shown in Figure 1.11, the anticholinergic, scopolamine, slightly steepens and the cholinergic, physostigmine, slightly flattens the theta-driving curve, but neither changes its basic shape (McNaughton, James and Gray, unpublished). In contrast, parachlorophenylalanine (PCPA), which blocks serotonin synthesis, abolishes the 7.7 Hz dip, and this is then restored by 5-hydroxytryptamine (5-HTP), a drug which by-passes the block and gives the rat the serotonin he needs (Stewart and Gray, unpublished). However, it will be noted (Figure 1.12) that PCPA abolishes the 7.7 Hz dip, not by raising the threshold at this frequency as do amytal, chlordiazepoxide, alcohol and THC, but by lowering the threshold at every other frequency except 7.7 Hz. Thus we had not succeeded in duplicating the

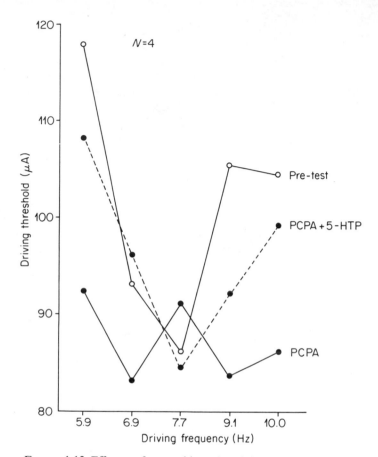

FIGURE 1.12 Effects of parachlorophenylalanine (PCPA) and 5-hydroxytryptamine (5-HTP) given after PCPA on the theta-driving curve.

effects of these 'minor tranquillizers' or 'anxiolytics' by blocking serotonin synthesis.

We next turned our attention to the catecholamines, dopamine and noradrenaline. While neither of these transmitter substances has been linked with behavioural inhibition before, noradrenaline at least has been implicated in emotion and response to stress (Schildkraut and Kety, 1967). We therefore investigated the effect on the theta-driving of haloperidol, a drug which acts as a receptor-blocker for both of the catecholamines. As shown in Figure 1.13, this drug produced a result which was qualitatively very similar to that produced by the four minor tranquillizers whose effects are shown in Figure 1.7. Haloperidol, however, does not distinguish between dopamine and noradrenaline. A treatment which does is to inject alpha-methyl-p-tyrosine (α-MPT), which blocks the synthesis of both dopamine and noradrenaline, and then to follow this with dihydroxyphenylserine (DOPS), which restores noradrenaline

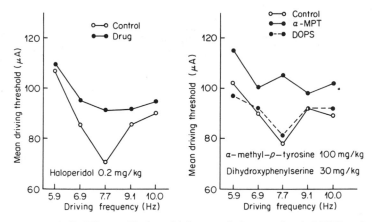

FIGURE 1.13 Effects of haloperidol, α-methyl-*p*-tyrosine (α-MPT) and dihydroxyphenylserine (DOPS) given after α-MPT.

but not dopamine levels. As shown in Figure 1.13, the first of these drugs had an amytal-like effect on the theta-driving curve, while subsequent treatment with the second restored the shape of the curve to normal. Thus, from this experiment, one can conclude that a normal theta-driving curve is compatible with severely impaired functioning of dopaminergic neurons; and that the amytal-like effects of haloperidol and α-MPT are almost certainly due to the interference produced by these drugs in the normal functioning of noradrenergic systems (McNaughton, James and Gray, unpublished).

Given this information, and the great advances made in recent years in our knowledge of the neuroanatomy of central noradrenergic pathways (Ungerstedt, 1971), it is possible to ask reasonable questions concerning the locus of action of the anxiolytics in the brain. Noradrenergic fibres all appear to originate in the midbrain and brainstem, and thence to ascend to higher structures. In their ascent they separate into two bundles. The ventral bundle collects fibres from many nuclei of origin and distributes them mainly to the hypothalamus. The dorsal bundle collects only from one nucleus, the locus coeruleus, and distributes in the main to the neocortex, the cerebellum and the hippocampus (Ungerstedt, 1971; Figure 1.14). It is this latter pathway, from the locus coeruleus to the hippocampus, which is the most obvious candidate for the site of action of the anxiolytic drugs with regard to their effects on the theta-driving curve, especially as there is already evidence from neurochemical studies that the benzodiazepines (including chlordiazepoxide) and the barbiturates reduce neuronal activity and noradrenaline turnover in this pathway (Corrodi, and coworkers, 1971; Lidbrink, and coworkers, 1972).

In order to examine this possibility, Kelly, McNaughton and I destroyed the dorsal bundle by injecting into it a neurotoxin, 6-hydroxydopamine (6-OHDA), which is specific for dopaminergic and noradrenergic fibres. Subsequent biochemical assay showed that this treatment reduced hippocampal levels of noradrenaline by 98 per cent, indicating a virtually complete lesion of

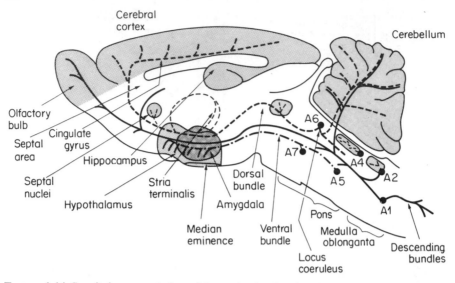

FIGURE 1.14 Saggital representation of the rat brain, showing the principal ascending and descending noradrenergic pathways. Shaded areas indicate regions of noradrenergic terminals. From Livett, *Br. Med. Bull.*, **29**, 1973, p. 96, Figure 3.)

the noradrenergic innervation of this structure, while there was no change in hypothalamic or striatal levels of dopamine (which would be expected to fall if the 6-hydroxydopamine had also destroyed the ventral bundle, since this carries the ascending dopaminergic neurons as well as other noradrenergic fibres). Animals treated in this way and subsequently implanted with hippocampal-recording and septal-stimulating electrodes showed a theta-driving curve with no sign of a minimum threshold at 7.7 Hz (Figure 1.15). Thus the noradrenergic innervation of the hippocampus from the locus coeruleus appears selectively to facilitate septal-driving of the hippocampal theta rhythm at a frequency of 7.7 Hz; and it seems very likely that the selective rise in the 7.7 Hz threshold produced by the anxiolytic drugs is due to an impairment produced by these agents in the activity of this pathway. From this conclusion, it is a small step to the hypothesis that the *behavioural* effects of the minor tranquillizers are also due to an action on the noradrenergic fibres which ascend from the locus coeruleus to the hippocampus (and neocortex). We are currently testing this hypothesis.

Although the results we have obtained by interfering with noradrenergic systems in the brain are clear-cut and offer, at least in embryo, a satisfying and coherent story, it would be a mistake to bury the possibility of serotonergic involvement in behavioural inhibition on the grounds that PCPA does not alter the theta-driving curve in the same way as does amytal. Indeed, if we put together the results shown in Figure 1.12 for this drug and in Figure 1.13 for α-MPT, we see that the shape of the theta-driving curve in the undrugged (male) animal depends on the joint action of serotonergic and noradrenergic

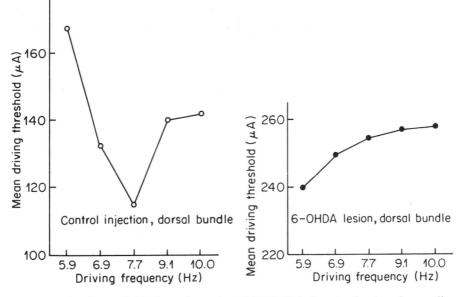

FIGURE 1.15 Effects of 6-hydroxydopamine (6-OHDA) lesions to the dorsal ascending noradrenergic bundle (Figure 1.14) on the theta-driving curve.

systems. Frequencies above and below 7.7 appear to be inhibited by a serotonergic system, while 7.7 Hz itself appears to be facilitated by a noradrenergic system (presumably travelling in the dorsal bundle). The question therefore arises whether the critical feature of the alteration produced in the theta-driving curve by the minor tranquillizers is (a) that they raise the threshold at 7.7 Hz or (b) that they alter the shape of the curve so that there is no longer a 7.7 Hz dip. If it is the former, PCPA should not have the same behavioural effect as these drugs; if it is the latter, it should.

We have so far conducted only one experiment on this point, but it is clear. We trained rats on continuous reinforcement to run an alley for food and then injected PCPA during extinction. One group of rats was given 5-HTP replacement therapy before the daily extinction session, a second group was given 5-HTP after this session, and there was a third control group given neither PCPA nor 5-HTP. The results showed that PCPA retarded extinction (thus acting like amytal) and that 5-HTP before the daily session reversed this effect (Gray, Rickwood and Stewart, unpublished). These initial results suggest that it may be the shape of the theta-driving curve (is there a 7.7 Hz dip or not?) which determines the level of behavioural inhibition; and the shape of the curve is dependent on a normally functioning serotonergic neural system as well as on the noradrenergic fibres originating in the locus coeruleus.

The known anatomy of serotonergic systems fits happily with the second of these conclusions. One major bundle of serotonergic neurons originates in the raphe nuclei of the midbrain and then ascends in the medial forebrain bundle to the septal area (Dahlström, Häggendal and Atack, 1973). The hippocampus is also a receiving area for serotonergic neurons, and, furthermore, the inhibition of serotonin synthesis by injections of PCPA is much greater in the forebrain (including both the septal area and the hippocampus) than it is in the midbrain (Aghajanian, Kuhar and Roth, 1973). It therefore seems reasonable to suggest that the alteration produced in the theta-driving curve by PCPA is due to an action of this drug on serotonergic terminals located in the medial septal area, the hippocampus or both. Furthermore, a role of these terminals in behavioural inhibition has been suggested recently by a number of other workers. For example, Mabry and Campbell (1974), who have been investigating the ontogeny of the inhibition of locomotor activity in the rat, have shown that there is a serotonergic system which is functionally separate from the cholinergic one and which matures a few days earlier than the latter. They also cite evidence from the work of Trimbach (1972) which suggests that the behaviourally inhibitory role of serotonin is exercised critically in the hippocampus. Also, Dominic (1973) has advanced evidence that a number of drugs used clinically to treat anxiety, such as chlordiazepoxide and diazepam ('Valium'), reduce the synthesis and metabolism of serotonin in the forebrain. There is, in addition, evidence, reviewed by Dominic (1973), that PCPA attenuates conflict behaviour and that treatments which elevate central serotonin levels increase conditioned suppression (Wise, Berger and Stein, 1970, 1972). Thus the hypothesis that serotonin is an important element in the septo-hippocampal neural chain which controls the kind of behavioural inhibition involved in the emotion of anxiety gains support from a number of different lines of work.

The picture which emerges, then, is that of a behavioural inhibition system including circuits in the septal area and the hippocampus, and with important ascending noradrenergic and serotonergic influences which reach the hippocampus (perhaps via the septal area) from the midbrain. It will be obvious that many of the arguments which have brought us to this point depend upon interpretations of our rather mysterious 'theta-driving' curves. These interpretations are by no means so clear-cut that additional support would not be welcome. Fortunately, such support is available. It comes from some experiments we have recently completed on the Maudsley Reactive (MR) and Maudsley Non-reactive (MNR) strains of rats (Broadhurst, 1960).

These strains have been selectively bred from an original Wistar population on criteria of either high (MR) or low (MNR) defecation in the open field. In consequence of this selective breeding, they have come to differ from each other in a variety of ways which are consistent with the hypothesis that the MR strain is more fearful than the MNR strain (Gray, 1971). These differences include one of the paradigmatic measures of behavioural inhibition, namely passive avoidance, which is, of course, weaker in the MNR strain (Ferraro and York, 1968; Weldon, 1967). Thus we might expect the 7.7 Hz dip to be less evident in MNR than in MR rats.

Accordingly, we measured the theta-driving curve in males of both these strains. The results of this experiment (Gray, James and McNaughton, un-

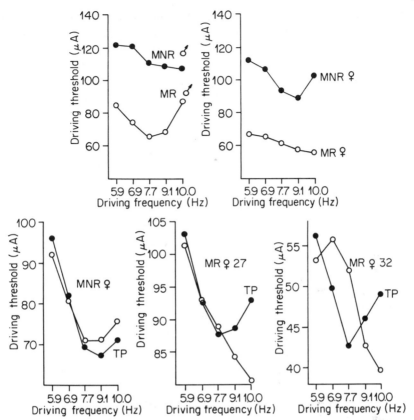

FIGURE 1.16 Theta-driving curves in untreated Maudsley reactive (MR) and non-reactive (MNR) males and females (above), and in a group of four MNR females and two individual MR females before and after daily injection of testosterone propionate (TP) (below).

published) bore this expectation out remarkably clearly: whereas males of the MR strain had essentially normal theta-driving curves, with a 7.7 Hz dip, males of the MNR strain lacked this dip completely (Figure 1.16). Even more striking, females of the MR strain responded in the same way as do Wistar females when injected with testosterone propionate, i.e. they displayed a 7.7 Hz dip; females of the MNR strain, on the other hand, showed no change from the normal female pattern, even when injected with massive doses of testosterone. Since MNR males also failed to respond to exogenous testosterone, we may conclude that the MNR strain has lost the capacity to respond to testosterone by producing a 7.7 Hz dip in the theta-driving curve. Furthermore, since we know how the MNR strain was produced (by selective breeding for low defecation scores in the open field), and since both the parental Wistar strain and the MR strain (which has had a comparable breeding regime, but for high defecation scores) retain the capacity to respond to testosterone, it is a reasonable conclusion that the change in the MNR strain is an actual *consequence* of breeding for low open field defecation, i.e. for low fearfulness. Thus these results offer strong support for the hypothesis that there is a functional link between the shape of the theta-driving curve and the level of fearfulness: the absence of a 7.7 Hz dip is an indication of low fearfulness, whether this is produced by pharmacological means (injection of amytal, alcohol or chlordiazepoxide) or by selective breeding.

CONCLUSION: THE BEHAVIOURAL INHIBITION SYSTEM AND ANXIETY

Suppose there is a behavioural inhibition system in the rat; even suppose that there is such a system, or one rather like it, in Man; and suppose that some individuals ('dysthymics') have a very low threshold for activity and/or a very high level of activity in this system: what kind of individuals would they be? We shall use the attempt to answer this question as a way of summarizing the series of linked hypotheses which constitutes the behavioural inhibition system as it has been presented in this paper.

(1) The stimuli which activate the behavioural inhibition system are of five kinds: novelty, stimuli associated with punishment, stimuli associated with frustrative non-reward, intense stimuli, and aggressive or dominance signals arising in the course of social interaction. These, then, are the kinds of stimuli to which we should expect dysthymics to be hypersensitive.

(2) The output of the behavioural inhibition system consists in the suppression of ongoing behaviour, especially ongoing behaviour which gives rise to an increase in the level of stimulation activating the system. Thus we would expect dysthymics to show restrained and cautious behaviour under conditions in which they were exposed to stimuli of the kind listed in (1).

(3) At the same time as the behavioural inhibition described in (2), there is an increment in the level of arousal. Thus, provided the dysthymic is exposed to stimuli of the kind listed in (1), we would expect him to display a high level of arousal.

(4) The emotional content of active states in the behavioural inhibition system can be described by such words as 'fear', 'anxiety' and 'frustration'. These, then, are the emotions which we would expect dysthymics particularly to display.

(5) The neural structures which are of most importance in the functioning of the behavioural system include the septal area, the hippocampus and the orbital frontal cortex (which we have not had space to discuss in this paper: see Gray, 1970a; Passingham, 1970). If recording were possible in these structures in Man, we would expect them to show a high level of activity in dysthymics (though not necessarily, of course, of the simple theta-type which is characteristic of hippocampal activity in the rat).

(6) The functioning of the behavioural inhibition system is impaired by low doses of barbiturates, benzodiazepines, alcohol and cannabis. We would

therefore expect (a) dysthymics to show particularly high resistance to these drugs and (b) dysthymic behaviour to be reduced by them.

(7) The behavioural inhibition system includes a critical component which is serotonergic. We would therefore expect antiserotonergic drugs to reduce dysthymic behaviour.

(8) The behavioural inhibition system includes a critical component which is noradrenergic, and which probably consists in the fibres travelling in the ascending dorsal noradrenergic bundle from the locus coeruleus to (among other structures) the hippocampus. We would therefore expect anti-noradrenergic drugs to reduce dysthymic behaviour. (However, it is clear that noradrenergic fibres also mediate other important behavioural functions perhaps via other routes, so such drugs are unlikely to be of any direct clinical value.)

Whether there are individuals in our species who conform to this description is obviously a matter for further debate; as is the question whether, assuming there are, they are the ones who fall into Eysenck's neurotic introvert quadrant. Relevant data may be obtained in the experimental laboratory, and we have begun the attempt to gather them (Nicholson and Gray, 1972). However, the final verdict on the theory presented in these pages must come from clinicians: I hope they will find it a useful framework within which to approach their patients' symptoms and to construct therapeutic stratagems.

REFERENCES

Aghajanian, G. K., Kuhar, M. J., and Roth, R. H. (1973). Serotonin-containing neuronal perikarya and terminals: differential effects of p-chlorophenylalanine. *Brain Research*, **54**, 85–101.

Amsel, A. (1958). The role of frustrative nonreward in noncontinuous reward situations. *Psychological Bulletin*, **55**, 102–119.

Amsel, A. (1962). Frustrative nonreward in partial reinforcement and discrimination learning: some recent history and a theoretical extension. *Psychological Review*, **69**, 306–328.

Broadhurst, P. L. (1960). Applications of biometrical genetics to the inheritance of behaviour. In H. J. Eysenck (Ed.), *Experiments in Personality*, Vol. 1: *Psychogenetics and Psychopharmacology*, Routledge and Kegan Paul, London.

Burgess, P. K. (1972). Eysenck's theory of criminality: a new approach. *British Journal of Criminology*, **12**, 74–82.

Carlton, P. L. (1963). Cholinergic mechanisms in the control of behaviour by the brain. *Psychological Review*, **70**, 19–39.

Cattell, R. B. (1965). *The Scientific Analysis of Personality*, Pelican, Harmondsworth, England.

Cattell, R. B. (1966). Anxiety and motivation: theory and crucial experiments. In C. D. Spielberger (Ed.), *Anxiety and Behavior*, Academic Press, New York.

Corcoran, D. W. J. (1972). Studies of individual differences at the Applied Psychology Unit. In V. D. Nebylitsyn and J. A. Gray (Eds.), *Biological Bases of Individual Behavior*, Academic Press, New York.

Corrodi, H., Fuxe, K., Lidbrink, P., and Olson, L. (1971). Minor tranquillizers, stress and central catecholamine neurons. *Brain Research*, **29**, 1–16.

38

Dahlström, A., Häggendal, J. and Atack, C. (1973). Localization and transport of serotonin. In J. Barchas and E. Usdin (Eds.), *Serotonin and Behavior*, Academic Press, New York.

Dominic, J. A. (1973). Suppression of brain serotonin synthesis and metabolism by benzodiazepine minor tranquillizers. In J. Barchas and E. Usdin (Eds.), *Serotonin and Behavior*, Academic Press, New York.

Douglas, R. J. (1967). The hippocampus and behavior. *Psychological Bulletin*, 67, 416–442.

Drewnowski, A., and Gray, J. A. (1975). Influence of $\triangle^9$ – tetrahydrocannabinol on partial reinforcement effects. *Psychopharmacologia*, 43, 233–237.

Eysenck, H. J. (1957). *The Dynamics of Anxiety and Hysteria*, Praeger, New York.

Eysenck, H. J. (1960). Classification and the problem of diagnosis. In H. J. Eysenck (Ed.), *Handbook of Abnormal Psychology*, Pitman, London.

Eysenck, H. J. (1967). *The Biological Basis of Personality*, C. C. Thomas, Springfield, Illinois.

Eysenck, H. J. (1970). *Crime and Personality*, 2nd ed., Granada, London.

Eysenck, H. J., and Eysenck, S. B. G. (1969). *Personality Structure and Measurement*, Routledge and Kegan Paul, London.

Eysenck, H. J., and Levey, A. (1972). Conditioning, introversion–extraversion and the strength of the nervous system. In V. D. Nebylitsyn and J. A. Gray (Eds.), *Biological Bases of Individual Behavior*. Academic Press, New York.

Ferraro, D. P., and York, K. M. (1968). Punishment effects in rats selectively bred for emotional elimination. *Psychonomic Science*, 10, 177–178.

Garattini, S., Mussini, E., and Randall, L. O. (Eds.) (1973). *The Benzodiazepines*, Raven Press, New York.

Gellhorn, E., and Loofbourrow, G. N. (1963). *Emotions and Emotional Disorders*, Hoeber, New York.

Glazer, H. I. (1974). Instrumental conditioning of hippocampal theta and subsequent response persistence. *Journal of Comparative and Physiological Psychology*, 86, 267–273.

Gray, J. A. (1964a). Strength of the nervous system as a dimension of personality in man, a review of work from the laboratory of B. M. Teplov. In J. A. Gray (Ed.), *Pavlov's Typology*, Pergamon, Oxford.

Gray, J. A. (1964b). Strength of the nervous system and levels of arousal: a reinterpretation. In J. A. Gray (Ed.), *Pavlov's Typology*, Pergamon, Oxford.

Gray, J. A. (1967a). Disappointment and drugs in the rat. *Advancement of Science*, 23, 595–605.

Gray, J. A. (1967b). Strength of the nervous system, introversion–extraversion, conditionability and arousal. *Behaviour Research and Therapy*, 5, 151–169.

Gray, J. A. (1969). Sodium amobarbital and effects of frustrative nonreward. *Journal of Comparative and Physiological Psychology*, 69, 55–64.

Gray, J. A. (1970a). The psychophysiological basis of introversion–extraversion. *Behaviour Research and Therapy*, 8, 249–266.

Gray, J. A. (1970b). Sodium amobarbital, the hippocampal theta rhythm, and the partial reinforcement extinction effect. *Psychological Review*, 77, 465–480.

Gray, J. A. (1971). *The Psychology of Fear and Stress*, McGraw-Hill, New York.

Gray, J. A. (1972a). Learning theory, the conceptual nervous system and personality. In V. D. Nebylitsyn and J. A. Gray (Eds.), *Biological Bases of Individual Behavior*, Academic Press, New York.

Gray, J. A. (1972b). The structure of the emotions and the limbic system: a theoretical model. In R. Porter and J. Knight (Eds.), *Physiology, Emotion and Psychosomatic Illness*. Ciba Foundation Symposium, 8 (new series), Associated Scientific Publishers, Amsterdam, pp. 87–120.

Gray, J. A. (1972c). Effects of septal driving of the hippocampal theta rhythm on resistance to extinction. *Physiology and Behavior*, 8, 481–490.

Gray, J. A. (1973). Causal theories of personality and how to test them. In J. R. Royce

(Ed.), *Multivariate Analysis and Psychological Theory*, Academic Press, New York.

Gray, J. A. (1975). *Elements of a Two-process Theory of Learning*, Academic Press, London.

Gray, J. A., Araujo-Silva, M. T., and Quintâo, L. (1972). Resistance to extinction after partial reinforcement training with blocking of the hippocampal theta rhythm by septal stimulation. *Physiology and Behavior*, **8**, 497–502.

Gray, J. A., and Ball, G. G. (1970). Frequency-specific relations between hippocampal theta rhythm, behavior and amobarbital action. *Science*, **168**, 1246–1248.

Gray, J. A., and Dudderidge, H. (1971). Sodium amylobarbitone, the partial reinforcement extinction effect, and the frustration effect in the double runway. *Neuropharmacology*, **10**, 217–222.

Gray, J. A., Quintâo, L., and Araujo-Silva, M. T. (1972). The partial reinforcement extinction effect in rats with medial septal lesions. *Physiology and Behavior*, **8**, 491–496.

Gray, J. A., and Smith, P. T. (1969). An arousal-decision model for partial reinforcement and discrimination learning. In R. M. Gilbert and N. S. Sutherland (Eds.), *Animal Discrimination Learning*, Academic Press, London.

Henke, P. G. (1974). Persistence of runway performance after septal lesions in rats. *Journal of Comparative and Physiological Psychology*, **86**, 760–767.

Hugelin, A., and Bonvallet, M. (1957). Etude expérimentale des interrelations réticulo-corticales: proposition d'une théorie de l'asservissement réticulaire à un système diffus cortical. *Journal de Physiologie*, **49**, 1201–1223.

Hull, C. L. (1943). *Principles of Behavior: An Introduction to Behavior Theory*, Appleton-Century, New York.

Ison, J. R., and Pennes, E. S. (1969). Interaction of amobarbital sodium and reinforcement schedule in determining resistance to extinction of an instrumental running response. *Journal of Comparative and Physiological Psychology*, **68**, 215–219.

Jonason, K. R., and Enloe, L. J. (1971). Alteration in social behaviour following septal and amygdaloid lesions in the rat. *Journal of Comparative and Physiological Psychology*, **75**, 286–301.

Kimble, D. P. (1969). Possible inhibitory functions of the hippocampus. *Neuropsychology*, **7**, 235–244.

Lader, M. H., and Wing, L. (1966). *Physiological Measures, Sedative Drugs, and Morbid Anxiety* (Maudsley Monographs, 18). Oxford University Press, London.

Levey, A. (1967). *Eyelid Conditioning, Extraversion and Drive: An Experimental Test of Two Theories.* Unpublished Ph.D. thesis, University of London.

Lewis, D. J. (1960). Partial reinforcement: a selective review of the literature since 1950. *Psychological Bulletin*, **57**, 1–28.

Lidbrink, P., Corrodi, H., Fuxe, K., and Olson, L. (1972). Barbiturates and meprobamate: decreases in catecholamine turnover of central dopamine and noradrenaline neuronal systems and the influence of immobilization stress. *Brain Research*, **45**, 507–524.

Livett, B. G. (1973). Histochemical visualization of peripheral and central adrenergic neurones. In L. Iversen (Ed.), *Catecholamines, British Medical Bulletin*, **29**, No. 2, 93–99.

Mabry, P. D., and Campbell, B. A. (1974). Ontogeny of serotonergic inhibition of behavioral arousal in the rat. *Journal of Comparative and Physiological Psychology*, **86**, 193–201.

McCleary, R. A. (1966). Response-modulating functions of the limbic system: initiation and suppression. In E. Stellar and J. M. Sprague (Eds.), *Progress in Physiological Psychology*, Vol. 1, Academic Press, New York.

McGonigle, B., McFarland, D. J., and Collier, P. (1967). Rapid extinction following drug-inhibited incidental learning. *Nature (London)*, **214**, 531–532.

Magoun, H. W. (1963). *The Waking Brain*, 2nd ed., C. C. Thomas, Springfield, Illinois.

Mangan, G. L. (1972). The relationship of strength-sensitivity of the visual system to extraversion. In V. D. Nebylitsyn and J. A. Gray (Eds.), *Biological Bases of Individual Behavior*, Academic Press, New York.

Marks, I. M. (1969). *Fears and Phobias*, Heinemann, London.

40

Millenson, J. R. (1967). *Principles of Behavioral Analysis*, MacMillan, New York.

Miller, N. E. (1959). Liberalization of basic S-R concepts: extensions to conflict behavior, motivation and social earning. In S. Koch (Ed.), *Psychology: A Study of a Science*, Study 1, Vol. 2, McGraw-Hill, New York.

Miller, N. E. (1964). The analysis of motivational effects illustrated by experiments on amylobarbitone. In H. Steinberg (Ed.), *Animal Behaviour and Drug Action*, Churchill, London.

Mowrer, O. H. (1960). *Learning Theory and Behavior*, Wiley, New York.

Nicholson, J. N., and Gray, J. A. (1972). Peak shift, behavioural contrast and stimulus generalization as related to personality and development in children. *British Journal of Psychology*, **63**, 47–62.

Passingham, R. E. (1970). The neurological basis of introversion–extraversion: Gray's theory. *Behaviour Research and Therapy*, **8**, 353–366.

Passingham, R. E. (1972). Crime and personality: a review of Eysenck's theory. In V. D. Nebylitsyn and J. A. Gray (Eds.), *Biological Bases of Individual Behavior*, Academic Press, New York.

Pawlik, K. (1973). Right answers to the wrong questions? A re-examination of factor-analytic personality research and its contribution to personality theory. In J. R. Royce (Ed.), *Contributions of Multivariate Analysis to Psychological Theory: Third Banff Conference on Theoretical Psychology*, Academic Press, New York.

Poplawsky, A., and Johnson, D. A. (1973). Open-field social behavior of rats following lateral or medial septal lesions. *Physiology and Behavior*, **11**, 845–854.

Rachlin, H. C. (1973). Contrast and matching. *Psychological Review*, **80**, 217–234.

Rescorla, R. A., and Solomon, R. L. (1967). Two-process learning theory: relationships between Pavlovian conditioning and instrumental learning. *Psychological Review*, **74**, 151–182.

Reynolds, G. S. (1961). Behavioral contrast. *Journal of the Experimental Analysis of Behavior*, **4**, 57–71.

Ross, R. R. (1964). Positive and negative partial-reinforcement extinction effects carried through continuous reinforcement, changed motivation, and changed response. *Journal of Experimental Psychology*, **68**, 492–502.

Schachter, S., and Singer, J. E. (1962). Cognitive, social and physiological determinants of emotional state. *Psychological Review*, **69**, 379–399.

Schildkraut, J. J., and Kety, S. S. (1967). Biogenic amines and emotion. *Science*, **156**, 21–30.

Shapland, J., and Rushton, J. P. (1975). Crime and personality: further evidence. *Bulletin of the British Psychological Society*, **28**, 66–67.

Sokolov, Ye. N. (1963). *Perception and the Conditioned Reflex*, Pergamon Press, Oxford.

Spence, J. T., and Spence, K. W. (1966). The motivational components of manifest anxiety: drive and drive stimuli. In C. D. Spielberger (Ed.), *Anxiety and Behavior*, Academic Press, New York.

Spence, K. W. (1956). *Behavior Theory and Conditioning*, Yale University Press, New Haven, Connecticut.

Stumpf, Ch. (1965). Drug action on the electrical activity of the hippocampus. *International Review of Neurobiology*, **8**, 77–138.

Terrace, H. S. (1972). Conditioned inhibition in successive discrimination learning. In R. A. Boakes and M. S. Halliday (Eds.), *Inhibition and Learning*, Academic Press, London.

Trimbach, C. (1972). Hippocampal modulation of behavioral arousal: mediation by serotonin. *Dissertation Abstracts International*, **33**, 1315.

Ungerstedt, U. (1971). Stereotaxic mapping of the monoamine pathways in the rat brain. *Acta Physiologica Scandinavica*, **82**, Suppl. 367, 1–48.

Vanderwolf, C. H. (1971). Limbic diencephalic mechanisms of voluntary movement. *Psychological Review*, **78**, 83–113.

Wagner, A. R. (1966). Frustration and punishment. In R. M. Haber (Ed.), *Current Research on Motivation*, Holt, Rinehart and Winston, New York.

Warburton, D. M. (1972). The cholinergic control of internal inhibition. In R. A. Boakes and M. S. Halliday (Eds.), *Inhibition and Learning*, Academic Press, London.

Weissman, A. (1973). Behavioral pharmacology of *p*-chlorophenylalanine (PCPA). In J. Barchas and E. Usdin (Eds.), *Serotonin and Behavior*, Academic Press, New York.

Weldon, E. (1967). An analogue of extraversion as a determinant of individual behavior in the rat. *British Journal of Psychology*, **58**, 253–259.

Wise, C. D., Berger, B. D., and Stein, L. (1970). Serotonin: a possible mediator of behavioral suppression induced by anxiety. *Diseases of the Nervous System*, **31** (suppl.), 34–37.

Wise, C. D., Berger, B. D., and Stein, L. (1972). Benzodiazepines: anxiety-reducing activity by reduction of serotonin turnover in the brain. *Science*, **177**, 180–183.

Zhorov, P. A., and Yermolayeva-Tomina, L. B. (1972). Concerning the relation between extraversion and the strength of the nervous system. In V. D. Nebylitsyn and J. A. Gray (Eds.), *Biological Bases of Individual Behavior*, Academic Press, New York.

2

PSYCHOPHYSIOLOGICAL VARIABLES

P. H. Venables

INTRODUCTION

Psychophysiological techniques may be thought to be of value in the field of behaviour modification in several ways. Firstly, they may be used as indicators of abnormal state, i.e. as diagnostic tools. Particularly, it is possible that psychophysiological techniques could be useful in detecting those individuals within a larger psychiatric diagnostic category who were most likely to benefit from the application of behaviour modification techniques.

Secondly, psychophysiological techniques may be potentially valuable as indicators of changes brought about during the course of behaviour modification. In this instance, the distinction is drawn between the gross indications of change which are changes in diagnostic indicators and the changes in measures which are thought to reflect aspects of the process of behaviour modification.

Thirdly, attempts may be made to modify the psychophysiological measures themselves and in doing so incidentally to modify the overt behaviour.

The distinction between the third and second categories is clearly that between bio-feedback techniques and the examination of the concomitants of behaviour modification. In what has first been said, however, the accent must remain on the 'may be' and the 'possibly'. The reason for this caution is that there is need to emphasize and reemphasize the lack of any close one-to-one relation between psychological state, or overt behaviour, and physiological variables commonly measured as indicants of more global psychological conditions. A general concept may be one which is in itself pseudo-physiological, such as 'arousal', or may be psychological, such as 'anxiety'; but since, still using the same examples, both 'arousal' and 'anxiety' are concepts of the same kind and, indeed, on occasions have been used almost as though they were interchangeable, the same lack of clear relation between them and the measures which are said to indicate them needs to be reexamined.

Difficulties appear to lie in the findings that the measures which have been used as indicants, for instance of arousal or anxiety, do not themselves correlate sufficiently highly together to give any feeling of confidence that they are

measuring the same thing. Furthermore, the relation of any one of the physiological measures to the behaviour to which they are supposed to be related is
seldom high and may not be linear. There is, furthermore, a lack of consistency
of relation between physiological indicators and behaviour across subjects.
Thus those subjects who say they are not disturbed by an emotional film may
be more reactive physiologically than those who admit their disturbance
(Lazarus and Alfert, 1964).

The question which must then be asked is how far are psychophysiological
variables of use in aiding the practice of behaviour modification? The answer
in the future probably is that, when we understand more about what we are
doing, psychophysiology will be of great importance. At the moment, however,
there is a tendency for the non-psychophysiologist to expect too simple an
answer from his psychophysiological colleague. Skin conductance, for example,
is not a simple measure of 'arousal'; changes in heart rate do not directly
reflect changes in anxiety.

In the end, there is probably no escape from a determined effort to understand
the physiological mechanisms of the indices that are of interest and the problems
involved in their measurement. In addition, there is the need to bear in mind
those 'extraneous' variables that have to be taken into account in the form,
for instance, of diurnal and seasonal variations, sex differences and the effects
of medication, smoking and alcohol intake. If we add to these the extent to
which the cognitive and social structure of the situation in which the measurements are taken needs to be considered, then it is not surprising that the more
naive applications of psychophysiological techniques lead to inconclusive
results.

This chapter will attempt to present a few of the major considerations that seem
to be important in the employment of psychophysiological variables. Attention
will be confined largely to two autonomic measures—electrodermal and
cardiovascular activity—to some extent because these are probably the most
used in this field, but also because their measurement and interpretation
throws up the problems outlined in the first part of this section. Additionally,
however, it is necessary to take into account other variables, e.g. respiration,
in the consideration of the two to which major treatment will be given.

ELECTRODERMAL ACTIVITY

Definitions

Electrodermal activity (EDA) can be divided into two general types. Firstly,
there is the endosomatic type, where the potential existing between two points
on the skin is measured and no external source of current is applied. In this
case, the measurement is of skin potential, either level (SPL) or response (SPR).
Secondly, and more commonly, the conductance between two points on the
skin is measured, exosomatically, by the use of an external current source.

Conductance level (SCL) or response (SCR) are measured. The use of the terms suggested in brackets above avoids ambiguities (Venables and Christie, 1973; Venables and Martin, 1967). The hitherto widespread use of the term GSR does not define what is being measured, and when terms like 'level of GSR' are found ambiguity reaches a maximum.

In the case of SPR which may take a biphasic or even multiphasic form, it is necessary to describe the component of the waveform being considered; hence phrases like 'the initial negative component' or 'the secondary positive component' of the SPR are required.

In the case of exosomatic activity, it is preferable to make measurements in terms of conductance units (conductance being the reciprocal of resistance). The reason for this convention is physiological and will be dealt with below ('Peripheral mechanisms of electrodermal activity').

Units of measurement and expected values

Amplitude measurements

Skin potential is usually measured in millivolts (mV). With electrodes conventionally placed on the palmar surface and on an abraded forearm site, skin potential levels will range from $+ 10$ mV to $- 70$ mV, the sign being that of the potential at the palmar electrode. Skin potential responses will probably range up to $- 2$ mV for the initial negative component and up to $+ mV$ for the secondary positive component.

Skin potential measurement is not dependent on electrode size. It is, however, dependent on the type and concentration of external electrolyte used. With physiological concentrations of NaCl or KCl, the figures above are those to be expected. If concentrated saline electrolytes are employed, such as those often commercially supplied for electrocardiograph (EKG) or electroencephalograph (EEG) work, wide-ranging and variable values of SPL and SPR will be found which cannot easily be related to underlying physiological states.

Skin conductance is measured in micromhos (μmho), although on occasions and for statistical convenience log micromhos are used. Values of skin conductance depend on the size of electrode used and should be quoted in terms of specific conductance as micromhos per square centimetre. With 1 cm^2 electrodes and bipolar placement (i.e. both electrodes on a palmar surface), the range of expected values for SCL will most likely be from 2 to 100 umho cm^{-2}. In the case of SCR the range of expected amplitudes is from .01 μmho to 5 umho cm^{-2}.

Temporal measurements

Not only have temporal measurements of SPRs and SCRs proved of diagnostic significance but knowledge of the extent of the 'temporal window' in which a stimulus may appear enables a response to a stimulus to be related to that stimulus in the context of a record with a high percentage of spontaneous responding.

In the case of SCR, three temporal measurements are of importance: latency, rise time and half recovery time. (As recovery of the SCR is exponential, it is convenient to measure its value in terms of the time taken for the response to return to half its peak amplitude (Edelberg, 1970)). Expected latency values will be from 1.3 to 2.5 secs, and this range may be suggested to give a conservative 'temporal window'. Time-to-peak response is usually less than 1 sec and half recovery time ($t/2$) will range from a minimum of 1 sec to 10 secs or longer.

In the case of SPR, the latency of the initial negative component is similar to that of SCR, namely 1.3 to 2.5 secs. No definitive figures are available for the latencies of the other components.

Other considerations

Because of the wide range of values within which SCR may vary between subjects, Lykken and coworkers (1966) advocated the use of a range correction technique for expressing changes in the SCL or SCR. Range-corrected SCL, ΦSCL is defined as:

$$\Phi SCL_x = \frac{SCL_x - SCL_{min}}{SCL_{max} - SCL_{min}}$$

where SCL_x refers to the SCL measured on a particular occasion and SCL_{min} and SCL_{max} those minimum and maximum values shown by the subject. Unfortunately, it is not always easy to obtain these values, particularly in patient subjects where a resting level may not be possible if the subject is anxious in the experimental situation; nor would it be desirable to achieve a maximum value by, for example, having the subject blow up a balloon until it bursts.

Possibly easier to obtain is the range-corrected value of SCR, ΦSCR, which is defined as:

$$\Phi SCR_x = \frac{SCR}{SCR_{max}}$$

In this instance, a maximum value of SCR may often be obtained by asking the subject to take a deep breath or may be achieved on the first occasion on which a novel stimulus is presented.

Peripheral mechanisms of electrodermal activity

In contrast to those electrophysiological measures where there is an internal source of electrical activity (e.g. EKG, EEG, EMG) and the main purpose of the electrode as a transducer of electrical activity is to transmit the underlying activity as faithfully as possible, in electrodermal measurement, the electrode–skin combination itself forms part of the system which determines the extent of electrical activity which is measured. This is particularly the case in the measurement of skin potential where, at least in part, the potential may be seen as a junction potential which obeys the Nernst equation (Christie and Venables, 1971a, 1971b). A detailed description of the peripheral mechanisms involved has been recently presented (Venables and Christie, 1973); only a summary will therefore be given here.

The effective peripheral mechanism of electrodermal activity at a palmar site may be considered to consist of the eccrine sweat glands and epidermal structures lying between them.

The epidermis is stratified and consists of soft deep layers and harder superficial layers. The outer layer, the stratum corneum, is hardest and thickest on the palmar and plantar surfaces, and immediately below it is the stratum lucidum which has been suggested to have a barrier function. It is possible, however, that the superficial layers act as a whole in the generation of aspects of electrodermal activity.

The eccrine sweat glands have their densest distribution on the palm and sole (< 2000 cm $^{-2}$); in contrast, the density in the axillae is 200–300 cm^{-2} and on the trunk, 100–200 cm $^{-2}$ (Weiner and Hellman, 1960).

The eccrine sweat glands may be considered as current paths through the otherwise relatively poorly conducting epidermis. These paths act as though they are resistors in parallel (e.g. Montagu and Coles, 1966) and as such provide the rationale for the advocacy of the measurement of exosomatic activity in conductance units (see 'Definitions', above).

This view is based on work by Thomas and Korr (1957) who showed a linear relation between numbers of active sweat glands and conductance, and is supported by work by Lader (1970) who showed that, after the inhibition of sweat gland activity by local iontophoresis of atropine, amplitude of SCRs showed a smooth decline. In contrast, when exosomatic activity was expressed in terms of skin resistance responses (SRRs) then the decline was variable and erratic.

The current path through the eccrine sweat glands has been the subject of some investigation over the past few years and reviews of the work may be had in Edelberg (1972b), Fowles (1973) and Venables and Christie (1973). The evidence suggests that there are two ductal pathways in the human eccrine sweat gland at dermal and epidermal levels; in consequence, a somewhat complicated set of relations exist which depend on the level of duct filling by sweat bringing into play one or the other mechanism.

As far as response amplitudes of SCR are concerned, consideration of the complexities of ductal activity is probably not too important. However, it is when other potentially interesting aspects are involved that knowledge of ductal function becomes more necessary. In so far as the recovery of the phasic SCR has shown itself to be prognostically (e.g. Mednick and Schulsinger, 1968) and diagnostically (e.g. Gruzelier and Venables, 1972) of importance in the study of schizophrenia, then its apparent reliance on the epidermal ductal reabsorption mechanism becomes a stimulus for further investigation. Venables (1974) has reviewed present knowledge in this area. The importance appears to lie in the extent to which the reabsorption is under innervative control or whether to some extent it can be the result of passive or secondary triggering by, for instance, ductal hydrostatic pressure.

The reason for this apparently rather narrow consideration of the minutiae of eccrine ductal reabsorption at this point is to emphasize the need to know the details of the indicators that are being used as measurement of behavioural change. If, as advocated by Edelberg (1972a), there is an active innervation of this epidermal reabsorption mechanism, then it is possible to expect that steps which are taken to change autonomic activity behaviourally may also have an effect on the ductal mechanism and this may be reflected more or less directly in the recovery limb of the SRC.

If, however, the triggering of epidermal ductal activity is relatively secondary, then we have other expectations. One possibility is that the myoepithelium around the duct is adrenergically innervated (Bligh, 1967; Goodall, 1970) (cf. the sweat secretory mechanism which is cholinergically innervated; Lader and Montagu, 1962) and that the mechanism of ductal reabsorption is triggered by hydrostatic pressure and/or sweat electrolyte concentration. In this instance, what the recovery limb of the SCR may reflect is (a) that there is enough sweat to reach the epidermal ductal mechanism (and hence we must also consider the amplitude of the response), (b) that sympathetic adrenergic activity, to produce the myoepithelial 'squeeze', has taken place, and (c) that the control of the sodium reabsorption mechanism in the ductal wall is set at a certain point by circulating mineralocorticoids such as aldosterone, in which case the recovery limb is reflecting longer-term (than just a few minutes) 'stress'.

Clearly, if points such as these have to be taken into account in the interpretation of the SCR, simple statements of psychological and physiological relations cannot be made.

So far only phasic aspects of exosomatic activity have been considered. At the present state of knowledge, it seems possible to make a fairly bald statement about phasic skin potential activity. That is, attempts to quantify SPRs other than in terms of latency of the initial component or the existence of different components are not likely to be productive. For instance, the amplitude of the initial negative component is a function of the presence and extent of the secondary positive component. In uniphasic negative responses the response proceeds to its maximum amplitude, in contrast to when there is a biphasic response, the response configuration is determined to a great extent by the secondary positive aspect and the negative component never reaches the maximum amplitude it might independently attain.

Knowledge of the SPR waveform is, however, of help in the interpretation of the SCR. At the moment, data (e.g. Edelberg, 1972a) seem to be fairly consistent in suggesting that a uniphasic negative SPR is the accompaniment of a slow recovery SCR, while a biphasic SPR is accompanied by a quick recovery SCR. It is possible, therefore, to use the form of the SPR as an alternative to the SCR where SCR recovery is the measure of particular interest.

Possibly the simplest of the electrodermal measures is SCL; provided that it is measured correctly, it is probably a reasonable measure of average sweat gland activity. However, it probably also is a function of epidermal hydration and is consequently influenced to a fairly substantial extent by ambient climatic conditions which have, therefore, to be subject to a degree of control. A measure which is relatively easy to obtain but which is subject to misinterpretation is that of skin potential level (SPL). Under conditions when sudorific activity is at a minimum, the SPL falls to a minimum value and then slowly rises again, while SPR measured at the same time continues to fall. This 'basal' SPL (BSPL) is an identifiable criterion point and is fairly stable for a stable individual subject under standard conditions. Data (Christie and Venables, 1971a, 1971b, 1971c, 1971d) suggest that BSPL is a junction potential and determined by the concentrations of the external 'electrode' electrolyte and the electrolyte in the skin surface. Because this latter value is probably a reflection of the history of mineralocorticoid activity of the subject, there is a suggestion that BSPL can be used as a measure of the stress experienced by the subject.

A viewpoint which has been put forward (Venables and Christie, 1974) is that the skin, and particularly that aspect of its activity which is reflected by BSPL, is an organ of adaptation (Yoshimura, 1964) and is a means whereby temporary storage of electrolytes is achieved. By looking at shifts in electrolytes in the skin (as reflected in SPL), it is possible to examine 'controlling' rather than 'controlled' physiological variables (Teichner, 1968; Venables, 1970) and hence readily see the influence of external stresses in Man's adaptive processes.

At the other 'aroused' end of the continuum of SPL where there is considerable sudorific activity, SPL is a function of eccrine sweat gland activity (Fowles and Venables, 1970). Schultz and coworkers (1965) showed that ductal potentials of about 50 mV negative relative to interstitial fluid were obtained even when the secretory portion of the duct was filled with non-conducting oil. Inhibition of the ductal wall sodium pump mechanism with g-strophanthin reduced the potential in the duct and increased the NaCl concentration of sweat.

The position hence seems to be that in two somewhat different ways SPL reflects the activity of the adrenal cortex. At the resting end of the scale, an increased recent history of stress is reflected as a *lower* reading of BSPL. This is because Selye's (1950) notion of hyperkalaemia resulting from the 'alarm' reaction of stress reduces the log of the ratio of external (electrode) to internal (skin) potassium and hence, via the Nernst equation, the BSPL. At the other end of the scale, increased stress results in more mineralocorticoid activity and hence more sodium reabsorption and a *higher* reading of SPL. This high-level SPL is, of course, also a function of adrenal–medullary–sympathetic activity in so far as reabsorption of sweat cannot take place without sweat being secreted in the first place.

This rather detailed exposition of the peripheral mechanisms of electrodermal activity has been presented here for several reasons. Firstly, because it would seem that a non-simplistic view of the system leads to the possibility of extracting more information from a recording channel than might otherwise be the case. Secondly, because it is evident that unless the determinants of electrodermal activity are more fully known a simplistic viewpoint may result in misleading conclusions.

Central mechanisms of electrodermal activity

In so far as the peripheral mechanisms of electrodermal activity are not fully understood, it becomes that much more difficult to make very definite statements about central activity. The only reasonable approach in these circumstances is to consider work on the central determinants of EDA in the light of whatever peripheral response system happens to have been measured.

It is important, however, in reviewing work which uses animals as subjects, to bear in mind some potentially relevant species differences. A considerable amount of work on central mechanisms has been undertaken with cats as the experimental subjects; the ductal reabsorption mechanisms which have been discussed in the last section are not present in the cats' foot pad. Hence, in general when SPRs are measured, uniphasic responses only are reported and those which suggest that biphasic responses are found may be suspect. Because of this, work on SCR recovery with cats is probably irrelevant. Rodents, however, having ductal reabsorption mechanisms do provide the possibility for comparative work on this topic as do, of course, the primates.

The other consideration to be borne in mind in this field is the extent of anaesthesia which is used in experimental studies. The general principle put forward by Wang (1957, 1958) of a 'hierarchy of suprasegmental controls' for EDA is potentially the subject of experimental confounding by a hierarchy of susceptibility to anaesthesia.

At a spinal level, pools of sympathetic neurons which control peripheral EDA exist separately for each limb and can discharge spontaneously. It is only control from higher centres that leads to simultaneous activity in each limb. At the next highest level, that of the bulbar reticular formation, the evidence from Wang and Brown (1956a, 1956b), Bloch and Bonvallet (1960) and Yokota, Sato and Fujimori (1963a) is that this system has an action which is inhibitory. Intercollicular decerebration results in an unmodulated inhibitory influence from the bulbar reticular formation and a diminution of peripheral EDA.

In contrast to Wang (1964) who minimized the role of mesencephalic reticular formation, Bloch and Bonvallet (1960) showed that low-voltage short-duration stimulation of the midbrain reticular formation gave rise to the same form of EDA which was normally elicited by an external stimulus. Within the region (which also gives EEG signs of wakefulness) between the bulbar reticular formation (RF) and the posterior hypothalamus the threshold for eliciting electrodermal activity is low; outside the region the threshold is much higher.

Within the limbic system, Yokota, Sato and Fujimori (1963b) showed that stimulation of the hippocampus produces inhibition of the SPR, while stimulation of the amygdala produces facilitation. A similar finding with respect to the amygdala is provided by Lang, Tuovinen and Valleala (1964). Bagshaw, Kimble and Pribram (1965) showed that in monkey amygdalectomy produces diminution of SCR to tones, while ablation of the hippocampus and inferotemporal cortex had no effect on SCR. Later analysis of the same data on a different time base (Bagshaw and Kimble, 1972) showed that, in the majority of animals, amygdalectomy produced complete abolition of responding. However, in two animals hyperresponsivity resulted. Hippocampectomy produced no changes in SCR-orienting. However, there was a diminution in the rate of habituation over the first fifteen evocations of the response. Hippocampectomy also produced changes in the SCR recovery limb, operated animals showing a shorter recovery time than normals. The mechanism whereby hippocampectomy had this influence on a complicated peripheral system is not known.

Darrow (1937) reported that stimulation of the anterior hypothalamus produced electrodermal activity, and this is also stated to be the case by Bloch and Bonvallet (1960). As the anterior hypothalamus is involved in thermoregulation, it may be that palmar and plantar sweating regulated from this area is part of this function.

The highest level of regulation of EDA is, of course, the cortex. Darrow (1937) showed that lesions of the pre-motor cortex, which resulted in loss of inhibitory control of motor movement and gave the condition of 'forced grasping', also gave rise to profuse sweating. Luria and Homskaya (1970), discussing orienting activity in general, say 'undoubtedly the neo-cortex of the cerebral hemispheres and above all the cortex of the frontal lobes of the brain take part in the regulation of the orienting reflex'.

In general, there has been nothing available since Wang's reviews (1957, 1958, 1964) to contradict the position he then stated that electrodermal activity is subject to 'a hierarchy of suprasegmental controls' with the cortex at the highest level.

The measurement of electrodermal activity

There are now several texts available which provide the necessary details of measurement techniques (Edelberg, 1967; Grings, 1973; Lykken, 1968; Lykken and Venables, 1971; Montagu and Coles, 1966, 1968; Venables and Christie, 1973; Venables and Martin, 1967). Starting from a wide range of recommended techniques, the range of methods now considered suitable has narrowed considerably. Nowadays, nearly everyone advocates the use of silver–silver chloride electrodes, the use of physiological levels of NaCl or KCl and, for the measurement of conductance, a constant voltage system measuring directly in micromhos. The arguments for standardization have been made by Lykken and Venables (1971) and Venables and Christie (1973).

At this point in the development of techniques, it is worthwhile, however, pointing to developments that need to be borne in mind over and above the recommendations in the works cited. A variety of different bases have been recommended over the years to produce electrolyte jellies. The three most common at this time are perhaps corn-starch (Edelberg, 1967), agar-agar (Venables and Sayer, 1968) and 'Unibase' (Lykken, 1968; Lykken and Venables, 1971). Recent work by Fowles and Rosenberry (1973) and Fowles and Schneider (1974) has shown the differences in recordings that can be obtained by the use of agar and 'Unibase'; these make the comparability of recordings using otherwise identical techniques extremely doubtful. Fowles and Schneider (1974), in addition to agar- and 'Unibase'-based electrolytes, used a glycol-based electrolyte, the effect of which is to minimize the hydration of the skin which is produced by the 'wet' agar electrolyte. 'Unibase' in general produces much larger SCRs than agar or glycol electrolytes, while with SCL the results are different depending on whether the subject is giving fast or slow recovery SCRs. The outcome is that the apparent equivalence of 'Unibase' and agar which is suggested by Lykken and Venables (1971) needs to be questioned. We are still not in a position to know which type of electrolyte base produces the 'real' electrodermal activity. We do know, however, that experiments using different types of electrolyte base cannot be compared.

CARDIOVASCULAR ACTIVITY

The main emphasis of this short discussion will be on the problems of understanding the measurement, analysis and mechanisms of heart rate. In contrast to the measurement of electrodermal activity which has just been described, major difficulties in work with heart rate do not lie in the area of electrode techniques and, for instance, decisions about the use of constant current or constant voltage systems. The basic principles of the process of obtaining indications of the electrical activity of the heart are relatively simple; it is rather the field of analysis of the record once it has been obtained that gives rise to problems and controversy.

Recording of the EKG

As far as the psychophysiologist is concerned, very little use has been made of analysis of components of the EKG; its recording, therefore, is largely for the purpose of measuring heart rate, and considerations in its recording should have optimization of this measurement in mind (Brener, 1967).

Exceptions to this general rule of the major interest being in heart rate have been concerned with the presentation of stimuli within a particular phase of the heart cycle (e.g. Birren, Cardon and Phillips, 1963; Engel, Thorne and Quilter, 1972; Saxon, 1970) and with the amplitude of the T-wave of the EKG as a measure reflecting plasma potassium concentration (Christie and Venables, 1971c).

When recording the EKG in order to measure heart rate, it is desirable to choose an electrode placement which normally provides a large QRS spike and a relatively small T-wave, in order that, when using a cardiotachometer or a computer for analysis, only one clear signal per heart beat is provided.

Unfortunately, the easiest lead configuration to use, i.e. right arm–left arm (Standard Lead I), is the lead which often gives rise to a large T-wave and a relatively small QRS complex; double counts may result from its use. The other leads often used by psychophysiologists are right arm–left leg (Lead II) and left arm–left leg (Lead III), both of which tend to give clear QRS complexes. Unfortunately, however, all these three convenient standard leads are prone to disturbance by movement artefacts. In consequence, in situations where the subject or patient is likely to move, and especially when telemetric techniques are used, chest electrode placements are to be advised.

A typical placement was suggested by Blanksby, Elliott and Bloomfield (1973) in a study of squash players: 'One of the electrodes was placed on the manubrium while the other was placed . . . at the fifth left intercostal space in the mid-clavicular line for right handed subjects'. For left-handed subjects 'and those carrying excessive amounts of adipose tissue', the second electrode was placed on the left, sixth intercostal space on the anterior axillary line. A similar placement is recommended by Schane and Slinde (1967) in a study of free-fall parachutists, with one electrode on the manubrium and the other over the corpus sterni at the level of attachment of the fifth costal cartilage. The other major requirement in obtaining a good signal, in addition to choice of electrode placement, is to achieve an adequate contact between body and equipment. Standard EKG electrodes are large silver-plated plates, generally attached to the limb by rubber straps. The skin underneath the electrode is prepared by rubbing with commercial electrode jelly which is a saturated saline solution and contains an amount of abrasive substance. In the use of chest leads it is more usual to use the same type of bio-potential electrodes used for measuring electrodermal phenomena. These may be attached by double-sided adhesive discs and held in place additionally by adhesive tape. The skin is best prepared by rubbing with acetone to remove grease; this enables the electrolyte to make a good contact and also helps with the adhesion of the electrodes.

In cases where it is undesirable to put electrodes on the subject, heart rate may be conveniently recorded by plethysmographic techniques. Detailed coverage of methods is given by Brown (1967), Lader (1967) and Weinman (1967). A recent paper by Stern (1974) shows that the ear-lobe provides an excellent site for attaching a photoplethysmographic transducer for the measurement of heart rate. This site shows little vasomotor activity, is convenient and, with careful use, is not prone to movement artefacts.

The measurement of heart rate and heart rate changes

Techniques used in the measurement of heart rate depend on the availability of hardware, on the need for immediate monitoring and on detailed considerations of the logic of the operation. At the cheapest end of the scale, photoplethysmographic monitors are available which give immediate readings of heart rate (HR) on a dial; with this system obviously no recording is available and in practice only levels of HR may be read with any accuracy. At the next stage, the simple recording of the EKG on a pen recorder will give a permanent record which can, by the use of hard work, provide all that is required for the most sophisticated analyses. An aid to minimize some of this hard work is a scale devised by Hayes and Venables (1972). One of the difficulties of this direct recording of EKG is that the experimenter is unable to appreciate immediately the appearance of small changes of cardiac rate and thereby gain insight into the responses of his subject to particular stimuli. However, this can be done using a cardiotachometer or rate meter where heart rate is indicated as a vertical deflection of the recording pen rather than as an interval between successive beats. Given an artefact-free primary record providing only a single signal on each beat, the use of a cardiotachometer provides a most useful record; however, it should be noted that the rate being indicated by the cardiotachometer on a particular heart pulse is the rate for the preceding beat interval and is not that current at the time when, for instance, the onset of a signal is marked on the paper record.

Given the use of a laboratory computer, either on-line or off-line, much greater flexibility is available, but this flexibility demands that greater thought be given to the question of what it is that it is important to measure. If tonic levels of HR or changes in tonic level are the measures of interest, then the decision is a twofold one: whether to express the data in terms of heart rate, or in terms of interbeat interval (IBI) or heart period (HP) which is reciprocally related to HR. The decision appears to be largely a statistical one.

Studies are not unanimous in preferring one or the other measure on the grounds of better approximation of the distribution of data to normality. Much appears to depend on whether the data are looked at within or between subjects. The latest contribution to this literature is that of Jennings, Stringfellow and Graham (1974) who advocate, on the basis of their analyses, the use of HP in measuring cardiac responses. One problem concerns the length of the sample which is taken as a measure of tonic heart rate. Empirically, work from these authors' laboratory showed correlation of 0.9 between the heart rates measured from ten-beat and thirty-beat samples of data. From another point of view, the length of sample should extend over at least one full respiratory period so that the effects of sinus arrhythmia may be averaged out. As respiration can range, in adult men, down to below 8 cycles per minute, a sample of 7 to 8 secs in temporal length, or covering about ten beats, is probably indicated.

It is in the measurement of phasic heart rate change that problems occur in a major way. The phasic heart rate response may be conveniently thought of as being graphically plotted with HR or IBI, or a derivative of either of these two measures on the ordinate and a measure on the abscissa in terms of physiological time (i.e. beats) or real time (i.e. second). The further problem is the length of time for which a sample of HR response should be taken post-stimulus and the length of the sample pre-stimulus against which to compare post-stimulus changes.

The decision on the ordinate measure is again fundamentally between HR and IBI, and this largely appears to be a distributional problem for the set of data from each particular experiment. However, further measures can be derived once, for instance, HR has been chosen as the measure to be used. The ordinate may be expressed in terms of 'raw' HR or it may be expressed in terms of HR deviations from a value which in some way exemplifies the pre-stimulus HR value. The most typical value for this, it might be suggested, on the basis of the arguments above, is a mean value of a sample ten beats in length. Other authors have used different conventions about the length of the pre-stimulus sample. Empirically, it can be shown that the post-stimulus sample probably needs to be about fifteen beats long in order to obtain all the information potentially available.

The decision about whether to use beats or seconds as the measure on the abscissa is similarly difficult. One factor making for a fairly clear decision is the existence of a stimulus situation where two stimuli are presented in real time, as in a classical conditioning procedure. In this case, it seems appropriate to suggest that the abscissa should record real time (i.e. seconds or other units as appropriate: half-seconds, for instance, if the subjects are young children). Expressing HR measured as beats in terms of seconds is, however, if accurate, not a procedure lightly undertaken. It is best performed by a computer, for example as in a program following an algorithm by Falconer (1971). This takes account of the likelihood of the stimulus falling in an interbeat interval. The average HR in a second is thus calculated from partial and whole beats weighted proportionately.

However, although HR can be calculated on a second-by-second basis, it must be recognized that in comparison to a beat-by-beat basis certain consequences arise. Some of these are discussed by Stratton (1970), who points out that misleading response curves can, for instance, be given by taking 5 secs of acceleration which might contain twelve beats and receive the same weight as 8 secs of deceleration containing the same number of beats. The difficulty is confounded where responses are averaged over subjects resulting in the possible obliteration of components in the process. Additionally, the question must be asked about whether it is reasonable to average by taking rates at successive beats with subjects having very different HR levels from which the responses start.

There is obviously a major problem in achieving 'typical' HR response curves. Averaging over subjects obliterates individual differences in response, while allowing the effects of habituation to appear and eliminating effects of sinus arrythmia. Averaging over responses within subjects again minimizes the effects of sinus arrythmia and allows the possibility of individual differences to appear, but tends to abolish information on habituation. In general, a compromise should be arrived at whereby the minimum number of responses are averaged to achieve a diminution of 'noise', with the effect of allowing other information in the signal to remain (Lang, 1971).

No easier is the problem of statistical analysis of the components of the HR response. The shape of the HR response curve depends markedly on the stimulus used to evoke it and the respiratory phase in which that stimulus is presented. It also varies widely between subjects.

In gross terms, many workers would agree with Graham and Clifton (1966) in holding that HR deceleration is indicative of orientation and acceleration indicative of a defensive response to stimulation. A further breakdown of the time scale is, however, probably required as in general the response curve can be thought to have a triphasic form (Connor and Lang, 1969). This takes the form of an early deceleration usually occurring in the first two beats, a secondary component, most usually acceleration occupying up to the next seven or eight beats, and a subsequent deceleration up to some fifteen beats. Given stimuli which elicit an orienting response, then the secondary component is one of deceleration rather than acceleration.

It is possible, following Connor and Lang (1969) to analyse this type of result using polynomial analysis of variance. However, it can be rightly objected that successive heart beats are not the independent samples of data required by analysis of variance and hence such a method may be invalid. An alternative method which has been proposed is that of Jones, Crowell and Kapuniai (1969), based on a prediction of expected values of mean and variance for post-stimulus data on the basis of pre-stimulus values. A test for deviation from predicted values may be made at each post-stimulus point. Jones, Crowell and Kapuniai (1969) provide a program for using this procedure.

The outcome of this discussion is that the usage of HR as a measure in therapeutic situations is by no means as simple as it first appears. Provided that tonic levels of heart rate and relatively long-term changes in those levels are studied, then use of the data is not too difficult. However, should it be required to use measures of phasic change, then some of the considerations detailed above must be recognized.

At all times, both in looking at slow tonic changes and at phasic changes, it is important to recognize the existence of the 'law of initial values' (Wilder, 1950, 1957), which states that the change in heart rate (or other psychophysiological measures) is a function of the value from which that change starts. The fact that heart rate is a result of interaction at the heart of dual innervation suggests that the law of initial values (LIV) is likely to be operative. The data are, however, by no means unanimous in supporting this expectation. The possibility of complications of this sort should alert the experimenter to examine his data to investigate level–response relations. Methods for analysing such data are presented by Lacey (1956), who advocated the use of an 'autonomic lability score' (Benjamin, 1963, 1967; Block and Bridger, 1962; Heath and Oken, 1962, 1965; Oken and Heath, 1963).

Heart rate variability

The discussion up to this point has been concerned with tonic and phasic aspects of heart rate. Heart rate variability has, however, increasingly become a measure of interest in its own right. Probably the first psychological work in this area was that of Lacey, Bateman and Van Lehn (1953) and Lacey and Lacey (1958), whose measure of cardiac 'bursts' (rates in 5 sec periods, greater by 6 b.p.m. than those in preceding 5 secs), although crude, was shown to be a relatively enduring individual characteristic. Cardiac lability was shown to be characteristic of the hyperkinetic-impulsive type of individual. Since that time, other measures have been advocated by Boyle, Dykman and Ackerman (1965), Burdick and Scarborough (1968), Obrist, Hallman and Wood (1964), Schacter and coworkers (1965) and Williams, Schacter and Rowe (1965), and these workers have in general noted behavioural patterns such as those described by Lacey and coworkers which differentiate cardiac labiles and stabiles.

Another direction of work was started by Kalsbeek and Ettema (1964) who showed that 'sinus arrythmia', or cardiac lability, decreased under 'mental load'. This line of investigation has been the subject of considerable investigation by ergonomists, resulting in a profusion of sophisticated methods of measurement (Luczak and Laurig, 1973; Opmeer, 1973). Perhaps the most potentially useful area of investigation is that of Sayers (1973, 1975) who has shown that spontaneous variability in heart rate is related to three major physiological factors: blood pressure control, thermal regulation and respiration. Frequency selective analysis of cardiac interbeat interval sequences allows the contribution of these factors to be isolated. Sayers' work suggests that mean heart rate and variance are unreliable indications of 'mental work' load, but variations in the cardiac interval spectrum do occur reliably.

It is recognized that some of the techniques which are recently advocated do demand facilities beyond those which are available in many laboratories. However, with the greater availabilities of cheaper laboratory computers it is important that the behaviour therapist should be aware of progress in this area.

Central mechanisms of cardiovascular activity

The pacemaker of the heart is the sino-atrial node which is innervated from the sympathetic and parasympathetic branches of the autonomic nervous system (ANS). Normally, both sets of nerves are tonically active. Sympathetic and parasympathetic tonus are controlled from cardio-acceleratory and cardio-inhibitory centres in the medulla. Section of the vagus nerves, i.e. the parasympathetic supply, increases HR by about 30 per cent.; cutting sympathetic nerves, however, decreases HR by only a few per cent. Vagus tonic control therefore on balance seems to be the more powerful.

It is not the place in this review to attempt to describe other physiological aspects such as local pH and partial pressures of carbon dioxide and oxygen in the blood which influence cardiac rate via centres in the medulla; it is, however, here where respiratory–cardiac interaction takes place. Changes in cardiac rate occur with stimulation of the hypothalamus, but it is possibly at the level of the limbic system that more interesting interactions can be seen to occur, bearing in mind those which have already been described in relation to electrodermal activity.

A number of studies (e.g. Bromley and Holdstock, 1969; Kaada, 1951; Malmo, 1961) have shown that septal stimulation results in HR deceleration. The septal area is apparently of crucial importance in pacing the hippocampal theta rhythm, which is an accompaniment of orientation (Grastyan and coworkers, 1966). It is possible that it is by this means that the HR deceleration characteristic of orienting and 'openness' to the environment (Lacey, 1967) is achieved. It should be noted, however, that Lacey espouses a mechanism whereby the attentional changes are achieved by the process of decrease in HR, lowering blood pressure, thereby lowering the pressure on carotid sinus receptors bringing about an increase in cortical activation (Bonvallet, Dell and Hiebel, 1954).

Although it has been suggested that the hippocampal signs of orientation and HR deceleration accompany septal stimulation, Sanwald and coworkers (1970) found that the decelerative HR orienting response of rats was not affected by hippocampal lesions. However, this lesion, in a similar way to that described for EDA, did appear to lessen habituation to repeated stimulus presentation. Lesions of the amygdala produce an elimination of the HR orienting reaction (Bagshaw and Benzies, 1968) in a similar way to that in which amygdalectomy abolishes SCRs.

In general, it can be said that the work on the central determinants of HR change tends to be sophisticated in its analysis of central mechanisms but less sophisticated in knowledge of the components of HR response that have been the subject of earlier discussion in this section. It is impossible, however, in the brief coverage available here to do more than cursorily cover some of the more salient and relevant points.

One type of research with considerable promise in this field is that of Scher and coworkers (1972), who attempted to distinguish between sympathetic and parasympathetic activity on the basis of latency. They state 'vagal responses are extremely fast: the response to a step increase in vagal activity may show a time constant of less than 1 second. Sympathetic responses are slower with time constants of the general order of 8 seconds'. This suggests that the short latency decelerative phase discussed in the previous section is vagally mediated and the later accelerative phase sympathetically mediated.

PSYCHOPHYSIOLOGICAL VARIABLES IN THE MEASUREMENT OF EMOTION

This section, of necessity, plunges the discussion centrally into the area of controversy of the James–Lange versus Cannon type theories of emotion in the light of more modern work in this field, which has shown that the controversy in a sense still exists (e.g. Fehr and Stern, 1970; Goldstein, 1968). However, as with the still bubbling nature–nurture argument in which contrasting groups take up untenable extreme positions, so the more exclusive and narrow ideas on the basis of the emotions are *ab initio* erroneous.

One piece of psychophysiological work which exemplifies the middle of the road, moderate, position but which unfortunately does so from rather poor experimental data is that of Edwards and Hill (1967). These authors point out that the James–Lange (1922) position holds that specific physiological patterns occur differentially during the experience of different emotions. On the other hand, the Cannon (1920) notion emphasizes that there is a state of general autonomic arousal during all emotions. Cannon's position is thus one holding the importance of the activating characterstic of the emotions in contrast to the James–Lange position which emphasizes the importance of visceral patterns. A third position, one perhaps most identified with the work of Lacey (1956), is that which holds that individuals exhibit characteristic response patterns as a result of stimulation, thus suggesting a person may on most occasions react as though he were exhibiting a certain single emotion.

Edwards and Hill (1967) set out to test the tenability of these positions by an experiment in which there were six stimulus conditions aimed at producing in the subjects a range of states from monotony to alertness. Six physiological measures were used to measure these states, and twenty-four subjects took part in the experiment, of which there were two replications.

All scores on the physiological measures were standardized and the whole experiment analysed by analysis of variance and covariance procedures. As the result of the analyses, a significant interaction between physiological measures and subjects regardless of condition or replication would be taken to support the Lacey position, a significant interaction between conditions and physiological measures would be taken to support the James–Lange position, and a conditions × subjects interaction could be taken as supportive of the Cannon position, i.e. that each subject gives a general unpatterned outflow of activation which varies in intensity with condition.

Analysis of the data showed that significant amounts of variance were attributable to each interaction term, and thus the theoretical basis of the emotions as tested in this experiment could not be ascribed to any one position. Objections to the experiment could, however, be raised in that the conditions used were insufficiently provocative of different emotional states and that the physiological measurements were insufficiently comprehensive. Nevertheless, the pattern of the experiment is one which deserves attention.

Throughout experimental work on emotions, one of the troubles, as exemplified by the Edwards and Hill experiment first discussed, is that of creating a situation which may be truly said to produce an identifiable situation. Thus the now classic experiment of Ax (1953) supporting a James–Lange position by showing a different pattern of psychophysiological response in fear-provoking and anger-provoking situations depends for its force on the extent to which the subjects were truly fearful or angry. Certainly, Ax's reports suggest that the desired emotions were achieved. Nevertheless, in another classic experiment, that of Schachter and Singer (1962) which is in part supportive of the Cannon position, the contrived emotional states of anger and euphoria seem open to misinterpretation.

It is because of this potential misidentification of emotions in contrived situations that experiments such as that of Fenz and Epstein (1967) on parachute jumping are most important. Their study nicely shows, in a 'real' situation, the physiological disturbance of the novice parachutist, his cognitive and motor disorganization, and his perceptual denial. More importantly, however, it shows how both the experience of fear and its physiological manifestations are modified in the course of experience.

In an initial study, Epstein and Fenz (1965) had novice and experienced parachutists rate the intensity of their feelings of fear at different points in time before and after a parachute jump. For the novice jumpers, the fear increased from the night before the jump, through reaching the aircraft, up to the point just before the jump. In contrast, with the experienced jumpers, for whom 'the absolute magnitude of fear at no time approaches the magnitude of fear experienced by novice parachutists shortly before a jump', the maximum experience of fear was well before the actual jump. In their main experiment Fenz and Epstein (1967) measured respiration, heart rate and skin conductance by portable apparatus, on a control day and at points leading up to the jump sequence. In all cases, the novices showed higher levels of physiological disturbance at the time of the goal act, the jump, than did the experienced jumpers. These latter showed, as with their fear ratings, their greater physiological disturbance at a time before the actual jump, the disturbance always being less than the novice jumpers' at their peak. Perhaps the most theoretically interesting aspect of the findings is that the extent to which the physiological disturbance is 'pushed back' in the jump sequence for the experienced parachutists is maximum for respiration, next for heart rate and least for skin conductance.

> If the assumption is made that an inhibitory process is responsible for the decline in response of the experienced parachutists, then respiration is inhibited first, skin conductance last, with heart rate more similar to respiration than to skin conductance. It is noteworthy that the order corresponds to what would be expected from the degree to which conscious control of and feedback from the different systems is possible (Fenz and Epstein 1967, p. 41).

These data do therefore suggest that modification of reported fear and its physiological concomitant is possible. Fenz and Epstein suggest that there is a hierarchy of alerting and inhibitory systems which provide a 'defense system in depth consisting of automatic warning signals at relatively low intensity levels'. This hierarchy 'corresponds to the degree to which the reactions can be recognized and consciously controlled'.

This work would appear to have particular consequences for theories of emotion and for behaviour therapy in particular. Firstly, it suggests that in the emotion of fear, at any rate, we have a categorizing process (Bindra, 1970) in which degree of physiological disturbance together with a circumstance recognized as fear-provoking are labelled as fearful (a similar process to that described by Schachter and Singer, 1962). Secondly, there would appear to be an interaction between the extent to which the subject gained (or wished to gain) mastery over his fear and the extent to which he was able to control the physiological concomitants of his fear. The other message which is derived from this study is that the degree of control of the physiological concomitants of fear depends on the extent to which they 'naturally' provide the necessary feedback. The study would, in fact, provide support for a bio-feedback approach to behaviour therapy, where feedback of those systems which do not naturally provide good signals is artificially provided. The study may also suggest that, if the effects of a therapeutic procedure are to be investigated, the most conservative measure of that procedure's effectiveness may be from that response system which is least prone to modification by the patient's own awareness of its status, for instance, as exemplified by this experiment, electrodermal activity.

One outcome of the Fenz and Epstein study was that in the groups of subjects studied there was a degree of parallelism between expressed emotion and the supposed physiological concomitants of that emotion. (It should, however, be noted that, in certain instances, there was in novice parachutists a dissociation between expressed emotion and perception of behavioural states. 'One novice parachutist reported that he was amazed how calm he was until he looked down and saw his knees knocking together' (Fenz and Epstein, 1967).)

A range of other studies, however, suggest that, depending on personality characteristics or disorders, there may be a dissociation between reported emotion and physiological state. The earliest of these studies would appear to be that of Landis (1932) who examined the electrodermal reactivity of a group of juvenile delinquents during work at a long 'unlearnable' pursuit rotor task. Some of the group became emotionally disturbed during the session; others remained calm. The emotional subjects showed *less* electrodermal reactivity than those who remained calm. Jones (1950) used independent ratings of children in playground situations and related these to SRR reactivity during free association tests. Subjects were divided into high reactives (upper 20 per cent. on SRR responsivity) and low reactives (lower 20 per cent. on SRR responsivity). Low reactives were rated as easily excitable, unstable and impulsive, while high reactives were rated as calm, deliberate and good-natured. More recently, work (Satterfield and Dawson, 1971) has taken place on 'hyperkinetic' children characterized by an abnormally high level of motor activity, short attention span, low frustration tolerance, and aggressive and impulsive behaviour—a more extreme version of Jones' (1950) low reactive group. Hyperkinetic children were found to have lower basal skin conductance, and fewer and smaller specific and non-specific SRRs than normal children. Interestingly, stimulant drugs produce a change toward normal electrodermal activity in the hyperkinetic children. A later study by Satterfield and coworkers (1972) showed that clinical improvement after methylphenidate treatment could be shown in those children whose EEG and EDA 'arousal' measures indicated low 'arousal', but not in those with pre-treatment high 'arousal'. The lower levels of electrodermal activity and reactivity in 'difficult' children are paralleled in a study by Davies and Maliphant (1971) of a lower level of resting HR and HR reactivity in a group of male adolescents exhibiting refractory behaviour at school. Again, therefore, the behaviourally more active subjects appear to be the physiologically least disturbed.

A further example of a dissociation between overt signs of behaviour indicating disturbance, but this time in the reverse direction, is from the field of schizophrenia. Venables and Wing (1962), for instance, showed that the higher the level of rated withdrawal among patients the higher their level of skin potential.

These studies suggest that the more physically active tend to show lower levels of measured physiological activity and vice versa. Various kinds of explanation are possible, suggesting that some physical behaviour, e.g. that of the hyperkinetic child, is 'stimulus seeking' and has the function of attempting to raise the subject's 'level of arousal' to something approaching the optimal. Another suggestion would be that the motor activity has the function of 'working off' high levels of arousal. As an example, Venables (1956) showed that, after a difficult task which acted to increase levels of skin conductance, normal subjects decreased that high level of conductance to the extent that they showed speedy performance on a subsequent easy task. Subjects rated high on 'neuroticism' were not able to do this. Data from a more recent study (Venables and Christie, 1974) suggested that, in a relaxation period after a noise avoidance stress period, normal subjects having personality scale values tending towards 'unstable introversion' had higher SPL values after the stress and showed a slower rate of decline of SPL during the relaxation period. It is possible, therefore, that to some extent the indicated low levels of arousal in the physically active, delinquent (and hence non-anxious?) group are a function of both their activity and their lack of anxiety.

These data and suggestions are not easily reconciled with other findings concerned with the dissociation between physiological and reported subjective disturbance. One very well-known study of this kind is that of Lazarus and Alfert (1964). Subjects watched a disturbing film of a painful initiation rite while their skin conductance and heart rate were measured. Those subjects denying that they experienced emotional disturbance showed greater physiological signs of disturbance than those that admitted they found the film upsetting. One measure used in this study was the represser–sensitizer scale of Byrne (1964). The repressers, who state that they are not disturbed by the threatening film but who show the greater physiological actuation, are described as calm and stable (although also as active, alert and quick), whereas the sensitizers, who say they are disturbed by the film and show least physiological disturbance, are described as easily disorganized by stress, aggressive and aloof. In another similarly relevant study, Dykman and coworkers (1963) found that subjects who reported high (test) anxiety on the Taylor scale were less reactive in heart rate than those scoring low on anxiety measures.

If primary psychopaths are taken to exemplify a group low on emotionality, as would clearly be the case from Cleckley's (1964) classic description, then it might be expected on the basis of the data reviewed above that they might show high rather than low signs of physiological activation.

The data have been extensively reviewed by Hare (1968, 1972, 1975). In brief, it can be said that, as far as electrodermal activity is concerned, the psychopath appears to be hyporeactive, particularly in the anticipation of aversive stimulation, suggesting that psychopaths experience little anticipatory fear arousal; however, in an experiment by Hare and Craigen (1974), psychopaths showed a greater phasic acceleratory HR response to anticipated shock then normals. They suggest that 'the anticipatory cardiac activity reflects an adaptive process that serves to reduce the emotional impact of the situation'. This experiment, therefore, shows the need to examine in a detailed fashion the nature of the response made in a particular situation before using psychophysiological measures uncritically as indicants of emotional behaviour.

A further example of more detailed examination of data proving useful is provided by work by Siddle, Nicol and Foggitt (1973). These workers investigated a group of antisocial adolescents, divided into three subgroups on the basis of high, medium and low antisocial behaviour. The high antisocial group showed smaller skin conductance orienting responses and faster OR extinction than the low antisocial group. So far, the data are in accord with those provided by other workers using delinquent and psychopathic groups. It was suggested, however, that these workers might rescore their data in terms of the half-recovery time of the skin conductance response (see above 'units of measurement, temporal'). It was found that the mean recovery half-times for the low, medium and high antisocial groups were 3.42, 4.82 and 6.48 seconds respectively, the difference between these values being significant (Siddle, 1972, personal communication). If, as suggested by Venables (1974), the length of the skin conductance recovery limb is possibly a measure of the extent to which the subject excludes stimulation by the process of gating (the longer the recovery limb, the greater the gating), then the long recovery shown by the high antisocial delinquents is a parallel finding to the acceleratory heart rate changes shown by Hare and Craigen (1974), discussed above.

PSYCHOPHYSIOLOGICAL MEASURES IN BEHAVIOUR THERAPY

The work reviewed up to this point has been particularly concerned to emphasize some of the areas of psychophysiology of potential importance to behaviour therapy where full knowledge of some of the difficulties of measurement and their bases in peripheral and central mechanisms might lead to a fuller understanding of therapeutic processes. Additionally there has been an examination of some of the experiments which indicate that the expectation of a close relation of psychophysiological variables and behavioural variables is possibly misconceived.

Nevertheless, psychophysiological measures are being used in behaviour therapy and it would not be in order to say that effort in this direction is misplaced. Recent reviews have covered in detail the work which has been done in the field of desensitization and other methods for the treatment of phobic anxiety (Katkin and Deitz, 1973; Lang, 1971; Mathews 1971), although the Katkin and Deitz paper is confined to work on electrodermal activity. It is interesting to note that Mathews begins his review with the statement which nicely summarizes much of what has been said earlier in this chapter: 'The importance of autonomic responses in the genesis and maintenance of fears and phobias is frequently taken for granted despite our continuing ignorance of the precise nature of the relationship between the physiological and psychological components of fear (Mathews, 1971, p. 73).'

The data reviewed earlier have suggested that no simple pattern of physiological background can be identified as giving rise to a particular emotion. Lacey's (1956) view of individual response stereotyping would suggest individual differences in response patterning. This and the view of the multifactor determination of emotional behaviour leads to the suggestion that successful therapy probably depends upon a broad-based approach, and even though a particular successful procedure may appear to employ a somewhat unitary technique it may work because that technique, of necessity, incorporates a variety of approaches. Thus the Jacobson (1938) deep muscle relaxation method employed in the Wolpe (1958) reciprocal inhibition procedure works not only because relaxation is incompatible with the expression of fear (a virtual restatement of the James–Lange position, i.e. we do not feel fear because we are too relaxed) but also because relaxation involves an overall reduction in 'arousal'. This reduction in arousal as a means of reducing fear is a statement of the Cannon position. It has been further elaborated as advantageous in desensitization in that it provides optimal conditions for habituation—extinction of response (Lader and Mathews, 1968). Given also that the reduction in arousal is induced in a therapeutic atmosphere, then the cognitive accompaniment is also appropriate and the Schachter and Singer (1962) type of experiment is repeated. More closely, however, perhaps there is a replication of the Schachter and Wheeler (1962) experiment, in which it was shown that a decrease in 'arousal' by the use of chlopromazine increased the rated enjoyment of a funny film, and pleasure is clearly incompatible with fear. As has been said earlier, however, not all subjects show the maximum physiological disturbance which accompanies their fear in the same response modality. Hence it seems important to attempt to measure activity by several channels of recording whenever possible. It is also necessary to attempt to account for the aetiology of phobic and anxious behaviour in order that perhaps a 'crutch' may be provided as a means to therapy.

Fenz and Epstein (1967), in their study of parachutists, spoke of the early warning from the feedback of systems like respiration providing a 'defense system in depth'. It is possible that such early warning is partially absent in the anxious patient and that it may be possible to provide it by bio-feedback techniques. In the psychopath, evidence has been cited earlier which suggests that the exaggerated acceleratory phasic heart rate response provides evidence of a highly tuned defensive system where anxiety is reduced to a stage where its social usefulness is minimized.

An extreme of lack of defensiveness of this kind is shown in work on schizophrenic patients (Lobstein, 1974), in which it is found that extreme heart rate deceleratory responses indicative of openness to the environment occur even to very loud noises which in normals produce the acceleration characteristic of a defensive response.

Psychophysiological measures are not of much value when taken as simple indicators of global states. However, when used to indicate aspects of the way in which the subject is coping with the environmental stimuli which are impinging on him, they may provide confirmation of insights which have been hypothesized to lie behind the mechanisms leading to the pathological behaviour which it is hoped to alleviate.

REFERENCES

Ax, A. F. (1953). The physiological differentiation between fear and anger in humans. *Psychosomatic Medicine*, **15**, 433–442.

Bagshaw, M. H., and Benzies, S. (1968). Multiple measures of the orienting reaction and their dissociation after amygdalectomy in monkeys. *Experimental Neurology*, **20**, 175–187.

Bagshaw, M. H., and Kimble, D. P. (1972). *Bimodal EDR Orienting Response Characteristics in Limbic Lesioned Monkeys: Correlates with Schizophrenic Patients.* Paper presented to a meeting of the Society for Psychophysiological Research, Boston, Massachusetts.

Bagshaw, M. H., Kimble, D. P., and Pribram, K. E. (1965). The GSR of monkeys during orienting and habituation and after ablation of the amygdala, hippocampus, and inferotemporal cortex. *Neuropsychologia*, **3**, 111–119.

Benjamin, L. S. (1963). Statistical treatment of the law of initial values (LIV) in autonomic research: a review and recommendation. *Psychosomatic Medicine*, **25**, 556–566.

Benjamin, L. S. (1967). Facts and artefacts in using analysis of covariance to undo the law of initial values. *Psychophysiology*, **4**, 187–206.

Bindra, D. (1970). Emotion and behavior theory: current research in historical perspective. In P. Black (Ed.), *Psychological Correlates of Emotion*, Academic Press, New York.

Birren, J. E., Cardon, P. V., and Phillips, S. L. (1963). Reaction time as a function of cardiac cycle in young adults. *Science*, **140**, 195–196.

Blanksby, B. A., Elliott, B. C., and Bloomfield, J. (1973). Telemetred heart rate responses of middle-aged sedentary males, middle-aged squash players and 'A' grade male squash players. *The Medical Journal of Australia* **2**, 477–481.

Bligh, J. A. (1967). A thesis concerning the processes of secretion and discharge of sweat. *Environmental Research*, **1**, 28–45.

Bloch, V., and Bonvallet, M. (1960). Le déclenchement des réponses électrodermales à partir du système réticulaire facilitateur. *Journal de Physiologie*, **52**, 25–26.

Block, J. D., and Bridger, W. H. (1962). The law of initial value in psychophysiology: a reformulation in terms of experimental and theoretical considerations. *Annals of the New York Academy of Sciences*, **98**, 1229–1241.

Bonvallet, M., Dell, P., and Hiebel, G. (1954). Tonus sympathique et activité électrique corticale. *Electroencephalography and Clinical Neurophysiology*, **6**, 119–144.

Boyle, R. H., Dykman, R. A., and Ackerman, P. T. (1965). Relationships of resting autonomic activity, motor impulsivity and EEG tracings in children. *Archives of General Psychiatry*, **12**, 314–323.

Brener, J. (1967). Heart rate. In P. H. Venables and I. Martin (Eds.), *A Manual of Psychophysiological Methods*, North Holland, Amsterdam.

Bromley, D. V., and Holdstock, T. L. (1969). Effects of septal stimulation on heart rate in vagotomised rats. *Physiology and Behavior*, **4**, 399–401.

Brown, C. C. (1967). The techniques of plethysmography. In C. C. Brown (Ed.), *Methods in Psychophysiology*, Williams and Wilkins, Baltimore.

Burdick, J. A., and Scarborough, J. T. (1968). Heart rate and heart rate variability: an attempt to clarify. *Perceptual and Motor Skills*, **26**, 1047–1053.

Byrne, D. (1964). Repression-sensitization as a dimension of personality. In B. A. Maher (Ed.), *Progress in Experimental Personality Research*, Vol. 1, Academic Press, New York.

Cannon, W. B. (1920). *Bodily Changes in Pain, Hunger, Fear and Rage*, Appleton-Century New York.

Christie, M. J., and Venables, P. H. (1971a). Sodium and potassium electrolytes and 'basal' skin potential levels in male and female subjects. *Japanese Journal of Physiology*, **21**, 659–668.

Christie, M. J., and Venables, P. H. (1971b). Effects on 'basal' skin potential level of varying the concentration of an external electrolyte. *Journal of Psychosomatic Research*, **15**, 343–348.

Christie, M. J., and Venables, P. H. (1971c). Basal palmar skin potential and the electrocardiogram T-wave. *Psychophysiology*, **8**, 779–786.

Christie, M. J., and Venables, P. H. (1971d). Characteristics of palmar skin potential and conductance in relaxed human subjects. *Psychophysiology*, **8**, 523–532.

Cleckley, H. (1964). *The Mask of Sanity*, 4th ed, Mosby, St. Louis.

Connor, W., and Lang, P. J. (1969). Cortical slow wave and cardiac responses in stimulus orientation and reaction time condition. *Journal of Experimental Psychology*, **82**, 310–320.

Darrow C. W. (1937). The equation of the galvanic skin reflex curve I. The dynamics of reaction in relation to excitation 'background'. *Journal of General Psychology*, **10**, 285–309.

Davies, J. G. V., and Maliphant, R. (1971). Autonomic responses of male adolescents exhibiting refractory behaviour in school. *Journal of Child Psychology and Psychiatry*, **12**, 115–127.

Dykman, R. A., Ackerman, P. T., Galbrecht, C. P., and Reese, W. G. (1963). Physiological reactivity to different stressors and methods of evaluation. *Psychosomatic Medicine*, **25**, 37–59.

Edelberg, R. (1967). Electrical properties of the skin. In C. C. Brown (Ed.), *Methods in Psychophysiology*, Williams and Wilkins, Baltimore.

Edelberg, R. (1970). The information content of the recovery limb of the electrodermal response. *Psychophysiology*, **6**, 527–539.

Edelberg, R. (1972a). Electrodermal recovery rate, goal-orientation and aversion. *Psychophysiology*, **9**, 512–520.

Edelberg, R. (1972b). The electrodermal system, In N. S. Greenfield and R. A. Sternbach (Eds.), *Handbook of Psychophysiology*, Holt, Rinehart and Winston, New York.

Edwards, A. E., and Hill, R. A. (1967). The effect of data characteristics on theoretical conclusions concerning the physiology of the emotions. *Psychosomatic Medicine*, **29**, 303–311.

Engel, B. T., Thorne, P. R., and Quilter, R. E. (1972). On the relationship among sex, age, response mode, cardiac cycle phase, breathing cycle phase and simple reaction time. *Journal of Gerontology*, **27**, 456–460.

Epstein, S., and Fenz, W. D. (1965). Steepness of approach and avoidance gradients in humans as a function of experience: theory and experiment. *Journal of Experimental Psychology*, **70**, 1–12.

Falconer, M. J. (1971). Program REDCAR (cardiac data reduction). Unpublished document, University of Wisconsin.

Fehr, F. S., and Stern, J. A. (1970). Peripheral physiological variables in emotion: the James–Lange theory re-visited. *Psychological Bulletin*, **74**, 411–424.

Fenz, W. D., and Epstein, S. (1967). Gradients of physiological arousal in parachutists as a function of an approaching jump. *Psychosomatic Medicine*, **29**, 33–51.

Fowles, D. C. (1973). Mechanisms of electrodermal activity. In R. F. Thompson and M. M. Patterson (Eds.), *Methods in Physiological Psychology*. Vol. 1: *Bioelectric Recording Techniques*. Part C: *Receptor and Effector Processes*. Academic Press, New York.

Fowles, D. C., and Rosenberry, R. (1973). Effects of epidermal hydration on skin potential responses and levels. *Psychophysiology*, **10**, 601–611.

Fowles, D. C., and Schneider, R. E. (1974). Effects of epidermal hydration on skin conductance responses and levels. *Biological Psychology*, **2**, 67–77.

Fowles, D. C., and Venables, P. H. (1970). The effects of epidermal hydration and sodium reabsorption on palmar skin potential. *Psychological Bulletin*, **73**, 363–378.

Goldstein, M. L. (1968). Physiological theories of emotion: a critical historical review from the standpoint of behavior theory. *Psychological Bulletin*, **69**, 23–40.

Goodall, McC. (1970). Innervation and inhibition of eccrine and apocrine sweating in man. *Journal of Clinical Pharmacology*, **10**, 235–246.

Graham, F. K., and Clifton, R. K. (1966). Heart rate change as a component of the orienting response. *Psychological Bulletin*, **65**, 305–320.

Grastyan, E., Karmos, G., Vereczkey, L., and Kellenyi, L. (1966). The hippocampal electrical correlates of the homeostatic regulation of motivation. *Electroencephalography and Clinical Neurophysiology*, **21**, 34–53.

Grings, W. W. (1973). Recording of electrodermal phenomena. In R. F. Thompson and M. M. Patterson (Eds.), *Methods in Physiological Psychology*, Vol. 1: *Bioelectric Recording Techniques*. Part C: *Receptor and Effector Processes*. Academic Press, New York.

Gruzelier, J. H., and Venables, P. H. (1972). Skin conductance orienting activity in a heterogeneous sample of schizophrenics. *Journal of Nervous and Mental Disease*, **155**, 277–287.

Hare, R. D. (1968). Psychopathy, autonomic functioning and the orienting response. *Journal of Abnormal Psychology*. (Monograph Supplement), **73**, Part 2, 1–24.

Hare, R. D. (1972). *Dissociation of Conditioned Electrodermal and Cardiovascular Responses in Psychopaths*. Paper presented to the Society for Psychophysiological Research, Boston, Massachusetts.

Hare, R. D. (1945). Psychopathology. In P. H. Venables and M. J. Christie (Eds.), *Research in Psychophysiology*, Wiley, London.

Hare, R. D., and Craigen, D. (1974). Psychopathy and physiological activity in a mixed-motive game situation. *Psychophysiology*, **11**, 197–206.

Hayes, R. W., and Venables, P. H. (1972). An accurate, direct reading, beat-by-beat, heart rate scale for measurement of the cardiac orientation reaction. *Psychophysiology*, **9**, 624–625.

Heath, H. A., and Oken, D. (1962). Change scores as related to initial and final levels. *Annals of the New York Academy of Sciences*, **98**, 1242–1256.

Heath, H. A., and Oken, D. (1965). The quantification of 'response' to experimental stimuli. *Psychosomatic Medicine*, **27**, 457–471.

Jacobson, E. (1938). *Progressive Relaxation*, University of Chicago Press, Chicago.

James, W. and Lange, C. G. (1922). *The Emotions*, Williams and Wilkins, Baltimore.

Jennings, J. R., Stringfellow, J. C., and Graham, M. (1974). A comparison of the statistical distributions of beat-by-beat heart rate and heart period. *Psychophysiology*, **11**, 207–210.

Jones, H. E. (1950). The study of patterns of emotional expression. In M. L. Reymert (Ed.), *Feelings and Emotions*, McGraw-Hill, New York.

Jones, R. H., Crowell, D. H., and Kapuniai, L. E. (1967). Change detection model for serially correlated data. *Psychological Bulletin*, **71**, 352–358.

Kaada, B. R. (1951). Somato-motor, autonomic and electrocorticographic responses to electrical stimulation of 'rhinencephalic' and other structures in primates, cat and dog. *Acta Physiologica Scandinavica*, **24**, Suppl. 83, 1–235.

Kalsbeek, J. W. H., and Ettema, J. H. (1964). Physiological and psychological evaluation of distraction stress. *Ergonomics*, **7**, 443–447.

Katkin, E. S., and Deitz, S. R. (1973). Systematic desensitization. In W. F. Prokasy and D. C. Raskin (Eds.), *Electrodermal Activity in Psychological Research*, Academic Press, New York.

Lacey, J. I. (1956). The evaluation of autonomic responses: toward a general solution. *Annals of the New York Academy of Science*, **67**, 123–164.

Lacey, J. I. (1967). Somatic response patterning and stress: some revisions of activation theory. In M. H. Appley and R. Trumbull (Eds.), *Psychological Stress*, Appleton-Century-Crofts, New York.

Lacey, J. I., Bateman, E. E., and Van Lehn, R. (1953). Autonomic response specificity. *Psychosomatic Medicine*, **15**, 8–21.

Lacey, J. I., and Lacey, B. C. (1958). The relationship of resting autonomic activity to motor impulsivity. In *The Brain and Human Behavior*, Williams and Wilkins, Baltimore.

Lader, M. H. (1967). Pneumatic plethysmography. In P. H. Venables and I. Martin (Eds.), *A Manual of Psychophysiological Methods*, North Holland, Amsterdam.

Lader, M. H. (1970). The unit of quantification of the GSR. *Journal of Psychosomatic Research*, **14**, 109–110.

Lader, M. H., and Mathews, A. M. (1968). A physiological model of phobic anxiety and desensitization. *Behaviour Research and Therapy*, **6**, 411–421.

Lader, M. H., and Montagu, J. D. (1962). The psycho-galvanic reflex: a pharmacological study of the peripheral mechanism. *Journal of Neurology, Neurosurgery and Psychiatry*, **25**, 126–133.

Landis, C. (1932). An attempt to measure emotional traits in juvenile delinquency. In K. S. Lashley, C. P. Stone, C. W. Darrow, C. Landis and L. L. Heath (Eds.), *Studies in the Dynamics of Behavior*, University of Chicago Press, Chicago.

Lang, H., Tuovinen, T., and Valleala, P. (1964). Amygdaloid afterdischarge and galvanic skin response. *Electroencephalography and Clinical Neurophysiology*, **16**, 366–374.

Lang, P. J. (1971). The application of psychophysiological methods to the study of psychotherapy and behavior modification. In A. E. Bergin and S. L. Garfield (Eds.), *Handbook of Psychotherapy and Behavior Change*, Wiley, New York.

Lazarus, R. S., and Alfert, E. (1964). Short circuiting of threat by experimentally altering cognitive appraisal. *Journal of Abnormal and Social Psychology*, **69**, 195–205.

Lobstein, T. J. (1974). Heart rate and skin conductance activity in schizophrenia, Unpublished *Ph.D. Thesis*, University of London.

Luczak, H., and Laurig, W. (1973). An analysis of heart rate variability. *Ergonomics*, **16**, 35–97.

Luria, A. R., and Homskaya, E. D. (1970). Frontal lobes and the regulation of arousal processes. In D. I. Mostofsky (Ed.), *Attention: Contemporary Theory and Analysis*, Appleton-Century-Crofts, New York.

Lykken, D. T. (1968). Neuropsychology and psychophysiology in personality research. In E. F. Borgatta and W. W. Lambert (Eds.), *Handbook of Personality Theory and Research*, Rand McNally, Chicago.

Lykken, D. T., Rose, R., Luther, B., and Maley, M. (1966). Correcting psychophysiological measures for individual differences in range. *Psychological Bulletin*, **66**, 481–484.

Lykken, D. T., and Venables, P. H. (1971). Direct measurement of skin conductance: a proposal for standardization. *Psychophysiology*, **8**, 656–672.

Malmo, R. B. (1961). Slowing of heart rate after self stimulation in rats. *Science*, **133**, 1123–1130.

Mathews, A. M. (1971). Psychophysiological approaches in the investigation of desensitization and related procedures. *Psychological Bulletin*, **76**, 73–91.

Mednick, S. A., and Schulsinger, F. (1968). Some pre-morbid characteristics related to breakdown in children with schizophrenic mothers. In D. Rosenthal and S. S. Kety (Eds.), *The Transmission of Schizophrenia*, Pergamon Press, New York.

Montagu, J. D., and Coles, E. M. (1966). Mechanism and measurement of the galvanic skin response. *Psychological Bulletin*, **65**, 261–279.

Montagu, J. D., and Coles, E. M. (1968). Mechanism and measurement of the galvanic skin response: an addendum. *Psychological Bulletin*, **69**, 74–76.

Obrist, P. A., Hallman, S. I., and Wood, D. M. (1964). Autonomic levels and lability and performance time on a perceptual task and a sensory motor task. *Perceptual and Motor Skills*, **18**, 753–762.

Opmeer, C. H. J. M. (1973). The information content of successive R–R interval times in the ECG. Preliminary results using factor analysis and frequency analysis. *Ergonomics*, **16**, 105–112.

Oken, D., and Heath, H. A. (1963). The law of initial values: some further considerations. *Psychosomatic Medicine*, **25**, 3–12.

Sanwald, J. C., Porzio, N. R., Deane, G. E., and Donovick, P. J. (1970). The effects of septal and dorsal hippocampal lesions on the cardiac component of the orienting response. *Physiology and Behavior*, **5**, 883–888.

Satterfield, J. H., Cantwell, D. P., Lesser, L. I., and Podosin, R. L. (1972). Physiological studies of the hyperkinetic child. I. *American Journal of Psychiatry*, **128**, 1418–1424.

Satterfield, J. H., and Dawson, M. E. (1971). Electrodermal correlates of hyperactivity in children. *Psychophysiology*, **8**, 191–197.

Saxon, S. A. (1970). Detection of mean threshold signals during four phases of the cardiac cycle. *Alabama Journal of Medical Sciences*, **7**, 427–430.

Sayers, B. McA. (1973). Analysis of heart rate variability. *Ergonomics*, **16**, 17–32.

Sayers, B. McA. (1975). Physiological consequences of informational load and overload. In P. H. Venables and M. J. Christie (Eds.), *Research in Psychophysiology*, Wiley, London.

Schachter, S., and Wheeler, L. (1962). Epinephrine, chlorpromazine and amusement. *Journal of Abnormal and Social Psychology*, **65**, 121–128.

Schachter, S., and Singer, J. E. (1962). Cognitive, social and physiological determinants of emotional state. *Psychological Review*, **69**, 379–399.

Schacter, J., Williams, T. A., Rowe, R., Schacter, J. S., and Jameson, J. (1965). Personality correlates of physiological reactivity to others: a study of forty-six college males. *American Journal of Psychiatry*, **121**, 12–24.

Schane, W. P., and Slinde, K. E. (1967). Continuous EKG recording during free-fall parachuting. *U.S. Army Aeromedical Research and Report*, **67**-7.

Scher, A. M., Ohm, W. M., Bumgarner, K., Boynton, R., and Young, A. C. Sympathetic and parasympathetic control of heart rate in the dog, baboon and man. *Federation Proceedings*, 1972, 31, 1219–1225.

Schultz, I, Ullrich, K. J., Frömter, E., Holzgreve, H., Frich, A., and Hegel, V. (1965). Mikropunktion und elektrische Potentialmesssung an Schweibdrusen des Menschen. *Pflügers Archiv für die gesamte Physiologie*, **284**, 360–372.

Selye, H. (1950). *The Physiology and Pathology of Exposure to Stress*, Acta Inc., Montreal.

Siddle, D. A. T., Nicol, A. R., and Foggitt, R. H. (1973). Habituation and overextinction of the GSR component of the orienting response in anti-social adolescents. *British Journal of Social and Clinical Psychology*, **12**, 303–308.

Stern, Z. M. (1974). Ear lobe photo plethysmography. *Psychophysiology*, **11**, 73–75.

Stratton, P. M. (1970). The use of heart rate for the study of habituation in the neonate *Psychophysiology*, **7**, 44–56.

Teichner, W. (1968). Interaction of behavioral and physiological stress reactions. *Psychological Review*, **75**, 271–291.

Thomas, P. E., and Korr, I. M. (1957). Relationship between sweat gland activity and electrical resistance of the skin. *Journal of Applied Physiology*, **10**, 505–510.

Venables, P. H. (1956). Some findings on the relationship between GSR and motor task variables. *Journal of General Psychology*, **55**, 199–202.

Venables, P. H. (1970). Electrolytes and behaviour in man. In R. Porter and J. Birch (Eds.), *Chemical Influence on Behaviour*, Churchill, London.

Venables, P. H. (1974). The recovery limb of the skin conductance response in 'high risk' research. In S. A. Mednick, F. Schulsinger, J. Higgins and B. Bell (Eds.), *Genetics, Environment, and Psychopathology*, North Holland, Amsterdam, and American Elsevier, New York.

Venables, P. H., and Christie, M. J. (1973). Mechanisms, instrumentation, recording techniques, and quantification of responses. In W. F. Prokasy and D. C. Raskin (Eds.), *Electrodermal Activity in Psychological Research*, Academic Press, New York.

Venables, P. H., and Christie, M. J. (1974). Neuroticism, physiological state and mood: an exploratory study of Friday/Monday changes. *Biological Psychology*, **1**, 201–211.

Venables, P. H., and Martin, I. (1967). Skin resistance and skin potential. In P. H. Venables and I. Martin (Eds.), *A Manual of Psychophysiological Methods*, North Holland, Amsterdam.

Venables, P. H., and Sayer, E. (1963). On the measurement of level of skin potential. *British Journal of Psychology*, **54**, 251–260.

Venables, P. H., and Wing, J. K. (1962). Level of arousal and the sub-classification of schizophrenia. *Archives of General Psychiatry*, **7**, 114–119.

Wang, G. H. (1957). The galvanic skin reflex: a review of old and recent works from a physiologic point of view. I. *American Journal of Physical Medicine*, **36**, 295–320.

Wang, G. H. (1958). The galvanic skin reflex: a review of old and recent works from a physiologic point of view. II. *American Journal of Physical Medicine*, **37**, 35–37.

Wang, G. K. (1964). *Neural Control of Sweating*, University of Wisconsin Press, Madison.

Wang, G. H., and Brown, V. W. (1956a). Changes in galvanic skin reflex after acute spinal transaction in normal and decerebrate cats. *Journal of Neurophysiology*, **19**, 446–451.

Wang, G. H., and Brown, V. W., (1956b). Suprasegmental inhibition of an autonomic reflex. *Journal of Neurophysiology*, **19**, 564–572.

Weiner, J. S., and Hellman, K. (1960). The sweat glands. *Biological Reviews*, **35**, 141–186.

Weinman, J. (1967). Photo plethysmography. In P. H. Venables and I. Martin (Eds.), *A Manual of Psychophysiological Methods*, North Holland, Amsterdam.

Wilder, T. (1950). The law of initial values. *Psychosomatic Medicine*, **12**, 392–401.

Wilder, T. (1957). The law of initial values in neurology and psychiatry. *Journal of Nervous and Mental Disease*, **125**, 73–86.

Williams, T. A., Schacter, J., and Rowe, R. (1965). Spontaneous activity, anxiety, and hyperkinetic implusivity. *Psychosomatic Medicine*, **27**, 9–18.

Wolpe, J. (1958). *Psychotherapy by Reciprocal Inhibition*, Stanford University Press, Stanford.

Yokota, T., Sato, A., and Fujimori, B. (1963a). Analysis of inhibitory influence of bulbar reticular formation upon sudomotor activity. *Japanese Journal of Physiology*, **13**, 145–154.

Yokota, T., Sato, A., and Fujimori, B. (1963b). Inhibition of sympathetic activity by stimulation of limbic system. *Japanese Journal of Physiology*, **13**, 137–143.

Yoshimura, H. (1964). Organ systems in adaptation: the skin. In D. B. Dill (Ed.), *Adaptation to the Environment. APS Handbook of Physiology*, section 4. Williams and Wilkins, Baltimore.

SECTION II

The Psychology of Learning

3

CLASSICAL CONDITIONING

Ian M. Evans

INTRODUCTION

Classical conditioning was the first of the twin pillars on which behaviour modification was constructed. Virtually all of the early clinical applications of learning principles were based on Pavlov's method of conditioning reflexes, the history of which has been well documented (Franks, 1969; Yates, 1970) and thus will not be pursued in this chapter. Similarly, the theoretical use in behaviour therapy of classical conditioning as an explanatory principle has been too ably argued in the past to bear repetition here: Dollard and Miller (1950) and Staats (1968a) on extensions of classical conditioning to cognitive processes; Eysenck (1957) on conditionability as a fundamental individual difference; Mowrer (1960, Wolpe (1958) and Eysenck and Rachman (1965) on classical conditioning accounts of psychopathology. The purpose of the present chapter is to survey some of the more recent empirical developments within classical conditioning in such a way as to help elucidate and preserve the mutual interpenetration of experimental research and clinical applications.

The term 'classical' conditioning was introduced by Hilgard and Marquis (1940) as an attempt to describe Pavlov's arrangement as neutrally as possible; the terms *Pavlovian* and *classical* can thus be used interchangeably, despite the fact that Pavlov used a variety of procedures not necessarily equivalent. Consider, for example, the possible differences between injecting acid directly into the dog's mouth and presenting the food dish some distance in front of him; furthermore, Gantt (1967) reports that, in all the experiments he saw in Pavlov's laboratory involving electric shock as the unconditioned stimulus (UCS), the dog was free to avoid pain by raising a paw. These three procedural differences are representative of the protracted debate that has been conducted on the separation and proper definition of classical and instrumental conditioning (Hilgard, 1967), a debate which has been sustained largely by the confusion between theoretical and procedural distinctions—as Hebb (1956), amongst others, pointed out years ago.

An excellent illustration of the difficulties with theoretically loaded distinctions between classical and instrumental is provided by classical appetitive conditioning in which the conditioned response (CR) is a motor response. In a study by Longo, Klempay and Bitterman (1964), a compound conditioned stimulus (CS) occurred prior to the discharge of grain. The CR observed in the pigeon subjects during CS-alone test trials was an increase in general activity level. Commenting on this study, Kimble (1964) objected to its being described as 'classical' conditioning, as that label 'applies only to responses of the sort which Skinner called elicited and the layman calls involuntary'. Bitterman (1964) replied that he did not see how such a definition could be feasible 'without continuous recourse to the advice of Skinner or of a consulting "layman"'. Gormezano (1972) asserted that because the CR in Longo, Klempay and Bitterman's (1964) study had to precede the UCS 'before it was received' by the subject, the response was established by instrumental conditioning, not classical. This may very well be true, but it is a *post hoc* analysis of the type he has specifically argued *against* in the case of eyelid conditioning (Gormezano and Coleman, 1973). And although classical appetitive conditioning has been common for years, when Brown and Jenkins (1968) carried out a similar procedure they called it 'autoshaping', implying that it was a new phenomenon. Staddon and Simmelhag (1971) have since admitted that 'the autoshaping procedure is operationally identical to Pavlovian conditioning'.

What, then, is the operational definition of Pavlovian conditioning? A common statement, found even in advanced texts, is that the Pavlovian paradigm is one in which the subject's behaviour has no effect on the presentation of the UCS. If this means that the CR cannot have an effect, the definition disqualifies eyelid conditioning and places under strong suspicion of eligibility even Pavlov's own favoured procedure:

> The great advantage to the organism of a capacity to react to the former stimuli [CSs] is evident, for it is by virtue of their action that food finding its way into the mouth immediately encounters plenty of moistening saliva, and rejectable substances, often nocuous to the mucous membrane, find a layer of protective saliva already in the mouth, which rapidly dilutes and washes them out (Pavlov, 1927, p. 14).

Such functional interpretations of classical conditioning have always been popular (Hull, 1929; Rescorla and Solomon, 1967; Schlosberg, 1937) and it is doubtless necessary to tease out the part played by CR consequences. But clearly, for definitional purposes, a statement must be found that makes no *a priori* assumptions. The most theoretically neutral, and the one adopted for this chapter, was put forward by Bitterman (1962); a Pavlovian arrangement may be defined as 'a sequence or conjunction of stimuli whose contiguity is independent of the animal's response'.

A common problem in behaviour therapy is the failure to distinguish clearly between classical conditioning as an explanatory mechanism and classical conditioning as a procedure, a conjunction of stimuli. A few years ago, to illustrate this problem, behaviour therapists were debating whether Mowrer and Mowrer's (1938) bell-and-pad treatment of enuresis was 'really' classical conditioning. The contingency (urination followed by ringing of the bell) is not Pavlovian by the definition above, so presumably the argument was a theoretical one: the Mowrers had hypothesized that proprioceptive cues from detrusor muscle contractions would be conditioned to waking or sphincter contraction. Without specifically testing that notion, or even running a simple non-contingent bell control group, Lovibond (1964) tried to reason that classical conditioning could not be the process and suggested instead that sphincter contraction (elicited by the bell) would be reinforced by the termination of the bell. Operationally, his resultant procedure was not much different from the Mowrers', except that the bell was changed to a more aversive hooter coming on for a shorter period of time. A comparison between the two procedures revealed no significant differences. With neither procedure was there a random bell/hooter control used.

More recently, the behaviour therapy literature has hosted a debate regarding 'classical conditioning' in Feldman and MacCulloch's treatment procedure with homosexuals (Feldman and MacCulloch, 1971). Operationally their procedure contained some Pavlovian trials and some trials having a standard avoidance contingency. Bucher and Lovaas (1968) pointed out that, given these mixed trials, it was possible that the effect was due to the Pavlovian trials. This seems to be a valid enough point and it has been frequently reiterated (Lovibond, 1970; MacDonough, 1972; Rachman and Teasdale, 1969; Thorpe, 1972). Feldman and MacCulloch's (1971) comparison between their standard treatment and a pure Pavlovian procedure is thus a comparison between Pavlovian trials mixed with avoidance and Pavlovian alone (no significant differences were found—reminiscent of Lovibond's experience in enuresis). Even if the Pavlovian trials in the original treatment package were eliminated, however, not every critic would be satisfied, because, it is argued (Rachman and Teasdale, 1969; Thorpe, 1972), classical conditioning is involved in the avoidance trials—here the theoretical begins to slip in—'the effective *process* operating in the Feldman and MacCulloch procedure ... is the *classical conditioning of anxiety*' (Rachman and Teasdale, 1969, p. 296, italics added). Before anticipatory responding develops, there are, in avoidance, CS–UCS pairings in which only UCS duration is controlled by the subject. The role of these pairings could be ascertained by a yoked control procedure in which control subjects received the sequence of CSs and UCSs (and UCS durations) received by the experimental subjects. Instead of this simple procedural control, Thorpe (1972) suggests that 'classical conditioning' would be 'unlikely' during avoidance training if the shock is delayed for 10 secs. On trials when the subject has failed to respond, the only operational difference between that suggestion and the standard avoidance trials used by Feldman and MacCulloch is the interstimulus interval (ISI)—20 as opposed to 8 secs—and a trace rather than delayed arrangement. Whatever effect these parameters might have, the Pavlovian conjunction of stimuli is the same in both procedures.

A strictly procedural definition says nothing about what response is to be considered the CR—this will be examined in the next section—but it does exclude response changes that are not a function of stimulus contiguity. Jensen (1961) has suggested that as control procedures, therefore, one should have groups receiving no stimulation, CS presentations alone, UCS presentations alone, and CS and UCS presented randomly. A more parsimonious procedure is to have one stimulus, the CS+, in contiguity with the UCS, and another stimulus, the CS−, randomly interspersed. This discrimination procedure is a within-subject control and conditioning is inferred from the difference in responding produced by the two stimuli, but the limitations become apparent when using variables conducive to flat generalization gradients. The exact procedure adopted depends to a large extent on the purposes of the study, but it is generally agreed that a minimal control requirement would be the random CS–UCS procedure.

It is extraordinary to realize that in none of the early group studies, supposedly illustrating classical conditioning applications, were controls employed. In studies involving conditioning with aversive stimuli, it would be especially important to control for pseudo-conditioning, a term coined by Grether (1938) when he observed fear responses elicited in monkeys by unpaired stimuli after the monkeys had been repeatedly exposed to a frightening explosion of flashlight powder. Backward presentation of the UCS and the CS, which some behaviour therapists have made use of, does not necessarily represent a suitable control, as human subjects show evidence of backward conditioning if they verbalize some kind of relationship between the two stimuli (see a later section).

An area that has generated considerable interest recently is the classical conditioning of sexual arousal; it provides some nice examples of problems with controls. Some studies have simply not used controls (Beech, Watts and Poole, 1971; Marshall, 1974; Rachman, 1966); others have used rather unsatisfactory ones. Barr and McConaghy (1971, 1974), for instance, used a discrimination procedure in which the CS− was paired with a moving film sequence of male nudes, the CS+ with female nudes; conditioning was inferred from the mean difference in penile volume between CS+ and CS−. The UCSs alternated at fixed intertrial intervals (ITI), so temporal cues rather than the visual CSs might have come to play a part. Herman, Barlow and Agras (1974) relied on a quite inappropriate control procedure apparently extrapolated from the operant laboratory. Three homosexual subjects were described; in each case the 'sensitization control' was backward pairing of the CS (female slide) with the UCS (homosexual film or slide) *before* the beginning of conditioning trials. In the absence of statistical analyses, it is not possible to decide whether the subjects showed systematic increase in heterosexual penile erections over conditioning trials. The procedure was confounded by instructing the subjects to imagine that they were having sexual relations with the CS and by the considerable sexual activity outside of the prolonged conditioning sessions.

Quite recently, the adequacy of classical conditioning controls was discussed by Rescorla (1967) in a very influential paper. His most important point pertains to the random and discrimination (CS+/CS−) procedures. The discrimination procedure has the problem that the CS− is likely to produce an inhibitory effect (Pavlov, 1927), and thus the difference between responding to the CS+ and the CS− is not due to associative as opposed to non-associative factors. Rescorla's identical objection to the random control is on less sure ground. He argued that the random control might also represent a negative contingency between CS and UCS, if the two stimuli are 'explicitly unpaired'. Rescorla advocated, instead, delivering the CSs (or the UCSs) for the control and the experimental subjects at the same times, but for the controls randomly distributing the UCSs (or CSs). Just how one programmes random UCSs is not entirely clear, as one must ensure that a set number of UCSs occur within a specified time interval (the duration of the study), and thus for most situations the *de facto* probability is that after a CS there will be, at some point in time, a UCS.

In defending the 'truly random procedure', Rescorla (1967) developed the view that one can describe the classical pairing not only in terms of the *contiguity* between CS and UCS but in terms of the *contingency* between the CS and UCS, and the latter is the fruitful dimension. By contingency is meant the probability of a UCS occurring, given the presence of the CS (excitatory conditioning) or the probability of a UCS not occurring (inhibitory conditioning). As, in a sequential arrangement, probabilities cannot be calculated without specifying the minimal time interval within which they must (or must not) occur, it turns out that the differences between the concept of contiguity and the concept of contingency are verbal, both being represented operationally by the traditional variables of interstimulus interval (ISI) and schedule of reinforcement.

There is empirical evidence for this position: Kremer and Kamin (1971) showed that the 'truly random' control *could* produce reliable conditioning, unattributable to non-associative effects, and that the outcome of the truly random control depended upon the average CS–UCS interval. Also, truly random control procedure can vary greatly in the actual density of stimulus events, althoug the contingency between CS–UCS remains constantly zero; density (i.e. number of random CSs and UCSs) was found to be a significant variable affecting conditioning by Kremer (1971). Burstein (1973), too, in the context of autonomic conditioning, pointed out that the random control involves no more than variable ISIs and interpolated UCSs. He further reasoned that the fixed ISIs of the conditioning procedure positively biases the likelihood of the experimenter classifying responses as conditioned. This would not, of course, be of concern to those who, like Rescorla, typically infer conditioning effects from other influence on other tasks (but see Sheldon's criticisms, 1973).

As one would expect, the manner in which conditioning is measured remains a concern irrespective of the controls used. There are advantages and disadvantages with the indirect method which will be taken up again later, because behaviour therapies usually have to rely on indirect measurement. Basic studies of classical conditioning, human autonomic conditioning in particular, are more likely to consider trial-by-trial changes in one or more response systems. As recent technical advances have been made in CR measurement, we must turn to this area and study form.

THE FORM OF THE CONDITIONED RESPONSE

The eyeblink CR

In order to decide what is the eyelid CR, certain kinds of eyelid activity must be clearly defined. Firstly, there is spontaneous blinking. The normal blink rate varies greatly, from one blink per minute to more than fifty; tension, fatigue, and most importantly the UCS, all influence blink rate. Various corrections have been suggested, but it remains likely that in most studies a number of spontaneous blinks will be scored as CRs. Secondly, beta (latency 100–250 msecs) blinks occur to light stimuli if the eye has been dark-adapted (Grant, 1945). Stimulus change will also elicit a startle type of blink—the 'alpha' blink—with a short latency of 10–100 msecs.

At the other end of the latency range occur the UCRs—20–60 msecs after the UCS, but longer latencies of 100–200 msecs are not uncommon. If UCSs are presented alone, the latency decreases over the first few trials and then starts to increase. Interestingly, one of the earliest consequences of CS–UCS pairings is a reduction in UCR latency (Martin and Levey, 1966), but this would not normally be scored as a CR unless the latency was shorter than the likely latency of the reflexive UCR, and in practice many experimenters require the blink to antedate the onset of the UCS. Evans (1970) reported that the first CR, using these latency criteria, was most frequently a small, slow, beginning eye closure; these would possibly have developed into discrete blinks had not the UCS intervened to produce the UCR, masking further potential developments. The only way to determine this is by means of test trials of CS presented alone. Findings from just such an analysis have recently been reported by Levey and Martin (1974). They show that the first CR to emerge could be either just prior to the UCS or shortly after the UCS—the latter they call the *UCR*. The important observation regarding the early CRs is that they differ from the UCRs in that they are substantially smaller and have slower recruitment times. And what is most interesting of all is that after the first CRs begin to emerge, their shape changes and develops with subsequent trials in the manner thoroughly documented by Martin and Levey (1969). Briefly, they have described how CR latency decreases and amplitude increases until eventually the CR is placed such that, at the moment the air-puff would strike the cornea, the eye is fully closed. Martin and Levey (1969) argue that the 'end-point of eyelid conditioning is a smooth, well blended CR that has not only done most of the work of the UCR but has upstaged it by actually attenuating the unpleasant air-puff'. So well integrated is this CR–UCR complex that if both CR and UCR components can be observed at the end of acquisition, both CR and UCR can be observed in extinction. The validity of this phenomenon has been corroborated by Evans (1973).

There is a great deal of circumstantial evidence that this blended form of the CR is shaped (Prokasy's term, 1965) by the avoidance contingency. For instance, the degree of eye-closure at air-puff impact time is more directly related to UCS intensity than CR frequency (Evans, 1970); if the ISI is lengthened the CRs occurring at the original latency begin to extinguish and CRs emerge at a latency that will allow them to overlap the UCS. (But note that this phenomenon occurs even when the CR is movement of the rabbit's nictitating membrane which closes only partially over the cornea; Smith, 1968. See also Gormezano and Coleman, 1973, for a critique of this issue.) In Spence's laboratory it became a common practice to separate those subjects whose CRs were short latency, had rapid recruitment, and overlapped with the UCR, from those that gave the characteristic long latency, discrete CR. The former were thought to be 'voluntary' responders (Vs) and the latter 'conditioned' responders (Cs). The V form of the CR might simply represent a later stage of CR development; Gormezano (1965) challenged the validity of the whole V–C distinction. Nevertheless, some subjects do just screw up their eyes, remove the air-puff nozzle, deflect the puff with a finger or simply leave the experiment. In eyelid conditioning, therefore, one must contend with a complex array of response changes as a function of CS–UCS pairings, from minor modifications of the UCR to complex CR–UCR integrations, to more obvious avoidance responses, any detail of which may be independently susceptible to the specific parameters of the study.

The heart beat CR

The form of the conditioned heart beat is in many ways a simpler problem than the eyeblink CR, as interest is focused on the change in response rate, rather than on the beat itself, i.e. the strength of the contraction. In human subjects, the heart rate UCR to a painful stimulus (electric shock, for instance) is acceleration followed by deceleration; the UCR is decelerative when the UCS is a sexual stimulus or a bout of exercise. Raskin, Kotses and Bever (1969) noted that if the auditory UCS was very intense, acceleration is immediate, whereas at lower decibel levels the first two heart beats following the stimulus were decelerative—they suggested the short latency deceleration was an oreinting response (OR) and the acceleration was a defensive reflex. The most frequently observed form of the heart rate CR is biphasic: acceleration following the CS, replaced by deceleration shortly before the time of the UCS, whether it is aversive or not. Rather long ISIs have to be used to observe this biphasic effect—something in the region of 7 secs. It might also be noted that cardiac deceleration occurs even when the UCS intensity is greatly increased. Obrist, Wood and Perez-Reyes (1965) compared groups receiving a painful, 2 mA shock with those receiving an almost unbearable 4 mA shock. Deceleration prior to UCS onset was observed in both cases.

A major complication in considering the form of the heart rate (HR) CR is that it is directly influenced by respiration and somatic movements. The significance of the latter will be discussed in the next section; the former problem, that of respiration, is usually considered a matter of control. Westcott and Huttenlocher (1961) required their subjects to breathe at a certain rate and depth and found initial rapid HR acceleration of about 8 b.p.m., followed by deceleration of 10 b.p.m. (see also Deane, 1964). Wood and Obrist (1964) and Obrist, Wood and Perez-Reyes (1965), however, found that if *depth* of respiration was carefully controlled, the initial acceleratory phase of the CR failed to appear. Another method of controlling breathing is to require subjects to maintain controlled inspiration during each conditioning trial; the problem here is that sustained inspiration increases HR over the basal level, which before tachometers were widely employed was the reference level used for showing HR increases at CS onset. Not only is tonic level changed by sustained inspiration, but if it is initiated at CS onset there are phasic changes as the heart responds, and then stabilizes, to the alteration in respiration.

As in the case of eyelid conditioning, the definition of *the* CR in cardiac conditioning is quite arbitrary. Beecroft (1966), writing some years ago, suggested measuring the rate in the interval from 2–5 secs following CS onset. In the light of what we now know about the general form of the changes taking place during the CS–UCS interval, one is obliged to consider all the modifications in response that result from the pairings of CS and UCS.

The skin resistance CR

Defining the form of the galvanic skin response (GSR) CR has been a matter of considerable debate, largely because of the fact that there is a healthy drop in skin resistance to the occurrence of any novel stimulus or the absence of a familiar one—a component of the general orienting reflex (OR). In a provocative and now classic paper, Stewart and coworkers (1961) challenged the validity of GSR conditioning studies up to that date. They argued that unless the ISI was quite long, one would simply be observing, once the conditioning trials were instituted, the reappearance of a habituated OR to the CS. Using a long (7.5 sec) ISI, Stewart and coworkers (1961) identified three different components of the conditioned GSR. They labelled these, perhaps prematurely, in the following manner: the first was the OR to the CS, the second was the anticipatory response, and the third (occurring on test trials) was the 'response to shock in the absence of shock'. As Lockhart and Grings (1963) were quick to point out, whether or not dishabituation of an OR represents pseudo-conditioning or true conditioning cannot be argued by fiat—the only way to tell is to use pseudo-conditioning comparison groups, which Stewart and coworkers (1961) did not do.

Studies using a differential conditioning procedure (Lockhart and Grings, 1963; Martin, 1965; Prescott, 1964) provide evidence that the short latency responses do occur to the CS+ at a greater frequency than to the CS−. Lockhart gave a description of the three-component GSR observed with adequate controls: a CS response (CS-R) of latency 1 to 4 secs after CS onset;

a pre-UCS response (Pre-UCS-R) occurring 4 secs after $\overline{\text{CS}}$ onset up to 1 sec post-UCS onset; and a post-UCS response (Post-$\overline{\text{UCS}}$-R) occurring 1 to 4 secs after UCS time when the UCS is not presented. A similar trio has been reported by Prokasy and Ebel (1967) with an 8 sec ISI. Dengerink and Taylor (1971) have claimed that the Pre-UCS-R component of the conditioned GSR occurs only when shock is the UCS and not when other stimuli such as loud noises are used. From this finding they argued that the Pre-UCS-R component is a protective reflex seen only where there is specific danger to the skin. However, there are studies showing this component *does* occur with loud noise UCSs (see, for example, Lockhart, 1973). If the Pre-UCS-Rs are not time-locked to the period immediately preceding the UCS, there may be increased spontaneous fluctuations. As for the Post-$\overline{\text{UCS}}$-R, the existence of this response (called the 'perceptual disparity' response by Grings, 1960) renders somewhat dubious the use of test trials or extinction procedures for the observation of CRs unless the various components are kept separate (Badia and Defran, 1970), and that requires long CS–UCS intervals. One solution is to use as a control group Badia and Defran's (1970) experimental group: two neutral stimuli, tone and light, were paired, which resulted in steady habituation until the tone was presented alone, at which point a large GSR was observed.

An important purpose in presenting this brief look at the form of three different CRs is to show how different response systems have quite different problems of measurement and interpretation, and how, despite substantial descriptive progress, there is still much disagreement regarding fundamental issues such as the criteria for a CR. If this is true for the time-honoured response systems such as eyeblinking, GSR and heart rate, then how much more problematic might one regard such recent interests in behaviour therapy as penile erection, where no groundwork has been done on the issues of spontaneous fluctuations, voluntary and involuntary response (see Zuckerman, 1971), rate of return to baseline and sensitization.

Agreed-upon criteria for the CR are also essential for any discussion of optimal variables. Behaviour therapists are often exhorted to arrange parameters to be optimal for conditioning. This sounds like very reasonable advice; unfortunately, these variables are not known, as they vary dramatically according to the species and the response system (see the next section), quite apart from inconsistencies in the scoring criteria. For these reasons, too, the concept of conditionability (Eysenck, 1957) cannot be based on the findings of one or two response systems. Eysenck (Eysenck and Levey, 1972) has refined his conditioning postulate to a superiority in conditioning for introverts over extraverts only when factors generally retarding conditioning are operative (e.g. weak UCS, long CS–UCS intervals and partial reinforcement); this refers only to eyelid conditioning under a masking procedure scored only as to frequency of CRs identified by preconceived criteria. In addition to seeing classical conditioning as a unitary phenomenon, behaviour therapists often assume that classical conditioning is a simple process which mediates more complex behaviours. As the relationship between classically conditioned responses and other behaviour has received a good deal of research attention in recent years, we shall turn next to that topic.

THE SOMATIC CORRELATES OF CLASSICAL CONDITIONING

Before considering the recent literature on somatic correlates of classical conditioning, it is worth recalling that the data have been generated by attempts to answer seemingly quite different questions. One of these has been the possibility that classically conditioned autonomic responses are simply by-products of somatic movements. The most extreme proponent of this view has been Smith (1954), who stated that 'every "conditioned visceral response" is in reality an artifact, an innate accompaniment of the skeletal responses inculcated by the conditioning process' (p. 217). Smith suggested that the CS causes the subject to brace himself against the forthcoming shock, a response likely to cause a GSR or change in HR. As shall be shown, there is little support for this extreme version, but there are considerable data showing the interdependence of the two types of responding.

Heart rate is a response system that is a particularly integral part of skeletal activity. It was shown earlier that HR bears some relation to respiration rate; however, studies by Obrist and his colleagues show that movement has the greatest influence. In dogs, for example, the cardiac CR is acceleration, and dogs, unlike human subjects, tend to struggle just before shock delivery. Using an aversive conditioning procedure, cardiac deceleration was associated with the cessation of background somatic activities; physiological (electromyograph) measures of such movements (EMG), reveal that their decrease corresponds closely to HR deceleration. When investigating the EMGs of human subjects in classical aversive conditioning situations, it was found that these subjects did not tense up just prior to shock. The few subjects who did respond in this way showed an accelerative cardiac CR (Obrist, 1968; Obrist, Webb and Sutterer, 1969). In a conditioned suppression paradigm involving rats, HR changes mirrored the somatic operant response, whereas electrodermal responses to the CS+ were similar whether the operant was suppressed, remained unchanged or increased in frequency (Roberts and Young, 1971).

Fitzgerald and Teyler (1970) pointed out that studies using unrestrained rats have tended to report HR acceleration as the CR, whereas studies using harnesses, attached electrodes, and so on, have typically reported deceleration. In cats, whether restrained or not, the HR CR is deceleration. This deceleration has been found to be closely related to an overall activity measure (activity decreases prior to the UCS in free-ranging cats), but does not correlate consistently with EMG and respiration. This is probably because HR adjusts to the sum of somatic movements, so a specific EMG measure from one group of muscles might or might not be related to the general somatic level (Howard and coworkers, 1974).

Obrist (Obrist, Sutterer and Howard, 1972) feels that the relationship between HR and somatic activity can be understood on simple metabolic grounds: the metabolic needs of striate muscles are met, in part, by adjustments of cardiac output such as alterations in heart rate. In general, Obrist and his associates speak of the 'coupling' of cardiac and somatic events; they argue that HR reflects variation in vagal, not sympathetic, activity, and they consider cardiovascular events cannot be linked in a direct or unidimensional way to emotionality. Black and de Toledo (1972) have adopted a very similar viewpoint based on the findings from an ingenious training procedure in which dogs were either trained to respond actively to avoid shock or to hold still to avoid shock. It was shown clearly that when the CS was an S^D for responding, both HR and EMG increased considerably. When the CS was a signal to refrain from movement, HR and EMG remained at baseline levels. The argument of these authors that HR does not provide an appropriate measure of conditioned fear has considerable implications for behaviour therapy, in which fear or anxiety tends to be equated with autonomic measures such as HR and GSR. In a study on phobic patients of the relationship between some overt escape response and HR in a contrived situation, Leitenberg and coworkers (1971) reported that 'therapeutic constraints' prevented the use of controls for interactions between skeletal activity and HR. But clearly, in the absence of such controls, no legitimate statement about anxiety, based on HR, could be made. Finding little systematic relationship between autonomic and behavioural measures of anxiety, behaviour therapists often interpret autonomic indices as one of three (together with cognitive and overt motor) behavioural 'systems' of anxiety (for general discussions, see Lang, 1969; Lazarus, 1968; Mathews, 1971; Venables, this volume); conditioning studies do not support an anxiety trinity of this kind.

Another way of approaching the problem is to record a number of responses concomitantly and examine their covariation over trials. The rabbit's nictitating membrane (NM) has provided a suitable somatic response as it can be elicited by electric shock delivered near the eye. It has been shown that the HR CR appears within ten trials or fewer, whereas the NM CR required more than seventy-five trials for its elaboration (Yehle, 1968). It should be noted that CR in this study refers to the appearance of differential responding between CS + and CS − ; the initial deceleration observed in HR decreased (reverted to the baseline) steadily over acquisition trials, whereas the frequency of NM CRs increased during acquisition. Schneiderman (1972), in a review of this and other studies from his laboratory, suggested that conditioned freezing occurred within a few trials, thus interfering with the development of the NM CR and resulting in early detection of HR deceleration. Some supporting evidence comes from a cat study by Bruner (1969): basically, he demonstrated that body tremors and HR both decreased within a few conditioning trials, whereas leg-flexions did not condition until later. Two things become immediately apparent from these findings. One is further evidence against studying autonomic responses concomitant with active avoidance responses to determine the validity of two-factor interpretations of avoidance learning. The other is additional proof that studies of conditionability (assessed by speed of CR acquisition) are likely to have serious flaws unless a number of response systems are recorded simultaneously or between-group comparisons are made under strictly identical conditions.

In discussing the form of the CR in the previous section, it was intimated that the CR may have some kind of direct consequence for the reception of the UCS. In considering the somatic correlates of autonomic conditioning, the same issue appears as an undercurrent to most of the studies just mentioned. Even if the autonomic response is not simply a correlate of preparatory skeletal responses, there may be subtler forms of preparation possible, e.g. preception. Preception is a term coined by Lykken (1959) to account for the observation that the pairing of a shock UCS with a warning signal (CS) serves to reduce the magnitude of the GSR elicited by the shock. Preception specifically refers to the hypothetical 'tuning out' of afferent input (that would be negative preception), which then supposedly reduces the noxiousness of the UCS, which in turn diminishes the UCR. One obvious problem is that the CS may elicit a GSR which directly interferes with the UCR—Lykken himself has reported that the phenomenon is greater with a 5 sec ISI than with a 30 sec ISI. Lykken, Macindoe and Tellegen (1972), however, reasoned that if the phenomenon was due simply to interference there should be a negative correlation between the magnitude of the CR and the UCR, which there was not; Furedy and Klajner (1974) pointed out that the lack of negative correlation may be due to the overriding change in electrodermal responsivity that occurs over trials.

Conditioned diminution of the UCR is a term that began to be used in the literature following observations, independent of Lykken's, that the magnitude of the eyelid UCR began to decrease once the CR was elaborated (Kimble and Dufort, 1956; Kimble and Ost, 1961). Demonstration of a similar effect in other response systems, such as salivation and HR, led to the interpretation of these effects by use of the concept of inhibition (see Kimmel, 1966). Inhibition of delay (Pavlov, 1927) is usually introduced to explain the increase in CR latency and the decrease in CR magnitude that occurs during conditioning with long ISIs. This inhibition is assumed then to spread, causing the UCR to decrease. Although response interference is a more parsimonious explanation, there are aspects of the phenomenon that might specifically interest the behaviour therapist. Kimmel (1970) has suggested that the diminution of the CR with reinforced trials reflects the inhibition of anxiety which is quite ineffective in dealing with the shock UCS. The subject is thought to 'manage' his conditioned fear. (Put crudely, there is no point having the discomfort of anxiety in addition to having to put up with the unpleasantness of the shock.) In addition, however, inhibiting anxiety has the extra benefit of, in turn, inhibiting the fear/anxiety to the shock (the UCR). If conditioned anxiety is effective in removing the shock altogether, then it might continue rather than be inhibited. Kimmel (e.g. Bishop and Kimmel, 1969) found that if the UCS is removed one or two trials after the CR has reached its peak magnitude, it takes a great length of time (over fifty trials) before the CR extinguishes; that is considerably larger than normally reported and might interest the applied conditioner who attempts to maximize resistance to extinction in aversion therapy. Further judgement regarding this phenomenon should be suspended until the influence of cognitive variables on GSR conditioning has been discussed.

In the preceding analysis, absence of CR (inhibition) is thought to attenuate discomfort, but it is more commonly argued that the presence of the CR has this effect (see 'Introduction'). In other words, the CR is some sort of preparatory adaptive response (PAR) of a subtle kind, and it is this which results in subjects preferring signalled over unsignalled shocks. In fact, the evidence for preference for signalled shocks remains doubtful. Furedy and Doob (1971a) asked their subjects whether they preferred the signalled or unsignalled shock; most reported that they did not care (this was true for high or low shock intensities). When these findings were replicated (Furedy and Doob, 1971b), Furedy argued that the original observations regarding such preferences (Lanzetta and Driscoll, 1966) may have been due to couching the question in emotionally loaded terms of 'information' versus 'no information'. In the case of animals, who care less about appearances, the preference was shown when shock was unscrambled and therefore modifiable (Perkins and coworkers, 1966); the phenomenon does not occur with scrambled grid electrodes (Biederman and Furedy, 1970).

Whether they prefer it or not, human subjects might nevertheless *experience* the signalled shock as less aversive. Furedy's admirably systematic research programme has repeatedly failed to find shock intensity or aversiveness ratings, taken throughout the duration of the study, to be higher for unsignalled shock (Furedy and Doob, 1971a, 1971b) or when the ratings were taken afterwards (Furedy and Chan, 1971). As Furedy and Doob (1972) remarked in their summary of these studies, the failure to find an effect has occurred with various ISIs, UCS intensities, UCS durations, subjects and indices of aversiveness, whether during or after the conditioning.

In view of the apparent absence of the two phenomena they are supposed to explain, the search for PARs would seem to be a trifle superfluous. Nevertheless, Furedy has approached this issue from a viewpoint that relates very closely to negative preception and conditioned diminution—he calls it the regression hypothesis—that there will be a negative correlation between CR magnitude and perceived intensity of the UCS if the CR somehow prepares the subject. Furedy and Doob (1971a, 1971b) disconfirmed the regression hypothesis with respect to both GSR and pulse volume change (VPC) CRs. Furedy favours his form of the hypothesis over the closely related form already discussed—that there will be a negative correlation between CR frequency (of magnitude) and UCR magnitude—for the reason that UCR is confounded with the CR, at least in the case of GSR conditioning. As one way around this problem, Furedy and Klajner (1972) used a secondary differential signal which indicated to the subject whether the subsequent shock would be signalled or not. In this, as in all the other Furedy studies, potential indicators of aversiveness of shock are independently validated according to their ability to differen-tiate UCS intensities of 1.0 as opposed to 2.5 mA. In this study, only GSR at CS offset and VPC at CS onset were validated, but neither of them reflected UCR differences between signalled and unsignalled UCSs. The major limita-tions of this study is that the 10 sec secondary signal might have been sufficient to reduce subjective aversiveness and the 0.5 sec primary signal might have been too short to allow preparatory responses to be conditioned.

Furedy's consistent findings regarding GSR conditioning do not necessarily run contrary to preparatory adaptive interpretations of other CRs, particularly motor responses (Culler, 1938; Loucks and Gantt, 1938; Wagner, Thomas and Norton, 1967), so while it is sometimes tempting to think that autonomic conditioning might be a by-product of such motor behaviour, the evidence indicates that this is not so. Nor does it seem that the reinforcement for the CR comes from more subtle protection from the UCS, such as negative preception. What is evident is that there is an inevitable interrelationship between bodily responses during conditioning. A useful research strategy, therefore, might be not to attempt to measure the CR directly but to examine the consequences, for subsequent motor responding, of introducing a CS that has previously been paired with a UCS in a Pavlovian procedure. This can be done with both positive and negative UCSs and with behaviours controlled both by positive and aversive stimuli, and are sometimes called 'transfer of control' studies. In the next section, we will look only at the special case in which the CS is paired with aversive UCSs or their termination.

THE CLASSICAL CONDITIONING OF FEAR AND RELIEF

There are several justifications for selecting fear conditioning as a research area for special examination. First of all, as mentioned above, fear is commonly equated with autonomic activation, yet GSR, HR and other such indices are not usually measured directly in the animal literature; fear is more typically inferred, as it so often must be clinically, from the impact of the CS on various ongoing activities of the subject. Then again, fear conditioning itself is of primary relevance to behaviour therapy and has for a long time provided the chief explanatory model for neurotic behaviour and the *raison d'être* for aversion therapy.

It should be made clear at this juncture that the active avoidance paradigm does *not* provide a good analogy to clinical neurosis, as is so often supposed in behaviour therapy (Eysenck and Rachman, 1965; Wilson and Davison, 1971); nor was it thought to do so in early behaviour therapy theorizing (Wolpe, 1971, discusses this further). The avoidance procedure involves two relationships: that between the warning signal and the shock and that between the avoidance response and the shock. Until the avoidance response occurs, the procedure is identical to the Pavlovian arrangement. Notice that this is a descriptive statement, not the two-factor theory of avoidance. In most studies, the response–shock avoidance contingency is clearly important, as revealed by the poorer performance of yoked controls who receive just the CS and UCS patterns of the avoidance group or by the poorer performance of groups receiving simply classical CS–UCS pairings (brief UCSs). Partial exceptions to the latter case are human eyelid conditioning (Gormezano, 1965) and shuttle responding in the goldfish (Scobie and Fallon, 1974; Woodard and Bitterman, 1973), in which the UCS to shock and the shuttle response are both increases in general activity. In general, however, the response–shock avoidance contingency is crucial. There is no such contingency, by definition, in human neurosis.

Given these observations, the value of the two-factor account of avoidance learning is of little *direct* interest to behaviour therapy, despite claims to the contrary (Costello, 1970; Franks and Wilson, 1973). Many studies of 'fear reduction' (Wilson and Davison, 1971; also Baum, this volume) in animals are of doubtful value to behaviour therapy, in this author's opinion, because their intent is usually to reduce *avoidance* behaviour, which can probably be done without affecting the 'fear'—reversing the response–shock avoidance contingency, for instance, or making the extinction contingency (shock removal) more highly discriminable. Working with human subjects in the author's laboratory, Montgomery (unpublished) noted rapid elimination of avoidance behaviour once the subject discovered the shock was disconnected. A rough analogy might be the client who firmly believes there will be some unpleasant consequences if he fails to avoid—such individuals should be persuaded to test reality to discover that there is no 'shock' contingency. But the general run of neurotic patients avoid anxiety, not shock, and so it is the effects on behaviour of classical fear conditioning that are most closely related to clinical neurosis.

In the experimental study of conditioned fear, there are four common behavioural measures which have been treated very well by McAllister and McAllister (1971) and so will be described here only briefly. The procedure that most resembles a clinical phobia is the escape from fear eliciting stimuli, a representative experiment being Miller's (1948) black–white compartment box, although in that particular study the UCS in each of the ten classical conditioning trials was terminated by the rat's escape response. It is also now clear that the nature of the fear response directly determines the ease with which an effect on escape behaviour may be shown; the rat's tendency to crouch (or freeze) in certain situations (Bolles, 1970) means that it is sometimes easier to show the effect on failure to approach a CS rather than on tendency to escape (Blanchard and Blanchard, 1968). A second procedure is to condition fear to a CS and then observe the effect, on a positively rewarded bar-press response, of contingent presentation of that CS. The procedure could be referred to as conditioned punishment, as it is logically identical to the empirical demonstration of conditioned reinforcement. A third general procedure is the well-known Estes and Skinner (1941) 'conditioned suppression' arrangement, in which the CS for fear disrupts the rate of an ongoing operant response, probably due to interference by competing overt fear responses (Miller, 1951). It is becoming increasingly common to observe the effects on Sidman avoidance schedules, in which *increases* in rate are taken as evidence of fear (this is not illogical as fear CSs retard *acquisition* of an avoidance response); the procedure is thus best referred to as a change of rate measure. The operant term 'conditioned emotional response' is most unfortunate as it suggests that this is the only method of determining emotional conditioning. The fourth method is to examine the effects of a fear CS on the magnitude of some unconditioned response (Brown, Kalish and Farber, 1951; Spence and Runquist, 1958); this is sometimes known as the probe stimulus method.

With the possible exception of the probe stimulus technique, these procedures used with human subjects tend to be very susceptible to experimenter demand and other social influence variables: see, for example, the problems with the escape from fear measure known as the direct behaviour avoidance test (Bernstein, 1973; Bernstein and Nietzel, 1974; Smith, Diener and Beaman, 1974). Staats (1968b), under the name A-R-D theory, has restated the argument on which the above-mentioned procedures were based: A refers to the attitudinal or hypothetical emotional response evoked by a given stimulus; R refers to the reinforcing value of a given stimulus—usually punishment when the emotion is fear (procedure 2); and D refers to the discriminative stimulus value—in the case of fear conditioning the fear CS is an S^D for escape (procedure 1). Again, the problem of conformity to demand characteristics remains a pressing problem. Studies relying on change of rate measures with human subjects have been unsuccessful because of large individual differences; Sachs and Keller (1972) found some subjects who showed almost complete suppression of a positively reinforced matching task and some who showed none. Although somewhat less murky, the animal research is also complicated by the fact that, particularly in the rate-change situation, the behaviour used to assess the CS effects has to be maintained by reinforcement, punishment and deprivation variables, which are often not consistent from study to study and which obviously affect the sensitivity and reliability of the measure. A very major limitation of the conditioned suppression situation is that the CS–UCS pairing is often superimposed on the operant training. There is conclusive evidence that fear can be conditioned to static apparatus cues and that this in turn would influence response rate (Brimer and Kamin, 1963; Kamin, 1965; McAllister and McAllister, 1971).

Having shown the similarity between procedures often encountered in behaviour therapy and those relied upon in the laboratory study of fear conditioning, it is necessary to confirm that in the animal literature (which has used the escape from fear and rate-change measures predominantly) the conventional empirical relationships between CSs and aversive UCSs have been observed and there are no special surprises. CS and UCS intensities are important determinants; however, quite long ISIs are effective (see Bitterman and Schoel, 1970). One interesting phenomenon, while not new, has been subject to recent experimental attack. Years ago, Harlow (1937) conditioned monkeys to fear a bell by pairing it with a snake blow-out (the party type). He then completely adapted the monkeys to the UCS by blowing it out slowly with bits of food on it. After this, however, the fear response to the bell was not only intact but extremely resistant to extinction. Rescorla (1973), relying on a conditioned suppression procedure, was able to show that 'habituation' trials (noise UCS alone) *did* affect subsequent responding to the CS: extinction was more rapid. (The 'habituation' trials seem odd, though, as when presented *before* conditioning they did not retard acquisition to the CS.) Partial confirmation of Harlow's finding did emerge, however, when it was found that a higher-order CS remained unaffected by UCS habituation (Rescorla, 1973; Rizley and Rescorla, 1972). Here there seem to be some possibly promising analogies of the origins of neurotic fear.

Probably the most influential contribution to fear conditioning in the past few years has been Rescorla's notion of 'contingency' discussed in the introduction. A CS which signals the non-occurrence, or reduced probability, of an aversive event should become an inhibitory stimulus for fear; operationally these arrangements are the ones supposed to produce conditioned relief, which will be mentioned again presently. In an early demonstration of conditioned inhibition, Rescorla and LoLordo (1965) trained dogs to shuttle to avoid shock delivered on a Sidman avoidance schedule. Increases in speed of shuttling were used to infer fear, on the assumption that the behaviour is fear-motivated. The classical conditioning procedure was CS_1 followed by either a shock or CS_2. According to Rescorla (1969) CS_1 tended to *predict* shock and CS_2 to *predict* no shock. CS_1 increased the rate of shuttling and CS_2 decreased it. In another study, CSs or shocks were each presented alone, but always separated by intervals of 1.5 to 2.5 minutes; occurrence of the CS was thus supposed to predict a shock-free period of at least 1.5 minutes and did, in fact, reduce shuttle-box response rate.

Seligman, Maier and Solomon (1971) have interpreted such phenomena somewhat differently. Just as CS+ is a signal for danger, so the inhibitory stimuli described above are safety signals (in Mowrer's terms). Assuming (incorrectly, as was shown earlier) that preference for signalled shock is a well-established phenomenon, these authors explain it as follows: general anxiety is reduced because the subject can relax between shocks if each one is signalled; in other words, 'safety' is signalled by the absence of the CS. If no safety signal is presented, the organism will remain in chronic fear. McAllister and McAllister (1971) argued that there is no such thing as *un*signalled shock, or free shock, as in these situations static apparatus cues become CSs for fear whenever the UCS is sufficiently intense. Thus the empirical observation that rats receiving 'unsignalled' shocks are under greater stress (produce more ulcers), show greater interference on other tasks and fail to develop conditioned fear to a CS when it *is* introduced (Seligman, 1968) can be accounted for by fear conditioning to apparatus cues, rather than to the 'relief' experienced by the signalled-shock animals.

The concept of relief goes back, of course, to Mowrer (1938) and Curtis (1937); the obvious question still remaining is the plausibility of the relief concept as opposed simply to conditioned inhibition of fear, which is really a more neutral theory referring mainly to the behavioural indices being of opposite sign to those of fear conditioning. (The conditioned inhibition concept—i.e. below zero CR strength—is supported directly in a study of rabbits by Marchant and Moore in 1974. This inhibitory stimulus retarded subsequent NMR acquisition.) Firstly, there are some reports that relief can be directly observed (e.g. heart rate in dogs decreases rapidly after shock termination: Church and coworkers, 1966; Leslie Weiss, however, in an unpublished work from the author's laboratory, was not able to find psycho-physiological evidence for the familiar 'sigh of relief', possibly because the shock was not sufficiently intense or prolonged). Denny (1971) claims that rats display short latency relief responses (5 sec latency, 10–15 sec duration), followed by, if there is no further aversive stimulation, easily detectable relaxation responses (latency 25–40 secs) when the animal begins to investigate, move around, manipulate, etc. Stimuli presented during either of these phases will later, when associated with the shock region of a new apparatus, retard acquisition of an avoidance response. In the same synthesis of his work, Denny speculates that, in chronically anxious individuals, circumstances may somehow have contrived to condition anxiety to proprioceptive relaxation cues—possibly aversive events delivered just about the time the individual is beginning to relax after the previous punishment.

Attempts to condition relief responses were reported very early in behavior therapy (Wolpe, 1958). Since then, numerous studies have appeared in the clinical literature, none of them, however, showing unequivocally either the specific value of the therapeutic strategy or the exact role of conditioned relief (Barlow, 1973). In the only treatment study to have had a random shock control, no outcome differences were found between the control and the aversion relief subjects (Solyom and coworkers, 1972). One of the most systematic uses of the aversion relief concept has been Feldman and MacCulloch's (1971) treatment of homosexuality. In their procedure, the female slide follows shock termination, though not on every trial. In Rescorla's terms this partial arrangement would reduce the predictive power of the female slide; temporal cues or the disappearance of the male slide are more predictive. The discussion is somewhat academic in that there has been no independent evaluation of the relief procedure and thus its role remains unknown.

In laboratory studies, the most traditional attempt to demonstrate conditioned relief has been to pair a neutral stimulus with shock termination and then to demonstrate that the neutral stimulus becomes a secondary reinforcer. In Beck's (1961) careful review of this literature, the major criticism was a procedural one—the difficulty of demonstrating that a stimulus was a secondary reinforcer rather than a cue, or S^D, for responding. On the whole, the evidence is still against the phenomenon (Siegel and Milby, 1969), and some studies that have responded to the procedural criticisms with corrections have found that stimuli paired with shock termination have aversive properties (Wahlsten, Cole and Fantino, 1967; Zelhart, 1972).

There is one feature of Zelhart's (1972) study that is problematic: although he varied shock duration, the stimulus was presented almost a second *after* shock had ended, so that while temporal cues did not 'predict' the end of the shock, neither did the stimulus. If the predictive, or signalling, function of the stimulus is at all important, perhaps a signal coming before shock offset would make a difference. In a human study, in which the CSs were evaluated indirectly by means of the semantic differential scale, Beck and Brooks (1967) and Sutterer and Beck (1970) reported that the stimulus occurring just prior to shock offset was rated more positively only if the onset of the shock was signalled by another stimulus. Perhaps this is because a stimulus preceding shock offset also precedes (predicts?) the onset of the next shock; but this prediction would be superseded if another stimulus more adequately predicted onset of the next shock. In attempting to programme examples of the possible arrangements that have been used, Leslie Weiss and the author began to realize the truly ephemeral quality of a signal's 'predictive value'. With a long CS preceding shock, the onset of the stimulus predicts a shock-free period (the ISI), while its offset predicts shock. Bobbitt and Beck (1971) found that the longer the CS the less unpleasant the subjects rated its onset, but one wonders how trace conditioning could ever be effective. We programmed one stimulus to come on, followed at a fixed interval by another which was paired with shock: does the first stimulus predict a shock-free interval or a wait before a signalled shock?

Interpretation of Rescorla's 'contingency' notion turns out to be highly subjective. For instance, Furedy and Schiffman (1973) compared a negative contingency CS− (nCS−) with a 'truly random' arrangement having zero contingency (zCS−). In the former case, no UCS followed within 30 secs of a nCS−; in the latter case, a certain percentage of zCS−s were followed within a few seconds by the UCS pairings. The authors, finding no difference between these two groups (confirmed in Furedy, 1974), opined that the contingency concept was faulty, at least with human electrodermal conditioning. It could be argued, however, that their procedure was not an adequate test as the prediction of the UCS could be done entirely from the CS+, so that the CS− was 'redundant' (Egger and Miller, 1962) no matter what it predicted. Thus the real error of the predictability concept is that it cannot be operationalized, and what the subject actually predicted can only be inferred, *post hoc*, according to how he behaves.

One other important topic must be mentioned before moving to the intricacies of cognition, namely the incubation of fear, or, more neutrally expressed, situations wherein one would expect fear to extinguish but where it does not. The tenacity of neurotic anxiety is not a new observation, but the incubation concept was introduced to behaviour therapy by Wolpe (1952, 1958) when he suggested that the evocation of anxiety was an effective source of second-order conditioning of the same response. Eysenck's more recent emphasis on the topic is similar: anxiety is both a response and a secondary drive; fear responses are themselves painful events. Eysenck (Eysenck and Beech, 1971) suggests using the term 'nocive response' (NR) to refer either to the UCR elicited by a painful stimulus or to the CR based thereon. Thus to the extent that an un-reinforced stimulus ($\overline{CS}$) elicits NR, there continues to be reinforcement. The specific evidence, either for the model or for the phenomenon, is not great. Napalkov's experiment (Eysenck, 1967) was inadequately described and lacked controls; so did Campbell, Sanderson and Laverty's (1964) apnœa study. On the other hand, Marukhanyan (1961) described how in certain dogs, the excitable ones, a conditioned motor response (the electrodes were attached) failed to extinguish. Rohrbaugh and Riccio (1970) have used the term 'paradoxical enhancement' to describe their demonstration that short (5 min) exposure to the $\overline{CS}$ resulted in the animals being more fearful than those that had had no exposure to $\overline{CS}$ at all (CS refers to static apparatus cues in this study). Fear was measured by a latency-to-drink-water parameter. In two studies they failed to find statistical significance between the non-exposure groups and the 5 min exposure group which were supposed to demonstrate enhancement; in another study exposure times of 30 and 60 secs produced more fear (escape from fear measure) than non-exposure; and in a fourth study (Rohrbaugh, Riccio and Arthur, 1972) the effect was found for a 15 sec exposure group when measured by *recovery* from suppression but not initial suppression. 'Paradoxical enhancement' will need more supporting data before it can be considered a replicable phenomenon. As for the clinical evidence, Eysenck gives some hypothetical situations that appear to fit more closely to a model proposed by Evans (1972) to describe only those situations in which anxiety, or some other emotional state, alters overt behaviour in such a way as to be socially embarrassing, and thus anxiety arousing, to the individual. In clinical situations, of course, cognitive and verbal factors are a prime consideration, and so it is to this area that we now turn.

COGNITIVE VARIABLES AND CLASSICAL CONDITIONING

One of the most venerable questions in classical conditioning has been the part played in conditioning by cognition. The question has been somewhat complicated by the fact that there are cognitive *variables* which influence human classical conditioning and cognitive *explanations* which have been put forward to account for classical conditioning in both humans and lower animals. It is the author's impression that contemporary theorists in behaviour therapy tend to confuse these two features, and are overly concerned about the admissibility of cognitive explanations rather than allowing, elucidating and incorporating cognitive variables—Hallam, Rachman and Falkowski (1972), for instance, use the terms 'cognitive theorist' versus 'conditioning theorist'.

Cognitive variables of crucial importance in behaviour therapy are those resulting in very rapid extinction of CRs once the UCS is removed. The rapidity of human CR extinction has been noted for years; its ubiquity led Spence (1966), in his latter years, to devote his talents to the study of cognitive variables in human conditioning. Hilgard, Campbell and Sears showed in 1938 that informing the subjects of the reinforcement contingencies in differential conditioning resulted in immediate (within twelve trials) conditioned discrimination, 'furnishing another instance of the significance in man of verbal controls over processes which have been supposed to be relatively automatic' (p. 506). The same point was made by Grant (1939) and Humphreys (1939), but the *pièce de résistance* was the Cook and Harris (1937) study, demonstrating that simply instructing the subject that shock would follow a green light was sufficient to produce a GSR to that stimulus. Of course, the GSR is remarkably sensitive to background events and, without the detailed response analysis advocated earlier, older reports might have been dealing with sensitized ORs which do wax and wane with circumstances—see Mowrer's (1938) observation that a neutral stimulus elicited a GSR when the subject was simply fitted with shock electrodes or Silverman's (1960) finding that the information 'from now on you will not be shocked' reduced GSRs in both a conditioning group *and* a pseudo-conditioning group.

The major point for behaviour therapists is that the extremely important influence of cognitive variables on human classical conditioning were known well before the 1940s. Although classical conditioners themselves often throw up their hands at the mention of cognitive variables, the experimental questions are not really all that complex, as almost all the studies have to do with knowledge of the situation revealed in ways other than by the appearance of the CR. There are, briefly, only three widely used designs to study cognitive variables: concurrent or retrospective measures of ability to verbalize the contingency; altering the experimental procedure in ways thought to decrease awareness; and seeking parameters of the CR which are thought to reveal anticipation, expectancy or awareness.

Verbalization of contingencies

Even when subjects are asked not to attempt to work out the sequence of events in an experiment, many of them, at the end of the study, can accurately describe the relationship between the CS and UCS, some seem not to be able to verbalize the relationship and some verbalize relationships that are quite incorrect. The more intensively the subjects are questioned, the more likely they are to be able to describe the contingencies (Creelman, 1966). Subjects frequently cannot describe their own behaviour, for instance reporting that they inhibited anticipatory blinking when they did not (Grant, 1973). Dawson (1973) has shown, by looking back over the literature, that the type of questioning is important—studies indicating that accurate verbal report is related to conditioning have used recognition questionnaires (i.e. select a contingency) rather than recall questionnaires. Dawson (1973) has also made the convincing point that one cannot just pick the measure that suits one's argument; recognition questionnaires, he proposes, are the truly valid measures of awareness as they relate best to degree of prior information given the subjects.

The upshot is that, when subjects are categorized according to success or failure in describing the contingencies, only the successful show differential GSR conditioning (Baer and Fuhrer, 1968, 1970; Fuhrer and Baer, 1965; Morgenson and Martin, 1969). This is true also when the knowledge measure is taken concurrently throughout acquisition (Baer and Fuhrer, 1968; Dawson and Biferno, 1973). On the other hand, studies by Furedy (Furedy, 1973; Furedy and Schiffman, 1971) failed to find a correlation between degree of conditioning and degree of verbally expressed probability that they would receive a shock. Turning a dial to express one's certainty regarding shock is obviously not the same as recognizing a CS–UCS relationship on a questionnaire; the author thus believes that discrepancies in the literature are due to different procedures. However, in a rather more positive vein, Dawson and Furedy have come together to reconcile the discrepancies in a very interesting paper (Dawson and Furedy, 1973). They propose a 'necessary-gate hypothesis', meaning that awareness of the CS–UCS relation is necessary, but not sufficient, for conditioning and that the effect is all or none—there must be some absolute level below which there is no conditioning, but above which conditioning is not influenced. The reader is again cautioned that what holds for autonomic conditioning may not be true for other response systems; Grant (1973) makes the point very strongly that in eyelid conditioning the subjects' cognitions rarely relate to their conditioning performance.

Masking procedures

The purpose of the masking task is to attempt to reduce the cognitive activity engaged in by the subject, and especially to disguise the fact that they are being conditioned. Conditioning laboratories (with the exception of the Maudsley group) use undergraduate psychology students as subjects, so the need to try to distract them is particularly acute. For behaviour therapists, the dilemma is, of course, that one usually does not want to interfere with conditioning by masking tasks, and yet frequently one would appreciate some sort of control for subjects simply conforming to the rather obvious demands of the conditioning task.

Certainly the effects of masking tasks upon conditioning are rather dramatic. In Spence's studies of rapid extinction mentioned earlier, the introduction of a probability matching cover task (the tones and air-puffs being described as 'distractions') slowed down extinction greatly, resulting in extinction curves resembling those from animal studies, and caused the disappearance of the partial reinforcement effect. Ross (1971) has provided a very detailed review of masking tasks. Some recent findings will give the reader a flavour of the issues involved. Nelson and Ross (1974), in a differential eyelid conditioning study, selected by questionnaire all subjects who had—at the end of the experiment—knowledge of the contingencies. Dividing these subjects into those who had been conditioned under a masking task and those who had not, they revealed that the masking task still reduced differential conditioning.

The authors argued that masking tasks have at least two components: interference with knowledge of the contingencies and altering attentional or cognitive activities involving the CSs and the UCS.

Related to masking tasks, but working in the opposite direction, so to speak, are those situations in which instructions regarding the contingencies are supplied right from the start of the experiment. (The ethical requirement of informed consent usually necessitates such a procedure in behaviour therapy.) Again, one can see the effect of cognitive activities over and above the knowledge factor. In a particularly valuable series of studies, Mandel and Bridger reported responding that was *not* in accord with expectancies established by instruction. They pointed out that such behaviour is characteristic in behaviour disorders where, for example, patients commonly acknowledge the foolishness and irrationality of their fears and attitudes. By the same reasoning, the studies are relevant to behaviour therapy where effects are supposed to continue despite the termination of the conditioning procedure. Early in their series, Bridger and Mandel (1964) showed that the acquisition of a GSR CR was similar whether subjects received shock as the UCS or simply threat of shock. When the electrodes were removed, however, the group that *had* received the shock showed a gradual extinction effect, whereas the CRs of the other group were eliminated immediately. A second study (Bridger and Mandel, 1965) confirmed the findings, even when suspicious subjects, who thought they might still get shocked via the GSR electrodes, were removed from the analysis.

Because subjects clearly respond contrary to their verbal expectancies, this design can be used to investigate cognitive involvement in traditional classical conditioning situations. Mandel and Bridger (1967a) gave all subjects information regarding the conditioning procedure (CS–UCS relationship) and in extinction gave only half of the subjects information by removing the electrodes—we will call these the informed subjects. One of the groups was a backward conditioning group, despite which differential conditioning was easily obtained. These subjects, however, extinguished immediately, whether informed or uninformed, indicating that the backward conditioning effect was due entirely to cognitive factors. The 0.5 sec and 5 sec forward ISI groups maintained a differential response over all ten extinction trials when uninformed, and over the first five or so extinction trials when informed. A second experiment (Mandel and Bridger, 1967b) used the same design and logic and investigated semantic and phonetic generalization—i.e. instead of extinction trials, generalization tests were presented: 'skip' for phonetic, 'boat' for semantic (the original CS in training being, of course, 'ship'). Phonetic generalization was shown to be present in all groups, whether actually shocked or just threatened and whether informed or not regarding the absence of shock in the generalization test. Semantic generalization, however, occurred only in shock-experienced subjects not informed either of the original contingencies or the switch to extinction.

The reader may wonder why the results from this series of studies appears to be so different from the previously cited work showing rapid extinction effects following information. Mandel and Bridger (1973) offer the high intensity of the shock UCS as an explanation; 10 per cent. of their subjects refused to continue after experiencing one or two shocks. 'We do not believe', they write (p. 90), 'that a UCS consisting of either a mildly uncomfortable shock or an air-puff to the cornea will permit demonstration of CRs *contrary* to cognitive expectancy'. Most human autonomic conditioning studies simply do not represent analogues of processes possibly involved in real-life traumatic experiences, aversion therapy or aversive conditioning in animals. Behaviour therapists who are able to justify highly unpleasant UCSs on treatment grounds are in a rather unique position to contribute to the experimental study of human aversive conditioning, if they would use adequate measures and controls.

CR measures

It was mentioned earlier that the response topography of the GSR CR allows identification of three components, and these three do not respond equally to information given the subject. For example, even if the subject has information regarding the contingencies, he typically does not know, from moment to moment, which stimulus will come up and whether it will be reinforced (especially in partial reinforcement, PR, arrangements), so that the CS-R is influenced only by advanced knowledge of the next trial. The Pre-UCS-R is a different kettle of fish. It does not occur in low-level retardates, it is easily disrupted by masking tasks and instructions, it tends to be absent when subjects cannot verbalize the contingencies and it is prominent when they can do so— all in all, Lockart (1973) has concluded, 'the Pre-UCS-R seems almost wholly mediated by cognitive factors'. The Post-UCS-R, while easily eliminated by instructions, is readily conditioned under masking tasks and is found in lower animals and retarded individuals.

A more direct method of investigating a subject's expectancies, also relying on the GSR, has been devised by Epstein. It is a count-up procedure leading to a stimulus event, and the method is thus something like conventional classical conditioning with a long CS, although the count-up procedure allows the subject more information prior to the actual moment when the UCS is delivered. When threatened with an extremely loud tone as a stimulus, subjects showed a large increase in skin conductance when the tone was presented, compared to subjects led to underestimate the same tone. The moment-to-moment changes in conductance during the count up showed an initial high level when the count began (in this situation, at least, the onset of a CS was *not* a 'safety signal'), which gradually decreased to the count of 8 (rather like the HR CR with long CSs) and then rose very sharply at the count of 9—the subjects had been told the event would occur on the count of 10 (Epstein and Clarke, 1970).

Epstein's relatively simple procedure has paid handsome dividends, as minor alterations in the parameters reveal some interesting effects. For instance, if subjects are told on what number the aversive event will occur, they react strongly at first but then habituate; subjects not given the information show a comparable initial reaction, but an *increased* reaction (incubation) on subsequent trials (Epstein, 1973). Epstein has concluded from this and similar studies that certainty regarding stimulus events does not reduce one's initial reaction to them, but does allow, in the longer term, eventual habituation to take place. Obviously, these ideas are significant for theories of neurotic anxiety not originating from painful, traumatic stimuli, but the more immediate practical application might be for aversion therapy in which habituation to the shock is a common problem.

Epstein's theory is based largely on the magnitude of the UCR; recently Öhman, Björkstrand and Ellström (1973) studied GSR CRs in a similar way. The CS used was an 8 sec slide announcing to the subject the probability and intensity of the shock UCS, e.g. '75% STRONG'. The results were presented separately for the three components of the GSR; only the relationship between Post-$\overline{\text{UCS}}$-R magnitude and UCS probability was an inverted U-function, but it was not statistically significant. The significance of this U-function is, as Epstein argues, that the most unpleasant thing about anticipating an aversive event is uncertainty. The 50 per cent. probability represents maximum uncertainty, as 25 per cent. makes it most probable there will not be a shock and 75 per cent. makes it most probable that there will be—in both cases the magnitude of the GSR, after the first few responses, should be less. In a comparable experiment, Grings and Sukoneck (1971) found monotonically increasing CRs with increasing shock probabilities as learned through direct experience, and found this for all three response components. Grings (1969) has predicted that the greater the probability of an aversive event, the stronger the anticipatory responses (Pre-UCS-R) and the larger the disparity (Post-$\overline{\text{UCS}}$-R) if the event fails to occur. The difference between Grings' and Epstein's positions is quite small, as Epstein predicts his effect only on later trials.

Also relying on the nature of the CR—in this case classifying subjects into Vs and Cs in eyelid conditioning as a moderator variable—Grant (see Grant, 1968) has been able to reveal something of the subjects' cognitive activities. The additional twist is the use of verbal CSs. If, for instance, four different CS+s are used which are all part of a conceptual set (e.g. river, sea, lake, ocean), differential conditioning is greater in Vs than if the words are unrelated or if there are only three, or two, different CS+s. So, despite the fact that the more words in a set the fewer UCS pairings each will have, terminal discrimination is greater the more words there are. In C-form responders, there is no greater discrimination when the words are related than when they are unrelated. If the CS+ is the command 'DON'T BLINK' and the CS− is 'BLINK' (a discrepancy between the command and its contingency with the UCS), C-form responders are able to disregard the evocation and respond appropriately; Vs show very poor differential conditioning under these circumstances. If one can agree with Grant that Vs are second-signal system dominant, then we begin to see the complexity of those procedures in behaviour therapy involving 'semantic' conditioning (Hekmat and Vanian, 1971) and we begin to realize the kind of verbal rule learning that may mediate the CRs of certain subjects. Even when different verbal UCSs (calm versus evaluative) have been compared, thus obviating social demand variables, the apparent anxiety reduction to the phobic CS words can be thought of as 'conditioning in only the loosest sense (Weiss and Evans, 1974).

PERCEPTION AND THE CHARACTERISTICS OF THE CS

One of the most striking differences between laboratory classical conditioning and clinical treatment procedures, supposedly derived therefrom, is the complexity of the stimuli in the latter situation. Fears may well be conditioned responses; clients do not fear buzzers or tones, however, but subtle, qualified stimuli complexes—the author recently treated the fear of a talented young singer whose performance anxiety was dependent on the probability of a former music teacher being in her audience and the extent to which she had rehearsed her piece. Practising behaviour therapists have countless such stories and the classical conditioning literature is hardly a useful guide to their analysis. Nevertheless, conditioning research has explored the variables related to stimulus selection and has clarified, in the process, important aspects of the classical conditioning paradigm.

Perhaps the most systematically developed research topic in this area has been conditioning with compound CSs, a topic, like so many considered in this chapter, first explored by Pavlov (1927). American interest in compound conditioning was given sustenance by Razran's research and interpretation of the Russian literature (for a recent review of his thought, see Razran, 1965). A major theme of Razran's writing has been that in the final stage of compound conditioning, the *configuration* becomes the CS; however, this is true mainly of simultaneous compounds and depends entirely on the experimental parameters. Wickens (1959, 1973), another leading contributor, has also seen the study of compound conditioning as a method for studying perception. In one investigation involving cats, CS_1 preceded a second CS_2 by 150 msecs during acquisition (sequential compound); test trials with the CSs alone revealed a greater percentage of CRs to the shorter stimulus (CS_2). When a CS_1 preceded a second CS_2 by 500 msecs, subsequent testing showed the longer stimulus to be the most effective. This is the common finding in sequential compounding—consider the famous study by Egger and Miller (1962), where stimulus A was followed 500 msecs later by stimulus B, followed 1500 msecs later by food. With just that experience, A became an effective secondary reinforcer, whereas B did not, because it was a redundant, non-informative cue for food, according to the authors. Wickens gives a rather different interpretation of his cat findings: through sensory preconditioning, CS_1 is capable of producing the sensory effect of the compound itself and thus eliciting a substantial response. Whichever type of theory one prefers, it must be able to handle the reversed effect when the interval between elements of the compound is only 150 msecs, as well as another strange reversal revealed in Wickens' work—when the interval between CS_1 and CS_2 was 2000 msecs, the short, second stimulus was again the more effective. Wickens interpreted this along the lines that such lengthy intervals result in the formation of two independent CRs and that the response to the more optimal 500 msec ISI would be larger. Latency or topographical measures of the two CRs would make this interpretation more convincing, but a dual CR has been observed in eyelid conditioning with shifting ISIs (Ebel and Prokasy, 1963).

Just as order of the elements in time is a significant but intricate variable, so the organism's past experience with the compound or its elements is a major factor determining conditioning. Most of the studies in this area rely on simultaneous compounds and a conditioned suppression or rate-change measure of conditioning. When the compound is a light and a tone presented together, the compound is significantly superior to either of the two elements presented alone in terms of producing suppression after fear conditioning. If in one group the animals are conditioned to the compound and then the noise alone, the subsequent suppression to the light is less than observed with a second group which have experienced the compound alone. Similarly, if some animals are conditioned to the noise alone and then to the compound, they show as little suppression to the light as the group that have had all their conditioning trials with the noise alone as the CS (Kamin, 1968, 1969). Kamin has called this a 'blocking' effect, and it has been observed within other response paradigms (e.g. rabbits' NMR, Marchant and Moore, 1973).

An unusual feature of the blocking effect is that it can be virtually eliminated by the presentation of an additional stimulus shortly after the compound CS–UCS pairing. Kamin (1969) called this additional stimulus a 'surprise' stimulus and argued, fancifully in this author's opinion, that it forces the animal to reassess the significance of the preceding compound. Clearly, much more detailed research needs to be done to determine the limits of the effect. At the moment, we know it occurs only if the 'surprise' stimulus comes 3–5 secs after the UCS; any longer (e.g. 10 secs) and the blocking phenomenon is observed as usual (Gray and Appignanesi, 1973).

A phenomenon related to blocking is what Lubow and Moore (1959) termed 'latent inhibition' (unreinforced pre-exposure to a stimulus retards subsequent acquisition with that stimulus). Pavlov (1927) had noted that conditioning would not proceed in the absence of an OR to the CS, and among autonomic conditioners it has become axiomatic that an OR is a prerequisite for normal conditioning. The phenomenon seems to run counter to Rescorla's claim that repeated non-reinforced presentations of a neutral stimulus does not convert it to an inhibitor and that only non-reinforcement in the presence of positive conditioning has that effect (Zimmer-Hart and Rescorla, 1974).

It is apparent that although conditioning to one CS element is asymptotic, the addition of the other element does not go unnoticed—there is, for instance, a lessened suppression effect when the second element is added to the first. Another way to show the influence of the added element is to make it significant—present an element followed by shock (CS+) and the compound alone (CS−). The animal quickly stops lever-pressing in the presence of the compound. In terms of danger and safety signals, one could then predict that the added element in a compound not followed by shock could become an inhibitory stimulus for fear. It turns out that this is the case. Pavlov (1927) had, of course, demonstrated this effect in salivary conditioning, and more contemporary Russian studies carry out a similar procedure called switching. In one study, cited by Asratyan (1965), a metronome beat of 120 per minute was conditioned to a salivary CR (UCS food) in the morning and to a paw flexion (UCS shock) in the afternoon. An even more complex procedure was to condition salivation to a buzzer and paw flexion to a tactile stimulus in one experimental chamber. When this was well established, the same dogs were placed in a different chamber and the conditioning procedure was reversed: the buzzer became the CS for paw flexion and the tactile stimulus the CS for salivation. Eventually the dogs were able to produce the correct response depending upon which chamber they were in. (This shows yet again the power of static apparatus cues as CSs.)

Thus far we have seen a 'blocking' effect and a 'qualifying effect'; there is also what has been called an 'overshadowing' effect—Pavlov (1927) demonstrated that the relative intensities of the stimuli in the compound are important. Kamin (1965) has shown that the overshadowing of the weak stimulus element by the strong one is a function of UCS intensity. If UCS intensity is greatly increased, a sound of 50 db, usually overshadowed by a bright light stimulus, comes to suppress responding very well when presented alone after being conditioned as part of a compound. It is not surprising that this general area of enquiry is referred to frequently as 'stimulus selection'.

Still another relevant variable regarding stimulus selection has emerged from studies by Wagner (1969a) and his colleagues. It will be recalled from an earlier section that the essence of Rescorla's argument was that the effectiveness of a CS depended upon the degree to which it predicted the UCS. This leads to the following type of investigation: Wagner and coworkers (1968) reported a study of eyelid conditioning in the rabbit in which the CS was a compound of light flashes (B) and either auditory clicks (A_1) or a tone (A_2). In what the authors called the correlated training procedure, all A_1B CSs were reinforced (4 mA shock to the cheek) and no A_2B trials were reinforced. Test trials to B alone showed there was little conditioning (and, obviously, test trials revealed good conditioning to A_1B, fair conditioning to A_1 alone and none to A_2). In the uncorrelated procedure, 50 per cent. of A_1B CSs were reinforced and so were 50 per cent. of A_2B trials. Here, it can be seen, A_1 and A_2 and B were equally valid in predicting forthcoming UCSs, and test trials revealed some conditioning to both A_1 and A_2 and considerable conditioning to B. When the correlated/uncorrelated conditions were reversed for the same subjects, it was shown that, when shifted from uncorrelated to correlated, the efficacy of B alone decreased and of A_1 increased slightly.

Summing up this and other studies, Wagner (1969b) writes (p. 110):

> ... a partially reinforced cue is much less likely to be an effective stimulus in isolation when it has been experienced in compounds containing elements more highly correlated

with reinforcement, than when it has been experienced in similar compounds which do not contain more valid elements.

The reversal conditions cited above also show that a cue will *lose* its 'signal value' when its correlation with reinforcement is unaltered, but other cues are made more 'valid', or highly correlated. Apparently, the same effect can occur in a sequential situation; Rescorla's (1973) study of UCS habituation, already described, could be interpreted as additional trials with a new CS (apparatus cues) and shock resulting in an attenuation of the suppression when the original CS is reintroduced.

It is not difficult to see why behaviour therapists should pay some attention to these aspects of classical conditioning. In the first place, the studies continue to develop the theme that the contiguity of any CS with any UCS is not sufficient for classical conditioning. Concern for the nature of the CS goes back a long way in behaviour therapy: Thorndike (1935), for example, thought that Watson and Rayner's (1920) demonstration was a 'very special case', as the CS, the rat, was itself potentially fear-arousing. Thorndike's colleague, Bregman (1934), in a controlled study, was unable to replicate Watson and Rayner's findings when CSs were inanimate objects. Secondly, the studies described in this section refer to what could loosely be called stimulus selection when the environment is complex. There are frequent accounts in the clinical literature of the CSs selected not being quite what the therapist bargained for: Quinn and Henbest's (1967) amusing account of the ten alcoholics who switched from whiskey to beer (or rum, gin, etc.) following aversion therapy (UCS apomorphine) is a good example. It would be relatively easy, however, following findings such as Wagner's, to set up cue-shock correlations which would result in, say, homosexual activity (rather than nude males) or the flavour of liquor (rather than its appearance) becoming the crucial CS for anxiety.

In recent years yet another variable has been put forward in stimulus selection; this has been variously known as the relationship of cue to consequence (Garcia and Koelling, 1966), biological preparedness (Seligman, 1970) or salience (Kalat and Rozin, 1970). Essentially this refers to the reported finding that not all stimuli are equally effective as CSs in studies in which edible substances have been associated with induced illness (X-rays, toxins, etc.) and electric shock. The specific claim has been that taste CSs are effective when the UCS is induced illness, but only exteroceptive stimuli, such as lights or noise, are effective when the rats are shocked during eating. Different relationships of this kind have been reported for different species. Another feature of these studies of taste aversions is that the time interval between CS and UCS is often extremely lengthy—typical classical conditioning laws do not appear to hold in these situations (selective reviews are available in Garcia, McGowan and Green, 1972; Rozin and Kalat, 1971; Seligman, 1970).

While these studies have aroused a good deal of interest, they tend to have serious methodological flaws which limit their credibility and their interpretation in terms of novel principles of behaviour. An excellent critique of these experiments has been presented by Bitterman (1975). The major points he makes are as follows: the studies are often weak in terms of pseudo-conditioning controls; when long CS–UCS intervals have been shown effective, the problem of after-taste (resulting from the nausea and illness) has not been adequately dealt with; when the efficacy of shock and illness induction are compared, differences in timing (ISI) are confounded; when taste cues and visual cues are contrasted, there is an inevitable order problem, not only in the conditioning procedure, but in the test situation; finally, there are many factors related to cue dominance, as discussed earlier, which are not taken into account in the taste-aversion studies. Attempts to generalize the animal findings to human clinical practice, especially aversion therapy (Danaher and Lichtenstein, 1974; Revusky, 1973; Wilson and Davison, 1969), have been examined by Evans and Busch (1974), who considered the logic of the extrapolation faulty. There is no evidence that human subjects fail to condition to taste CSs when shock is the UCS.

CONCLUSIONS

Classical conditioning, I have endeavoured to show, is a vital and lively field of study. It is also a rather fragmented one; not impossibly so, but sometimes the technological complexities of one area seem to mask the significance of the findings for another. The experimenter who must worry about the log transformations of the range-corrected magnitudes of the second segment of the GSR rarely mentions the significance of the findings for the one who worries about changed suppression ratios being artefacts of the response maintenance schedule. It is, then, especially encouraging that more and more classical conditioners are mentioning the significance of thier findings, both animal and human, for clinical practice.

Here, however, one cannot help but feel that the direct value of these studies for behaviour therapists has declined. For years, behaviour therapists have relied on a simple, textbook kind of account of classical conditioning, and it has fared them quite well. The major message of the current survey is that classical conditioning is complex; little can be generalized from one response system to another or from one species to another. The basic parameters of classical conditioning turn out to be dependent not only on the general method-ology for that study but even on such basic features as the criteria for defining a CR. Laboratory classical conditioning with humans, especially autonomic conditioning, proves to be extremely influenced by a myriad of cognitive variables—attitude, set, verbal mediation, instructions, and so forth. What, then, is the basis for the 'classically conditioned' responses that theorists have supposed *mediate* complex behaviour such as cognition? Similarly, the direct derivation of clinical methods from classical conditioning principles is rather naïve. Behaviour therapists may have to abandon their earlier traditions and comfort themselves with a gain in the general knowledge of behaviour principles as a substitute for an oversimplified reliance upon an explanatory analogue—classical conditioning.

REFERENCES

Asratyan, E. A. (1965). *Compensatory Adaptations, Reflex Activity and the Brain*, Pergamon, Oxford.

Badia, P., and Defran, R. H. (1970). Orienting responses and GSR conditioning: a dilemma. *Psychological Review*, 77, 171–181.

Baer, P. E., and Fuhrer, M. J. (1968). Cognitive processes during differential trace and delayed conditioning of the GSR. *Journal of Experimental Psychology*, 78, 81–88.

Baer, P. E., and Fuhrer, M. J. (1970). Cognitive processes in the differential trace conditioning of electrodermal and vasomotor activity. *Journal of Experimental Psychology*, 84, 176–178.

Barlow, D. H. (1973). Increasing heterosexual responsiveness in the treatment of sexual deviation: a review of the clinical and experimental evidence. *Behavior Therapy*, 4, 655–671.

Barr, R. F., and McConaghy, N. (1971). Penile volume responses to appetitive and aversive stimuli in relation to sexual orientation and conditioning performance. *British Journal of Psychiatry*, 119, 377–383.

Barr, R. F., and McConaghy, N. (1974). Anxiety in relation to conditioning. *Behavior Therapy*, 5, 193–202.

Beck, R. L. (1961). On secondary reinforcement and shock termination. *Psychological Bulletin*, 58, 28–45.

Beck, R. C., and Brooks, C. I. (1967). Human judgments of stimuli associated with shock onset and termination. *Psychonomic Science*, 8, 327–328.

Beech, H. R., Watts, F., and Poole, A. D. (1971). Classical conditioning of a sexual deviation: a preliminary note. *Behavior Therapy*, 2, 400–402.

Beecroft, R. S. (1966). *Classical Conditioning*, Psychonomic Press, Goleta, California.

Bernstein, D. A. (1973). Situational factors in behavioral fear assessment: a progress report. *Behavior Therapy*, 4, 41–48.

Bernstein, D. A., and Nietzel, M. T. (1974). Behavioral avoidance tests: the effects of demand characteristics and repeated measures on two types of subjects. *Behavior Therapy*, 5, 183–192.

Biederman, G. B., and Furedy, J. J. (1970). The preference-for-signalled-shock phenomenon: signalling shock is reinforcing only if shock is modifiable. *Quarterly Journal of Experimental Psychology*, 22, 681 685.

Bishop, P. D., and Kimmel, H. D. (1969). Retention of habituation and conditioning. *Journal of Experimental Psychology*, 81, 317–321.

Bitterman, M. E. (1962). Techniques for the study of learning in animals: analysis and classification. *Psychological Bulletin*, 59, 81–93.

Bitterman, M. E. (1964). Comment. *Psychonomic Science*, 1, 94.

Bitterman, M. E. (1975). Issues in the comparative psychology of learning. In R. B. Masterton, M. E. Bitterman, C. B. G. Campbell and N. Hotten (Eds.), *The Evolution of Brain and Behavior in Vertebrates*, Erlbaum, New York.

Bitterman, M. E., and Schoel, W. M. (1970). Instrumental learning in animals: parameters of reinforcement. *Annual Review of Psychology*, 21, 367–436.

Black, A. H., and de Toledo, L. (1972). The relationship among classically conditioned responses: heart rate and skeletal behavior. In A. H. Black and W. F. Prokasy (Eds.), *Classical Conditioning II: Current Research and Theory*, Appleton-Century-Crofts, New York.

Blanchard, R. J., and Blanchard, D. C. (1968). Escape and avoidance responses to a fear eliciting stimulus. *Psychonomic Science*, 13, 19–20.

Bobbitt, R. G., and Beck, R. C. (1971). Semantic differential judgments of single and multiple conditioned stimuli with an aversive delay conditioning paradigm. *Journal of Experimental Psychology*, 89, 398–402.

Bolles, R. C. (1970). Species-specific defense reactions and avoidance learning. *Psychological Review*, 71, 32–48.

Bregman, E. (1934). An attempt to modify the emotional attitude of infants by the conditioned response technique. *Journal of Genetic Psychology*, **45**, 169–198.

Bridger, W. H., and Mandel, I. J. (1964). A comparison of GSR fear responses produced by threat and electric shock. *Journal of Psychiatric Research*, **2**, 31–40.

Bridger, W. H., and Mandel, I. J. (1965). Abolition of the PRE by instruction in GSR conditioning. *Journal of Experimental Psychology*, **69**, 476–482.

Brimer, C. J., and Kamin, L. J. (1963). Disinhibition, habituation, sensitization, and the conditioned emotional response. *Journal of Comparative and Physiological Psychology*, **56**, 508–516.

Brown, P. L., and Jenkins, H. M. (1968). Auto-shaping of the pigeon's key-peck. *Journal of the Experimental Analysis of Behavior*, **11**, 1–8.

Brown, T. S., Kalish, H. I., and Farber, I. E. (1951). Conditioned fear as revealed by magnitude of startle response to an auditory stimulus. *Journal of Experimental Psychology*, **41**, 317–328.

Bruner, A. (1969). Reinforcement strength in classical conditioning of leg flexion, freezing and heart rate in cats. *Conditional Reflex*, **4**, 24–31.

Bucher, B., and Lovaas, O. I. (1968). Use of aversive stimulation in behavior modification. In M. R. Jones (Ed.), *Miami Symposium on the Prediction of Behavior, 1967: Aversive Stimulation*, University of Miami Press, Coral Gables, Florida.

Burstein, K. R. (1973). On the distinction between conditioning and pseudoconditioning. *Psychophysiology*, **10**, 61–66.

Campbell, D., Sanderson, R. E., and Laverty, S. G. (1964). Characteristics of a conditioned response in human subjects during extinction trials following a simple traumatic conditioning trial. *Journal of Abnormal and Social Psychology*, **68**, 627–639.

Church, R. M., LoLordo, V. M., Overmier, J. V. B., Solomon, R. L., and Turner, L. H. (1966). Cardiac responses to shock in curarized dogs: effects of shock intensity and duration, warning signal and prior experience with shock. *Journal of Comparative and Physiological Psychology*, **62**, 1–7.

Cook, S. W., and Harris, R. E. (1937). The verbal conditioning of the galvanic skin reflex. *Journal of Experimental Psychology*, **21**, 202–210.

Costello, C. G. (1970). Dissimilarities between conditioned avoidance responses and phobias. *Psychological Review*, **77**, 250–254.

Creelman, M. B. (1966). *The Experimental Investigation of Meaning: A Review of the Literature*, Springer, New York.

Culler, E. (1938). Recent advances in some concepts of conditioning. *Psychological Review*, **45**, 134–153.

Curtis, Q. F. (1937). *The Experimental Neurosis in the Pig*. Paper presented at the meeting of the American Psychological Association, September, 1937.

Danaher, B. G., and Lichtenstein, E. (1974). Aversion therapy issues: a note of clarification. *Behavior Therapy*, **5**, 112–116.

Dawson, M. E. (1973). Can classical conditioning occur without contingency learning? A review and evaluation of the evidence. *Psychophysiology*, **10**, 82–86.

Dawson, M. E., and Biferno, M. A. (1973). Concurrent measurement of awareness and electrodermal classical conditioning. *Journal of Experimental Psychology*, **101**, 55–62.

Dawson, M. E., and Furedy, J. J. (1973). *The Role of Relational Awareness in Human Autonomic Discrimination Classical Conditioning*. Paper presented at the meeting of the Society for Psychophysiological Research, October, 1973.

Deane, G. E. (1964). Human heart rate responses during experimentally induced anxiety: a follow-up with controlled respiration. *Journal of Experimental Psychology*, **67**, 193–195.

Dengerink, H. A., and Taylor, S. P. (1971). Multiple responses with differential properties in delayed galvanic skin response conditioning: a review. *Psychophysiology*, **8**, 348–360.

Denny, M. R. (1971). Relaxation theory and experiments. In R. F. Brush (Ed.), *Aversive Conditioning and Learning*, Academic Press, New York.

Dollard, J., and Miller, N. E. (1950). *Personality and Psychotherapy: An Analysis in Terms of Learning, Thinking, and Culture*, McGraw-Hill, New York.

Ebel, H. C., and Prokasy, W. F. (1963). Classical eyelid conditioning as a function of sustained and shifted interstimulus intervals. *Journal of Experimental Psychology*, **65**, 52–58.

Egger, M. D., and Miller, N. E. (1962). Secondary reinforcement in rats as a function of information value and reliability of the stimulus. *Journal of Experimental Psychology*, **64**, 97–104.

Epstein, S. (1973). Expectancy and magnitude of reaction to a noxious UCS. *Psychophysiology*, **10**, 100–107.

Epstein, S., and Clarke, S. (1970). Heart rate and skin conductance during experimentally induced anxiety: effects of anticipated intensity of noxious stimulation and experience. *Journal of Experimental Psychology*, **84**, 105–112.

Estes, W. K., and Skinner, B. F. (1941). Some quantitative properties of anxiety. *Journal of Experimental Psychology*, **29**, 390–400.

Evans, I. M. (1970). *The Effects of Unconditioned Stimulus Intensity on the Conditioned Eyelid Response*. Unpublished doctoral dissertation, University of London.

Evans, I. M. (1972). A conditioning model of a common neurotic pattern—fear of fear. *Psychotherapy: Theory, Research and Practice*, **9**, 238–241.

Evans, I M. (1973). An unusual phenomenon in classical eyelid conditioning—the double conditioned response. *South African Journal of Psychology*, **3**, 83–89.

Evans, I. M., and Busch, C. J. (1974). The effectiveness of visual and gustatory cues in classical aversive conditioning with electric shock. *Behaviour Research and Therapy*, **12**, 129–140.

Eysenck, H. J. (1957). *The Dynamics of Anxiety and Hysteria*, Routledge and Kegan Paul, London.

Eysenck, H. J. (1967). Single-trial conditioning, neurosis and the Napalkov phenomenon. *Behaviour Research and Therapy*, **5**, 63–65.

Eysenck, H. J., and Beech, H. R. (1971). Counter conditioning and related methods. In A. E. Bergin and S. L. Garfield (Eds.), *Handbook of Psychotherapy and Behavior Change*, Wiley, New York.

Eysenck, H. J., and Levey, A. (1972). Conditioning, introversion–extraversion and the strength of the nervous system. In V. D. Nebylitsyn and J. A. Gray (Eds.), *Biological Bases of Individual Behavior*, Academic Press, New York.

Eysenck, H. J., and Rachman, S. (1965). *The Causes and Cures of Neurosis*, Routledge and Kegan Paul, London.

Feldman, M. P., and MacCulloch, M. J. (1971). *Homosexual Behaviour: Therapy and Assessment*, Pergamon, New York.

Fitzgerald, R. D., and Teyler, T. J. (1970). Trace and delayed heart-rate conditioning in rats as a function of US intensity. *Journal of Comparative and Physiological Psychology*, **70**, 242–253.

Franks, C. M. (1969). Behavior therapy and its Pavlovian origins: review and perspectives. In C. M. Franks (Ed.), *Behavior Therapy: Appraisal and Status*, McGraw-Hill, New York.

Franks, C. M., and Wilson, G. T. (1973). Systematic desensitization, flooding, modeling, and behavior rehearsal: commentary. In C. M. Franks and G. T. Wilson (Eds.), *Annual Review of Behavior Therapy, Theory and Practice, 1973*. Brunner/Mazel, New York.

Fuhrer, M. J., and Baer, P. E. (1965). Differential classical conditioning: verbalization of stimulus contingencies. *Science*, **150**, 1479–1481.

Furedy, J. J. (1973). Some limits on the cognitive control of conditioned autonomic behavior. *Psychophysiology*, **10**, 108–111.

Furedy, J. J. (1974). Experimental assessments of the importance of controlling for contingency factors in human classical differential electrodermal and plethysmographic conditioning. *Psychophysiology*, **11**, 308–314.

Furedy, J. J., and Chan, R. M. (1971). Failures of information to reduce rated aversiveness of unmodifiable shock. *Australian Journal of Psychology*, **23**, 85–94.

Furedy, J. J., and Doob, A. N. (1971a). Autonomic responses and verbal reports in further tests of the preparatory-adaptive-response interpretation of reinforcement. *Journal of Experimental Psychology*, **89**, 258–264.

Furedy, J. J., and Doob, A. N. (1971b). Classical aversive conditioning of human digital volume-pulse change and tests of the preparatory-adaptive-response interpretation of reinforcement. *Journal of Experimental Psychology*, **89**, 403–407.

Furedy, J. J., and Doob, A. N. (1972). Signalling unmodifiable shocks: limits on human informational cognitive control. *Journal of Personality and Social Psychology*, **21**, 111–115.

Furedy, J. J., and Klajner, F. (1972). Unconfounded autonomic indexes of the aversiveness of signaled and unsignaled shocks. *Journal of Experimental Psychology*, **92**, 313–318.

Furedy, J. J., and Klajner, F. (1974). On evaluating autonomic and verbal indices of negative preception. *Psychophysiology*, **11**, 121–124.

Furedy, J. J., and Schiffman, K. (1971). Test of the propriety of the traditional discriminative control procedure in Pavlovian electrodermal and plethysmographic conditioning. *Journal of Experimental Psychology*, **91**, 161–164.

Furedy, J. J., and Schiffman, K. (1973). Concurrent measurement of autonomic and cognitive processes in a test of the traditional discriminative control procedure for Pavlovian electrodermal conditioning. *Journal of Experimental Psychology*, **100**, 210–217.

Gantt, W. H. (1967). Pavlovian, classical conditional reflex—a classic error? *Conditional Reflex*, **2**, 255–257.

Garcia, J., and Koelling, R. A. (1966). The relation of cue to consequence in avoidance learning. *Psychonomic Science*, **4**, 123–124.

Garcia, J., McGowan, B. K., and Green, K. F. (1972). Biological constraints on conditioning. In A. H. Black and W. F. Prokasy (Eds.), *Classical Conditioning II: Current Research and Theory*, Appleton-Century-Crofts, New York.

Gormezano, I. (1965). Yoked comparisons of classical and instrumental conditioning of the eyelid response; and an addendum on 'voluntary responders'. In W. F. Prokasy (Ed.), *Classical Conditioning*, Appleton-Century-Crofts, New York.

Gormezano, I. (1972). Investigations of defense and reward conditioning in the rabbit. In A. H. Black and W. F. Prokasy (Eds.), *Classical Conditioning II: Current Research and Theory*, Appleton-Century-Crofts, New York.

Gormezano, I., and Coleman, S. R. (1973). The law of effect and CR contingent modification of the UCS. *Conditional Reflex*, **8**, 41–56.

Grant, D. A. (1939). The influence of attitude on the conditioned eyelid response. *Journal of Experimental Psychology*, **25**, 333–346.

Grant, D. A. (1945). A sensitized eyelid reaction related to the conditioned eyelid response. *Journal of Experimental Psychology*, **35**, 393–402.

Grant, D. A. (1968). Adding communication to the signalling property of the CS in classical conditioning. *Journal of General Psychology*, **79**, 147–175.

Grant, D. A. (1973). Cognitive factors in eyelid conditioning. *Psychophysiology*, **10**, 75–81.

Gray, T., and Appignanesi, A. A. (1973). Compound conditioning: elimination of the blocking effect. *Learning and Motivation*, **4**, 374–380.

Grether, W. F. (1938). Pseudo-conditioning without paired stimulation encountered in attempted backward conditioning. *Journal of Comparative Psychology*, **25**, 91–96.

Grings, W. W. (1960). Preparatory set variables related to classical conditioning of autonomic responses. *Psychological Review*, **67**, 243–252.

Grings, W. W. (1969). Anticipatory and preparatory electrodermal behavior in paired stimulus situations. *Psychophysiology*, **5**, 597–611.

Grings, W. W. (1972). Compound stimulus transfer in human classical conditioning. In A. H. Black and W. F. Prokasy (Eds.), *Classical conditioning II: Current Research and Theory*. Appleton-Century-Crofts, New York.

Grings, W. W., and Sukoneck, H. I. (1971). Prediction probability as a determiner of anticipatory and preparation electrodermal behavior. *Journal of Experimental Psychology*, **91**, 310–314.

Hallam, R., Rachman, S., and Falkowski, W. (1972). *Subjective, attitudinal and physiological effects* of electrical aversion therapy. *Behaviour Research and Therapy*, **10**, 1–13.

Harlow, H. F. (1937). Experimental analysis of the role of the original stimulus in conditioned responses in monkeys. *Psychological Record*, **1**, 62–68.

Hebb, D. O. (1956). The distinction between 'classical' and 'instrumental'. *Canadian Journal of Psychology*, **10**, 165–166.

Hekmat, N., and Vanian, D. (1971). Behavior modification through covert semantic desensitization. *Journal of Consulting and Clinical Psychology*, **36**, 248–251.

Herman, S. H., Barlow, D. H., and Agras, W. S. (1974). An experimental analysis of classical conditioning as a method of increasing heterosexual arousal in homosexuals. *Behavior Therapy*, **5**, 33–47.

Hilgard, E. R. (1967). Classical and instrumental conditioning. Do single-process or two-process theories exhaust the alternatives? In D. B. Lindsley and A. A. Lumsdaine (Eds.), *Brain Function*, Vol IV: *Brain Function and Learning*. University of California Press, Berkeley.

Hilgard, E. R., Campbell, R. K., and Sears, W. N. (1938). Conditioned discrimination: the effect of knowledge of stimulus relationships. *American Journal of Psychology*, **51**, 498–506.

Hilgard, E. R., and Marquis, D. G. (1940). *Conditioning and Learning*, Appleton-Century-Crofts, New York.

Howard, J. L., Obrist, P. A., Gaebelein, C. J., and Galosy, R. A. (1974). Classical aversive conditioning in the cat. *Journal of Comparative and Physiological Psychology*, **87**, 228–236.

Hull, C. L. (1929). A functional interpretation of the conditioned reflex. *Psychological Review*, **36**, 498–511.

Humphreys, L. G. (1939). The effect of random alternation of reinforcement on the acquisition and extinction of conditioned eyelid reactions. *Journal of Experimental Psychology*, **25**, 141–158.

Jensen, D. D. (1961). Operationism and the question 'Is this behaviour learned or innate?'. *Behaviour*, **17**, 1–8.

Kalat, J. W., and Rozin, P. (1970). 'Salience': a factor which can override temporal contiguity in taste-aversion learning. *Journal of Comparative and Physiological Psychology*, **71**, 192–197.

Kamin, L. J. (1965). Temporal and intensity characteristics of the conditioned stimulus. In W. F. Prokasy (Ed.), *Classical Conditioning*, Appleton-Century-Crofts, New York.

Kamin, L. J. (1968). 'Attention-like' processes in classical conditioning. In M. R. Jones (Ed.), *Miami Symposium on the Prediction of Behavior, 1967: Aversive Stimulation*, University of Miami Press, Coral Gables, Florida.

Kamin, L. J. (1969). Selective association and conditioning. In N. J. Mackintosh and W. K. Honig (Eds.), *Fundamental Issues in Associative Learning*, Dalhousie University Press, Halifax.

Kimble, G. A. (1964). Comment. *Psychonomic Science*, **1**, 40.

Kimble, G. A., and Dufort, R. H. (1956). The associative factor in eyelid conditioning. *Journal of Experimental Psychology*, **52**, 386–391.

Kimble, G. A., and Ost, J. W. P. (1961). A conditioned inhibitory process in eyelid conditioning. *Journal of Experimental Psychology*, **61**, 150–156.

Kimmel, H. D. (1966). Inhibition of the unconditioned response in classical conditioning. *Psychological Review*, **73**, 232–240.

Kimmel, H. D. (1970). Essential events in the acquisition of classical conditioning. *Conditional Reflex*, **5**, 156–164.

Kremer, E. F. (1971). Truly random and traditional control procedures in CER conditioning in the rat. *Journal of Comparative and Physiological Psychology*, **76**, 441–448.

Kremer, E. F., and Kamin, L. J. (1971). The truly random control procedure: associative or nonassociative effects in rats. *Journal of Comparative and Physiological Psychology*, **74**, 203–210.

Lang, P. J. (1969). The mechanics of desensitization and the laboratory study of human fear. In C. M. Franks (Ed.), *Behavior Therapy: Appraisal and Status*, McGraw-Hill, New York.

Lanzetta, J. T., and Driscoll, J. M. (1966). Preference for information about an uncertain but unavoidable outcome. *Journal of Personality and Social Psychology*, **3**, 96–102.

Lazarus, R. (1968). Emotions and adaptation: conceptual and empirical relations. In W. J. Arnold (Ed.), *Nebraska Symposium on Motivation*, University of Nebraska Press, Lincoln, Nebraska.

Leitenberg, H., Agras, S., Butz, R., and Wincze, J. (1971). Relationship between heart rate and behavioral change during the treatment of phobias. *Journal of Abnormal Psychology*, **78**, 59–68.

Levey, A. B., and Martin, I. (1974). Sequence of response development in human eyelid conditioning. *Journal of Experimental Psychology*, **102**, 678–686.

Lockhart, R. A. (1973). Cognitive processes and the multiple response phenomenon. *Psychophysiology*, **10**, 112–118.

Lockhart, R. A., and Grings, W. W. (1963). Comments on 'An Analysis of GSR Conditioning'. *Psychological Review*, **70**, 562–564.

Longo, N., Klempay, S., and Bitterman, M. E. (1964). Classical appetitive conditioning in the pigeon. *Psychonomic Science*, **1**, 19–20.

Loucks, R. B., and Gantt, W. H. (1938). The conditioning of striped muscle responses based upon faradic stimulation of dorsal roots and dorsal columns of the spinal cord. *Journal of Comparative Psychology*, **25**, 415–426.

Lovibond, S. H. (1964). *Conditioning and Enuresis*, Pergamon, Oxford.

Lovibond, S. H. (1970). Aversive control of behavior. *Behavior Therapy*, **1**, 80–91.

Lubow, R. E., and Moore, A. U. (1959). Latent inhibition: the effect of nonreinforced pre-exposure to the conditional stimulus. *Journal of Comparative and Physiological Psychology*, **52**, 415–419.

Lykken, D. T. (1959). Preliminary observations concerning the 'preception' phenomenon. *Psychophysiological Measurement Newsletter*, **5**, 2–7.

Lykken, D. T., Macindoe, I., and Tellegen, A. (1972). Preception: autonomic response to shock as a function of predictability in time and locus. *Psychophysiology*, **9**, 318–333.

McAllister, W. R., and McAllister, D. E. (1971). Behavioral measurement of conditioned fear. In R. F. Brush (Ed.), *Aversive Conditioning and Learning*, Academic Press, New York.

MacDonough, T. S. (1972). A critique of the first Feldman and MacCulloch avoidance conditioning treatment for homosexuals. *Behavior Therapy*, **3**, 104–111.

Mandel, I. J., and Bridger, W. H. (1967a). Interaction between instructing and ISI in conditioning and extinction of the GSR. *Journal of Experimental Psychology*, **74**, 36–43.

Mandel, I. J., and Bridger, W. H. (1967b). *Cognitive Factors in GSR Generalization to Verbal Stimuli*. Paper presented at the meeting of the American Psychological Association, September, 1967.

Mandel, I. J., and Bridger, W. H. (1973). Is there classical conditioning without cognitive expectancy? *Psychophysiology*, **10**, 87–90.

Marchant, H. G., III, and Moore, J. W. (1973). Blocking of the rabbit's conditioned nictitating membrane response in Kamin's two-stage paradigm. *Journal of Experimental Psychology*, **101**, 155–158.

Marchant, H. G., III, and Moore, J. W. (1974). Below-zero conditioned inhibition of the rabbit's nictitating membrane response. *Journal of Experimental Psychology*, **102**, 350–352.

Marshall, W. L. (1974). The classical conditioning of sexual attractiveness: report of four therapeutic failures. *Behavior Therapy*, **5**, 298–299.

Martin, I. (1965). Discriminatory GSRs. *Activitas Nervosa Superior*, **7**, 217–223.

Martin, I., and Levey, A. B. (1966). Latency of the eyelid UCR during conditioning. *Life Sciences*, **5**, 17–26.

Martin, I., and Levey, A. B. (1969). *The Genesis of the Classical Conditioned Response*, Pergamon, Oxford.

Marukhanyan, E. V. (1961). The resistance of motor defensive conditioned reflexes to extinction in dogs. *Pavlov Journal of Higher Nervous Activity*, **11**, 492–500

Mathews, A. (1971). Psychophysiological approaches to the investigation of desensitization and related procedures. *Psychological Bulletin*, **76**, 73–91.

Miller, N. E. (1948). Studies of fear as an acquirable drive: I. Fear as a motivation and fear-reduction as reinforcement in the learning of new responses. *Journal of Experimental Psychology*, **38**, 89–101.

Miller, N. E. (1951). Learnable drives and rewards. In S. S. Stevens (Ed.), *Handbook of Experimental Psychology*, Wiley, New York.

Morgenson, D. F., and Martin, I. (1969). Personality, awareness and autonomic conditioning. *Psychophysiology*, **5**, 536–549.

Mowrer, O. H. (1938). Preparatory set (expectancy)—a determinant in motivation and learning. *Psychological Review*, **45**, 62–91.

Mowrer, O. H. (1960) *Learning Theory and Behavior*, Wiley, New York.

Mowrer, O. H., and Mowrer, W. A. (1938). Enuresis: a method for its study and treatment. *American Journal of Orthopsychiatry*, **8**, 436–447.

Nelson, M. N., and Ross, L. E. (1974). Effects of masking tasks on differential eyelid conditioning: a distinction between knowledge of stimulus contingencies and attentional or cognitive activities involving them. *Journal of Experimental Psychology*, **102**, 1–7.

Obrist, P. A. (1968). Heart rate and somatic-motor coupling during classical aversive conditioning in humans. *Journal of Experimental Psychology*, **77**, 180–193.

Obrist, P. A., Sutterer, J. R., and Howard, J. L. (1972). Preparatory cardiac changes: a psychobiological approach. In A. H. Black and W. F. Prokasy (Eds.), *Classical Conditioning II: Current Research and Theory*, Appleton-Century-Crofts, New York.

Obrist, P. A., Webb, R. A., and Sutterer, J. R. (1969). Heart rate and somatic changes during aversive conditioning and a simple reaction task. *Psychophysiology*, **5**, 696–723.

Obrist, P. A., Wood, D. M., and Perez-Reyes, M. (1965). Heart rate during conditioning in humans: effects of UCS intensity, vagal blockade and adrenergic block of vasomotor activity. *Journal of Experimental Psychology*, **70**, 32–42.

Öhman, A., Björkstrand, P., and Ellström, P. (1973). Effects of explicit trial-by-trial information about shock probability in long interstimulus interval GSR conditioning. *Journal of Experimental Psychology*, **98**, 145–151.

Pavlov, I. P. (1927). *Conditioned Reflexes: An Investigation of the Physiological Activity of the Cerebral Cortex*, Oxford University Press, London.

Perkins, C. C., Jr., Seymann, R. G., Levis, D. J., and Spence, H., Jr. (1966). Factors affecting preference for signal-shock over shock-signal. *Journal of Experimental Psychology*, **72**, 190–196.

Prescott, J. W. (1964). *A Factor Analysis of Electrodermal Response Measures. A Study in Human Conditioning*. Unpublished doctoral dissertation, McGill University.

Prokasy, W. F. (1965). Classical eyelid conditioning: experimenter operations, task demands and response shaping. In W. F. Prokasy (Ed.), *Classical Conditioning*, Appleton-Century-Crofts, New York.

Prokasy, W. F., and Ebel, H. C. (1967). Three distinct components of the classically conditioned GSR in human subjects. *Journal of Experimental Psychology*, **73**, 247–256.

Quinn, J. T., and Henbest, R. (1967). Partial failure of generalization in alcoholics following aversion therapy. *Quarterly Journal of Studies on Alcohol*, **28**, 70–75.

Rachman, S. J. (1966). Sexual fetishism: an experimental analogue. *Psychological Record*, **16**, 293–296.

Rachman, S. J., and Teasdale, J. (1969). Aversion therapy: an appraisal. In C. M. Franks (Ed.), *Behavior Therapy: Appraisal and Status*, McGraw-Hill, New York.

Raskin, D. C., Kotses, H., and Bever, J. (1969). Autonomic indicators of orienting and defensive reflexes. *Journal of Experimental Psychology*, **80**, 423–433.

Razran, G. H. S. (1965). Empirical codifications and specific theoretical implications of compound-stimulus conditioning: perception. In W. F. Prokasy (Ed.), *Classical Conditioning*, Appleton-Century-Crofts, New York.

Rescorla, R. A. (1967). Pavlovian conditioning and its proper control procedures. *Psychological Review*, **74**, 71–80.

Rescorla, R. A. (1969). Conditioned inhibition of fear. In N. J. Mackintosh and W. K. Honig (Eds.), *Fundamental Issues in Associative Learning*, Dalhousie University Press, Halifax.

Rescorla, R. A. (1973). Effect of US habituation following conditioning. *Journal of Comparative and Physiological Psychology*, **82**, 137–143.

Rescorla, R. A., and LoLordo, V. M. (1965). Inhibition of avoidance behavior. *Journal of Comparative and Physiological Psychology*, **59**, 406–412.

Rescorla, R. A., and Solomon, R. L. (1967). Two-process learning theory: relationships between Pavlovian conditioning and instrumental learning. *Psychological Review*, **74**, 151–182.

Revusky, S. (1973). Some laboratory paradigms for chemical aversion treatment of alcoholism. *Journal of Behavior Therapy and Experimental Psychiatry*, **4**, 15–17.

Rizley, R. C., and Rescorla, R. A. (1972). Associations in second-order conditioning and sensory preconditioning. *Journal of Comparative and Physiological Psychology*, **81**, 1–11.

Roberts, L. E., and Young, R. (1971). Electrodermal responses are independent of movement during aversive conditioning in rats but heart rate is not. *Journal of Comparative and Physiological Psychology*, **77**, 495–512.

Rohrbaugh, M., and Riccio, D. C. (1970). Paradoxical enhancement of learned fear. *Journal of Abnormal Psychology*, **75**, 210–216.

Rohrbaugh, M., Riccio, D. C., and Arthur, A. (1972). Paradoxical enhancement of conditioned suppression. *Behaviour Research and Therapy*, **10**, 125–130.

Ross, L. E. (1971). Cognitive factors in conditioning: the use of masking tasks in eyelid conditioning. In H. H. Kendler and J. T. Spence (Eds.), *Essays in Neobehaviorism: A Memorial Volume to Kenneth W. Spence*, Appleton-Century-Crofts, New York.

Rozin, P., and Kalat, J. W. (1971). Specific hungers and poison avoidance as adaptive specialization of learning. *Psychological Review*, **78**, 459–486.

Sachs, D. A., and Keller, T. (1972). Intensity and temporal characteristics of the CER paradigm with humans. *Journal of General Psychology*, **86**, 181–188.

Schlosberg, H. (1937). The relationship between success and the laws of conditioning. *Psychological Review*, **44**, 379–394.

Schneiderman, N. (1972). Response system divergencies in aversive classical conditioning. In A. H. Black and W. F. Prokasy (Eds.), *Classical Conditioning II: Current Research and Theory*, Appleton-Century-Crofts. New York.

Scobie, S. R., and Fallon, D. (1974). Operant and Pavlovian control of a defensive shuttle response in goldfish (*carassius auratus*). *Journal of Comparative and Physiological Psychology*, **86**, 867–874.

Seligman, M. E. P. (1968). Chronic fear produced by unpredictable shock. *Journal of Comparative and Physiological Psychology*, **66**, 402–411.

Seligman, M. E. P. (1970). On the generality of the laws of learning. *Psychological Review*, **77**, 406–418.

Seligman, M. E. P., Maier, S. F., and Solomon, R. L. (1971). Unpredictable and uncontrollable aversive events. In R. F. Brush (Ed.), *Aversive Conditioning and Learning*, Academic Press, New York.

Sheldon, M. H. (1973). Contingency theory and the distinction between associative and non-associative effects in classical conditioning. *Quarterly Journal of Experimental Psychology*, **25**, 124–129.

Siegel, P. S., and Milby, J. B. (1969). Secondary reinforcement in relation to shock termination: second chapter. *Psychological Bulletin*, **72**, 146–156.

Silverman, R. E. (1960). Eliminating a conditioned GSR by the reduction of experimental anxiety. *Journal of Experimental Psychology*, **59**, 122–125.

Smith, K. (1954). Conditioning as an artifact. *Psychological Review*, **61**, 217–225.

Smith, M. C. (1968). CS–US interval and US intensity in classical conditioning of the rabbit's nictitating membrane response. *Journal of Comparative and Physiological Psychology*, **66**, 679–687.

Smith, R. E., Diener, E., and Beaman, A. L. (1974). Demand characteristics and the behavioral avoidance measure of fear in behavior therapy analogue research. *Behavior Therapy*, **5**, 172–182.

Solyom, L., McClure, D. J., Heseltine, G. F. D., Ledwidge, B., and Solyom, C. (1972). Variables in the aversion relief therapy of phobias. *Behavior Therapy*, **3**, 21–28.

Spence, K. W. (1966). Cognitive and drive factors in the extinction of the conditioned eyeblink in human subjects. *Psychological Review*, **73**, 445–458.

Spence, K. W., and Runquist, W. N. (1958). Temporal effects of conditioned fear on the eyelid reflex. *Journal of Experimental Psychology*, **55**, 613–616.

Staats, A. W. (1968a). *Learning, Language and Cognition*, Holt, Rinehart and Winston, New York.

Staats, A. W. (1968b). Social behaviorism and human motivation: Principles of the attitude-reinforcer-discriminative system. In A. G. Greenwald, T. C. Brock and T. M. Ostrom (Eds.), *Psychological Foundations of Attitudes*, Academic Press, New York.

Staddon, J. E. R., and Simmelhag, V. L. (1971). The 'superstition' experiment: a reexamination of its implications for the principles of adaptive behavior. *Psychological Review*, **78**, 3–43.

Stewart, M A., Stern, J. A., Winokur, G., and Fredman, S. (1961). An analysis of GSR conditioning. *Psychological Review*, **68**, 60–67.

Sutterer, J. R., and Beck, R. C. (1970). Human responses to stimuli associated with shock onset and termination. *Journal of Experimental Research in Personality*, **4**, 163–170.

Thorndike, E. L. (1935). *The Psychology of Wants, Interests and Attitudes*, Appleton-Century-Crofts, New York.

Thorpe, G. L. (1972). Learning paradigms in the anticipatory avoidance technique: a comment on the controversy between MacDonough and Feldman. *Behavior Therapy*, **3**, 614–618.

Wagner, A. R. (1969a). Incidental stimuli and discrimination learning. In R. M. Gilbert and N. S. Sutherland (Eds.), *Animal Discrimination Learning*, Academic Press, London.

Wagner, A. R. (1969b). Stimulus validity and stimulus selection in associative learning. In N. J. Mackintosh and W. K. Honig (Eds.), *Fundamental Issues in Associative Learning*, Dalhousie University Press, Halifax.

Wagner, A. R., Logan, F. A., Haberlandt, K., and Price, T. (1968). Stimulus selection in animal discrimination learning. *Journal of Experimental Psychology*, **76**, 171–180.

Wagner, A. R., Thomas, E., and Norton, T. (1967). Conditioning with electrical stimulation of motor cortex. *Journal of Comparative and Physiological Psychology*, **64**, 191–199.

Wahlsten, D., Cole, M., and Fantino, E. (1967). Is a stimulus associated with the escape from shock a positive or negative reinforcer? *Psychonomic Science*, **8**, 283–286.

Watson, J. B., and Rayner, R. (1920). Conditioned emotional reactions. *Journal of Experimental Psychology*, **3**, 1–14.

Weiss, A. R., and Evans, I. M. (1974). *The Semantic Counter-conditioning of Anxiety*. Unpublished manuscript, University of Hawaii.

Westcott, M. R., and Huttenlocher, J. (1961). Cardiac conditioning: the effects and implications of controlled and uncontrolled respiration. *Journal of Experimental Psychology*, **61**, 353–359.

Wickens, D. D. (1959). Conditioning to complex stimuli. *American Psychologist*, **14**, 180–188.

Wickens, D. D. (1973). Classical conditioning, as it contributes to the analyses of some basic psychological processes. In F. J. McGuigan and D. B. Lumsden (Eds.), *Contemporary Approaches to Conditioning and Learning*, V. H. Winston and Sons, Washington, D.C.

Wilson, G. T., and Davison, G. C. (1969). Aversion techniques in behavior therapy: some theoretical and metatheoretical considerations. *Journal of Consulting and Clinical Psychology*, **33**, 327–329.

Wilson, G. T., and Davison, G. C. (1971). Processes of fear-reduction in systematic desensitization: animal studies. *Psychological Bulletin*, **76**, 1–14.

Wolpe, J. (1952). Experimental neurosis as learned behaviour. *British Journal of Psychology*, **43**, 243–268.

Wolpe, J. (1958). *Psychotherapy by Reciprocal Inhibition*, Stanford University Press, Stanford, California.

Wolpe, J. (1971). The behavioristic conception of neurosis: a reply to two critics. *Psychological Review*, **78**, 341–343.

Wood, D. M., and Obrist, P. A. (1964). Effects of controlled and uncontrolled respiration on the conditioned heart rate response in humans. *Journal of Experimental Psychology*, **68**, 221–229.

Woodard, W. T., and Bitterman, M. E. (1973). Pavlovian analysis of avoidance conditioning in the goldfish (*carassius auratus*). *Journal of Comparative and Physiological Psychology*, **82**, 123–129.

Yates, A. J. (1970). *Behavior Therapy*, Wiley, New York.

Yehle, A. L. (1968). Divergence among rabbit response systems during three-tone classical discrimination conditioning. *Journal of Experimental Psychology*, **77**, 468–473.

Zelhart, P. F., Jr. (1972). Conditioned reinforcement based on shock termination. *Journal of General Psychology*, **86**, 131–139.

Zimmer-Hart, C. L., and Rescorla, R. A. (1974). Extinction of Pavlovian conditioned inhibition. *Journal of Comparative and Physiological Psychology*, **86**, 837–845.

Zuckerman, M. (1971). Physiological measures of sexual arousal in the human. *Psychological Bulletin*, **75**, 297–329.

INSTRUMENTAL LEARNING: COMPARATIVE STUDIES

Morrie Baum

Behaviour therapy is based on the assumption that maladaptive behaviour patterns are established via the laws of learning and that treatment to change these behaviour patterns must also operate according to these same laws. Much of the theory of behaviour therapy is based on learning laws elucidated in animal studies. The present chapter reviews some recent developments in the field of animal instrumental learning and their implications for behaviour therapy. Five topics are reviewed: (1) flooding, (2) learned helplessness, (3) drug fusion, (4) biological factors in instrumental learning and (5) frustration tolerance.

FLOODING

Flooding consists of forcibly exposing an organism to cues which it fears (the CS) in the absence of any trauma, and it has been shown to hasten avoidance extinction in animals and to eliminate phobias in Man. This section of the chapter discusses the correct nomenclature for the flooding procedure and describes the various ways in which it can be carried out. Recent research on parameters which influence how well flooding works is reviewed, as are methods for increasing its effectiveness. The issue of the effect of flooding on fear (as distinct from the overt avoidance behaviour) is discussed, as are the implications of flooding studies with animals for the use of flooding in Man.

Nomenclature and techniques of administering flooding

Flooding involves forced exposure to the stimuli which the organism fears, in the absence of any trauma and with the avoidance contingency rendered inoperable. Various labels which have been used to describe this basic procedure include 'flooding', 'response prevention', 'response blocking', 'detainment' or 'forced reality-testing'. Baum (1971a) has suggested that in the interests of standardization the term 'flooding' should be adopted. When the avoidance response involves an element of active flight, then flooding may entail thwarting or blocking the avoidance response, detaining the organism in the presence of the feared stimuli for some length of time. Hence the labels 'response prevention' or 'detainment' for this technique. However, the technique can also be employed in the case of the extinction of passive avoidance responding as well. Thus, an animal can be trained to run down an alley-way for food and then punished for responding. This animal will learn to avoid punishment passively by ceasing its alley-running behaviour. When punishment has been removed and we wish the passive avoidance response to extinguish, flooding would entail forcing the animal to move down the runway in the absence of any punishment, so that its previous behaviour of alley-running for food would be reestablished. Obviously, the terms 'response prevention' or 'detainment' would be misleading in this case. Flooding is thus the term which is most appropriate, since it is applicable to the extinction of both active and passive avoidance responding alike. Most phobias in Man seem to be of the passive avoidance variety, with the patient refusing to approach some object rather than actively fleeing it. Flooding would thus consist of encouraging confrontation with the feared stimuli rather than a prevention of an active avoidance response.

The term 'forced reality testing' has also been used interchangeably with the term 'flooding'. However, the former term has some clinical connotations which may be inappropriate in purely experimental work. Side-stepping these connotations, the term flooding also conveys the notion that it must be an unusually strong emotional experience for an organism to undergo forced exposure to something it fears and has been accustomed to fleeing or avoiding in some way. In the clinical treatment of phobias or human avoidance behaviour, the forced exposure often occurs through the use of the patient's imagination rather than in real life. For such 'flooding in imagination', the much-used term 'implosion' has been suggested as the standard term (Baum and Poser, 1971).

Flooding actually refers to several different techniques, all of which have in common that they expose the organism to the feared cues or CS underlying the behaviour while no trauma are presented. While flooding is undoubtedly effective in hastening avoidance extinction (e.g. Baum, 1966), there are several ways in which the procedure can be applied. One method of administering flooding involves allowing the avoidance response to be made at will by the animal, but seeing to it that the CS is not terminated (e.g. Bankart, 1971; Heath, 1968; Polin, 1959; Shearman, 1970). This flooding (type 1) has been what is conventionally referred to as flooding (initially named by Polin, 1959). In the shuttlebox, flooding-1 involves simply keeping the CS on while the subject is permitted to respond by hurdle-jumping as frequently as it desires; in the ledgebox, a one-way avoidance situation (see Baum, 1966), flooding-1 involves beginning a new trial as soon as the response is made; thus it entails reducing the intertrial interval to zero.

Another type of flooding, flooding-2, involves blocking or thwarting the avoidance response while exposing the organism to the feared CS or cues. This form of flooding has been conventionally referred to as response prevention (Page and Hall, 1953) or response blocking. In the shuttlebox or one-way Miller-type avoidance task, flooding-2 typically involves placing a barrier across the middle of the apparatus, thus physically rendering impossible the response of crossing to the other side of the apparatus (Bersh and Keltz, 1971; Kamano, 1968; Linton and coworkers, 1970; Schiff, 1971).

A third type of flooding, flooding-3, involves removing a part of the avoidance apparatus and in this way making it impossible for the animal to perform the avoidance response. In the case of lever-press avoidance, the lever is simply withdrawn from the chamber while the CS is presented without shock for a period of time (Reid, Taylor and Rassel, 1971). In the ledgebox of Baum (1966), flooding-3 entails removing the safety ledge from the apparatus so that it is impossible for the animal to climb onto it.

Since there are at least three distinctly different techniques of flooding, the question arises as to which is the most effective in hastening avoidance extinction in animals. This problem has received considerable attention in recent research. Baum and Oler (1968) compared a technique similar to flooding-1 with flooding-3 in the ledgebox, and found flooding-1 to be superior. Shearman (1970) found flooding-1 and flooding-2 to be equally effective in hastening the extinction of shuttlebox avoidance. Polin (1959) claimed to have demonstrated the superiority of flooding-1 over flooding-2, while Berman and Katzev (1972), in a more carefully controlled study, found flooding-2 was the more effective of the two. In a little-known experiment, Akiyama (1969) found flooding-1 to be superior to flooding-2. The last three experiments also employed the shuttlebox avoidance situation, and all of the above experiments involved rat subjects. Baum (1973a) compared all three techniques under comparable conditions in his one-way ledgebox and found flooding-1 and flooding-2 to be equally effective, both being superior to flooding-3. In general, it can be said that all techniques of administering flooding are effective in hastening the subsequent extinction of the avoidance response. Contradictory findings have clouded the issue of which flooding technique is the most effective, with differences in apparatuses, procedures and particular parameters seeming to determine the outcome of these comparison-type experiments.

Flooding in man can also involve various procedures. It can be carried out in the patient's imagination, where we have suggested that it be termed 'implosion'. When flooding in Man is carried out *in vivo*, it may often involve modelling and observation where the patient observes the therapist approaching and in contact with the object of the phobia. It may also involve verbal reinforcement by the therapist of the patient's approach to the phobic object or stimulus. Flooding may thus involve one or several procedures and often a combination of more than one, all having in common a contact with the feared stimulus in the absence of any trauma.

Parameters affecting the efficacy of flooding

The extent to which flooding is effective in eliminating avoidance behaviour is dependent on various parameters. As reviewed by Baum (1970), these include intensity of the shock trauma used in avoidance learning, the degree to which the response has been overtrained, the amount of shock trauma received prior to avoidance acquisition and the duration of the flooding treatment. Duration of flooding seems a critical parameter since, no matter how strong or well established the avoidance behaviour, it can still be extinguished via flooding if the flooding period is sufficiently long in duration. In recent years, new parameters have been found to influence the effectiveness of any given constant duration of flooding.

One parameter is that of massed versus distributed (spaced) flooding. That is, a given duration of flooding may be administered in a single, prolonged session or in several brief sessions spaced out in time. In the systematic desensitization of human phobias and avoidance behaviour, there is some evidence that short periods of therapy spaced out over several days are more effective in eliminating phobic reactions than is an equal duration of therapy massed together all at one time (Ramsay and coworkers, 1966), although the effect is sometimes found to be a small one, with massed therapy also being effective (Lanyon, Manosevitz and Imber, 1968). Using flooding in rats, Baum and Myran (1971) found distributed flooding to be superior (leading to faster extinction) when compared to massed flooding. This experiment involved type 3 flooding having a total duration of 9 min, administered in either a single session (massed) or in three 3 min sessions, given one per day. Using both flooding-1 and flooding-2 procedures, Shearman (1970) found no difference between one massed and one spaced flooding condition. Schiff (1971) systematically varied number and duration of flooding sessions in a 3×5 factorial design, and like Shearman found no difference between massed versus spaced flooding, concluding that the only significant variable was total flooding time. Thus, the massed versus distributed parameter in flooding yields results similar to those obtained using systematic desensitization of human phobias; sometimes the distributed procedure yields better results, but often there is no difference between massed and spaced procedures.

A second parameter is that of immediate versus delayed flooding following avoidance acquisition, based on the possibility that flooding might be more effective if the subject to whom it was administered was in a quiescent state at the beginning of flooding rather than being agitated. If this notion is correct, then one reason why a brief period of flooding may be ineffective in eliminating an avoidance response learned under strong shock may be that the animal is too highly agitated, even before flooding is administered. This seems quite likely since a frequent experimental procedure employed in flooding studies is to administer flooding immediately upon completion of acquisition. Perhaps if the animal were given a rest period after acquisition, in order that the agitation resulting from the recent shock trauma subside, then the brief period of flooding would be more effective in leading to subsequent extinction. In a recent study (Baum, 1972a), this was indeed found to be the case, since a 5 min flooding session was more successful in eliminating an avoidance response when the flooding session was given 30 minutes following acquisition than immediately after acquisition. Appropriate control groups showed that this effect was not simply a result of the 30 min delay prior to extinction testing, but rather was due to an interaction between the delay period and the flooding session.

A third parameter recently explored involves the repeated administration of flooding, i.e. the acquisition–flooding–extinction sequence is repeated. A control group receives repetitions of acquisition-interval in a neutral situation-extinction. Using this paradigm, Baum (1972b) found that a flooding session quickly became ineffective as it was repeatedly given daily over 5 days, when compared to the control time period equal in duration to the flooding period but spent in a neutral situation. Akiyama (1968, 1969) found a similar result when, using a rat shuttlebox situation, the acquisition–flooding–extinction sequence was repeated once and flooding was found to be less effective on the second administration.

Increasing the efficacy of flooding

Baum (1970) has reviewed various means of making flooding more effective under any given set of parameters. These include 'social facilitation', where naïve rats are present along with the fearful subject during flooding, and 'mechanical facilitation', where physically disrupting the subject during flooding and forcing it to move around and explore the experimental chamber increases the efficacy of flooding in hastening avoidance extinction. Recent work has added additional techniques for enhancing the action of flooding.

Baum and Gordon (1970) showed that the application of a loud buzzer during flooding served to increase greatly the amount of general exploratory activity displayed during flooding (with the subject exploring rather than freezing or making abortive attempts to avoid), and this was correlated with a greater efficacy of flooding. An even more powerful effect was obtained by Gordon and Baum (1971), who showed that the administration of pulsing, rewarding brain stimulation to the posterior lateral hypothalamus of the frightened rat during flooding, greatly increased the efficacy of flooding. Both of these experiments involved training the rats to avoid intense shock (1.3 mA), after which a 5 min flooding period was administered, followed by an extinction session. The facilitating extra stimulation (loud buzzer or electrical brain stimulation) was administered only during the flooding period.

The powerful facilitating effect of rewarding brain stimulation during flooding has been confirmed by Reid, Taylor and Rassel (1971). Baum, Leclerc and St.-Laurent (1973) replicated the effect with stimulation to the posterior lateral hypothalamus, but showed that aversive brain stimulation to the reticularis pontis caudalis had no significant effect on the efficacy of flooding. In another study, Leclerc, St.-Laurent and Baum (1973) showed that rewarding brain stimulation to the *anterior* lateral hypothalamus failed to facilitate flooding. Since brain stimulation can be precisely controlled as to intensity, frequency, affective result and placement in the brain, the study of brain stimulation administered during flooding is a promising new development.

Changes in stimulation in other sensory modalities will, if introduced during flooding, also make the procedure more effective. This follows from a suggestion of R. L. Solomon (personal communication) that extraneous stimuli during flooding distract the animal's attention away from the fear stimulus, and this makes the procedure more effective. In keeping with this notion, Baum (1972a) has shown that a change in visual stimulation (altering the illumination conditions by darkening the experimental room while the animal is undergoing flooding) increases the efficacy of flooding. This experiment followed the general paradigm employed in the Baum and Gordon (1970) and Gordon and Baum (1971) studies, but the facilitating effect obtained by changing illumination conditions seemed to be relatively weak. Whether or not stimulus changes in other modalities introduced during flooding will also make the procedure more effective is open to further research.

As suggested by Baum (1970), another way of facilitating the action of flooding might be to administer relaxing drugs prior to flooding so that the subject can achieve a more relaxed state while confronting the object of its fears. The use of chlorpromazine (Nelson, 1967) and amobarbital sodium (Kamano, 1968) in this way has failed to yield positive results (as discussed in Baum, 1970). Kamano (1972) has even found that administering relaxing drugs in conjunction with flooding can diminish the effectiveness of the procedure, probably via drug dissociation of the effects of flooding. However, Baum (1973b) has shown that chlorpromazine can diminish the apparent stressfulness of the flooding procedure in rats, without adversely affecting its efficacy. In general, there have been no published reports of relaxing drugs increasing the effectiveness of flooding in animals.

In recent work on flooding in Man, Hussain (1970, 1971) has obtained improved efficacy in treating human phobias via flooding by employing intravenous injections of thiopental, designed to induce relaxation during flooding. Marks and coworkers (1972) observed a similar trend using diazepam in conjunction with flooding. In another recent study, Johnston and Gath (1973) also found improved efficacy using diazepam-assisted flooding. At present, it is not possible to explain why using drugs in conjunction with flooding has yielded positive results in Man but negative results in animals.

Enhancement of fear due to flooding

While flooding has been shown to be an effective means of eliminating avoidance behaviour, there is some question as to what happens to the underlying fear state when flooding is administered. For example, Page (1955) found that flooding led to increased residual fear and that, although a rat's active avoidance response of removing itself from a chamber had extinguished via flooding, the rat would nonetheless exhibit pronounced passive avoidance of that situation (by taking an exceptionally long time to approach food that had been placed in the chamber). Werboff, Duane and Cohen (1964) found that when rats had undergone extinction of avoidance via flooding, their heart rates were greatly elevated, indicating a high level of fear in the absence of any avoidance responding. Recent studies by Riccio and his associates, using rats in a one-way shuttlebox situation, have also found that underlying fear was augmented by flooding, despite the fact that the active avoidance response had been extinguished (Coulter, Riccio and Page, 1969; Linton and coworkers, 1970). In these studies, as in Page's original study, residual fear was measured via increased latency of approach to food.

However, using Page's measure of residual fear, Bersh and Paynter (1972) have demonstrated that flooding *does* reduce fear as well as avoidance behaviour, explaining the contradiction with Riccio's and Page's findings on the grounds that the latter studies had involved a confounding of variables (with flooding animals actually receiving less exposure to the CS than control animals receiving extinction trials without prior flooding). Baum (1971b) also found no greater residual fear following flooding than following extinction of the avoidance response without flooding. This study involved introducing a loud buzzer after the response had extinguished, and recovery from extinction was found for all groups to roughly the same extent, regardless of whether flooding had been used to hasten extinction or not. In summary, there is evidence for the existence of residual fear following the cessation of avoidance responding induced by flooding. Whether or not such residual fear is enhanced following flooding (when compared to extinction without flooding) remains in some dispute.

A related issue is that of enhancement of fear of a signal following unreinforced exposure to that signal. This process, termed 'incubation' by Eysenck (1968), predicts that flooding procedures would exacerbate or strengthen avoidance behaviour rather than weaken it, and Eysenck cites fragmentary supporting data on the problem by Napalkov (1963) and others. The theory behind this possible phenomenon emphasizes the nocive nature of the CR in aversive conditioning, and suggests that, if sufficiently strong, this CR may serve as a reinforcement for the CS–CR link, even if no UCS is presented (Eysenck and Beech, 1971). Since the publication of Eysenck's paper, several investigators have demonstrated that flooding or unreinforced exposure to a feared CS exacerbates fear and avoidance behaviour. Rohrbaugh and Riccio (1970) demonstrated this in rats using short CS exposures, terming their finding 'paradoxical enhancement of learned fear'. Solyom (1969) apparently demonstrated a similar effect in rats, while in Man, Miller and Levis (1971) found exacerbation of fear of a phobic test stimulus following a short period of unreinforced exposure. In general, it can be said that usually flooding has not been observed to strengthen fear or avoidance behaviour in laboratory investigations, but on the contrary serves to extinguish the avoidance behaviour. Conditions under which Eysenck's 'incubation' effect is produced may involve avoidance behaviour based on very traumatic experiences (e.g. very intense shock) and flooding periods that are relatively short in duration.

Applications in Man of animal flooding studies

Perhaps the most important role of animal research with flooding is to provide an overall theoretical and experimental framework for the use of flooding in man. Indeed, the pioneering research of Isaac Marks and his associates into flooding as a means of treating phobias in man (reviewed by Marks, 1972) was triggered by demonstrations of the efficacy of flooding in eliminating avoidance behaviour in animals. Phobias in man involve an element of fear as well as flight from some object or situation (both in the absence of any trauma), making phobias analogous to the extinction of avoidance behaviour in animals. The validity of this analogy, while it has not gone unquestioned (e.g. Costello, 1970), makes it possible to develop new theories and suggestions for increasing the efficacy of flooding in man based on animal studies.

Animal studies have given rise to various specific refinements of the flooding technique in man. The relaxation theory of flooding suggested by Baum (1970) to explain flooding studies in animals led to the successful use of relaxing drugs in conjunction with flooding in man (Hussain, 1970, 1971). As discussed earlier, this development is expanding at the human level, despite the ironic lack of success in more recent animal studies. Animal work has shown that distracting the animal's attention (e.g. with a loud buzzer) during flooding increases the procedure's efficacy (Baum and Gordon, 1970). This has led to successful clinical use where the patient was distracted by being required to perform some manual task during flooding (Naud, Boisvert and Lamontagne, 1973; E. G. Poser, personal communication).

The close links between animal and human research on flooding is something not found in the case of systematic desensitization (Wilson and Davison, 1971). A clear example of these links is found in the studies of 'irrelevant fear' or 'irrelevant stress' and flooding. Watson and Marks (1971) found that flooding was equally effective in treating phobias, regardless of whether the confrontation during flooding was with the feared object of the phobia or with another 'irrelevant fear' stimulus. This suggests that flooding may be effective in eliminating avoidance behavior because it leads to a generalized habituation to fear and stress, which is later reflected in weakened avoidance responding in extinction. This study by Watson and Marks with humans triggered an animal study by Baum and Leclerc (1974). They compared flooding with forced swimming (irrelevant stress), either treatment being interpolated between avoidance acquisition and extinction in rats. The results showed that the irrelevant stress did eliminate avoidance responding as well as did flooding if the extinction test occurred immediately after flooding or irrelevant stress. However, if the extinction test took place some hours after treatment, only flooding was effective in reducing avoidance behaviour. This suggests that habituation to irrelevant stress or irrelevant fear leads only to a short-term, temporary diminution of avoidance behaviour (a sort of transient, 'contrast' effect), while only flooding has a long-term, permanent effect. Thus, there has been a mutual enrichment between animal and human studies involving flooding.

LEARNED HELPLESSNESS

The first reference to the notion of learned helplessness comes in a paper by Overmier and Seligman (1967), who reported that dogs exposed to unavoidable, inescapable electric shocks in a Pavlovian harness were subsequently impaired in acquiring an escape avoidance response in the shuttlebox. More specifically, dogs exposed to the prior inescapable shocks would, when confronted with the instrumental task in the shuttlebox, show a passive acceptance of severe shock. Even if an escape response was occasionally made by the 'helpless' dogs, it did not reliably predict the further occurrence of escape responses, which was the normal pattern for dogs not preexposed to inescapable shock. Furthermore, the dogs 'helpless' in the face of shock had not been physically debilitated by the prior inescapable shock in the Pavlovian harness, since they occasionally jumped the barrier in the shuttlebox between trials and some jumped the barrier at the end of the session in order to leave the shuttlebox.

Overmier and Seligman (1967) also ruled out the possibility of a superstitiously learned, incompatible, motor response being acquired during exposure to the inescapable shock which would later interfere with instrumental learning in the shuttlebox. This possibility was excluded by carrying out the inescapable shock treatment while the dog was paralyzed with curare, a neuromuscular blocking agent. This was not found to alter the helplessness phenomenon. Curiously, this early research (Overmier, 1968; Overmier and Seligman, 1967) demonstrated that helplessness was a transient, time-dependent phenomenon. Inescapable shocks interfered with avoidance learning in the shuttlebox one day later, but not if the gap between the two experiences was several days or a week. The helplessness phenomenon was alleged to involve a learning that shock was uncontrollable and that responding was ineffective, and this undermined the incentive to learn to escape or avoid in the subsequent shuttlebox test. It was not clear why this learned helplessness should be so time-dependent. However, in a later study, Seligman and Groves (1970) demonstrated that the learned helplessness could be more permanent in nature if the initial inescapable shocks were given in a series of sessions distributed over a number of days.

Prevention and alleviation of learned helplessness

Seligman and Maier (1967) showed that it was not exposure to shock per se that caused helplessness, but only exposure to uncontrollable shock that was responsible. If the dog were merely given escapable shock in the Pavlovian hareness (the escape response being to press a panel by means of a head movement), then there was no interference with subsequent instrumental escape avoidance in the shuttlebox task. Animals which received the same pattern of shocks in a yoked-control design but had no control over the shocks were subsequently 'helpless'. Furthermore, in this same study, Seligman and Maier (1967) showed that if dogs were first given escapable shock in the shuttlebox, they became 'immunized' to the detrimental effects of subsequent inescapable shocks. That is, escape training followed by inescapable shocks did not produce helplessness. Thus helplessness in the face of shock can be prevented if, in the dog's initial experience with shock, he learns to escape it. In a sense, this is a kind of 'mastery training' which enables the animal to endure subsequent uncontrollable trauma without deleterious effects.

Seligman, Maier and Geer (1968) studied techniques of alleviating learned helplessness in dogs. They found that the chronic failure of helpless dogs to escape shock can be eliminated by physically compelling them to engage repeatedly in the response which terminates shock. Such 'directive therapy' was accomplished by dragging the dog from one side of the shuttlebox to the other by means of long leashes, forcing the dog to expose himself to the response reinforcement (shock-termination) contingency. Such repeated forced responding ultimately led to the restoration of normal instrumental behaviour.

Clinical relevance of learned helplessness

The maladaptive failure of dogs to escape shock resembles human behaviour disorders in which individuals passively accept aversive events without resistance or attempts to escape, as observed by Seligman, Maier and Geer (1968). Bettelheim (1960) described certain prisoners of Nazi concentration camps as ' . . . people so deprived of affect, self-esteem, and every form of stimulation, so totally exhausted, both physically and emotionally, that they had given the environment total power over them (pp. 151–152)'. Bleuler (1950) also described the behaviour of some of his patients who were very passive in the face of danger and whose sense of self-preservation was often reduced to zero. More recently, Seligman (1972, 1974) has drawn the analogy between learned helplessness in dogs to depression in Man. In helplessness in dogs, there is a passivity in the face of trauma and a lack of escape response initiation combined with a negative expectation that instrumental responding is to no avail. According to Seligman, helplessness can be cured by repeated exposure to responding that produces relief, and changing the patient's perception of himself as helpless to a set in which he believes that he can control reinforcement may be central to the successful treatment of depression. Learned helplessness can be prevented by immunizing experiences with control over trauma, and it is speculated that a life history of control over reinforcers may make individuals more resilient to depression.

DRUG FUSION

The object of this section is to discuss the properties of behaviour which is learned under more than one drug state. A previous study (Baum, 1971c) suggests that such behaviour is stronger and more persistent than behaviour learned only in the non-drug state. This 'drug fusion effect', wherein experiences from both drug and non-drug conditions are fused and lead to stronger conditioned behaviour, was demonstrated using alcohol. More specifically, the experiment involved giving rats two instrumental avoidance training sessions. One group was given both sessions while undrugged; the second group received one session while drugged with alcohol and the second while undrugged. After the two training sessions, the avoidance response underwent extinction, i.e. the shock motivating the response was disconnected and the experimenter observed how long the animals persisted in responding. This resistance to extinction of the avoidance response was taken as a measure of the response's strength. The results showed that animals receiving training in both alcohol and non-drugged states persisted in responding for a much longer time in extinction. That is, behaviour learned under more than one drug state is stronger—this is the 'drug fusion effect'. There is very little other experimental literature on drug fusion in animals apart from the initial experiment with rats (Baum, 1971c).

The practical implications of drug fusion for behaviour therapy are great. If the phenomenon of stronger behaviour following learning in more than one drug state is reliable, then it would suggest that therapy should be administered to patients while they are in several drug states. In this way the behaviour change induced by therapy would be more lasting and less susceptible to relapse. Ernest G. Poser (personal communication) at the Douglas Hospital in Verdun, Quebec, has already begun to administer aversion therapy to alcoholics while they are both sober and inebriated, in order to make the conditioned aversion to alcohol more persistent and resistant to extinction. Preliminary results are encouraging. Marks and coworkers (1972) have carried out flooding sessions during waning diazepam treatment. In this way, they ensured that flooding was experienced under both drug and non-drug conditions. Their results indicated a drug fusion effect, with flooding being rendered more effective.

Drug fusion and drug dissociation

Behaviour learned while an organism is drugged sometimes fails to appear during subsequent non-drug conditions. Conversely, if the same behaviour is learned while the organism is not drugged, it may then be performed only as long as the organism remains undrugged. For some reason, the ability to perform appears to be conditional upon the drug conditions present during initial acquisition of learning (Overton, 1964). This phenomenon is generally referred to as 'drug dissociation'.

A considerable literature exists on drug dissociation, primarily from animal studies (e.g. as reviewed in Overton, 1970, 1972). Drug dissociation seems to occur only with drugs that act on the central nervous system and not with peripheral agents. As summarized by Overton, strong drug dissociation effects have been obtained with anesthetic drugs (pentobarbital, alcohol) and minor tranquillizers (chlordiazepoxide, meprobamate). Moderately strong drug dissociation effects have been obtained with antimuscarinic drugs, nicotinic drugs, narcotics and miscellaneous psychedelic drugs, such as mescaline, tetrahydrocannabinol (THC) and lysergic acid diethyl amide (LSD). Only weak effects have been obtained with other drugs, such as the phenothiazines.

It is important to distinguish between drug dissociation and drug fusion. In the former, behaviour learned under one drug state fails to transfer to the second state. In drug fusion, the behaviour is learned separately under both states and is made stronger in either state. While the two phenomena are clearly different conceptually, there may be a pharmacological relationship between the drugs which can produce both kinds of effects. Thus, alcohol yields strong dissociation as well as a strong fusion effect (Baum, 1971c). Additional research is required to establish the drug fusion effect with more certainty and also to relate drug fusion to drug dissociation.

BIOLOGICAL FACTORS IN INSTRUMENTAL LEARNING

Early work on conditioning was characterized by the assumption that all events and responses were equipotential in their associability in the learning process. Thus, in the field of classical conditioning, Pavlov (1927) suggested that any CS or signalling stimulus could be linked with any inborn or unconditioned reflex (UCR). In the field of instrumental learning, Skinner (1938) argued that any motor response could be established through reward and that the dynamic properties of any instrumental behaviour could be studied via a single response, the lever-press. Recent work, however, has called into question this assumption of equipotentiality.

Seligman (1970) has summarized recent findings that some events are more easily associated than others in the learning process. He has delineated a dimension of preparedness, wherein, in the case of instrumental learning, responses are either prepared, unprepared or contraprepared for being learned in association with reward or avoidance of punishment. If a response is 'prepared', it will be learned quickly, i.e. its acquisition will be rapid and reliable. If it is unprepared, its acquisition will be less reliable and will require many more trials or pairings with the reinforcer. If the response is contraprepared, the response is acquired only after a great many trials or not at all.

An example of a contraprepared response is seen in some of Thorndike's work on the puzzlebox in 1911 (Thorndike, 1964). The classic puzzlebox basically consisted of a confinement chamber into which a cat was placed. In order to escape from the box, the cat was required to perform some arbitrary response such as pulling a string or pressing a button. Thorndike observed that if the arbitrary escape response required was scratching or licking itself, then the cat would have great difficulty in learning to escape. In Seligman's terms, the cat is unprepared or contraprepared to associate the ordinarily frequent response of scratching or licking with instrumental escape. Similarly, dogs have trouble in acquiring the response of yawning when it is followed by food (Konorski, 1967).

Some responses are acquired very readily. Thus, rats learn readily to press a lever with their paws in order to obtain food in the Skinner box. This is an example of relatively prepared learning, presumably because the rat innately or biologically relates manipulations of objects with its paws to food-getting. An example of even more prepared learning is seen in the phenomenon of autoshaping in pigeons (Brown and Jenkins, 1968). In autoshaping, there is a Pavlovian contingency between the illumination of a key on the wall of the experimental chamber and the delivery of food to the magazine. Faced with such a classical conditioning paradigm, the pigeon begins to peck spontaneously at the key whenever it is illuminated. This illustrates how the pigeon is biologically prepared to use key-pecking as a food-obtaining response, and it is small wonder that the most frequently studied rewarded-operant response in pigeons is the key-peck (while in rats it is the lever-press).

Avoidance learning

Bolles (1970) has analysed the acquisition of avoidance behaviour in animals in terms of innate biological factors. According to Bolles, animals possess 'species-specific defense reactions' such as fleeing, freezing or fighting. These are highly probable responses displayed instinctively when the animal is faced with danger. The extent to which an arbitrarily selected instrumental avoidance reponse is readily acquired depends on the degree to which it resembles a species-specific defense reaction (SSDR). This is how Bolles accounts for the fact that avoidance learning is very rapid in the jump-out or ledgebox (see Baum, 1966), where the avoidance response resembles flight. On the other hand, training rats to avoid by pressing a lever is extremely difficult (e.g. Meyer, Cho and Wesemann, 1960), because bar-pressing is not similar to any SSDR.

This analysis also explains species differences in the ease with which a given avoidance response is learned, e.g. avoidance in the shuttlebox. According to Bolles (p. 35):

> ... whereas the rat and other small rodents flee from predators by getting completely away from them, an animal such as the dog needs to, and typically does, only stand off at some distance. From such observations the SSDR hypothesis suggests the inference that dogs might be much better than rats at learning to run in the shuttle box.

This indeed appears to be the case.

Implications for behaviour therapy

The importance of biological factors in both instrumental learning and classical conditioning has been recognized only recently. Consequently, attempts to relate these factors and the notion of preparedness to behaviour therapy are only just beginning. Seligman (1971) analyses phobias in terms of these notions, suggesting that phobic stimuli are those which people are biologically prepared to fear. For behaviour therapy, the origin of phobias may be a classical conditioning experience, as, for example, Watson established the famous phobia of rats in Little Albert (Watson and Rayner, 1920). There, the traumatic event was the frightening noise produced by the clanging of two metal bars—unconditioned stimulus (UCS—when the child saw the rat—conditioned stimulus (CS). Seligman (1971) observes that it was possible to condition a phobia of a small, moving, furry animal by classical conditioning, but that later attempts to condition phobias to common household CS like curtains and blocks using this technique were unsuccessful (Bregman, 1934). According to Seligman, man is biologically predisposed or prepared to learn to fear small animals (or living things in general). In general, phobias are held to be *not* merely arbitrary associations of CS with traumatic UCS (as proposed by Wolpe and Rachman, 1960, for example), but rather to involve a biologically prepared classical conditioning.

Many instances of instrumental learning serve as models for the origin of maladaptive behaviour. Alcohol is consumed because it reduces tension and anxiety; thus alcoholism can be likened to an escape response, according to behaviour therapists. Similarly, patterns of homosexual behaviour can be established by accident when such behaviour is reinforced by sexual gratification, according to behaviourist principles. The notion of preparedness suggests that certain elements of the population are more susceptible than others in acquiring these instrumentally learned patterns of behaviour. Thus, the alcoholic or the homosexual requires a biological predisposition or preparedness to learn certain behaviour, as well as the actual instrumental learning experience in order to develop his symptomatology. While this is still at the stage of speculation, it does suggest how the notion of preparedness can bring together previously disparate models of psychopathology—those emphasizing organic and constitutional factors and those emphasizing experience.

The role of biological factors serves to alter not only the models of the origin of symptology for behaviour therapy but also treatment techniques. Little is known about biological propensities for learning in man as they relate to treatment via behaviour therapy. However, it is entirely possible that, for example, sexual fetishes are more amenable to aversion therapy than is alcoholism because of biological predispositions. Numerous other examples could be cited, but at the moment these would only be highly speculative.

FRUSTRATION TOLERANCE

Frustration and lack of frustration tolerance have been linked to psychopathology. Dollard and Miller related aggression to frustration. Jenkins (1950, 1952) concluded that continuous and severe frustration in interpersonal relations was the main cause of schizophrenia. Clearly, techniques which could be used to increase frustration tolerance would be important in both preventing and treating frustration-based disorders. Examination of the concept of frustration in the field of instrumental learning suggests such techniques.

Yates (1962) discusses the concept of frustration at length, and Kimble (1961) also reviews the use of frustration in instrumental learning. Frustration can be an energizing or motivating force in instrumental learning, as was unambiguously demonstrated by Amsel and Roussel (1952). They trained rats in two runways placed end to end so that the goalbox of the first served as the startbox for the second. After training the rats to traverse the runways with continuous reward in both goalboxes, reward in the first goalbox was presented on an intermittent schedule. It was found that on trials when the reward was omitted in the first goalbox (frustration trials), animals ran more quickly down the second runway (than they did on trials when reward was present in the first goalbox). Thus, frustration caused by the omission of an expected reward energized subsequent behaviour. Other experiments showed that frustration could also have a cue value as well as an energizing function, and that it acted like an aversive drive whose termination was reinforcing (see Kimble, 1961).

Demonstration of the frustration effect by Amsel and Roussel led to the application of frustration theory to such instrumental learning phenomena as extinction and the partial reinforcement effect. Extinction, wherein the absence of reward leads to a decline in performance of the instrumental response, was held to be due to frustration. The lack of the anticipated reward led to the causing of frustration, which was held to act as a negative drive. By ceasing the instrumental response in extinction, the organism came to avoid or reduce frustration.

The partial reinforcement effect (PRE) in extinction refers to the fact that, following a history of intermittent reinforcement, an instrumental response persists very much longer in extinction than does a previously continuously rewarded instrumental response. The explanation of the PRE in terms of frustration theory maintains that partial or intermittent reward builds up frustration tolerance, wherein the organism learns to perform the behaviour in the face of periodic frustration (non-rewarded trials). Thus, in the face of continuous frustration (extinction), the organism persists longer, following a history of partial reinforcement.

The PRE in extinction as interpreted by frustration theory suggests techniques for the prevention and treatment of frustration-based disorders in man. The procedure suggested follows that used to build up high fixed- or variable-ratio performance in animal instrumental learning. At first the organism is rewarded after each response (continuously); then rewards are omitted more and more frequently following some responses, until eventually rewards for the instrumental response are only rare. If the procedure has been followed gradually enough, the net result will be a high frustration tolerance or ability to perform the response well in the face of frequent non-reward. Experience with such a procedure in Man may serve as a form of 'behavioural prophylaxis' (Poser, 1970) for frustration-based disorders, or even as treatment.

REFERENCES

Amsel, A., and Roussel, J. (1952). Motivational properties of frustration: I. Effect on a running response of the addition of frustration to the motivational complex. *Journal of Experimental Psychology*, **43**, 363–368.

Akiyama, M. (1968). Effects of extinction techniques on avoidance response. *Bulletin of the Faculty of Education, Hiroshima University*, **17**, 163–173.

Akiyama, M. (1969). Relation between extinction techniques and extinction of avoidance response in albino rats. *Annual of Animal Psychology*, **19**, 1–16.

Bankart, B. (1971). *An Investigation of Techniques used to Facilitate the Extinction of Avoidance Behavior*. Paper presented at the Eastern Psychological Association Convention, New York City.

Baum, M. (1966). Rapid extinction of an avoidance response following a period of response prevention in the avoidance apparatus. *Psychological Reports*, **18**, 59–64.

Baum, M. (1970). Extinction of avoidance responding through response prevention (flooding). *Psychological Bulletin*, **74**, 276–284.

Baum, M. (1971a). Flooding or response prevention or detainment or forced reality-testing: a note on nomenclature. *Psychological Reports*, **28**, 558.

Baum, M. (1971b). Extinction of an avoidance response in rats via response prevention (flooding): a test for residual fear. *Psychological Reports*, **28**, 203–208.

Baum, M. (1971c). Avoidance training in both alcohol and non-drug states increases the resistance-to-extinction of an avoidance response in rats. *Psychopharmacologia*, **19**, 87–90.

Baum, M. (1972a). Flooding (response prevention) in rats: the effects of immediate versus delayed flooding and of changed illumination conditions during flooding. *Canadian Journal of Psychology*, **26**, 190–200.

Baum, M. (1972b). Repeated acquisition and extinction of avoidance in rats using flooding (response prevention). *Learning and Motivation*, **3**, 272–278.

Baum, M. (1973a). Extinction of avoidance behavior: comparison of various flooding procedures in rats. *Bulletin of the Psychonomic Society*, **1**, 22–24.

Baum, M. (1973b). Extinction of avoidance in rats: the effects of chlorpromazine and methylphenidate administered in conjunction with flooding response (prevention). *Behaviour Research and Therapy*, **11**, 165–169.

Baum, M., and Gordon, A. (1970) Effect of a loud buzzer applied during response prevention (flooding) in rats. *Behaviour Research and Therapy*, **8**, 287–292.

Baum, M., and Leclerc, R. (1974). Irrelevant stress vs response prevention (flooding) interpolated between avoidance acquisition and extinction in rats. *Journal of Psychiatric Research*, in press.

Baum, M., Leclerc, R., and St.-Laurent, J. (1973). Rewarding vs aversive intracranial stimulation administered during flooding (response prevention) in rats. *Psychological Reports*, **32**, 551–558.

Baum, M. and Myran, D. D. (1971). Response prevention (flooding) in rats: the effects of restricting exploration during flooding and of massed vs distributed flooding. *Canadian Journal of Psychology*, **25**, 138–146.

Baum, M., and Oler, I. D. (1968). Comparison of two techniques for hastening extinction of avoidance-responding in rats. *Psychological Reports*, **23**, 807–813.

Baum, M., and Poser, E. G. (1971). Comparison of flooding procedures in animals and man. *Behaviour Research and Therapy*, **9**, 249–254.

Berman, J. S., and Katzev, R. D. (1972). Factors involved in the rapid elimination of avoidance behavior. *Behaviour Research and Therapy*, **10**, 247–256.

Bersh, P. J., and Keltz, J. R. (1971). Pavlovian reconditioning and the recovery of avoidance behavior in rats after extinction with response prevention. *Journal of Comparative and Physiological Psychology*, **76**, 262–266.

Bersh, P. J., and Paynter, W. E. (1972). Pavlovian extinction in rats during avoidance response prevention. *Journal of Comparative and Physiological Psychology*, **78**, 255–259.

Bettelheim, B. (1960). *The Informed Heart*, Free Press of Glencoe, New York.

Bleuler, E. (1950). *Dementia Praecox or the Group of Schizophrenias*, International Universities Press, New York.

Bolles, R. C. (1970). Species-specific defense reactions and avoidance learning. *Psychological Review*, **77**, 32–48.

Bregman, E. (1934). An attempt to modify the emotional attitude of infants by the conditioned response technique. *Journal of Genetic Psychology*, **45**, 169–198.

Brown, P., and Jenkins, H. (1968). Autoshaping of the pigeon's key-peck. *Journal of the Experimental Analysis of Behavior*, **11**, 1–8.

Costello, C. G. (1970). Dissimilarities between conditioned avoidance responses and phobias. *Psychological Review*, **77**, 250–254.

Coulter, X., Riccio, D. C., and Page, H. A. (1969). Effects of blocking an instrumental avoidance response: facilitated extinction but persistence of 'fear'. *Journal of Comparative and Physiological Psychology*, **68**, 377–381.

Eysenck, H. J. (1968). A theory of the incubation of anxiety/fear responses. *Behaviour Research and Therapy*, **6**, 309–321.

Eysenck, H. J., and Beech, H. R. (1971). Counter conditioning and related methods. In A. E. Bergin and S. L. Garfield (Eds.), *Handbook of Psychotherapy and Behavior Change: An Empirical Analysis*, Wiley, New York.

Gordon, A., and Baum, M. (1971). Increased efficacy of flooding (response prevention) in rats through positive intracranial stimulation. *Journal of Comparative and Physiological Psychology*, **75**, 68–72.

Heath, G. H. (1968). *A Comparison of Reciprocal Inhibition and Flooding in Decreasing the Strength of a Conditioned Avoidance Response.* Paper presented at the Eastern Psychological Association Convention, Washington, D.C.

Hussain, M. Z. (1970). Thiopentone-facilitated implosion in treatment of phobic disorders. *Canadian Medical Association Journal*, **103**, 768–769.

Hussain, M. Z. (1971). Desensitization and flooding (implosion) in treatment of phobias. *American Journal of Psychiatry*, **127**, 85–89.

Jenkins, R. L. (1950). The nature of the schizophrenic process. *Archives of Neurology and Psychiatry*, **64**, 243–262.

Jenkins, R. L. (1952). The schizophrenic sequence: withdrawal, disorganization, psychotic reorganization. *American Journal of Orthopsychiatry*, **27**, 738–748.

Johnston, D., and Gath, D. (1973). Arousal levels and attribution effects in diazepam-assisted flooding. *British Journal of Psychiatry*, **123**, 463–466.

Kamano, D. K. (1968). Joint effect of amobarbital and response prevention on CAR extinction. *Psychological Reports*, **22**, 544–546.

Kamano, D. K. (1972). Using drugs to modify the effect of response prevention on avoidance extinction. *Behaviour Research and Therapy*, **10**, 367–370.

Kimble, G. A. (1961). *Hilgard and Marquis' Conditioning and Learning*, Appleton-Century-Crofts, New York.

Konorski, J. (1967). *Integrative Activity of the Brain*, University of Chicago Press, Chicago.

Lanyon, R. I., Manosevitz, M., and Imber, R. R. (1968). Systematic desensitization: distribution of practice and symptom substitution. *Behaviour Research and Therapy*, **6**, 323–329.

Leclerc, R., St.-Laurent, J., and Baum, M. (1973). Effects of rewarding, aversive, and neutral intracranial stimulation administered during flooding (response prevention) in rats. *Physiological Psychology*, **1**, 24–28.

Linton, J., Riccio, D. C., Rohrbaugh, M., and Page, H. A. (1970). The effects of blocking an instrumental avoidance response: fear reduction or enhancement? *Behaviour Research and Therapy*, **8**, 267–272.

Marks, I. M. (1972). Flooding (implosion) and allied treatments. In W. S. Agras (Ed.), *Behavior Modification: Principles and Clinical Applications*, Little, Brown and Co., Boston.

Marks, I. M., Viswanathan, R., Lipsedge, M. S., and Gardner, R. (1972). Enhanced relief of phobias by flooding during waning diazepam effect. *British Journal of Psychiatry*, **121**, 493–505.

Meyer, D. R., Cho, C., and Wesemann, A. F. (1960). On problems of conditioning discriminated lever-press avoidance responses. *Psychological Review*, **67**, 224–228.

Miller, B. V., and Levis, D. J. (1971). The effects of varying short visual exposure times to a phobic test stimulus on subsequent avoidance behavior. *Behaviour Research and Therapy*, **9**, 17–21.

Napalkov, A. V. (1963). Information process of the brain. *Progress of Brain Research*, **2**, 59–69.

Naud, J., Boisvert, J. M., and Lamontagne, Y. (1973). Traitement de la peur des armes à feu et autres stimuli associés par immersion 'in vivo' combinée à une tâche manuelle. *Bulletin de l'Association pour l'Analyse et la Modification du Comportement*, **3**, 33–38.

Nelson, F. (1967). Effects of chlorpromazine on fear extinction. *Journal of Comparative and Physiological Psychology*, **64**, 496–498.

Overmier, J. B. (1968). Interference with avoidance behavior: failure to avoid traumatic shock. *Journal of Experimental Psychology*, **78**, 340–343.

Overmier, J. B., and Seligman, M. E. P. (1967). Effects of inescapable shock upon subsequent escape and avoidance learning. *Journal of Comparative and Physiological Psychology*, **63**, 23–33.

Overton, D. A. (1964). State-dependent or 'dissociated' learning produced with pentobarbital. *Journal of Comparative and Physiological Psychology*, **57**, 3–12.

Overton, D. A. (1970). Discriminative control of behavior by drug states. In T. Thompson and R. Pickens (Eds.), *Stimulus Properties of Drugs*, Appleton-Century-Crofts, New York.

Overton, D. A. (1972). State dependent learning produced by alcohol and its relevance to alcoholism. In B. Kessen and H. Begleiter (Eds.), *The Biology of Alcoholism*, Vol. 2: *Physiology and Behavior*. Plenum Press, New York.

Page, H. A. (1955). The facilitation of experimental extinction by response prevention as a function of the acquisition of a new response. *Journal of Comparative and Physiological Psychology*, **48**, 14–16.

Page, H. A., and Hall, J. F. (1953). Experimental extinction as a function of the prevention of a response. *Journal of Comparative and Physiological Psychology*, **46**, 33–34.

Pavlov, I. P. (1927). *Conditioned Reflexes*, Dover, New York.

Polin, A. T. (1959). The effect of flooding and physical suppression as extinction techniques on an anxiety-motivated avoidance locomotor response. *Journal of Psychology*, **47**, 253–255.

Poser, E. G. (1970). Toward a theory of 'behavioral prophylaxis'. *Journal of Behavior Therapy and Experimental Psychiatry*, **1**, 39–43.

Ramsay, R. W., Barends, J., Breuker, J., and Kruseman, A. (1966). Massed versus spaced desensitization of fear. *Behaviour Research and Therapy*, **4**, 205–207.

Reid, L. D., Taylor, C. L., and Rassel, L. M. (1971). *Efficient Deconditioning of avoidance*. Paper presented at the Psychonomic Society Convention, St. Louis.

Rohrbaugh, M. and Riccio, D. C. (1970). Paradoxical enhancement of learned fear. *Journal of Abnormal Psychology*, **75**, 210–216.

Schiff, R. (1971). *Effect of Length and Number of Blocked Trials on Extinction of an Avoidance Response*. Paper presented at the Eastern Psychological Association Convention, New York City.

Seligman, M. E. P. (1970). On the generality of the laws of learning. *Psychological Review*, **77**, 406–418.

Seligman, M. E. P. (1971). Phobias and preparedness. *Behavior Therapy*, **2**, 307–320.

Seligman, M. E. P. (1972). Learned helplessness. *Annual Review of Medicine*, **23**, 407–412.

Seligman, M. E. P. (1974). Depression and learned helplessness. In R. J. Friedman and M. M. Katz (Eds.), *The Psychology of Depression: Contemporary Theory and Research*, Wiley, New York.

Seligman, M. E. P., and Groves, D. (1970). Non-transient learned helplessness. *Psychonomic Science*, **19**, 191–192.

Seligman, M. E. P., and Maier, S. F. (1967). Failure to escape traumatic shock. *Journal of Experiment of Psychology*, **74**, 1–9.

Seligman, M. E. P., Maier, S. F., and Geer, J. H. (1968). Alleviation of learned helplessness in the dog. *Journal of Abnormal and Social Psychology*, **73**, 256–262.

Shearman, R. W. (1970). Response-contingent CS termination in the extinction of avoidance learning. *Behaviour Research and Therapy*, **8**, 227–239.

Skinner, B. F. (1938). *The Behavior of Organisms*, Appleton-Century-Crofts, New York.

Solyom, C. (1969). *Effects of Re-exposures to Components of an Early Fear Conditioning Situation*. Unpublished M. A. Thesis, Sir George Williams University.

Thorndike, E. L. (1964). *Animal Intelligence*, Hafner, New York. (Originally published by MacMillan, New York, 1911.)

Watson, J. B., and Rayner, R. (1920). Conditioned emotional reactions. *Journal of Experimental Psychology*, **3**, 1–14.

Watson, J. P., and Marks, I. M. (1971). Relevant and irrelevant fear in flooding—a crossover study of phobic patients. *Behavior Therapy*, **2**, 275–293.

Werboff, J., Duane, D., and Cohen, B. D. (1964). Extinction of conditioned avoidance and heart rate responses in rats. *Journal of Psychosomatic Research*, **8**, 29–33.

Wilson, G. T., and Davison, G. C. (1971). Processes of fear reduction in systematic desensitization: animal studies. *Psychological Bulletin*, **76**, 1–14.

Wolpe, J., and Rachman, S. (1960). Psychoanalytic 'evidence': a critique based on Freud's case of Little Hans. *Journal of Nervous and Mental Disease*, **131**, 135–148.

Yates, A. J. (1962). *Frustration and Conflict*, Methuen, London.

5

OPERANT CONDITIONING AND CLINICAL PSYCHOLOGY

Glyn V. Thomas and Derek E. Blackman

In this chapter we shall examine some extensions of operant conditioning methods to clinical psychology, methods which are currently exciting interest in a variety of contexts (e.g. Franks, 1969; Ullman and Krasner, 1975).

Within experimental psychology, operant conditioning has long been associated with the radical behaviourism of B. F. Skinner. Strictly speaking, operant conditioning (the modification of behaviour by reinforcement) and behaviourism (as a way of seeing behaviour) are logically independent and can be distinguished. Indeed, some clinical psychologists advocate the use of operant conditioning methods without Skinner's behaviourism (e.g. Davison, 1969). This view is also implied by Watson (1973), where he introduces his manual on child behaviour modification as a 'practical "cookbook" type of text'.

We think, however, that the methods of operant conditioning should not be applied merely as set of 'cookbook' techniques. It is our contention that, ultimately, the successful application of operant conditioning methods requires behaviourism. We believe that to use operant conditioning well requires us to adopt an alternative concept of behaviour to that traditionally held by many clinicians. In a sense, we need a different way of seeing behaviour. To explain more clearly what we mean by this, it may be helpful first to consider an example from the visual arts. Impressionist painters used a method of painting which emphasizes coloured reflections and coloured shadows. At first, many people did not find paintings of this kind convincing. They had to learn to see them, and in doing so they also learned to recognize coloured shadows and reflections in nature, perhaps for the first time. The impressionist method of painting, in fact, suggested a new and different way of seeing which was not always accepted without opposition (Gombrich, 1969).

Further examples of different ways of seeing can also be found in the history of science. Indeed, Kuhn (1961) has argued that major progress in science is characterized not by the accumulation of new facts but by fundamental changes in ways of seeing (paradigms). For example, before Darwin, an organism might have been said to have a well-developed ear for the purpose of hearing better. In contrast, Darwin's theory of evolution by natural selection proposes that organisms with well-developed ears were descended from those which were able to hear better, who as a consequence possessed a survival advantage and so produced more descendents. Darwin's major contribution to science was not the facts and data that he collected but the new and different way of seeing phylogenetic purpose which he constructed out of the facts.

In psychology, the traditional conception of the behaving organism has been characterized by Woodworth (1929) and by Keehn (1969) as S-O-R. The arrangement of the symbols expresses the view that behaviour (R) is a product of internal contents and processes (O) and that such content is affected by stimuli (S). This formulation resembles our 'everyday' understanding of behaviour when we explain actions by referring to inner intentions, purposes and wishes. Keehn (1969) argues that such formulations put behaviour into second place as a mere reflection of these inner processes: 'Although it is now more fashionable to attribute neurological rather than mentalistic properties to O, traditional dualistic conceptions still prevail (p. 277).'

A similar dualistic view is represented in the traditional conception of abnormal behaviour as mental illness. This view, sometimes called the medical model, proposes that, when an individual's behaviour is called abnormal or deviant, it is because of some underlying pathology or cause. This model of mental illness developed in the nineteenth century by analogy with physical medicine, in which germs or lesions led to the appearance of symptoms. The causes of abnormal behaviour implied by the medical model are apparently not always physical disturbances. There may also be inferred 'psychological' causes of abnormal behaviour (e.g. anxiety), for which no physiological counterpart is necessarily identified. At this point, the medical model becomes almost indistinguishable from the traditional ways of seeing all behaviour described above. The basic similarity lies in the view that a person's actions are mere reflections or symptoms of inner causal events.

However, a different way of seeing behaviour has emerged in Skinner's behaviourism. Here the focus shifts away from inner processes to the behaviour itself. Behaviour is assigned primary importance and explanations of behaviour are sought largely in the organism's environment (both past and present). Inner processes receive much less attention and explanations of behaviour that refer to inner causes are criticized on the grounds that they may deflect our attention away from more important variables (Skinner, 1950).

Operant conditioning, of course, refers to the direct modification of behaviour by environmental events (reinforcers). It is natural, therefore, that operant conditioning should appear to be of central importance from the standpoint of radical behaviourism and, perhaps, appear to be merely a peripheral phenomenon from the standpoint of traditional S-O-R formulations.

Some versions of traditional S-O-R psychology have also been described as behaviouristic (e.g. Hull, 1943). However, it is important to distinguish between such formulations as these, which preserve inner causes (by defining them operationally), and Skinner's behaviourism, which excludes them altogether. To avoid confusion, we shall refer to Skinner's position as *radical* behaviourism.

A natural extension of radical behaviourism is to attempt explanations of abnormal behaviour in terms similar to those invoked to explain normal behaviour (e.g. Skinner, 1956; Ullmann and Krasner, 1975). These attempts to explain disordered behaviour emphasize environmental conditions (past and present) rather than inferred, pathological, inner states (such as anxiety). This change in conception has a number of implications for clinical practice which, if widely accepted, could fundamentally change our approach to the problems we now describe as mental illness. In the following sections, we attempt to examine the use of operant conditioning techniques against the background of alternative ways of seeing behaviour.

TECHNIQUES

In the previous section, we argued that operant conditioning techniques are closely related to an attempt to understand behaviour which differs from the traditional S-O-R model. In this section, we go on to review briefly the ways in which some of these experimental techniques have been used in clinical psychology.

It is, of course, a well-established empirical fact that behaviour can be changed by manipulating its consequences. The prototypical example is provided by the laboratory demonstration that an arbitrarily chosen behavioural act may be increased in frequency by arranging certain consequences for such acts. The arbitrary act may frequently take the form of lever-pressing in rats, and the consequence of this behaviour is often the presentation of either food or water. A simple demonstration might be arranged in three phases. First, the frequency of lever-pressing is measured before any consequences are differentially related to it. This provides a control baseline against which the effects of the experimental conditions may be assessed. Next, each lever-press is followed by food, and the frequency of lever-pressing engendered by this procedure is measured. Finally, it is possible to check that any differences in the first two phases are not merely a sequence effect. This can be done by reverting to the original condition. Notice that this demonstration is based on the study of individual rats, each of which is exposed to experimental conditions in an ABA design (see Blackman and Thomas, in press).

It is possible to say, then, that in certain circumstances food will act as a reinforcer, i.e. that food will increase and control the frequency of behaviour which immediately precedes it. The rat may be said to press the lever because of its consequences. Note, however, that food is not necessarily a reinforcer in all situations. We wish to stress that it is a purely empirical matter to determine in what circumstances the food does act as a reinforcer. One important, if obvious, limitation is provided by the subject's immediate past history; food may act as a reinforcer only if the subject has not recently eaten.

Demonstrations such as that discussed above also show that behaviour maintained at high frequencies (as in the second phase of the experiment) may be reduced by discontinuing any reinforcing consequences (as in the third phase). This is technically described as an extinction procedure.

One of the earliest papers to examine the implications of these findings in clinical psychology was written by Ayllon and Michael (1959). They suggested that in the typical hospital ward for psychotic patients, the psychiatric nurse might be a source of reinforcement in terms of his social interaction with the patients. Thus the patients might behave in certain ways because of the differential consequences for such behaviour provided by nurses. Ayllon and Michael provide a number of demonstrations that this can be the case. Briefly, it is easy to see that in many wards the nurse can find himself interacting with patients mainly when their behaviour is in some sense undesirable, for such behaviour may be dangerous to the patient or may force the attention of the nurse. Ayllon and Michael show that attempting *not* to provide social interactions for certain undesired behaviour may lead to a reduction in the frequency of those behaviours, technically an extinction procedure. The case of Lucille illustrates this: the frequency with which the patient interrupted or interfered with the necessary work of nurses was reduced markedly by no longer pleading with her to stop and by not interacting with her when she appeared in the nurses' office.

The above should certainly not be taken simply as a recipe for ignoring undesirable behaviours, for it is obvious that this cannot always be done. The implications of Ayllon and Michael's (1959) paper are more wide-ranging, and are strictly emphasized by their title: 'The psychiatric nurse as a behavioral engineer'. The paper suggests that the psychiatric nurse is in a very real sense *responsible* for the behaviour of the patients in his charge. If he fails to recognize the ways in which his behaviour may selectively strengthen and maintain the patient's behaviour, he may inadvertently generate abnormal or undesirable behaviour. Bigelow (1972) has described this as a 'behavioural accident', and suggests that such accidents occur very frequently in the context of institutionalized care for patients whose behaviour is retarded. If, however, the psychiatric nurse is made aware of these dynamics, he is placed in a position where he may systematically relate the reinforcers at his disposal to desirable or normal patterns of behaviour on the part of the patients, and thus may increase and maintain (engineer) the frequency of such behaviours. The ward staff thus are encouraged to change their role from that of custodians to that of educators. Note, however, that reinforcement is not just a teaching tool; it must be used to keep behaviour occurring even after an initial change has been produced (Bigelow, 1972). Conditioning techniques are not simply ways of generating new behaviours; they provide the conditions in which behaviour is maintained as a function of the environment.

The literature is now marked by repeated demonstrations that relating consequences to behaviour in a systematic way may lead to decreases in undesirable behaviour and increases in appropriate behaviour, and examples may be cited from the general behavioural problems discussed above to very specific behavioural abnormalities or deficits. Some of these may be seen in Ulrich, Stachnik and Mabry (1966, 1970) and Ullmann and Krasner (1965). Conditioning (relating reinforcers to certain behaviour) and extinction (preventing a relationship between reinforcers and specified behaviours) may be seen as basic techniques. However, when they are associated with the way of seeing which we discussed in the previous section, that of radical behaviourism, it is important to note that these procedures are not thought to be introduced into behavioural situations *de novo*. Relationships between behaviour and its consequences (contingencies of reinforcement) are important in determining behaviour, whether they were planned, as in a therapeutic intervention, or whether they were left to chance. In the former case, they may be exploited to the benefit of a patient; in the latter, they may conspire together to his detriment.

When abnormal behaviour is seen in terms of contingencies of reinforcement, it is clearly important to search vigorously for events which may be reinforcers and to relate these as directly as possible to desirable behaviour. The typical reinforcers from the animal laboratory, food and water, cannot always be easily related to behaviour in a systematic way, and the circumstances which are associated with the reinforcing effectiveness of these events, namely prior deprivation history, may often not seem acceptable procedures outside the experimental laboratory. As we have seen, social interactions can be powerful reinforcers, but this can vary widely from person to person, can be dependent on interpersonal relations, and the circumstances associated with their reinforcing effectiveness may be hard to identify and difficult to manipulate.

Recently, attempts have been made to maximize the dynamics of reinforcement and extinction by using what are described as 'generalized conditioned reinforcers'. These often take the form of tokens which are of little behavioural importance in themselves, but which acquire reinforcing effectiveness by being exchanged for other events which might be reinforcing. There are many advantages in using tokens in this way: they are easy to deliver, can be closely related to appropriate behaviours, can permit reinforcement at any time and for extended periods, and are relatively unaffected by specific recent deprivations or situation effects. A wide range of back-up reinforcers can be exploited, and frequently take the form of additional privileges such as cigarettes or sweets, additional choice of food or clothes, and such things as privacy, excursions, better sleeping accommodation, etc. A comprehensive account of such a scheme, called a 'token economy', has been provided by Ayllon and Azrin (1968). More recently, Kazdin and Bootzin (1972) have considered the wide use of these token economy schemes. They show that token schemes can be used successfully with psychiatric patients in ward-wide schemes, retardates, children in classroom settings, delinquents and autistic children.

Kazdin and Bootzin also identify a number of problems that have emerged. First, nurses need considerable skill in administering the schemes, for they must take decisions quickly and constantly about the behaviour of individuals while trying to ensure consistency with each individual in terms of the behavioural objectives decided for him. The nurse must actively seek out appropriate behaviour to reinforce, for, of course, the tokens can only be reinforcers if they are given. This more positive surveillance of the ward has been mentioned already, and token economies do no more than accentuate the problems of generating and maintaining appropriate non-custodial behaviours in nurses. Since this is, of course, itself a behavioural problem, it is not surprising that some have suggested that the behaviour of the nurses might also, in turn, be maintained by structured consequences for appropriate token-giving behaviours. Other problems identified by Kazdin and Bootzin are described as 'client resistance' (where the individuals subjected to token economies object, complain, seek transfers, etc.), 'circumvention of contingencies' (where patients develop alternative modes of exchange of tokens, among themselves, so that black market and other distressing factors begin to operate) and 'non-responsiveness' (it being the case that many token economies fail to change and maintain appropriate behaviour in a minority of patients—Kazdin, 1973).

Such problems can be interpreted in two ways. Within an S-O-R framework, such difficulties could be taken as evidence for the fundamental failure of the system. However, within radical behaviourism it could be argued that difficulties of this kind arise from inefficient or inappropriate schemes. This helps to emphasize that the acceptability or otherwise of operant conditioning treatments can depend on one's way of seeing behaviour as much as on the effectiveness of the techniques they include.

This brings us to the next technique which we wish to consider, namely, punishment. Essentially it is an empirical fact that in certain circumstances a stimulus which follows behaviour will *reduce* the future frequency of similar behaviour. In fact, painful stimuli will often act as punishers. A simple laboratory demonstration might be arranged in which rats' lever-presses are maintained by intermittent food reinforcement. The additional presentation of a brief electric shock after each response usually produces an immediate fall in the rate of responding. It has therefore been argued (Baer, 1970) that this technique should be included as a way of reducing inappropriate behaviour in patients.

Punishment is probably the most controversial of operant conditioning procedures, and its use and justification depend a great deal on how behaviour is seen. In terms of the medical model, abnormal behaviour is seen as the result of illness, and nothing could then be more inappropriate than punishment. In behaviouristic terms, however, the question of punishment is not so easily resolved. First, unplanned punishment contingencies exist, as anyone who has burnt their fingers on a hot object will be able to testify. So there is nothing unnatural about punishment. Second, punishment can quickly eliminate undesirable behaviour, so that when it is employed to treat self-mutilating behaviour in autistic or retarded children it almost certainly involves less suffering than alternative treatments, which are invariably much slower or consist of mere physical or chemical restraint (Baer, 1970;

Goldiamond, 1974). When we consider that self-mutilating behaviour can be shaped inadvertently by the attention it commands (Bachman, 1972), it is not easy to sustain objections to punishment on moral grounds alone. It is also essential to recognize that, in behavioural terms, punishment should not be identified simply with the administration of pain. It is an inescapable fact that painful stimuli, such as electric shocks or loud noise, do not inevitably decrease the frequency of behaviours upon which they are made dependent. Indeed, there is evidence that an electric shock can actually function like a (positive) reinforcer (see, for example, Stubbs and Silverman, 1972). Such an effect may arise because of the way in which shock is related to positive reinforcers.

It is also important to note that for a punishing stimulus to have the desired effect it should be presented *immediately* after the response to be eliminated. Azrin (1958) found that blasts of white noise which suppressed subjects' responding, when they were response-contingent, had only transient effects when presentation of the white noise was made independent of responding.

In many clinical settings, it may frequently be impractical to arrange immediate consequences for many inappropriate behaviours. Azrin's results can be taken to imply that for these problems punishment will be relatively of little help. For practical purposes, punishment can seldom be successfully used in isolation simply to reduce undesirable and inappropriate behaviour. For example, token economies should not exact penalties (perhaps by taking tokens away from patients) for undesirable behaviour without considering what alternative behaviour would be more appropriate. Therapeutic strategies that pay attention only to the elimination of undesirable responses (by punishment), thus producing a behavioural void, often create new problems and tend to justify criticisms that behaviour modification inevitably leads to symptom substitution (Ullmann and Krasner, 1975). The elimination of inappropriate responses, whether by punishment or extinction, can frequently be expedited by the simultaneous reinforcement of desirable and appropriate behaviour, which should preferably be physically incompatible with the undesirable response (Azrin and Holz, 1966).

Painful stimuli may create special difficulties because they frequently produce strong emotional distress reactions in the patient which may interfere with the progress of treatment. In many cases, we also should not be too surprised that the extensive use of punishment may generate hostility towards both treatment and therapists (see Ulrich and coworkers, 1972). As we have seen, painful stimuli do not always act as punishers, perhaps because of the context in which they occur. However, for related reasons, stimuli such as a green light, which are not intrinsically painful, can be used to punish behaviour if they are scheduled appropriately. Azrin and Holz (1966) report a laboratory experiment in which a green light functioned as a punisher when it was correlated with the withdrawal of positive reinforcement (technically, extinction).

There might, clearly, be advantages with a punishment procedure that was non-painful. For example, Wolf, Risley and Mees (1964) placed an autistic child in his room for a brief period every time a temper tantrum occurred. The result was a very satisfactory reduction in the frequency and severity of tantrums. The child was, naturally, deprived of the reinforcing activities and social interaction of the ward during these brief periods, so that they may be interpreted as response-produced extinction periods. (Note that extinction on its own, though it may result in reduced responding, is not a punishment procedure. Only response-produced extinction periods which suppress responding can be termed punishment.)

Inappropriate behaviour, then, can often be eliminated by punishment, but we feel that punishment procedures in particular should not be used without considering the context in which the problem behaviour occurs. It may be crucial, for example, to consider why the problem behaviour is present in the first instance. Action to change the reinforcement conditions responsible for maintaining the problem may be more desirable than simple punishment. Further, many feel that the side-effects and implications of punishment (see above) preclude its introduction into most settings.

We have been able to discuss only a very few examples of the clinical use of operant conditioning techniques. In themselves, the techniques involve manipulating the context and consequences of behaviour, and sometimes may appear very simple. We feel that this simplicity is deceptive and have tried to show that there are not just a few 'cookbook' techniques which provide general answers to a wide range of problems. Reinforcers and punishers are often idiosyncratic, and their effectiveness can depend on their context and may change over time.

The most effective procedures appear to accommodate the individual characteristics of each patient or client, are planned to meet his particular needs and set individual behavioural goals. Such procedures, we feel, can only be derived from a behaviouristic analysis of a person's interactions with his environment. Furthermore, this analysis should not end once preliminary procedures have been developed. As behaviour and circumstances change, then the procedures should be revised.

ANALYSIS

In the previous section, we argued that consistently effective operant conditioning procedures can be devised only by making an overall analysis of each clinical problem in behaviouristic terms. Let us take the case of Helen (a psychotic patient discussed by Ayllon and Michael, 1959) as an illustration. Helen's psychotic talk had become so annoying that other patients had beaten her in an attempt to silence her. Her conversation centred on an illegitimate child and the men that she claimed were pursuing her. In traditional ways of seeing behaviour, the psychotic talk would be viewed as symptoms of an underlying illness, and treatment would be aimed at the latter. In contrast, radical behaviourism prompts a search for factors in her environment and history of reinforcement which could be responsible. Reports from nursing staff suggested that Helen's psychotic talk may have been shaped and maintained by the nurses' reaction to it, e.g. listening to her to try to get to the 'roots of her problem'. The relative frequency of psychotic talk was dramatically reduced by a programme in which psychotic talk was ignored (extinguished) and sensible talk was reinforced with attention from the nurses. Demonstrations like this one do not force acceptance of radical behaviourism as a way of seeing behaviour. Davison (1969), for example, has criticized a number of studies (which included the case of Helen) on the grounds that inferences to patients' feelings, cognitions and inner states were neglected. He argued that 'such inferences are *necessary* and *appropriate* to behaviour modification (p. 265)'. In the same article, Davison also claimed 'that there are many alternatives (to the kind of treatment given to Helen) not the least of which is to take care initially to find out what is wrong and only then to proceed with behaviour modification techniques (p. 245)'. Davison is arguing here against the paradigm of radical behaviourism rather than specific operant conditioning procedures. Against this view, we would suggest that the use of operant conditioning within traditional S-O-R paradigms as Davison recommends could lead to muddled treatments and inconsistencies. For example, how can reinforcement of healthy talk and extinction of sick talk really help a patient, if the real problem is the 'illness' underlying the psychotic talk? But the fact remains that there are few successful alternatives to operant conditioning for treating and changing the psychotic behaviour of chronically hospitalized patients.

In our view, it may also prove useful to examine traditional approaches, e.g. psychotherapy, from the standpoint of radical behaviourism. In terms of radical behaviourism, reinforcement should operate in every verbal interaction with or without the blessing of the therapist. There is, in fact, evidence that, even when the therapist is deliberately trying not to 'direct' the patient, the effects of reinforcement and verbal conditioning can be observed (Truax, 1966). 'As Molière's character discovered that he had been speaking prose all his life, so the conventional psychotherapist has discovered that he has always used reinforcement on his patients (Salzinger, 1969, p. 394)'. The lack of success of conventional psychotherapy (Eysenck, 1952; Truax and Carkhuff, 1967) may be taken to mean that any reinforcement implicit in such therapy is not being arranged in the most helpful ways. Perhaps psychotherapy would become more effective if the dynamics of verbal conditioning were more widely recognized (see Salzinger, 1969). However, we wish to suggest that such a reorientation may ultimately require therapists to abandon traditional ways of seeing abnormal behaviour in favour of behaviouristic analyses. To take a simple illustration, it is not immediately obvious how to apply operant conditioning treatments if the patient's problems are represented in the S-O-R terms of, let us say, personal construct theory or Freudian psychodynamics. The patient's problems must be reformulated in behavioural terms before operant conditioning procedures can be applied.

It must be admitted, however, that radical behaviourism is highly controversial (Wheeler, 1973) and many people clearly do not find in it an acceptable way of seeing behaviour. Some of the opposition seems to stem from misapprehensions of radical behaviourism (see Wiest, 1967), some of which we now attempt to clarify.

Radical behaviourism emphasizes operant conditioning as an important behavioural process, and this emphasis has sometimes been interpreted as a denial of other influences on behaviour. Of course, the degree to which behaviour can be modified by operant conditioning is sometimes limited by constitutional and genetic factors (Seligman, 1970). Subnormal children may never be able to learn as much as other children, but we should not be too pessimistic about what can be achieved with skilfully designed training programmes (Thompson and Grabowski, 1972). The fact that operant conditioning is sometimes constrained and that conditioning is not the only influence upon behaviour does not mean either that operant conditioning is unimportant (Seligman, 1973) or that radical behaviourism, as a way of seeing behaviour, is limited in scope. There is nothing about radical behaviourism that depends upon operant conditioning being the only influence upon behaviour.

Some authors also appear to be under the impression that behaviourism inevitably excludes 'consciousness', 'feelings' and 'thinking' from consideration (e.g. Burt, 1962). It is true that some kinds of behaviourism (methodological behaviourism—Mace, 1957) restrict their subject matter to directly observable, public behaviour. But this is more of a research strategy than a way of seeing behaviour. Many traditional S-O-R formulations are behaviouristic in this sense (e.g. Hull, 1943; Tolman, 1932). Of course, we are conscious and have experiences which are private. The crucial difference between radical behaviourism and many traditional views is that in radical behaviourism 'being conscious', 'thinking' and 'feeling' are activities which are neither in a special mental world of their own nor are they assigned any special status as primary causes of overt behaviour. A psychotic patient's feelings are not held to cause his overt psychotic behaviour; both his feelings and overt behaviour are seen as the results of his history, environment and current situation. Feeling and thinking are still important in radical behaviourism, but they are not regarded as causes of overt behaviour—rather they are more behaviour to be explained (Skinner, 1974).

Radical behaviourism is also often believed to involve a denial of the importance of physiology. As with feeling and thinking, however, it is the role assigned to physiological processes that distinguishes radical behaviourism from traditional S-O-R ways of seeing. Physiology is concerned with events within the skin. Many of these events may turn out to be just more behaviour which can be conditioned. The nervous system, we assume, is also changed by events such as reinforcements, and these changes are important in determining how the organism will behave in the future. 'Something is done today which affects the behaviour of an organism tomorrow. No matter how clearly that fact can be established, a step is missing, and we must wait for the physiologist to supply it (Skinner, 1974, p. 215)'. Thus physiology, in radical behaviourism, is the study of the 'bridge' between past environmental (and evolutionary) causes and the current behaviour of an organism. Unlike some S-O-R formulations, radical behaviourism assigns no special causal or explanatory status to physiological processes.

Many people also find radical behaviourism hard to accept because of its implications for our traditional ideas of freedom and personal responsibility. For example, if a person's actions are explained in terms of his environment and history, then his freedom and responsibility seem to be reduced. First, we should not identify behaviourism in any way with fatalistic philosophies of predestination (Grünbaum, 1952). Such philosophies imply that, whatever a person does, it will make no difference to his fate. The interpretation of the causes of behaviour in radical behaviourism, however, is quite different; the person himself is involved as a crucial part of the sequence of cause and effect, and environmental influences are not seen as necessarily forcing a person to act 'against his will'. This view is really very close to common sense. For example, when we make a supposedly 'free' choice, we can often, on reflection, identify factors which have influenced our decision, but we seldom feel coerced in such circumstances.

Radical behaviourism, in emphasizing the environment, also seems to minimize the contribution of the person himself. Thus Skinner argues that a poet 'has a poem' rather than creates it out of nothing. That is to say, the poet is a locus where certain variables interact.

> A poem seldom makes its appearance in a completed form. Bits and pieces occur to the poet who rejects them or allows them to stand, and who puts them together to *compose* a poem. But they come from his past history, verbal and otherwise, and he has to learn how to put them together. The act of composition is no more an act of creation than 'having' the bits and pieces composed (Skinner, 1973, p. 352).

From the standpoint of traditional ways of seeing behaviour, this view of ourselves is superficially unflattering and appears to offer little to induce many people to abandon familiar, traditional ways of seeing behaviour. We feel, however, that radical behaviourism does have a very important advantage: it often permits us to reformulate problems in more tractable ways.

Some indication of the usefulness of radical behaviourism and operant conditioning procedures for education and therapy can be gained by surveying the extent of their applications. Much early clinical use of operant conditioning took place with institutionalized patients whose behaviour was severely disordered, partly because new treatments are often tried out on problems that have not yielded to traditional methods. However, the degree of environmental control possible within institutions also made them an appropriate first step in extrapolating operant conditioning from the laboratory. Many successful attempts have been made subsequently to extend operant conditioning procedures to the home and other non-institutional milieus (Tharp and Wetzel, 1969). Training programmes using operant conditioning procedures have been developed in prisons, schools and subnormality hospitals (Ulrich, Stachnik and Mabry, 1970). The same principles of behaviour analysis and operant conditioning have been used in designing prosthetic environments for the elderly and handicapped (Lindsley, 1964). The principles themselves have also been taught to patients to enable them to gain control over problem behaviours such as overeating, smoking and poor study habits (Goldiamand, 1965; Rachlin, 1974; Skinner, 1974). This is not an exhaustive review by any means, but the very range of applications suggests that a new way of seeing behaviour is involved which is proving fruitful.

A distinctive feature of all behaviouristic analyses is the emphasis placed on direct observation and measurement of behaviour. We can contrast this approach with psychological tests of personality, intelligence and psychopathology that have been developed to assess patients in various ways. We shall not attempt to judge the relative values of these two approaches because, in our view, they try to accomplish two quite different things. Psychological tests are, perhaps, best understood in S-O-R terms since they attempt to measure 'traits', 'tendencies' or 'abilities' which are thought to underly behaviour. As such, psychological tests are consistent with the medical model of abnormal behaviour and appear to be used primarily to diagnose 'illness' or to predict behaviour in a general way.

By way of contrast, the direct measurement of the behaviour of individuals is a characteristic of quite a different tradition—that of the single-subject research which has long been used to investigate operant conditioning in the laboratory. Like radical behaviourism, single-subject methodology is logically quite independent of operant conditioning and should be distinguished from it. There may, however, be practical reasons why a single-subject research strategy should have become so closely identified with behaviourism and operant conditioning.

In general terms, such research aims to investigate the effects of a given independent variable on the dependent variable provided by the behaviour of an individual subject. Instead of applying different experimental treatments to different groups of subjects and evaluating the outcome with statistics, the same subject is usually exposed to all the treatments in order. Each treatment is maintained until the subject's behaviour has become highly predictable (a steady state of behaviour); then the next treatment is introduced. The differences between the steady states can be related to the different treatments; in effect, the steady state has replaced the control group as a basis for comparison.

The aim of this approach, then, is the demonstration of behavioural control in individuals rather than populations. Clinicians are, of course, accustomed to dealing with patients as individuals, and its association with single-subject research designs may have facilitated the extension of operant conditioning from the laboratory to clinical problems. Several features of single-subject research also appear to be in sympathy with a behaviouristic approach to abnormal behaviour. Direct observation and measurement of what an individual does tends to focus our attention on the behaviour itself (rather than on an underlying illness) and may encourage us to think in terms of actively changing specific behaviours. The use of steady states as the basis for evaluating treatment may also draw our attention to the maintenance of behaviour as well as the initial production of behavioural change.

In this section, we have tried to show how many different kinds of behaviour can be analysed from a behaviouristic standpoint. We feel that this approach can be very useful in clinical psychology, but we do not claim that other orientations may not be valuable too. Should we then conclude that clinicians may have to adopt different, perhaps conflicting, theoretical frameworks for different problems? Certainly, operant conditioning seems to be successful at treating a wide range of problems, but some behavioural problems appear to have medical causes and respond well to medical treatment (e.g. phenylketonuria). Some authors (e.g. Franks, 1969) have argued from this that no single approach, such as radical behaviourism, can 'go it alone' in clinical psychology. The selection of the most helpful approach for each problem is possibly a skill that develops with increasing practical experience. Our main concern here is to emphasize yet again that the choice of operant conditioning as a treatment should not be made without an appreciation of its theoretical and philosophical context.

CONCLUSION

We have tried to show how a particular way of seeing behaviour (radical behaviourism) is necessary for an adequate technology of operant conditioning. We should like to stress, however, that we regard radical behaviourism as primarily an attempt to understand behaviour. It seeks explanations of behaviour without referring to inner causes, and there is now much evidence that a surprising number of our actions can be understood in terms of their environmental consequences. Because environmental conditions are so much more accessible and so much easier to manipulate than inner factors, the approach is confronted, perhaps more than any other in psychology, with questions of how its techniques should be used. For example, concern is often expressed over the morality of behavioural control and over possible misuses of the techniques.

Unfortunately, there has been recently a small number of distressing reports from the U.S.A. which suggest that frankly cruel treatments are being justified in terms of operant conditioning (Reppucci and Saunders, 1974). These treatments have in almost every case been administered by non-psychologists with apparently very little understanding of the techniques that they were using. Of course, we do not want to imply that non-psychologists are generally incapable of administering operant conditioning programmes—nor in any way to defend cruelty. However, untrained people are, perhaps, particularly likely to apply operant conditioning procedures as 'cookbook' techniques, and thus fail to recognize the disadvantages, side-effects and implications of, say, punishment which an adequate behavioural analysis would reveal (see above). In fact, treatments that we would describe as cruel in traditional terms are seldom successful in achieving appropriate behavioural changes.

Sometimes much less extreme treatments are criticized because they seem to infringe patients' rights. In a most interesting recent paper, Wexler (1973) has argued that many token economies make what the law will increasingly regard as patients' unconditional rights dependent on specified patterns of behaviour. He argues that only idiosyncratic back-up reinforcers may be allowed in future. We do not dispute that this may be so, but would argue that it is based on a failure to appreciate the philosophical context of behaviouristic treatments.

First, an event can only be a reinforcer if it is delivered; the whole point of any token economy is to deliver reinforcers, not to withhold them. Second, the items often made contingent upon behaviour in token economies (food, good clothes, entertainment, and so forth) are not seen just as examples of the creature comforts that a humane society should provide for the sick and the handicapped. Instead, these items are regarded as potential reinforcers which, when made contingent upon behaviour, can be said, in one sense, to give a reason or purpose to the behaviour. We should beware that in providing patients with everything quite freely and in placing few, if any, demands upon them that we are not creating a more subtle kind of deprivation—that of reasons to do anything. We may suspect that such 'humane' but unstructured treatments may inadvertently contribute to the 'apathy' that is all too often a characteristic of patients in long-term custodial care (see above).

The interpretation of the justification for token economies is also of very great importance. For example, it is easy to think of them in a superficial way as similar to the money economies in which we all live. If we want something, we must pay for it, and payment is dependent on performing certain (often unexciting) tasks. But the token economy should not just be seen as a way of making patients work for their living. For example, by 'paying' patients with tokens for domestic chores, the primary aim should always be to specify appropriate behavioural objectives for individuals and for groups, and to ensure that such behaviours are engendered by the delivery of reinforcing tokens.

A fairly frequent reaction of a more general nature to the use of operant conditioning is to question the morality of any behavioural control at all. In our view, however, the question of controlling others can be misleading. In a sense we all control each other all the time, whether by design or accident. We do this by supplying differential consequences for other peoples' behaviour, and they control us in the same way. In our discussion of Helen (above) we tried to show how unplanned events could engender her psychotic talk. If we are aware of this possibility and yet fail to restructure her environment can we be said to be responsible for her psychotic behaviour?

Our experience suggests that there are widely differing views on such questions; these will clearly be related to the way of seeing behaviour that is adopted. In our opinion, the real issue centres on what behaviours we should seek to control rather than whether to introduce control techniques. It is not just a matter of diagnosing and then curing an illness; in adopting a behaviouristic view, we must consider why our patients' behaviour is undesirable and then try to engender more appropriate behaviours. This leads to questions of how the desirability (or otherwise) of behaviour should be assessed. In fact, patients in mental hospitals often find themselves there because their relatives or friends can no longer cope with their unusual behaviour. Radical behaviourism is in sympathy with the idea that what is deemed abnormal behaviour is usually a social judgement, a view which has come greatly to the fore in a different context as a result of the writings of Szasz (e.g. Szasz, 1961). This view emphasizes yet more starkly the problem of whether a pattern of behaviour which others judge to be undesirable (not sick) should be changed.

We shall not attempt to resolve such issues here. Clearly they raise questions which should be considered by everyone. Our main concern, in conclusion, is to argue again for an appreciation of the theoretical and philosophical context of operant conditioning techniques. A behaviouristic approach, we feel, has much to offer in clinical psychology, but we certainly do not claim that it is the only possible approach or that other orientations are not valuable.

REFERENCES

Ayllon, T., and Azrin, N. H. (1968). The measurement and reinforcement of behavior of psychotics. *Journal of the Experimental Analysis of Behavior*, **8**, 357–383.

Ayllon, T., and Michael, J. (1959). The psychiatric nurse as a behavioral engineer. *Journal of the Experimental Analysis of Behavior*, **2**, 323–334.

Azrin, N. H. (1958). Some effects of noise on human behavior. *Journal of the Experimental Analysis of Behavior*, **1**, 183–200.

Azrin, N. H., and Holz, W. C. (1966). Punishment. In W. K. Honig (Ed.), *Operant Behavior: Areas of Research and Application*, Appleton-Century-Crofts, New York.

Bachman, J. A. (1972). Self-injurious behavior: a behavioral analysis. *Journal of Abnormal Psychology*, **80**, 211–224.

Baer, D. M. (1970). A case for the selective reinforcement of punishment. In C. Neuringer and J. L. Michael (Eds.), *Behavior Modification in Clinical Psychology*, Appleton-Century-Crofts, New York.

Bigelow, G. (1972). The behavioral approach to retardation. In T. Thompson and J. Grabowski (Eds.), *Behavior Modification of the Mentally Retarded*, Oxford University Press, New York.

Blackman, D. E. and Thomas, G. V. (in press). Single-subject methodology in operant conditioning. In C. W. Deckner (Ed.), *Perspectives in Behavioral Research Methodology*, C. C. Thomas, Springfield, Illinois, in press.

Burt, C. (1962). The concept of consciousness. *British Journal of Psychology*, **53**, 329–342.

Davison, G. C. (1969). Appraisal of behavior modification techniques with adults in institutional settings. In C. M. Franks (Ed.), *Behavior Therapy: Appraisal and Status*, McGraw-Hill, New York.

Eysenck, H. J. (1952). The effects of psychotherapy: an evaluation. *Journal of Consulting Psychology*, **16**, 319–324.

Franks, C. M. (Ed.) (1969). *Behavior Therapy: Appraisal and Status*, McGraw-Hill, New York.

Goldiamond, I. (1965). Self-control procedures in personal behavior problems. *Psychological Reports*, **17**, 851–868.

Goldiamond, I. (1974). Toward a constructional approach to social problems. *Behaviorism*, **2**, 1–84.

148

Gombrich, E. H. (1969). Visual discovery through art. In J. Hogg (Ed.), *Psychology and the Visual Arts*, Penguin Books, Harmondsworth.

Grünbaum, A. (1952). Causality and the science of human behavior. *American Scientist*, **40**, 665–676.

Hull, C. L. (1943). *Principles of Behavior*, Appleton-Century-Crofts, New York.

Kazdin, A. E. (1973). Methodological and assessment considerations in evaluating reinforcement programs in applied settings. *Journal of Applied Behavior Analysis*, **6**, 517–531.

Kazdin, A. E., and Bootzin, R. (1972). The token economy: an evaluative review. *Journal of Applied Behavior Analysis*, **5**, 343–372.

Keehn, J. D. (1969). Consciousness, discrimination and the stimulus control of behaviour. In R. M. Gilbert and N. S. Sutherland (Eds.), *Animal Discrimination Learning*, Academic Press, London.

Kuhn, T. S. (1961). *The Structure of Scientific Revolutions*, University of Chicago Press, Chicago.

Lindsley, O. R. (1964). Geriatric behavioral prosthetics. In R. Kastenbaum (Ed.), *New Thoughts on Old Age*, Springer, New York.

Mace, C. A. (1957). Behaviourism. In A. V. Judges (Ed.), *Education and the Philosophic Mind*, Harrap, London.

Rachlin, H. (1974). Self control. *Behaviorism*, **2**, 94–107.

Reppucci, N. D., and Saunders, J. T. (1974). Social psychology of behavior modification: problems of implementation in natural settings. *American Psychologist*, **129**, 649–660.

Salzinger, K. (1969). The place of operant conditioning of verbal behavior in psychotherapy. In C. M. Franks (Ed.), *Behavior Therapy: Appraisal and Status*, McGraw-Hill, New York.

Seligman, M. E. P. (1970). On the generality of the laws of learning. *Psychological Review*, **77**, 406–418.

Seligman, M. E. P. (1973). Reply to Malone. *Psychological Review*, **80**, 306.

Skinner, B. F. (1950). Are theories of learning necessary? *Psychological Review*, **57**, 193–216.

Skinner, B. F. (1956). What is psychotic behavior? In F. Gildea (Ed.), *Theory and Treatment of the Psychoses: Some Newer Aspects*, Washington University Studies, Washington.

Skinner, B. F. (1973). *Cumulative Record: A Selection of Papers*, 3rd ed. Appleton-Century-Crofts, New York.

Skinner, B. F. (1974). *About Behaviorism*, A. A. Knopf, New York.

Stubbs, D. A., and Silverman, P. J. (1972). Second-order schedules: brief shock at the completion of each component. *Journal of the Experimental Analysis of Behavior*, **17**, 201–212.

Szasz, T. S. (1961). *The Myth of Mental Illness*, Hueber-Harper, New York.

Tharp, R. G., and Wetzel, R. J. (1969). *Behavior Modification in the Natural Environment*, Academic Press, New York.

Thompson, T., and Grabowski, J. (Eds.) (1972). *Behavior Modification of the Mentally Retarded*, Oxford University Press, New York.

Tolman, E. C. (1932). *Purposive Behavior in Animals and Men*. Appleton-Century, New York.

Truax, C. B. (1966). Reinforcement and non reinforcement in Rogerian psychotherapy. *Journal of Abnormal Psychology*, **71**, 1–9.

Truax, C. B., and Carkhuff, R. R. (1967). *Toward Effective Counselling and Psychotherapy*, Aldine, Chicago.

Ullmann, L. P., and Krasner, L. (Eds.) (1965). *Case Studies in Behavior Modification*, Holt, New York.

Ullmann, L. P., and Krasner, L. (1975). *A Psychological Approach to Abnormal Behavior* (2nd. ed.), Prentice-Hall, Englewood Cliffs, New Jersey.

Ulrich, R., Dulaney, S., Kucera, T., and Colasacco, A. (1972). Side-effects of aversive control. In R. M. Gilbert and J. D. Keehn (Eds.), *Schedule Effects: Drugs, Drinking and Aggression*. University of Toronto Press, Toronto.

Ulrich, R., Stachnik, T., and Mabry, J. (Eds.) (1966). *Control of Human Behavior*, Scott, Foresman Co., Glenview, Illinois.

Ulrich, R., Stachnik, T., and Mabry, J. (Eds.) (1970). *Control of Human Behavior II*, Scott, Foresman Co., Glenview, Illinois.

Watson, L. S., Jr. (1973). *Child Behavior Modification: A Manual for Teachers, Nurses, and Parents*, Pergamon, New York.

Wexler, D. B. (1973). Token and taboo: behavior modification, token economies and the law. *Behaviorism*, **1**, 1–24.

Wheeler, H. (Ed.) (1973). *Beyond the Punitive Society*, Wildwood House, London.

Wiest, W. M. (1967). Some recent criticisms of behaviorism and learning theory. *Psychological Bulletin*, **67**, 214–225.

Wolf, M., Risley, T., and Mees, H. (1964). Application of operant conditioning procedures to the behavior problems of an autistic child. *Behavior Research and Therapy*, **1**, 305–312.

Woodworth, R. S. (1929) *Psychology*, Holt, New York.

6

THE EXPERIMENTAL ANALYSIS OF RETARDED BEHAVIOUR AND ITS RELATION TO NORMAL DEVELOPMENT

James Hogg

INTRODUCTION

Studies in the experimental analysis of the behaviour (EAB) of retarded individuals range from laboratory investigations of reinforcement and stimulus control to functional analysis of behaviour and its modification in home, school, work and hospital settings. In addition, some studies involve laboratory investigations of analogues of the behaviour in such social settings. The relations between the various kinds of study, particularly between the EAB at a laboratory level and behaviour modification, may be conceived of in two ways. First, the basis for behaviour modification may be said to rest upon the EAB as exemplified by Skinner (1966a) and as explored by a variety of representative authors in Honig (1966). This simple relation between principles and practice is asserted by several writers. Thus:

> Many behavior modification practitioners apply clinically the learning theory principles of Skinnerian operant psychology. Operant theory is bottomed on the principle, amply demonstrated by empirical data, that behavior is strengthened or weakened by its consequences (Wexler, 1973, p. 2).

Second, there is the view that the extension of the EAB does not involve the simple application of principles, but the development of research within the EAB framework in areas of increasingly complex behaviour. Thus Skinner (1966b) writes:

> Criticism (of the EAB) often takes the line that analysis is oversimplified, that it ignores important facts, that a few obvious exceptions demonstrate that its formulations cannot possibly be adequate and so on. ... An understandable reaction might be to stretch the available facts and principles in an effort to cover more ground, but the general plan of research suggests another strategy (p. 217).

Skinner goes on to advocate continued and progressive use of the EAB, extending what is encompassed by the method: 'Patience with respect to unexplored parts of a field is particularly important in a science of behavior because, as part of our own subject matter, we may be overwhelmed by the facts which remain unexplained (p. 218).'

This gradual process of extension is exemplified in the studies referred to above that have undertaken an experimental analysis of retarded behaviour. The main aim of this chapter is to illustrate this diversity and to consider some of the problems of method and interpretation in such studies. Retarded behaviour, however, as the term implies, is considered such because the individual fails to meet some normative standard that is considered developmentally typical. This fact has a number of consequences for those undertaking experimental studies or educational intervention with the retarded. For this reason, studies of young normal children have been included as well as studies of mentally retarded people. Both populations are here subsumed under the term 'developmentally young individuals'. It is hoped that by including studies of normal children, the conditions under which such information is relevant to understanding the behaviour of retarded people will be clarified.

In the first section, the definition of mental retardation is considered, and it will be seen that criteria are invoked that implicate the performance of developmentally normal individuals. In addition, the experimental designs that have been advocated as relevant to the study of retardation, often involving formal comparison of developmentally contrasted subjects, are reviewed. The second section is concerned with the explanation of normative development through the procedure of functional analysis, and recent reformulations of retarded behaviour within this framework are described. Then comes a section dealing with laboratory studies of reinforcement and stimulus control in developmentally young individuals. The fourth section is concerned with behaviour modification—its evaluation and content. With regard to the content of such programmes, the relevance of information on normal development to intervention with retarded individuals is considered. The final section draws together a number of the main points in the preceding sections by considering the EAB of a selected area of complex behaviour, namely the imitation of motor and verbal models by both retarded and normal children. Finally, some concluding comments are made.

CLASSIFICATION AND CHARACTERIZATION OF RETARDED INDIVIDUALS

Clarke and Clarke (1973) and Mittler (in press) have summarized the main criteria for classifying subnormal or retarded individuals and have indicated the varying terminology in different systems. The following summary draws upon these authors' reviews. The Mental Health Act, 1959, distinguishes between severe subnormality and subnormality. Severe subnormality involves 'a state of arrested or incomplete development of mind which includes subnormality of intelligence and is of such a nature or degree that the patient is incapable of living an independent life or guarding himself against serious exploitation, or will be so incapable when of an age to do so'. Subnormality is defined as a similar state of arrested or incomplete development, less in degree to severe subnormality, and ' ... susceptible to medical treatment or other special care or training of the patient'. The explicit use of intelligence as a criterion for classification represents an addition to, and an advance on, previous definitions, and lends itself to assessment through standardized IQ tests. These may used to place the subnormality boundaries at IQs between 55 and 70 and severe subnormality at IQs below 55. Recently both groups have been designated educationally subnormal (ESN), sometimes with the prefix or suffix 'S' to indicate 'severely' and 'M' to indicate 'moderately', i.e. SESN or ESN(S), and MESN or ESN(M).

In contrast, the American Association on Mental Deficiency (Grossman, 1973) has produced a highly differentiated classification system. Again, social and intellectual criteria are employed: 'Mental Retardation refers to significantly sub-average general intellectual functioning existing concurrently with deficits in adaptive behaviour, and manifested during the development period'. 'Sub-average' refers to performance on an objective test resulting in an IQ score that is more than two standard deviations (SDs) below the population mean. The developmental period may be regarded as extending up to 18 years of age. Adaptive behaviour is defined in terms of (a) maturation, (b) learning and (c) social adjustment, and the AAMD have issued rating scales to facilitate the objective assessment of relevant areas of functioning. In addition, four grades of retardation are specified for each of the two areas of assessment, i.e. adaptation and intelligence. Here we shall limit ourselves to the IQ ranges on a test of SD = 15 points associated with these: mild retardation, IQ = 69–55; moderate retardation, 54–40; severe retardation, 39–25; profound retardation, 24–0. In addition, the AAMD system includes classification based upon differential diagnosis of presumed 'biomedical' causes of the retardation. The term 'familial' is employed to indicate, in the American literature, retardation resulting from normal polygenetic variation.

The majority of research designs involving comparisons of retarded and non-retarded subjects employ contrasts based on chronological age (CA), mental age (MA) and intelligence quotient (IQ). The most obvious group of deficits in the behaviour of retarded individuals reflects a discrepancy between the subject's performance at a given CA and what is normatively expected for the population at large at that CA. Thus, the deficit is defined in developmental terms. This has lead Ellis (1969) to advocate studies of retarded functioning employing two groups of CA-matched subjects in which the retarded group has a lower MA and IQ than the normal group. Ellis also suggests that aetiology of the retarded group be disregarded and that aetiologically heterogeneous samples should be used. Thus, from Ellis's position, aetiological homogeneity, even where such a sample can be composed, does not imply behavioural homogeneity.

In contrast, Zigler (1969) advocates the separation of familial and organic subjects for the purpose of study. He concurs with Ellis in regarding the discrepancy between actual performance and normative performance as a feature of retardation. He chooses to use the term 'deficit', however, in a highly restricted way. A deficit exists for Zigler if a group of *familial* retarded subjects performs more poorly than a group of MA-matched normal subjects on a task in which variables such as motivation are adequately controlled. An absence of any difference between two such MA-matched groups of subjects supports what Zigler calls a developmental view of familial retardation, i.e. the position he espouses in the light of the available evidence.

We may see, then, that both the terms 'deficit' and 'development' have somewhat differing meanings in terms of the conceptualizations of retardation underlying studies employing CA and MA matching. It follows from this that, if in an operant study a deficit or developmental difference is to be demonstrated, a two-group design meeting the requirements of one of these authors must be employed, a requirement that has typically not been met in studies purporting to show such differences in operant behaviour between normal and retarded groups.

Both Ellis and Zigler allow two out of the three developmental variables, i.e. CA, MA and IQ, to vary while the third is held constant. To avoid this, Denny (1964) advocated three-group designs with the retarded group matched in MA and CA to two normal groups. Subsequently, Kappauf (1973) has suggested that more extensive sampling from the whole developmental domain is called for if inferences regarding the effect of developmental variables are to be drawn. Since two of the variables predict the third, he has suggested on statistical grounds that CA and IQ be extensively sampled as well as several levels of the task variable. However, the existence of the concept of MA is determined by the failure of CA to predict ability adequately for the section of the population referred to as retarded, and writers such as Harter (1965), while also employing IQ, have preferred MA to CA.

Generally, the experimental analysis of behaviour has followed Baumeister's (1967) suggested research design employing groups of retarded subjects, each of the same CA, MA and IQ, but subjected to differential treatments. Results from such designs, Baumeister suggests, are no less important, meaningful or reliable because normative comparisons are not made. Baumeister's position seems of more relevance to the EAB of retarded behaviour than comparative studies for two reasons. First, the technical and practical problems of establishing adequate meaningful subject group matches have not been fully resolved, in the wider experimental literature, sufficiently to warrant the expansion of experimental effort that would be called for in a time-consuming operant study. Second, it is doubtful that comparative information, in its own right, increases the relevance of information to intervention procedures with retarded people other than in the most general prescriptive fashion. This is not to say, however, that studies of normal subjects (also considered in their own right) are necessarily irrelevant to those concerned with retarded subjects. Both the technology and procedures of research with normal subjects may provide direction to operant research with the retarded.

THE FUNCTIONAL ANALYSIS OF RETARDED BEHAVIOUR

Baumeister's (1967) suggestion regarding the study of retarded behaviour in its own right is most fully realized in the use of functional analysis with this population. Here an experimental analysis of the behaviour of an individual retarded person is undertaken in line with the fundamental approach of such an analysis (Skinner, 1966a). There are two related aspects to this procedure. First, retarded behaviour may be analysed in terms of an individual's lifespan, or a significant phase within it. The behaviour is dealt with in the context of developmental psychology, through behavioural analysis of development as exemplified by Bijou (1968) and Bijou and Baer (1966). Second, an experimental analysis of retarded behaviour may be undertaken over a shorter phase without recourse to the wider developmental significance of the individual's behaviour in his total lifespan. Such functional analysis may be seen as relating to specific components of educational and training procedures (Kiernan, 1973, pp.277–279). In this situation, functional analysis has been described by Kiernan as ' . . . the application of the Skinnerian theory of behaviour to the analysis of particular problems in applied behaviour analysis (p. 263)'. Clearly, the distinction drawn here is not a rigid one, though the differing objectives in any given study are quite distinct. In terms of specific procedures, however, no distinction may be drawn. Here we shall deal with the wider conceptual analysis of behavioural development. Specific short-term analyses are described in studies reviewed below.

The functional analysis of behavioural development has been evolved in the main by Bijou and Baer (1961, 1965, 1966). The development of the child's motor, perceptual, linguistic, intellectual, emotional, social and motivational repertoires is conceived in terms of the developing child's objective interactions with his environment (both internal and external). Behaviour evolves through both respondent and operant conditioning, some responses sharing components of both functions and the balance shifting between them. Intellectual development reflects the control of behaviour through classes of events via discrimination and generalization. Individual differences reflect variations in the discriminative stimulus history, i.e. the past experience of stimuli in the presence of which operant behaviour was reinforced and in the absence of which that behaviour was not reinforced, and reinforcement schedule history. Social development and personality both depend in particular on the development of discriminative stimuli as conditioned reinforcers, i.e. stimuli that acquire reinforcing effects through their association with an already effective reinforcer. Motivation itself, clearly of central importance to an understanding of many aspects of child development, may be considered in terms of the motivating effects of reinforcement (e.g. Teitelbaum, 1966) or in terms of setting factors or events. The latter term refers to stimulus conditions that have a specific effect on a range of respondent and operant functions. Thus, deprivation, physical or sensory, might be such a setting event, having wide-ranging and long-term effects. However, complex interactions are not regarded as simply sums of less complex pieces of behaviour. When complex behaviour is exhibited, it is necessary to analyse this in its totality.

Bijou (1966) has considered retarded behaviour in terms of this model of development. Such behaviour is accounted for without recourse to hypothetical mental constructs such as 'defective intelligence' or hypothetical biological abnormalities such as 'clinically inferred brain damage'. The development of retarded behaviour is seen in the context of objective stimulus–response interactions between the child and his environment. A limited repertoire of behaviour evolves in contrast to that of the child engaging in a normal, i.e. culture typical, set of interactions as a result of these exchanges being slowed down by deviant social, biological and physical conditions.

This position is illustrated by Bijou with reference to four classes of child–environment interactions that lead to retarded behaviour. First, abnormal anatomical and physiological functioning can lead to interactions with others that are abbreviated as a result of avoidance or merely dutiful behaviour by other people. Second, the child's history of reinforcement and the discriminative situations to which he has to respond may be restricted, leading to retarded development. Ferster (1961) has emphasized the consequence of extinction and intermittent reinforcement for social and language development in particular. Bijou points to evidence derived from studies such as that of Dennis and Najarian (1957) in institutions, and notes the implications drawn for intervention by Sayegh and Dennis (1965). Other advocates of intervention to offset the effects of cultural deprivation have made a similar case, notably Hunt (1966). Third, inappropriate punishment or punishment that is too severe may distort serviceable responses, impairing their usefulness in future learning. Severe punishment may not only suppress ongoing behaviour but may generalize to other stimulus situations in an inappropriate way. Fourth, undesirable behaviour may be reinforced, for example, by parents attending to such behaviour. The termination of the undesirable behaviour is in turn negatively reinforcing for the parent, thus maintaining the non-adaptive intervention. Concomitantly, educational interactions will be discouraged.

To date the analysis of behavioural development is still in its infancy, and hence the movement from the extensive study of laboratory behaviour and educational and training studies with retarded individuals has barely begun. Nevertheless, Bijou, Peterson and Ault (1968) have clearly pointed the way by suggesting techniques for the integration of descriptive and experimental field studies at the level of data and empirical concepts. Similarly, Baer (1973) has proposed a strategy that moves from what has been shown to be possible in a behaviour modification setting into the modification of developmental sequences, as a hypothesis-testing technique for investigating development in the natural environment.

An interesting example of both the strengths and weaknesses of this approach may be found in Gavalas and Briggs' (1966) reconstruction of the concept of dependency in terms of the concurrent schedule paradigm (see below). These authors define dependent behaviour as ' . . . persistently recurring behaviour characterized by the seeking of others and by a lack of achievement or success, which has been caused by an earlier history of reinforcement for seeking others, concurrent with a lack of reinforcement for competence (p. 101)'. Typically, in normal development, it is proposed that concurrent schedules function in which reinforcement is received for approaches to other people, notably a child's parents, and is also received in other situations in which competent behaviour, e.g. manipulatory behaviour, is also reinforced. Dependent behaviour is hypothesized as being generated when approaches to the parent are reinforced but competent behaviour in other areas is not. In the latter situation, neutral stimuli associated with the competence response will come to act as discriminative stimuli for periods of non-reinforcement. The hypothesis is that lack of reinforcement for competent behaviour will increase behaviour directed to gratification from other people at the expense of obtaining gratification through accomplishment. Gavalas and Briggs (1966) elaborate the various outcomes for development of a variety of different concurrent schedules involving dependency and competence behaviour.

The advantage of the approach is that non-behavioural concepts that have traditionally played an important part in both learning-based and psychoanalytic theories of dependency, such as anxiety, frustration, displacement and inhibition, etc., become redundant, and observable behaviour replaces them. However, the disadvantages of the approach are also clear, and the authors draw attention to several—among them the fact that the schedule of reinforcement is in operation in the home and therefore difficult to evaluate. To deal with this, they suggest that (a) reports from parents might be employed, (b) direct observation in the home used, (c) miniature experiments attempted in which the concurrent schedule is directly investigated with the child and (d) hypotheses might be made concerning what schedules were in operation in the childhood of an adult. Predictions based on these hypotheses concerning the person's behaviour in an experimental setting might then be evaluated.

REINFORCEMENT AND STIMULUS CONTROL OF DEVELOPMENTALLY YOUNG INDIVIDUALS

We have seen above that normal and retarded behaviour may be considered by functionally analysing its development. We have also seen that at present such an account, while being theoretically tenable, has yielded little of empirical substance. The direct investigation of reinforcement and stimulus control has received more consideration in laboratory and behaviour modification studies. It is to the former that we turn here.

In the following sections, significant experiments on reinforcement and stimulus control in developmentally young individuals are described. The purpose of these reviews is (a) to summarize some of the main findings from such studies; (b) to indicate the basic designs employed in terms of subject characteristics, in order to; (c) draw conclusions on what kind of comparisons may legitimately be made and their limitations; and (d) to enable us to suggest certain directions that such research might most usefully take in future.

Single schedule studies with developmentally normal children

The major focus of the EAB is operant behaviour, i.e. behaviour whose future occurrence is determined by its consequences. A number of responses that differ in various ways may actually produce the same consequence, and hence the operant is defined not by a single response but by a class of responses, all of which produce the same outcome. Thus a manipulandum may be pressed with the left or right hand or the subject's nose. If the consequence is the same, then these responses make up the response class defining that operant. The relation between an operant and its consequences is described by the schedule of reinforcement.

Reinforcement schedules may be defined in terms of response requirements, temporal requirements, or both. In addition, any given reinforcement schedule may be considered in terms of the typical pattern of responding, or characteristic performance, that it produces. In order to clarify the following discussion of work with developmentally young subjects, some of the main simple schedules that have been studied will be described. For fuller accounts, the reader may turn to Ferster and Skinner (1957) or Thompson and Grabowski (1972).

When every occurrence of an operant is followed by an event that leads to an increase in its future occurrence, i.e. an event that is therefore positively reinforcing, a continuous reinforcement schedule (CRF) is in operation. If no such event follows the occurrence of the operant, then an extinction (EXT) schedule is in operation.

Both CRF and EXT involve non-intermittent reinforcement, in contrast to schedules in which reinforcement occurs intermittently, i.e. does not follow every occurrence of the operant. When the schedule specifies that a fixed number of responses must be made after the last reinforcement before a further reinforcement occurs, then a fixed ratio (FR) schedule is operating. The number of responses required follows the abbreviation, e.g. FR-5 indicates that five responses must be made before reinforcement occurs. Similarly, the variable ratio (VR) schedule specifies the number of responses that must occur on average following the previous reinforcement. The number of responses varies around some average from reinforcement to reinforcement. The mean ratio of reinforcers to responses follows the abbreviation, e.g. VR-6 indicates an average of six responses. In addition, the lowest and highest number of responses may be specified, as may the arithmetic or geometric series used to generate the ratio employed.

In contrast to schedules that relate number of responses to reinforcement, fixed interval (FI) and variable interval (VI) schedules relate the reinforcement of an operant to its occurrence following a given interval of time. The FI schedule specifies that the first response after a fixed duration from either the last reinforcement, or the time at which the last reinforcement was available, is reinforced. The actual interval, usually in minutes, is specified after the abbreviation, e.g. FI-2 indicates that the interval is 2 minutes. If other than a minute is employed as the unit then this is specified, e.g. FI-45 sec. Similarly, the variable interval (VI) reinforcement schedule also specifies that the occurrence of reinforcement depends upon temporal duration. However, this varies from interval to interval in a random or near-random way. The mean interval is therefore specified following the abbreviation with the same conventions as the FI specification, e.g. VI-2 for an average interval of 2 minutes or VI-10 sec for an average interval of 10 sec. The limits of the intervals (highest and lowest) and the arithmetical or geometrical progression employed to generate the intervals may also be stated.

With the exception of extinction schedules, those described above involve positive reinforcement and have received more attention than schedules involving response reduction or aversive stimuli in studies of developmentally young subjects. Thus, less work has been carried out on punishment, avoidance and escape procedures with such subjects in a laboratory setting. Punishment schedules involve the operant being followed by a reduction in future responding. Azrin and Holz (1966) indicate that no assumptions need be made about the consequent event being aversive to the subject, the reduction in responding attributable to a specific consequent stimulus being sufficient to characterize the operation of punishment. The aversiveness of a stimulus may be demonstrated employing an avoidance or an escape schedule. Thus, in a Sidman (free-operant) avoidance schedule, a stimulus that is known to be negatively reinforcing is programmed to occur at the end of a given interval. However, an appropriate response will put off the event for the full duration again, i.e. the subject will avoid it. In contrast, an escape schedule necessitates that the subject actually terminates an ongoing aversive event. It is the increase in the future probability of the operant resulting from the termination of the aversive stimulus that characterizes the stimulus as a negative reinforcer.

Finally, schedules have been developed that are designed to generate high or low rates of responding. Thus a schedule that involves differential reinforcement of low rates of responding (DRL) specifies that no response must occur before a given duration has elapsed. The first response after that interval will be reinforced. A response before the interval has elapsed will reinstate the full duration. Similarly, differential reinforcement of high rates (DRH) entails the subjects in responding before a specified duration has elapsed. such schedules have also been referred to as involving differential reinforcement of interresponse times (IRT) schedules. As with FI schedules, the abbreviations DRL and DRH may be followed by a specification of the actual IRT demanded by the schedule.

The study of these schedules with young children developed rapidly following Skinner's early work with infrahuman subjects (Skinner, 1938). While Long (1940) employed operant behaviour to investigate the concept of roundness in children, it appears that Warren and Brown (1943) carried out the first study which explicitly considered operant behaviour and the generality of 'Skinner's unique behavioural system' across species. With children of CA = 2–5 years, they investigated acquisition and extinction of a response, its spontaneous recovery (i.e. reappearance during extinction after a decline in its occurrence), disinhibition of responding and periodic reconditioning in a lever-pressing task. Strong parallels with the infrahuman literature are apparent. The main impetus for operant studies with children occurred during the mid-1950s with Bijou's (1955) advocacy of the experimental analysis of child behaviour and his brief study of simple schedule effects with normal pre-school children (Bijou, 1957a). It is, however, the work of Long and coworkers (1958) with 200 children of CA = 4–8 years that constitutes the major study in this area. These authors report on the characteristics of responding in their sample on FR, FI, VR and VI schedules. Though they conclude, as did Warren and Brown (1943), that some measure of comparability with infrahuman studies exists, they also point to less orderliness in responding, especially with reference to FI schedules. Relative weakness of the reinforcers, social interactions between child and experimenter, variability of intersession intervals, the effects of holidays and presents, and the shortness of sessions are all suggested as possible causes of lack of schedule control. Weisberg and Fink (1966), with younger children of from 14 to 19 months, reach similar conclusions regarding the effects of limited food deprivation on performance under an FR schedule. In this study, Weisberg and Fink attempt to overcome some of the specific shortcomings of earlier experiments that involve only brief sessions (Simmons, 1964) and long intersession intervals (Rheingold, Stanley and Doyle, 1964).

Much of the infrahuman literature has demonstrated that resistance to extinction is increased by intermittent reinforcement in contrast to CRF. The practical significance of this finding for maintaining responding in human subjects is clear, and a number of laboratory studies with young children have been undertaken. Bijou (1957b) contrasted VR and CRF, as did Kass and Wilson (1966). Cowan and Walters (1963) studied FR and CRF. All confirmed that resistance to extinction was greater following intermittent reinforcement. Bijou (1958) found that the duration of the interval in FI schedules was inversely related to rate of extinction. Though Bijou (1957b) indicates that not all studies with children support the findings that intermittent reinforcement increases resistance to extinction relative to CRF, there is some consistency in this finding. Though infrahuman studies of intermittent reinforcement effects are complex (Sutherland and Mackintosh, 1971), a strong parallel between these and child studies does exist.

The broadening of schedule studies may take at least two directions. First, schedule effects may be related to subject variables. Second, schedule effects may be related to procedures of educational significance. The former leads the experimenter into design considerations of the kind raised above. The latter raises questions regarding the relevance of the effect to criteria external to the operant study itself, i.e. educational objectives of the kind to be discussed below.

Subject variables were studied by Bijou and Oblinger (1960). They considered decrease in responding in normal children (CA = 2.6–6.6 years) in relation to the general social milieu that the child experienced. Children from a university laboratory school made fewer responses on a manipulative task in which there was no 'extrinsic' reinforcement than those from a cooperative and a private day-care centre. Bijou and Oblinger interpret this in relation to the difference between the relatively higher socioeconomic status of the university group children and the lower (but actually average) socioeconomic status of the day-care groups. Social and material experiences at home were suggested as factors affecting the relative rate of responding, the university group being exposed to a richer environment at home than the day-care groups. Similarly, the university group experienced greater social contact and more elaborate equipment in the school setting than the day-care groups. Assumedly, these factors reduced the effectiveness of reinforcement in the experimental setting. In addition, the authors suggest that the fact that the study was carried out in a mobile laboratory in the day-care setting, but not in the university school group, maintained the behaviour for more trials as the total experience was relatively more attractive. Similarly Thor (1972) demonstrates that boys are more resistant to extinction than girls (mean CA = 8.7 years), a difference that is attributed to a cultural emphasis on perseverative behaviour being desirable in boys, and alleged greater 'intrinsic' reinforcement in manipulative behaviour for boys than girls. In contrast, Frederiksen and Peterson (1974) found no difference between nursery school boys (CA = 5.0 years) and girls (CA = 5.125 years) in aggressive behaviour towards a doll during periods of extinction following CRF. However, several subjects did hit the doll and the authors suggest that individual differences are more relevant in accounting for this than sex differences.

The study of schedule effects in situations more complex than those involving lever-pressing may be illustrated through Davidson and Osborne's (1974) matching-to-sample experiment with children of CA = 4–7 years. In conditions where matching was delayed, FR and FI schedules gave rise to systematic (though differing) errors in contrast to VR and VI schedules in which errors were not systematic. Close parallels to infrahuman studies were found.

Experimental studies of punishing or aversive events are more restricted than those involving positive reinforcement. Baer (1960) established withdrawal of a cartoon film as aversive and employed it in the study of avoidance and escape schedules with pre-school children. Subsequently, Baer (1962) used the withdrawal of attention by a talking puppet as an aversive event establishing avoidance behaviour to this contingency. In this study, individual differences in schedule control were found to be related to the degree of attention-seeking exhibited by the child in the classroom. Rainey (1965) (reported by Moffat and Miller, 1971) also used interruption of cartoons as an aversive event and established avoidance behaviour in half the subjects in both a normal and a retarded sample, using a discrete trial procedure (i.e. a situation in which the subject responds only once, if at all, on any given trial, in contrast to the free-operant procedure where several responses may be made in the presence of the stimulus on any one of its presentations). Similarly, Moffat and Miller (1971) themselves used omission of nursery rhymes and demonstrated that pre-training—systematic exposure to the stimulus conditions and instructions—affected performance. Robinson and Robinson (1961) also employed a discrete trial procedure, but failed to establish control of avoidance behaviour.

Single schedule studies with developmentally retarded individuals

Studies involving single schedules with developmentally retarded individuals are more limited in their sampling and details of reporting than that of Long and coworkers (1958). In addition, much of the evidence has been derived from institutionalized subjects and may not be generalizable to non-institutionalized individuals. Thus, Ellis, Barnett and Pryer (1960) investigated institutionalized adult retarded subjects. In the first group of IQ < 30, FR responding was typically stable, smooth and linear, while FI records were characterized by erratic responding. In a second group of MA = 3–9 years, rate of responding under FR was positively related to MA. Also working with institutionalized subjects of CA = 9–21 years and IQ = 23–64, Orlando and Bijou (1960) found stable responding under FR and increasing rate as the ratio was increased. Variable rate responding was similar, though pauses in responding after a reinforcement were more irregular than under FR. Variable internal perform-ance was similar to VR, though interresponse times were more variable in the former, i.e. they showed rougher 'grain'. As in Long and coworkers' (1958) study with normal children, FI responding was most erratic and exhibited marked individual differences varying between low and very high response rates. Spradlin, Girardeau and Corte (1965) extended these studies to pro-foundly retarded institutionalized subjects, investigating FR and FI schedules. Again, high-rate responding under FR and individual differences in the extent to which temporal control was exhibited under FI emerged.

It is perhaps the occurrence of individual differences under FI responding as well as its significance for temporal discrimination that has lead to some specific studies on this schedule in the light of earlier work. Orlando (1961) has attempted to analyse the factors controlling responding in an FI situation with retarded subjects, in an effort to account for the individual differences. His result suggests that a low rate of responding depends upon at least two factors, i.e. use of the temporal interval as a discriminative stimulus and with-holding responding in the presence of non-reinforced stimuli. Headrick (1963) implicates the procedure employed in establishing schedule control as an important group of variables affecting responding. She investigated the effects of instructions and ambiguity of reinforcement on FI schedule control with twenty-five institutionalized retarded subjects of CA = 11–29 years and IQ = 31–76. She suggests that these variables directly affect the degree of control gained by reinforcement *per se*. Clearly, the importance of such stimulus conditions cannot be overemphasized, whatever the objectives of the individual study. We shall see that in more complex situations their relative contribution in relation to reinforcement is significant.

Bijou and Oblinger's (1960) study also included a group of institutionalized retarded subjects (CA = 6.1–11.7 years and mean MA = 3.3 years). This group made on average three times as many responses as the normal group, who were closest in performance. Older retarded children made more responses than younger ones, while retarded girls made more responses than retarded boys. However, the fact that the retarded group consisted of institutionally-based children precludes direct comparison with the home-based normal children. Here responding was to a manipulandum, operation of which had never been reinforced by the experimenter. Thor (1972), however, looked at extinction following experimentally manipulated reinforcement. Here, girls extinguished more rapidly than boys. This occurred whatever task, or reinforcer, was used and was independent of IQ and CA. In addition, non-institutionalized boys in the retarded group (mean CA for both sexes = 15.4 years and mean IQ = 62) responded for longer during extinction than institutionalized boys (mean CA for both sexes = 15.1 years and mean IQ = 65.8). Thor's result supports that of Noonan and Barry (1967a). He draws attention to their observation (Noonan and Barry, 1967b) that success deprivation may be as motivating for non-institutionalized subjects as social deprivation is for those who are institutionalized. In line with this, Spradlin and Fixen (personal communication) have suggested that the failure of two institutionalized retarded girls to extinguish responding might have reflected a generalized compliance response.

The extent to which the reinforcer acquires discriminative properties, i.e. becomes itself a stimulus for responding, has been investigated by considering the effect of its presentation during extinction. Spradlin, Girardeau and Hom (1966) tested Jenkins' (1965) contention that such properties develop, using six institutionalized retarded female adolescents (CA = 12.7–14.9 years and IQ = 26–54). Following performance on FR-50, extinction was instituted. When reinforcement was freely delivered, responding increased relative to control periods. Spradlin, Fixen and Girardeau (1967) confirmed this finding with nine comparable subjects (CA = 11.6–15 years and IQ = 25–54), but also found that for two subjects a novel stimulus presented during extinction increased responding relative to the increase following reinforcement presentations. In addition, for four subjects, novel stimuli continued to lead to an increase of responding after the stimulus properties of reinforcement had ceased.

Sequential and concurrent schedule studies with developmentally normal children

The simple schedules described above may be related in sequential and concurrent reinforcement schedules. Several such schedules have been investigated with developmentally young individuals and these will now be briefly described. In a sequential schedule, simple schedules occur in sequence and are said to be its components. The four schedules to be considered here are the multiple, mixed, chain and tandem schedules. Two features differentiate these. First, a specific stimulus change may or may not be associated with the various components, i.e. differential discriminant stimuli (SDs) may or may not be present. Second, unconditioned reinforcement may or may not occur in all components. Thus, in a multiple schedule (MULT), each component is associated with a specific SD, and reinforcement occurs in each component (unless the component is associated with EXT). In a MULT FR-10 FI-2, a red light may be on when the FR schedule is in operation and a green light when the FI component is in operation. When a schedule requirement is met, e.g. ten responses in the FR component, reinforcement occurs. The components may change, following a response requirement being met or following some pre-set period of time. Components may alternate or change randomly, and more than two components may be involved. A mixed (MIX) schedule is the same in all respects to the multiple schedule except that no differential discriminant stimuli are associated with the components. A mixed schedule analogous to the multiple schedule just noted is specified by MIX FR-10 FI-2. A chain (CHAIN) schedule, like the multiple schedule, has SDs associated with its component schedules. However, completion of the response requirement in the first component is not reinforced, except by a change to a second component in which reinforcement is available on completion of the response requirement. Such a schedule would be specified in the following form, e.g. CHAIN FI-2 VR-15. The tandem (TAND) schedule is comparable to the mixed schedule in that no SDs are correlated with the components, but is like the chain schedule in that reinforcement in the first component is followed only by a change to the second component, in which unconditioned reinforcement occurs following completion of the response requirement. Because multiple and mixed schedules differ only in their stimulus conditions, but not in their reinforcement schedules, their contrast provides information on the extent to which behaviour is under stimulus control, a concept explored in more detail later. A similar contrast may be made between chain and tandem schedules.

In the above schedules, a single operant occurs under schedules that change sequentially. If the subject can at any time make more than one operant response, then a concurrent (CONC) schedule is in effect. Here the subject might be reinforced by food on an FR-10 schedule on lever A and with water on VR-20 on lever B. Such a schedule would be designated CONC FR-10 VR-20. In some cases, a response on either lever would count towards the ratio requirement for that lever event if the subject alternated between A and B. This is referred to as a reversible option. If, however, the ratio or interval requirement had to be met on A before B became operative, a non-reversible option would be in effect. Concurrent schedules are therefore sometimes referred to as 'options'.

The step from simple to sequential schedule studies with children is clearly large in terms of the procedures that must be adopted to gain control. Not only is the use of standard infrahuman procedures time-consuming (Bijou and Orlando, 1961), but considerable ingenuity is called for in modifying them. Though Bijou (1961) reported some measure of schedule control (i.e. differential responding related to the components) with three children of CA = 3:10–4:10 years on a MULT VR-50 EXT schedule, none of thirty-two children showed differential responding between the components of a MULT FI FR schedule after eight sessions in a study by Long (1959). A variety of modifications had therefore to be employed. Eventually some schedule control was achieved with eighteen of the sample. Increased control was achieved on this multiple schedule in an extensive study by Long (1962) with 132 children of CA = 4–7 years. Again, additional procedures were generally required. A similar pattern emerges in Long (1963), in which chain and tandem schedules were explored and 102 subjects in the same CA range were involved. CHAIN DRL FR led to stimulus control and differential responding between the components. Additional techniques were necessary for CHAIN FI FR, however, as they were for TAND FI FR. Weisberg (1969) successfully extended the study of multiple and chain schedules to children of CA = 15–25 months using as the discriminant stimulus a flashing light of varying cycles per second in contrast to Long's use of hue.

There is little information as yet on the significance of specific schedules of reinforcement on behaviour outside the laboratory, as we noted in our discussion of Gavalas and Briggs' (1966) analysis of dependency. It is questionable that their importance can be deemphasized as Kiernan (1974) implies. Whatever the case proves to be, it is reasonable to suggest that sequential schedules represent a closer approximation to natural conditions than simple schedules. An important study that attempts to bridge the laboratory–natural environment gap was carried out by Brigham and Sherman (1973). A laboratory analogue to a token reinforcement system was created, involving a two-component multiple schedule with pre-school children. Here performance on a MULT FR FR schedule involving different ratios was assessed. Reinforcement conditions in the components were varied, e.g. whether the candy to be received for a token was selected by the experimenter or child. In a concurrent schedule condition, the child could then select the component of the multiple schedule in which to respond. Though differences in response rate between the multiple components did not emerge, significant preferences were revealed by the choice of the two for components in the concurrent schedule, e.g. showing a preference for child-selected versus experimenter-selected candy. Brigham and Sherman suggest their findings have direct application in token economies.

Sequential and concurrent schedule studies with developmentally retarded individuals

More restricted work directly comparable to that of Long's with normal children and Weisberg's with normal infants has been carried out with retarded individuals by Bijou and Orlando (1961), Orlando (1965b) and Orlando and Bijou (1960). The first two studies used the same sample of institutionalized retarded individuals with CA = 9–21 years and IQ = 23–64. In the 1961 study the authors point to the time-consuming nature of establishing multiple schedule control, i.e. differential responding in the individual components. It is clear that techniques are required over and above those involved in standard infrahuman studies and a detailed account of the instructional procedures to induce responding to the manipulandum is also given. This is followed by a four-phase procedure consisting of (1) rate evaluation and strengthening; (2) pause-building; (3) rate recovery; and (4) final multiple schedule training. Exact details of the procedures are specified. Sample data for MULT VR-25 EXT, MULT FR-25 EXT, MULT FI-1 EXT, MULT CRF VI-30 sec and MULT VR-100 EXT are presented. Despite the effectiveness of the procedure, Orlando (1965b) alludes to a significant number of subjects in the sample who showed no evidence of differential responding in the components. Although he invokes both situational and central nervous system defects to account for this, he also calls attention to inadequacies of the shaping technique. The objective of the 1965 study was therefore to improve the technique and to arrive at stable control under MULT VR-25 EXT. The procedure described was undertaken with sixteen experimentally naïve institutionalized subjects with CA = 14–21 years and MA = 2.2–14.2 years. The problem of establishing multiple schedule control was clearly indicated by the outcome. Five subjects completed the shaping procedure in less than 60 minutes and performed adequately for 12 minutes on MULT VR-25 EXT. An additional two subjects completed the shaping procedure, but failed to show multiple schedule control. Nine subjects failed to complete the shaping procedure. Of the seven successful subjects, only two performed satisfactorily on the multiple schedule in the second session. The other fourteen subjects underwent an intensive demonstration by the experimenter performing on the multiple schedule. Nine of these subjects then showed schedule control. With the remaining five subjects, a variety of procedures was employed, including programming an aversive noise contingent on responding to the stimulus associated with the extinction component of the schedule, changes in the type of reinforcement, changes in the VR schedule and the experimental situation. The criteria for adequate schedule control were all subsequently met by the five subjects. Those who met criterion under the initial shaping procedures did not differ significantly in CA or MA from those who failed to do so, but the former had been institutionalized for longer. The subjects requiring the special procedures beyond the demonstration were significantly lower on CA and MA than subjects who showed control following or before the demonstration.

Hom (1967) employed a situation involving concurrent performance on two VI schedules with token reinforcement to study the effect of amount of reinforcement on responding and acquisition. Twenty institutionalized children (described as mildly retarded; CA = 12.2–17.1 years and IQ = 34–81) were employed. In line with the finding of Hom and coworkers (1966) with two such subjects, an increase in the number of tokens, in contrast to a decrease, led to a higher rate of responding. This difference was maintained in extinction, though the decrement in responding under high reinforcement was greater than under low reinforcement.

Smeets and Striefel (1974) report a particularly interesting investigation employing a chain schedule in which a correct response on an oddity learning task (the first component) initiated the second component which consisted of a match-to-sample task, a correct response on which was reinforced. Improvement on the oddity task attributable to the reinforcement in the second component is shown for two of three institutionalized mildly-to-moderately retarded boys (CAs 10.3–14.1 years). The relevance of such tasks to curriculum activities is apparent, and the result points the way to structuring learning sequences in an optimal fashion.

Stimulus control with developmentally normal children

As Ray and Sidman (1970) have suggested, sudden changes in the environment outside the laboratory leading to abrupt changes in behaviour are the rule. The study of the effect of changes in stimulus conditions in and out of the laboratory is therefore an essential complement to studies of reinforcement. This relation between stimulus change and behaviour is termed stimulus control, and Terrace (1966) suggests that the term refers to the extent to which an antecedent stimulus determines the probability of a conditioned response occurring. Thus stimulus control is measured as a change in response probability, resulting from a change in stimulus value.

It is Terrace's work (Terrace, 1963a, 1963b, 1963c, 1964, 1966, 1969) that has given impetus to the study of stimulus control in both infrahuman and developmentally young subjects. Many of Terrace's findings have been extended to the latter population. Moore and Goldiamond (1964) used a fading procedure with normal pre-school children of CA = 3–6 years in a matching-to-sample task. With subjects acting as their own controls, it was shown that the use of a fading procedure reduced errors in contrast to the situation where the stimuli were at full intensity from the outset. A similar demonstration of the effectiveness of the fading procedure, again with normal pre-school children of CA = 3.5–5.0 years, is reported by Powers, Cheyney and Agostino (1970). The use of fading procedures has been extended beyond these experimental demonstrations by its direct application in educational programming. Corey and Shamow (1972), for example, considered the effect of fading on the acquisition and retention of oral reading with nursery school children (CA = 4.0–5.8 years) and showed that oral reading was learnt better and retained longer following fading in contrast to non-fading procedures.

In studies in which learning involves the use of relational aspects of the stimulus array, e.g. in a conditional discrimination or oddity learning task, rather than simple discriminations, fading techniques have not to date been effective. Gollin and Savoy (1968) found that young children learnt a conditional discrimination with fewer errors following use of a non-fading procedure than those who had been exposed to a fading procedure. Similarly, Cheyney and Stein (1974), using material similar to that employed by Powers, Cheyney and Agostino (1970), found that a variety of fading procedures were no more effective in teaching an oddity learning task to normal pre-school children of CA = 5.95 years than non-fading methods. The implication of these studies is that stimulus control may be restricted by the fading procedure in such a way that the probability of appropriate stimulus control in the relational task is diminished.

These experiments on the transfer of stimulus control across dimensions represent starting points for detailed analyses of the exact conditions under which stimulus control is acquired. It is well established that reinforcement is not a sufficient condition to guarantee control by stimuli of the experimenter's choice. Thus Ray and Sidman (1970) describe the performance of a normal child of CA = 5.2 years in a matching-to-sample task. Stimulus control by an orientation dimension is apparently shown until at a specific point in the programme it becomes clear that some other aspect of the stimulus configuration is actually exercising control. More detailed information on this aspect of stimulus control is given below on retarded individuals.

Studies of special significance in analysing the conditions under which stimulus control is established, maintained, removed and restored appear in Sidman and Stoddard (1966) with normal (as well as retarded) children. A further detailed analysis appears in Stoddard and Sidman (1967) with normal children of CA = 3:10–10:11 years. Here the effect of errors generated by the sequencing of stimuli are determined, and the stimuli that come to control responding under such conditions are established by analysis of response patterns.

Direct measurement of stimulus control may be established through the use of stimulus generalization procedures. It is important to note that stimulus generalization in this context does not refer to an organismic process variable, but to the technique of measuring stimulus control (Prokasy and Hall, 1963; Ray and Sidman, 1970; Terrace, 1966). The technique, which in the infrahuman literature may be applied to both free-operant and discrete trial procedures, consists in training a discrimination and then presenting several stimuli that vary in some respect from the training stimuli, in order to establish what is the controlling dimension. Dimensional control is indicated by differential and orderly responding on the dimension. The exact procedures involved in training and testing vary across studies, as may be seen from Mostofsky (1965) and Switalski, Lyons and Thomas (1966).

The paradigm that has been mainly used with normal children is the intra-dimensional paradigm. Here a reinforced stimulus, the S+, and a non-reinforced or less reinforced stimulus, the S−, are drawn from the same stimulus dimension. Generalization testing is then carried out around these stimuli using other stimulus values on the same dimension. Thus, Weisberg

(1969) established differential rates of responding in children of from 15 to 25 months to S + and S − stimuli differing on a steady light–flickering light continuum. Generalization stimuli consisted of differing cycles per second of flicker. Reliable decremental gradients were established around the S+ stimulus, i.e. responding decreased with progressively greater stimulus differences from the S+. Gradients around the S− were typically flatter than the S+ gradients. Nicholson and Gray (1971), with older children of from 7:1 to 10:6 years, employed a dimension of line-tilt, also establishing reliable decremental gradients around S+ and somewhat flatter gradients around S−. In a subsequent study, Nicholson and Gray (1972) related various parameters of these gradients to individual differences in the children's personality and development, thus relating a basic and well-explored operant technique to wider psychological issues.

Nicholson and Gray's procedure involving reinforcement and extinction of free-operant responding produced results that were more consistent with the infrahuman literature than did a discrete trial study also involving line-tilt and post-discrimination generalization testing by Landau (1968a). Here nursery school children (CA = 3.5–4.5 years) and normal adults made verbal responses to the stimuli and received verbal feedback on correctness of response. Landau suggests that his results for children and adults reflect mediation by conceptual categorization of the line stimuli. In other work with children in the 3.5 to 5.5 years age range, Landau (1968b, 1969) has explored the effect of training and testing procedures on stimulus generalization.

Stimulus control with developmentally retarded individuals

Parallel studies on stimulus control with normal children have also been undertaken with developmentally retarded subjects. Indeed, in some cases more information is available on stimulus control in the latter group. It may be the case that the similarity of Terrace's experimental situation to those employed in the classroom of the mentally retarded, and the ease with which his operations may be extended to standard teaching procedures such as match-to-sample, have made this a more natural extension of animal procedures than has been the case with schedule studies.

The superiority of fading versus non-fading as a training method for teaching a simple discrimination was confirmed by Sidman and Stoddard (1967) in a group design involving match-to-sample. Here retarded boys of CA = 9.9–14.4 years were placed in a traditional training or a programmed (fading) group. Similarly, Lambert (1974) confirmed Terrace (1963a) by transferring control across dimensions more effectively with a fading than a traditional procedure. Here retarded children (CA = 7.6–14.3 years and IQ = 43–58) were involved. In addition, the fading group showed better retention than that exhibited by the traditional group. Additional confirmation for Sidman and Stoddard (1967) also comes from Touchette's (1968) study with retarded boys (CA = 9–16 years and IQ = 27–45). Lambert (1974) has also replicated

Terrace (1969) on the effect of errorless learning on extinction. In Terrace's experiment, pigeons that learnt an errorless discrimination in a discrete trial procedure with CRF were disrupted in their performance during extinction in contrast to those who learnt in a free-operant situation under intermittent reinforcement. Lambert's retarded subjects showed the same effects. Most studies on fading have employed visual stimuli, though Harvey and Bornstein (1974) have confirmed the superiority of fading versus non-fading training using auditory stimuli. In a study of twenty severely retarded subjects (mean $CA = 9.0$ years), however, when they extended the situation from a one- to a two-stimulus discrimination task, fading techniques did not reduce trials to criterion from that of the non-fading group.

A variety of studies on the use of fading procedures has also been undertaken in more complex situations. Dorry and Zeaman (1973) demonstrated the superiority of fading over a non-fading procedure in paired associate (word-picture) learning with retarded children ($MA = 4{:}2{-}6{:}11$ years and $IQ = 23{-}55$). Kern (1972) studied number conservation in mildly and moderately retarded boys ($CA = 7.2{-}14.5$ years and $IQ = 41{-}66$), and found that fewer errors were made during learning than when traditional (non-fading) procedures were employed.

Ray and Sidman's (1970) contention that reinforcement does not guarantee stimulus control by the aspects of the stimuli chosen by the experiment is fully demonstrated by Touchette (1969) with retarded boys of $CA = 12{-}17$ years and $IQ = 28{-}38$. Using a technique developed in an earlier study (Touchette, 1968), he trained an orientation discrimination, and with suitable probes found that responding was controlled by different features of stimuli for different subjects. Thus, apparently simple bars were functioning as complex stimuli, i.e. parts of a unitary stimulus controlled behaviour independently of the whole. The exact moment of transfer of control from one dimension to another has also been established by Touchette (1971), working with retarded boys of $IQ < 40$.

The ineffectiveness of fading procedures in teaching relational learning does not appear to have been investigated with retarded subjects, other than in an unpublished study by Lambert (personal communication). Here the general finding with normal subjects was confirmed, i.e. that fading techniques did not facilitate learning of a conditional discrimination relative to non-fading procedures.

The most detailed account of stimulus generalization following intra-dimensional training with developmentally retarded individuals appears in Paulson, Orlando and Schoelkopf (1967). Their technique was initially elaborated in a study of a rat (Orlando, 1965a) in the light of earlier experiments establishing multiple schedule control in human subjects (Orlando and Bijou, 1960). Paulson, Orlando and Schoelkopf's procedure led to orderly and stable gradients in three retarded subjects ($CA = 10.9{-}14.8$ years and $IQ = 35{-}50$), though it is implied that some subjects failed to complete the procedure. The continuum employed was an auditory frequency dimension.

In a somewhat different situation involving responding to two tones of differing volume on two different levers, Lane and Curran (1963) also established orderly gradients between the two tones. Here three blind retarded children of CA = 7:2–9:11 years and IQ = 10–30 were studied. Similar results with sighted retarded adolescents were found by Risley (1964) on an auditory frequency dimension, again employing two manipulanda. These workers produced results that are similar to studies with normal human adults (Cross and Lane, 1962) and infrahuman subjects (Honig and Day, 1962).

Visual dimensions have also received attention in free-operant and response rate studies of stimulus generalization. Smith (1960), employing a free-operant technique and employing hue as the generalization gradient, established reliable generalization gradients in one study but failed to replicate his finding subsequently. Evans (1974) also employed hue as the generalization dimension in a discrete trial go/no-go discrimination. Reliable gradients were established around both the S+ and S− following intradimensional discrimination training in ESN(S) subjects (CA = 162.04 months; verbal age (VA) = 54.22 months) and ESN(M) subjects (CA = 168.9 months; VA = 98.10 months). As in the Nicholson and Gray (1972) study, Evans relates an aspect of the generalization gradient, notably steepness of the gradient around S−, to the extent to which teachers rate the child as inhibitable in his or her classroom behaviour. Thus a flatter gradient around S−, indicative of greater inhibitory control than a relatively steeper gradient, is positively associated with how inhibitable the child's classroom behaviour is. Hogg and Evans (1975) have also investigated attentional control in ESN(S) children (experimental group CA = 163.0 months; VA = 72.10 months), using an extradimensional training procedure. Here the subject is trained on an orientation discrimination but generalization tested on a hue dimension. Attentional transfer across dimensions was demonstrated and evidence for the effect of colour-naming on the shape of the gradient reported.

Conclusions

In the introduction to this section we indicated that the information presented would enable us to draw conclusions on comparative information derived from the studies, and also to suggest useful directions for research in this area. In terms of 'hard' comparisons involving contrasting subjects of varying CA or MA within an experiment, little has been done. Even in those cases where a formal contrast is made, as in the case of Bijou and Oblinger (1960), the normal–retarded contrast is confounded by the institutionalization of the latter group. Thor (1972) provides a notable exception to this state of affairs. At the 'weak' level of comparison, i.e. the replication of studies on differing samples on differing occasions, explicit attempts to replicate an earlier experiment are also absent, and choice of subjects appears to have been made on the basis of availability rather than with a view to contrasting subjects differing on a specific independent variable. Indeed, reference to infrahuman studies often appears most pertinent simply because of the established degree of replicability between animal experiments. The best that can perhaps be said is that in the reinforcement studies some replication of findings in both normal and retarded samples has been demonstrated, e.g. high rates of responding under FR schedules and marked individual differences under FI. More direct replications are noted in the study of stimulus control, notably in similar studies of fading techniques with both normal and retarded children.

We have indicated above that Baumeister's (1967) strategy of contrasting groups within a given developmental range constituted an approach to retarded functioning that in EAB terms was useful and realistic. If we abandon comparative objectives and approach the material reviewed from this stand-point, then the possibility of employing EAB techniques to elucidate both normal and retarded functioning has been clearly demonstrated. It may also be argued that the persistent implicit or explicit attempt to replicate infrahuman studies has imposed a limitation on this work. This results from both practical considerations and also the potentially wider application of the EAB in a developmental framework. Control of deprivation level, the extraexperimental environment and setting conditions (such as demonstrations or verbal instruc-tions) all influence the performance of developmentally young individuals in such studies. As Woods (1974) has indicated, these difficulties do not suggest the abandonment of the laboratory EAB of human subjects, but a wider exploration of the controlling conditions. Extraexperimental variables may be admitted to the design in a formal fashion, as in Headrick's (1963) study of instructional effects.

The potentially wider framework referred to has already begun to be explored in the studies reviewed. At least five approaches suggest themselves:
(1) The laboratory replication of an effect that is directly analogous to some relevant environmental situation. Gavalas and Briggs (1966) suggest miniature experiments to test their operant model of dependency. Brigham and Sherman (1973) have investigated schedule control that parallels such control in token economies.
(2) Schedules may be investigated employing tasks that are similar to, or the same as, those employed in the classroom, as carried out by Smeets and Striefel (1974).
(3) Individual differences may be related to more traditional or specially developed personality theories, as in the case of the studies noted by Evans (1974) and Nicholson and Gray (1972).
(4) The interaction of operant behaviour and language merits special considera-tion. The influence of language on the form of generalization gradients has been demonstrated by Doll and Thomas (1967) and Thomas and Mitchell (1962) with human adults. Hogg and Evans (1975) suggest that similar effects operate in ESN(S) children. Such procedures may be used to investigate traditional areas of concern in child development, such as the extent to which motor behaviour is under verbal regulation.
(5) The traditional concern with lever- or panel-pressing in operant studies

appears to have informed the work with developmentally young individuals to an excessive extent. A number of behaviours may usefully be considered that would not only serve as operants in their own right, but would also enable us to elucidate areas of special interest such as attention. Thus there is an extensive literature on operant control of eye movements and visual fixation (e.g. Auge, 1973a, 1973b; Schroeder, 1969a, 1969b; Schroeder and Holland, 1968a, 1968b) which has direct relevance to studying and controlling attention in developmentally young individuals, as in Maier and Hogg's (1974) study of visual fixation in ESN(S) hyperactive children. Similarly, reading responses merit further consideration as operants. Staats and coworkers (1962, 1964) have investigated simple and multiple schedules employing reading. More recently, Gonzalez and Weller (1974) have studied handwriting as an operant in normal human adults. A progressive broadening of the type of operants studied would not only give more immediate relevance to education and training but could be achieved without any sacrifice in the rigour of the studies.

Finally, caution must always be observed in extrapolating findings of the kind reviewed to more complex situations. Replication of findings in some form must be the ultimate target. Nevertheless, we should not be overcautious in that some general prescriptions in the light of research, interpreted in a sensitive fashion, may be of help to those working directly with children. Indeed, such general prescriptions might in some cases be the practical optimum. In the case of stimulus control, for example, Ray and Sidman (1970) have suggested that techniques for acquiring stimulus control may not generalize across species or even across dimensions within species. Perhaps the best that can be hoped for, they suggest, is a combination of techniques that are known individually to encourage stimulus control.

BEHAVIOUR MODIFICATION: EVALUATION AND CONTENT

The use of the EAB in contexts in which the study is informed by criteria external to the EAB is sometimes referred to as the applied analysis of behaviour. Here an experimental analysis is undertaken, but objectives are set by situational demands about which value judgements have been made. Thus social and educational criteria affect the objectives of the study, though not the fundamental conceptual framework in which the analysis is undertaken. It is the use of the experimental analysis of behaviour in such contexts that is referred to as 'behaviour modification'. Kiernan (1974) has indicated that this is a specially restricted use of the term, since there is no reason why all attempts to modify behaviour should constitute behaviour modification in this sense. Nevertheless, if we take behaviour modification to mean the experimental analysis of behaviour with reference to specified objectives extrinsic to the EAB, then we may use the term in a consistent fashion.

It follows from such a view that it is neither technique nor rigour that distinguishes the EAB from behaviour modification. Both may or may not take place in laboratory settings with careful control. Thus, the development of operant audiometry (Bricker and Bricker, 1969; Fulton, 1972) or operant testing of visual functioning (Friedlander and Knight, 1973; Macht, 1970) may relate in a specific fashion to an educational procedure. Conversely, a discrimination learning task in a classroom using 'real' money may not be relevant to an educational objective. A number of studies may overlap between the EAB and behaviour modification in a significant fashion. Those of Brigham and Sherman (1973) and Sidman and Stoddard (1966), both described above, are such examples. At this point, then, we may remind ourselves of Skinner's (1966b) recommendation, noted in the introduction, regarding the patient exploration of increasingly complex areas of behaviour. The EAB and behaviour modification represent two facets of this process, not merely an application of the former to the latter.

The setting of objectives in behaviour modification studies with retarded individuals raises three questions, none of which are specific to this population. The first relates to the nature of evaluation and control; the second to choice of objectives; and the third to choice of techniques. Here we shall restrict ourselves to the first two aspects. Relevant information regarding the last area may be found in Blackham and Silberman (1971), Gardner (1971) and Watson (1973). Kiernan and Riddick (1973) have produced a training programme in operant techniques, while Kiernan and coworkers (1973a, 1973b) provide specific programme materials based on material developed by Panyan, Boozer and Morris (1970).

Evaluation and control

Any change in the selected response in a behaviour modification programme must be evaluated in relation to the stimulus conditions (antecedent and consequent) hypothesized to be controlling the behaviour. Thus, what Sherman and Baer (1969) refer to as the 'functional core' of the technique must be established. Such an analysis will typically be undertaken for an individual subject and may involve either the use of a reversal technique or multiple baseline procedure. A reversal procedure involves withdrawing the contingency to which a systematic change in the behaviour under consideration has been attributed. The withdrawal and reintroduction of the contingency may be carried out several times in order to establish the reliability of the effect. The multiple baseline procedure involves establishing baselines for several behaviours that occur concurrently in the experimental situation. Reinforcement is applied to occurrences of only one of these behaviours. A change in this behaviour and no change in the concurrent behaviours is accepted as a demonstration of the specific effect of the contingency. The reliability of the effect may be further established by subsequently reinforcing other behaviours for which baselines have been established and noting change in those behaviours.

Gelfand and Hartmann (1968) also suggest alternatives to reversal where this is not feasible, such as the use of a yoked control, schedule changes and contingency reversal for a limited aspect of the target behaviour and/or for the target behaviour under limited discriminable conditions. As Gelfand and Hartmann emphasize, all such procedures are only valid against an adequate initial baseline assessment.

Such approaches are characteristic of the Skinnerian tradition, though as Kiernan notes, behaviour modifiers are becoming increasingly willing to employ more traditional procedures involving group evaluation. Thus, Maier and Hogg (1974), while considering individual response records, also apply analysis of variance to group data. Such a development meets Gardner's (1969) call for more adequate control procedures in behaviour modification studies. Specifically he calls for the appropriate use of 'no treatment' groups, citing Bensberg, Colwell and Cassell (1965), and the use of 'conventional treatment' groups, as in Kimbrell and coworkers (1967). Kiernan (1974), however, considers that the no-treatment procedure is 'meaningless' within the context of behaviour modification, and different treatment comparisons are less valuable than comparisons of effects within different behaviour modification studies. Nevertheless, however convincing the internal adequacy of a behaviour modification programme's success may seem to its proponents, it is questionable whether such isolationism can survive indefinitely. Wexler (1973), a lawyer, has discussed the need for comparisons of alternative therapies in specific relation to token economies if the latter are to avoid ' ... both legal and behavioural extinction (p. 23)'. He suggests that ' ... unless systematic comparative studies of alternative therapies are performed soon, the law will be unable to incorporate the results in developing a sensible package of patient rights, and expected legal developments may ultimately preclude such studies (p. 23).' While Wexler is here referring to the American scene, his caution would appear to have wider generality.

An important criticism of many behaviour modification studies is the inadequacy of the specification regarding both independent and dependent variables. Gardner (1969) demands clear specification of subject and experimenter variables in order to facilitate valid generalizations and increase the accuracy of predictions. The nature of the sampling procedures in behaviour modification studies with the mentally retarded also calls for comment. Gardner (1969) has criticized the choice of the 'worst' subjects in many studies, as this biases the results in favour of improvement being demonstrated. Bricker (1970) has called for extensive phases of programme evaluation which will establish the applicability of a given programme with a specified population. A further indirect influence on apparent sampling emerges from the tendency to publish only positive results (Kiernan, 1974).

The whole question of generalization of training effects in behaviour modification with the retarded has also become a central issue in considering evaluation. Baer, Wolf and Risley (1968) call for the programming of generalization rather than merely expecting or lamenting it. Kazdin (1973) has suggested relevant procedures for such programming. At a wider level of evaluation, Bricker (1970) and Kiernan (1974) have drawn attention to several contextual aspects of behaviour modification. Thus, the evaluation of so-called side-effects, the specification and monitoring of situational variables, the economics of implementing programmes evolved in a research setting and the generalized effects on development all merit assessment, evaluation and detailed reporting in the literature.

Content

Historically, behaviour modification with retarded individuals has evolved from the development of piecemeal programmes, usually conducted in an institutional setting, towards comprehensive programmes dealing with a variety of areas of behaviour. In an educational context, this has brought the behaviour modifier into contact with the field of curriculum development. It is generally accepted that behaviour modification itself is without curriculum content and that the development of a curriculum entails a series of value judgements. Writing of pre-school education in general, Spodek (1973) states that the source of a curriculum ' . . . is the set of goals which are the aims of education for children. This in essence is a value statement about what children ought to be (p. 89)'. Cunningham (1974) makes a similar assertion with specific reference to retarded children. How far, then, will objectives for normal children serve for retarded children?

First, it is important to note that this question is independent of the development versus deficit issue raised above. Even if, in an adequate experimental evaluation of the kind demanded by Zigler, it were shown that retarded children exhibit a specific deficit, this would not influence overall educational aims. It might, however, affect subgoals in that behaviour relevant to overcoming or circumventing the deficit must be developed. Thus, despite the possibility of deficits in retarded children, this does not of itself rule out a common curriculum with normal children. Second, if retarded behaviour may be viewed as development at a rate slower than normal, then clearly educational goals for normal children are equally applicable to retarded children. Cunningham (1974) cites a variety of studies that do indicate that for many subpopulations of the retarded, such as Down's syndrome individuals, developmental sequences follow a normal pattern but at a slower rate. This effectively represents Ellis's position. Here the significant feature of retarded behaviour is its occurrence in a child whose CA would predict a higher level of performance.

This developmental standpoint has led a number of behaviour modifiers to by-pass formal curricula for normal children and concentrate on modifying developmentally significant behaviours with a view to decreasing the CA–MA discrepancy. Such a 'developmental curriculum' draws directly upon developmental theory. However, 'developmental theory', like 'learning theory', consists of a wide range of varying positions. They differ not only in the variables they emphasize but in their fundamental conceptualizations regarding the nature of the interaction between child and environment. Cooke and Cooke (1973) review a variety of theories of child development (e.g. Piaget, Erikson, Bijou and Baer), and point towards their relevance to what they term 'educational programming' for normal and retarded pre-school children. However, the inadequacy of such generalizations in setting specific objectives is obvious, and it is to more detailed aspects of development theories that we must turn if specific objectives are to be set.

Bricker (1970) comments that ' ... behavior has a structure and that the components of that structure change in the various stages of development (p. 18)'. He suggests that there is little disagreement in this among behaviourist and cognitive psychologists. Such structure and orderly change may be seen in sensory motor, conservation and language behaviour among others. The problem, then, becomes one of specifying goals and subgoals which will enable the behaviour modifier to teach the requisite components of a terminal skill. This may be exemplified by the use of developmental psycholinguistics in the evolution of a programme. Following a review of recent work in linguistics and operant psychology, Lynch and Bricker (1972) observe that 'the starting point for a possible synthesis of the two supposedly divergent positions might be that if the linguist can define it properly the behaviorist can shape it (p. 14)'. This they regard as the 'fulcrum for interaction', and elsewhere (Bricker and Bricker, 1974) dismiss problems as to whether language is innate or learnt, and the 'natural' importance of reinforcement and imitation in language learning as pseudo-issues in so far as early language intervention is involved. From this position, they are then able to draw upon psycholinguistic data to develop a suitably sequenced programme which may be represented as a lattice specifying terminal procedures and programme steps. In a similar way, other developmental lattices such as a sensory motor lattice may be developed, drawing upon information from Piagetian studies.

It is possible that the distinction drawn above, between a normal academic curriculum and a special developmental curriculum for retarded children, is an artificial one stemming from the dearth of curriculum statements for retarded individuals. Thus Resnick, Wang and Kaplan (1973) show how a mathematics curriculum for normal pre-school children implicates abilities described by Piaget (1965), such as seriation, in a formal curriculum setting. Indeed, it is the relevance of a developmentally significant behaviour to an academic curriculum that implicates such behaviour as an objective, rather than the fact that it happens to have been studied by developmental psychologists or psycholinguists. Behaviours that change in childhood in a systematic and developmentally significant fashion may not necessarily be relevant or even desirable targets in a curriculum. We have therefore suggested elsewhere that developmental behaviours cannot of themselves be set as educational objectives (Hogg, 1975) and that behaviour modifiers must face up to a more thorough analysis of the environmental demands on a given child in determining objectives for him.

FUNCTIONAL ANALYSIS AND INTERVENTION: AN EXAMPLE

We shall now attempt to bring together the main features of the experimental analysis of retarded behaviour that have been described so far. This is to be done by a description of work on generalized imitation, an area regarded by Bijou (1968) as making a significant contribution to the study of complex behaviour. The use of imitation training procedures has, first, generated a variety of procedural innovations in behaviour modification, and has employed most of the non-aversive standard procedures. It has also constituted an experimental focus for a variety of theories of imitative behaviour. Second, it has evolved as a particularly effective procedure in educational settings for retarded people, especially in the area of language development. Clearly, choice of this example is not intended to suggest that this is the only area that merits such consideration, the breadth of application of the techniques under consideration being extensive. Kiernan (1974) lists a variety of other behaviours of special interest in retardation research.

Procedural aspects of imitative training

Many of the significant features of imitation training may be illustrated by Baer, Peterson and Sherman's (1967) study of three profoundly and severely retarded children of CA = 9–12 years. None exhibited any imitative behaviour. Presentation of a discriminative stimulus, i.e. the model to be imitated, was preceded by 'Do this' and a correct imitation reinforced by food preceded by 'Good'. In the case of subject 1, raising of the left arm constituted the first response. This was established by the experimenter moving the subject's limb passively (i.e. 'putting through') and then reinforcing her. This support was faded by withdrawing manual guidance at increasingly earlier points in the sequence. In this, as in all such studies, a time limit within which a correct response had to be exhibited was imposed. The complexity of the model tended to increase throughout training. Following such training, both old and new responses were chained and trained. In the case of subject 1, verbal imitation was initiated by incorporating a vocal response, e.g. 'Ah', into a motor chain. Reinforcement of successive approximations was employed in this stage to establish more complex vocalizations. Subject 3, on the other hand, was trained in motor responses that moved progressively closer to vocalizations, e.g. moving from blowing out a match to blowing with an initial plosive 'p'. Similarly, Lovaas and coworkers (1966) employed physical manipulation of the lips to initiate imitation.

Within the training procedure just described, an assessment is also made as to whether generalized imitation has developed. The significance of generalized imitation is that in conditions where such control has developed, it is not necessary to train each individual response in the manner just described. Typically, probe items are included in the sequence of training items, and correct imitations of these items are not reinforced. It is usually found that as training progresses generalized imitation does occur, as shown by correct imitation of the probe items as well as maintenance of such responding in the absence of reinforcement. Numerous studies have demonstrated this, e.g. Baer and Sherman (1964), Brigham and Sherman (1968), Burgess, Burgess and Esveldt (1970), Lovaas and coworkers (1966), Metz (1965), Schumaker and Sherman (1970) and Whitehurst (1972).

Imitation has been considered in relation to both reinforcement schedule control and stimulus control. Under certain conditions, it is clear that generalized imitation is dependent upon reinforcement of correct imitation of training items. Following stable performances on both reinforced and unreinforced imitative responses, Baer, Peterson and Sherman (1967) introduced non-reinforcement of all imitative behaviour through a contingency change involving differential reinforcement of other behaviour (DRO). Here any behaviour other than imitation that occurred at least 20 seconds after the last imitation was reinforced. The same procedure was employed by Risley and Wolf (1967). During DRO there was no change in the contingency for correct imitation of a probe, the change being limited to the reinforced imitations. Two of the subjects showed rapid reductions in and complete removal of responding. The third subject, however, maintained responding. This was reduced by the introduction of what Baer, Peterson and Sherman refer to as DRO-0 sec. Here reinforcement was given immediately after the model, before any response could be made. A return to contingent reinforcement supported by some shaping returned imitative performance to its originally high level. The authors conclude that the imitative repertoire was clearly dependent on reinforcement of at least some of its members. Brigham and Sherman (1968) and Lovaas and coworkers (1966) demonstrate the same result.

A variety of studies, however, has shown the importance of antecedent stimulus conditions in both the elicitation of an imitation and the occurrence of generalized imitation. In the former area, Risley and Reynolds (1970) demonstrated with three 5.0-year-old disadvantaged children that stress affects imitation. It was effective in influencing which parts of a sentence were imitated, though only in those cases where relatively few words were stressed. In the latter area, Peterson and coworkers (1971), working with normal pre-school children of CA = 4.3–5.1 years, investigated the inter-relations between the presence or absence of the person modelling, discrimination training and complexity of the stimulus situation on the maintenance of non-reinforced responding. Thus the experimenter would change the game and leave the room before the subject was to imitate. The importance of antecedent events is shown by the general trend in the findings that in the presence of the modeller no difference in responding to reinforced and non-reinforced stimuli is shown, whereas in the absence of the modeller subjects respond differentially. In a similar demonstration with normal children of CA = 4.8–5.2 years, Peterson and Whitehurst (1971) conclude that the presence of an experimenter can be a setting event for responding, defining such an event as an antecedent environmental change that alters the probability of a large number of subsequent responses. As indicated by these authors, such a finding illustrates the position adopted by Bijou and Baer (1961) regarding setting events in child development. Burgess, Burgess and Esveldt (1970) call for a more systematic study of experimenter-related variables such as instructions and coincidental experimenter cues. Steinman (1970), working with older children (CA = 7.2–9.0 years), presents convincing support for the view that social setting events are of special importance in generalized imitation by having separate modellers associated with reinforced and non-reinforced stimuli. All models were imitated, but in a choice procedure reinforced stimuli were imitated in preference to non-reinforced stimuli. Similarly, instructions not to respond to non-reinforced stimuli also led to discriminated behaviour. In addition, specific techniques of presentation of the models have also been studied. For example, Schroeder and Baer (1972) have found the concurrent presentation of models in contrast to serial presentation increases generalized imitation.

In the foregoing, we have discussed functional aspects of stimulus and reinforcement in the development and maintenance of imitative control. Many of the studies noted in elucidating variables affecting imitation also provide tests of theories of generalized imitation that have been developed. It is beyond the scope of this chapter to discuss the relevant findings that bear upon the main theories, namely (a) the conditioned reinforcement hypothesis of Baer, Peterson and Sherman (1967); (b) the failure to discriminate hypothesis of Bandura (1968); and (c) the generalization of components position of Bricker and Bricker (1972). The development and testing of such theories illustrate the way in which detailed experimental analysis calls for conceptual unification rather than the proliferation of unrelated studies.

Imitation and education

We have indicated that information derived from normal development may have relevance to the content of behaviour modification programmes with retarded individuals. Bricker and Bricker (1974) point out that there is disagreement as to how far imitation of language is necessary for its acquisition. They go on to say, however, that the crucial issue is whether the use of imitation training is effective in developing skills, especially language skills, with retarded children. The relevance of imitation, therefore, is not in terms of the form the acquisition of behaviour takes in the natural environmental situation, but in its use in developing content within a programme.

Detailed discussions of the development of linguistic training programmes in the context of behaviour modification will be found in Bricker and Bricker (1972, 1974) and Lynch and Bricker (1972). Within such programmes, imitation procedures have a wide-ranging application to a variety of behaviours. This may be illustrated from studies dealing with normal, retarded and low-functioning children. Guess and coworkers (1968) trained the productive use of plural morphemes in a 10-year-old severely retarded girl. Guess (1969) replicated and extended this study with two more similar subjects. Schumaker and Sherman (1970) trained generative verb usage in three retarded boys. Wheeler and Sulzer (1970), working with a language deficient child, developed the use of complete sentences in relation to pictures, while Bricker (1972) facilitated word-object associations in low-functioning children. Whitehurst (1972) taught normal pre-school children (22 to 24 months) employing imitation training to develop adjective–noun pairings, while Whitehurst and Novak (1973) with older normal subjects (3.5 to 4.7 years) trained participle, preposi- tional, appositive or infinitive phrases. Lutzker and Sherman (1974) taught the appropriate use of singular and plural in such a way that subject–verb agreement was maintained. Imitation and reinforcement procedures were functional in teaching such structures to both retarded children and normal pre-schoolers. Thus, the application of imitation procedures is far-reaching in its implications for training and education, though economic aspects of the techniques have yet to be studied in detail. Programme efficiency certainly merits special attention given to the observation (Baer, 1973) that it takes between 50 and 200 hours to establish tight imitative control in a profoundly retarded person.

CONCLUSIONS

The studies of the EAB of retarded individuals reviewed in this chapter amply demonstrate the feasibility and usefulness of investigating the behaviour of such subjects in an operant framework. Reinforcement and stimulus control has been demonstrated in situations involving not only simple manipulative responses but complex verbal behaviour. It is suggested, however, that less concern with the direct replication of infrahuman studies and a broadening of the framework in which such work is conceptualized, especially with reference to laboratory studies, is called for. Trends in this direction may already be discerned.

The fact that retarded development may be considered in relation to normal development suggested that studies of young normal individuals are pertinent to work with retarded people. It emerges that direct comparative operant studies are few and far between, and 'hard' comparative conclusions restricted. However, such a state of affairs would be of little importance if replications across populations in various studies had been undertaken. Such replications are characteristic of the EAB of infrahuman subjects. In general, however, replication with developmentally young individuals of different MAs are few. What conclusions can be drawn are limited to some simple schedule effects or to common difficulties in establishing sequential schedule control. The situation is somewhat better for studies of stimulus control, especially with reference to the use of fading procedures. If, then, comparative findings are to be employed to illuminate important features of retarded behaviour, more systematic replication is called for. This is especially so if we are to pursue a behavioural approach to the development of retarded behaviour through functional analysis of its development. The reference point of normative development, also considered within a functional analysis framework, is essential if our account is to be anything other than descriptive.

With regard to the content of intervention programmes, two points emerge.

182

First, the comparison of normal and retarded development does not of itself provide content for such programmes. Content must be determined within a broader framework of educational theory. However, when such content has been established, then information on both normal and retarded development may be implicated in guiding procedures and providing specific behavioural objectives. Second, in the area reviewed—imitation training—the application of directly comparable techniques to both retarded individuals and normal children was described. At this level, there would seem to be no constraint on the transfer of techniques and their evaluation on different populations, other than the level of development of the subject group at the start of any given programme.

REFERENCES

Auge, R. J. (1973a). Effects of stimulus duration on observing behavior maintained by differential reinforcement magnitude. *Journal of the Experimental Analysis of Behavior*, **20**, 429–438.

Auge, R. J. (1973b). Extinction of observing behavior. *Psychological Reports*, **33**, 603–609.

Azrin, N. H., and Holz, W. C. (1966). Punishment. In W. K. Honig (Ed.), *Operant Behavior: Areas of Research and Application*, Appleton-Century-Crofts, New York.

Baer, D. M. (1960). Escape and avoidance response of pre-school children to two schedules of reinforcement withdrawal. *Journal of the Experimental Analysis of Behavior*, **3**, 155–159.

Baer, D. M. (1962). A technique for the study of social reinforcement in young children: behavior avoiding reinforcement withdrawal. *Child Development*, **33**, 847–858.

Baer, D. M. (1973). The control of development process: why wait? In J. R. Nesselroade and H. W. Reese (Eds.), *Life-span Developmental Psychology: Methodological Issues*, Academic Press, New York and London.

Baer, D. M., Peterson, R. F., and Sherman, J. A. (1967). The development of imitation by reinforcing behavioral similarity to a model. *Journal of the Experimental Analysis of Behavior*, **10**, 405–416.

Baer, D. M., and Sherman, J. A. (1964). Reinforcement control of generalized imitation in children. *Journal of Experimental Child Psychology*, **1**, 37–49.

Baer, D. M., Wolf, M. M., and Risley, T. R. (1968). Some current dimensions of applied behavior analysis. *Journal of Applied Behavior Analysis*, **1**, 91–97.

Bandura, A. (1968). Social-learning theory of identificatory processes. In D. A. Goslin and D. D. Glass (Eds.), *Handbook of Socialization Theory and Research*, Rand McNally, Chicago.

Baumeister, A. A. (1967). Problems in comparative studies of mental retardates and normals. *American Journal of Mental Deficiency*, **71**, 869–875.

Bensberg, C. J., Colwell, C. N., and Cassell, R. H. (1965). Teaching the profoundly retarded self-help skill activities by behavior-shaping techniques. *American Journal of Mental Deficiency*, **69**, 674–679.

Bijou, S. W. (1955). A systematic approach to an experimental analysis of young children. *Child Development*, **26**, 161–168.

Bijou, S. W. (1957a). Methodology for an experimental analysis of child behavior. *Psychological Reports*, **3**, 243–256.

Bijou, S. W. (1957b). Patterns of reinforcement and resistance to extinction in young children. *Child Development*, **28**, 47–54.

Bijou, S. W. (1958). Operant extinction after fixed interval schedules with young children. *Journal of the Experimental Analysis of Behavior*, **1**, 25–29.

Bijou, S. W. (1961). Discrimination performance as a baseline for individual analysis of young children. *Child Development*, **32**, 163–170.

Bijou, S. W. (1966). A functional analysis of retarded development. In N. R. Ellis (Ed.), *International Review of Research in Mental Retardation*, Vol. 1. Academic Press, London and New York.

Bijou, S. W. (1968). Child behavior and development: a behavioral analysis. *International Journal of Psychology*, **3**, 221–238.

Bijou, S. W., and Baer, D. M. (1961). *Child Development: A Systematic and Empirical Theory*, Vol. I. Appleton-Century-Crofts, New York.

Bijou, S. W., and Baer, D. M. (1965). *Child Development: Universal Stage of Infancy*, Vol. 2. Appleton-Century-Crofts, New York.

Bijou, S. W., and Baer, D. M. (1966). Operant procedures and child behavior and development. In W. K. Honig (Ed.), *Operant Behavior: Areas of Research and Application*, Appleton-Century-Crofts, New York.

Bijou, S. W., and Oblinger, B. (1960). Responses of normal and retarded children as a function of the experimental situation. *Psychological Reports*, **6**, 447–454.

Bijou, S. W., and Orlando, R. (1961). Rapid development of multiple-schedule performances with retarded children. *Journal of the Experimental Analysis of Behavior*, **4**, 7–16.

Bijou, S. W., Peterson, R. F., and Ault, M. H. (1968). A method to integrate descriptive and experimental field studies at the level of data and empirical concepts. *Journal of Applied Behavior Analysis*, **1**, 175–191.

Blackham, G. J., and Silberman, A. (1971). *Modification of Child Behavior*, Wadsworth, Belmont, California.

Bricker, D. D. (1972). Imitative sign training as a facilitator of word-object association with low-functioning children. *American Journal of Mental Deficiency*, **76**, 509–516.

Bricker, W. A. (1970). Identifying and modifying behavioral deficits. *American Journal of Mental Deficiency*, **75**, 16–21.

Bricker, W. A., and Bricker, D. D. (1969). Four operant procedures for establishing auditory stimulus control with low-functioning children. *American Journal of Mental Deficiency*, **73**, 981–987.

Bricker, W. A., and Bricker, D. D. (1972). *The Use of Programmed Language Training as a Means for Differential Diagnosis and Educational Remediation among Severely Retarded Children*. Final Report: Project No. 7–0218, Contract No. OEG2–7–07218–1639. U.S. Department of Health, Education, and Welfare.

Bricker, W. A., and Bricker, D. D. (1974). An early language training strategy. In R. L. Schiefelbusch and L. L. Lloyd (Eds.), *Language Perspectives—Acquisition, Retardation, and Intervention*, University Park Press, London.

Brigham, T. A., and Sherman, J. A. (1968). An experimental analysis of verbal imitation in pre-school children. *Journal of Applied Behavior Analysis*, **1**, 151–158.

Brigham, T. A., and Sherman, J. A. (1973). Effects of choice and immediacy of reinforcement on single response and switching behavior of children. *Journal of the Experimental Analysis of Behavior*, **19**, 425–435.

Burgess, R. L., Burgess, J. M., and Esveldt, K. C. (1970). An analysis of generalized imitation. *Journal of Applied Behavior Analysis*, **3**, 39–46.

Cheyney, T., and Stein, N. (1974). Fading procedures and oddity learning in kindergarten children. *Journal of Experimental Child Psychology*, **17**, 313–321.

Clarke, A. M., and Clarke, A. D. B. (1973). Mental subnormality. In H. J. Eysenck (Ed.), *Handbook of Abnormal Psychology*, 2nd ed. Pitman Medical, London.

Cooke, S., and Cooke, T. (1973). Implications of child development theories for pre-school programming. *Education*, **94**, 112–116.

Corey, J. R., and Shamow, J. (1972). The effects of fading on the acquisition and retention of oral reading. *Journal of Applied Behavior Analysis*, **5**, 311–315.

Cowan, P. A., and Walters, R. H. (1963). Studies of reinforcement of aggression: I.

Effects of scheduling. *Child Development*, **34**, 543–551.

Cross, D. V., and Lane, H. L. (1962). On the discriminative control of concurrent responses: the relations among response frequency, latency, and topography in auditory generalization. *Journal of the Experimental Analysis of Behavior*, **5**, 487–496.

Cunningham, C. C. (1974). The relevance of 'normal' educational theory and practice for the mentally retarded. In J. Tizard (Ed.), *Mental Retardation: Concepts of Education and Research*, Butterworth, London.

Davidson, N. A., and Osborne, J. G. (1974). Fixed-ratio and fixed-interval schedule control of matching-to-sample errors by children. *Journal of the Experimental Analysis of Behavior*, **21**, 27–36.

Dennis, W., and Najarian, P. (1957). Infant development under environment handicap. *Psychological Monograph*, **71**, No. 7 (Whole No. 436).

Denny, M. R. (1964). Research in learning and performance. In H. A. Stevens and R. Heber (Eds.), *Mental Retardation: A Review of Research*, University of Chicago Press, Chicago.

Doll, T. J., and Thomas, D. R. (1967). Effects of discrimination training on stimulus generalization for human subjects. *Journal of Experimental Psychology*, **75**, 508–512.

Dorry, G. W., and Zeaman, D. (1973). The use of a fading technique in paired-associate teaching of a reading vocabulary with retardates. *Mental Retardation*, **11**, 3–6.

Ellis, N. R. (1969). A behavioral research strategy in mental retardation: defense and and critique. *American Journal of Mental Deficiency*, **72**, 557–566.

Ellis, N. R., Barnett, C. D., and Pryer, M. W. (1960). Operant behavior in mental defectives: exploratory studies. *Journal of the Experimental Analysis of Behavior*, **3**, 63–69.

Evans, P. L. C. (1974). Attentional and inhibitory transfer in the ESN(M) and ESN(S) child. *Bulletin of the British Psychological Society*, **27**, No. 95, 161–162.

Ferster, C. B. (1961). Positive reinforcement and behavior deficits of autistic children. *Child Development*, **32**, 437–456.

Ferster, C. B., and Skinner, B. F. (1957). *Schedules of Reinforcement*, Appleton-Century-Crofts, New York.

Frederiksen, L. W., and Peterson, G. L. (1974). Schedule-induced aggression in nursery school children. *Psychological Record*, **24**, 343–351.

Friedlander, B. Z., and Knight, M. S. (1973). Brightness sensitivity and preference in deaf-blind retarded children. *American Journal of Mental Deficiency*, **78**, 323–330.

Fulton, R. J. (1972). A program of developmental research in audiologic procedures. In R. L. Schiefelbusch (Ed.), *Language of the Mentally Retarded*, University Park Press, London.

Gardner, J. M. (1969). Behavior modification research in mental retardation: search for an adequate paradigm. *American Journal of Mental Deficiency*, **73**, 844–851.

Gardner, W. I. (1971). *Behavior Modification in Mental Retardation*, Aldine Atherton, New York.

Gavalas, R. J., and Briggs, P. F. (1966). Concurrent schedules of reinforcement: a new concept of dependency. *Merrill-Palmer Quarterly of Behavior and Development*, **12**, 97–121.

Gelfand, D. M., and Hartmann, D. P. (1968). Behavior therapy with children: a review and evaluation of research methodology. *Psychological Bulletin*, **69**, 204–215.

Gollin, E. S., and Savoy, P. (1968). Fading procedures and conditional discrimination in children. *Journal of the Experimental Analysis of Behavior*, **11**, 443–451.

Gonzalez, F. A., and Waller, M. B. (1974). Handwriting as an operant. *Journal of the Experimental Analysis of Behavior*, **21**, 165–175.

Grossman, H. J. (1973). *Manual on Terminology and Classification in Mental Retardation*. American Association on Mental Deficiency, Special Publication Series No. 2.

Guess, D. (1969). A functional analysis of receptive language and productive speech: acquisition of the plural morpheme. *Journal of Applied Behavior Analysis*, **2**, 55–64.

Guess, D., Sailor, W., Rutherford, G., and Baer, D. M. (1968). An experimental analysis of linguistic development: the productive use of the plural morpheme. *Journal of Applied Behavior Analysis*, **1**, 297–306.

Harter, S. (1965). Discrimination learning set in children as a function of IQ and MA. *Journal of Experimental Child Psychology*, **2**, 31–43.

Harvey, E., and Bornstein, R. (1974). The effects of visual cue fading and task complexity on auditory discrimination in severely retarded children. *Psychological Record*, **24**, 109–117.

Headrick, M. W. (1963). Effects of instructions and initial reinforcement on fixed interval behavior in retardates. *American Journal of Mental Deficiency*, **68**, 425–432.

Hogg, J. (1975). Normative development and educational programme planning for severely educationally subnormal children. In C. C. Kiernan and P. Woodford (Eds.), *Behavior Modification in the Severely Retarded: Study Group 8, Institute for Research into Mental and Multiple Handicap.* Associated Scientific Publishers; Amsterdam, in press.

Hogg, J., and Evans, P. L. C. (1975). Stimulus generalization following extra-dimensional training in educationally subnormal (severely) children. *British Journal of Psychology*, **66**, 211–224.

Hom, G. L. (1967). Effects of amount of reinforcement on the concurrent performance of retardates. *Psychological Reports*, **20**, 887–892.

Hom, G. L., Corte, E., Spradlin, J. E., and Michael, J. (1966). Effects of amount of reinforcement on the performance of mildly retarded adolescent girls. *Psychological Reports*, **19**, 1191–1194.

Honig, W. K. (Ed.) (1966). *Operant Behavior: Areas of Research and Application*, Appleton-Century-Crofts, New York.

Honig, W. K., and Day, R. W. (1962). Discrimination and generalization on a dimension of stimulus differences. *Science*, **138**, 29–31.

Hunt, J. McV. (1966). The psychological basis for using preschool enrichment as an antidote for cultural deprivation. In O. J. Harvey (Ed.), *Experience, Structure and Adaptability*, Springer, New York.

Jenkins, H. M. (1965). Measurement of stimulus control during discriminative operant conditioning. *Psychological Bulletin*, **64**, 365–376.

Kappauf, W. E. (1973). Studying the relationship of task performance to the variables of chronological age, mental age, and IQ. In N. R. Ellis (Ed.), *International Review of Research in Mental Retardation*, Vol. 6. Academic Press, London and New York.

Kass, N., and Wilson, H. (1966). Resistance to extinction as a function of percentage of reinforcement, number of training trials, and conditioned reinforcement. *Journal of Experimental Psychology*, **71**, 355–357.

Kazdin, A. E. (1973). Issues in behavior modification with mentally retarded persons. *American Journal of Mental Deficiency*, **78**, 134–140.

Kern, H. J. (1972). The effects of fading, feedback, and feedback plus instruction on the performance of institutionalized retarded children in number retention exercises. *Psychologische Forschung*, **35**, 243–262.

Kiernan, C. C. (1973). Functional analysis. In P. Mittler (Ed.), *Assessment for Learning in the Mentally Handicapped*, Churchill Livingstone, Edinburgh and London.

Kiernan, C. C. (1974). Behaviour modification. In A. M. Clarke and A. D. B. Clarke (Eds.), *Mental Deficiency: The Changing Outlook*, 3rd ed. Methuen, London.

Kiernan, C. C., Harlow, S., Saunders, C., and Riddick, B. (1973a). *Programme Materials 1: Research Paper No. 3*. Thomas Coram Research Unit, Institute of Education, University of London, London.

Kiernan, C. C., Harlow, S., Saunders, C., and Riddick, B. (1973b). *Programme Materials 2: Research Paper No. 4*. Thomas Coram Research Unit, Institute of Education, University of London, London.

Kiernan, C. C., and Riddick, B. (1973). *A Draft Programme for Training in Operant Techniques. Vol. 1: Theoretical Units*. Institute of Education, University of London, London.

Kimbrell, D. L., Luckey, R. E., Barbuto, P. F. P., and Love, J. G. (1967). Operation dry pants: an intensive habit-training program for severely and profoundly retarded. *Mental Retardation*, **5**, 32–36.

Lambert, J.-L. (1974). Errorless learning and retarded children. *Bulletin of the British Psychological Society*, **27**, No. 95, 169.

Landau, J. S. (1968a). Line-orientation generalization in children and adults as a function of the number of training trials. *Psychonomic Science*, **13**, 219–220.

Landau, J. S. (1968b). Post-discrimination generalization in human subjects of two different ages. *Journal of Experimental Psychology*, **76**, 656–663.

Landau, J. S. (1969). Size generalization in children as a function of test method and age. *Psychonomic Science*, **16**, 57–58.

Lane, H., and Curran, C. (1963). Gradients of auditory generalization for blind, retarded children. *Journal of the Experimental Analysis of Behavior*, **6**, 585–588.

Long, E. R. (1959). Mutliple scheduling in children. *Journal of the Experimental Analysis of Behavior*, **2**, 268.

Long, E. R. (1962). Additional techniques for producing multiple schedule control in children. *Journal of the Experimental Analysis of Behavior*, **5**, 443–455.

Long, E. R. (1963). Chained and tandem scheduling with children. *Journal of the Experimental Analysis of Behavior*, **6**, 459–472.

Long, E. R., Hammack, J. T., May, F., and Campbell, B. J. (1958). Intermittent reinforcement of operant behavior in children. *Journal of the Experimental Analysis of Behavior*, **1**, 315–339.

Long, L. (1940). Conceptual relationships in children: the concept of roundness. *Journal of Genetic Psychology*, **57**, 289–315.

Lovaas, O. I., Berberich, J. P., Perloff, B. F., and Schaeffer, B. (1966). Acquisition of imitative speech by schizophrenic children. *Science*, **151**, 705–707.

Lutzker, J. R., and Sherman, J. A. (1974). Producing generative sentence usage by imitation and reinforcement procedures. *Journal of Applied Behavior Analysis*, **7**, 447–460.

Lynch, J., and Bricker, W. A. (1972). Linguistic theory and operant procedures: toward an integrated approach to language training for the mentally retarded. *Mental Retardation*, **10**, 12–17.

Matcht, J. (1970). Examination and re-evaluation of prosthetic lenses employing an operant procedure for measuring subjective visual acuity in a retarded child. *Journal of Experimental Child Psychology*, **10**, 139–145.

Maier, I., and Hogg, J. (1974). Operant conditioning of sustained visual fixation in hyperactive severely retarded children. *American Journal of Mental Deficiency*, **79**, 297–304.

Metz, J. R. (1965). Conditioning generalized imitation in autistic children. *Journal of Experimental Child Psychology*, **2**, 389–399.

Mittler, P. J. (in press). *Problems and Policies in Mental Handicap*, Methuen, London.

Moffat, G. H., and Miller, F. D. (1971). Effects of pretraining and instructions on avoidance conditioning in preschool children. *Journal of Experimental Child Psychology*, **11**, 133–138.

Moore, R., and Goldiamond, I. (1964). Errorless establishment of visual discrimination using fading procedures. *Journal of the Experimental Analysis of Behavior*, **7**, 269–275.

Mostofsky, D. I. (Ed.) (1965). *Stimulus Generalization*, Stanford University Press, Stanford, California.

Nicholson, J. N., and Gray, J. A. (1971). Behavioural contrast and peak shift in children. *British Journal of Psychology*, **62**, 367–373.

Nicholson, J. N., and Gray, J. A. (1972). Peak shift, behavioural contrast and stimulus generalization as related to personality and development in children. *British Journal of Psychology*, **63**, 47–62.

Noonan, J. R., and Barry, J. R. (1967a). Differential effects of incentives among the retarded. *Journal of Educational Research*, **61**, 108–111.

Noonan, J. R., and Barry, J. R. (1967b). Performance of retarded children. *Science*, **156**, 171.

Orlando, R. (1961). Component behaviors in free temporal discrimination. *American Journal of Mental Deficiency*, **65**, 615–619.

Orlando, R. (1965a). A discriminated-operant baseline procedure for analysis of stimulus generalization in individuals. *Perceptual and Motor Skills*, **20**, 247–254.

Orlando, R. (1965b). Shaping multiple schedule performances in retardates: establishment of baselines by systematic and special procedures. *Journal of Experimental Child Psychology*, **2**, 135–153.

Orlando, R., and Bijou, S. W. (1960). Single and multiple schedules of reinforcement in developmentally retarded children. *Journal of the Experimental Analysis of Behavior*, **3**, 339–348.

Panyan, M., Boozer, H., and Morris, N. (1970). Feedback to attendants as a reinforcer for applying operant techniques. *Journal of Applied Behavior Analysis*, **3**, 1–4.

Paulson, D. G., Orlando, R., and Schoelkopf, A. M. (1967). *Experimental Analysis and Manipulation of Auditory Generalization in Three Developmental Retardates by Discriminated-operant Procedures*. Institute on Mental Retardation and Intellectual Development, George Peabody College for Teachers, Nashville. Papers and Reports, IV (13).

Peterson, R. F., Merwin, M. R., Moyer, T. J., and Whitehurst, G. J. (1971). Generalized imitation: the effects of experimenter absence, differential reinforcement and stimulus complexity. *Journal of Experimental Child Psychology*, **12**, 114–128.

Peterson, R. F., and Whitehurst, G. J. (1971). A variable influencing the performance of generalized imitative behaviors. *Journal of Applied Behavior Analysis*, **4**, 1–9.

Piaget, J. (1965). *The Child's Conception of Number*, W. W. Norton, New York.

Powers, R. B., Cheyney, C. C., and Agostino, N. R. (1970). Errorless training of a visual discrimination in preschool children. *Psychological Record*, **20**, 45–50.

Prokasy, W. F., and Hall, J. F. (1963). Primary stimulus generalization. *Psychological Review*, **70**, 310–322.

Rainey, J. D. (1965). *Escape, Avoidance and Discriminated Learning in Normal and Mentally Retarded Children Matched for Mental Age*. Doctoral dissertation, Western Reserve University, University Microfilms, No. 60–8024, Ann Arbor, Michigan.

Ray, B. A., and Sidman, M. (1970). Reinforcement schedules and stimulus control. In W. N. Schoenfeld (Ed.), *The Theory of Reinforcement Schedules*, Appleton-Century-Crofts, New York.

Resnick, L. B., Wang, M. C., and Kaplan, J. (1973). Task analysis in curriculum design: a hierarchically sequenced introductory mathematics curriculum. *Journal of Applied Behavior Analysis*, **6**, 679–710.

Rheingold, H. L., Stanley, W. C., and Doyle, G. A. (1964). Visual and auditory reinforcement of a manipulatory response in the young child. *Journal of Experimental Child Psychology*, **1**, 316–326.

Risley, T. R. (1964). Generalization gradients following two-response discrimination training. *Journal of the Experimental Analysis of Behavior*, **7**, 199–204.

Risley, T. R., and Reynolds, N. J. (1970). Emphasis as a prompt for verbal imitation. *Journal of Applied Behavior Analysis*, **3**, 185–190.

Risley, T. R., and Wolf, M. M. (1967). Establishing functional speech in echolalic children. *Behaviour Research and Therapy*, **5**, 73–88.

Robinson, N. M., and Robinson, H. R. (1961). A method for the study of instrumental avoidance conditioning with young children. *Journal of Comparative and Physiological Psychology*, **54**, 20–23.

Sayegh, Y., and Dennis, W. (1965). The effect of supplementary experiences upon the behavioral development of infants in institutions. *Child Development*, **36**, 81–90.

Schroeder, G. L., and Baer, D. M. (1972). Effects of concurrent and serial training on generalized vocal imitation in retarded children. *Developmental Psychology*, **6**, 293–301.

Schroeder, S. (1969a). Effects of cue factors on selective eye movements and choices during

188

successive discrimination. *Perceptual and Motor Skills*, **29**, 991–998.

Schroeder, S. (1969b). Fixation and choice selectivity during discrimination transfer. *Psychonomic Science*, **17**, 324–325.

Schroeder, S. R., and Holland, J. G. (1968a). Operant control of eye movements. *Journal of Applied Behavior Analysis*, **1**, 161–166.

Schroeder, S. R., and Holland, J. G. (1968b). Operant control of eye movements during human vigilance. *Science*, **161**, 292–293.

Schumaker, J. and Sherman, J. A. (1970). Training generative verb usage by imitation and reinforcement procedures. *Journal of Applied Behavior Analysis*, **3**, 273–287.

Sherman, J. A., and Baer, D. M. (1969). Appraisal of operant therapy techniques with children and adults. In C. M. Franks (Ed.), *Behavior Therapy Appraisal and Status*, McGraw-Hill, New York.

Sidman, M., and Stoddard, L. T. (1966). Programming perception and learning for retarded children. In N. R. Ellis (Ed.), *International Review of Research in Mental Retardation*, Vol. 2. Academic Press, New York.

Sidman, M., and Stoddard, L. T. (1967). The effectiveness of fading in programming a simultaneous form discrimination for retarded children. *Journal of the Experimental Analysis of Behavior*, **10**, 3–15.

Simmons, M. W. (1964). Operant discrimination learning in human infants. *Child Development*, **35**, 737–748.

Skinner, B. F. (1938). *The Behavior of Organisms*, Appleton-Century-Crofts, New York.

Skinner, B. F. (1966a). Operant behavior. In W. K. Honig (Ed.), *Operant Behavior: Areas of Research and Application*, Appleton-Century-Crofts, New York.

Skinner, B. F. (1966b). What is the experimental analysis of behavior? *Journal of the Experimental Analysis of Behavior*, **9**, 213–218.

Smeets, P. M., and Striefel, S. (1974). Oddity and match-to-sample tasks as the components of a chained schedule with retarded children. *American Journal of Mental Deficiency*, **78**, 462–470.

Smith, J. (1960). Discrimination learning and stimulus generalization in mental defectives. In D. Zeaman (Ed.), *Learning and Transfer in Mental Defectives*. Progress Report No. 2, NIMH USPHS Research Grant M-1099 to the University of Connecticut.

Spodek, B. (1973). What are the sources of early childhood curriculums? In B. Spodek (Ed.), *Early Childhood Education*, Prentice-Hall, Englewood Cliffs, New Jersey.

Spradlin, J. E., Fixen, D. L., and Girardeau, F. L. (1967). *Stimulus Properties of Reinforcement During Extinction*, Working Paper 158. Parsons Research Center (Kansas).

Spradlin, J. E., Girardeau, F. L., and Corte, E. (1965). Fixed ratio and fixed interval behavior of severely and profoundly retarded subjects. *Journal of Experimental Child Psychology*, **2**, 340–353.

Spradlin, J. E., Girardeau, F. L., and Hom, G. L. (1966). Stimulus properties of reinforcement during extinction of a free operant response. *Journal of Experimental Child Psychology*, **4**, 369–380.

Staats, A. W., Finley, J. R., Minke, K. A., and Wolf, M. M. (1964). Reinforcement variables in the control of unit reading responses. *Journal of the Experimental Analysis of Behavior*, **7**, 139–149.

Staats, A. W., Staats, C. K., Schutz, R. E., and Wolf, M. M. (1962). The conditioning of textual responses using 'extrinsic' reinforcers. *Journal of the Experimental Analysis of Behavior*, **5**, 33–40.

Steinman, W. M. (1970). The social control of generalized imitation. *Journal of Applied Behavior Analysis*, **3**, 159–167.

Stoddard, L. T., and Sidman, M. (1967). The effects of errors on children's performance on a circle–ellipse discrimination. *Journal of the Experimental Analysis of Behavior*, **10**, 261–270.

Sutherland, N. S., and Mackintosh, N. J. (1971). *Mechanisms of Animal Discrimination Learning*, Academic Press, London and New York.

Switalski, R. W., Lyons, J., and Thomas, D. R. (1966). Effects of interdimensional training on stimulus generalization. *Journal of Experimental Psychology*, **72**, 661–666.

Teitelbaum, P. (1966). The use of operant methods in assessment and control of motivational states. In W. K. Honig (Ed.), *Operant Behavior: Areas of Research and Application*, Appleton-Century-Crofts, New York.

Terrace, H. S. (1963a). Discrimination learning with and without 'errors'. *Journal of the Experimental Analysis of Behavior*, **6**, 1–27.

Terrace, H. S. (1963b). Errorless discrimination learning in the pigeon: effects of chlorpromazine and imipramine. *Science*, **140**, 318–319.

Terrace, H. S. (1963c). Errorless transfer of a discrimination across two continua. *Journal of the Experimental Analysis of Behavior*, **6**, 223–232.

Terrace, H. S. (1964). Wavelength generalization after discrimination learning with and without errors. *Science*, **144**, 78–80.

Terrace, H. S. (1966). Stimulus control. In W. K. Honig (Ed.), *Operant Behavior: Areas of Research and Application*, Appleton-Century-Crofts, New York.

Terrace, H. S. (1969). Extinction of a discriminative operant following discrimination learning with and without errors. *Journal of the Experimental Analysis of Behavior*, **12**, 571–582.

Thomas, D. R., and Mitchell, K. (1962). Instructions and stimulus categorizing in a measure of stimulus generalization. *Journal of the Experimental Analysis of Behavior*, **5**, 375–381.

Thompson, T., and Grabowski, J. G. (1972). *Reinforcement Schedules and Multioperant Analysis*, Appleton-Century-Crofts, New York.

Thor, D. H. (1972). Sex differences in extinction of operant responding by educable retarded and non-retarded. *American Journal of Mental Deficiency*, **77**, 100–106.

Touchette, P. E. (1968). The effects of graduated stimulus change on the acquisition of a simple discrimination in severely retarded boys. *Journal of the Experimental Analysis of Behavior*, **11**, 39–48.

Touchette, P. E. (1969). Tilted lines as complex stimuli. *Journal of the Experimental Analysis of Behavior*, **12**, 211–214.

Touchette, P. E. (1971). Transfer of stimulus control: measuring the moment of transfer. *Journal of the Experimental Analysis of Behavior*, **15**, 347–354.

Warren, A. B., and Brown, R. H. (1943). Conditioning operant response phenomena in children. *Journal of General Psychology*, **28**, 181–207.

Watson, L. S. (1973). *Child Behavior Modification: A Manual for Teachers, Nurses and Parents*, Pergamon Press, Oxford.

Weisberg, P. (1969). Operant procedures for the establishment of stimulus control in two-year-old infants. *Journal of Experimental Child Psychology*, **7**, 81–95.

Weisberg, P., and Fink, E. (1966). Fixed ratio and extinction performance of infants in the second year of life. *Journal of the Experimental Analysis of Behavior*, **9**, 105–109.

Wexler, D. B. (1973). Token and taboo: behavior modification, token economies, and the law. *Behaviorism*, **1**, 1–24.

Wheeler, A. J., and Sulzer, B. (1970). Operant training and generalization of a verbal response form in a speech-deficient child. *Journal of Applied Behavior Analysis*, **3**, 139–147.

Whitehurst, G. J. (1972). Production of novel and grammatical utterances by young children. *Journal of Experimental Child Psychology*, **13**, 502–515.

Whitehurst, G. J., and Novak, G. (1973). Modelling, imitation training and the acquisition of sentence phrases. *Journal of Experimental Child Psychology*, **16**, 332–345.

Woods, P. A. (1974). Schedule effects in the operant behavior of ESN(S) children. *Bulletin of the British Psychological Society*, **27**, No. 95, 188.

Zigler, E. (1969). Developmental versus difference theories of mental retardation and the problem of motivation. *American Journal of Mental Deficiency*, **73**, 536–556.

SECTION III

Social Psychology and the Psychology of Decision-making

7

OBSERVATIONAL LEARNING AND THERAPEUTIC MODELLING

S. J. Rachman

INTRODUCTION

Although the subjects of observational learning, imitation and modelling are of widespread psychological significance, the present analysis deals mainly with the therapeutic implications of these three related phenomena. So far, most progress has been made in applying the concepts and methods of observational learning and modelling to problems of fear-reduction, or, to put it another way, the acquisition and/or facilitation of fearless behaviour. We do, however, have good reason to anticipate progress in the application of these ideas to other therapeutic problems.

This chapter begins with a brief history of the subject and an attempt to clarify some problems of definition. The most influential and ambitious modern theory, proposed by Bandura, is described and evaluated. The research on therapeutic modelling is analysed and then related to other therapeutic methods. Finally, the prospects are adumbrated.

Any therapeutic method which is said to produce results superior to desensitization merits close inspection. The first comparative experiment to give rise to such a claim was reported by Bandura, Blanchard and Ritter (1969), who found that the technique of live modelling followed by participation produced a significantly larger reduction of fear than did systematic desensitization. The outcome of this important study on snake-phobic volunteer subjects was noteworthy for the striking magnitude of the change obtained with modelling plus participation; in 92 per cent. of subjects, the snake phobia was virtually eliminated. Although the modelling procedure has now been joined by other competitors (most recently, by the flooding method which has also been claimed to be potentially more powerful than desensitization—e.g. Marks, 1972), it is one of the most interesting alternatives because of its wide implications and long pedigree. In addition to the potential therapeutic value of modelling, the underlying process of observational learning is important in theorizing about the aetiology and course of certain types of behavioural abnormality. For example, it has been found necessary to revise and extend the traumatic theory of phobias in order to encompass findings on observational learning (Rachman, 1968, 1974). As a consequence, the theory was elaborated in a way that enables it to accommodate some awkward findings, such as the occurrence of fears in people who have no recollection of any direct contact with the feared object. In the light of the findings on observational learning, it now seems likely that many of these fears were acquired by vicarious experience. The research on observational learning also goes part of the way to explaining the unduly common fears, such as snake phobia, and the equally interesting fact that there are some objects which seemingly never become items of fear-provoking quality (e.g. lambs). The possible role of observational learning in the prevention of behavioural abnormalities, while recognized, has not yet been the subject of intensive study. Nevertheless, there are some fairly obvious applications which might already be signposted. It might, for example, prove to be useful for promoting satisfactory social behaviour, preparing children for their first attendance at school (e.g. films of the school and school activities, the attachment of each new child to an experienced and confident attender), and so on.

The study of observational learning, more especially imitation, has a long history. In their classic work, published thirty years ago, Miller and Dollard (1941) summarized and discussed over a dozen distinct theories of imitation, but with the exception of their own work none of the contributions are directly relevant to the present topic. There are, however, two interesting precedents worth mentioning. Nearly fifty years ago the prescient Mary Cover Jones (1924) described the results of a series of attempts to eliminate circumscribed fears of children. She obtained 'unqualified success with only two (p. 390)' out of the seven methods used. 'Direct conditioning' (a forerunner of Wolpe's concept of reciprocal inhibition therapy) was successfully used in the famous case of Peter and the rabbit. The other beneficial method was 'social imitation (in which) we allowed the subject to share, under controlled conditions, the social activity of a group of children especially chosen with a view to prestige effect (p. 390)'. She also reported that under certain conditions fears were socially *transmitted* rather than eliminated—socially-induced fear 'is perhaps the most common source of maladjustive fear trends'. Another pioneering effort was the work of Jersild and Holmes (1935), who conducted a good deal of research on children's fears and other difficulties. As part of their research programme, they interviewed the parents of forty-seven children, aged 1 to 7 years, about the methods which they used for dealing with their children's fears. 'The most effective techniques in overcoming fear are those that help the child to become more competent and skilful and that encourage him to undertake active dealings with the thing he fears (p. 102)'. The least effective methods included attempts to ignore the fear, coercion, retreat, etc. It was felt that demonstrations of fearlessness were of some small value, but the addition of verbal expressions of reassurance made little impact. In general, their conclusion was that both for the prevention and treatment of children's fears, the best way of proceeding is to find methods of bringing the child into 'direct, active contact with or participation in the situation he fears (p. 88)'. These quotations show that two of the currently most promising procedures for overcoming fears, modelling and participation, had early supporters. As is often the case, however, the full significance of findings of this type was not appreciated until other advances had been made. Recognition of the importance of observational learning and its revival and development during the past decade must be attributed in great measure to the work of Bandura.

Miller and Dollard (1941) made it clear that we can learn a variety of things by imitation—new skills, information, fears or their reduction. Their explanation of this type of learning was based on a reinforcement theory of the Hullian type. They proposed that the four fundamental factors, which at that time were felt to be involved in all forms of learning, were equally applicable to imitation learning. It was argued that the relevant drive impels responses which are themselves shaped by cues; responses which are followed by drive reduction are strengthened. They drew attention to the advantages of imitation: it enables one to learn in large units of behaviour and, by precluding the need for laborious trial-and-error learning, it becomes possible to acquire new behaviour rapidly and economically. On the basis of a number of simple and satisfying experiments, Miller and Dollard drew a number of generalizations about imitation learning, and some of the more important ones will be noted. They concluded that one more readily imitates a prestigious model, that we generalize between models, that imitation learning is assisted by verbalizing responses and that directing the subject's attention to the vital cues is a help. Failures to imitate occur if any of the major conditions are not met, i.e. if rewards are not provided or if low status models are used, etc.

Although many of their findings and ideas find a ready echo in modern work, the contribution of Miller and Dollard is limited by their understandable adherence to the influential learning theory of the time. Moreover, as Bandura (1969) has pointed out, the value of the experiments is circumscribed because they dealt primarily with what he calls 'place learning'. The subjects learnt *where* to respond, but little or no new behaviour was developed. He strengthens this criticism by pointing out, quite correctly, that the same results could have been obtained by direct instruction.

DISTINCTIONS

Turning to Bandura's own work, he shows little interest in distinguishing between the various terms used in discussions of observational learning, other than to subsume imitation and observational learning under the concept of modelling (Bandura, 1971a, p. 5). Is there, in fact, anything to be gained by distinguishing between the numerous terms? It would seem to be worth attempting because one can find examples of what appear to be observational learning that are not imitative and yet other examples of modelling which do not involve observation or, indeed, examples of observational learning which involve no modelling.

To take a few examples, observational learning can result in clear and significant changes in which the observer's behaviour does not move in the same direction as that which he has seen, and may even move in an opposite direction. That is, observational learning can result in counterimitative behaviour. Observers who watch a model transgressing some convention may subsequently demonstrate behaviour which is quite the reverse of that they have observed—particularly if the model's transgression is seen to be followed by punishment. This same illustration serves as an example of the divergence between observational learning and modelling. Although the observer's behaviour will alter after seeing the consequences for the actor, the restraints or inhibitions that the observer subsequently displays are not approximations of the actor's behaviour. As to the difference between imitation and modelling, one can imitate the swaying of a willow tree or the sighing of the wind, but in neither instance is one modelling. While there is no absolute reason for doing so, it seems to be useful to restrict that term to approximations of human behaviour.

Before providing further illustrations of the distinctions between observational learning, imitation and modelling, it is necessary to attempt a definition of each. Observational learning is taken to mean a change in behaviour which is acquired as a result of observing the behaviour of another person(s)—it is by definition, then, a social phenomenon. Imitation is taken to mean a change in behaviour acquired as a result of observing the behaviour of a person or an animal or of an inanimate occurrence (e.g. a sound); imitative behaviour is marked by its similarity to the observed event or experience and is often a deliberate attempt to approximate to that event or experience. Modelling is taken to mean social imitation—i.e. it is a subclass of both imitation and of observational learning, but not synonymous with either.

The potential advantage of these proposed definitions is that they mark out the similarities and then provide distinctions between the three related phenomena in a manner that specifies observable and manipulable conditions. If, as seems likely, the three phenomena exhibit corresponding similarities and differences in their growth, maintenance and elimination, then the definitions are worth retaining. However, a failure to find any differences of importance will of course ensure their demise.

Before moving on to consider some of the issues raised by research on these topics, some definitional problems need to be anticipated. In the case of observational learning, for example, whether defined broadly or as in this analysis, narrowly, there is no simple test to apply in deciding whether observational learning is the correct term to use. If the subject's behaviour alters appropriately after he has observed a videotape of an actor or model, does this qualify as an instance of observational learning? In some of the important studies on aggression in children reported by Bandura and Walters (1963), the observational learning experience was in fact presented on videotape. After observing a model behave aggressively, the subjects were seen to display similar behaviour. There will be little hesitation about accepting this as an example of observational learning. However, if the observational learning experience consisted of merely an audiotape recording, would one agree quite so readily? And if the audio recording is acceptable, then we are left little reason for rejecting an audiotape in which the model's behaviour is described by a third party. In other words, we can anticipate that in extreme cases there will be some difficulty in agreeing on the range of the term observing. There are other semantic problems which will arise, but one hopes that they will not be too troublesome or discouraging (e.g. how do we define whether in marginal cases the observer's behaviour is moving in a similar direction to that of the model?)

FUNCTIONS

Bandura argues that modelling serves three important psychological functions: models transmit new patterns of behaviour, inhibit or disinhibit unnecessary responses, and facilitate the expression of already established responses. One of the distinctive features of his view is that Bandura has moved away from the reinforcement theory of observational learning on the grounds that new responses can be acquired in 'no-trials' and, second, new behaviour can develop in the absence of reinforcement and can be extinguished without negative reinforcement. He also draws attention to the frequently observed delay in the overt expression of newly acquired observational responses. He conceives of the role of reinforcement as being secondary and applicable to the *expression* of a learned response (i.e. in performance). The acquisition of new behaviour does not require the operation of reinforcers.

Bandura argues that there are four subprocesses involved in observational learning. The first is attentional, meaning the need to register the new learning by attending. Second, one needs to retain the new learning and here he posits two main forms of retention, imaginal and verbal, the latter bring the more durable. The third subprocess involves motoric reproduction, which refers to the necessity for practice, particularly when complex motor behaviour is being acquired. Fourth, as noted above, reinforcement ensures the translation of the observed learning into overt performance.

Although the general schema and some of the constituent parts proposed by Bandura are open to critical examination (see below), for the moment, the emphasis will be on the clinical applications of the theory and research. It should be noted in passing, however, that his use of attentional factors can be questioned on the grounds that a great deal of apparently unwitting learning occurs by observation. In addition, his explanation of the retention phase of observational learning is in the early stages of development and has only begun to come to grips with some of the intricate and difficult problems involved in analyses of, for example, verbal coding (e.g. Bandura and Jeffery, 1973; Bandura, Jeffery and Bachicha, 1974).

MODELLING TREATMENT

Before turning to an examination of the empirical evidence relating to therapeutic modelling, it may be of some interest to provide a description of what appears to be 'the full package' as proposed by Bandura in various of his writings. This compendium is based on several sources, but may be incomplete. He recommends clear pre-therapy instructions, perhaps supplemented by relaxation training; repeated modelling experiences; multiple models; a progressive increase in the difficulty of the modelled approaches; the use of models who resemble the observers; and that the model should describe his progress. In relation to the use of supplementary *participant* modelling he recommends repeated practice; the provision of guidance during practice; gradual increases in exposure time; encouragement during practice; graduation of practice exercises; provision of feedback during practice; provision of favourable conditions for practice; and attenuation of fear stimuli in the early stages. By way of a general recommendation, he urges that attempts be made to arrange for the regular reinforcement of newly acquired behaviour in order to ensure that it endures. Lastly, he recommends that the reinforcement and control of the new behaviour be placed on a self-regulating system as early as possible.

Therapeutic modelling is being adopted fairly widely. In view of the fact that it will be some time before we have detailed empirical answers to questions of the relative contribution made by each of the factors mentioned above (and others which may yet emerge), an account follows of the evidence available at present. Needless to say, this account will need to be modified as additional research is completed.

The bulk of the research has followed the style of analogue experiments developed for the investigation of systematic desensitization (Lang and Lazovik, 1963; Rachman, 1967). In the main, this involves the selection of non-psychiatric volunteer subjects who have a demonstrable but circumscribed fear of at least moderate intensity. In most cases, the final selection of subjects is made on the basis of their performance in behavioural avoidance tests. The selected subjects are divided into experimental and control groups in the customary manner. The effects of the therapeutic modelling procedure, or its variants, are then assessed by the outcome of the behavioural avoidance tests. The *behavioural* consequences of the modelling procedure feature in all but five of the experiments reported so far; moreover, this criterion is frequently supplemented by psychiatric or other assessments. As a minimum aim, all of the experiments on phobic subjects attempt to demonstrate the fear-reducing properties of modelling. Two other broad aims can also be ascertained—a search for the effective variables in the treatment 'package' and some attempts to determine the relative contributions of what are assumed to be the main elements in the treatment procedure.

Table 7.1 sets out the main features of the research findings. The 'norm' used for purposes of tabular presentation is the symbolic form of modelling (i.e. where the observer observes a real or recorded version of the model performing in the fearful situation, but does not come into live contact with the situation or therapist). In studies of fear reduction, there is only one (relatively minor) exception (the third experiment of Spiegler and coworkers, 1969) to the finding that modelling is superior to no-treatment types of control procedure. In the exception, only a very small modelling effect was obtained and, because of the pure relaxation effect, symbolic modelling was found to be inferior to the relaxation control. It is difficult to place too much reliance on this finding because, like the two other preliminary studies contained in the Spiegler report, it indicates that they were able only to produce a small therapeutic modelling effect. It seems quite probable that the main reason for the relative ineffectiveness of the modelling procedure in these three connected studies is that the experimenters used only a brief amount of modelling (a 14 minute film, with and without narrative). Another disappointing result was reported by Ritter (1969) in the second of her studies. Although she was able to demonstrate substantial therapeutic effects from modelling supplemented by subsequent participation in the real situation, the symbolic modelling procedure yielded an unusually poor outcome with the five acrophobic subjects. In this experiment, too, the duration of symbolic modelling was comparatively brief—barely 35 minutes in duration. Moreover, this study was unfortunately plagued by problems of baseline comparability. Lastly, O'Sullivan, Gilner and Krinski (1973) confirmed the therapeutic modelling effect for male but not for female subjects. With these exceptions, the substantial evidence on the effects of therapeutic modelling is encouraging in a high degree; we appear to have a mighty strong fact.

Before drawing attention to some of the limitations of this research on fear-reduction, it might be helpful to attempt a summary of the main conclusions one can draw from the data. In most circumstances, symbolic modelling produces some reduction of fear. This fear-reduction is lasting. It also generalizes to similar situations and stimuli. Supplementing the symbolic modelling by participant modelling increases the extent of fear reduction substantially. These statements can be accepted with a reasonable amount of confidence. My clinical experiences, supported by the general thrust of the research findings obtained so far, lead me to lay special emphasis on the therapeutic powers of *participant* modelling.

There are also some conclusions which, while quite reasonable, will require additional support before they are acceptable at a high level of certainty. Therapeutic modelling can be conducted successfully as a group treatment. The provision of verbalized guidance and/or reinforcement during modelling is facilitative. Models who are observed to overcome their own fear and acquire mastery in the situation are more effective in producing reductions of fear in the observer.

Next we turn to some summary statements which must be regarded as tentative, but are nevertheless likely to be borne out by future research. The therapeutic modelling effect is facilitated by a combination of audio and visual presentations and by repeated practice, by prolonged exposure times (both

TABLE 7.1 Experiments on therapeutic modelling

Authors	Date	Aims	Subjects	Comparisons with symbolic modelling (MDL)	No-treatment control
Bandura, Grusec and Menlove	1967	Effects of live progressive MDL (8 × 10 min sessions)	4 × 12 nursery children; one-third dog-phobic	Neutral versus positive context	Two groups
Geer and Turtletaub	1967	Effects of fearless and fearful models	3 × 20 students; half snake-phobic	Fearless versus fearful subjects and models	Yes
Bandura and Menlove	1968	Value of multiple models	3 × 16 dog-phobic 3–5 year-olds	Single versus multiple models	Yes
Hill, Liebert and Mott	1968	Effects of brief audiofilm MDL	2 × 9 dog-phobic Ss.	—	Yes
Ritter	1968	Effects of MDL and participant MDL in groups	3 × 15 snake-phobic children	Two group sessions of 35 min live modelling versus two of live + participation	Yes
Bandura, Blanchard and Ritter	1969	Effects of MDL on phobias	4 × 12 snake-phobic adults	Versus desensitization versus participant MDL	Yes
Mann and Rosenthal	1969	Effects of vicarious desensitization	5 × 10 school children and 21 controls	1. Desensitization (group/individual) 2. Group versus individual vicarious desensitization	Yes
O'Connor	1969	Reduction of social withdrawal	6 + 7 isolated nursery children	—	Yes

Outcome measures	Modelling (MDL) versus control	Modelling (MDL) versus comparisons	Conclusions	Problems
Behaviour tests	Superior to both types of control	Positive context adds nothing	MDL produces generalized, lasting increases in approach (MDL 67% completed terminal versus 33% controls)	Only 1/3 Ss were phobic
Behaviour tests	Evidence of superior fear reduction	Fearful model does not increase fear of observers	Exposure to fearless model reduces fear	Durability?
Behaviour tests	Both types superior to control but not on terminal tests until Follow-up	Multiple superior to single	Multiple MDL superior	Models of differing ages; multiple fear stimuli. Follow-up changes. MDL wholly successful with only 40% Ss
Behaviour tests	MDL superior 8/9 did terminal test (versus 3/9)	—	Brief symbolic MDL reduces fear	Short account
Behaviour tests	Both forms of MDL superior	Participant superior (80% versus 53% achieved terminal test)	Participant group MDL powerful method	
Behaviour test, attitudes, fear survey and fear estimates	Superior on all measures	Participant best, desensitization = MDL on behaviour test but not attitudes	Improvements were lasting and generalized; relaxation not facilitative	MDL wholly successful with 40% Ss
Test-anxiety scale	Superior to no-treatment	All methods equally effective	Individual/group vicarious, desensitization effective	More outcome measures?
Behaviour frequencies in class	23 min sound film of multiple models superior	Immediate effects show significant effects of MDL	Multiple MDL + narration produced immediate improvement in social behaviour	No satisfactory measures of durability

TABLE 7.1 (*Contd.*)

Authors	Date	Aims	Subjects	Comparisons with symbolic modelling (MDL)	No-treatment control
Rimm and Mahoney	1969	Effects of brief part-icipant MDL	2 × 6 snake-phobic students	—	Yes
Ritter	1969	Contributions of participant and therapist contact	3 × 5 acro-phobics	Versus participant MDL versus parti-cipant MDL + thera-pist contact	No
Spiegler and coworkers (Expt. I)	1969	Effects of visual/audi-tory parts of MDL film	4 × 5 snake-phobic students	14 min film versus film + narrative versus narrative only	Yes
(Expt. II)		Replication of main effect of Expt. I	2 × 5 snake-phobic students	Film + narrative sole method	Yes
(Expt. III)		Value of add-ing relaxation	21 snake-phobic adults	Versus relaxation only versus relaxation + MDL	No
Blanchard	1970	Contributions of information and of participation	4 × 12 snake-phobic adults	Versus participant MDL versus MDL + information	Yes
Rimm and Medeiros	1970	Effects of relaxation on participant MDL	4 × 10 snake-phobic students	Versus relaxation + participant MDL versus relaxa-tion alone	Yes
Friedman	1971	MDL and role-playing students	6 × 17 unassertive students	Live MDL + role-playing	Yes

Outcome measures	Modelling (MDL) versus control	Modelling (MDL) versus comparisons	Conclusions	Problems
Behaviour test and fear esti- mates	Superior on both measures	—	Improvements large and generalized after single session + relaxation.	
Behaviour tests	—	Both com- parisons superior to MDL	35 min of MDL produced unusually poor outcome	Too brief? Baseline problems
Behaviour tests	Only film + narrative was superior, including 1 month follow-up	—	Visual/auditory components are necessary	Brevity of treatment; small effect?
Behaviour tests	MDL superior, but no follow-up	—	Film modelling + narrative reduces fear	Brevity of treatment; no follow-up; small effect?
Behaviour tests	—	MDL + relaxation best; relaxation only superior to film + narrative	Relaxation facilitates MDL effects	Unaccounted for relaxation effect; small MDL effect
Behaviour tests, fear survey, atti- tude and fear estimates	Superior on all measures	Participant best, then MDL	Improvements were mainly due to MDL factor; infor- mation not facilitative	
Behaviour test and fear esti- mates	Superior on both measures	Relaxation + participant MDL = participant MDL and both superior to relaxation alone	Large general- ized effects, but relaxation non-facilitative	
Self, behaviour test	Superior	MDL + role superior to MDL or role alone	MDL boosted by role- playing	Brief; in complete; follow-up measures?

TABLE 7.1 (*Contd.*)

Authors	Date	Aims	Subjects	Comparisons with symbolic modelling (MDL)	No-treatment control
McFall and Lillesand	1971	Coaching + MDL versus rehearsal	3 × 11 unassertive students	Covert versus overt rehearsal in MDL to audiotapes	Attention
Meichenbaum	1971	Effects of coping, verbal MDL	4 × 8 snake-phobic students	Coping model versus mastery model; verbal versus non-verbal model	No
Rachman, Hodgson and Marks	1971	Treatment of chronic obsessional neuroses	2 × 5 obsess-ional inpatients	*In vivo* MDL versus flooding	Own control, relaxtion treatment
Hall and Hinkle	1972	Symbolic effect	4 × 13 test anxious students	Group desens-itization	Yes
Mann	1972	Symbolic MDL effect; relaxation?	4 × 20 test anxious students	No relaxation, desensitization, MDL	Yes
O'Connor	1972	Film MDL versus shaping	33 withdrawn young children	Combined MDL + shaping	Yes
Bandura and Barab	1973	Model similarity, child versus adult	3 × 22 snake-phobics	Irrelevant MDL control	None
Eisler, Hersen and Miller	1973	MDL versus practice	3 × 10 unasser-tive psychiatric patients	Versus practice only	Yes
Goldstein (Expt. I)	1973	MDL independent behaviour	3 × 30 depen-dent psychiatric patients	One session tapes, dependent/ independent control MDL	Yes
(Expt. II)		Ditto for warm/cold therapist	3 × 20 depen-dent psychiatric patients	As above, with warm/ cold therapist	Yes

Outcome measures	Modelling (MDL) versus control	Modelling (MDL) versus comparisons	Conclusions	Problems
Self, behaviour test	Superior	MDL superior on behaviour test, all equal on self	MDL + rehearsal + coaching effective	One week follow-up; brief, confounds pre-test differences; measures?
Behaviour test and fear estimates	—	Coping > superior to mastery; verbal > non-verbal	Coping models and verbali-zations facilitate fear-reduction	
Self and independent ratings, behaviour tests, attitudes	MDL superior on all measures	MDL and flooding equally effective	Substantial and lasting im-provements with some failures	Small sample size
Psychometric	Superior	MDL = desens-sitization	MDL equals desensitization; confirms Mann and Rosenthal	One outcome test; durability?
Self, reading test	Superior	All equally effective	Desensitization main effect	
Behaviour test	Superior	MDL = shaping	MDL effective, more durable	Three week follow-up; brief shaping; one test
Behaviour test, attitudes, GSR, self report	Superior	Not applicable	Models different but equal	Brief; mainly correlational; needs replication
Behaviour test	Superior 5/8 indices	MDL + practice superior to practice	MDL main contribution	Acute study; durability? extent?
Self report type	Superior	Not applicable	MDL effective	Confound instruc-tion and reinforce-ment; measures? brief; acute experi-ment
As above	Superior	Warm superior	Therapist effect	As above

TABLE 7.1 (*Contd.*)

Authors	Date	Aims	Subjects	Comparisons with symbolic modelling (MDL)	No-treatment control
Goldstein Expt. I Expt. III)	1973	MDL + instruction	4 × 14 dependent psychiatric patients	One session tapes, dependent/ independent control MDL, with and without instruction	Yes
Hersen, Eisler and Miller	1973	MDL versus practice versus instruction	5 × 10 unassertive psychiatric patients	Versus instructions versus practice	Yes
Kazdin	1973	Covert MDL effect	4 × 16 snake-phobics	Coping versus mastery versus no model	Yes
McFall and Twentyman (Expt. I)	1973	Coaching versus MDL versus rehearsal	6 × 12 unassertive students	MDL ± coaching ± rehearsal	Yes
(Expt. II)		Rehearsal ± MDL ± coaching	3 × 30 unassertive students	Rehearsal ± MDL	Yes
(Expt. III)		Role of specific audio model	8 × 60 unassertive students	New model versus old	Yes
(Expt. IV)		Audio versus audiovisual model	3 × 18 unassertive students	Audiovisual versus audio	Yes
Murphy and Bootzin	1973	Passive versus active	67 snake-fearful children	Participant MDL only	Yes
O'Sullivan, Gilner and Krinksi	1973	Sex differences	8 × 10 snake-phobics	Male versus female models, Ss, assessors	Attention control
Rachman, Hodgson and Marks	1973	Combined MDL + flooding effects	10 obsessional patients	None	Own relaxation control
Rathus	1973	MDL versus practice	78 unassertive students (coeds.)	MDL versus practice	Yes

Outcome measures	Modelling (MDL) versus control	Modelling (MDL) versus comparisons	Conclusions	Problems
Self report type	Superior	MDL, instruction and MDL + instruct : equally effective	Instruction effective; no distinctive MDL advantage	Confound instruction and reinforcement; measures' brief; acute experiment
Behaviour test, self report	MDL superior	Instruction ± MDL superior	Value of instructions	Acute experiment no follow-up
Self, behaviour test, attitude test	MDL superior except on attitude test	MDL superior no model	Covert MDL effective	Brief; durability? mild fears
Self, behaviour test	Superior	Rehearsal + coaching effective	MDL adds nil	Lowered selection criteria; brief $(2 \times 20$ min); measures? follow-up?
Self, behaviour test, plus	Not applicable	Rehearsal − MDL = rehearsal + MDL	MDL adds nil	As above
Self, behaviour test, plus	Superior	New—old audio model	Confirms Expts. I and II	As above + outcome problems
Self, behaviour test, plus	Superior	Audio − audiovisual	Confirms Expts. I–III	As above
Behaviour test	MDL superior	Passive = active	Passive participant MDL effective	Mildly fearful Ss; only one test
Behaviour test	Only for males	Male factor superior	Sex difference	
Ratings, behaviour test, attitudes	Superior	None	Combined treatment effective	Some failures
Self, psychometric	Superior on self	MDL = practice alone	Practice ± MDL effective	No follow-up; MDL confounded

TABLE 7.1 (*Contd.*)

Authors	Date	Aims	Subjects	Comparisons with symbolic modelling (MDL)	No-treatment control
Young, Rimm and Kennedy	1973	MDL versus reinforcement	4 × 10 unassertive students	MDL versus MDL + reinforcement	Yes
Bandura, Jeffery and Wright	1974	Value of support aids— participation MDL	3 × 12 snake-phobics	High, moderate, low support	None
Kazdin	1974a	Multiple covert models and stimuli	4 × 13 snake-phobics, 16 snake-phobic controls	Multiple models versus single versus multiple snakes	Attention
Kazdin	1974b	Covert coping/ mastery; covert self/other	84 snake-phobics, 5 groups	Coping versus mastery/self versus other	Yes
Roper, Rachman and Marks	1975	Effects of symbolic MDL	10 obsessional patients	Relaxation + MDL	Own control

within a session and overall), by the use of multiple models and multiple fear situations or stimuli. The supplementary use of participant modelling facilitates the generalization of improvements and the transfer from 'internal' learning to manifest behaviour change. The use of relaxation training prior to or during the modelling sessions facilitates therapeutic change. Covert modelling can be effective. In sum, modelling treatment (particularly of the participant type) is capable of producing significant, generalized and lasting therapeutic improvements in psychiatric patients. Other things being equal, participant modelling appears to be significantly more effective than vicarious modelling. At this stage, two of the main determinants of the therapeutic modelling effect appear to be (a) the number of successful exposures to the model(s) and (b) the total time of successful exposures to the model(s).

It may be thought a little puzzling that some of the findings are regarded in the present account as tentative. For example, it can be argued that multiple modelling is more effective than single modelling. Nevertheless, it is included in the tentative list because the research on the use of multiple models has so far not succeeded in separating out the effect of numerous models from the separate and perhaps more important effects of exposing the observers to a wider range of fear stimuli (e.g. the experiments on dog-phobic nursery children reported by Bandura and Menlove, 1968). My reservation about the possible facilitative value of relaxation training arises from the fact that there have been two published failures to demonstrate such an effect (Bandura, Blanchard

Outcome measures	Modelling (MDL) versus control	Modelling (MDL) versus comparisons	Conclusions	Problems
Self, behaviour test	Superior	MDL groups equal	Reinforcement adds nil	Brief; no follow-up; no generalization
Behaviour test, attitudes, self report	Not applicable	High and moderate aids equally superior	Supportive aids facilitation of treatment	Durability?
Self, behaviour test, attitudes	MDL superior	Multiple superior on some measures	Multiple MDL small advantage	Brief; mild fears; scanty generalization
Self, behaviour test, attitudes	MDL superior	Self-mastery weakest	Coping/other MDL advantage	Brief; mild fears; scanty generalization
Ratings, behaviour test, attitudes	Slightly superior	Weaker than participant MDL	Participant MDL most powerful	Sample size small

and Ritter, 1969; Rimm and Medeiros, 1970) and only one finding in support of the idea (Spiegler and coworkers, 1969, second experiment). The unexpected and unexplained effects of relaxation in the Spiegler study, coupled with the fact that the reductions in fear were of a small magnitude, recommend a cautious attitude towards the potential value of relaxation training.

The intrinsic interest of the subject will, of course, ensure that research into the statements listed here, and a wide variety of others, will be carried out in the coming years. It may be of some interest to bear in mind the following suggestions which arise out of the available evidence and from shortcomings in the research already completed. It seems advisable in this type of research to carry out and report on the effects of therapeutic modelling in terms of the subjects' success with a terminal test of some kind, e.g. ability to handle the snake. Closely allied to this recommendation is the one that arises from experience with analogue research on desensitization. Interpretation of some of the findings is bedevilled by the fact that there is no standard measure of therapeutic outcome. Because of this deficiency, unfortunate misunderstandings arose when some writers failed to make allowances for experimental findings based on a weak test of outcome.

For the most part, the research dealt with in this chapter has reported the outcome of modelling in terms of behaviour avoidance tests or, more precisely, increases in approach behaviour. The desirability of this type of measure is obvious, but it would be helpful if in future a wider range of outcome measures was added to the behavioural tests. As there are indications in the early findings that modelling treatments which are too brief fail to produce any significant effect, every attempt should be made to provide a reasonable amount of treatment over more than a single session. Where a strong effect is required, participant modelling is to be preferred. The use of mildly phobic subjects, or, to put it bluntly, subjects who are not phobic at all but simply fall short of the final step in an approach test, should be avoided. Lastly, the *clinical* value of therapeutic modelling should be investigated more widely.

MODELLING OF ASSERTIVE, INDEPENDENT BEHAVIOUR

Although the reduction of fear still attracts a great deal of scientific attention, no less than eight reports on the value of modelling assertive behaviour have appeared within the past two years. With the major exception of the work of McFall and Twentyman (1973) and the partial exception of Goldstein's (1973) studies, the available evidence shows that modelling is capable of promoting assertive (or independent) behaviour in subjects who are socially overinhibited (see Table 7.1: e.g. Eisler, Hersen and Miller, 1973; Hersen, Eisler and Miller, 1973; Rathus, 1973; etc.). Progress has also been made in the determination of methods which can boost this modelling effect—e.g. practice (Eisler, Hersen and Miller, 1973; Rathus, 1973), rehearsal (Young, Rimm and Kennedy, 1973; McFall and Lillesand, 1971; McFall and Twentyman, 1973), instructions (Goldstein, 1973; Hersen, Eisler and Miller, 1973) and role-playing (Friedman, 1971). Obviously, there is some overlap between 'practice', 'rehearsal' and 'role-playing', but the general message is clear—and also consistent with my earlier emphasis on the value of *participation* in the therapeutic modelling of fear-reduction.

The quality of the evidence appears to be sound as far as it goes, but there is a strong tendency for research workers to rely entirely on demonstrations of an acute (short-term) effect. The longer-term value of modelling has rarely been studied, but surely needs to be examined. Another weakness of the overall research is the brevity of the treatment or modification exposure provided— rarely more than an hour. Then, too, some experiments have confounded treatment interventions. Others have used weak selection criteria when choosing their subjects. Lastly, the problem of poor generalization from the experimental situation to the natural environment must be overcome; particular attention must be paid to the extent and duration of transfer effects.

Although therapeutic modelling is capable of promoting assertive behaviour, it may not be the most efficacious method. The recent report by McFall and Twentyman (1973) of four experiments on unassertive students sounded a mild caution and was supported to some extent by Goldstein's (1973) third experiment. In these instances, modelling added nothing distinctive; indeed, rehearsal, coaching and instruction carried almost all of the weight. These mildly disappointing results were, however, obtained in acute studies, on subjects not entirely suitable and after only a brief amount of modelling.

Nevertheless, it is as well to keep their reports in mind if for no other reason than to temper any inclinations to exaggerate the value of therapeutic modelling.

FEAR-REDUCTION PROCESSES

The overriding theoretical questions concern the nature and determinants of therapeutic modelling. A related question is whether or not modelling can achieve more than other therapeutic procedures. Or, can modelling achieve improvements in conditions which are resistant to other therapeutic techniques?

In considering the relation between behavioural methods, it is tempting to assume that there may be an underlying process which is common to many or all of the fear-reduction techniques (Rachman, 1974). While following this possibility, it is as well to remember the confounding implicit in many comparisons between techniques. For example, in virtually all *in vivo* forms of treatment, modelling will play a part if only because of the therapeutic presence of the psychologist acting in a calm fashion. Modelling appears to play a major part in much of the operant training of children where the importance of imitation is so often emphasized (e.g. Lovaas and coworkers, 1967). In addition, modelling is likely to play a considerable part both in flooding treatment which is best administered *in vivo* and also in desensitization treatment when it is carried out *in vivo*.

Modelling also appears to play a part, if only a minor one, in some of the operant reinforcement schemes such as token economy systems and classroom modification procedures. It is also likely that a measure of vicarious modelling occurs as part of imaginal desensitization treatment. In one sense, the therapist is encouraging imaginal modelling by the patient of himself. Similarly, a small amount of therapeutic modelling may be implicit in imaginal flooding treatment.

It cannot be argued that modelling is a *necessary* condition for therapeutic change. It is evident that some methods can produce successful results despite the seeming absence of any modelling experiences. For example, the successful desensitization of snake-phobic subjects by automated desensitization (Lang, Melamed and Hart, 1970) involves only a very small amount of modelling—if any. In other behavioural methods of treatment such as aversion therapy, modelling plays no part in the suppressive stage of the treatment but may in future be used with success in the second stage of restoring (or developing) satisfactory alternative behaviour, e.g. new sexual habits and performances. Of course, it could be argued by the more enthusiastic proponents of therapeutic modelling that those behavioural techniques which make little use of this method might well be augmented by the deliberate introduction of modelling.

This brief listing of the contribution of modelling to various behavioural techniques serves to indicate its wide and pervasive role. The question of greater theoretical interest, however, remains.

The fact that flooding and modelling methods have proved to be equally successful in the treatment of chronic obsessional patients (Rachman, Hodgson and Marks, 1971) suggests that the possibility of a single underlying process is worth considering. While retaining a cautious view of the conclusions drawn in that study (because of the small sample size), it is nevertheless striking that the methods produced similar results. The possibility of a common underlying process is further supported by the earlier findings of Bandura and Menlove (1968) in which symbolic modelling and symbolic (i.e. imaginal) desensitization were found to be equally effective. Leaving aside the additional contribution made to therapeutic outcome by *in vivo* practice, we are left with the possibility that all three fear-reduction techniques—modelling, desensitization and flooding—are variations on a single theme.

A fairly obvious candidate for consideration in this connection is the phenomenon of extinction. In all three forms of treatment, the patient or subject is repeatedly or enduringly exposed to the fear-provoking stimuli. And in all three types of treatment, attempts are made to prevent the subject from making escape or avoidance responses. It seems reasonable, therefore, to consider the possibility that the three methods are different therapeutic examples of the operation of treatment by extinction and the prevention of escape and avoidance. Another possibility, closely related, is that the underlying processes in all three procedures is one of habituation to sensitized or sensitizing stimulation.

In all three forms of treatment, the subject is exposed to the sensitized stimuli on a number of occasions and/or for prolonged periods. In view of the relative success of applying an habituation model to desensitization therapy (Lader and Mathews, 1968; Lader and Wing, 1966; Rachman, 1974; Watts, 1971), this possibility is worth developing in experimental undertakings.

The possibility that all *three* methods are effective because of the operation of the process of reciprocal inhibition—Wolpe's theory constructed to account for the operation of desensitization treatment—seems unlikely to succeed. While it is not too difficult to conceive of ways in which the presence of the model may act as a powerful counterconditioning agent (and thereby satisfy an important requirement of the reciprocal inhibition model), it is more difficult to encompass the flooding methods within this theory.

One other contender which bears examination is the possibility that all three methods might be accounted for in terms of reinforcement theory. The desensitization treatment works because each successful reduction of fear reported by the patient or subject is rewarded by the therapist; unsuccessful consequences, such as a failure to experience a reduction in fear to an imaginal item, tend to be ignored by the therapist (i.e. he makes no comment, but merely repeats the item). In therapeutic modelling of the participant type, it is also relatively easy to recast the events in terms of powerful social and self-reinforcement. Each successful approach made by the subject is immediately and amply rewarded by the attendant therapist. Moreover, the patient is also receiving immediate feedback of his successful approaches and these, too, might serve to reinforce increasingly courageous behaviour. Symbolic, passive modelling is more difficult to encompass within a reinforcement model because no responses are made during the modelling period and consequently no clear-cut reinforcements can be delivered. It will not escape notice that the main objection to a reinforcement interpretation of symbolic modelling treatment is precisely that which Bandura has used in explaining the inadequacy of a reinforcement theory to account for observational learning in general. Although the speed of its action might be awkward to explain, flooding treatment can be encompassed within reinforcement theory by placing major emphasis on the socially reinforcing value of the therapist's presence, his directional and guiding function, and the promptness of the reinforcements which he delivers. In all, the reinforcement theory has attractive aspects but falls short in some ways, most notably in the case of symbolic modelling. Reinforcement theory also has difficulty in accounting for automated desensitization, one of the procedures in which modelling plays virtually no part. To explain the effects of this form of treatment, it appears to be essential to adopt some form of extinction hypothesis or Wolpe's theory of reciprocal inhibition.

GENESIS OF FEAR

The main clinical significance of modelling is to be found in its therapeutic strength, both for the elimination of fearful and other types of unwanted behaviour and also because of its potential ability to promote adequate behaviour, such as social responding. The aetiological significance of research on observational learning remains to exploited and may prove to be immensely fruitful. It is abundantly clear that just as fearful and fearless behaviour can be socially transmitted so normal and abnormal behaviour can be socially transmitted. The early research of Bandura and Walters (1963) provided numerous examples of the social transmission of aggressive behaviour, for example. However, this discussion is restricted to the relevance of observational learning for a theory of the genesis of phobic disorders. It has been remarked that the conditioning theory of phobias has difficulty in accounting for some of the observations. For example, Rachman (1968, 1974) has argued that the frequency of occurrence of certain kinds of phobic disorders, such as snake phobia, is far greater than one might expect to arise on the basis of traumatic or subtraumatic conditioning experiences. For this and other reasons, it was proposed that the theory be expanded to incorporate the genesis and transmission of phobic disorders by observational learning. If this extension is successful, then it helps to overcome some of the unsatisfactory aspects of conditioning theory. At the same time, it makes more explicable the observation that many patients, and indeed non-patient subjects, report that their phobic disorders had no clearly remembered time of onset. This apparent failure of recall is more easily understood if the fears are predominantly acquired by a slow process, perhaps over many years, of observational learning experience, direct and indirect. It has been remarked by clinicians that certain kinds of fears and phobias appear to be common in certain families. More recently, Bandura and Menlove (1968) described the information they collected during the course of one of their fear-reduction experiments. Their interviews with the parents of dog-phobic

3–5 year-olds showed that they had more dog fears than the parents of non-fearful children from the same group. Similarly, May (1950) reported that there is 'a good deal of correspondence between frequency of fears of children of the same family', with the correlations between fears displayed by siblings ranging from 0.65 to 0.74. Hagman (1932) reported a correlation of 0.67 between the total number of fears exhibited by children and their mothers.

It might be worth pointing out that exposure to fearful models will not necessarily produce fear in the observers (e.g. Geer and Turtletaub, 1967). We do have evidence of a general kind which supports the proposition that negative emotions may be transmitted vicariously (see the discussions by Aronfreed, 1969; Bandura, 1969; Berger, 1962), but there is as yet little experimental evidence which bears on the direct transmission of fear. The growing importance of observational learning in theorizing about abnormal behaviour is certain to ensure a good deal of research activity in the coming years—we may, in fact, see a revival of interest in the topic of experimental neuroses, but this time they will be socially induced rather than traumatically induced. An interesting example of the type of investigation which may prove fruitful is provided by Miller, Murphy and Mirsky (1959). They reported three experiments on rhesus monkeys which showed that fear can be transmitted from a fearful model to an observer monkey. It was also found that fear can be transmitted by pictorial representations of fearful monkeys. In all the experiments, the observers, although calm during the modelling session, had themselves been subjected to the fearful situation at some time in the past. Moreover, the transmission of *fear* was deduced from the occurrence of avoidance behaviour. The authors also noted in passing that their monkeys appeared not to respond fearfully when exposed to fearful models of other species. Further research into the how, when and why of socially transmitted fear (and other types of abnormal behaviour) should prove to be extremely interesting.

BANDURA'S SOCIAL LEARNING THEORY

This is a useful point at which to turn towards theoretical problems. Bandura (1969, 1971a, 1971b) has developed an elaborate theory to account for observational learning and related phenomena. He describes it as a *social* learning theory because of his belief that 'human behavior is transmitted ... largely through exposure to social models (Bandura, 1971b, p. 1)'. He is careful to point out that although a great deal of social learning occurs through direct observation of the behaviour of people, much is also learnt through the direct and indirect observation of symbolic models (including television, pictorial representations, and so on). It is important to bear in mind that modelling is not confined to simple matching behaviour but is capable of promoting skilful performances and complex behaviour. Modelling can be extended to higher-order forms of learning, including the abstraction and formulation of rules for generating behaviour. Particularly clear-cut examples of the modelling of higher-order learning (e.g. grammatical speech, conservation, etc.) are provided in the experiments by Rosenthal and his colleagues (Rosenthal and Carroll, 1972; Rosenthal and Whitebrook, 1970; Rosenthal and Zimmerman, 1972).

It can, of course, be objected that Bandura is begging the question. No one doubts that abstraction and generalization occur and few psychologists will deny that these abilities can be learned. Hence, to add that they can be and, indeed, often are learned by modelling the behaviour of other people does not take us too far forward. The most intriguing questions remain—*how* do people abstract? Although the objection is, I think, a fair one, the fact remains that Bandura has successfully drawn attention to the occurrence of higher-order modelling; formerly, 'imitative' behaviour was regarded as being confined to simple matching behaviour, typically childish and rather *infra dig*.

Just as in the psychology of learning it became necessary to distinguish between *learning* and *performance* (to account for phenomena such as latent learning or extinction, among others), Bandura finds it necessary to distinguish between observational learning and the manifestation of imitative behaviour. 'In evaluating the role of reinforcement in modelling processes, it is essential to distinguish between response acquisition and performance because these events are determined by different variables (Bandura, 1969, p. 128)'. The acquisition of matching behaviour 'results primarily from stimulus contiguity (p. 128)', whereas the performance of the learned response will 'depend to a great extent upon the nature of reinforcing consequences to the model or to the observer (p. 128)'. The contiguity element in the theory has been supported in a series of experiments carried out by Rosenthal (1973), who concluded that 'in short, we have found no improvement in conceptual social learning from various reinforcement manipulations'.

It will be seen from these quotations that although Bandura places a great deal of emphasis on the role of reinforcement in eliciting and maintaining the *performance* of modelled behaviour, he leaves the door open (slightly) to the possibility of other influences. The emphasis on reinforcement is evident in a number of his contributions. For example, 'the learning will rarely be activated into overt performance if negative sanctions or unfavourable incentive conditions obtain. In such circumstances, the introduction of positive incentives promptly translates observational learning into action (Bandura, 1971b, p. 22)'. And again, 'Both operant conditioning and social learning theories assume that performance of acquired matching behavior is strongly controlled by the consequences. But in social learning theory, behavior is regulated by not only directly experienced consequences arising from external sources, but also by vicarious reinforcement and self-reinforcement (Bandura, 1971b, p. 46)'. The place of these various forms of reinforcement in his scheme of things is neatly illustrated in Figure 7.1. It should be mentioned, however, that although the figure clarifies some points, it is open to misinterpretation (see below).

It is, of course, necessary for Bandura's theory, as for those proposed by other theorists, to explain why it is that we do not learn everything we observe—

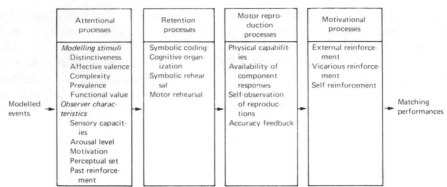

FIGURE 7.1 Bandura's schema of the subprocesses in observational learning. (From Bandura, 1971b.).

i.e. it is incumbent on all theorists to explain the *selectivity* which operates in social and other forms of learning. In common with other theories, social learning theory postulates that people will selectively attend to those modelled events that are perceptually striking or have personal reinforcement value. In Bandura's theory, 'reinforcement variables not only regulate the overt expression of matching behavior, but they can also affect observational learning by exerting selective control over the types of modelled events to which people are most likely to attend (Bandura, 1971b, p. 23)'. He goes further to say that reinforcement variables also 'facilitate selective retention by activating deliberate coding and rehearsal of modelled behaviors that have functional value (p. 23)'.

Referring back to Figure 7.1, the reinforcement variables should be shown to operate at each of the four stages—attention, retention, reproduction, motivation—and not merely at the last stage. The figure is misleading to the extent that it suggests, incorrectly, that Bandura assigns purely retroactive actions to reinforcement. He could have given a more accurate schema of his theory by indicating the putative contributions made by reinforcement at each of the four stages—I am not willing to expose my own visuomotor deficiencies by offering a revised sketch—but a Mark II version should draw attention to the proactive effects of reinforcement. In Bandura's theory, reinforcement focuses attention, enhances stimuli and strengthens retention—as well as governing the performance of modelled behaviour (Bandura, 1971b, p. 45).

CAN THE THEORY BE REFUTED?

As we have seen, Bandura places a great deal of weight on the importance of reinforcement in eliciting and maintaining the performance of modelled behaviour. He does, however, leave the door slightly ajar. What if modelled behaviour is *not* always governed by its consequences? While allowing that it often is so governed, perhaps even *usually* so governed, there remains a possibility that some instances of modelled behaviour are not governed in this way. Now the problem is that, even if exceptions of this type do arise (i.e. modelled behaviour which is not governed by its consequences), they are quite likely to pass unnoticed if we apply Bandura's theory to its natural limits.

Consider the problem of non-reinforced modelled behaviour. Bandura says that 'imitative behavior is often performed without explicit external reinforcement . . . . This phenomenon may be partly attributable to discrimination processes. It has been demonstrated that people regulate their behavior to a large extent on the basis of anticipated consequences (Bandura, 1971b, p. 52)'. Later he explains that non-reinforced modelled behaviour 'can be rendered partially independent of its external consequences through self-reinforcement of imitative performances and this 'self-reinforcement' can include the earlier referred to 'anticipated consequences' (p. 53).

Thus there are three outlets—three alternative explanations open to us:
(1) The behaviour is maintained by self-reinforcement.
(2) The behaviour is maintained by anticipatory reinforcement.
(3) The behaviour is maintained by vicarious reinforcement.

In elucidating these possibilities it will be helpful at times to refer to an experimental example chosen from Bandura's own work. In 1965 he reported an experiment in which observers were shown a film of a model engaging in novel aggressive behaviour that was either rewarded, punished or 'unaccompanied by any consequences'. The results revealed that observers who witnessed aggression being punished performed fewer modelled responses than either the subjects who observed the aggressive model being rewarded or the subjects who watched the model who experienced no consequences. The results of this experiment are conveniently summarized in Figure 7.2. The effects of offering the observers a positive incentive are also shown in the graph (rewards were given contingent upon the observers reproducing the aggressive responses exhibited by the model).

For our purposes, the important experimental group comprises the boys and girls who were exposed to the model 'unaccompanied by any consequences'. Notice their high rate of responding notwithstanding. Moreover, they continued to respond, although not as vigorously, even when no external incentives were provided. Is this a clear example of non-reinforced modelled behaviour?

Now, returning to the three possible explanations listed above, we can test each of them against this example. Extrinsic reinforcement is, of course, excluded in the 'no-incentive' group. Vicarious reinforcement is excluded by the experimental conditions—the relevant observers were shielded from the consequences for the model.

This leaves only two outlets—self-reinforcement or anticipated reinforcement. As there are no grounds for postulating the occurrence of anticipatory reinforcement in this example, we are left with self-reinforcement in general (i.e. not merely anticipatory self-reinforcement). This residual problem is one of finding a basis for discerning the presence or absence of self-reinforcement. If it cannot be solved, and there does not seem to be a simple solution, then we may be faced with an immortal theory. Unless we have satisfactory

218

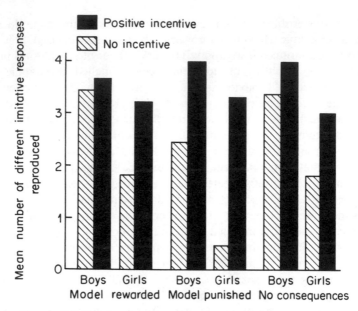

FIGURE 7.2 Results from an experiment by Bandura (1965, p. 589). They show the mean number of matching responses performed by children as a function of response consequences to the model (i.e. rewarded, punished or no consequences) *and* the influence of positive incentives which were offered for reproducing the model's behaviour. For present purposes, the most significant group comprises the children who observed the model who experienced no consequences; even in the absence of incentives, they performed matching responses.

grounds for deciding in particular cases (and, preferably, in advance) whether to accept or reject each of the four possible 'governing consequences' of modelled behaviour, the theory may become inoperable.

In those cases where apparently non-rewarded modelling behaviour persists, we can say that reinforcement is present but obscure (e.g. vicarious, anticipated or self-administered) *or* allow the possibility that non-rewarded behaviour can persist. Why not?

There is no doubt that reinforcement is capable of substantially facilitating the performance of modelled behaviour. The question is whether or not reinforcement is a *necessary* condition.

VICARIOUS REINFORCEMENT

The concept of vicarious reinforcement has an important part in Bandura's theory, and for good reason. He starts with two propositions: 'behavior is controlled by its consequences' and 'most human behavior, of course, is not controlled by immediate external reinforcement (Bandura, 1971a, p. 229)'. The two most important reinforcement processes in social learning theory are vicarious reinforcement and self-reinforcement. For present purposes, it is the first of these that is most pertinent and it has to be admitted that Bandura's treatment of the concept of vicarious reinforcement falls short of his own high standards. The difficulty starts with his definition: 'vicarious reinforcement is applied to changes in the behavior of observers that result from witnessing a model's actions being rewarded or punished (Bandura, 1971b, p. 47)'. But he then adds that 'it should be noted that vicarious reinforcement is simply a descriptive term (p. 48)'. Elsewhere, he has written that vicarious positive reinforcement is 'a function of observing rewarding consequences to a model (Bandura, 1971a, p. 233)'. Now it is evident that a definition which states that reinforcement 'results from' or is 'a function of' something is not simply descriptive. It implies a causal connection. As we shall see, the postulated connection is open to argument.

According to the theory, several 'mechanisms may be responsible for the changes accompanying vicarious reinforcement (Bandura, 1971a, p. 239ff.)'. Vicarious reinforcement may accomplish its effects through any one of the following means or a combination of them. In the first place, it may have an informational function, and closely allied to this an attention-directing function. As a third (and compatible) possibility, it may produce motivational changes. Fourth, emotional conditioning acquired through vicarious experiences is said to be a mechanism responsible for vicarious reinforcement (Bandura, 1971a, p. 243). Although there is abundant evidence of the occurrence of vicarious emotional arousal (and, equally important, suppression of emotional responses), it is not clear why these occurrences are called in to explain vicarious *reinforcement*.

Each of his interpretatons has something to be said for it and the evidence is well assembled by Bandura, but the total picture is not satisfactory. Although there is little doubt that vicarious experiences (simply, observing the behaviour of someone else) can be informative, can direct attention, influence motives and cause emotional reactions, there does not seem to me to be any compelling reason for attempting to tie all of these phenomena together by the concept of reinforcement. Might it not be much simpler to state, as matters of confirmed observation, that vicarious experiences can be informative, directive, emotional and motivating? Nor does this list exhaust all of the possibilities. Vicarious experiences can, of course, be followed by other behavioural and cognitive changes, and these can be added to the list of vicarious effects more easily when the 'cement' of the reinforcement concept is dropped.

The problems raised by Bandura's view of vicarious reinforcement can also be illustrated, perhaps paradoxically, by referring to his critique of one of best of the Skinnerian-type explanations. Gewirtz and Stingle (1968) and Baer, Peterson and Sherman (1967) argued skilfully that apparently non-reinforced imitative behaviour persists because of the operation of conditioned reinforcement (not, as in Bandura's case, by *vicarious* reinforcement and/or *self*-reinforcement). They pointed out that we are regularly reinforced for carrying out matching, imitative behaviour—especially in childhood. This gives rise to habits of generalized imitation ('conditioned reinforcement', if you will). Bandura's main objection is that 'the theory explains more than has ever been observed (Bandura, 1971b, p. 52)'. People should imitate everyone they see, but in fact they are 'highly selective'.

Presumably, Gewirtz and his colleagues could answer that 'generalized imitation' does not mean indiscriminate imitation. So, for example, models associated with reinforcing consequences will become positive discriminative stimuli and those associated with unpleasant consequences will become negative discriminative stimuli. In this way, reinforcement theorists can explain both the generality and the selectivity of imitative behaviour.

Does this sound too facile and is it beyond possible disproof? In my opinion it comes close to both of these. If a person emits a new imitative response, it can be attributed to the operation of a generalized habit of imitation; if the same person *fails* to emit the (expected) imitative response, it can be attributed to the absence of the appropriate discriminative stimulus. Are there any conceivable instances of imitative behaviour (or indeed the non-occurrence of expected imitations) which might fall outside this explanatory scheme? Can the theory ever be embarrassed and, if not, does it hold any value? (In passing it might be mentioned that although the reinforcement view of imitation appears able to cope with a lot of the available data, it is highly improbable that it could have *predicted*, rather than postdicted, the occurrence of phenomena such as no-trial learning).

Regrettably, Bandura's own alternative is, as I have tried to show, also open to the objection that it precludes the possibility of disproof. In fact, his dismissal of the reinforcement theory is closely followed by this alternative: 'In everyday life behavior is often performed without explicit external reinforcement ... this may be partly attributable to discrimination process ... people regulate their behavior to a large extent on the basis of *anticipated* (my italics) consequences'. These anticipated consequences 'are established on the basis of differential reinforcements that individuals have previously experienced in relation to different behavior, different people and different situations (Bandura, 1971b, p. 52–53)'.

This alternative resembles the discrimination part of the reinforcement theory, but adds or substitutes *anticipated* consequences for contingent consequences. Perhaps because this lacks conviction, Bandura also adds that 'such behavior can be rendered partially independent of its external consequences through *self-reinforcement* (my italics) of imitative performances (p. 53)'.

And so we seem to have come full circle. If extrinsic reinforcement cannot meet the case, it might be vicarious reinforcement. If that fails, it might be anticipated reinforcement. If that fails, it might be self-reinforcement. And if that fails, *how will we know*?

I am in no position to provide a satisfactory means of dealing with these problems, but it may help to clarify matters if we start by acknowledging some statements to be highly probable. Extrinsic, vicarious and self-reinforcement are all capable of exerting a powerful influence on imitative behaviour—*but* none of them is necessary for either the elicitation or maintenance of imitative behaviour. Similarly, observational learning can be powerfully influenced by these varieties of reinforcement, but none of them is necessary for the occurrence of such learning (Bandura's view, of course).

It will take time to unravel these theoretical problems, but fortunately the therapeutic application of modelling procedures continues at a satisfactory peace in the interim. With that agreeable thought, we can leave these heady questions for the present.

THERAPEUTIC ADVANTAGES AND LIMITATIONS OF MODELLING

Returning to practical matters, we can look forward to an increasing use of therapeutic modelling for reducing fear, investigations into the aetiological contributions of observational learning and new applications of modelling procedures. Attempts at modelling more satisfactory social behaviour will, of course, continue (perhaps with more success in future) and we can expect modelling procedures to play an increasingly prominent part in the training and education of children (e.g. speech and social training, prevention and overcoming of fears, etc.). Modelling will also play a valuable part in training parents to improve the quality of their child-care—parent-training is of course a rapidly growing branch of applied psychology (Berkowitz and Graziano, 1972).

Although significant advances have been made, it will not do to exaggerate how much can be achieved. We are already in possession of examples in which symbolic modelling made little or no impact (e.g. Roper, Rachman and Marks, 1975) and others in which even participant modelling is insufficient. The research of Lovaas and coworkers (1967) is an example of how weak a tool modelling can be (even in combination with other methods) when pitted against the speech and other deficits of autistic children. In our research into the treatment of patients with severe obsessional problems, we have had some clinical failures (Rachman, Hodgson and Marks, 1973); for example, some of them were unable to approach their dreaded situations despite intensive modelling treatment. My impression is that this type of failure is largely the result of extraordinarily high levels of fear. Another disappointing result comes from the analogue research of McFall and Twentyman (1973), who achieved scant success in modelling for unassertive volunteers.

I can discern four obstacles to the successful use of therapeutic modelling, but they are not insuperable problems. First, as mentioned earlier, there are some people who simply do not experience fear-reduction. Second, there are those who learn the necessary skill or bravery during the sessions of modelling, but fail to translate the learning into performance (thereby supplying Bandura with support for his position). So far the most blatant and worrying clinical examples of this type of failure (also failures to transfer from clinic to the natural environment) have occurred in social skills training programmes (e.g. J. Marziller, personal communication, 1974). Third, some people acquire skills or bravery through modelling and it even transfers to the natural environment for a short spell, but they then experience a failure of maintenance—not a new clinical problem, of course, but one for which therapeutic modelling confers no immunity. Fourth, failures have occurred in instances where the observer lacks the necessary capacities to learn or to perform; in the case of Lovaas's autistic sample it was inadequate learning, while in sexual problems the person may lack the necessary drive.

The advantageous features of therapeutic modelling include the following. It is capable of acting rapidly. It can transmit large and complex units of behaviour. It is easily accepted by most patients—the problems of non-cooperation are ones of scepticism rather than reluctance or distaste. It is easily explained and easily understood. Lastly, it is easy to provide advice, practical advice at that, for further management.

From a practical point of view, it can be anticipated that large individual differences in responsivity to modelling will be encountered. Leaving aside the question of situational determinants, such as the specific attributes of the relevant model, the observed consequences for the model, and so on, we are left with some general factors which will facilitate or impede the social transmission of abnormal or of therapeutic behaviour. In estimating the potential value of therapeutic modelling, it must be remembered that certain types of imitation (or non-independent) behaviour are disapproved of. In children, for example, there are strong socially learned influences acting against attempts to 'copy' other children. An experimental illustration of this phenomenon is reported by Luchins and Luchins (1961) where their child subjects were reluctant to admit having copied a problem solution from a 'confederate' of the experimenter. Another widespread and powerful set of taboos surround the imitation of crossgender behaviour—boys in particular will go to great lengths in order to avoid the imitation of feminine (sissy) behaviour. Lanzetta and Kanareff (1959) described several experimental failures to show that reward increases imitative behaviour and concluded that it generally fails when there are negative sanctions applied for behaviour which is not independent. A more general discussion of the factors that determine imitation and its failures is provided by Aronfreed (1969).

WHO RESPONDS?

In clinical practice, it has already been observed that autistic children are unresponsive to the influence of models (e.g. Lovaas and coworkers, 1967). Comparable problems have been encountered (or will be encountered) in work with schizophrenic patients, alcoholics, addicts and, more generally, patients with personality disorders. The early indications are that, by and large, children are particularly responsive to modelling influences and there is reason to believe that dysthymic (neurotic introverted) subjects may also show high levels of responsiveness. The characteristics of responsive subjects in experiments are discussed by Flanders (1968) and by Bandura (1969). It is likely that differences in personality (Eysenck, 1967) will have a bearing on the subject's responsiveness to modelling experiences. For example, one may anticipate that extraverts will be more responsive to *socially* transmitted models or influences. Another interesting possibility is that a modelling paradigm might provide a useful testing ground for some of the postulates of Gray's (1971) theory. It might, for example, be possible to assess the predicted differences in responsiveness to socially transmitted experiences of reward, punishment, frustrative non-reward, and so on.

CODA

It is plain that modelling, theory and practice, is going to play an increasingly useful part in clinical psychology. On the theoretical side, the recent advances can be traced to the original work of Miller and Dollard (1941), who drew attention to the importance of the phenomenon, the role of attentional and verbal factors, and who emphasized the importance of observational learning as a means for learning large units of behaviour in a relatively short time. The more recent contributions of Bandura (1969, 1971a) have expanded this work in a remarkable manner. He has improved the concept of observational learning by showing its increased value once one drops the insistence on direct reinforcement. Bandura also pointed out that observational learning can occur even when the observer refrains from carrying out the model's behaviour until a considerable time has passed. And such learning occurs even in the absence of reinforcement. He led the way to the development of a new treatment method and the possibility of establishing a more reasonable and useful aetiological theory of certain types of abnormal behaviour (e.g. phobias). The empirical research will take expected directions and can look after itself. On the theoretical side, Bandura has provided a framework for further research, but we need to know more about the processes of vicarious reinforcement, imaginal and verbal encoding, among others. The outstanding problems of generative speech, jumbled speech, translation, and so on, remain to be dealt with. In addition, although the processes of attention and verbalization almost certainly facilitate modelling, they are not apparently essential. It is also to be hoped that there will be attempts to come to grips with the role of individual differences in observational learning and, particularly, the part they play in abnormal behaviour.

REFERENCES

Aronfreed, J. (1969). The problem of imitation. In L. Lipsitt and H. Reese (Eds.), *Advances in Child Development and Behavior*, Vol. 4. Academic Press, New York.

Baer, D., Peterson, R., and Sherman, J. (1967). The development of imitation by reinforcing behavioral similarity to a model. *Journal of Experimental Analysis of Behavior*, **10**, 405–416.

Bandura, A. (1965). Influence of model's reinforcement contingencies on the acquisition of imitative responses. *Journal of Personality and Social Psychology*, **1**, 589–595.

Bandura, A. (1969). *Principles of Behavior Modification*, Holt, Rinehart and Winston, New York.

Bandura, A. (1971a). Vicarious and self-reinforcement processes. In R. Glaser (Ed.), *The Nature of Reinforcement*, Academic Press, New York.

Bandura, A. (Ed.) (1971b). *Psychological Modeling*, Aldine-Atherton, Chicago.

Bandura, A., and Barab, P. (1973). Processes governing disinhibitory effects through symbolic modelling. *Journal of Abnormal Psychology*, **82**, 1–9.

Bandura, A., Blanchard, E. B., and Ritter, B. (1969). The relative efficacy of desensitization and modelling approaches for inducing bheavioral, affective, and attitudinal changes. *Journal of Personality and Social Psychology*, **13**, 173–199.

Bandura, A., Grusec, J. E., and Menlove, F. L. (1967) Vicarious extinction of avoidance behavior. *Journal of Personality and Social Psychology*, **5**, 16–23.

Bandura, A., and Jeffery, R. (1973). Role of symbolic coding and rehearsal processes in observational learning. *Journal of Personality and Social Psychology*, **26**, 122–130.

Bandura, A., Jeffery, R., and Bachicha, D. L. (1974). Analysis of memory codes and cumulative rehearsal in observational learning. *Journal of Research in Personality*, **7**, 295–305.

Bandura, A., Jeffery, R. W., and Wright, C. (1974). Efficacy of participant modeling as a function of response induction aids. *Journal of Abnormal Psychology*, **83**, 56–64.

Bandura, A., and Menlove, F. L. (1968). Factors determining vicarious extinction of avoidance behavior through symbolic modeling. *Journal of Personality and Social Psychology*, **8**, 99–108.

Bandura, A., and Walters, R. H. (1963). *Social Learning and Personality Development*, Holt, Rinehart and Winston, New York.

Berger, S. M. (1962). Conditioning through vicarious instigation. *Psychological Review*, **69**, 450–468.

Berkowitz, B. P., and Graziano, A. M. (1972). Training parents as behavior therapists: a review. *Behaviour Research and Therapy*, **10**, 297–318.

Blanchard, E. B. (1970). Relative contributions of modeling, informational influences, and physical contact in extinction of phobic behavior. *Journal of Abnormal Psychology*, **76**, 55–61.

Eisler, R., Hersen, M., and Miller, P. (1973). Effects of modelling on components of assertive behavior. *Journal of Behavior Therapy and Experimental Psychiatry*, **4**, 1–6.

Eysenck, H. J. (1967). *The Biological Basis of Personality*, Thomas, Springfield, Illinois.

Flanders, J. P. (1968). A review of research on imitative behavior. *Psychological Bulletin*, **69**, 316–337.

Friedman, P. H. (1971). The effects of modeling and role-playing on assertive behavior. In R. Rubin, H. Fensterheim, A. A. Lazarus and C. M. Franks (Eds.), *Advances in Behavior Therapy*, Academic Press, New York.

Geer, J., and Turtletaub, G. (1967). Fear reduction following observation of the model. *Journal of Personality and Social Psychology*, **6**, 327–335.

Gewirtz, J., and Stingle, K. (1968). Learning of generalized imitation as a basis for identification. *Psychological Review*, **75**, 374–397.

Goldstein, A. (1973). The use of modeling to increase independent behavior. *Behaviour Research and Therapy*, **11**, 31–42.

Gray, J. A. (1971). *The Psychology of Fear and Stress*, Weidenfeld and Nicholson, London.

Hagman, R. (1932). A study of fears in children of pre-school age. *Journal Experimental Psychology*, **1**, 110–115.

Hall, R. A., and Hinkle, J. E. (1972). Vicarious desensitization of test anxiety. *Behaviour Research and Therapy*, **10**, 407–410.

Hersen, M., Eisler, R., and Miller, P. (1973). Effects of practice, instructions and modeling on components of assertive behavior. *Behaviour Research and Therapy*, **11**, 443–452.

Hill, J. H., Liebert, R. M., and Mott, D. E. W. (1968). Vicarious extinction of avoidance behavior through film: an initial test. *Psychological Reports*, **12**, 192–196.

Jersild, A. T., and Holmes, F. B. (1935). Methods of overcoming children's fears. *Journal of Psychology*, **1**, 75–104.

Jones, M. C. (1924). The elimination of children's fears. *Journal of Experimental Psychology*, **7**, 383–390.

Kazdin, A. E. (1973). Covert modeling and the reduction of avoidance behavior. *Journal of Abnormal Psychology*, **81**, 87–95.

Kazdin, A. (1974a). Multiple covert models, variation of fear stimuli, and avoidance reduction. *Behaviour Research and Therapy*, in press.

Kazdin, A. (1974b). The effect of model identity and fear-relevant similarity on covert modeling, *Behaviour Therapy*, **5**, 624–635.

Lader, M. H., and Mathews, A. M. (1968). A physiological model of phobic anxiety and desensitization. *Behaviour Research and Therapy*, **6**, 411–421.

Lader, M. H., and Wing, L. (1966). *Physiological Measures, Sedative Drugs and Morbid Anxiety*, Maudsley Monograph No. 14. Oxford University Press, London.

Lang, P., and Lazovik, A. (1963). Experimental desensitization of phobia. *Journal of Abnormal and Social Psychology*, **66**, 519–525.

Lang, P. J., Melamed, B. G., and Hart, J. (1970). A psychophysiological analysis of fear modification using an automated desensitization procedure. *Journal of Abnormal Psychology*, **76**, 220–234.

Lanzetta, J. T., and Kanareff, V. T. (1959). The effects of a monetary reward on the acquisition of an imitative response. *Journal of Abnormal and Social Psychology*, **59**, 120–127.

Lovaas, I., Freitas, L., Nelson, K., and Whalen, C. (1967). The establishment of imitation and its use for the development of complex behavior in schizophrenic children. *Behavior Research and Therapy*, **5**, 171–182.

Luchins, A. S., and Luchins, E. H. (1961). Imitation by rote and by understanding. *Journal of Social Psychology*, **54**, 175–187.

McFall, R. M., and Lillesand, D. B. (1971). Behavior rehearsal with modeling and coaching in assertion training. *Journal of Abnormal Psychology*, **77**, 313–323.

McFall, R., and Twentyman, C. (1973). Four experiments on the relative contributions of rehearsal, modeling, and coaching to assertion training. *Journal of Abnormal Psychology*, **81**, 199–218.

Mann, J. (1972). Vicarious desensitization of test anxiety through observing videotaped treatment. *Journal of Counseling Psychology*, **19**, 1–7.

Mann, J., and Rosenthal, T. L. (1969). Vicarious and direct counterconditioning of test anxiety through individual and group desensitization. *Behaviour Research and Therapy*, **7**, 359–367.

Marks, I. M. (1972). Flooding (implosion) and allied treatments. In W. S. Agras (Ed.), *Learning Theory: Applications of Principles and Procedures*, Little, Brown and Co., Boston.

May, R. (1950). *The Meaning of Anxiety*, Ronald Press, New York.

Meichenbaum, D. (1971). Examination of model characteristics in reducing avoidance behavior. *Journal of Personality and Social Psychology*, **17**, 298–307.

Miller, N. E., and Dollard, J. (1941). *Social Learning and Imitation*, Yale University Press, New Haven.

Miller, R., Murphy, J., and Mirsky, I. (1959). Non-verbal communication of affect. *Journal of Clinical Psychology*, **15**, 155–158.

Murphy, C., and Bootzin, R. (1973). Active and passive participation in contact desensitization. *Behavior Therapy*, **4**, 203–211.

O'Connor, R. D. (1969). Modification of social withdrawal through symbolic modeling. *Journal of Applied Behavior Analysis*, **2**, 15–22.

O'Connor, R. D. (1972). Relative efficacy of modeling, shaping, and the combined procedures for modification of social withdrawal. *Journal of Abnormal Psychology*, **79**, 327–334.

O'Sullivan, M., Gilner, F., and Krinski, R. (1973). The influence of sex of experimenter on modeling in the reduction of fear. *Behavior Therapy*, **4**, 535–542.

Rachman, S. (1967). Systematic desensitization. *Psychological Bulletin*, **67**, 93–103.

Rachman, S. (1968). *Phobias: Their Nature and Control*, Thomas, Springfield, Illinois.

Rachman, S. (1972). Clinical applications of observational learning. *Behavior Therapy*, **3**, 379–397.

Rachman, S. (1974). *The Meanings of Fear*, Penguin Books, Middlesex.

Rachman, S., Hodgson, R., and Marks, I. M. (1971). The treatment of chronic obsessive–compulsive neurosis. *Behaviour Research and Therapy*, **9**, 237–247.

Rachman, S., Hodgson, R., and Marks, I. M. (1973). The treatment of obsessive–compulsive neurotics by modelling and flooding *in vivo*. *Behaviour Research and Therapy*, **11**, 463–471.

Rathus, S. (1973). Instigation of assertive behavior through videotape-mediated assertive models and directed practice. *Behaviour Research and Therapy*, **11**, 57–66.

Rimm, D. C., and Mahoney, M. J. (1969). The application of reinforcement and participant modeling procedures in the treatment of snake-phobic behavior. *Behavior Therapy*, **1**, 369–376.

Rimm, D. C., and Medeiros, D. C. (1970). The role of muscle relaxation in participant modeling. *Behaviour Research and Therapy*, **8**, 127–132.

Ritter, B. (1968). The group desensitization of children's phobias. *Behaviour Research and Therapy*, **6**, 1–6.

Ritter, B. (1969). The use of contact desensitization, demonstration-plus-participation and demonstration-alone in the treatment of acrophobia. *Behaviour Research and Therapy*, **7**, 157–164.

Roper, G., Rachman, S., and Marks, I. M. (1975). Participant modelling treatment of obsessive–compulsive neurosis. *Behaviour Research and Therapy*, in press.

Rosenthal, T. L. (1973). *Some Design Options: Inert and Active Alternatives*. Paper presented at Rocky Mountain Psychological Association, Nevada, May, 1973.

Rosenthal, T. L., and Carroll, W. R. (1972). Factors in vicarious modification of complex grammatical parameters. *Journal of Educational Psychology*, **63**, 174–178.

Rosenthal, T. L., and Whitebrook, J. S. (1970). Incentives versus instructions in transmitting grammatical parameters with experimenter as model. *Behaviour Research and Therapy*, **8**, 189–196.

Rosenthal, T. L., and Zimmerman, B. (1972). Modeling by exemplification and instruction in training conservation. *Developmental Psychology*, **6**, 392–401.

Spiegler, M. D., Liebert, R. M., McMains, M. J., and Fernandez, L. E. (1969). Experimental development of a modeling treatment to extinguish persistent avoidance behavior. In R. D. Rubin and C. M. Franks (Eds.), *Advances in Behavior Therapy*, Academic Press, New York.

Watts, F. (1971). Densitization as a habituation phenomenon: I. Stimulus intensity as determinant of the effects of stimulus lengths. *Behaviour Research and Therapy*, **9**, 209–217.

Young, E. R., Rimm, D. C., and Kennedy, T. D. (1973). An experimental investigation of modeling and verbal reinforcement in the modification of assertive behavior. *Behaviour Research and Therapy*, **11**, 317–319.

8

SOCIAL PSYCHOLOGY AND THE BEHAVIOUR THERAPIES

M. Philip Feldman

INTRODUCTION

In this chapter, I shall draw on the theoretical and experimental literature of social psychology to consider two questions of relevance to all psychological therapies and of particular relevance to the behaviour therapies, which appear to be more effective than the psychotherapies and may largely or even wholly replace them.

Both questions concern the therapist and his behaviour during the course of the therapy, from the initial interview to the end of treatment. The first is about the effect of social influence variables on the outcome of treatment by behavioural methods. The major variables are the form and content of the messages conveyed to the patient concerning the likely outcome of therapy, and the effectiveness of the therapist as a dispenser of approval and other forms of social reinforcement for the client. Thus, the first question concerns the possibility of the therapist making a *positive* contribution to therapy, over and above the formal techniques employed. The second question relates to the opposite possibility: because of his laudable desire for success and his dislike of failure the therapist may *reduce* the effectiveness of the techniques employed. The results of laboratory studies of cognitive dissonance theory are drawn on to derive a theory of therapist behaviour in response to discrepancies experienced between intention (successful result of treatment) and outcome (failure of treatment).

SOCIAL INFLUENCE PROCESSES

Background

My interest in the effect of social influence variables on therapeutic change started when I attended ward rounds as one of the entourage accompanying the Director of a Department of Psychiatry. The 'round' consisted of a tour of about twenty inpatients; it always took place at the same hour every Monday morning and was regarded as an 'occasion', particularly by the patients and the nursing staff. The Director always wore the attire of the old-fashioned upper professional—black waistcoat and jacket, striped trousers and starched collar. He had wings of silver hair, a rubicund complexion and his manner was in keeping. He appeared to be conveying to the patients, by both verbal and non-verbal means, the following persuasive communication: 'I am a highly experienced and compassionate psychiatrist; my team of assistants is well trained and alert; if you will cooperate and follow our advice all will be well'. At the level of uncontrolled observation his social influence effect was rather powerful. After a few moments of conversation, the patients (most of whom were suffering from depression of mood) *looked* more cheerful. Frequently, patients who were contemplating taking their own discharge, because of apparent slow progress in response to electroconvulsive therapy (ECT) or chemotherapy, postponed their departure following the formula: 'I want you to put up with it (i.e. your depression of mood) a little longer and continue to take your tablets (have the shock treatment)'.

This anecdote illustrates and introduces the major thesis of this section: social influence processes may be of considerable therapeutic relevance to an effective therapy such as behaviour therapy; they are likely to *enhance* the efficiency of formal therapeutic procedures, rather than to account for them wholly; their major effects are to persuade the patient that the therapist is competent and that the chances of success are good; therefore, the patient should come into therapy and having done so should remain in therapy, and attend to and carry out fully the instructions of the therapist.

It has been argued (e.g. Liberman, 1972) that social influence variables would have little additional impact on 'strong' therapies, e.g. the behaviour therapies. By contrast, 'weak' therapies, such as the various forms of psycho-therapy, might be considerably enhanced. Yet if the therapeutic activities carried out by a patient *are in themselves ineffective*, persuading him to carry them out regularly and in the manner prescribed will have little additional effect. It is only effective therapies which are worth the effort of enhancement.

As Bandura (1969) points out: ' . . . even though the change agent has planned an optimal sequence of activities, his efforts will be of little avail unless the individual carries out the necessary procedures that have been prescribed for him (p. 397)'. Such procedures may be unpleasant. For example, entering a fear-provoking situation and performing fear-provoking responses are precisely the behaviours which constitute the patient's avoidance problem. Bandura suggests that the approach behaviour of the patient will be assisted by a number of variables. These include the social rewards supplied by the therapists, the incentives offered to maintain the patient in therapy, explicit and realistic feedback concerning progress, and proceeding at the right speed. (If too much distress is suffered because of too great a pace, the patient may terminate therapy prematurely.) Social influence procedures may also enhance the efficiency of behavioural methods by ensuring regular attendance and the optimal sequence of activities. This is a most important point, and one usually neglected by therapists of all persuasions (Lanyon, 1972). The more efficient a procedure is in reaching a given therapeutic goal, the greater the number of patients who may be helped in any given unit of time. (This is an argument which will, perhaps, commend itself less to those in private practice than to those in the public service.) It is possibly most important of all that the patient should remain in therapy. Otherwise even the most effective and efficient therapy will be of no avail.

There is no doubt of the high rate of drop-out from psychotherapy (Garfield, 1971). There appear to be no similar data for behaviour therapy (studies of patient attributes and behaviours, in general, are lacking), but it would be surprising if all patients who began a course of behaviour therapy completed it. The systematic use of social influence variables may, in addition to enhancing efficacy and efficiency, reduce the proportion of patients who leave treatment prematurely.

There is a voluminous literature on the importance of placebo effects in chemotherapy, frequently with respect to subjectively experienced and reported pain (Liberman, 1962), which is clearly relevant to desensitization, concerned as it is with the amelioration of subjectively experienced and reported distress. Therapeutic stimuli in the placebo process, as listed by Liberman on the basis of an extensive literature survey, include the credibility and expertise of the doctor (as experienced by the patient) and his attitude towards the therapy and towards the patient, the therapeutic setting and the mode of administration of the placebo (e.g. an intravenous solution had a greater placebo effect than tablets). Involving subjects in the task of reporting 'drug' effects is more productive of placebo effects than simple suggestion (Knowles and Lucas, 1960), as is a positive previous reinforcement history with doctors. Attention to the therapeutic communications and imaginal rehearsal of them also increase the placebo effect.

Liberman considers that there are marked individual differences in placebo responsiveness. For example, Jellinek (1946) administered a placebo on five separate occasions to 121 patients with headache. Forty-nine were never relieved of pain, nineteen were relieved on one to three occasions and fifty-three on four or five occasions. Thus, some people are consistently never placebo reactors, some are sometimes but not at other times, depending on the specific occasion, and yet others are consistently placebo reactors, possibly irrespective of the situation. Liberman suggests that the latter are characterized by a personality constellation of chronic low self-esteem, immaturity, extraversion and social gregariousness, all of which enhance dependency on the therapist and responsiveness to his communications. Therapist influence is also enhanced by a high level of current distress and a relatively low educational level.

Paul (1967) made one of the few formal attempts to study the placebo effect in the behaviour therapy context. Two years after termination of the treatment of fear of public speaking, 85 per cent. of his desensitization group were improved as compared to 50 per cent. of those treated by 'insight' therapy, 50 per cent. of a group whose treatment was designated 'placebo' and 22 per cent. of an untreated control group. The increased effectiveness of the placebo as compared to the control group is of considerable interest. In general, the placebo literature supports the conclusion that the response to therapy of at least a proportion of patients will be improved by the systematic manipulation of social influence variables. However, both the placebo literature and the theoretical arguments concerning the relevance of social influence processes to the behaviour therapies fail to consider separately the two major sets of variables: the therapist as a social reinforcer responding to the behaviour of the patient and the therapist as a source of messages to the patient intended to influence his beliefs concerning outcome and his response to requests to carry out the necessary sequence of activities.

The therapist as a social reinforcer

The central question is: 'Does the behaviour of the therapist, particularly his approval or disapproval of the client and the client's behaviour, whether expressed through verbal or non-verbal channels of communication, significantly affect the process of the therapy and the outcome of the therapy?' It is part of an issue which has provided one of the main controversies in the history of therapy, both medical or psychological, namely the importance of the therapist–patient relationship (how each evaluates the other), over and above the objective features of the technique employed. If the behaviour of the therapist, other than his ability to manage the technique correctly, is unimportant in affecting both process and outcome, then the patient–therapist relationship is also unimportant and the general style of behaviour of the therapist throughout treatment may safely be ignored as a relevant outcome variable.

There are two aspects of the therapist as a social reinforcer: his approval/disapproval of those responses of the patient which are relevant to therapy and his approval/disapproval of the patient as a person, as revealed by the patient's general manner and appearance and by his behaviours other than those strictly relevant to the process of therapy. It is necessary to analyse the importance of each aspect separately, so as to explore the extent to which they operate independently or have an interactive effect. The published literature to date consists largely of assertion and counterassertion. At one extreme, Wolpe (1969) has consistently argued against the importance of the therapist as a social reinforcer: 'The responsibility for the patient's recovery is placed unequivocally on the therapist . . . (carrying out) the correct assessment and the correct techniques (p. 18)'. What Wolpe meant may be inferred from an earlier report (Wolpe, 1962) in which he claimed to have demonstrated specifically the lack of importance of the patient–therapist relationship. He handed over the treatment of a phobic patient half-way through to a junior psychiatrist and the patient made a complete recovery. Wolpe interpreted this as indicating the irrelevance of the relationship between himself and the patient to the outcome of treatment. However, the patient was in contact with *a* therapist throughout. The extent to which Wolpe's *charisma* was important in the early stages of therapy, and to which it was perceived by the patient as devolving on Wolpe's assistant, are both quite unknown.

Apparent support for Wolpe's view is provided by an analogue study by Lang, Melamed and Hart (1970). They reported automated desensitization to be at least as effective as a therapist-controlled procedure. However, the machine-treated group underwent the usual pre-treatment procedures of detailed interviewing as well as relaxation training, both of which may have established a favourable evaluation by the patient of the therapist. Moreover, the physiological recordings which were carried out were monitored continuously by an operator. It is not stated whether the subjects knew of his presence and, if so, whether this made any difference to their behaviour. A further, apparently paradoxical feature may have been of importance; it concerns the extent to which the subject believed himself to be in control of the situation. Lang's DAD (device for automated desensitization) allows the subject to control his rate of progress along stimulus hierarchies by signalling his experience of anxiety, ability to visualize without anxiety and the clarity of the imaginal scene. Variations in the ability of the therapist to attend vigilantly to the patient's responses and to interpret them accurately are both cut out. For some individuals, who value highly the attribution of causality to the self (Kelley, 1967), the degree of *patient control* allowed by the DAD system may more than outweigh the absence of the live therapist; the reverse may be true for other individuals. When combined, the two levels of response to the DAD situation—one *better* than the live system, one *worse*—may cancel each other out. This interpretation would be supported if the heterogeneity of subject response to the DAD situation was greater than that to the live therapist situation. At the level of raw data this would be indicated by a significantly larger variance in post-session avoidance tests for the DAD than for the live-therapist subjects. Unfortunately, Lang, Melamed and Hart (1970) did not supply such data in their report. At a higher level of analysis, it would be hypothesized that personality scores on the locus of control measures (Rotter, 1966) would predict the differential response to the two techniques. The highly 'internal' subject who values the self-attribution of improvement may respond better to DAD; the highly 'external' subject may respond better to the live therapist. A similar argument applies to an analogue study by Kahn and Baker (1968), which reported no difference in outcome between a therapist-treated desensitization group and a self-treated one which had received initial training in relaxation and hierarchy construction and then maintained contact by weekly telephone calls. Studies by Davison and Valins (1969) and Davison, Tsujimoto and Glaros (1973) on the maintenance of self-attribution of behaviour change might have yielded clearer results if the locus of control scores of the subjects had been measured.

One of the results of an analogue study of systematic desensitization (SD), client-centred and rational emotive therapy (Di Loreto, 1971) was that, whereas there was no difference in outcome between the two therapists using SD, there were significant differences between the pairs of counsellors using the other two approaches. This has been interpreted by one reviewer as indicating that 'personal attributes of the therapist . . . are less important when a potent method such as desensitization is used than when more unstructured verbal psychotherapies are used (Liberman, 1972, p. 649)'. Two comments may be made. First, the two non-behaviour therapy approaches both emphasize therapist–patient relationship variables; differences in the ability of the therapists to manipulate such variables would be expected to show up in outcome differences, although the efficacy even of the more effective one would be less than that of SD. This was the case. Second, in conventional SD as used in the Di Loreto study, no attempt is made to enhance outcome by manipulating the therapist variable. Had this been done, therapist differences in outcome might have emerged. It is hardly conventional scientific practice to infer the lack of effect of a variable when it has not been systematically manipulated.

Lazarus (1971), another of the founding fathers, occupies an intermediate position, suggesting that both technique and relationship are important: 'An explicit assumption is that genuine rapport and a good therapeutic relationship are usually necessary, but often insufficient, for profound and durable behaviour change'. He continues, 'One should be on the lookout for evidence and exceptions to these general rules' (i.e. the importance of 'therapeutic conditions'—warmth, accurate empathy and genuineness—Truax and Carkhuff, 1967; see below). 'Cases who react adversely (to high therapeutic conditions) require a distant business-like approach (p. 38).' The last quotation may be interpreted as supporting the need for research into methods of adapting therapy to the patient's habitual attribution of causality, discussed above.

Bandura (1969) cites reports which suggest the possibly *greater* importance of the therapist–patient relationship in the clinical situation as opposed to the laboratory. They indicate that increased distress enhances the therapist as a reinforcing agent (Bentler, 1962; Chu, 1966; Dabbs and Leventhal, 1966; Estabrooks, 1930). Bandura argues that non-contingent social reinforcement has a 'hit-or-miss' effect in inducing the desired changes in behaviour. However, there is a difference between non-contingent acceptance of the patient as a human being and non-contingent reinforcement of his responses to therapeutic stimuli. This distinction may be what Rachman (1972) has in mind when he suggests that the Rogerian emphasis on warmth, empathy and genuineness (Traux and Carkhuff, 1967) can be recast in learning theory terms. The *patient* is to be responded to with 'unconditional, positive regard'; his *behaviour* is to be reinforced, positively or negatively, as therapeutic goals decree. (In passing, it should be noted that workers outside the immediate Truax and Carkhuff group have not yet been able to confirm the claims of the group, either for the psychometric aspects of the therapeutic conditions or their detailed relevance to therapeutic outcome—see Garfield and Bergin, 1971; Shapiro, 1969.)

At the opposite extreme from the view that social influence variables are irrelevant to behaviour therapy techniques is a study by Ryan and Gizynski (1971). They questioned fourteen patients (recruited by advertisements and paid for their participation in the study) concerning their evaluation of the behaviour therapists, who had previously treated them. A successful outcome was significantly correlated with a positive mutual evaluation by therapist and patient, the patient's confidence in the treatment, his perception of the therapist as confident and persuasive, and the therapist's fostering of expectations of a successful outcome. A low correlation was found between outcome and 'the proportions of behaviour modification techniques in the therapy'. The authors conclude that type of technique is not as important as 'the general features of the therapist and the therapeutic climate'. However, several serious faults prevent this study from adding anything of value to the present discussion:

(1) The evaluations of the therapist by the patients were *post hoc*. Patients with a personal commitment to the importance of the relationship variables would be inclined to attribute success to such variables.
(2) Related to the above is the likelihood that patients with the currently fashionable aversion to being 'manipulated' would similarly emphasize relationship variables.
(3) A 'variety of techniques' said to be 'based on the manipulation of social variables to effect behaviour change' were used. No further description is provided.
(4) Five of the six therapists involved are described as 'social workers', three of whom were of 'limited experience' (as behaviour therapists).
(5) Most important of all, the study is retrospective; thus, no comparisons were possible between pre- and post-treatment indices of distress and of evaluation of therapists by patients. Only a prospective study with independent assessments of severity and outcome can answer the questions posed by Ryan and Gizynski.

The next section surveys briefly the variables involved in the social context within which reinforcement by the therapist occurs, namely the therapist–patient relationship, together with methods of influencing this in a favourable direction. The term 'relationship' refers to the sum total of mutual evaluations, both positive (attraction) and negative (rejection).

It is important to distinguish between the therapist's attraction to a patient as a person with whom he will enjoy spending his time and attraction to the patient as someone who is likely to make a good response to therapy. Psychotherapists tend to prefer YAVIS patients (young, attractive, verbal, intelligent and successful) to those of the HOUND variety (homely, old, unattractive, non-verbal and dumb), with the result that the latter tend to be neglected by psychotherapists or even actively rejected (Goldstein and Simonson, 1971). Behaviour therapists have paid little attention to the topic of patient selection (Paul, 1969). In analogue studies (the staple diet of the behaviour therapy literature), therapist–patient attraction may not be maximal because of the general failure to manipulate social influence variables, but neither will it be minimal due to the therapist's communicated dislike of his subjects. The subjects of analogue studies tend to be perceived by experimenters rather like

Thurber's wolfish doctor saw his patient: 'You're Not My Patient, You're My Meat, Mrs. Quist!' They are the passports to a supervisor's commendation, a Ph.D., a more impressive *curriculum vitae*, the support of one's own theory or the discomfiture of a rival's—even to the disinterested advance of science. The same may be true of the attitude of therapists to clinical patients when the results of the treatment are for publication, or a successful record of treatment may strengthen one's political influence in the employing institution. Patients to whom none of these reasons apply may be considerably less attractive to their therapists.

A detailed review of the social psychological research relevant to enhancing the evaluation of the therapist by the patient, and vice versa, has been carried out by Goldstein, Heller and Sechrest (1966). On the basis of their review, the variables they expected to be relevant to the outcome of therapy included deliberately arranging matters so that one participant relates negatively or positively to the other, the provision of models expressing different degrees of attraction to the therapist, and arranging different levels of interpersonal compatibility or attitude similarity in patient–therapist pairs. Goldstein and Simonson (1971) report several studies arising from the 1966 review. Their basic notion was that the initial therapist–patient relationship would be related indirectly to the outcome of psychotherapy, by potentiating, or acting as a catalyst to, a favourable outcome. From studies with clinical patients, it was found that when the attraction of the patient to the therapist was high, the patient talked more, suppressed less information and admitted more distress. Similar consequences followed when the attraction of the therapist to the patient was high, This is a finding of considerable relevance to behaviour therapy. Patients frequently do not reveal all their problems, particularly the most distressing ones, at the initial interview, but do so later in treatment, resulting in changes of therapeutic strategy and a greater expenditure of time than would have been necessary following a complete initial disclosure.

Goldstein and Simonson found that patients led to believe that their therapist was warm and experienced were more responsive to his influence attempts than those led to believe the opposite. In another study, alcoholic subjects listened to tape-recordings of interviews in which a patient, always described as having a good treatment outcome, displayed high or low attraction to a therapist. The same subjects then had the same interview themselves. Those who heard the high attraction tape displayed more attraction to their interviewer, indicating the importance of modelling in the enhancement of social influence.

It should be noted that, in the above and other studies by this group, the method of assessment of responsiveness to therapist influence was a set of attitude statements, each purporting to show the position adopted by the therapist and administered to the subjects post-manipulation rather than the outcome of the therapy itself. The position adopted in this chapter is that the manipulations being studied by Goldstein and his colleagues are more relevant to behaviour therapy than to psychotherapy; a basically effective technique can be enhanced, a basically ineffective one cannot. If this general approach is correct, then it would be ironic that a considerable and in many ways admirable research effort should have been applied to the wrong school of therapy.

Berscheid and Walster (1969) set out some of the theoretical antecedent conditions for increasing the 'rewardingness' of one individual for another, which may be relevant to enhancing the attraction of the patient to the therapist. These include both the capacity to reward and the relative rarity of rewards. Homans (1961) argued that mutual social approval is a function of the profit each obtains from the interaction. This is rather similar to the position of Thibaut and Kelley (1959) who considered that attraction, within an interaction, is a function of the extent to which each participant receives a reward–cost outcome in excess of some minimum level, termed the comparison level (CL). This is the average value of all the outcomes known to the person—the actually experienced, the vicarious and the current. In the therapy situation, this may boil down to the therapist asking himself: 'Is this patient worth my time (i.e. would relieving his distress be more rewarding than relieving that of another; is the case an interesting one; is it publishable; is it politically prestigious; and so on)?'

Although researchers frequently concentrate on only one or other aspect of it, the therapist–patient relationship is a reciprocal one, each participant influencing the other. The interdependent nature of the psychotherapist–patient evaluation is demonstrated by several reports, those by Moos and Clemes (1967) and Houts, MacIntosh and Moos (1969) making it particularly clear that much of the variance is accounted for by interaction rather than by either component separately. McLaughlin (1971) cites evidence that interpersonal attraction is increased by 'consensual validation', i.e. each discovers the other is in agreement with his views on certain salient topics. This implies that a behaviour therapist will respond more favourably to patients who accept a broadly determinist view of Man than one who does not, and vice versa. A colleague working in a student-counselling centre states that a great many students are strongly opposed to the 'manipulative' therapies—by which they mean the behaviour therapies (Veasey, personal communication, 1972). Bandura (1969) has pointed out that all therapies are manipulative, the more crucial questions being whether therapeutic goals are set by the patient or by the therapist, and the relative efficacy and efficiency of therapists in reaching those goals. The 'public image' of the behaviour therapies is certainly worthy of study.

Manipulation of the attraction of the patient to the therapist is an exercise which should continue throughout therapy (drop-out may occur at any stage). Unfortunately, this is difficult because the necessity for repeated measurements of attraction (so that deficiencies may be corrected) may interfere with the process of therapy. It follows that methods of assessing attraction should be as unobtrusive as possible (Webb and coworkers, 1966). This suggests the relevance of such non-verbal indicants of attraction as gaze direction and eye contact (Argyle and Kendon, 1965), distance apart and angle of lean in the sitting position (Mehrabian, 1968, 1971), and changes in facial expression (Ekman and Friesen, 1969).

Attitude formation and attitude change

Assertions

Murray and Jacobson (1971) consider attitudinal variables to be of major importance for the behaviour therapies. They argue: 'There is serious doubt that systematic desensitization can be described as a counter conditioning process. Neither muscular relaxation, a progressive hierarchy, or imaginal rehearsal seem essential ... systematic desensitization may be viewed most adequately as a method of modifying beliefs and attitudes by the use of social influence (p. 727).' They see the 'crucial factor' as an expectation of change, and the major subsidiary need 'giving the patient enough hope to carry him over the crisis period'. Thus, they argue that systematic desensitization can be best understood in terms of attitude change—which *then* produces behaviour change—rather than the alternative, which has been, and still is, the conventional wisdom of behaviour therapists. In support of their view they cite evidence from reviews of laboratory studies of conditioning: 'Cognitive and perceptual variables remain to complicate the human conditioning scene (Grings, 1965, p. 85)'; 'In ... the absence of formal instructions S often provides self instructions that may facilitate or interfere with the acquisition of CRs ... Similarly in the absence of objective criteria E feed-back may markedly alter the classical conditioning paradigm (Gormezano, 1966, p. 387)'. Murray and Jacobson find particularly telling a statement by Kenneth Spence: 'It is strongly suspected that complex processes, call them cognitive factors, sets, mediating processes, or what you will, have greatly affected the extinction data heretofore reported for human subjects (Spence, 1966, p. 445).'

However, it is one thing to assert the importance of the preparatory, enhancing and maintaining effects of attitude manipulation procedures as accounting for part of the variance in laboratory conditioning studies, and quite another to argue that behaviour therapy is entirely to be understood in cognitive terms.

Wilkins (1971) also analyses systematic desensitization in largely cognitive terms, a view which has been vigorously rebutted by Davison and Wilson (1972) and equally vigorously defended by Wilkins (1972). The debate has now been joined by Morgan (1973) and the latest instalment is a rejoinder to Morgan (Wilkins, 1973).

In fact, the studies about which the above protagonists are debating—studies of the effects of manipulating the expectancy of outcome, and the feedback of therapeutic progress—are not very suitable as a basis for a theoretical discussion. Although they directly concern social influence variables, their design appears to have been largely uninfluenced by the extensive body of experimental research into social psychology. Despite the considerable pay-off which might result from adding systematically performed social influence procedures to established behavioural techniques (an argument put forward some years ago by Wilson, Hannon and Evans, 1968), behaviour therapists have shown little interest in such research. In contrast, a major research programme on the contribution of social influence processes to psychotherapy (Goldstein, 1962, 1971; Goldstein, Heller and Sechrest, 1966) has based itself very firmly on the methods and findings of experimental social psychology.

Analogue studies

Borkovec (1973) has reviewed nineteen studies of the effects of manipulating expectancy on the outcome of treatment of fears by desensitization. Nine of the studies demonstrated an expectancy effect; ten failed to do so. On the basis of a careful reading of the studies Borkovec suggests:
(1) Manipulated expectancy of improvement (which he terms more precisely 'external demand characteristics for improved overt behaviour') in outcome studies has a greater effect on low-fearful subjects than on high-fearful subjects *within* (his italics) the analogue phobic population.
(2) In the case of highly fearful subjects it will be necessary to reduce effectively the internal physiological components of fear behaviour in order that responses in other systems (verbal, cognitive, motor) may be reduced by treatment components enhanceable by a manipulated expectancy.

If Borkovec's first conclusion is correct then manipulated expectancy is unlikely to enhance the outcome of treatment of *clinical* cases (assuming that they would be high, rather than low, on fear), unless the physiological component is dealt with effectively. However, there are three major criticisms of the studies which were reviewed by Brokovec. First, as pointed out, all of them are analogue studies, using undergraduates as subjects, usually volunteer females with reported animal phobias, none of which had previously needed professional help. Bernstein and Paul (1971) have reviewed in detail the very limited generalizability to clinical practice of small animal analogue studies, carried out on non-complaining females in their late teens and early twenties. The contribution to this book by Cochrane and Sobol (this volume) amply reinforces this point. Second, the studies reviewed by Borkovec (1973) failed to measure the effectiveness of the attitude manipulations, the beliefs of the manipulated subjects concerning the outcome of treatment. This is an elementary but essential feature of an experiment on attitude change. Third, no attempt was made to draw on the extensive research literature concerning attitude change, which demonstrates that the effect of attitude manipulations depends on several components of a persuasive communication. Until these have been employed in the most effective manner according to current research and their effects studied on patients as opposed to analogue subjects, no conclusion can be drawn as to the effect of attitude manipulation on therapeutic outcome. A selective overview follows of some of the major variables and findings in the social psychology literature of attitude formation and change. It is provided as an essential preliminary to any systematic programme of research into the effects of persuasive communications on the clinical outcome of behaviour therapy procedures.

Research findings

In his review of research on attitudes and attitude change, McGuire (1969) concentrated largely on the effects of persuasive verbal communications on the affective (evaluative) component of attitudes. The summary which follows lists only aspects of clinical relevance. McGuire divided the matrix of persuasive communications into five components: the source, the message, the channel, the receiver and the destination. Each component consists of a number of variables, variations in most of which have been shown to influence the evaluative component of an attitude.

Source factors The major components of variation in the source (the speaker or writer) of a message are credibility, attractiveness and power. Under the heading of credibility, perceived competence adds more to the persuasiveness of the message than trustworthiness. Competence means perceived expertise, status and intelligence. Trustworthiness is related to disinterestedness, objectivity and apparent lack of persuasive intent. Attractiveness has three aspects, familiarity, similarity and liking, which tend to be interrelated and to support and strengthen each other. General 'liking' emerges as particularly important.

Power is an important component of source variance, provided that the source of the message is seen as able to administer positive and negative sanctions, concerned about the receiver's compliance, and able to scrutinize compliance effectively.

Message factors McGuire lists three types of persuasive appeal: emotional (*ad hominem*, etc.), rational, relating to the persuasiveness of different types of logical argument (on which there has been little work), and fear appeals. There is an inverted U-shaped function between the level of evoked fear and persuasiveness, although McGuire suggests an increasingly higher level of fear arousal to be optimal as the simplicity and clarity of the persuasive message increases (this is reminiscent of work relating motivation, task difficulty and task performance—Feldman, 1964; Yerkes and Dodson, 1908). Generally, positive reinforcement associated with the communication of the message increases the amount of attitude change (e.g. eating a highly appreciated food while listening to the message). McGuire refers to clinical reports of greater compliance if the patient is left to find the conclusion of an argument for himself, whereas the laboratory evidence is equivocal or even opposite, and suggests the greater motivation of clinical patients as accounting for the discrepancy. He also mentions clinical evidence that the impact of a strong message may be greater given more time for consideration; laboratory studies usually measure message effects rather soon after delivery. This seems an important point worth clinical investigation; does it make a difference to general cooperation to ask a patient to indicate immediately his response to an offer of treatment, following a detailed appraisal of the likely outcome, or to do so after an interval of time, e.g. at the next interview? The possibility of an 'incubation' of the effect of a persuasive message during the intervening period will be discussed again later. Concerning order of presentation, it is generally more effective to give the agreeable information first.

The discrepancy of the message from the receiver's initial position is of obvious clinical relevance, but one ignored in behaviour therapy studies. McGuire states that, while subjects tend to expose themselves selectively to supportive information, the literature is much less clear concerning the selective avoidance of disconfirming information. Selective avoidance seems to occur less when the subject feels very confident. Up to extreme discrepancies the amount of change is a negatively accelerated function of the discrepancy between the receiver's initial position and that of the message, particularly if the message contains arguments for the position rather than simply source endorsements. The credibility of the source is of major importance. Bergin (1962) compared subjects receiving, from two different sources, ratings of their standing on a masculinity–femininity dimension which were discrepant from their ratings of themselves. A 'highly credible' source was seen in an impressively furnished office; a 'low credible' source in a nondescript office. Following the receipt of the discrepant message, subjects rerated themselves. For the high-credibility source, the change in self-rating was greater the greater the discrepancy; the results were opposite for the low-credibility source. To spell out the clinical implications: in order to persuade into therapy a patient who believes success to be unlikely, but whose prognosis is objectively good, a highly credible therapist (source) will be required; the same applies to changing in the desired direction a patient's prior estimate of the amount of his time he will be required to give up. Another possible response to a large discrepancy is to derogate the source, so that he will be disbelieved.

Channel factors Channel factors concern the mode of presentation of the persuasive communication. Heard speech is more persuasive than read speech, as is a message delivered face to face compared to one delivered through an artificial channel, such as a tape-recorder or closed-circuit television.

Receiver factors These are largely concerned with differences between the persons to whom the message is addressed. Mischel (1968) has argued that the search for consistent individual differences in many areas of behaviour has been both misguided and fruitless, behaviour being a function of the current specific stimulus situation and the previous experiences of the individual in similar situations. His review of the areas in which consistency has been sought, including several of relevance to the topic of social influence in the treatment context, found little evidence for the consistency view. However, there may well be relatively stable individual differences in consistency of response in any particular area (Alker, 1972), a view supported by Hartshorne and May's (1928) well-known study of moral behaviour in children. When observed in a large number of situations in which cheating was possible, some children consistently cheated, some never cheated; the majority were inconsistent, sometimes cheating, sometimes not, as the situation varied. In short, the children, several thousand in number, *varied in the consistency of their behaviour*. Conventional measures of personality might well make accurate behavioural predictions for *some* individuals, but inaccurate ones for the majority. It follows that people do not contribute equally to the variance accounted for by general factors of, for example, persuasibility. The implication of this attempt at a resolution between the consistency and the specificity views is that predictions of situational behaviour will be most accurate for some people from a knowledge of *both* personality measures and the specifics of the situation, and for others of the situation alone. We will return later in this chapter to an overview of the personality literature relevant to the patient–therapist interaction in general, as opposed to the specific area of persuasive communications. The above analysis would suggest that, for example, some persons are rather easy to persuade and others very difficult to persuade, largely irrespective of the situational factors (source, message, and so on); for the majority, variations in the situation will be crucial in determining the impact of the message.

McGuire notes the effect of three other individual difference variable: mental age, self-esteem and sex. Persuasibility is largely unrelated to mental age, but there is a suggestion of a small positive relationship where the material is subtle and complex. Persons chronically low in self-esteem tend to be slightly more persuasible and those situationally manipulated by failure experiences to be temporarily low in self-esteem are highly responsive to persuasion. This suggests that individuals temporarily low in self-esteem (such as many of those in psychological distress) will be much more responsive to persuasive communications than those higher in self-esteem.

Females tend, on average, to be more persuasible than males, irrespective of the sex of the source. This suggests the doubtful generalizability to male patients of analogue studies of social influence carried out on females reporting small animal phobias. McGuire speculates that the greater persuasibility of females could be related to more effective message reception due to the greater verbal ability of females, so that the sex difference would be greater for more complex messages. The greatest sex differences in persuasibility are found in early adolescence, when there is also the greatest sex difference in verbal skills.

Destination factors As might be expected from memory studies, there is usually a post-session temporal decay, but with much persistence of the induced change. Attitude change is less long-lasting the higher the credibility and likeability of the source. This apparently contradictory finding suggests that, *providing* change has been induced, a negatively perceived source may be more effective in maintaining persistent change, possibly because maintenance becomes the self-attributed responsibility of the individual himself. A slower rate of decay has been noted for more complex and subtle messages, as well as for those in the initial receipt of which the active participation of the receiver was required.

As well as temporal decrements there have been reports of temporal *increments*, of a greater impact after a delay of time following message reception than immediately afterwards. This is termed by McGuire a 'sleeper effect', a phrase which implies a passive role on the part of the receiver. Feldman and MacCulloch (1971) suggest that there are individual differences in the active cognitive rehearsal of behavioural experiences, which help to account for the success or failure of treatment by aversive techniques; the theory, if correct, would also be relevant to the explanation of psychological therapies in general. Meichenbaum has adopted a not dissimilar approach in training individuals to 'talk to themselves' as a means of developing self-control (e.g. Meichenbaum and Goodman, 1971). Thus, the effect of overt behaviour rehearsal, both within the therapy situation and *in vivo*, may be enhanced by covert (cognitive) rehearsal, a view supported by an analogue study by McFall and Lillesand (1971). The interaction between existing attitudes and a newly received message has been studied by Greenwald (1967). He hypothesized that the persisting effects of a communication are partially accounted for by an individual rehearsing and learning his own cognitive reactions to the communication, and that learning existing content may be more important than learning the new communication *per se*. In Greenwald's study, the subject was required to list his thoughts about the communication ten minutes after it was received. The result was more 'recipient-generated' cognitions than externally oriented ones. Attitude change towards the communicated position was more correlated with the favourability of the recipient-generated conditions than with that of externally generated ones. It follows that therapy studies of persuasive communications should assess existing attitudes as well as the effect of the new communications in arousing them. The final outcome will be an amalgam of the new and old attitudes. The time allowed for rehearsal, whether or not a rehearsal set is induced, and individual differences in habitually comparing new with old information are also likely to be relevant.

Immunization against persuasion McGuire uses the term 'immunization' by which he means preparatory treatments which make the receiver less prone to change his attitude when subsequently exposed to a persuasive communication. The analogy is with the injection of a low level of a toxic agent which immunizes the recipient against the harmful effects of much higher subsequent doses. In the behaviour therapy context, immunization against persuasion might be particularly relevant following the treatment of problem behaviours from which individuals derive pleasure as well as distress, such as sexual deviations and addictions to drugs and alcohol. Preparing them against a renewed exposure to 'persuasive communications'—to recommence deviant behaviours or purchase drugs or alcohol—might markedly reduce the relapse rate in these problem areas. The resistance of an induced change of attitude against a subsequent persuasive communication designed to restore the original attitude is enhanced more by the receipt of weak counter-arguments, together with their refutations, than by the presentation of additional supporting arguments. There is some generalization to associated counter-arguments (e.g. Greenwald, 1967; see above) and such refutational arguments tend to persist. A public commitment to an attitude confers more resistance than a private commitment; the effect is still greater if the individual carries out overt behaviours on the basis of the induced attitude, particularly if he does so for small, rather than large, rewards. The immunization approach may be seen as an additional method of reducing generalization decrement, one of the persisting problems of the behaviour therapies.

The learning approach Conventional learning techniques have also been applied to the formation and change of attitudes. They tend to use rather brief and simple stimuli in contrast to the sometimes long and complex messages of the verbal communication approach reviewed above. Orwell's famous 'four legs good, two legs bad' would be eminently suitable for presentation as discriminative stimuli in an attitude-conditioning experiment. Staats and his colleagues have classically conditioned a wide variety of attitudinal responses (Staats, 1966; Staats and Staats, 1958) and have demonstrated stimulus generalization (Das and Nanda, 1963). Staats (1972) argued for the application of his general 'social behaviourism' approach to behaviour therapy, an assertion supported by reports by Hekmat (1972) and Hekmat and Vanian (1971) of the reduction of spider-avoidance by classically conditioning positive words to the negative verbal representations of the behaviour. A replication with a group of self-referring patients would be of considerable importance (A. Broadhurst, personal communication, 1974, reports a single-case failure). Attitudes have also been regarded as operant responses which may be shaped, like any other behaviours, by the appropriate variation of reinforcement contingencies. The incidence of attitude statements is increased by verbal reinforcement, the effects of which generalize to other attitudes and tasks. The effectiveness of reinforcement is partially a function of the subject's evaluation of the reinforcing agent (Krasner, 1965).

Finally, although little direct work has been carried out, it would be surprising if observational learning were not of major importance in the acquisition and modification of attitudes. There is good evidence (Bandura, 1969) that changes in verbal statements following psychotherapy are largely due to modelling and reinforcement by the therapist. A similar role might be possible for the behaviour therapist, prior to and following the evocation and reinforcement of the behavioural responses appropriate to the problem concerned.

Attitude–behaviour consistency

It has been asserted (Fishbein, 1967) that seventy-five years of research have produced little consistent evidence that attitudes to an object necessarily predict the behaviour towards that object, a view supported by a detailed review by Wicker (1969). It should be noted that many of the behaviours to which attitudes predict poorly are considerably more complex than those related to the behaviours of attending therapy regularly and carrying out instructions faithfully. Moreover, the more specific is an attitude and its concomitant behaviour, the better the prediction. In the present context, this implies that it is more important for the patient to have a favourable attitude to his own therapist, and to regular attendance and faithful adherence to relevant activities in respect of his particular course of therapy, than to hold them towards therapists and therapy in general.

Fishbein (1967) has produced a detailed theoretical analysis of the attitude–behaviour relationship, emphasizing the crucial importance of behavioural intention as an intermediate stage between attitude and behaviour. Both the intention to behave and the performance of the behaviour itself are considered to be a function of the attitudes towards performing the behaviour in a given situation, the norms (both personal and social) governing behaviour in that situation and the motivation to comply with those norms. In the context of a Prisoners' Dilemma Game, Ajzen (1971) has found strong support for Fishbein's analysis. However, Fishbein made little or no reference either to the opportunity to carry out the behaviour or to knowing how to carry it out, both probably of crucial relevance to therapy. The importance of Fishbein's work is that it begins to delineate and fill in the gap between attitude and behaviour and to suggest how to answer the question, 'Will the patient behave in therapy so as to maximize the chances of a successful response after I have told him the prognosis is good?' One of the factors involved in that question may be the valuation placed by the patient on the positive and negative reinforcements administered by the therapist in response to the patient's behaviour in therapy. We have discussed earlier the therapist as a social reinforcer.

Social influence variables and extratherapy behaviour

The active participation of the patient may be increased by providing him with activities to carry out between sessions of therapy or even by replacing the attention of an individual therapist with a prescribed set of tasks, both overt and imaginal. Another variation is for others significant in the patient's environment to act as para-therapists, having received from the therapist detailed instructions as to their role. The likelihood of such extraclinic treatment prescriptions being adhered to may be increased by a public commitment to their tasks by both para-professionals and patients, and further still by drawing up a formal contract. Stuart (1971) has given an operational definition of a behavioural contract as that which 'schedules the exchange of positive reinforcement between persons'. It specifies the reinforcements which individuals will receive in return for emitting, or suppressing, particular responses. Single case reports have appeared on the application of behavioural contracting to several problem areas: eating (Ferster, Nurnberger and Levitt, 1962), adolescent female delinquency (Stuart, 1971), (mild) alcoholism (Miller, 1972) and amphetamine abuse (Boudin, 1972). Entering into a contract is initiated by an 'intention statement' (Kanfer and Karoly, 1972), a term which is probably close to Fishbein's (1967) notion of 'behavioural intention'. It is defined by Kanfer and Karoly as 'a class of verbal operants which specify behavioural outcomes'; e.g. 'I am going to give up tobacco'. It would be useful to investigate the role of social influence variables in affecting both the probability of an intention statement being made and the likelihood that the behaviours laid down will be carried out.

Contracted behaviours may be covert, as well as overt; it is a truism that people spend much of their time emitting 'sub-vocal speech' (Skinner, 1957), an older name for which is 'thinking'. The likelihood of overt behaviours being emitted may be markedly affected by the level of covert (cognitive) rehearsal of those behaviours. The extent to which cognitive rehearsal increases overt behaviour is a heuristic approach which deserves systematic investigation (the work of Meichenbaum in this context has already been referred to). If it receives experimental support, the next step would be to study the role of social influence variables in promoting cognitive rehearsal.

Demand characteristics

Experimenter effects on the outcome of laboratory research have been extensively investigated (Rosenthal, 1966), one of the major concerns being the generalizability of laboratory findings to the field situation. A detailed review by Weber and Cook (1972) concludes: ' ... the roles subjects adopt can threaten both the interpretation of the independent variable and the external validity of the experiments (p. 291).' They identify as a crucial problem that caused by subjects who adopt the 'apprehensive role', one which is particularly threatening to valid causal inferences (i.e. from the laboratory to real life). The notion of 'evaluation apprehension' (developed by Weber and Cook into the apprehensive role) is due largely to Rosenberg (1965), who postulated that subjects are apprehensive about how they will be evaluated, as well as being motivated to present themselves favourably to experts on human behaviour, such as psychologists. Because their awareness of the problem under study will have been enhanced and made more salient by selection as subjects, participants in analogue studies of behaviour therapy may be particularly likely to adopt the role of the apprehensive subject. Thus, they may be even more responsive to cues from the experimenter about how they 'should' respond than subjects participating in studies in which they are less personally involved. This speculation is supported by a study by Miller and Bernstein (1972) which used an own-control design to test the effects of demand characteristics on the avoidance responses of volunteer female undergraduates self-described as fearful of enclosed spaces. Subjects spent two periods, each of ten minutes, in an enclosed space following one of two different sets of instruction. The first set stated they could leave when they felt uncomfortable, the second required them to stay the full ten minutes. Under 'high demand' subjects stayed significantly longer than under 'low demand'. Miller and Bernstein suggest that these results have considerable implications for the use as dependent measures of outcome of behavioural avoidance tests, which they consider to be complex social situations. Bernstein (personal communication, 1973) is engaged in a broad programme of research into the demand characteristics involved in analogue studies, the results of which will be of considerable relevance to the generalizability of analogue findings to the clinic.

Personality variables

Several dimensions of current interest to personality researchers may interact with the effects of situationally manipulated social influence variables on the outcome of behaviour therapy techniques. If they prove to do so, the personality scale scores of the influencing individual (therapist or experimenter) and of the individual subjected to the influence attempt (patient or subject) will *both* be relevant. Three dimensions of personality are of interest: field dependence—independence (Witkin, Goodenough and Karp, 1965), locus of control (Rotter, 1966) and Machiavellianism (Christie and Geis, 1970). A considerable body of research exists on all three; space considerations allow only brief outlines.

Field dependence–independence

Individuals are considered to display stable styles of cognitive functioning which cut across diverse psychological areas. In the field-dependent style, perception and cognition are strongly dominated by the overall organization of the field; in the field-independent style, parts of the field are experienced as separate from the background. A number of perceptual tasks are used to assign persons to a position on the hypothesized dimension. Witkin, Goodenough and Karp (1965) summarize evidence to the effect that the psychological problems experienced by field dependents are likely to include alcoholism, psychosomatic conditions and the 'hysterias', and those of field independents to include paranoid delusions and obsessional behaviour. Witkin suggests that field-dependent persons are more likely to accept the social influence attempts of therapists and to report early improvement, but are also more likely to fail to maintain that improvement, the opposite being true of field independents (slower improvement, but better maintenance of it). Pollack and Kiev (1963) report that highly field-independent psychiatrists favoured a directive approach to patients, the more field-dependent ones favouring a more 'relationship'-oriented approach (cited by Witkin, Goodenough and Karp, 1965, p. 330).

Locus of control

As a general principle, internal control refers to the perception of environmental events, whether positive or negative, as being a consequence of one's own actions and therefore under personal control; external control refers to the perception of events as unrelated to one's own behaviour. A questionnaire (Rotter, 1966) is used to select groups differing in perceived locus of control. A large number of studies have been reviewed by Lefcourt (1966). Psychological distress appears to increase self-perceived externality of control, suggesting an increased responsiveness to social influence attempts. Biondo and MacDonald (1971) reported data suggesting that internals will strongly resist perceived influence attempts, particularly resenting those which the influencing agent has unsuccessfully attempted to disguise. However, it seems that internals attend better to instructional cues, thereby partially compensating for their markedly lesser responsiveness to influence attempts. Felton (1971) studied the effect of one individual on the extent to which another will shift his ranking of a set of photographs (Rosenthal, 1963). The greatest amount of shift was achieved by the combination of an 'internal' influencing agent (termed the 'experimenter') and an 'external' recipient of influence (the 'subject'); the opposite combination achieved the least amount of shift. This further supports the importance of the *interaction* of patient–therapist/experimenter–subject personality attributes in determining the outcome of the situational manipulation of social influence variables.

Machiavellianism

This is an area of personality research which is explicitly concerned with the effectiveness of manipulation of others as a function of the *relative* scores of the participants on the Machiavellianism scale. As described by Christie and Geis (1970), the high-Mach person displays a relative lack of concern with conventional morality, a lack of gross psychopathology and a low ideological commitment. They summarize the main results of a number of studies as indicating that 'high Machs manipulate more . . . are persuaded less . . . and persuade others more', the opposite being true for low Machs. These differences emerged most clearly in experimental situations characterized by face-to-face interaction, latitude for improvization and the arousing of irrelevant affect (all of which seem to apply to the clinical situation). English (1972) has repeated the Felton study, mentioned above in the context of locus of control, but using high- and low-Mach pairs of experimenters and subjects, and obtained results in the direction expected. An interesting finding concerns the relationship between the Mach scores of medical students and their intended area of specialization. In all eleven medical schools surveyed (Christie and Geis, 1970), intending psychiatrists obtained the highest scores (i.e. they were the most describable as 'high Machs'). No data have been reported on trainee clinical psychologists.

Little work has been carried out on the correlations between the personality measures reviewed above, although Daniels, cited by Christie and Geis (1970), reported that high Machs also tended to be internals on the locus of control measure. Further correlational studies would be of value. Moreover, personality variables may be multidimensional rather than unidimensional and of relevance only to certain situations. (The strength of the Machiavellianism research is that those situations have been spelled out.) It is possible that high correlations will be found between the above measures and the pervasive dimensions of introversion–extraversion and neuroticism–stability. Finally, it is important to reiterate that dispositional (personality) scores are likely to be of more predictive value for extreme scorers than for moderate scorers.

The time span of effect of social influence variables

A systematic programme of research into the relevance for the behaviour therapies of the situational and personality determinants of social influence effects must have a *temporal dimension*. Campbell (1963) suggests as a central observation in the field of attitudes that 'a person retains a residue of experience to guide, bias or otherwise influence later behavior (p. 94)'. Laboratory studies tend to regard the experimental subject as if he were a *tabula rasa*, responsive only to the stimuli employed in the current experiment, and have frequently used stimuli such as nonsense syllables, deliberately chosen so as to minimize the instigating effects of previous associations. Campbell reminds us that the real world is simply not like that: clinical patients will undoubtedly have encountered one variety or other of helping agents—usually physicians or nurses; and they may have also encountered psychiatrists, or psychologists, personally, through the description of others or through the communication media. They will bring with them into therapy expectations of all kinds which will interact with the complex of social stimuli, programmed and unprogrammed, provided by the therapist (see Greenwald, 1967, referred to earlier). In his turn, the therapist will have encountered many other patients; from his previous experience he will derive expectations against which he will match the information provided by his impression of the new patient. Next, the *perceived* responses each displays to the other will affect their mutual evaluation, and will do so, session by session, as therapy progresses. It will not be a simple matter to devise and carry out research techniques which will both do justice to the complex situation outlined above and provide controlled and repeatable findings. Yet if social influence research is to benefit the behaviour therapies, the temporal dimension will need to be taken fully into account.

A COGNITIVE DISSONANCE-BASED THEORY OF BEHAVIOUR IN THE CLINICAL SITUATION

The previous section of this chapter discussed the relevance to behaviour therapy procedures of social influence variables, relating to situations, to persons and to the interaction between them. It was argued that such variables may exert important *facilitating* effects on both the efficiency and efficacy of the behaviour therapies, and some of the ways were sketched in which the findings of experimental social psychology might contribute to a systematic programme of research into the general effects of social influence variables in behaviour therapy.

This section draws on another area of experimental social psychology, cognitive dissonance studies, to develop a theory concerning the behaviour of helping agents which is applicable to all psychological therapies, including both the behaviour—and psycho-therapies, but more so to the former because of their greater demonstrated effectiveness. In general, it will be proposed that in order first to escape and later to avoid the cognitive dissonance which results from the discrepancy between helping attempts which are intended to be successful, and their outcomes, which not infrequently are those of failure, therapists develop strategies of behaviour which *reduce* the potential efficacy of available treatment techniques.

Cognitive dissonance theory

No attempt will be made to give a comprehensive review of the findings of research influenced by dissonance theory (see, for example, Brehm and Cohen, 1962; Zimbardo, 1969) or of the critical commentaries that have been produced (e.g. Chapanis and Chapanis, 1964). Briefly, dissonance theory, formulated by Festinger (1957), is concerned with the assertion that persons seek consistency, between two attitudes or two behaviours in the same related area, or between an attitude and its behavioural concomitant. Dissonance, the consequence of inconsistency, has the theoretical status of an aversive stimulus. The arousal of dissonance is considered to lead to attempts at dissonance-reduction, several mechanisms being used, usually involving attitude change rather than behaviour change. Provided that the dissonance-reduction mechanisms are successful in reducing the dissonance experienced, what may appear to an observer to be a continued inconsistency will be acceptable to the individual concerned.

Dissonance theory and learning theory

To interpret the findings of dissonance research within a learning framework, various attempts have been made, that of Bem (1967) being of particular interest. Bem argues that dissonance phenomena relate to self-descriptive statements of attitudinal beliefs. Self-perception is a special case of interpersonal perception, enabling the individual to respond both to his own behaviour and to the variables controlling it. Members of the social community teach individuals the correct responses to impinging verbal stimuli. An observer can infer from the overt behaviour of the subject the external stimulus conditions as well as the private stimuli accompanying the external behaviour of the subject. It follows, according to Bem, that people act *as if* they were external observers, inferring their attitudes from their own behaviour, as in the phrase: 'I must like cheese, I eat so much of it'.

Bem was able to carry out successful 'interpersonal replications' (by using observers) of three major dissonance phenomena—forced compliance, free choice and exposure to discrepant information—and to interpret the results within his self-perception framework. Nevertheless, as McLaughlin (1971) points out, Bem's avowed Skinnerian framework has a considerable cognitive flavour: 'judgements are made' and 'inner states are inferred by an observer'. Moreover, the latter 'duplicates the phenomenology of the subjects in the experiment'. The observers in Bem's experiments used inferences about their *own subjective experiences*, in response to the external behaviour of the observed subject, to make inferences about the subjective experiences of the subject. The final arbiter of the accuracy of the matching is thus the cognitive phenomena experienced by the observer which he, as it were, reports to himself. While Bem's approach gives a satisfactory behavioural account of the *development* of cognitive phenomena—external validation (reinforcement) by the social community being required for individuals to label their own cognitive experiences—once such labelling has occurred, further social confirmation is of little value. If it is confirmatory, as in the Bem studies, it is superfluous; if disconfirmatory, it only muddies the issue. The individual then has to choose between his own subjective experience and that reported by others. Depending on both the situation and relevant individual differences, some subjects will 'yield' and conform, while others will follow the evidence of their own senses (Asch, 1952). It follows that in order to index 'cognitive' phenomena we have no recourse at the present time other than to self-report, using some form of attitudinal measure. This should not disturb behaviour therapists unduly. The operations carried out during desensitization depend largely on the ongoing self-reports of the patient, and the various fear schedules used before, during and after therapy, also depend on self-report. Provided that the stimuli used to elicit self-reports are standard in form, and administration and scoring are independent of the scorer, the results of self-report measures may be treated with a fair degree of confidence. Finally, if rigorous behaviourists are unhappy (another cognitive term!) with the term 'cognitive dissonance', they may prefer 'a verbal statement concerning a subjective experience of psychological discomfort'.

Antecedent conditions and the arousal of dissonance

Variations in several antecedent conditions have been shown to influence the amount of attitudinal change following the occurrence of a behavioural response discrepant with previous behaviour. Attitude change is taken to indicate the arousal of varying levels of dissonance; the greater the change of attitude, the greater the dissonance aroused. The antecedent conditions for high-dissonance arousal include small incentives, minimal threat, low justification, high perceived freedom of choice, high effort and high self-esteem of the influenced individual (McLaughlin, 1971). The methods by which dissonance is reduced are varied, but all tend to involve the denial of some aspect of the physical situation or the derogation of the other person in a two-person situation.

Dissonance-based research with clinical implications

Effort

Lewis (1965) reviewed studies mainly carried out with children and concluded that increased effort enhanced the value of stimuli associated with the expenditure of effort, a generalization which accords well with dissonance theory, as does the associated finding that when the rewards are judged insufficient for the effort expended, the activity itself becomes more highly regarded. In the clinical context, these two findings would suggest that for some clinicians the disappointment at working within a problem area for which there are no current solutions may be assuaged by enhancing the value of such activities as careful history-taking or studying the patient's behaviours for research purposes.

Goldstein, Heller and Sechrest (1966) suggested that the degree of effort required to secure entrance to a therapy group would positively enhance the subsequent attractions of membership, once this was attained, and hence the reward of approval by other members of the group and their effectiveness as social reinforcers. The studies on which they based this view included one by Aronson and Mills (1959), which showed that subjects justified to themselves the unpleasantness of experiences necessary to secure group membership by evaluating the group more highly and adhering more closely to its norms. Goldstein and Simonson (1971) report the importance of 'effort consolidation'. The attraction of the therapist was enhanced more when patients returned after their initial interview, to hear and discuss a tape-recording of it, than when they returned to hear an irrelevant tape. The effect of the latter on attraction was greater than no post-interview visit.

The possible enhancement of treatment efficacy by increased effort lies behind several references to the therapeutic value of fee-paying for psychotherapy. For example, Davids (1964) argues that, if the patient is charged nothing for what he believes to be worth nothing, there would be no dissonance and hence no attitude change in response to therapy. If he paid nothing for what he believed to be worth something, dissonance would be aroused but would be reduced in the wrong direction—by devaluing the therapy—so that again no change would occur. When a fee is charged, the patient may expect substantial and immediate therapeutic gain. If so, and improvement manifestly fails to occur quickly, the patient will drop out. However, if the patient both believes that what is expensive must be good and is prepared to wait for benefits to accrue, he will both try hard for therapeutic gain and remain in therapy.

Davids considers that the poor and the rich both make little therapeutic gain, the former because they do not pay, the latter because the money involved is an unimportant fraction of their income; in both cases, effort is low. It follows that the greatest gains should be made by those intermediate in economic status; they can and do pay, the money involved is a noticeable proportion of their income and, therefore, they make more effort. The relevance of fee-paying to the effort variable is likely to be greater in a society in which the quality of personal care services is generally considered to be higher when they are provided by the private enterprise, rather than by the public service, section of the economy. A study within the behaviour therapy context of fee-paying and other effort variables would be of interest, and may have important practical consequences.

Interview behaviour

Walster and Presthold (1966) had two groups of social work trainees listen to the case histories of two clients being discussed by experienced social workers, and then asked them to evaluate each client accurately. The first group was told that the taped discussion was misleading and would lead them to be overgenerous in their evaluations. The second group was not warned. The manipulation was effective in influencing the content of the trainees' reports. Half of each group then made a 'commitment' to the views expressed by signing their evaluations and then reading them to a psychiatrist. The other half simply handed in their evaluations. All subjects heard a second taped discussion, which contradicted the first, following which they made their final evaluation. 'Committed' subjects tended to adhere to their original evaluation. 'Uncommitted' subjects were much more likely to change their minds. This study suggests the importance of delaying decisions about the nature of a presenting problem and of its prognosis, until all the information is available, as well as of not making public any early 'snap' judgements.

Aggression and helping

At first sight, studies of altruism and aggression, carried out in laboratories within the framework of dissonance theory, seem very far from the clinic. It will be argued that this is not the case. A typical situation is one in which one subject is apparently able to inflict electric shocks (usually simulated) on another subject. The effects of a wide range of antecedent manipulations have been studied (Krebs, 1970; Macaulay and Berkowitz, 1970). The responses of the aggressing subject to the 'distress' displayed by the victim on being shocked have included denying the severity of his distress and derogating the victim, both being greater in intensity the greater the responsibility assigned to the subject for the victim's fate (Lerner and Mathews, 1967; Lerner and Simmons, 1966).

Berscheid and Walster (1969) cite evidence to suggest that restitution may be made to a victim, but only if the restitution available is neither too much nor too little but exactly appropriate. Public commitment to the course of action adopted reduces the likelihood of restitution (e.g. admitting the error). Restitution may be made to the next person encountered in the same situation (Berscheid, Boye and Darley, 1968). However, if the situation is perceived as one of relative equity between the participants, then aggression may be displayed in the next encounter, particularly if the other person shares features, even irrelevant ones, with the previously frustrating partner. The subjects of an ingenious study by Berkowitz (1968) were prevented from winning in a competitive game by the apparent incompetence of their partners. They attributed more unfavourable characteristics to an innocent bystander and, given the opportunity, inflicted more shocks on him if he happened to possess the same first name as the frustrating partner than if he had a neutral name. Interviewers tend to attribute to a new interviewee personality features and expected behaviours on the basis of a superficial similarity to previously encountered interviewees (Vernon, 1964). It may be speculated that clinicians may displace the aggressive response elicited by a failing (and hence frustrating) patient on to another patient similar in some way to the first. An aversion to taking on any more of the particular type of clinical problem, or to making serious efforts with such a type, may thus develop.

The above studies exemplify the cognitive consequences of aggressing against a dependent victim, the interest being in the frequent use of derogation and denial as means of reducing the dissonance aroused by behaviours which are inconsistent with the social norm of not aggressing. The opposite dissonance-reducing mechanism, *self*-blame, is considered by Berscheid and Walster (1969) as likely to be an unusual reaction, found only in the clinical literature. However, there is evidence that self-blame can be elicited in the laboratory, given the appropriate antecedent conditions. Feldman (1970) has described a laboratory arrangement adapted from the cooperative avoidance situation studied in monkeys by Miller, Banks and Ogawa (1963) in which one subject is dependent on the help afforded by another. Qualitative assessments of the 'helper's' attitude to the 'victim' indicated that a quantitative study would be of value. A second study, by Feldman and Callister (1971), assessed the different mechanisms of dissonance-reduction which were resorted to as a function of the type of justification available for behaviours discrepant with the social norm of helping. In tackling this question, they made their starting point Zimbardo's (1969) extension of dissonance theory. According to Zimbardo, whether people blame themselves or blame external causes for their own discrepant behaviours depends on the availability of external justification for such behaviour and the degree to which they were free to choose the discrepant behaviour or were not free to do so. A combination of high freedom of choice and low external justification was predicted to be the antecedent condition most likely to result in self-derogation rather than that of the other person or an outside authority, etc., when a behaviour discrepant with accepted social norms has both been carried out and cannot be denied because it was on public display.

The experimental arrangements used were as follows. The simulated facial expressions of relief and distress of a display (D) subject, a trainee actor, were watched on close-circuit television by observer (O) subjects, all of whom were non-psychology undergraduates. The latter were offered £1 ($2.40) for participating in 'a study of cooperative behaviour'. The situation was set up so that the actor always took the D role, although it appeared to O that he was equally likely to do so. The observer subject was told that a light signal, visible only to D, would indicate to D that he would receive an electric shock (previously demonstrated to O), unless O operated a response lever to enable D to avoid shock, and did so within eight seconds of the light coming on. Half of the O subjects (termed high-loss = high external justification) were told that they would lose five pence (5 p ≃ 12 cents) each time they enabled D to avoid the shock. The other half (low-loss = low external justification) were told that they would lose one penny (1p) each time. Both groups were told that there would be twenty trials. In this context, 'external justification' meant the availability of an 'external' reason—significant monetary loss—for departing from the assumed social norm of helping a person in distress. During the whole of the twenty trials O had a clear head-and-shoulders view of D. The changes in facial expression of the latter left no doubt that the performance, or the omission, of an avoidance response by O had direct, and either pleasant or unpleasant, consequences for D.

A large number of behavioural, cognitive and personality measures were taken. The results of interest at present concern the correlations between the evaluative ratings of the D and O subjects (made by the latter before the justification variable was manipulated, and again at the end of the twenty trials) and two behavioural measures: the number of trials on which O avoided and the latency of the response on those trials. The results indicated that high-loss subjects who avoided infrequently, or slowly, or both, evaluated D *worse* after the session than prior to the session, but left unchanged their self-evaluation. In contrast, infrequently helping low-loss subjects tended to evaluate *themselves worse* and left their evaluations of D unchanged. The corollaries of these results also occurred: frequently helping high-loss subjects evaluated D *better* and left themselves unchanged; frequently helping low-loss subjects tended to evaluate *themselves better* and left D unchanged. It should be noted that the changes in the evaluation of the self and of the other person in this experiment took place *after* the behaviour of helping or failing to help.

The results, which were predicted from Zimbardo's (1969) explication of the justification concept, indicated different methods of achieving dissonance-reduction for the two groups. High external justification (high-loss) subjects, who helped infrequently, dealt with the dissonance between the social norm of helping and their own behaviour by devaluing the other person. Those who helped frequently increased the consonance between helping and evaluation. Self-evaluations were unaffected because behaviour took place in a context in which the responsibility for one's behaviour could be attributed to an external source—the loss of a sum of money which was appreciable to undergraduates at that time. In the case of the low justification subjects (the low-loss group), responsibility rested squarely on the self, failure to meet socially accepted standards led to self-derogation and meeting those standards improved further the evaluation of the self. When external justification for discrepant behaviour is low, the self-administered cognitive rewards for socially approved behaviour are high, but so are the self-administered cognitive punishments for failing to display socially approved behaviour.

Dissonance research and the clinical situation

In order to generalize readily from the laboratory study described above to the clinic, we have to assume that the roles of potential helper (observer) and actual victim (display) are relatively parallel with those of therapist and patient. In the laboratory situation, the interest lies in the dissonance (inconsistency) between the assumed social norm of helping and the actual behaviour of not helping; in the clinical setting, in which a treatment attempt has failed, the inconsistency is between the *apparently intended* and the *actual* outcomes of the attempt. The central question is: '*How do clinicians cope with the cognitive consequences of helping attempts which fail?*' (It is hardly necessary to remind ourselves that not every problem behaviour is successfully treated.) The question broadens into: 'What are the significant cognitive features of the helping situation, from the points of view of both therapist and patient, and how can the theory of cognitive dissonance be used to predict and account for them?' The discussion which follows will be centred largely on the failure of therapeutic efforts (leading to cognitive dissonance) rather than on success (leading to consonance).

The laboratory–clinic analogy just outlined enables us to extend dissonance theory into an area into which it has not hitherto been employed, with the exception of a brief paper by Innes (1972, see later). If we can accept that the extension is possible, it will follow, as we argue below, that the consequences of cognitive dissonance in the clinic will be considerably greater than in the laboratory, so that the cognitive phenomena demonstrated in the laboratory are likely to exert much more powerful effects when they occur in the clinic.

Following his discrepant behaviour, the experimental subject may never again see either the victim or the observing experimenter. The therapist may encounter again the patient with whom treatment has failed and colleagues who are aware of both his intention to treat successfully and his failure to do so. The therapist is well aware that he is being observed by others or, at least, that observation is possible.

A second factor which suggests that dissonance phenomena will be more powerful in the clinic relates to the temporal dimension. Laboratory subjects participate in a single study; therapists repeat many scores, even hundreds, of times their experience of the sequence of helping-attempt and outcome. They are thus enabled to develop *long-term strategies* for coping with cognitive dissonance.

The speculative theory which follows was set out in a brief and preliminary form by Feldman (1971). It covers both the short- and the long-term aspects of dissonance-arousal and -reduction following therapeutic failure. It has echoes of instrumental avoidance learning, in which escape trials are followed by trials on which the subject *anticipates* and *avoids* the noxious stimulus. I shall begin with the antecedent conditions which are most likely to arouse high dissonance in therapists, following therapeutic failure, and proceed to the various mechanisms which might be resorted to in order to reduce dissonance. Next, I shall set out the therapist behaviours which enable dissonance to be avoided altogether, rather than the more painful process of escape. This will lead to a consideration of the general strategies which therapists might adopt in structuring their long-term professional role vis-a-vis patients. The theory is offered as a heuristic set of speculations which are readily testable. Its major theme is that, because of their painful experience of the dissonance which occurs in instances of therapeutic failure, between intention (a successful result of therapy) and outcome (an unsuccessful result), many therapists will be found to behave towards many patients in ways which reduce the potential effectiveness of their therapeutic techniques when applied to these patients.

A theory of behaviour in the clinical situation

Therapist behaviour

1. *High-effort conditions* The antecedent conditions which dissonance theory suggests would lead to the maximum output of effort by therapists in the implementation of therapeutic techniques include the following: (a) a public commitment to the technique chosen and explicit freedom of choice in selecting it, (b) a public statement of the worthiness of the patient to receive help and of the high likelihood of the treatment being successful and (c) the planned and systematic use of the social influence procedures discussed earlier. They would all be expected to enhance the efficacy and the efficiency of techniques of demonstrated effectiveness. Unfortunately, such high-effort conditions are also the antecedent conditions for the maximum arousal of cognitive dissonance, following the failure of a helping attempt. The most painful method of reducing dissonance, possibly leading to a frank depression of mood, is to blame oneself; it is one which most therapists would not adopt, particularly if other mechanisms for dissonance-reduction were available. Such 'external justifications' for the failure of the helping attempt include the following: attributing to a superior the selection of the helping technique used and hence responsibility for its failure; seeking social support from one's colleagues or the published literature 'for having done the best I possibly could under the circumstances'; denying the severity of the problem treated ('there wasn't much wrong with him anyway'); denying the possibility of any method solving the problem; and denying the worthiness of the patient to receive either effective help or a substantial investment of therapist time ('he was a bit of a psychopath

anyway'). A further alternative, discussed above under the heading of the experimenter expectancy effect (Rosenthal, 1966), is to deny that the treatment did fail completely, perhaps even to the extent of asserting a marked degree of success; this is assisted by using outcome criteria which are so vague that failure may be misrepresented as success. Innes (1972) has suggested that aversion therapists may reduce the dissonance they experience because they inflict painful electric shocks on patients (discrepant with social norms of not injuring others) by exaggerating the degree of success obtained in treatment. He suggests independent assessment of treatment outcomes by persons other than the therapist. Innes' point is well taken, but both the possibility of therapist exaggeration and the need for objective assessment apply to *all* therapies and not only to the aversive techniques. Feifel and Eels (1963) reported statistically significant differences between therapist's and patient's estimations of the benefits obtained from psychotherapy, both for symptom relief and social behaviours, those of the therapist being more optimistic. A final method of dissonance-reduction, which may particularly appeal to the more research-oriented among behaviour therapists, is to admit failure but to extol the advance of knowledge gained even from failure. Knowledge is indeed advanced by failure, but only if all patients who seek help are accepted for treatment and full information is recorded throughout treatment so that unsuccessful outcomes may be used to improve future attempts.

2. *Low-effort conditions* In order to avoid having to deal with high levels of dissonance-reduction after failure, therapists may adopt behaviours which are the opposite of those associated with high effort: no public commitment to the technique; attributing to others the choice of technique; publicly evaluating the patient as an unworthy candidate for help; and stating publicly the low probability of treatment being successful. Because failure under low-effort conditions arouses less dissonance, the reduction of dissonance following failure will be considerably easier and less painful than under high-effort conditions. Moreover, if justifications for possible failure are stated beforehand, much less 'face' is lost. The therapist may even gain prestige as an accurate prophet.

An even more effective method is to structure the situation so that dissonance is *avoided* in advance, by one or both of two methods.

3. *Anticipatory avoidance of dissonance* Festinger (1957) states:

Under certain circumstances there are ... strong and important tendencies ... to avoid an increase of dissonance ... or to avoid the occurrence of dissonance altogether. [Festinger cites the example of avoiding a discussion with someone who might agree with the cognitive element one is trying to change.]
Past experience may lead a person to fear, and hence avoid, the initial occurrence of dissonance .... The fear of dissonance would lead to a reluctance to take action ... or to commit oneself .... Where decision and action cannot be indefinitely delayed, the taking of action may be accompanied by a cognitive negation of the action (e.g. a

person who buys a new car, then announces he did the wrong thing). . . . Personality differences with respect to the fear of dissonance, and the effectiveness of dissonance reduction are important in determining whether such avoidance of dissonance is likely to occur (pp. 29–31).

Festinger's theoretical formulations can be applied to the clinical context. It is evident that a particularly effective method of avoidance is to structure the therapeutic situation so that dissonance is avoided in advance. The strategies of dissonance-avoidance include a careful selection of patients, and either not assessing outcome or (a more subtle version) setting outcome criteria which are so vague they can be interpreted as the therapist wishes.

A review by Garfield (1971) makes it clear that psychotherapists turn away a great many prospective patients. The more sophisticated an agency or a therapeutic method and the more highly qualified its workers, the more highly selected and higher in status the population it serves. Moreover, Garfield states, the higher the status of an agency, the less flexible are its methods of operation and the greater the tendency to label clients as unsuitable or immature. A considerable proportion of patients, in some reports the majority, had left treatment by the eighth interview, the average length of stay being greater for middle-class persons. 'Verbal, intelligent, introspective, interested and educated clients with relatively little disturbance are eagerly sought after by therapists (Garfield, 1971, p. 293)', particularly by the more prestigious clinics and therapists.

The furore which greeted Eysenck's well-known critique (1952) of the ability of psychotherapy to exceed the base rate of improvement without treatment is too well known to need much documenting here. Several critics, surveyed by Astin (1961), asserted that the efficacy of psychotherapy was beyond doubt. Therefore, Eysenck was wrong *ipso facto*. Others argued, as did Freud (1922) many years earlier, that the clinician's own estimate of his therapy was to be preferred to that of the controlled experiment:

> Friends of analysis have advised us to counterbalance a collection of failures by drawing up a statistical enumeration of successes. I have not taken up this suggestion either. I brought forward the argument that statistics would be valueless if the units collated were not alike, and the cases which had been treated were, in fact, not equivalent in many respects. Further, the period of time that would be reviewed was too short for one to be able to judge of the permanence of the cures; and in many cases it would be impossible to give any account (p. 175).

A variation of the above is to assert that the only test of efficacy is 'actual clinical involvement'. It is suggested the variables are too 'subtle' to be measured, so that subjective experience, as therapist, of the therapy under consideration is the only true guide. Inevitably, this confuses the roles of advocate and judge. The most effective strategy of all, from the point of view of ensuring dissonance-avoidance, is to argue that the assessment of outcome, particularly by follow-up some time after treatment, is actually *undesirable*, representing an intrusion into privacy. This turns what would be a vice for the scientist into a virtue for the 'humanist'.

It is to be hoped that behaviour therapy does not suffer from such maladies, from which, to be fair, psychotherapy has made vigorous attempts to recover (see the review of a considerable number of clinical outcome studies by Bergin, 1971). Yet the literature of behaviour therapy contains rather few controlled clinical trials, as opposed to analogue studies of small animal phobias of American female undergraduates, uncontrolled clinical series and single case reports.

As yet, there are no published reports of how the average clinical behaviour therapist (i.e. outside university and other research clinics) operates with respect to patient selection. Behaviourist critics have frequently suggested that psychotherapists select their patients for reporting in journals. How true is this of behaviour therapists? How likely are editors to publish reports of treatment failures submitted to them? A bibliography of the behaviour therapy literature published between 1950 and 1969 (Morrow, 1971) stated as one of its explicit criteria for inclusion ' . . . (papers which) describe the successful modification of target behaviours in the desired direction', and added ' . . . (these) criteria exclude . . . unsuccessful attempts at modification (p. 2)'.

4. *Therapist strategies* It will be evident from the above that the set of therapist behaviours referred to as high-effort carry a high pay-off for both therapist and patient (a high probability of a successful outcome of treatment) but also a high risk to the therapist, in that treatment failure means the painful process of dissonance-reduction. The low-effort set of behaviours is characterized by a lower pay-off for both but also a lower risk to the therapist (post-failure dissonance-reduction is easier because less dissonance is aroused). The strategy which may be most attractive to clinicians consists of a combination of the two: adopt the former with patients judged highly likely to respond well (hence select carefully) and the latter with patients judged unlikely to do so. As a back-up for both, use vague criteria of outcome or avoid measuring outcome at all. Both strategies enable the anticipatory avoidance of the dissonance which follows failure despite high effort.

An early example of the combined approach, possibly only applicable to physical illness, is cited by Ullmann and Krasner (1969, p. 78): 'On departing, the physician promises the patient he shall recover; to those who are about the sickbed, however, he must affirm that the patient is very ill; if the patient recovers the physician's reputation will be enhanced; should he die, the physician can state that the outcome was as he predicted (Packard, in Harington, 1922, pp. 18–20, ascribed to Archimatheus of Salerno *ca.* 1100)'.

Which strategy is more likely to be adopted in any particular professional setting? As an initial speculation, it is suggested that the high-effort strategy will be adopted by psychologists carrying out research into treatment, or by newcomers to institutions in which a spectacular and predicted success would enhance the prestige of clinical psychology. The low-effort strategy will be adopted by those working in institutional settings, the *mores* of which they do not seek to change. Those in private practice may be inclined to adopt the combined approach, particularly when they are well established and can select their patients as they wish.

Provided that the matching of strategies and patients is accurate, the combined approach might have much to commend itself; in practice it seems likely that therapists will play safe, both by rejecting would-be patients who might have responded well to high-effort therapy and by adopting a low-effort strategy for patients who might well have responded successfully if treated within the context of high-effort conditions.

5. *Decision-taking* I have dealt so far with the predicted, overt behaviours of therapists aiming to achieve the most pleasurable, or at any rate the least distressing, cognitive outcomes for themselves. I have suggested that in order to achieve this goal therapists may behave towards some patients in ways which result in less than the optimum outcome of therapy. Dissonance theory suggests a number of mechanisms which therapists can use in order to avoid being confronted with the clear and inescapable evidence of inadequate therapeutic effort, and I have detailed some of these above. Thus, therapists can 'have their cake and eat it'; less than optimal therapeutic efficacy and efficiency can be combined with a general sense of high professional self-esteem. In short, there is a range of cognitive mechanisms which enable therapists to justify to themselves behaviours which benefit them rather than their patients.

The process of justification is made easier if discrepant and, hence, inconvenient information may be *avoided*. This is exactly what happens, according to dissonance theory, following any decision. Dissonance is assumed to arise following all decisions due to 'the undischarged tension of the rejected alternative (Festinger, 1957)'. Dissonance-reduction is achieved in several ways, including enhancing the attractiveness of the chosen alternative and derogating that of the non-chosen alternative. It follows that, in order to make easier both the process of decision-taking and the reduction of post-decision dissonance, there will be selective self-exposure to the information on which the decision is based, a process enhanced by the cumulative effects of successive decisions in the same area of behaviour. The implications for therapist behaviour are clear. If it has been decided not to treat a particular patient, further information supportive of that decision will be welcomed, contrary information will not. The same selective bias will be applied to the case of a patient accepted for therapy. Information supportive of the choice of therapy and of the predicted outcome is more likely to be attended to than information suggesting that the wrong decision was made or that the prognosis was inaccurate. Finally, at the stage of assessment of outcome, the therapist will engage in selective self-exposure to information, being attentive to information confirming that the predicted outcome did, in fact, occur and tending to ignore information indicating a different outcome. The more habitual the use of selective exposure in the past and the weaker the attempts made by colleagues, subordinates, etc., to direct the therapist's attention to contrary information, the more likely is it that the therapist will engage in selective self-exposure on any given new occasion. It follows also that the therapists most likely to behave in this way include those working single-handed and those too senior for subordinates to annoy (by pointing out inconvenient facts) without great risk.

6. *Patient behaviour*   We can apply dissonance theory to the behaviour of patients, as well as to that of therapists. Patients would be expected to use both self-justificatory mechanisms and selective exposure to supportive information. Once a decision *not* to seek help has been made, the (subjectively experienced) distress will be eased and the problems attendant on seeking help will be enhanced. In everyday terms, 'putting up with it' becomes easier.

Conversely, a decision to seek help will be buttressed by evaluating the distress as even more severe and the likelihood of successful treatment as more favourable. The help-seeking patient, therefore, will be more amenable to the use of social influence procedures to enhance systematic treatment techniques. It would be expected that many patients will enhance the influence of the 'therapist effect' on the overestimation of the success of therapy, discussed above, by a 'patient effect', the *direction* of the effect being the same.

Finally, some patients will avoid the disappointment of an unsuccessful response to treatment by cooperating with the therapist in not assessing outcome, or at least in postponing the day when such an assessment has to be made.

The effect of individual differences in personality

It is an implicit assumption of cognitive dissonance theory that *all* persons both experience dissonance when inconsistencies exist and seek consistency. A detailed examination of the implication for social psychology research of individual variations, both in the experience of inconsistency and in the use of dissonance-reduction mechanisms, is well beyond the scope of this chapter, and in any event empirical research to date is limited. However, two studies have provided results of relevance to the present theory. Bogart and coworkers (1969) reported that those scoring high on the Machiavellianism scale (Christie and Geis, 1970) showed less attitude change, indicating less dissonance-arousal following discrepant behaviour, than those scoring low on the scale. Thus, high Machs may continue to adopt 'high-effort' conditions despite previous treatment failures, because inconsistency between intention and outcome arouses less dissonance than for low Machs, so that escape from dissonance is easier. It would also follow that the anticipatory avoidance of dissonance would be less likely. In this connection, a report by Christie and Geis (1970) that future psychiatrists scored higher on the Mach scale than any other group of medical students is of interest.

Subjects manipulated to be high in self-esteem show greater attitude change, indicating greater dissonance-arousal following discrepant behaviour (aggression), particularly towards derogation of the victim, than those manipulated to be low in self-esteem (Glass and Wood, 1969). This suggests that well-known and highly prestigious therapists (presumed to be high in self-esteem) would be more likely to avoid dissonance by careful selection of patients than will those who are less well known. Garfield (1971) has reported that the more prestigious the psychotherapy agency, the more carefully it selects potential patients.

Although there appear to be no relevant studies as yet, it is a reasonable prediction that subjects scoring at the internal end of the locus of control dimension (Rotter, 1966) would experience greater dissonance-arousal than those scoring at the external end of the dimension. The latter habitually attribute the causation of their behaviour to events external to themselves, so that inconsistency is both a very frequent experience and one which has not followed from their 'own' actions. Hence, inconsistency is less dissonance-arousing than for those who do attribute causality to the self.

Feldman and MacCulloch (1971) have suggested that patients may differ, not only in the frequency which they rehearse (cognitively) their experiences in treatment but also in the type of experience habitually rehearsed, with some being more likely to rehearse pleasant, others unpleasant, experiences. They related the above possibilities both to the repression–sensitization (RS) dimension (Byrne, 1964) and to the Eysenckian personality dimensions, persons at the R end being equated with neurotic extraverts and considered likely to rehearse pleasant experiences, and those at the S end being equated with neurotic introverts and seen as more likely to rehearse unpleasant experiences. To extend the speculation: neurotic introverts/sensitizers may find it more difficult than neurotic extraverts/repressors both to avoid discrepant (and hence unpleasant) information and to escape/avoid dissonance by the use of dissonance-reduction mechanisms. Since dissonance-related behaviour of both clinician and patient is relevant to the present discussion, it follows, other things being equal, that the greatest mutual self-deception will occur in a therapist–patient pairing in which both are high on E and N, the least in which both are high on N but low on E.

Some of the implications for clinical practice of the assault on trait (consistency) notions of personality launched by Mischel (1968) were noted in the previous section. It was suggested that a resolution between the consistency and the specificity views is achieved by assuming that behavioural outcomes always represent a varying interaction between situational and dispositional (personality) variables. For most persons, current situational stimuli and previous outcomes in similar situations will exert a much greater effect than dispositional variables. For a minority, scoring at the extremes of personality dimensions, relatively stable individual differences will exert a greater effect than in the case of the majority. This attempt at a resolution of the apparently diametrically opposed consistency and specificity positions should be borne in mind when testing the present theory in terms of the personality variables discussed above. It implies that personality questionnaire scores will be much more relevant for extreme-scoring persons than for those scoring in the middle ranges.

The temporal dimension

Studies which take place over a substantial span of time will be needed in order to explore fully the complex interactions between attitudes and behaviours, and the patterns of changes in both, which are predicted by the theory outlined in this chapter. It follows that the theory can be tested completely only in the real world of the clinic, although laboratory analogue studies may be useful in the initial ground-clearing stage. Such a use of the clinical situation would fit in well with current emphases on the need to establish external validity by using both laboratory and field settings within the same research programme, and the desirability of carrying out research on human populations other than undergraduates (Carlson, 1971).

Concluding comment

It is appreciated that the theory outlined in this section has a somewhat unusual aspect: the more usual assumption would be that all therapists, at all times, operate in ways which are calculated to serve the best interests of all their patients, both prospective and actual. What the theory suggests is that many therapists, at least some of the time, place their own interests, specifically the need to maintain cognitive consistency, before those of their patients.

Although the theory is applicable to the therapies and therapists of all varieties, it is of greater practical relevance to therapeutic techniques of demonstrated efficacy. Patients deprived of *ineffective* help, or given an ineffective therapy under conditions of low effort, are obviously suffering a lesser deprivation than those who are either deprived of *effective* help, or receive it under suboptimal conditions.

Cognitive dissonance theory has been successful in predicting similarly non-obvious outcomes in several areas of experimental social psychology. The present theory has been proposed in the hope that it will prove equally successful in the applied area of clinician and patient behaviour. Moreover, as even the present very brief review of clinically relevant dissonance research indicates, the theory outlined far from exhausts the range of potential clinical applications of cognitive dissonance and other cognitive consistency theories.

CONCLUSIONS

The two previous sections of this chapter yield a set of predictions and a set of prescriptions. The predictions are concerned with the enhancement of therapeutic efficacy and efficiency in clinical practice by the systematic application of social influence variables and the adoption of high-effort conditions. Conversely, it is predicted that therapeutic efficacy will be reduced by failing to use social influence procedures and by adopting low-effort conditions.

The prescriptions concern the implication of social influence and dissonance research for the design of studies of outcome. If it emerges that social influence variables significantly enhance efficacy and efficiency, such variables must be rigorously controlled in outcome research. Similarly, if evidence is obtained that therapists deceive themselves as to outcome and that patients connive in the deception, outcome measures must be carried out by those unaware of the treatment received, and in such a way as to estimate accurately the outcome of all patients participating in the study, irrespective of treatment.

Perhaps the most overriding suggestion of all is that both therapists (even behaviour therapists) and patients are human beings. When they enter the clinic, neither of them ceases to exert, or to be responsive to, social influence effects or to seek cognitive consistency. We should both study these phenomena objectively and use the results for the maximum benefit of patients. So far as the distress of therapists following failure is concerned, the best short-term remedy is to accept that some failures are unavoidable despite the best possible efforts. The best long-term remedy is to develop increasingly effective therapies and therapeutic adjuncts.

REFERENCES

Ajzen, I. (1971). Attitudinal versus normative messages: an investigation of the differential effects of persuasive communications on behaviour. *Sociometry*, **34**, 263–280.

Alker, H. A. (1972). Is personality situationally specific or intra psychically consistent? *Journal of Personality*, **40**, 1–16.

Argyle, M., and Kendon, A. (1965). The experimental analysis of social performance. In L. Berkowitz (Ed.), *Advances in Experimental Social Psychology*, Academic Press, New York.

Aronson, E., and Mills, J. (1959). The effect of severity of initiation on liking for a group. *Journal of Abnormal and Social Psychology*, **59**, 177–181.

Asch, S. E. (1952). *Social Psychology*, Prentice-Hall, New York.

Astin, D. W. (1961). The functional autonomy of psychotherapy. *American Psychologist*, **16**, 75–78.

Bandura, A. (1969). *Principles of Behavior Modification*, Holt, Rinehart and Winston, New York.

Bem, D. (1967). Self-perception: an alternative interpretation of cognitive dissonance phenomena. *Psychological Review*, **74**, 183–200.

Bentler, P. M. (1962). An infant's phobia treated with reciprocal inhibition therapy. *Journal of Child Psychology and Psychiatry*, **3**, 185–189.

Bergin, A. E. (1962). The effect of dissonant persuasive communications upon changes in a self-referring attitude. *Journal of Personality*, **30**, 423–438.

Bergin, A. E. (1971). The evaluation of therapeutic outcomes. In A. E. Bergin and S. L. Garfield (Eds.), *Handbook of Psychotherapy and Behaviour Change: An Empirical Analysis*, Wiley, New York.

Berkowitz, L. (1968). *Roots of Aggression: A Re-examination of the Frustration–Aggression Hypothesis*, Atherton Press, New York.

Bernstein, D. A., and Paul, G. L. (1971). Some comments on therapy analogue research with small animal phobias. *Journal of Behaviour Therapy and Experimental Psychiatry*, **2**, 225–239.

Berscheid, E., Boye, D., and Darley, J. M. (1968). Effects of forced association upon voluntary choice to associate. *Journal of Personality and Social Psychology*, **8**, 13–19.

Berscheid, E., and Walster, E. (1969). *Interpersonal Attraction*, Addison Wesley, Reading, Massachusetts.

Biondo, J., and MacDonald, A. P., Jr. (1971). Internal–external locus of control and response to influence attempts. *Journal of Personality*, **39**, 407–419.

Bogart, K., Geis, F., Levy, M., and Zimbardo, P. G. (1969). No dissonance for Machiavellians? In P. G. Zimbardo (Ed.), *The Cognitive Control of Motivation*, Scott Foresman and Co., Glenview, Illinois.

Borkovec, T. D. (1973). The role of expectancy and physiological feedback in fear research: a review with special reference to subject characteristics. *Behavior Therapy*, **4**, 491–505.

Boudin, H. M. (1972). Contingency contracting as a therapeutic tool in the deceleration of amphetamine use. *Behavior Therapy*, **3**, 604–608.

Brehm, J., and Cohen, A. R. (1962). *Explorations in Cognitive Dissonance*, Wiley, New York.

Byrne, D. (1964). Repression-sensitization as a dimension of personality. In B. A. Maher (Ed.), *Progress in Experimental Personality Research*, Vol. 1. Academic Press, New York.

Campbell, D. T. (1963). Social attitudes and other acquired behavioral dispositions. In S. Koch (Ed.), *Psychology: A Study of a Science*, Vol. 6. McGraw-Hill, New York.

Carlson, R. A. E. (1971). Where is the person in personality research? *Psychological Bulletin*, **75**, 203–220.

Chapanis, N. P., and Chapanis, A. (1964). Cognitive dissonance: five years later. *Psychological Bulletin*, **61**, 1–23.

Christie, R., and Geis, F. (1970). *Studies in Machiavellianism*, Academic Press, New York.

Chu, C. G. (1966). Fear arousal, efficacy and imminency. *Journal of Personality and Social Psychology*, **4**, 517–524.

Dabbs, J. M., Jr., and Leventhal, H. (1966). Effects of varying the recommendations in a fear arousing communication. *Journal of Personality and Social Psychology*, **4**, 525–531.

Das, J. P., and Nanda, P. C. (1963). Mediated transfer of attitudes. *Journal of Abnormal and Social Psychology*, **66**, 12–16.

Davids, A. (1964). The relation of cognitive-dissonance theory to an aspect of psychotherapeutic practice. *American Psychologist*, **19**, 329–332.

Davison, G. C., Tsujimoto, R. N., and Glaros, A. G. (1973). Attribution and the maintenance of behavior change in falling asleep. *Journal of Abnormal Psychology*, **82**, 124–133.

Davison, G. C., and Valins, S. (1969). Maintenance of self-attributed and drug-attributed behavior change. *Journal of Personality and Social Psychology*, **11**, 25–33.

Davison, G. C., and Wilson, G. T. (1972). Critique of 'Desensitisation: social and cognitive factors underlying the effectiveness of Wolpe's procedure.' *Psychological Bulletin*, **78**, 28–31.

Di Loreto, A. O. (1971). *Comparative Psychotherapy: An Experimental Analysis*, Aldine-Atherton, Chicago.

Estabrooks, G. H. (1930). The psycho-galvanic reflex in hypnosis. *Journal of General Psychology*, **3**, 150–157.

Ekman, P., and Friesen, W. V. (1969). Nonverbal leakage and clues to deception. *Psychiatry*, **32**, 88–106.

English, F. B. (1972). *The Experimenter Expectancy Effect as a Function of the Differential Ability of Individuals to Influence Others*. Unpublished M.Sc. thesis, University of Birmingham.

Eysenck, H. J. (1952). The effects of psychotherapy: an evaluation. *Journal of Consulting Psychology*, **16**, 319–324.

Feifel, H., and Eels, J. (1963). Patients and therapists assess the same psychotherapy. *Journal of Consulting Psychology*, **27**, 310–318.

Feldman, M. P. (1964). Motivation and task performance: a review of the literature. In H. J. Eysenck (Ed.), *Experiments in Motivation*, Pergamon Press, Oxford.

Feldman, M. P. (1970). *Situational and Cognitive Aspects of Helping Behaviour*. Paper read at the Second Annual Conference on Behaviour Modification, Kilkenny, Eire.

Feldman, M. P. (1971). *Cognitive Aspects of the Therapeutic Situation: An Extrapolation from the Theory of Cognitive Dissonance*. Paper read at the Third Annual Conference on Behaviour Modification, Wexford, Eire, September, 1971.

Feldman, M. P., and Callister, J. (1971). *Interpersonal Helping Behaviour: Cognitive and Situational Aspects*. Research report: December, 1971. Social Science Research Council of Great Britain, Grant HR 536/1.

Feldman, M. P., and MacCulloch, M. J. (1971). *Homosexual Behaviour: Therapy and Assessment*, Pergamon Press, Oxford.

Felton, G. S. (1971). The experimenter expectancy effect examined as a function of task ambiguity and internal-external control. *Journal of Experimental Research in Personality*, **5**, 286–294.

Ferster, C. B., Nurnberger, J. I., and Levitt, E. B. (1962). The control of eating. *Journal of Mathetics*, **1**, 87–109.

Festinger, L. (1957). *A Theory of Cognitive Dissonance*, Stanford University Press, Stanford, California.

Fishbein, M. (1967). Attitudes and the prediction of behavior. In M. Fishbein (Ed.), *Readings in Attitude Theory and Measurement*, Wiley, New York.

Freud, S. (1922). *Introductory Lectures in Psychoanalysis*, Allen and Unwin, London.

Garfield, S. L. (1941). Research on client variables in psychotherapy. In A. E. Bergin and S. L. Garfield (Eds.), *Handbook of Psychotherapy and Behavior Change: An Empirical Analysis*, Wiley, New York.

Garfield, S. L., and Bergin, A. E. (1971). Therapeutic conditions and outcome. *Journal of Abnormal Psychology*, **77**, 108–114.

Glass, D. C., and Wood, J. D. (1969). The control of aggression by self-esteem and dissonance. In P. G. Zimbardo (Ed.), *The Cognitive Control of Motivation*, Scott Foresman and Co., Glenview, Illinois.

Goldstein, A. P. (1962). *Therapist–Patient Expectancies in Psychotherapy*, Pergamon Press, New York.

Goldstein, A. P. (1971). *Psychotherapeutic Attraction*, Pergamon Press, Oxford.

Goldstein, A. P., Heller, K., and Sechrest, L. B. (1966). *Psychotherapy and the Psychology of Behavior Change*, Wiley, 1966.

Goldstein, A. P., and Simonson, N. R. (1971). Social psychological approaches to psychotherapy research. In A. E. Bergin and S. L. Garfield (Eds.), *Handbook of Psychotherapy and Behavior Change: An Empirical Analysis*, Wiley, New York.

Gormezano, I. (1966). Classical conditioning. In J. B. Sidowski (Ed.), *Experimental Methods and Instrumentation in Psychology*, McGraw-Hill, New York.

Greenwald, A. C. (1967). *An Amended Learning Model of Persuasion*. Paper read at American Psychological Association, Washington, D.C., September, 1967.

Grings, W. W. (1965). Verbal-perceptual factors in the conditioning of autonomic responses. In W. F. Prokasy (Ed.), *Classical Conditioning*, Appleton-Century-Crofts, New York.

Hartshorne, H., and May, M. A. (1928). *Studies in Deceit*, MacMillan, New York.

Hekmat, H. (1972). The role of imagination in semantic desensitization. *Behavior Therapy*, **3**, 223–231.

Hekmat, H., and Vanian, D. (1971). Behavior modification through covert semantic desensitization. *Journal of Consulting and Clinical Psychology*, **36**, 248–251.

Homans, G. C. (1961). *Social Behavior: Its Elementary Forms*, Harcourt, Brace and World, New York.

Houts, P. S., MacIntosh, S., and Moos, R. H. (1969). Patient–therapist interdependence: cognitive and behavioral. *Journal of Consulting and Clinical Psychology*, **33**, 40–45.

Innes, J. M. (1972). Dissonance reduction in the therapist and its relevance to aversion therapy. *Behavior Therapy*, **3**, 441–443.

Jellinek, E. M. (1946). Clinical tests on comparative effectiveness of analgesic drugs. *Biometrics*, **2**, 67–71.

Kanfer, F. H., and Karoly, P. (1972). Some additional conceptualisations. In R. C. Johnson, P. R. Dokecki and O. H. Mowrer (Eds.), *Conscience, Contract and Social Reality*, Holt, Rinehart and Winston, New York.

Kelley, H. N. (1967). Attribution theory in social psychology. In D. Levine (Ed.), *Nebraska Symposium on Motivation*, University of Nebraska, Lincoln, Nebraska.

Khan, M., and Baker, B. (1968). Desensitization with minimal therapist contact. *Journal of Abnormal Psychology*, **73**, 198–200.

Knowles, J. B., and Lucas, C. J. (1960). Experimental studies of the placebo response. *Journal of Mental Science*, **106**, 231–240.

Krasner, L. (1965). Studies of the conditioning of verbal behavior. *Psychological Bulletin*, **55**, 148–171.

Krebs, D. L. (1970). Altruism: an examination of the concept and a review of the literature. *Psychological Bulletin*, **73**, 258–302.

Lang, P. J., Melamed, B. G., and Hart, J. (1970). A psychophysiological analysis of fear modification using an automated desensitization procedure. *Journal of Abnormal Psychology*, **76**, 220–234.

Lanyon, R. I. (1972). Technological approach to the improvement of decision making in mental health services. *Journal of Consulting and Clinical Psychology*, **39**, 43–48.

Lazarus, A. (1971). *Behavior Therapy and Beyond*, McGraw-Hill, New York.

Lefcourt, H. M. (1966). Internal versus external control of reinforcement: a review. *Psychological Bulletin*, **65**, 206–220.

Lerner, M. J., and Mathews, G. (1967). Reactions to suffering of others under conditions of indirect responsibility. *Journal of Personality and Social Psychology*, **5**, 319–325.

Lerner, M. J., and Simmons, C. (1966). Observer's reaction to the 'innocent victim'. Compassion or rejection. *Journal of Personality and Social Psychology*, **4**, 203–210.

Lewis, M. J. (1965). Psychological effect of effort. *Psychological Bulletin*, **64**, 183–190.

Liberman, R. P. (1962). An analysis of the placebo phenomenon. *Journal of Chronic Diseases*, **15**, 761–783.

Liberman, R. P. (1972). Review of A. O. Di Loreto, 'Comparative psychotherapy: an experimental analysis'. *Behavior Therapy*, **3**, 647–649.

Macaulay, J. R., and Berkowitz, L. (Eds.) (1970). *Altruism and Helping Behavior*, Academic Press, New York.

McFall, R. M., and Lillesand, D. B. (1971). Behavior rehearsal with modelling and coaching in assertion training. *Journal of Abnormal Psychology*, **77**, 313–323.

McGuire, W. J. (1969). The nature of attitudes and attitude change. In G. Lindzey and E. Aronson (Eds.), *Handbook of Social Psychology*, Vol. 3, 2nd ed. Addison-Wesley, Reading, Massachusetts.

McLaughlin, B. (1971). *Learning and Social Behavior*, The Free Press, New York.

Mehrabian, A. (1968). Inference of attitudes from the posture, orientation, and distance of a communicator. *Journal of Consulting and Clinical Psychology*, **32**, 296–308.

Mehrabian, A. (1971). Nonverbal betrayal of feeling. *Journal of Experimental Research in Personality*, **5**, 64–73.

Meichenbaum, D. H., and Goodman, J. (1971). Training impulsive children to talk to themselves: a means of developing self-control. *Journal of Abnormal Psychology*, **77**, 115–126.

Miller, B. N., and Bernstein, D. A. (1972). Instructional demand in a behavioural avoidance test for claustrophobic fears. *Journal of Abnormal Psychology*, **80**, 206–210.

Miller, P. M. (1972). The use of behavioral contracting in the treatment of alcoholism: a case report. *Behavior Therapy*, **3**, 593–596.

Miller, R. E., Banks, J. H., Jr., and Ogawa, N. (1963). Role of facial expression in 'cooperative-avoidance conditioning' in monkeys. *Journal of Abnormal and Social Psychology*, **67**, 14–30.

Mischel, W. (1968). *Personality and Assessment*, Wiley, New York.

Moos, R. H., and Clemes, S. R. (1967). Multi-variate study of the patient–therapist system. *Journal of Consulting Psychology*, **31**, 119–130.

Morgan, W. G. (1973). Non-necessary conditions or useful procedures in desensitization: a reply to Wilkins. *Psychological Bulletin*, **79**, 373–375.

Morrow, W. R. (1971). *Behavior Therapy Bibliography: 1950–1969*, University of Missouri Press, Columbia, Missouri.

Murray, E. I., and Jacobson, L. I. (1971). The nature of learning in traditional and behavioral psychotherapy. In A. E. Bergin and S. L. Garfield (Eds.), *Handbook of Psychotherapy and Behavior Change: An Empirical Analysis*, Wiley, New York.

Packard, F. R. (1922). History of the School of Salernum. In J. Harington (Trans.), *The School of Salernum*, Humphrey Milford, London.

Paul, G. L. (1967). Insight versus desensitization in psychotherapy two years after termination. *Journal of Consulting Psychology*, **31**, 333–348.

Paul, G. L. (1969). Outcome of systematic desensitization. II: Controlled investigations of individual treatment, technique variations, and current status. In C. M. Franks (Ed.), *Behavior Therapy: Appraisal and Status*, McGraw-Hill, New York.

Pollack, I. W., and Kiev, A. (1963). Spatial orientation and psychotherapy: An experimental study of perception. *Journal of Nervous and Mental Disease*, **137**, 93–97.

Rachman, S. J. (1972). *The Effects of Psychotherapy*, Pergamon Press, Oxford.

Rosenberg, M. (1965). When dissonance fails: on eliminating evaluative apprehension from attitude measurement. *Journal of Personality and Social Psychology*, **1**, 28–42.

Rosenthal, R. (1963). On the social psychology of the psychological experiment: the experimenter's hypothesis as unintended determinant of experimental results. *American Scientist*, **51**, 268–283.

Rosenthal, R. (1966). *Experimenter Effects in Behavioral Research*, Appleton-Century-Crofts, New York.

Rotter, J. B. (1966). Generalised expectancies for internal versus external control of reinforcement. *Psychological Monographs*, **80**, No. 1.

Ryan, V. L., and Gizynski, M. N. (1971). Behavior therapy in retrospect: patients feelings about their behavior therapies. *Journal of Consulting and Clinical Psychology*, **37**, 1–9.

Shapiro, D. (1969). Empathy, warmth and genuineness in psychotherapy. *British Journal of Social and Clinical Psychology*, **8**, 350–361.

Skinner, B. F. (1957). *Verbal Behavior*, Appleton-Century-Crofts, New York.

Spence, K. W. (1966). Cognitive and drive factors in the extinction of the conditioned eye-blink in human subjects. *Psychological Review*, **73**, 445–458.

Staats, A. W. (1966). An integrated-functional approach to complex human behavior. In B. Kleimmuntz (Ed.), *Problem Solving: Research Method and Theory*, Wiley, New York.

Staats, A. W. (1972). Language behavior therapy: a derivative of social behaviorism. *Behavior Therapy*, **3**, 165–192.

Staats, A. W., and Staats, C. K. (1958). Attitudes established by classical conditioning. *Journal of Abnormal and Social Psychology*, **57**, 37–40.

Stuart, R. B. (1971). Behavioral contracting within the families of the delinquents. *Journal of Behavior Therapy and Experimental Psychiatry*, **2**, 2–11.

Thibaut, J. W., and Kelley, H. H. (1959). *The Social Psychology of Groups*, Wiley, New York.

Truax, C., and Carkhuff, R. (1967). *Toward Effective Counselling and Psychotherapy: Training and Practice*, Aldine, Chicago.

Ullmann, L. P., and Krasner, L. (1969). *A Psychological Approach to Abnormal Behavior*, Prentice-Hall, London.

Vernon, P. E. (1964). *Personality Assessment*, Methuen, London.

Walster, E. H., and Presthold, p. (1966). The effect of misjudging another. Overcompensation or disssonance reduction? *Journal of Experimental Social Psychology*, **2**, 85–97.

Webb, E. J., Campbell, D. T., Schwartz, R. D., and Sechrest, L. (1966). *Unobtrusive Measures: Nonreactive Research in the Social Sciences*, Rand McNally, Chicago.

Weber, S. J., and Cook, T. D. (1972). Subject effects in laboratory research: an examination of subject roles, demand characteristics, and valid inference. *Psychological Bulletin*, **77**, 273–295.

Wicker, A. W. (1969). Attitudes versus actions: the relationship of verbal and overt behavioural responses to attitude objects. *Journal of Social Issues*, **25**, 41–78.

Wilkins, W. (1971). Desensitization: social and cognitive factors underlying the effectiveness of Wolpe's procedure. *Psychological Bulletin*, **76**, 311–317.

Wilkins, W. (1972). Desensitization: getting it together with Davison and Wilson. *Psychological Bulletin*, **78**, 32–36.

Wilkins, W. (1973). Desensitization: a rejoinder to Morgan. *Psychological Bulletin*, **79**, 376–377.

Wilson, G. T., Hannon, A. E., and Evans, W. I. M. (1968). Behavior therapy and the therapist–patient relationship. *Journal of Consulting and Clinical Psychology*, **32**, 103–109.

Witkin, H. A., Goodenough, D. R., and Karp, S. A. (1965). Psychological differentiation and forms of pathology. *Journal of Abnormal Psychology*, **70**, 317–336.

Wolpe, J. (1962). Isolation of a conditioning procedure as the crucial psychotherapeutic factor: a case-study. *Journal of Nervous and Mental Disease*, **134**, 316–329.

Wolpe, J. (1969). *The Practice of Behaviour Therapy*, Pergamon, Oxford.

Yerkes, R. M., and Dodson, J. D. (1908). The relation of strength of stimulus to rapidity of habit-formation. *Journal of Comparative Neurology and Psychology*, **18**, 459–482.

Zimbardo, P. G. (Ed.), (1969). *The Cognitive Control of Motivation*, Glenview, Ill.: Scott Foresman and Co., Glenview, Illinois.

9

APPLICATIONS OF THE PSYCHOLOGY OF DECISIONS

Anne Broadhurst

INTRODUCTION

In everyday life man is constantly called upon to make decisions. The same is true, of course, for animals. According to . . . game theory, man chooses the most utilitarian mode of behavior from among the many possibilities open for him. This decision-making process can be expressed in mathematical formulas, in which the available possibilities, probabilities, and the 'utility value' of each choice are contained in their relationship to each other. To account by mathematical formulas for the extreme range of values that motivate human behavior and influence human decision . . . presents obstacles, but these may not be insuperable.

   Game theory recognizes that there are probabilities of choice alternatives that are also important in psychotherapy. Neurotic individuals too often behave as though they have only one choice—a self-defeating one—and all too often accept this choice. The psychotherapeutic process for these people is to allow them to gain understanding of alternative choices measured in terms of risks and gains (Alexander and Selesnick, 1966, p. 316).

In these words decision theory is briefly and simply outlined, together with a view of neurosis which, though little discussed, is perhaps generally acceptable. It comes as no novelty to suggest that the neurotic individual is indecisive where choice is offered or prone to limit his choices arbitrarily or, when aware of wider choices, inclined to make choices on the basis of inadequate information. Indeed, some would even go further and view neurosis as primarily a disorder of decision-making. And in so far as this is true, among the many deleterious consequences of the medical model as applied to psychiatric patients is the creation of an atmosphere or situation, such as hospitalization, which discourages decision-making by the patient at a point in his life when he most requires training in this important function. The ramifications of decision-making can be seen at every stage of behaviour disorder, including the client's choice of certain aspects of his environment, his development of certain (selected?) maladaptive behaviours, his decision to seek help, to cooperate (however weakly) with the therapist and the therapist's selection of techniques and explanatory verbalizations. The importance of decisions in the therapeutic setting is now fully established with the advent of 'direct decision therapy' (Greenwald, 1973), in which the patient is confronted with the choices life offers and made aware of his many past decisions and future decision opportunities.

Yet the inclusion of a chapter on decision psychology is an innovation among books which link general psychology with its clinical applications. On one hand, it is difficult to account for this meagre published association between academic psychology and clinical practice. There is so often a time lag between theoretical developments and applications, but in this case the academic study, even the experimental study, of decisions is old, even older than experimental psychology itself. Decision theory historians trace its inception back to the mathematical philosophers (e.g. Bernoulli) and economists (e.g. Jeremy Bentham) of the eighteenth century (Edwards, 1954). The literature is already extensive and the theories varied and sophisticated. One might have expected more influence by now on psychological concern with behaviour disorders.

Further puzzlement over the lack of previous interest in decision study and its clinical application stems from the obvious advantages in many areas. Decisions, we may conclude, are ubiquitous. If decision processes are weak or faulty, as they evidently may be in the 'normal' as well as in the neurotic individual, then decision study, analysis, theory and research must surely offer hope for behaviour change—the work of the applied scientist, the clinical psychologist.

Finally, among grounds on which one might have expected earlier demonstration of concern with the theory of decisions by clinical editors, there is, as already indicated, the clear interest of clinicians in decision processes. In addition to those already mentioned (Alexander and Selesnick, 1966; Greenwald, 1973), Jones (1970), for example, is evidently aware of the wide applicability of decision theory although he emphasizes its relevance to statistical and diagnostic decisions of the clinician. Much interest has indeed attached to this important area (e.g. Aitchison, 1970; Arthur, 1969, 1972; Edwards and Berry, 1974; Edwards and Tversky, 1967; Kozielecki, 1972; Nathan, 1967) and the reader is directed to Lanyon (this volume) for further details. Clinicians have by no means been slow to view their problems and their clients' problems in terms of decisions.

On the other hand, two main reasons could be put forward to account for the failure of decision psychology to influence psychologists in applied fields. First, there is the undoubted deterrent of the aforementioned sophistication of decision theory itself, particularly the philosophical and mathematical sophistication (probability has been said to be 'common sense reduced to calculation'—Laplace, 1951) of many of the presentations in the area of decisions, and also the apparent aridity of many of the prevailing controversies. Neither of these factors encourage entry into the arena by the clinician pressed with a too heavy case load; and the dedication required for expertise in these matters equally precludes concomitant development of clinical skills. Second, there exists a discrepancy in the views of decision theorists themselves as to how far their thinking can have practical implications. While decision theorists have not lacked proponents of the view that application is possible and desirable (e.g. Raiffa, 1970), there have been others who appear to argue themselves out of real situations. Savage (1967), for example, believes that multistage (sequential) decision theory has little usefulness in psychology. Then, too, we find such statements as the following:

> A large part of the confusion seems to have come about because probability theory was . . . discussed in terms of beliefs, and thus it *sounded as if* the theory dealt with beliefs (i.e., with real people). A close reading of these theories, however, indicates that they actually dealt with consistent, logically related beliefs—not with the actual beliefs of people . . . . The body of work developed over the past several centuries known as probability theory does not concern actual beliefs (Lee, 1971, p. 42, italics added).

However, whatever the intentions of the theorists, there have already been attempts to relate decision theory and research to real situations. Industrial and managerial applications have perhaps been most noticeable (e.g. Heneman and Schwab, 1972; Vroom, 1964); personality theorists have taken an occasional interest (Block and Petersen, 1955; Deutsch, 1960; Rotter, 1954); and Kleiter (1974) relates multistage decision-making to the psychology of thinking and motivation. It is the writer's purpose to draw attention to the clear relationship between behaviour disorder, especially (but not solely) neurotic disorder, and decision-making; to point out the availability in decision theory of a source of concepts and approaches for dealing with decision problems, as yet largely untapped by the clinician; to examine some of the early attempts to apply decision psychology to behaviour problems; and to suggest some possible lines for further development in clinical psychology.

CLASSICAL DECISION THEORY

While there is a limited amount of work on superficial correlates of decision-making (e.g. Busse and Love, 1973), as propounded by Edwards (1954) or Raiffa (1970) for example, behavioural decision theory (probability theory or game theory) is directed at quite fundamental explanation of the decision behaviour of Man. (These authors ably present the decision theory approach, but, for those who seek an even more straight-forward introduction with a minimum of assumptions, the text by Bross (1953) can be recommended.) However, the meaning of decision is always to some extent unclear and hence the boundaries of discussion are equally unclear (Lee, 1971). Decision theory work is often categorized according to whether it deals with a normative (prescriptive) model (how one should behave) or with a descriptive model (how one actually behaves) (Becker and McClintock, 1967). However, Rapoport and Wallsten (1972) find this distinction difficult and refer in particular to the possibly misleading philosophical implications. There may be difficulties, too, in dichotomizing decision behaviour as individual or group decisions, depending on the source of the information provided for the individual. In many circumstances, this may be a useful distinction, however, and since the clinician is primarily concerned with individual decision behaviour this is in the main our subject matter in this chapter. Decision tasks may also be classified as single- or multi-stage, depending on the number of decisions to be made sequentially by the decision maker (DM). Multistage decision-making is more than a series of single-stage decisions, since it is assumed that each decision alters the 'state of the world' in which the next decision is to be made. Thus multistage decision-making approximates real life in many situations. For example, the client's first decision to mention his problem to his general practitioner will result in an alteration to his records such that it may later be easier for him to convince (decide to intensify the manipulation of) this same doctor to arrange (decide upon) referral to another agency.

Where a range or repertoire of behavioural outcomes is available, rational man—the DM—is assumed to choose on the basis of probabilities of consequences and preferences for or values of consequences, according to one of several decision principles, e.g. the Maximin principle by which the maximizes the minimum possible gain or utility outcome of his choice and minimizes the maximum disutility (loss) from his decision. Considerable difficulties follow, however, from this analysis, since it involves the measurement of utilities. While in many economic choice situations the utility can be roughly equated with monetary value (expected monetary value—EMV), this will clearly not hold for all situations, especially clinical situations, nor even for the economic situation when the decision maker (DM) may be either a pauper or a millionaire whose views of the value of money are bound to differ. Hence, for example, the concept of subjectively expected utility (SEU) has been developed to help in accounting for decision-making, and although little used in other fields of psychology than decision theory it has been argued (Pollard and Mitchell, 1972) that the concept is related to Lewinian levels of aspiration (Lewin and coworkers, 1965) and Fishbein's (1967) work on motivation, and that learning theories (Hull, 1943; Tolman, 1952) and personality theories (Atkinson, 1964; Rotter, 1954) can be interpreted in such decision theory terms. (In this connection, see Feather (1959) for an illuminating table of relationships between Lewin, Tolman, Rotter, Edwards and Atkinson.)

It must not be thought, however, that decision theory is limited to the concept of SEU. Risk is an alternative basic concept with the advantage that it is much easier to apply than SEU to situations with a large range of possible decisions to be made. In any case, since data incompatible with SEU theory have been reported (Slovic and Lichtenstein, 1968), there are those who regard the concept as inadequate. There must be further investigation of the conditions under which the SEU concept has validity and those in which it has none (Rapoport and Wallsten, 1972). It may be some time before this is established since, because of the subjectivity of his values, every DM must be regarded as a separate experiment and hence the gathering of adequate data entails subjecting him to the boredom of making vast numbers of decisions. This is an unfortunate experimental requirement, especially as there is already evidence of changes in decision strategy under conditions of boredom or fatigue (Slovic, Lichtenstein and Edwards, 1965). The SEU concept has to face such problems before it is fully established.

Nevertheless, the concept of SEU has appealed to various workers in the field of real decisions as well as to experimenters and theoreticians (e.g. Mitchell and Biglan, 1971). Several workers have looked at the influence of evidence in forming SEUs (Kleiven, Fraser and Gouge, 1974; Wright, 1974). In the following section, some early applications of the SEU model will be presented.

APPLICATIONS OF SUBJECTIVELY EXPECTED UTILITY

Smoking behaviour is now generally recognized as behaviour associated with risk (to health) and hence appropriately dealt with by the SEU model (Vinokur, 1971a). In this area, Mausner and Platt (1971) introduced a measure of SEU in which subjects rate (evaluate) a wide variety of possible outcomes from smoking and from not smoking, and give an estimate of their expectation that these outcomes would, in fact, occur in the conditions of smoking or not smoking (see Figure 9.1). Scores for SEU are then found by multiplying value by expectancy and summing separately for the two behaviours in question (smoking or not smoking).

This scale was first validated on a group of smokers and non-smokers (i.e. populations that have already made a behavioural choice) and later on groups subjected to behaviour change techniques. Change in SEU was related to actual changes in later smoking behaviour. Subjects who succeeded in cutting down their smoking did not differ in their SEU for *smoking* from those who made no change in their smoking consumption. Where they did differ, however, was in their SEU for *not smoking*, and hence in the overall difference between utilities, in which the reducers/abandoners showed a much higher value than the continuers. These results suggest strongly that behaviour change in the smoking area depends less on fear of the consequences of continuing to smoke than on benefits expected from abstinence. The desirable direction of antismoking propoganda is clear from these findings. It may even be that this finding is generalizable to other behaviours—it has been shown, for example, that horrific dental hygiene communications were less effective than more moderate ones (Evans and coworkers, 1970)—but this would need to be further tested.

Despite its crudity (and more refined devices are awaited), such a measure of SEU as Mausner's enables us to assess the value to the individual or the group of any suggested behaviour change and hence to approach the task of bringing about change with full appreciation of the difficulties ahead. Studies are already in progress to develop similar measures of SEU among college students learning statistics and among high school students exposed to training in dental hygiene, the prediction in both cases being that the initial SEU and the change in SEU after manipulation will account for the major

274

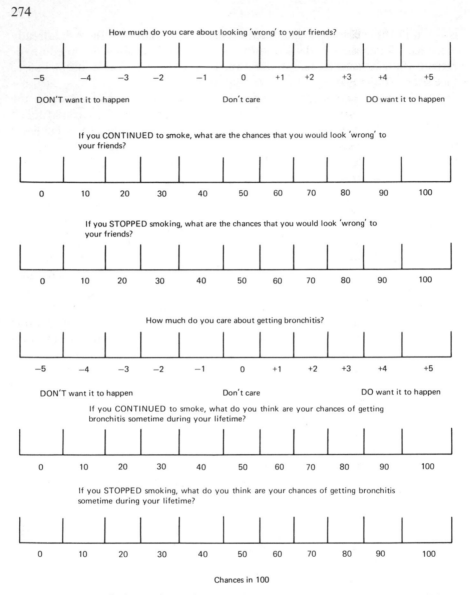

How much do you care about looking 'wrong' to your friends?

| -5 | -4 | -3 | -2 | -1 | 0 | +1 | +2 | +3 | +4 | +5 |

DON'T want it to happen   Don't care   DO want it to happen

If you CONTINUED to smoke, what are the chances that you would look 'wrong' to your friends?

| 0 | 10 | 20 | 30 | 40 | 50 | 60 | 70 | 80 | 90 | 100 |

If you STOPPED smoking, what are the chances that you would look 'wrong' to your friends?

| 0 | 10 | 20 | 30 | 40 | 50 | 60 | 70 | 80 | 90 | 100 |

How much do you care about getting bronchitis?

| -5 | -4 | -3 | -2 | -1 | 0 | +1 | +2 | +3 | +4 | +5 |

DON'T want it to happen   Don't care   DO want it to happen

If you CONTINUED to smoke, what do you think are your chances of getting bronchitis sometime during your lifetime?

| 0 | 10 | 20 | 30 | 40 | 50 | 60 | 70 | 80 | 90 | 100 |

If you STOPPED smoking, what do you think are your chances of getting bronchitis sometime during your lifetime?

| 0 | 10 | 20 | 30 | 40 | 50 | 60 | 70 | 80 | 90 | 100 |

Chances in 100

FIGURE 9.1 Sample items from the test of (smoking) subjectively expected utility (From Mausner, B., An ecological view of cigarette smoking, *J. abnorm. Psychol.*, 1973, **81**, 115–126. Copyright 1973 by the American Psychological Association. Reported by permission.).

part of the variance of actual behaviour change (Mausner, personal communication, 1974).

An intriguing variation on the SEU model is provided in Steiner's (1970) and Steiner, Rotermund and Talaber's (1974) model of the choice ascribed to a DM either subjectively, by himself, or by others aware of his decision problem.

Three experiments (Steiner, Rotermund and Talaber, 1974) essentially confirmed the prediction that greatest choice is attributed when available options seem equally attractive. While not wishing to go fully into the philosophical arguments for and against the determinist position, it is clear that theory and findings in the area of ascribed choice will at least throw light on the protagonists in the wider debate and may eventually free us to work for improved decision-making by individuals rather than accepting the myth that human nature is immutable.

STAGES IN DECISION-MAKING: JANIS' MODEL

Decisions once made are not irrevocable. As Mausner (1973) points out, even after smokers have officially 'stopped smoking', they may have to replay many of the anxious moments which preceded that 'decision' each time they are faced with the temptation to smoke. It is here that the work of Janis (Janis, 1968b; Janis and Mann, 1968) is of such importance to the practising clinician. Concerned with decision-making of a vital, personal kind rather than the trivial and largely verbal content of much experimentation on decision-making, Janis has investigated decisions to undergo recommended surgery (Janis, 1958), to give up smoking (Janis and Terwilliger, 1962) and to keep to a reducing diet (Sofer, Wishlade and Janis, 1964), and from many observations before, during and after actual decisions has analysed decision-making and provided a 'conflict-theory' testable in many other decision situations.

Janis (1968b) suggests that there is a sequence of five stages in the decision process. Stage 1, *appraisal of a challenge*, is initiated when the individual encounters and seriously considers a challenge to his present mode of action. Such a challenge would be likely to be one that provided information on probable loss to the individual if he does not change his attitude or behaviour. The new information is inconsistent with earlier information on the subject and, when confronted with such inconsistent input, the individual at first tries to dismiss it in a prejudiced fashion. But if he accepts the challenge as a real one and personally relevant, then he will be ready to progress to Stage 2.

In Stage 2, *appraisal of recommended courses of action*, the person who has accepted a challenge to his present attitudes and *modus vivendi* becomes susceptible to arguments and suggestions of methods of coping with the challenge. He will keep to present policy if possible, but, if the challenge of Stage 1 is strong, he will be actively curious about other possibly superior courses of action. He will seek information and will start to consider carefully the SEUs of various proposed changes. Thus, costly means of coping with the threat will be put aside and the DM ends with a series of possible courses of action.

Next, at Stage 3, *tentative selection of a course of action*, the DM passes through a phase of intense consideration of each viable possibility. Each possible course of action is tried out in imagination for what Janis calls 'goodness of personal fit'. At the same time, the possibility of continuing as before (the no-change course of action) is still actively considered. This last course, always presuming that no other has actually been tried in the past, acts as the comparison against which new courses are judged. It offers many attractions in terms of familiarity and ease. But again SEUs for each possible course of action will be the deciding factor, and, having tentatively selected one candidate from the group of possibles, this stage will include also some attempt to increase the SEU for that one by additional plans of action, such as devising means of explaining the change to avoid or minimize ridicule from former associates.

At this point, having made his personal decision, the DM now moves towards actual change. This is Stage 4, *commitment to a decision*, and it will involve behaviour change and, in all probability, a statement to important others that the change has been made. Thus, at this stage any failure to carry through the new policy will involve some loss of self-esteem, while, on the other hand, success will bring added esteem. The more people who know of the commitment, the greater the possible loss or gain of esteem, as the case may be. However, the DM is aware at this stage of some vulnerability for he is found to be welcoming supportive evidence and avoiding people and evidence counter to his decision.

And if there are many people or items of information which go counter to the decision, then the DM will be to some extent shaken in his resolve. The extent of the negative feedback will be an important feature here and we might observe a reversal of the decision at this stage if the reaction of the DM's environment is sufficiently adverse, as, for example, would be anticipated when a young heroin addict returns to the society of addicts after 'kicking' the habit for a short time. For a fully developed decision, however, the DM, rather than going back on his decision, enters instead Stage 5, *adherence to new policy despite negative feedback*, in which he perseveres against all social and personal difficulties. At first sight, the DM who has reached Stage 5 is in a strong position. Experiments such as those of Leventhal and Watts (1966) have confirmed that resistance to counterproposals is characteristic of this stage. However, we must remember that Stage 1 is described as one in which a challenge to existing action is received and considered. Thus Janis' model encourages the investigator to prepare for a reopening of the whole decision-making process. Stage 5, in fact, may be the Stage 1 of another decision and the decision-making process may then go through another cycle.

Janis' analysis of decision-making carries implications for attitude change at each stage, as can be seen in Table 9.1 (from Janis, 1968b) which shows the stages of decision-making and the predicted behaviour and attitude change with each stage. The DM, it is suggested, will show gradual change in the attitude components of the left-hand column as he progresses from one stage to the next of the decision. Janis points out that the analysis predicts further that the pattern of attitude change will form a unitary Guttman-type scale. We would not expect, for example, behaviour conforming to the decision (components 1 and 2) until all other components had changed to positive. It can be seen, too, that changes are progressively more frequent from Stage 1 to Stage 5 when all the expected changes have taken place.

TABLE 9.1 Types of attitude change accompanying each stage in making a decision to adhere to a recommended policy. (Inferred from studies of heavy smokers who decided to stop smoking after being exposed to publicity about the (U.S.) Surgeon-General's Report on smoking and lung cancer.) (From Janis, I. L., Stages in the decision-making process, in Robert P. Abelson, et al., (Eds.) *Theories of Cognitive Consistency: A Source book*, © 1968 by Rand McNally & Company, Chicago, table on p. 582. Reprinted by permission of Rand McNally College Publishing Company)

Components of attitude change, new beliefs, value judgements, and dispositions toward recommendation (R)	Initial attitude of complacency	Stage 1 Positive appraisal of challenge	Stage 2 Positive appraisal of recommendation (R)	Stage 3 Selection of R as the best alternative	Stage 4 Commitment to decision to adopt R	Stage 5 Adherence to R despite negative feedback
	(1)	(2)	(3)	(4)	(5)	(6)
Overt behavior						
1. Acts in accordance with R following major challenges to the new attitude?	No	No	No	No	(?)	Yes
2. Acts in accordance with R under normal circumstances?	No	No	No	No	Yes	Yes
Verbal evaluation of R						
3. Feels willing to act in accordance with R?	No	No	No	No	Yes	Yes
4. Believes R is best available means?	No	No	No	Yes	Yes	Yes
5. Believes R is a satisfactory means, worth considering?	No	No	Yes	Yes	Yes	Yes
6. Selectively responsive to subsequent communications about R? (Accepts assertions that R is an effective means and rejects assertions opposing assertions.) Verbal evaluation of threat	No	No	Yes	Yes	Yes	Yes

Table 9.1 (*Contd.*)

Components of attitude change, new beliefs, value judgements, and dispositions toward recommendation (R)	Initial attitude of complacency	Stage 1 Positive appraisal of challenge	Stage 2 Positive appraisal of recommendation (R)	Stage 3 Selection of R as the best alternative	Stage 4 Commitment to decision to adopt R	Stage 5 Adherence to R despite negative feedback
7. Believes the threat is serious?	No	Yes	Yes	Yes	Yes	Yes
8. Selectively responsive to subsequent communications about the threat. (Accepts assertions that the threat is serious and rejects those that minimize the threat.)	No	Yes	Yes	Yes	Yes	Yes

In addition, this model suggests that therapeutic change would be more permanent in those clients who had most opportunity to make a change decision with full knowledge of the positive and negative consequences (Janis, 1968a). Without assessing SEU in the manner of Mausner (1973), Toomey (1972) tested this hypothesis in the area of alcoholism where behaviour change has always been thought to rest heavily on the patient's own decision. Fifty-eight hospitalized alcoholic men and women were allocated at random to one of three treatment conditions. The first group attended two group meetings in which they were taken through the stages of the decision-making process and encouraged to consider the advantages and disadvantages of drinking and not drinking, and to make a decision, with a public commitment, to give up drinking. The second group similarly met for two group sessions, but in these groups only the negative consequences of drinking were discussed and there was no positive encouragement of decision-making one way or the other. The third group was a control group and received only the regular hospital treatment of 'drying out' for one or two weeks, followed by discharge from hospital. Results were in the expected direction, showing the superiority of decisions based on positive and negative factors, though they did not differentiate the two treatment groups significantly. It may be that 'the work of worrying' or the decision process is adequately advanced merely by a forceful presentation of the negative consequences (from which the positives can always be inferred). Discussion of the consequences, whether negative only (condition 2) or positive and negative (condition 1), led to increased optimism at discharge and decreased drinking at follow-up relative to the control group. However, it must be noted that this control did not control for experimenter time. This and several other difficulties of experimentation on a clinical population in hospital are discussed. The issue of decision analysis and its power for the benefit of alcoholics therefore remains open. Nor has it been further advanced by Goldman (1974), who reports a confused attempt to investigate the effects of group and individual decisions on the actual drinking behaviour of four chronic, male alcoholics. The questions posed in this study are unclear. Hence, it is not surprising to find that instructions to subjects and measures taken are both equally ambiguous. Results are not reported in such a manner that we can differentiate between group and individual decisions as regards strength for maintenance of abstention. This disappointing study notwithstanding, the method of decision analysis is still applicable to problems of alcoholism and to many other perhaps less recalcitrant problems of behaviour change.

The same analysis—that decisions made or behaviour changed with full awareness of positive and negative features would be more permanent than less thorough decisions made by short-cutting the stages—has been more effective in predicting resistance to counterpropaganda when the propaganda itself includes a statement of both sides of the argument (Lumsdaine and Janis, 1953). Similarly, a group of college students given training (following the strategy outlined by Bross, 1953) in decision-making, including discussion of the values or advantages of certain decisions, was found to be further advanced on a vocational decision checklist than a group given simple vocational guidance by the same counsellors and a third group given no assistance in their vocational development (Smith and Evans, 1973).

Further, the Janis model of decisional stages leads to the hypothesis that commitment in the form of role-playing will strengthen decisions already taken or encourage the individual along the decision-making path. While Janis and King (1954) found this true of opinion change in a traditional experimental setting, the experiment of Janis and Mann (1965) demonstrates the point in a more real situation. Subjects who were smokers were asked to play the role of a patient showing symptoms associated with smoking. The experimenter, playing the role of doctor, informed the 'patient' that he had lung cancer and would be operated on immediately. Subjects were considerably disturbed by this role-playing session and more of them decided to give up smoking in this group than from a control group who received the same information without role-playing. At an eighteen month follow-up, this was found to have a continued effect (Mann and Janis, 1968).

Interestingly, Janis' analysis of the conflict resulting from challenge to existing behaviour leads to similar predictions to those from Festinger's (1964) cognitive dissonance model when post-decisional challenges are weak— the decision maker will tend to bolster his decisions and is presumably at Stage 5 in Janis' model. However, when the challenge is strong, then, contrary to any consequence from dissonance theory, it is hypothesized that regret can become pre-potent and the decision maker goes into a new pre-decisional conflict (Janis, 1968b). (Note that regret is here used in its decision theory technical sense—a non-emotional concept representing a measurable difference between gains expected from a decision made on the basis of incomplete knowledge of the relevant true 'state of the world' and gains actually achieved from the decision.) Mann (1971), however, found no post-decisional bolstering of children's decisions and it may be that the development of decision-making in children follows a pattern rather different from the adult pattern. He found children, warned that their decision was final, approached the task with care and decisiveness, thus again demonstrating the importance of commitment in decision-making.

While there are undoubted ethical arguments against 'therapeutic' endeavours for a patient coerced in some way (legal, penal, social, etc.) into the treatment situation, Janis' five-stage conflict theory of decision processes also gives us some theoretical basis for predicting failure for such an endeavour with an individual who has presumably progressed no further than Stage 1 (Janis, 1968b).

FURTHER APPLICATIONS

It has already been noted that decision theory has been applied to industry and to vocational guidance, and related to learning and personality studies. Looking for applications in other areas of behaviour of particular interest to the clinician, we might with advantage consider decision theory in relation to criminal behaviour (see also Feldman, 1976). (Parenthetically, we note that, although gambling behaviour is the essence of much decision theory and associated experimentation, the approach has not yet been systematically applied to pathological gamblers who gamble to their own and others' destruction, and who may very likely overlap with the criminal group. This would be an obvious area for decision theorists to turn to and it is to be hoped that they will indeed consider the compulsive gambler whose decision to gamble has never been reversed despite high subjective and statistical probabilities of loss. It may be noted that pathological gambling has not escaped the attention of other psychological theoreticians. Skinner (1953, 1973), for example, suggested that such behaviour could result from a variable ratio (VR) reinforcement schedule. Dickerson (1974) investigated whether such a schedule was, in fact, operating to create or maintain actual gambling behaviour in betting shop customers and in a group from Gamblers Anonymous. He found the betting shop situation more likely to offer a fixed interval (FI) schedule combined with VR reinforcement (winnings), i.e. a conjunctive schedule. Skinner's analysis therefore is correct up to a point, but considerable further complexities are developed in Dickerson's modification. Plymen (1974) also takes the analysis of reinforcement schedules a stage further with her experiment to assess the effects of a gambling ratio (G), consisting of a VR schedule combined with a pay-off ratio (POR). The gambling ratio, while always less than unity, produced more gambling when large than when small.)

However, returning to criminal behaviour, i.e. behaviour of those guilty of violating the criminal law, Cohen (1970) shows that the criminal decision depends neither on the certainty of being caught, nor on the severity of the punishment—both of which can to some extent be estimated from official statistics—but on the interaction of *subjective* probability of being caught, *subjective* probability of punishment if caught and convicted, *subjective* severity of expected punishment and *subjective* probability of enjoyment of the loot irrespective of discovery, detention and punishment, making in all a complex SEU. As Cohen points out, this does not exhaust the factors determining the decision to commit crime. However, despite the well-known difficulties of experimentation and, particularly, of obtaining appropriate control groups, this analysis does optimistically point to the possibility of testing the hypothesis that the criminal offender is taking a gamble, staking his freedom and reputation against his subjective probabilities of gain and punishment, and hence his behaviour is susceptible to analysis in decision theory terms. Though staking less, the minor offender may with advantage be regarded in a similar light.

While the time taken to make decisions may be, at present, more a matter of neurophysiology than of decision theory—Surwillo (1964) has shown that subjects with slow brain waves require more time to decide between two alternatives than subjects with fast brain waves—it can readily be envisaged that speed of decision is a factor of importance to the professional DM. Hence, we would wish to know more of the electroencephalographic (EEG) correlates of decision-making, especially as the slower decision-making of increasing age was found to vanish when EEG brain wave period was partialled out (Surwillo, 1964). If decisions are not slower with age, as was at one time seriously maintained, our ageing populations can be more optimistic. This is also a conclusion to be drawn from work showing that older groups as readily make risky decisions as do younger (Spencer, Williams and Oldfield-Box, 1974). Such work provides glimpses of potential areas of investigation and their importance for the clinician.

A further development of decision psychology, and the closely allied work of detection theory, to the problems of discrimination and psychophysics familiar to psychologists is provided by Swets (1973). His relative operating characteristic (ROC) is an analytic technique for quantifying the relative magnitudes of discrimination biases and decision process biases (due to perceived probabilities and utilities of the total situation) in the study of making discriminations—rightly the concern of general and clinical psychologist alike. While numerous studies of vigilance have shown a decrement in performance after as little as half an hour of work (observation) and investigators (e.g. Broadbent, 1971) have examined the variables thought to affect alertness (e.g. fatigue, knowledge of results, drugs, introversion, age and sex), the ROC analysis suggests that the sole change over time is in the decision criterion or SEU for one decision rather than another. Swets (1973) deals at length with applications of this analysis for the clinician (memory studies, perceptual studies, especially subliminal perception studies and studies of perceptual defence need reinterpretation), and the clinician searching for evidence of disorder may be influenced by his judgements of the value of a particular treatment or of the prognosis of a certain medical disorder. The biases entering into our discriminations of right/wrong, yea/nay, red/green, treatable/untreatable, go/no-go, withdraw/approach, etc., must be understood before we can comprehend the fundamental behaviours. The field, as always, is open for the enterprising applied scientist to pick out further relevance. In the next section, we suggest some further domains of particular interest to the clinician in which decision analysis could add to the depth of our functional analyses of behaviour problems.

DECISIONS OF THE CLIENT

Relevant decisions of the client include general life decisions—both major decisions producing changes in life history, such as the decision to marry or divorce or the decision to abort (Bracken, Hachamovitch and Grossman, 1974; Millard, 1971) and simple and ordinary decisions (such as where to buy the sugar or whom to consult when puzzled) where these present difficulties which may in themselves constitute the disorder. The indecision of the neurotic is well known and may be most apparent in anxiety states and obsessional disorder. It has already been demonstrated (Carr, 1970; Steiner, 1972) that compulsive neurotics show an abnormally high subjective expectation of unfavourable outcome, although no hypothesis has as yet been put forward as to how this arises. Carr (1974), however, develops from this a theory of threat—expectation (of harm) times value as in Mausner and Platt's (1971) estimate of SEU—and concomitant anxiety being high in compulsive neurotics but reduceable by superstitious or ritual behaviours which subjectively lower the probability (expectation) of harm. This is an interesting model to explain compulsions but, as Carr himself notes, the therapeutic techniques for modification of subjective estimates of the probability of harm have yet to be worked out. Carr's is a promising theoretical model on which therapeutic endeavours could in the future be built. Analysis of other disorders in decision terms may similarly suggest therapeutic strategies.

It is possible also that behaviour modifications through training in decision processes (e.g. after Bross, 1953; Hopson and Hough, 1973; or Raiffa, 1970, p. 34) could benefit not only the indecisive but also those individuals who recognize in themselves a tendency to rush into action (decide?) precipitately and show themselves to be foolhardy or tactless. In this connection, it is promising to note that decision process training has been found to have some transfer of effect (Evans and Cody, 1969).

The decision to seek help for a behaviour problem is no mean decision for many, involving, as it may do, first the overcoming of desires for independence and, second, the potent remnants of the social stigmata of lunacy. Psychologists with an interest in publicity and public relations may with advantage look to decision models for ideas to facilitate such decisions of the client.

Then again, the decision to get better must be differentiated from the decision to ask for help (Greenwald, 1973) and might fruitfully be subject to a separate analysis of subjective utilities in individual cases. Psychiatrists have long considered the secondary gains of disorder and these, when stripped of 'unconscious' elements, are clearly subjectively expected utilities. This suggests the testable hypothesis of a relationship between SEU for behaviour change and (a) improvement or actual behaviour change, (b) symptom substitution or (c) later relapse after improvement, if any.

Still considering the relationship of decision and therapy, Goldfried and Merbaum (1973) believe that where self-control methods are employed the patient must himself decide on the desired goal, although this can and should be a matter for prior discussion with the therapist.

An interesting area only beginning to be studied is the relationship between personality variables and decision-making (Atkinson, 1957). Some people, for example, are thought to be risk-averse. Given a choice, they would prefer not to participate in a lottery (Raiffa, 1970). This might possibly account for patients not coming into therapy. Psychologists should perhaps turn their attention to the assessment of risk-aversion as a personality characteristic. Perhaps it is obversely related to the stimulus-seeking personality (Zuckerman and Link, 1968). Edwards (1961) found no coherent picture emerging in his study of decision-making and personality. However, the idea of risk-aversion versus stimulus-seeking as a focus of personality research is but one example

284

of the possible future developments, and we must retain our optimism here also.

DECISIONS OF GROUPS

The importance of decision-making in groups has been a major feature of decision theory (Vinokur, 1971b). Davis (1973) provides a theory of social decision schemes which could be developed to have relevance for group therapy or for family interaction situations. Group decisions with political consequences have been investigated (Scioli, Dyson and Fleitas, 1974). Pollard and Mitchell (1972) apply decision theory to the analysis of social power which might appear peripheral to our concerns until it is recognized, as it generally is now, that the therapist is willy-nilly in a situation of social power vis-à-vis his clients. The nature of decision-making as an activity which can divide or bind the group is recognized by Levinger and Breedlove (1966) in their study of marriage partners, and the facilitating effect of a partner in strengthening a decision has been noted (Janis and Hoffman, 1970).

Decision-making by the important decision makers of society, such as judges and arbitrators in industrial disputes, has appropriately been the subject of study (Shaw, Fischer and Kelley, 1973). While interesting findings have emerged concerning attitudes before and after decision-making, further analysis using perhaps the decision theory concept of regret in this connection would seem worthwhile.

Decision-making, however, is ubiquitous and there is no apologia for its inclusion here. I submit that clinical psychologists must and will in future consider behaviour change in terms of utilities or the reward cost approach to the explanation of clinical behaviour, and that the further study of decisions will throw interesting light on our clinical decisions and the life decisions of our clients, always remembering that 'the creative stage (of a decision analysis) is ... the stage in which the decision maker decides he has a problem and decides to consider it in earnest (Raiffa, 1970, p. 262)'.

REFERENCES

Aitchison, J. (1970). Statistical problems of treatment application. *Journal of the Royal Statistical Society*, **133**, 206–238.
Alexander, F. G., and Selesnick, S. T. (1966). *The History of Psychiatry*, Harper and Row, New York.
Arthur, A. Z. (1969). Diagnostic testing and the new alternatives. *Psychological Bulletin*, **52**, 372–376.
Arthur, A. Z. (1972). Theory and action-oriented research. *Journal of Consulting and Clinical Pathology*, **38**, 129–133.
Atkinson, J. W. (1957). Motivational determinants of risk-taking behavior. *Psychological Review*, **64**, 359–372.
Atkinson, J. W. (1964). *An Introduction to Motivation*, Van Norstrand, Princeton.
Becker, G. M., and McClintock, C. G. (1967). Value: behavioral decision theory. *Annual Review of Psychology*, **18**, 239–286.

Block, J., and Petersen, P. (1955). Some personality correlates of confidence, caution, and speed in a decision situation. *Journal of Abnormal and Social Psychology*, **51**, 34–41.

Bracken, M. B., Hachamovitch, M., and Grossman, G. (1974). The decision to abort and psychological sequelae. *Journal of Nervous and Mental Disease*, **158**, 154–162.

Broadbent, D. E. (1971). *Decision and Stress*, Academic Press, London.

Bross, I. D. J. (1953). *Design for Decision*, Macmillan, New York.

Busse, T. V., and Love, C. (1973). The effect of first names on conflicted decisions: an experimental study. *Journal of Psychology*, **84**, 253–246.

Carr, A. T. (1970). *A Psychophysiological Study of Ritual Behaviours and Decision Processes in Compulsive Neurosis*. Unpublished Ph.D. thesis, University of Birmingham.

Carr, A. T. (1974). Compulsive neurosis: a review of the literature. *Psychological Bulletin*, **81**, 311–318.

Cohen, J. (1970). Uncertainty and risk-taking in crime. *Bulletin of the British Psychological Society*, **23**, 293–296.

Davis, J. H. (1973). Group decision and social interaction: a theory of social decision schemes. *Psychological Review*, **80**, 97–125.

Deutsch, M. (1960). Trust, trustworthiness and the F scale. *Journal of Abnormal and Social Psychology*, **61**, 138–140.

Dickerson, M. G. (1974). *The Effect of Betting Shop Experience on Gambling Behaviour*. Unpublished Ph.D. thesis, University of Birmingham.

Edwards, D., and Berry, N. H. (1974). Psychiatric decisions: an actuarial study. *Journal of Clinical Psychology*, **30**, 153–159.

Edwards, W. (1954). The theory of decision making. *Psychological Bulletin*, **51**, 380–417.

Edwards, W. (1961). Behavioral decision theory. *Annual Review of Psychology*, **12**, 473–498.

Edwards, W., and Tversky, A. (1967). *Decision Making: Selected Readings*, Penguin, Harmondsworth.

Evans, J. R., and Cody, J. J. (1969). Transfer of decision-making skills learned in a counseling-like setting to similar and dissimilar situations. *Journal of Counseling Psychology*, **16**, 427–432.

Evans, R. I., Rozelle, R. M., Lasater, T. M., Dembroski, T. M., and Allen, B. P. (1970). Fear arousal, persuasion, and actual versus implied behavioral change. *Journal of Personality and Social Psychology*, **16**, 220–227.

Feather, N. T. (1959). Subjective probability and decision under uncertainty. *Psychological Review*, **66**, 150–164.

Feldman, M. P. (1976). *Criminal Behaviour: A Psychological Analysis*, Wiley, London.

Festinger, L. (Ed.) (1964). *Conflict, Decision and Dissonance*, Stanford University Press, Stanford, California.

Fishbein, M. (1967). Attitude and the prediction of behavior. In M. Fishbein (Ed.), *Readings in Attitude Theory and Measurement*, Wiley, New York.

Goldfried, M. R., and Merbaum, M. (1973). *Behavior Change through Self-control*, Holt, Rinehart and Winston, New York.

Goldman, M. S. (1974). To drink or not to drink: an experimental analysis of group drinking decisions by four alcoholics. *American Journal of Psychiatry*, **131**, 1123–1130.

Greenwald, H. (1973). *Decision Therapy*, Wyden, New York.

Heneman, H. G., and Schwab, D. P. (1972). Evaluation of research on expectancy theory prediction of employee performance. *Psychological Bulletin*, **78**, 1–9.

Hopson, B., and Hough, P. (1973). *Exercises in Personal and Career Development*, Careers Research and Advisory Centre (CRAC), Cambridge.

Hull, C. L. (1943). *Principles of Behavior*, Appleton-Century-Crofts, New York.

Janis, I. L. (1958). *Psychological Stress*, Wiley, New York.

Janis, I. L. (1968a). Attitude change via role playing. In R. P. Abelson, E. Aronson, W. J. McGuire, T. M. Newcomb, M. J. Rosenberg and P. H. Tannenbaum (Eds.), *Theories of Cognitive Consistency: A Source Book*, Rand McNally, Chicago.

Janis, I. L. (1968b). Stages in the decision-making process. In R. P. Abelson, W. J. McGuire, T. M. Newcomb, M. J. Rosenberg and P. H. Tannenbaum (Eds.), *Theories of Cognitive Consistency: A Source Book*, Rand McNally, Chicago.

Janis, I. L., and Hoffman, D. (1970). Facilitating effects of daily contact between partners who make a decision to cut down on smoking. *Journal of Personality and Social Psychology*, **17**, 25–35.

Janis, I. L., and King, B. T. (1954). The influence of role playing on opinion change. *Journal of Abnormal and Social Psychology*, **49**, 211–218.

Janis, I. L., and Mann, L. (1965). Effectiveness of emotional role-playing in modifying smoking habits and attitudes. *Journal of Experimental Research in Personality*, **1**, 84–90.

Janis, I. L., and Mann, L. (1968). A conflict theory approach to attitude change and decision making. In A. Greenwald, T. Brock and T. Ostrom (Eds.), *Psychological Foundations of Attitudes*, Academic Press, New York.

Janis, I. L., and Terwilliger, R. (1962). An experimental study of psychological resistance to fear-arousing communications. *Journal of Abnormal and Social Psychology*, **65**, 403–411.

Jones, H. G. (1970). Principles of psychological assessment. In P. Mittler (Ed.), *The Psychological Assessment of Mental and Physical Handicaps*, Tavistock, London. pp. 1–25.

Kleiter, G. D. (1974). Multistage decision models in psychology. *Psychologische Beitrage*, **16**, 93–127.

Kleiven, J., Fraser, C., and Gouge, C. (1974). Are individual and group decisions dependent on the available information? *Scandinavian Journal of Psychology*, **15**, 178–184.

Kozielecki, J. (1972). A model for diagnostic problem solving. *Acta Psychologica*, **36**, 370–380.

Laplace, P. S. (1951). *A Philosophical Essay on Probabilities*. Trans. by F. W. Truscott and F. L. Emory. Dover, New York.

Lee, W. (1971). *Decision Theory and Human Behavior*, Wiley, New York.

Leventhal, H., and Watts, J. C. (1966). Sources of resistance to fear-arousing communications on smoking and lung cancer. *Journal of Personality*, **34**, 155–175.

Levinger, G., and Breedlove, J. (1966). Inter-personal attraction and agreement: a study of marriage partners. *Journal of Personality and Social Psychology*, **3**, 367–372.

Lewin, K., Dembo, T., Festinger, L., and Sears, P. (1965). Level of aspiration. In J. McV. Hunt (Ed.), *Personality and the Behavior Disorders*, Ronald Press, New York.

Lumsdaine, A. A., and Janis, I. L. (1953). Resistance to 'counter propaganda' produced by one-sided and two-sided 'propaganda' presentations. *Public Opinion Quarterly*, **17**, 311–318.

Mann, L. (1971). Effects of a commitment warning on children's decision behavior. *Journal of Personality and Social Psychology*, **17**, 74–80.

Mann, L., and Janis, I. L. (1968). A follow-up study on the long-term effects of emotional role playing. *Journal of Personality and Social Psychology*, **8**, 339–342.

Mausner, B. (1973). An ecological view of cigarette smoking. *Journal of Abnormal Psychology*, **81**, 115–126.

Mausner, B., and Platt, E. S. (1971). *Smoking: A Behavioral Analysis*, Pergamon, New York.

Millard, D. W. (1971). The abortion decision. *British Journal of Social Work*, **1**, 131–148.

Mitchell, T. R., and Biglan, A. (1971). Instrumentality theories: current uses in psychology. *Psychological Bulletin*, **76**, 432–454.

Nathan, P. (1967). *Cues, Decisions and Diagnoses*, Academic Press, New York.

Plymen, E. A. (1974). *The Effect of Gambling Ratio on Gambling Behaviour*. Unpublished M.Sc. thesis, University of Birmingham.

Pollard, W. E., and Mitchell, T. R. (1972). Decision theory analysis of social power. *Psychological Bulletin*, **78**, 433–446.

Raiffa, H. (1970). *Decision Analysis: Introductory Lectures on Choices Under Uncertainty*, Addison-Wesley, Reading, Massachusetts.

Rapoport, A., and Wallsten, T. S. (1972). Individual decision behavior. *Annual Review of Psychology*, **23**, 131–176.

Rotter, J. B. (1954). *Social Learning and Clinical Psychology*, Prentice Hall, New York.

Savage, L. J. (1967). Difficulties in the theory of personal probability. *Philosophy of Science*, **34**, 305–332.

Scioli, F. P., Dyson, J. W., and Fleitas, D. W. (1974). The relationship of personality and decisional structure to leadership. *Small Group Behavior*, **5**, 3–22.

Shaw, J. I., Fischer, C. S., and Kelley, H. H. (1973). Decision making by third parties in settling disputes. *Journal of Applied Social Psychology*, **3**, 197–218.

Skinner, B. F. (1953). *Science and Human Behavior*, Free Press, New York.

Skinner, B. F. (1973). *Beyond Freedom and Dignity*, Penguin, Harmondsworth.

Slovic, P., and Lichtenstein, S. (1968). Relative importance of probabilities and payoffs in risk taking. *Journal of Experimental Psychology Monographs*, **78**, 1–18.

Slovic, P., Lichtenstein, S., and Edwards, W. (1965). Boredom-induced changes in preference among bets. *American Journal of Psychology*, **78**, 208–217.

Smith, R. D., and Evans, J. R. (1973). Comparison of experimental group guidance and individual counseling as facilitators of vocational development. *Journal of Counseling Psychology*, **20**, 202–208.

Sofer, C., Wishlade, L., and Janis, I. L. (1964). Social and psychological factors in changing food habits. In J. Yudkin and J. MacKenzie (Eds.), *Changing Food Habits*, McGibbon and Kee, London, pp. 90–108.

Spencer, C., Williams, M., and Oldfield-Box, H. (1974). Age, group decisions on risk-related topics and the prediction of choice shifts. *British Journal of Social and Clinical Psychology*, **13**, 375–381.

Steiner, I. D. (1970). Perceived freedom. In L. Berkowitz (Ed.), *Advances in Experimental Social Psychology*, Vol. 5. Academic Press, New York.

Steiner, I. D., Rotermund, M., and Talaber, R. (1974). Attribution of choice to a decision maker. *Journal of Personality and Social Psychology*, **30**, 553–562.

Steiner, J. (1972). A questionnaire study of risk-taking in psychiatric patients. *British Journal of Medical Psychology*, **45**, 365–374.

Surwillo, W. W. (1964). The relation of decision time to brain wave frequency and to age. *Electroencephalography and Clinical Neurophysiology*, **16**, 510–514.

Swets, J. A. (1973). The relative operating characteristic in psychology. *Science*, **182**, 990–1000.

Tolman, E. C. (1952). A cognition motivation model. *Psychological Review*, **59**, 389–400.

Toomey, M. (1972). Conflict theory approach to decision making applied to alcoholics. *Journal of Personality and Social Psychology*, **24**, 199–206.

Vinokur, A. (1971a). Cognitive and affective processes influencing risk taking in groups: an expected utility approach. *Journal of Personality and Social Psychology*, **20**, 472–486.

Vinokur, A. (1971b). Review and theoretical analysis of the effects of group processes upon individual and groups decisions involving risk. *Psychological Bulletin*, **76**, 231–250.

Vroom, V. H. (1964). *Work and Motivation*, Wiley, New York.

Wright, P. (1974). The harassed decision maker: time pressures, distractions, and the use of evidence. *Journal of Applied Psychology*, **59**, 555–561.

Zuckerman, M., and Link, K. (1968). Construct validity for the sensation-seeking scale. *Journal of Consulting and Clinical Psychology*, **32**, 420–426.

10

BEHAVIOURAL ASSESSMENT AND DECISION-MAKING: THE DESIGN OF STRATEGIES FOR THERAPEUTIC BEHAVIOUR CHANGE

Richard I. Lanyon and Barbara J. Lanyon

INTRODUCTION

The domain of behaviour therapy continues to grow rapidly and to become increasingly complex. To attempt a definition that would satisfy everybody would be a difficult task, and one that perhaps should not be attempted. From the authors' perspective, behaviour therapy involves primarily the application of principles derived from research in the psychology of learning to the alleviation of human suffering and the enhancement of human functioning. An essential component of behaviour therapy is a systematic monitoring and evaluation of the effectiveness of these applications. Behaviour therapy typically involves direct intervention through environmental change and social or interpersonal interaction. The techniques are generally intended to facilitate improved self-control by expanding the skills, abilities, and independence of the individuals.

It is useful to view behaviour therapy as a specialized professional service for personal behaviour change. There is always an initial period of assessment and decision making, which consists of the following steps. First, potential clients or patients are helped to describe the current situation and also the goal or end-product as they would like it. Next, the therapist collects the information that is needed to develop alternative outlines of what might be done, and to make estimates of the resources that are likely to be required of the client. Negotiation then takes place until a contract, explicit or implicit, is agreed upon. It is this initial period of assessment and decision-making that constitutes the topic for the present chapter.

The chapter is not intended to be a practical guide for behaviour therapists as they attempt to set up a problem for treatment by behaviour therapy. Rather, it is a theoretically and empirically based conceptual overview of the process of designing strategies for therapeutic behaviour change. However, the chapter can be useful practically to readers who possess the following additional skills: a working knowledge of behavioural learning theory; basic clinical skills, including those that are specific to behaviour therapy (e.g. negotiating a behavioural contract); a working knowledge of psychopathology; and a working knowledge of psychometric methods.

In setting out to review the process of assessment in behaviour therapy, one cannot help but be impressed by the potential for rapid development in this area of knowledge and skill. As implied in the title, it is the authors' belief that the theoretical and research foundations of behaviour therapy are rapidly becoming sophisticated enough that problems of therapeutic behaviour change can be approached primarily as problems in *design*—the design of strategies, programmes or systems for changing behaviour in the manner requested. As these developments occur, the actual carrying out of behaviour change procedures will tend to become a technical rather than a professional level task. The ethical dilemmas posed by the widespread training of persons with technical but not professional competence in behaviour change procedures are many, and psychologists should continue actively in their attempts to resolve them, lest government controls hamper the ultimate public interest. Although few persons would argue against the continued application of behaviour principles in the area of relieving human distress, those who accept the challenge of developing and improving them also accept a responsibility for guarding against their misuse.

It should be emphasized from the beginning that the design of behaviour change strategies must be viewed as a *process*, and one that usually continues well beyond the formal assessment period and into the period when behaviour change procedures are being actively applied. Perhaps the ultimate in sophistication would be a technology of behaviour change that enabled the major design aspects to be carried out first, much in the manner of the engineer, architect or surgeon. Whether or not this will prove an appropriate model for the future cannot yet be determined; for the present, only simple behaviour change procedures designed by skilled behavioural clinicians can be planned ahead of time with any degree of certainty. The need to regard planning as a continuous process is particularly important now that behaviour therapists are increasingly working with patients whose problems are complex and extensive, as compared to the simple, unitary disorders that were once the sole material for this treatment modality.

The development of procedures for the design of behaviour change strategies has lagged somewhat behind the development of behaviour change technology itself. There are two major reasons for this lag. The first relates to the fact that behaviour therapy originated as a series of procedures for altering unitary, easily defined behaviours under circumstances where other therapeutic procedures had been ineffective. Examples are the reduction of phobic anxiety through systematic desensitization, and the development of speech and other social behaviours in chronic psychotic patients and severely disturbed children.

In these situations, which involved the extension of simple behaviour change principles developed in the animal laboratory to discrete behaviours in humans, the question of 'assessment' was more or less redundant. It is only as behaviour therapy has sought to emerge as a viable treatment modality in its own right, dealing with problems that require the sequential or simultaneous application of a variety of behaviour change techniques, that questions of planning, design, assessment and evaluation have become more significant.

The second reason for the lag in the development of behavioural assessment procedures has to do with the attitudes of behaviour therapists toward the whole topic of assessment for therapeutic purposes. In the view of most behaviour therapists, the traditional assessment battery administered routinely by the psychologist or the intern to the patient awaiting psychodynamic therapy, and consisting of some combination of tests such as the Rorschach, TAT, Bender and human figure drawings, did not produce much information that was centrally relevant to the practical decisions that had to be made. Further, the uncertain validity of many of these techniques, even in optimal circumstances, tended to lead the more scientifically oriented clinicians away from assessment altogether.

Another important related influence, defined by Goldfried and Pomeranz (1968), is that personality assessment has traditionally been based on what Murray (1938) has called the 'centralist' orientation in the study of Man. In this approach, the basic concepts to be assessed and understood as the determinants of behaviour are dynamics, needs, expectations and underlying motivational forces. The orientation of the behaviour therapist implies a rejection of the centralist philosophy, and there is little use for such concepts in the design of behaviour change procedures. It has only been rather recently (e.g. Goldfried and Pomeranz, 1968; Goldfried and Sprafkin, 1974; Kanfer, 1972; Kanfer and Saslow, 1969; Wolff and Merrens, 1974) that systematic attempts have been made to delineate the nature, rôle and functions of assessment in behaviour therapy.

It is to be hoped that the heavy criticism directed at traditional assessment procedures by psychometrically oriented researchers in the 1950s and 1960s, while perhaps delaying the full integration of assessment procedures into the field of behaviour therapy, will prove to have had a salutory effect. What infusion of psychometric techniques there has so far been into behavioural assessment methods appears to be having a greater impact than previous similar infusions into projective assessment methods, for example. In the same vein, problems such as validity, instructional bias and observer reliability are now beginning to be approached on a wider scale in behavioural assessment. Perhaps these developments may be taken as favourable signs that behaviour therapists will eventually be fully open to the incorporation of whatever can be utilized from psychometric technology.

Views of behavioural assessment

In attempting to determine what the area of behavioural assessment includes, or should include, it is useful to survey the views of other writers on this topic. Peterson (1968) has stated the question as follows:

> What, in specific detail, is the nature of the problem behavior? What is the person doing, overtly or covertly, which he or someone else defined as problematic and hence changeworthy behavior? What are the antecedents, both internal and external, of the problem behavior and what conditions are in effect at the time the behavior occurs? What are the consequences of the problem behavior? In particular, what reinforcing events, immediate as well as distant, appear to perpetuate the behavior under study? What changes might be made in the antecedents, concomitants, or consequences of behavior to effect behavior change? (Donald R. Peterson, *The Clinical Study of Social Behavior*, © 1968. Reprinted by permission of Prentice-Hall Inc, Englewood Cliffs, N. J., U.S.A.)

A similar view is taken by Mischel (1968), who stated that 'the most urgent goal in assessment is to design the treatments required by the client's problems (p. 235)'. To enlarge upon this statement:

> The problem behaviors and the desired objectives have to be defined with clear behavioral referents. Next it is necessary to describe the exact circumstances provoking the problem behaviors and to identify the conditions maintaining them. In light of this information the particular behavior-change operations most likely to produce the desired objectives must be selected. (p. 236).

The view taken by Kanfer and Phillips (1970) is also similar:

> Behavioral diagnosis or analysis can be used for several purposes: (1) identification of therapeutic target responses and their maintaining stimuli; (2) assessment of functional relationships among response classes and among discriminative and reinforcing stimuli; (3) determination of available social resources, personal assets, and skills for use in a therapeutic program, as well as of limitations and obstacles in the person and the environment; and (4) availability of specific therapeutic strategies or behavioral techniques most consonant with the personal and environmental factors in the patient's life situation (p. 504).

A more elaborate rationale and framework for behavioural assessment has been given by Kanfer elsewhere (Kanfer and Saslow, 1969).

A fourth source of writings on behavioural assessment has been Goldfried and his colleagues (Goldfried and Kent, 1972; Goldfried and Pomeranz, 1968; Goldfried and Sprafkin, 1974). In their view, the most appropriate uses of assessment for behaviour therapy are 'to delineate those target areas where change should take place, and to offer some information about the specific therapeutic technique which would be best suited for bringing about change with this particular individual (Goldfried and Pomeranz, 1968, p. 78)'.

Examination of these statements shows common elements in five respects:

(1) The basic task of defining the problem behaviour or behaviours in concrete, observable terms.

(2) Observation and description of the events that are maintaining the current state of affairs—antecedents, concomitants and consequences.

(3) Behavioural formulation, in which an attempt is made to determine what

events are maintaining the problem behaviours in their present state and by what behavioural processes.

(4) Survey of available treatment resources, including those of the environment and those of the patient.

(5) Design of an optimal treatment strategy, given the nature of the problem and the operating resources and constraints.

To these five points the present authors would add several emphases. First, it is important to appreciate the active, deliberate and planful nature of the assessment process, in which the treatment procedures are *designed* and *constructed*. Second is the very real possibility that assessment might show that the available resources are simply inadequate to bring about any of the desired changes, in which case nothing further would be attempted. Third, as emphasized earlier, assessment is, in practice, very much a continuous process, so that even though the procedures are set forth as a series of consecutive steps, assessment in practice will usually be tentative and the design will be subject to revisions. Economy is a factor here; while it may be theoretically possible at times to design the complete behaviour change system in advance, it will often be quicker and cheaper to initiate behaviour change procedures as soon as the first steps have been decided upon and to acknowledge that changes and further planning will be necessary after more complete information is gathered and some progress has been made.

Traditional versus behavioural assessment

In order to appreciate fully the conceptual nature of assessment within the framework of behaviour therapy, it is useful to make a comparison with traditional assessment procedures, which are typically viewed within the framework of psychodynamic therapy. A number of authors (Cautela, 1968; Goldfried and Kent, 1972; Goldfried and Pomeranz, 1968; Kanfer and Phillips, 1970; Kanfer and Saslow, 1968; Wallace, 1966, 1967) have already written on this topic.

One important difference lies in basic theoretical views about human nature. The psychodynamic approach to human nature includes the basic assumptions that specific behaviour patterns, or at least dispositions toward specific behaviour patterns, are relatively independent of the environment, that they are rather stable over long periods of time and that changing them requires prolonged and in-depth attention to underlying attributes or personality characteristics. This view, as we have already stated, is consistent with the centralist orientation in the study of Man. Actions are determined by underlying predispositions or personality structure, in which concepts such as traits, needs, drives and defences are central. Assessment, therefore, focuses on the study of these underlying predispositions.

In the behavioural view, by contrast, behaviours are held to be much more directly under the control of environmental cues, both external and internal to the person, and are considered capable of being changed by the same processes as those by which the person learns other competencies and skills. Thus, assessment within a behavioural approach focuses on response capability or performance. It is oriented toward what people *do* and under what environmental conditions, not what they 'have' or 'are'. Behavioural assessment can be seen as much more similar to the assessment of abilities or skills than to predispositions (Wallace, 1966, 1967).

An examination of the differences between traditional tests of ability and traditional tests of personality highlights another important aspect of behavioural assessment (Wernimont and Campbell, 1968). In ability assessment, the behaviours of interest are typically sampled in a standardized situation under conditions of high motivation. A representative example would be the assessment of vocabulary level by asking about the meanings of selected words and scoring the responses according to pre-set criteria, such as in the vocabulary subsets of the WAIS or the Stanford-Binet. It is assumed that the individual's performance on the test reflects his performance *capability* or performance level in other situations of high motivation. An analogous sampling approach is employed in the assessment of behavioural problems, except that the stimulus situation is kept constant, not by eliciting the maximum possible level of response but by making the assessment under the particular stimulus conditions that are normally associated with the problem behaviour. In determining the validity of direct behaviour sampling as an assessment procedure, emphasis is placed on the degree to which the *content* of the behaviour sample and of the stimulus situation are representative of the behaviours and situations to which the assessment is to be generalized.

Traditional assessment, on the other hand, does not involve direct sampling, but employs test data as signs, or indicators, of the underlying predispositions that are the basic target for assessment. Illustrative examples might include Piotrowski's (1937) 'organic signs' or Klopfer's 'schizophrenic signs' on the Rorschach (Klopfer and Kelley, 1942), the Meehl-Peterson 'psychotic signs' on the MMPI (Peterson, 1954) and the search for 'paranoid signs' or 'anxiety signs' in human figure drawings. The model is the centralist one, in which dispositions can never be observed directly but must be assessed through the presence of their indirect signs. In establishing the utility of these procedures, *empirical* (predictive or concurrent) validity must be demonstrated. This approach tends to be consistent with the traditional medical or illness model of psychological disorder (e.g. Ullmann and Krasner, 1965).

It is worth noting that the weight of research evidence now shows that content validity is of critical importance in traditional assessment also. The traditional view that empirical validity was sufficient led to the inclusion of many 'subtle' items in the MMPI, for example. More recent studies (e.g. Duff, 1965) and an extended review by Jackson (1971) have clearly demonstrated that it is those inventory items with greatest content validity that carry most of the predictive weight. Even more significant, the findings of Goldberg and Slovic (1967) clearly imply that inventory items that refer to actual data (e.g. 'I have fewer than three close friends') are more predictive than items that are worded in a more global manner (e.g. 'I have few close friends').

Another important difference between traditional and behavioural assessment regarding the 'locus of interest' has already been implied, but should be stated explicitly. Traditional assessment is essentially a matter of the individual patient; i.e. it focuses on the individual and attempts to assess qualities that are 'within' him. The assumption is made that the causes of the patient's difficulties are internal or 'intrapsychic', and that treatment should proceed by dealing with these internal problems in relative isolation from the external environment. Another implicit assumption is that these internal characteristics have been stable over a lengthy period of time and that it is important to develop a historical understanding of how they came about. The behavioural model, on the other hand, takes the view that behaviour (including problem behaviour) is determined to a significant extent by the conditions of the current environment. Thus, there is a greatly increased focus of assessment on the environment and much less on internal qualities of the individual. Further, it is the present environment that is considered important rather than the past environment.

The subject matter of behaviour therapy

A topic that has received little systematic attention is the dual question of deciding what psychological or mental health problems are amenable to behaviour therapy, and for what problems behaviour therapy should constitute the treatment of choice. In other words, does behaviour therapy have a specific 'turf' and, if so, how should it be described? Ten years ago, when behaviour therapy was in its infancy, problems were only considered for this treatment modality if one of the specific techniques that were then available appeared to be appropriate. As behaviour therapy has gradually gained the status of a 'movement' (some might say a 'religion'), it has become fashionable to take the position that all mental health problems are best treated by behavioural means. To hold this view is to fall into the same trap as the adherents of other movements in the past, the most celebrated being psychoanalysis. A distinction should be made between the position that the treatment of all problems can, in principle, be conceptualized in behavioural terms and the position that all problems are *best* treated behaviourally. The former position can be legitimately debated, but only the most radical of behaviour therapists would attempt to defend the latter.

Another defensible view might be that behavioural procedures should nearly always constitute one or more *components* of an appropriate treatment strategy. Also important is the fact that a problem might be amenable to a behavioural approach in principle but not in practice, because the necessary treatment resources are not available. In fact, the limitation of inadequate treatment resources is probably the single most important factor in the inability of therapists to design a behavioural programme and in the failure of many programmes that are designed.

As would be expected, the greatest reported success to date for behavioural treatment has been with disordered behaviours that are readily observable and can be clearly described in specific terms. A partial list would include phobias, sexual disorders, the management of problem behaviours in children, obesity and other specific anxieties and avoidance behaviours such as shyness, unassertiveness and difficulty in studying, plus certain instances of problems such as alcoholism, stuttering, depression, obsessive-compulsive disorders and hysterical conversion reactions. The present chapter is written within the context of relatively specific problems such as these, and it is suggested that this fact be kept in mind in reading the remainder of the chapter. Behaviour therapists who attempt to work with complex problems that involve a large variety of difficulties, or where the components are vague or difficult to specify, generally try to analyse them into a series of discrete problems of the kind listed above. It is still too early in the development of behaviour therapy as a field to know how often behavioural procedures will prove to be the method of choice for complex problems, although informal clinical evidence does tend to support a favourable view.

Covert behaviours

The term 'covert' behaviours in the context of behaviour therapy refers to events that are internal to the individual and therefore not directly observable. Loosely speaking, it can be regarded as referring to cognitive behaviours (thoughts) and affective behavours (feelings of anxiety, anger, etc.). Behavioural psychologists have traditionally ignored such events as not having a legitimate place in the edifice of behaviour theory, except in the guise of correlated events that are publicly observable (e.g. trembling, sweating). The status of overt *verbal* responses as a legitimate source of behavioural data has also been in doubt.

In the last few years, it has become rather well established that many covert behaviours, as determined from an individual's verbal report, conform to the same behavioural principles that govern overt behaviours. Thus, a thought can function as a response, as an antecedent stimulus or as a reinforcer. Research supporting such a position has been recently reviewed by Thoreson and Mahoney (1974). There are obviously a great many complexities to this view of covert behaviours, and they are well beyond the scope of the present chapter. The important point in the present context is that it is often possible to regard a covert state, as defined by self-report, as behaviour within the framework of behaviour therapy. Attention is drawn to the three different ways in which covert behaviours can be relevant to behaviour therapy: (a) as actual problem behaviours; (b) as maintaining stimuli (antecedents or consequences) of problem behaviour; and (c) as events that are introduced as part of the behaviour change strategy. As with overt behaviours, covert events can be both voluntary (e.g. a deliberate thought) or involuntary (e.g. a hallucination).

Beyond the presenting complaint

A persistent topic of disagreement between behaviour theorists and psychodynamic theorists has been the importance of non-immediate events in determining and maintaining problem behaviours. Classical psychoanalytic theory holds that disordered behaviour is maintained largely by the residue of childhood experiences, the significant aspects of which are 'unconscious' or unavailable to voluntary designation by the patient and are visible only in symbolic, or displaced, or generalized form. As discussed above, behaviour therapists believe that the significant events maintaining the problem behaviour are currently present in the patient's environment, although they may not be at all obvious. Also, the events that originally caused the development of the problem behaviour may, in the behavioural view, be quite different from the events that are currently maintaining it.

These beliefs have direct relevance for behavioural assessment because they dictate what should or should not be assessed. First, they indicate that behavioural assessment and treatment should focus on the problem behaviour *as presented*, and not on other behaviours that traditionally would be regarded as the 'real' or 'underlying' problem. Second, they lead to the view that a behavioural analysis need not attempt to piece together the conditions of original learning of a problem behaviour, no matter how interesting such an analysis might be. Third, if the patient declares that the 'real' problem behaviour is not what the therapist has been working on, but another one that is now becoming more evident, there is no reason to take the view that the second behaviour has somehow been 'uncovered' by removing the protective function of the first. Individuals with complex difficulties will have many problem behaviours—some they can verbalize and some not, some immediately evident to the therapist and some not, and some serving as discriminative or reinforcing events for others.

It is not meant to imply that historical or biographical data are of no relevance in behavioural assessment and treatment, but simply that the *critical* data will generally not be found there. Behavioural assessment procedures typically include a comprehensive self-report biographical questionnaire, designed as a general survey of past events that might have some relevance to the current problem behaviour. The increasing popularity and endorsement of this approach gives some subjective support to its appropriateness and utility.

Nor is it meant to imply that the behaviour therapist will always focus on the problem exactly as presented by the patient. For example, behavioural analysis may indicate that the events serving to maintain the problem behaviours are not those that the patient thinks. A common example can be seen in married couples who present as a problem their children's unmanageable behaviour, when it is their own behaviours that are primarily maintaining the children's difficulties. Further, there may be instances in which patients are quite unable to specify their problem behaviours, which are nevertheless capable of a precise formulation by the therapist. An example would be the patient who complains that life has 'lost its meaning' for him and is unable to specify his difficulties any further. The behaviour therapist may discover that the patient's current environment offers neither stimuli nor reinforcement for behaviours that the patient considers 'meaningful', but instead stimulates and reinforces meaningless, repetitive behaviours and punishes any attempts by the patient to initiate new activities.

Framework for behavioural assessment

We now summarize the process of assessment for behaviour change as it applies in an ongoing clinical situation of the kind experienced by most mental health professionals. This four-step sequence is essentially the same as the five elements of behavioural assessment that were stated earlier in the chapter, with the first two (definition and observation) considered together. The organization of the remainder of the chapter follows this outline. It should be emphasized that the behaviour therapist does not attempt to assess all the different problems that the patient might have, but only the portion of the patient's functioning that is directly relevant to the problem for which change is being sought. However, the patient might not know how limited or extensive the problem is, and the therapist must make this determination.

1. Definition and observation

The therapist defines the behaviour or behaviours of specific concern and then gathers direct information about (a) their current frequency; (b) their consequences; and (c) their antecedents—the stimulus conditions under which they occur. In the case of behaviours whose frequency is deficient, he gathers similar information about the stimulus conditions under which they would normally occur and the consequences that would normally be expected to maintain them. It should be emphasized that no amount of sophistication in behavioural technology can substitute for good clinical skills on the part of the behaviour therapist as he works with the patient toward formulating the problems within a behavioural framework. Also, as stated above, not all problems presented to a mental health professional are best conceptualized within a behaviour change framework.

2. Behavioural formulation

The therapist devotes some effort to a formulation or analysis of the problem in behavioural terms. That is, he makes an attempt to identify the specific antecedents or consequences that are maintaining the problem behaviours or are preventing the development of new behaviours. Implementation of behaviour change procedures can begin in the absence of a conceptual formulation, but the more accurately the relevant characteristics of the problem are delineated from the observational data, the more efficient can be the design of a behaviour change strategy.

3. Assessment of available treatment resources

The behaviour therapist assesses the means available for bringing about behaviour change, including: the patient's self-observation and self-regulation skills, and the degree to which these skills can be learned; the degree of control available to the therapist; the patient's imagery skills; the availability of workable reinforcers; the therapist's own skills and resources; and the availability of other human change agents.

4. Design of optimal treatment strategy

Armed with a behavioural analysis of the patient's difficulties and an assessment of the available treatment resources, the therapist surveys the possible methods of bringing about the desired changes, discusses them with the patient, explains the responsibilities of each person and attempts to negotiate an agreement as to what procedures will be followed. The negotiation includes agreement as to what end-products, or terminal behaviours, can realistically be achieved. The therapist, as a specialist in behaviour change, takes responsibility for bringing about the agreed changes provided the patient fulfils his responsibility, which is to follow the therapist's instructions in the agreed manner.

DEFINING AND OBSERVING BEHAVIOURAL PROBLEMS

The basic thrust of behaviour therapy is in working on discrete, easily identifiable units of behaviour. As we have already noted, the contemporary definition of behaviour includes 'covert' as well as overt behaviours and involuntary as well as voluntary behaviours. As a first step toward the design of strategies for therapeutic behaviour change, it must be understood how to *define* behaviours in the appropriate manner. Definition is closely associated with *observation*, since in the modified logical positivist philosophy that underlies behaviour therapy, definition is itself operationally defined as public and reliable observation.

The emphasis on definition and observation that has characterized behaviour therapy from its inception has been one of its most solid foundations. It has placed behaviour therapy procedures in a prime position for verification through laboratory research and has permitted the possibility of clear conclusions being drawn from the results. It has permitted therapists to negotiate with their patients clear goals for behaviour change, and to know precisely when these goals have been reached. It has enabled therapists to state clearly which problem behaviours are amenable to change through behavioural means and which ones are not. Finally, and perhaps most important in the future development of behaviour therapy as a field, it puts the therapist in the role of planner, who can list the possible courses of action and the likely outcome of each, and can later evaluate the accuracy of the planning and the quality of the conceptualization.

In approaching the topic of defining a behavioural event for purposes of behaviour therapy, it must be emphasized that we are not referring only to the unadaptive or adaptive behaviour itself. Behaviours of interest occur within the context of antecedents and consequences, many of which can be regarded as events in much the same manner as the problem or target events. Indeed, it frequently happens that one unadaptive behaviour serves as an antecedent for another or as a reinforcer for a third. Thus, there are many similarities among antecedent, target and reinforcing events in regard to definition and observation.

One practical difference between these three kinds of events is in the amount of information about each that is usually necessary in order to design a treatment strategy. In general, one needs comprehensive information about the target behaviour, including a topographical description and an assessment of antecedents, and concomitants, and consequences. On the other hand, it is often unnecessary to describe all antecedents and consequences so precisely, since effective behaviour change procedures can often be designed without doing so. Because of the lesser emphasis on the precise details of the antecedents and consequences as compared with the target behaviour, rather little attention has been given in the literature to the former. Notable exceptions include the work of Stuart and Davis (1972) on obesity, in which major emphasis is placed on discovering relevant antecedents to eating, and the work of Lewinsohn (1973) and his students on depression, which emphasizes the identification and development of new reinforcers.

The reader should not underestimate the importance to successful behaviour therapy of a clear definition of relevant antecedents and consequences. In the short history of behaviour therapy, the most successful applications have been to those problem behaviours for which antecedents and consequences *have* been most clearly specified. This is true both for problems in which behaviours are to be eliminated and those in which new behaviours are to be initiated. An excellent example can be seen in the treatment of circumscribed phobias by systematic desensitization, now widely recognized as the procedure of choice for this disorder. The definition of a circumscribed phobia automatically carries with it a designation of both the antecedent, such as snake, airplane or examination, and also of the consequence, which consists of anxiety plus avoidance behaviour followed by the anxiety reduction that serves as a negative reinforcer for the avoidance. Another common example, of a behaviour deficit rather than an excess, is the development of social-interpersonal behaviours, such as speech, in chronic state hospital patients or autistic children. Here, an appropriate reinforcer is selected and prepared, and the appropriate antecedent conditions are presented to the patient in the form of the therapist who makes a request for speech. In disorders for which behavioural procedures have been slow in developing, such as compulsive ritualistic behaviours, it is often true that neither the antecedents nor the consequences are readily apparent, and may in fact prove impossible to specify with any clarity. One view of such situations is that antecedents and/or consequences might be mainly covert, consisting, for example, of self-statements about the 'need' to perform the behaviour and the dangers of failing to do so.

Methods of definition

Behaviours that are most commonly considered for behaviour therapy are those that involve easily observable events. A partial list of such behaviours has been given above. Although one might expect that the definition of most of these behaviours would be obvious, numerous writers have stressed the utmost importance of formulating a precise definition and applying it concretely and consistently. Even such an apparently obvious behaviour as fingernail biting requires careful definition, as shown by the following case. A young married woman, when given a simple event counter and asked to record every instance of fingernail biting per day for one week, reported that she was not certain as to what should qualify as biting. Sometimes she would inspect a finger, wondering whether or not to bite. Sometimes she would put a finger to her mouth but not to her teeth. Sometimes she would close her teeth over a nail but not bite off any nail. After discussion it was decided that fingernail biting should be defined to include all times when a finger touched the mouth, for any reason whatever except while eating or washing.

Frequency counts serve several important functions. First, as illustrated above, they compel the therapist and patient to formulate precise definitions of the problem behaviour. Second, they force the patient to give careful and systematic attention to the problem behaviour, thus increasing awareness and familiarity with the behaviour. Third, they provide baselines against which to evaluate changes. Fourth, they help focus the patient's attention on the associated antecedents and consequences that may be triggering and maintaining the behaviour. The practical technology of instructing patients in keeping frequency counts and of formulating ways to surmount practical difficulties is beyond the scope of this chapter. Excellent accounts are given by Watson and Tharp (1972) and by Schaefer and Martin (1969).

For certain problem behaviours, such as subjectively experienced anxiety and depression, it is often more useful to record the duration of the behaviour rather than, or in addition to, discrete instances. Thus, the patient who reported that she often felt depressed 'for no reason' was instructed to note systematically the time at which depressive feelings began and when they disappeared. A college student who desired to increase the amount of time spent in studying was likewise instructed to keep a record of the actual time currently spent in this behaviour.

Antecedents and consequences

As stated above, observing the frequency of problem behaviours orients the individual toward observing antecedents and consequences. Because individuals will not know what information is relevant and what is not, the therapist usually instructs them initially to keep records that may be somewhat redundant. Relevant antecedents could be a specific place, a specific time, people or objects, verbal statements, a specific thought, and a great many other kinds of events or chains of events. Some are easily identified, while others may defy the most assiduous behavioural detective. The identification of some is essential—some not. Some problem behaviours are maintained entirely by their consequences; some are under powerful stimulus control and maintained by reinforcing events that are highly intermittent and/or obscure. Identifying the events that maintain unadaptive behaviours is still very much of an art, and few systematic rules can yet be offered. Fortunately, there are usually several different options available for changing a particular behaviour, so that failure to identify precisely all the antecedents and reinforcers does not preclude treatment success. However, it sometimes means that a more roundabout strategy must be adopted, such as punishing an unadaptive behaviour whenever it occurs or teaching an incompatible behaviour.

Behavioural observation: review of procedures

Many of the procedures discussed below are similar to certain traditional 'behavioural tests' or 'situational tests' which were used for many years before the popular advent of behaviour therapy. The major techniques of this nature have been reviewed by Lanyon and Goodstein (1971). One difference between them and the procedures reviewed below is that the latter have been developed specifically for use in the context of therapeutic behaviour change, and are presumably better suited to that purpose. The reader should also be aware of the extensive review of unobtrusive procedures for behavioural observation by Webb and coworkers (1966).

It should be borne in mind that procedures for the observation and recording of behaviour within the framework of behaviour therapy have been developed in two rather different types of settings: clinical practice, on the one hand, and research programmes, on the other. Research workers are usually interested in single, easily specifiable behaviours, and because of the demands of scientific rigour observation procedures are often multiple and rather elaborate. In clinical practice, however, the practical constraints of the situation usually make it impossible to achieve the rigour that a research effort would demand; also, the nature of the patient's difficulties are often imprecise and rather complex. The following discussion is meant to include both types of settings. Researchers should bear in mind that their work is to be consumed by clinicians, and clinicians should remember that the more clearly and precisely they are able to conceptualize a clinical problem, the better the understanding that can be gained and the more sophisticated the treatment strategy that can be developed.

There is a developing literature on procedures for the definition and assessment of a variety of behaviours that are commonly presented to the behaviour therapist. These procedures can be grouped into four categories: (a) naturalistic observation, (b) self-observation, (c) laboratory observation and (d) written self-reports. As already stated, current assessment procedures focus mainly on characteristics of the problem behaviour itself, and there is as yet little available technology for assessing antecedents and consequences, except on an informal or intuitive basis. It should also be pointed out that many of the behavioural assessment procedures that have been developed within research contexts are not yet readily available to the individual clinician.

Naturalistic observation

Naturalistic observation refers to the observing and recording of the behaviour of interest by an independent observer exactly as it occurs in real life. There is a substantial advantage to this approach over laboratory observation in that the real-life antecedent stimuli and the consequences of the behaviour can also be observed directly. If the problem is a behavioural deficit, then observation would also include the stimulus conditions under which the behaviour would normally be expected, plus whatever information is available regarding the probable consequences.

A major disadvantage of naturalistic observation is its cost. However, it is often argued that, particularly in a clinical situation, anything other than naturalistic observation. is of limited value, since it is only there that the relevant antecedents and consequences can be detected. Unfortuantely, scientific methodologists in psychology have traditionally regarded data gathered by naturalistic observation as an unsatisfactory basis for the development of knowledge (e.g. Underwood, 1966), even though it has been frequently pointed out (e.g. Sarason, 1974, p. 56) that the antecedents and consequences for behaviours in the laboratory are usually different from those in the natural environment. This is particularly important in the assessment of real-life problem behaviours for which the antecedents and/or consequences are obscure. In such situations, which are frequently encountered by practising behaviour therapists, naturalistic rather than laboratory observation is essential, at least until sufficient knowledge is gained so that an appropriate 'contrived' situation can be designed.

Problems in naturalistic observation

The various methodological difficulties encountered in naturalistic observation have been recently reviewed in several places (Goldfried and Sprafkin, 1974; Lanyon and Goodstein, 1971; Lipinski and Nelson, 1974). Four kinds of problems are identified: (a) the effect of the observer on the frequency of the behaviour to be observed, often termed 'reactive effects of measurement'; (b) bias due to the observer's own expectancies; (c) problems of reliability; and (d) problems in the recording of complex behaviours.

The effect of the observer's presence in causing a change in the frequency of behaviour is well known. Webb and coworkers (1966) have devoted an entire book to a discussion of ways for obtaining 'nonreactive' measures. The presence of an observer could be regarded by the individual under observation either as an aversive stimulus, leading to escape and avoidance behaviour (e.g. Bechtel, 1967), or as a potential reinforcer, so that the individual 'puts his best foot forward'.

The observer's expectancies regarding what is to be observed have also been shown to affect significantly the reported frequency of behaviour. This effect is closely related to the better known effect of expectancies on the outcome of psychological research (e.g. Orne, 1962; Rosenthal, 1966). Lipinski and Nelson (1974) have listed three factors that appear to exert an influence upon observers' reports: knowledge of expected results, evaluative feedback from another person and knowledge that reliability measurements are being made. In a study that experimentally manipulated observers' expectancies of therapeutic change, Kent and coworkers (1974) demonstrated that expectancies were not a significant factor when a highly structured observational procedure was employed, but that the observers' subjective impressions about the behaviour being observed nevertheless did show significant bias.

Problems of reliability are not unique to assessment in behavioural settings. It is significant, however, that despite the tendency of behaviour therapists to derogate or ignore traditional psychological assessment procedures as methodologically inadequate, they have often been willing to accept rather low standards of psychometric adequacy for their own procedures. Two kinds of reliability problems can be noted: those having to do with obtaining an adequate sample of the behaviour and those involving observer accuracy. Obtaining adequate samples involves devoting sufficient time to permit a full awareness of the range of variability of the behaviour under different stimulus and reinforcement conditions and then designing a time-sampling procedure that adequately incorporates this variability. Observer reliability may be developed through specific training. Of considerable interest is the fact that the process of measuring reliability is itself reactive, so that different results may be obtained depending on the contingencies available to the observer. Thus, Romanczyk and coworkers (1973) showed that not only was reliability higher when the observers knew that they were to be monitored but it increased even more when they knew against whose work it would be checked.

Recording complex behaviours, such as family interactions, is a difficult and time-consuming process, no matter what theoretical framework is employed. Any system that is designed to collect such data must necessarily abstract or 'code' it, and some data are unavoidably lost during the process. Because coding is a judgmental process, and because coders or observers must be specifically trained in the system to be used, formal demonstrations of·reliability are particularly important here.

Self-observation

The view that self-reports can contain useful information about actual behaviour has had a stormy history. Individuals' own reports about their behaviour have usually been regarded with considerable suspicion, both by psychodynamically oriented psychologists and by traditional behaviourists. It has been fashionable to believe that self-observation does not usually correlate adequately with observation made by independent observers, and that it is therefore not a valid assessment procedure. Such a view is expressed, for example, in the review by Wolff and Merrens (1974). Recently, however, there has been increasing support for the view that accurate and reliable self-observation is a learnable skill that can be efficiently taught by behavioural methods such as modelling and shaping. One very important factor gives overriding support to the practical use of self-observation: its *economy*. The self-observer is always ready and available, and is free of charge.

Methods of self-observation

The importance of self-observation as an integral part of behavioural evaluation and change is only now beginning to be appreciated, and its technology is still primitive (Thoreson and Mahoney, 1974). As indicated above, one important aspect is the training of individuals to engage in self-observation. Many beginning behaviour therapists have failed in specific cases over their inability to get the patient to keep usable records.

Most methods of self-observation involve systematic written note-taking, either on index cards or in a notebook. Special tally sheets have also been prepared for specific behaviours, such as eating (Stuart and Davis, 1972) and children's activities (Wahler and Cormier, 1970). Wrist counters (Lindsley, 1968) and other similar devices such as golf or supermarket counters can also be used, although they only enable the recording of frequencies and not the antecedent stimulus conditions (e.g. time and place) under which the behaviour

TABLE 10.1 One day's self-observation sheet for a depressed patient, recording all changes in depressive feelings together with their time and place. On the right are shown the therapist's notes after questioning the patient concerning correlated events.

Time	Circumstances	Additional information elicited by therapist
8 a.m.	Woke up feeling depressed; sat on side of bed	
10:15 a.m.	Felt less depressed; got dressed and made coffee	Telephone rang; patient hates its sound and answered it to stop the ringing
10:30 a.m.	Depressed again; sat in kitchen	
11:45 a.m.	Less depressed; got ready for work and left apartment	Patient became anxious about being late, which would result in a reprimand and possibly being fired
5:30	Became depressed when arrived home; depressed all evening; watched TV	

occurs—nor its consequences. Obviously, a patient who is recording instances of nailbiting, which may occur one hundred times per day, requires a different recording technique from one who is recording instances of depression, which may occur only once or twice per day but last several hours. Watson and Tharp (1972) have presented an excellent discussion of a wide variety of practical self-observation techniques. One common procedure is for the behaviour therapist to have the patient construct his own recording sheet, as illustrated in Table 10.1 for a depressed patient. Taken over a one-week or two-week time interval and expanded through inquiry by the therapist, such observations provide an overall frequency count of depressive episodes and their length, plus a listing of the stimuli associated with their onset and termination.

Covert behaviours

As discussed above, it is now fairly well accepted that behaviour therapy procedures can be used to change the frequency of behaviours that are covert, such as thoughts and feelings, as well as publicly observable behaviours. The basic premise, that internal or private phenomena correspond in relevant respects to external behaviour, is termed the 'continuity assumption'. Thoreson and Mahoney (1974) emphasize that covert behaviours may, in addition to constituting problem areas, serve at various times both as antecedents (triggering stimuli) and as consequents (reinforcement and punishment) for problem behaviour that itself may be either covert or overt. Bandura (1969) has extensively documented the use of cognitive events as mediators or antecedents of complex behaviour. The use of internal events as consequents has been developed by a number of investigators, prominent among whom is Cautela (1967, 1971). Since self-observation provides the only means to obtain an assessment of covert events, the development of viable technology in this area will be critical for future advances in behaviour therapy.

Teaching self-observation

Procedures for the teaching of self-observation skills are not systematized at the present time. As pointed out by Thoreson and Mahoney (1974), individuals are not 'naturally' accurate self-observers, so that specific training is in most instances essential. These authors have listed a number of factors that have been shown to enhance the learning of self-observation: modelling, immediate accuracy feedback, systematic reinforcement and the gradual transfer of the responsibility for recording from an external source to oneself.

Problems in self-observation

Many of the methodological difficulties encountered in self-observation are similar to those encountered when naturalistic observations are made by an independent observer. However, one specific type of problem, the reactive effects of measurement, takes on additional complexities. The reactive effect of self-observation has itself been successfully used as a behaviour change procedure (e.g. McFall, 1970), although unsuccessful outcomes have also been reported (e.g. Berecz, 1972). A simple operant explanation of this effect might be given in terms of either self-punishment or self-reward. Thus, recording one's problem behaviours might call forth a self-statement such as 'This is bad; I should do it less often' or 'I'm doing a good job of cutting back'. Kazdin (1974) has analysed the behaviour change properties of self-observation in considerable detail and has shown that its behaviour change effects are highly varied and usually temporary, and that a variety of theoretical explanations are possible in addition to a simple operant view.

Laboratory observation

The term 'laboratory observation' refers to any situation that is specifically created for the purpose of observing the behaviour of interest. Such assessment procedures have been widely used in research on the utility of behavioural treatment. One well-known laboratory observation procedure is the 'experimental analogue', as exemplified in the behavioural avoidance or look–touch–hold test used by Lang and Lazovik (1963), Cooke (1966), Lanyon, Manosevitz and Imber (1968) and other researchers in the assessment of small animal fears, and by Paul (1966), Karst and Most (1973) and others in the assessment of public speaking anxiety.

A second group of procedures involves the direct assessment of interpersonal skills. McFall and Marston (1970) and McFall and Lillesand (1971), for example, developed a tape-recorded behavioural role-playing test to assess assertive behaviour. Subjects were required to respond as though in real life to hypothetical situations requiring assertiveness, and the degree of assertiveness that they displayed was determined by independent judges. A somewhat different kind of example is found in the work of Bernal and coworkers (1968) with uncontrollable children and their mothers. Bernal made video tapes of the mothers interacting with their children in the clinic situation, and then used the tapes as teaching materials to help the mothers learn more appropriate behaviours.

A third group of laboratory observation procedures involves the use of physiological measures, either as a direct assessment of a problem behaviour such as blood pressure (Shapiro, Schwartz and Tursky, 1972) or degree of penile tumescence (Bancroft, Jones and Pullan, 1966; Freund, 1965, 1967), or as an indirect assessment of a state such as anxiety, as reflected in GSR or heart rate (Lang, 1968).

The use of contrived observational settings for the assessment of problem behaviours was popular well before behavioural treatment reached its current vogue. An important question concerns the degree to which such situations provide adequate data for purposes of behavioural evaluation and change. A partial answer to this question has been given above: laboratory observation is valid to the extent that the antecedents and consequences that maintain the problem behaviour in real life are also present in the laboratory situation. In research situations, this criterion should be deliberately used as a condition of satisfactory experimental design. In clinical treatment situations, if the environment in which new behaviours have been initially taught is a contrived setting, such as a laboratory or office, then the individual must also be systematically taught to generalize the new behaviour to the natural environment, where different stimuli are presumably present. It is possible that the limited success of traditional therapies for problem behaviours that are to a considerable degree under stimulus control (e.g. obesity, alcoholism, stuttering) can be accounted for, in part, by the failure of those methods to deal fully and systematically with the wide variety of relevant stimuli.

Written self-reports

The term 'written self-reports' is used here to refer to structured self-report inventories and questionnaires. Such instruments have traditionally occupied a central position in the assessment of complex interpersonal behaviours. They originated as simple labour-saving devices (Symonds, 1931), but were soon pressed into service by trait-oriented psychologists, who drew upon the evolving psychometric technology to develop measures of such characteristics as dominance, introversion and thoughtfulness.

One type of structured questionnaire that has been commonly used in behaviour therapy is the 'fear survey schedule'. These instruments are essentially checklists of stimuli that frequently evoke fear, such as blood, high places and spiders. Respondents rate each item on a five- or seven-point scale according to 'how afraid it makes you nowadays', and a mean fear rating can be calculated, both for the overall checklist and also for specific content areas such as 'interpersonal'. Early developers of these instruments included Wolpe and Lang (1964), Geer (1965) and Manosevitz and Lanyon (1965). More recently, fear survey schedules have been extended to children (Scherer and Nakamura, 1968), and have been scaled (Tasto, Hickson and Rubin, 1971), factor analysed (Bernstein and Allen, 1969; Rubin and coworkers, 1969) and reviewed for validity and reliability (Hersen, 1973).

The early belief was that self-report fear questionnaires would serve a broad and basic purpose in the behaviour therapy of neurotic problems, based on the reasoning that it was ' . . . a necessary preliminary to have a full picture of the stimulus antecedents of the neurotic reactions (Wolpe and Lang, 1964, p. 27)'. This belief has not been fulfilled, and fear survey schedules have often tended to serve the function of providing insecure behaviour therapists with test data to hide behind, just as insecure psychoanalytic therapists have hidden behind projective tests. More recently, several attempts have been made to develop standardized behavioural questionnaires to assess other characteristics that are of frequent interest in behaviour therapy, such as social competence (Arkowitz and coworkers, 1975; Lanyon, 1967), assertiveness (Galassi and coworkers, 1974) and degree of sexual experience in males (Bentler, 1968a; Brady and Levitt, 1965; Podell and Perkins, 1957) and in females (Bentler, 1968b).

All these instruments are similar in that they attempt to go beyond the assessment of a single behaviour and, instead, yield a score that represents the respondent's frequency of performing a whole class of behaviours. As such, they should be regarded as similar to traditional personality questionnaires, although items refer more to actual behaviours and less to attitudes, beliefs and preferences. This continuing attempt to use the well-developed field of psychometric technology in behavioural assessment should be encouraged, although it is too early to predict how useful these and other questionnaires will ultimately be in behaviour therapy.

Behaviour therapists are, of course, interested in factual reports of behaviour, and the use of simple written procedures for gathering basic factual data is currently enjoying a resurgence of interest. One important example is the increasing use of self-report biographical data questionnaires (e.g. Lazarus, 1971), which serve to elicit a large amount of routine information in an economical manner. The reader is reminded of studies such as those of Kostlan (1954) and Sines (1959), who demonstrated the superiority of case history data over traditional psychological tests for personality description and prediction. Also relevant is the fact that individuals' written self-reports of factual data tend to be reasonably accurate, even under conditions where there are incentives to distort (Walsh, 1967, 1968).

Comment

Although the above survey of behavioural observation procedures is obviously not exhaustive, it does offer a framework for structuring knowledge in this field and a perspective on the current state of the art. Two additional topics should be mentioned.

Complex behaviours

A number of attempts have been made to bring under the rubric of behavioural assessment certain problem complaints that subsume a whole variety of behavioural events. One of the most important, and perhaps the most troublesome, is anxiety, a concept that has so far defied behavioural psychologists' attempts at a unitary definition and a unitary assessment procedure. A representative treatment of the difficulties involved can be found in Lang's (1968) paper 'Fear reduction and fear behavior: problems in treating a construct', in which anxiety is regarded as an inclusive concept for certain behaviors expressed within three different behavioural systems: verbal (cognitive), overt-motor and somatic. Attempts to show meaningful correlations between quantitative measures of anxiety in these three domains, and even in some cases within the same domain, have been consistently disappointing (Hersen,

1973). More satisfactory progress will probably be made if cases and research studies in which anxiety is involved concentrate on whatever individual components of this concept are of specific concern.

Other attempts to deal with complex concepts under a single behavioural assessment umbrella appear to be more promising. One is Lewinsohn's (1973) approach to depression; another is the work of Goldfried and D'Zurilla (1969) on the assessment of social competence. In general, behaviour therapists have approached complex problem areas piecemeal, dealing separately with each identifiable behaviour and tending to avoid the traditional diagnostic terminology of mental health practice.

Reliability and validity

In their eagerness to develop workable assessment procedures within their own framework, many behaviour therapists have given inadequate attention to the two basic necessities of measurement—reliability and validity. Thus, as stated by Evans and Nelson (1974), 'behaviour therapists seem to be in the awkward position of coming to depend on (procedures) that are less psychometrically sophisticated than those they have spurned (p. 602)'. Since most behavioural assessment procedures involve direct sampling, questions of validity in the usual sense of correlations with concurrent or future criteria are not a primary concern. As stated above, the most relevant consideration is the representativeness of the sample with respect to the stimulus conditions and the consequences that are normally associated with the problem behaviour. In regard to reliability, the same aspects that are important in traditional personality assessment (Lanyon and Goodstein, 1971) are also important in behavioural assessment. The fact that psychometric adequacy has not been emphasized, to date, in behavioural observation can perhaps be taken to suggest, in conjunction with the extremely rapid growth rate of behaviour therapy as a field, that even rather careless assessment procedures can often result in successful interventions. Thus, it could be that careful observations are often unnecessary and add little to therapeutic success, or that higher success rates can be expected as behavioural observation procedures become more sophisticated.

BEHAVIOURAL FORMULATION

Behavioural formulation, or behavioural analysis, begins with the observational data that have been collected in the manner described above, and draws upon the framework of behavioural learning theory to determine (or to make an educated guess about) events that are maintaining the problem behaviours in their present state. Possible strategies for bringing about the desired change are then identified.

It is important to understand that it is not always necessary to know what is maintaining a problem behaviour (either an excess or a deficit) in order to change it. Whether such knowledge is going to be necessary often cannot be determined in advance, however. Thus, some behaviour therapists take a trial-and-error approach, either from ignorance or as a calculated gamble, and attempt to bring about behaviour change without a complete formulation. It should also be clearly understood that the task of behavioural formulation is, in practice, ongoing throughout treatment. While it would be elegant to state that the behavioural formulation is performed after the period of observation and before treatment begins, real-life problems are rarely so simple.

Although behavioural learning theory nowadays constitutes rather a sophisticated body of knowledge and there is an extensive literature on behaviour therapy, writings on behavioural formulation and analysis as applied to complex clinical problems of actual patients are making their appearance rather slowly. Certain problems of patients in institutional settings have, of course, been subjected to rather complete behavioural analysis, e.g. basic social and self-help behaviour of chronic psychiatric patients (Ayllon and Azrin, 1968; Schaefer and Martin, 1969), and toilet functions in the retarded (Foxx and Azrin, 1973). Behavioural analysis of certain specific problems have also been proposed, e.g. depression (Ferster, 1973; Lewinsohn, 1973), obesity (Stuart and Davis, 1972), sexual dysfunction (Masters and Johnson, 1970) and autism (Kozloff, 1973). In another area, speech pathologists have for a number of years used procedures that are similar to what is now called behavioural analysis (e.g. Williams, 1957).

What is still lacking at the present time is a systematic formulation of principles for the process of using basic observational data plus a working knowledge of learning theory and behavioural technology to develop a theoretically sound practical plan of action. The relevant information currently on this topic would include the frameworks for detailed theoretical analysis of behavioural problems presented in the writings of Kanfer (Kanfer and Phillips, 1970; Kanfer and Saslow, 1969), and stepwise procedures for conducting simple behaviour analysis of concrete unitary behaviours (e.g. Krumboltz and Krumboltz, 1972; Watson and Tharp, 1972). Not yet available are principles and procedures for the detailed analysis of complex problems based on the constraints present in actual clinical practice.

As stated above, it is not always necessary to develop a thorough behavioural formulation before attempting behaviour change. There are three classes of problems where such an exception might apply. The first is where the problem is a simple behaviour deficit that is potentially amenable to a positive reinforcement procedure. Such situations have been frequently reported in work with chronic psychiatric patients (e.g. Baker, 1971) and with retarded children (e.g. Goldstein and Lanyon, 1971). In both of these examples, food reinforcement was used in conjunction with modelling and shaping to increase speech production and improve articulation. Thus, if a rather simple procedure exists that has potential applicability, it is often most economical to apply it first and ask questions later.

The second situation in which a complete behavioural analysis might not be conducted is with complex but standardized problems for which adequate behavioural formulations have already been reported in the literature. A good example is the Stuart and Davis (1972) approach to obesity, which holds that:

(1) A major stimulus for overeating is the ready presence of food in the individual's environment.
(2) The environment strengthens the eating habit by offering many different reinforcers for eating but not for dieting behaviour.
(3) Food serves as a major source of pleasure for the individual.
(4) The individual may be deficient in the skills needed to elicit other kinds of reinforcement from the environment.
(5) The individual does not attend carefully either to eating behaviour or to the weight problem and therefore is relatively unaware of many of its aspects.

Behaviour therapists who accept the Stuart and Davis formulation would not conduct their own complete behavioural analysis. Rather, they would proceed directly to:

(1) Have the individual systematically remove food cues from the day-to-day environment;
(2) Structure the environment to reinforce non-eating behaviour;
(3) Identify other sources of pleasure;
(4) Teach behaviours that will be spontaneously reinforced in the natural environment;
(5) Have the individual monitor systematically all aspects of the eating problem, including food intake, weight, clothing and exercise.

The third type of situation occurs when researchers have been unable to agree as to how a particular class of problem behaviour is usually maintained, but a certain technique is known to be successful in alleviating the problem. An example is found in the treatment of compulsive rituals, a problem that has traditionally shown a high degree of resistance to change. Recent research (e.g. Mills and coworkers, 1973) has demonstrated that response prevention is a promising approach, even though the antecedents and consequences of this class of problem behaviour remain obscure.

Table 10.2 presents an example of a behavioural formulation. The patient was a 24-year-old homosexual man who requested help in becoming fully heterosexual in his orientation. His decision to change had been made after careful deliberation, and at the time of the first interview he had already refrained from most homosexual contacts for a period of one month. The initial data base for the formulation consisted of three interviews, a series of structured self-observations by the patient, a self-report biographical data sheet and the MMPI. The patient's problems were formulated in terms of the following deficits and excesses. Deficits: social and sexual interaction with women; positive social and sexual thoughts about women; and certain masculine overt motor behaviours. Excesses: sexual interactions with men; thoughts about sexual interaction with men; anxiety about social and sexual

TABLE 10.2 Behavioural deficits and excesses constituting the problem behaviours of a 24-year-old homosexual man, and ways in which these behaviours are maintained.

Problem behaviour	Way in which problem behaviour is maintained
Behaviour deficits	
1. Social interaction with women	(a) Avoidance behaviour currently maintained by anxiety reduction (b) Lacks knowledge of social skills (c) Social interaction with women and men punished by mother
2. Sexual interaction with women	Same as for social interaction; in addition, lack of social interaction precludes sexual interaction
3. Positive social and sexual thoughts toward women	Avoidance behaviour maintained by anxiety reduction
4. Certain masculine overt motor behaviours	Incompatible behaviours currently reinforced
Behaviour excesses	
1. Sexual interaction with men	Reinforced by affection and sexual pleasure
2. Thoughts about sexual interaction with men	Reinforced with sexual excitement and thoughts of pleasure
3. Anxiety about social and sexual interaction with women	Response to self-punishing thoughts of unskillfulness and being rejected and ridiculed, and to verbal punishment from mother
4. Certain effeminate overt motor behaviours	Reinforced by attention from other homosexual men; probably learned originally through modelling
5. Passive, ineffectual interpersonal behaviour with mother (including whining, crying, tantrums)	Negatively reinforced by terminating mother's abusive verbal behaviour

interaction with women; certain effeminate overt motor behaviours; and passive and ineffectual interpersonal behaviour with his mother. Although this formulation was not completed before treatment was begun, its major aspects were developed after three interviews, based on the information indicated. Therapeutic contacts totalled twenty-five one-hour sessions over seven months.

It is noteworthy that the particular behaviour that was changed first in this patient was not one of the problem behaviours as initially presented. As a general rule, new adaptive behaviours should be taught before unadaptive behaviours are reduced. Thus, attention was focused upon increasing the patient's social approach skills with women. However, it was considered necessary to reduce the patient's anxiety over social and sexual interaction with women before these skills could be taught. This anxiety and the related avoidance behaviour was being actively maintained by the behaviour of the patient's mother. Therefore, the first step in treatment was to have the patient decrease the frequency of his mother's abusive verbal behaviour by teaching him to make assertive and realistic statements about his own needs and intentions. The reader should be cautioned that behaviour therapists do not make a practice of searching for hidden but 'key' behaviours; however, there will be occasions, as described above, when the behaviour that requires attention first is not immediately obvious.

ASSESSMENT OF TREATMENT RESOURCES

The systematic collection of practical information about the nature and range of viable treatment options is of basic importance in designing strategies for behaviour change. This topic has not been given much formal recognition in traditional psychodynamic assessment, although it is clear that the psychoanalytic therapist performs analogous assessments before embarking on treatment. Thus, certain information is implicit in the diagnostic category to which the patient is assigned; for example, 'uncovering' therapy is generally not attempted with a patient whose psychiatric diagnosis includes the mention of psychotic disorder. Relevant predictions are also made from projective techniques; e.g. human movement responses on the Rorschach are traditionally regarded as conveying important information about patients' ability to develop insight. Another source of information used in designing a psychodynamic treatment strategy is the first few interviews, during which the therapist assesses the ability of the patient to develop an adequate therapeutic relationship.

Because the procedures that constitute behaviour therapy are both more specific and more varied than those of psychodynamic therapy, it is reasonable to expect that factors influencing success or failure would be more readily identifiable in behaviour therapy. The present section identifies the different kinds of 'tools' or resources that are needed in order for successful behaviour change to be arranged, and reviews the available procedures for assessing these resources. As with a number of other areas within the field of behavioural assessment, such procedures are as yet highly limited in their development.

There is generally more than one way to bring about any given set of desired behaviour changes. Thus, it becomes the therapist's responsibility to select the optimal, or most economical, of the feasible strategies. The more resourceful the therapist is in locating treatment resources, the wider will be the range of available options. The survey of treatment resources should therefore be as comprehensive as possible, even if there is a possible treatment strategy that is immediately apparent, since a little extra time devoted to this task by the therapist might well result in the identification of less obvious but more economical possibilities. A good example is seen in the 8-year-old encopretic son of a family on welfare. The therapist spent a considerable amount of time teaching the mother basic pinciples of reinforcement and then trying to locate events that were both reinforcing to the boy and readily available to the parents.

After a number of frustrating sessions with the mother, the therapist took the trouble to consider reinforcers that might be available to him but not to her. As a result, he had the boy visit the clinic each afternoon on the way home from school if he was 'clean', and collect a 'quarter' from the clinic secretary. The problem disappeared in two weeks, at a total cost, including follow-up, of approximately five dollars.

The following survey of possible treatment resources is loosely organized into two sections. In the first section are discussed resources that are part of the patient's own functioning. Included are the patient's self-observation and self-regulation skills, willingness to follow instructions and to permit the therapist control over the patient's behaviour and environment, availability of friends and family members to function as change agents, the patient's imagery skills and the range of events that can function as reinforcers for the patient. The second section reviews those resources that belong to, or can be arranged by, the therapist, such as the therapist's own range of skills, both conceptual and practical, the availability of professional supervision and/or consultation, the therapist's flexibility to make home visits or to hospitalize the patient, adjunctive electrophysiological equipment, individuals to model new behaviours for the patient, those reinforcers that are under the therapist's control and traditional psychodiagnostic instruments. An overriding consideration is the issue of *financial* resources, which can in principle be translated into many of the specific resources listed above. Thus, the same money could be used to hire a consultant, an observer, a model or a piece of equipment.

Patient resources

Self-observation and self-regulation

Perhaps the most basic and important treatment resource of all in behaviour therapy, apart from the availability of adequate time by both patient and therapist, is patients' ability to observe and regulate their own behaviour. Since patients in behaviour therapy are essentially students, their ability to perform work assignments and to report accurately on them is paramount. Discussed earlier in this chapter was the importance of self-observation, which is usually the most economical means, and in many instances the only available means, for gathering needed assessment information.

The term 'self-regulation' is used here in a broader sense than its usage by such authors as Kanfer and his students (e.g. Kanfer and Karoly, 1972), and refers to all instructed assignments that the patient carries out between therapy sessions. Examples would be practice in deep muscle relaxation, the obese patient's instructions to put out of sight all food in the home that is freely visible and to rearrange the contents of the refrigerator, and the socially anxious man's assignment of observing other men making social contacts at a party or dating bar.

The absolute necessity for the patient to 'get his work done' cannot be overemphasized. As yet, however, there is practically no literature on the management of this most important aspect of behaviour therapy. As stated above, there is now considerable agreement that self-observation skills can be taught, and a number of recent studies attest to the fact that self-regulation can also be taught (e.g. Mahoney and Thoreson, 1974). What is still lacking is a systematic listing of general principles and methods for teaching these skills, and literature on assessing patients' initial skills in self-regulation and their ability to learn them.

The usual method that is employed for assessing these skills involves a subjective trial-and-error behaviour sample approach. The therapist samples the patient's ability to do assignments by setting some assignments, and if the patient does not do them, the therapist then samples the patient's ability to learn to do assignments by attempting to teach this skill. Unknown factors at the present time include the therapist's role in setting expectancies, the patient's own prior expectations about therapy and the patient's history in regard to self-regulation skills.

Willingness to permit control

The aspect in which behaviour therapy perhaps differs most from psycho-dynamic therapy is that behaviour therapists literally tell their patients what to do. Behaviour therapists take active control of the situation and, with their patients' full approval, ask them to perform specific activities and change specific aspects of their daily living. Obviously, the more readily patients will agree to do exactly what is asked, no matter whether they believe it will do any good, the more likely they are to achieve the desired changes. The greater the amount of the environment that the patient is willing to make available for therapeutic involvement, the more flexibility the therapist has for designing strategies to bring about change. This point is clearly seen in the work of Masters and Johnson (1970) on sexual dysfunction. These authors have insisted on the necessity for having the control that is provided by the availability of both members of a marital unit, and have generally declined to work with one spouse alone. The need to have more of the patient's environment available to the therapist than just the patient alone is also recognized, of course, in family therapy and other types of mental health intervention.

Once again, there is essentially no formal literature on the effects of the therapist having more versus less control over the patient's environment, nor have methods been developed for assessing the extent to which the patient is likely to make (or has made) control available. Physicians in hospital practice have traditionally been much more comfortable about assuming control than psychologists have been, telling patients, for example, that their bodies have to be cut open if they wish to have continued good health. When compared with medical practice, the public discomfort at having behaviour therapists exercise a somewhat lesser degree of control in order to bring about desired changes is indeed noteworthy.

Imagery skills

Another patient resource that forms the basis of a number of behavioural techniques is the ability to engage therapeutically in imagery. In view of the significant contribution made by imagery procedures to behaviour change technology (e.g. Wilkins, 1974), it is surprising that so little attention has been given to the assessment of imagery skills within the context of behaviour therapy.

The published research to date on the assessment of imagery has been mainly concerned with the question of a unitary dimension of 'imagery ability'. In general, however, relationships among different measures of imagery ability have been found to be low. For example, Rimm and Bottrell (1969) intercorrelated four measures that could be related to visual imagining ability: self-rating of ability to imagine; enhancement in recall when employing imagery; respiratory changes during fearful images; and memory for pictures. The highest of these correlations was only 0.33. Similar findings have been reported in more recent studies (Danaher and Thoreson, 1972; Rehm, 1973).

In making assessments of imagery, researchers and clinicians currently tend to rely upon direct self-report procedures. One such procedure for assessing ability to imagine is the Betts (1909) Questionnaire Upon Mental Imagery (Sheehan, 1967a, 1967b). Another simple practical procedure for evaluating the vividness of an image is to have the individual give ratings of clarity, either on a specifically defined scale (McCullough and Powell, 1972) or by subjective description. Perhaps the most common procedure for gauging the extent of a patient's imagery skills, however, is to determine empirically whether they are sufficient to enable the desired therapeutic changes to be achieved, independent of the patient's self-report.

In view of the increasing importance of imagery in behavioural treatment and its widespread recognition as a significant concept in other major areas of psychology (e.g. Paivio, 1971; Singer, 1974), it is obvious that more satisfactory measures should be developed. One possible approach would be the development of standardized behaviour sample procedures similar to measures of hypnotizability (e.g. Hilgard, 1965), a concept that appears to be closely related. Another would be the identification of different variables that could be significant for the specific uses that are made of imagery in behaviour therapy. For example, there appear to be reliable differences in the degree to which different individuals experience spontaneous shifts in the content of their imagery (Lanyon, 1974). Another variable of possible significance might be the degree of reality distortion in free imagery (Beck, 1970).

One unanswered question of considerable significance is the degree to which useful imagery skills can be learned. This question does not refer to the usual few sessions in which patients are taught how to use their existing imagery skills, but to basic learning procedures for those individuals who appear to be unable to engage in visual imagery to any significant extent. A related question would concern the extent to which an individual's potential for learning imagery skills could be predicted.

Availability of reinforcers

The use of simple positive reinforcement was identified by Krasner in 1971 as the most widely used procedure in behaviour therapy at that time. Two questions frequently arise:

(1) What events are reinforcing for a particular patient?
(2) What reinforcers can, from a practical viewpoint, be arranged for a particular patient?

Different individuals find different events to be reinforcing, and it cannot be automatically assumed that even the most usual of reinforcers, such as food, money or attention, will be suitable in a particular instance.

Several writers have developed lists that can be used in assessing the potential reinforcing power of different events. One such list is the reinforcement survey schedule of Cautela and Kastenbaum (1967), a comprehensive catalogue of common reinforcers plus a number of multiple choice and open-ended questions. Respondents are asked to rate each item in the main part of the instrument for degree of pleasure on a five-point scale. Another instrument is the pleasant events schedule of MacPhillamy and Lewinsohn (1971), a 320-item true/false questionnaire that was originally developed for use in research on depression, but which serves essentially the same purpose as the reinforcement survey schedule. A third listing of potential reinforcers, specifically relevant to children, can be found in the volume by Madsen and Madsen (1970). Other techniques for assessing the utility of different events as reinforcers, again used primarily with children, are the questionnaire (Tharp and Wetzel, 1969) and the reinforcer 'cabinet' or 'menu' approach (e.g. Browning and Stover, 1971), in which the child is permitted to select from among a variety of reinforcing options that are offered.

The practical question as to what reinforcers are actually available for use is related to the extent to which the patient is willing to make his environment available to the therapist, a topic discussed above. The wider the range of available reinforcers, of course, the more flexible the therapist can be in designing procedures for behaviour change. While there are no formal guidelines for evaluating the extent or range of reinforcing events that the patient is willing to have the therapist employ in influencing his behaviour, it is clear that such an assessment is, in fact, made in most clinical situations.

Therapist resources

Therapist's skills

It is by no means trite to consider the therapist's particular range of skills as a treatment resource. For example, if the patient's problem is a simple phobia of a stimulus that is not readily available in real life (e.g. thunderstorms), progress will be significantly hampered if the therapist is not familiar with the use of imaginal desensitization. On the other hand, this skill would be of little use in school consultation on hyperactive children. In other words, what the therapist knows (or can learn quickly) will be one limiting factor in determining the behaviour change procedures to be employed.

Models

Many writers believe that modelling is, in general, the most effective procedure for initiating new behaviours, either alone or in combination with reinforcement (e.g. Bandura, 1971). In order to employ a modelling procedure, an appropriate model for the desired behaviour must obviously be available. The main practical alternatives are usually the use of the therapist to model the desired behaviours or the use of some available person in the patient's environment. In some cases, the behaviour may be initially modelled by the therapist (e.g. social approach responses for a shy adult), after which the patient is assigned to observe the behaviour in its natural environment, such as a social gathering or dating bar. If direct observation of the behaviour is difficult to arrange, models can be shown on film. Increasing use is being make of this approach in the treatment of sexual inadequacy, for example (Lassen and Held, 1974). Sometimes the behaviour to be initiated is known to the patient but not to the therapist. This situation might occur, for example, where the behaviour is interpersonal and is specific to the patient's own cultural subgroup, which is not shared by the therapist. As is true with most of the treatment resources discussed in the present section, no formal assessment procedures are currently available to assist in the identification of appropriate models.

Electronic equipment

Rather recent developments in the field of electronics and related fields have made available quite a range of sophisticated devices for assessing physiological responses that constitute problem behaviours or that are related to them. Included are electromyograph (EMG) equipment to assess muscle tension states that are basic to certain instances of headache (Budzynski and coworkers, 1973) and other problems, the measurement of penile erection through blood volume (Freund, 1967) or strain gauge transducers (Bancroft, Jones and Pullan, 1966), electroencephalograph (EEG) patterns in epileptic patients (Sterman, 1973) and an increasing number of other uses. These developments are closely associated, of course, with the technology of bio-feedback, in which a formerly indiscriminable physiological response is made discriminable through instrumentation, enabling small changes to be reinforced in a shaping process.

The opportunity for aligning behaviour therapy with the 'harder' sciences through the use of instrumentation is difficult for behaviour therapists to resist, and it can be reasonably predicted that this is one area of research and development which will be active for some time to come. Since the use of electronic devices requires the availability of the appropriate device plus supporting technology and adequate training, it is likely that their major use will continue to be confined mainly to specific research institutions. It would be premature to speculate on their potential impact on behaviour therapy as a field or to offer a list of disorders whose preferred behavioural treatment may eventually involve instrumentation. Excellent reviews of the state of the art can be found in the annually published set of readings entitled *Biofeedback and Self-control* (e.g. Miller and coworkers, 1973).

Traditional psychological tests

Little has been published on the use of traditional psychological tests in behaviour therapy. This lack can perhaps be understood in terms of behaviour therapists' disenchantment with traditional procedures for evaluating and treating psychological disorders. The development of certain psychometric instruments (e.g. fear survey schedules) that are seen as specific to the needs of the behaviour therapist has been discussed earlier in this chapter. Whether more traditional tests might be useful under certain circumstances, however, is a legitimate question that has not been dealt with as yet.

Some rather obvious examples can be given of the use of traditional tests in behaviour therapy. A standardized intelligence test administered to a child could enable a choice to be made between accepting his slow rate of learning as optimal for him or exploring behavioural (and other) factors that might be interfering with learning. An MMPI administered to a patient who presents a simple shyness problem might yield a 'normal' profile, in which case the therapist might decide to conduct only a brief inquiry about other problems that could affect therapeutic progress, or a clearly 'disturbed' profile, in which case the therapist might conduct a detailed inquiry with the expectation of identifying additional problems that would interfere with treatment. The use of the MMPI or other instruments to assess the generality and permanence of therapeutic behaviour change has also been reported (e.g. Arkowitz, 1974; Baker, 1969).

Mention should also be made of the possible utility of performance on common conditioning tasks as predictors of outcome in behaviour therapy. In one study, Morganstern, Pearce and Rees (1965) investigated standardized eyeblink conditioning and verbal conditioning tasks as predictors of the outcome of a drug-aversion conditioning procedure for eliminating transvestism. No conclusive results were found. In another, Brady and coworkers (1962) examined the correlations between MMPI scores and a number of indices of operant behaviour derived from a button-pressing task. A number of significant correlations were reported, though once again there were no conclusive findings.

DESIGNING THE OPTIMAL TREATMENT STRATEGY

The basic purpose of behavioural assessment, as defined by the present authors, is to design the best possible strategy for bringing about the changes requested by the patient. The tasks to be performed by the therapist and patient in this final state of the behavioural assessment process involve an integration of the steps described in the previous sections of this chapter, including an agreement about the specific terminal behaviours to be developed, a consideration of the various alternative strategies that are available for bringing about the desired changes and negotiation as to the most feasible procedures to be followed. At this point in the assessment and design process, the therapist should have accumulated the following information: a description of the specific changes requested by the patient; a description of the specific unadaptive behaviours now being performed or adaptive behaviours not being performed; some hypotheses about the ways in which the current state of affairs are being maintained; and the resources available for bringing about change.

Behaviour design and engineering design

There are many similarities between the activities of behaviour therapists in designing strategies for producing a behavioural product and the activities of engineers in designing procedures for producing a physical product. The term 'behavioural engineer' has sometimes been used, in fact, to describe the use of learning principles in modifying behaviour (e.g. Ayllon and Michael, 1959; Homme and coworkers, 1968). The analogy proposed here, however, is broader in scope, referring to the entire process of using basic observations plus research and theoretical knowledge to design and put into operation a complex process for producing a desired end-product.

Let us review the specific steps that would be involved in a typical engineering design project, such as the design of a chemical plant (e.g. Lanyon, 1957). First, the desired product is specified. Second, a review of the empirical (and perhaps theoretical) literature is done to determine the different possible methods of making this product. Associated with each method is a particular set of initial materials; a specific set of physical and chemical processes involving specific requirements of energy, labour costs, physical plant, and time; and a specific set of undesired by-products, such as chemical residues, impurities, and air and noise pollution. If insufficient prior knowledge exists about processes for manufacturing the desired product, pilot research-and-development work may be done in order to determine the feasibility of different methods. Third, the advantages and disadvantages of the available processes are evaluated in conjunction with the available resources, and a decision is made as to the process that is optimal. Fourth, the selected process and the plant are designed in detail.

The use of this four-step scheme for approaching and carrying out a complex design task is not confined to engineering, but has wider applicability to other complex planning situations. A statement of these steps in more general terms might be made as follows:
(1) Decide on the exact state of affairs that constitutes the desired goal or product.

(2) Review each of the different possible avenues or methods for reaching the goal, including an evaluation of initial states, costs and side-effects.

(3) Review all the available resources, evaluate them in conjunction with the available methods and select the optimal method.

(4) Develop detailed plans using the chosen method.

The design of strategies for therapeutic behaviour change differs from this general plan only in matters of emphasis. In planning behaviour changes, one constraining variable of overriding importance is the behaviour initially present. The behaviour therapist is called upon not simply to make something but to change one existing state of affairs into another. Thus, the first step in the framework for behavioural design as presented in this chapter involves a careful assessment of the situation as it initially exists. There is also the very real question of determining whether the job can be accomplished at all, plus the difficulty of having as collaborators individuals whose functioning capacity to participate may be somewhat restricted. Another difference in emphasis concerns the setting of goals. In behaviour therapy, particularly with complex problems, although an immediate specification can be made of the patient's ideal goals, specification of the goals that are actually attainable must often be postponed until later in the assessment process.

The point to be emphasized is that behaviour therapy involves the planful and active consideration of resources and alternatives, the deliberate selection of the most appropriate procedures and the careful monitoring of progress with the full collaboration of the patient as the plan is carried out. In these respects, the procedure is rather unlike other forms of psychological therapy, such as non-directive or psychoanalytic therapy, and more like a series of consultations with a competent specialist in a field such as orthodontics, finance or architecture, whose help has been sought for the purpose of accomplishing a specific goal. The degree to which clinical behaviour therapy procedures currently fit this framework is debatable; however, the fact that they have the potential for doing so gives the field the possibility for developing a technology whose sophistication and effectiveness is on a higher plane than other psychological treatment procedures.

Principles and flowcharts

In better developed fields of technology there are usually recognized sets of basic principles which underlie the activities of planning and design. It would be premature at this time to attempt a specification of such principles for the design of therapeutic behaviour changes. However, the following list is offered as illustrative guesses as to what some of these principles might ultimately be.

(1) New behaviours should generally be developed before removing unwanted behaviours.

(2) It is not necessary to identify the stimuli originally involved in generating an unadaptive behaviour, assuming they are not the same as the stimuli that currently trigger the behaviour.

(3) New behaviours should be planned to be under the eventual control of either naturally occurring stimuli and/or contingencies, or stable self-regulation.

(4) It should be recognized that the available resources will in some instances not permit the desired changes to be made.

(5) It will often be impossible to design the therapeutic strategies completely before embarking on them.

It should eventually be possible to formalize such rules into flowcharts for decision-making and to develop standardized instructions for carrying out specific tasks. Figures 10.1 and 10.2 show hypothetical partial flowcharts that illustrate what might be done in this regard. They are offered for illustrative purposes only and not for technical accuracy. Figure 10.1 illustrates a rather global aspect of the design procedure—selecting a strategy for reducing or eliminating unwanted behaviour. Figure 10.2 represents a much more specific task—the removal of an overt aversive contigency. Inspection of the box labelled A in Figure 10.1 shows that Figure 10.2 represents the questions to be asked and decisions to be made in that particular step.

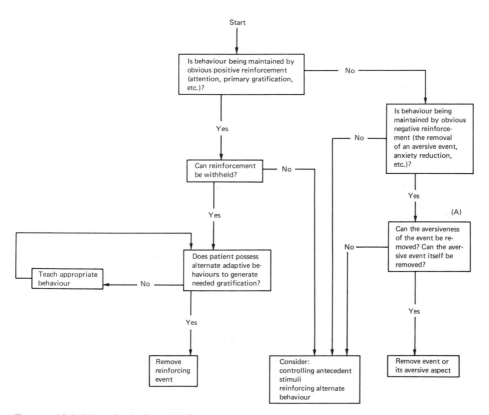

FIGURE 10.1 Hypothetical partial flowchart for selecting a procedure to reduce or remove an unwanted behaviour.

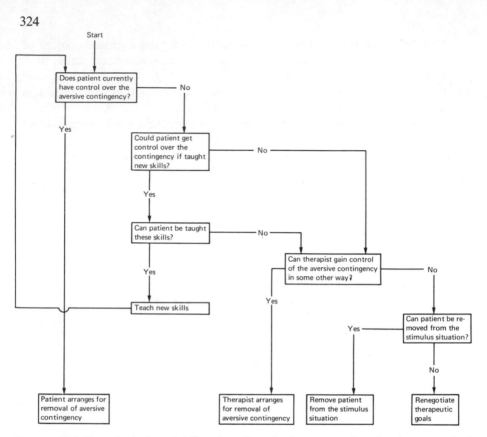

FIGURE 10.2 Hypothetical partial flowchart for selecting a procedure for the removal of an overt aversive contingency.

Neither of these flowcharts specifies the actual behaviours to be engaged in by the patient or therapist. Rather, they represent a formalization of the steps involved in decision-making. Each operation that is specified (e.g. 'Teach new skills', 'Remove reinforcing event') would require an instructional manual of its own. Such procedural manuals are, in fact, available for certain operations under certain circumstances; e.g. the shaping of speech in autistic children, the imaginal desensitization of anxiety and the reduction of tension in the frontalis muscle. Because more and more of these specific procedures are now being made available, the availability of adequate conceptual frameworks would seem of considerable importance, in order that the procedures can be placed in some overall perspective and further procedures can be more easily planned. A second reason for developing conceptual frameworks is to facilitate the student's task of learning behaviour therapy and putting into practice as effectively as possible the most appropriate procedures for each individual situation.

Concluding comment

In concluding this chapter, the authors wish to reemphasize a point that can easily be overlooked in the present enthusiasm for developing sophisticated behavioural technology. Although the literature of behaviour therapy does not cover the learning of basic clinical skills, it is simply not possible to be a good behaviour therapist without also being a good clinician. This point has been illustrated by the strong impact made by Lazarus' (1971) book *Behavior Therapy and Beyond*. While this book purports to be about behaviour therapy, it does not emphasize the unique technology of the field, but describes and attempts to teach general clinical skills. As such, it should be construed as a timely caution that neither good clinical skills alone nor a sophisticated grasp of behavioural technology alone are sufficient to produce a competent behaviour therapist.

REFERENCES

Arkowitz, H. (1974). Desensitization as a self-control procedure: a case report. *Psychotherapy: Theory, Research, and Practice*, **11**, 172–174.

Arkowitz, H., Lichtenstein, E., McGovern, K., and Hines, P. (1975). The behavioral assessment of social competence in males. *Behavior Therapy*, **6**, 3–13.

Ayllon, T., and Azrin, N. (1968). *The Token Economy: A Motivational System for Therapy and Rehabilitation*, Appleton-Century-Crofts, New York.

Ayllon, T., and Michael, J. (1959). The psychiatric nurse as a behavioral engineer. *Journal of the Experimental Analysis of Behavior*, **2**, 323–344.

Baker, B. (1969). Symptom treatment and symptom substitution in enuresis. *Journal of Abnormal Psychology*, **74**, 42–49.

Baker, R. (1971). The use of operant conditioning to reinstate speech in mute schizophrenics. *Behaviour Research and Therapy*, **9**, 329–336.

Bancroft, J. H., Jones, H. G., and Pullan, B. R. (1966). A simple transducer for measuring penile erection, with comments on its use in the treatment of sexual disorders. *Behaviour Research and Therapy*, **4**, 239–241.

Bandura, A. (1969). *Principles of Behavior Modification*. Holt, Rinehart and Winston, New York.

Bandura, A. (1971). *Psychological Modeling: Conflicting Theories*, Aldine-Atherton, Chicago.

Bechtel, F. B. (1967). The study of man: human movement and architecture. *Transaction*, **4**, 53–56.

Beck, A. T. (1970). Role of fantasies in psychotherapy and psychopathology. *Journal of Nervous and Mental Disease*, **150**, 3–17.

Bentler, P. M. (1968a). Heterosexual behaviour assessment—I. Males. *Behaviour Research and Therapy*, **6**, 21–26.

Bentler, P. M. (1968b). Heterosexual behaviour assessment—II. Females. *Behaviour Research and Therapy*, **6**, 27–30.

Berecz, J. (1972). Modification of smoking behavior through self-administered punishment of imagined behavior: a new approach to aversive therapy. *Journal of Consulting and Clinical Psychology*, **38**, 244–250.

Bernal, M. D., Duryee, J. S., Pruett, H. L., and Burns, G. J. (1968). Behavior modification and the brat syndrome. *Journal of Consulting and Clinical Psychology*, **32**, 447–455.

Bernstein, D. A., and Allen, G. J. (1969). Fear survey schedule (II): normative data and factor analyses based upon a large college sample. *Behavior Research and Therapy*, **7**, 403–407.

Betts, G. H. (1909). The distribution and functions of mental imagery. *Columbia University Contributions to Education*, **26**, 1–99.

Brady, J. P., and Levitt, E. E. (1965). The scalability of sexual experiences. *Psychological Record*, 15, 275–279.

Brady, J. P., Pappas, N., Tausig, T. N., and Thornton, D. R. (1962). MMPI correlates of operant behavior. *Journal of Clinical Psychology*, 18, 67–70.

Browning, R. M., and Stover, D. O. (1971). *Behavior Modification in Child Treatment*, Aldine-Atherton, Chicago.

Budzynski, T. H., Stoyva, J. M., Adler, C. S., and Mullaney, D. J. (1973). EMG biofeedback and tension headache: a controlled outcome study. *Psychosomatic Medicine*, 35, 484–496.

Cautela, J. R. (1967). Covert sensitization. *Psychological Reports*, 20, 459–468.

Cautela, J. R. (1968). Behavior therapy and the need for behavioral assessment. *Psychotherapy: Theory, Research, and Practice*, 5, 175–179.

Cautela, J. R. (1971). Covert conditioning. In A. Jacobs and L. B. Sachs (Eds.), *The Psychology of Private Events: Perspectives on Covert Response Systems*, Academic Press, New York.

Cautela, J. R., and Kastenbaum, R. (1967). A reinforcement survey schedule for use in therapy, training, and research. *Psychological Reports*, 20, 1115–1130.

Cooke, G. (1966). The efficacy of two desensitization procedures: an analogue study. *Behaviour Research and Therapy*, 4, 17–24.

Danaher, B. G., and Thoreson, C. E. (1972). Imagery assessment by self-report and behavioral measures. *Behaviour Research and Therapy*, 10, 131–138.

Duff, F. L. (1965). Item subtlety in personality inventory scales. *Journal of Consulting Psychology*, 29, 565–570.

Evans, I. M., and Nelson, R. O. (1974). A curriculum for the teaching of behavior assessment. *American Psychologist*, 29, 598–606.

Ferster, C. B. (1973). A functional analysis of depression. *American Psychologist*, 28, 857–870.

Foxx, R. M., and Azrin, N. H. (1973). *Toilet Training the Retarded*, Research Press, Champaign, Illinois.

Freund, K. (1965). Diagnosing heterosexual pedophilia by means of a test for sexual interest. *Behaviour Research and Therapy*, 3, 229–234.

Freund, K. (1967). Diagnosing homo- or hetero-sexuality and erotic age-preference by means of a psychophysiological test. *Behaviour Research and Therapy*, 5, 209–228.

Galassi, J. P., DeLo, J. S., Galassi, M. D., and Bastien, S. (1974). The college self-expression scale: a measure of assertiveness. *Behavior Therapy*, 5, 165–171.

Geer, J. H. (1965). The development of a scale to measure fear. *Behaviour Research and Therapy*, 3, 45–53.

Goldberg, L. R., and Slovic, P. (1967). Importance of test item content: an analysis of a corollary of the deviation hypothesis. *Journal of Counseling Psychology*, 14, 462–472.

Goldfried, M. R., and D'Zurilla, T. J. (1969). A behavior-analytic model for assessing competence. In C. D. Spielberger (Ed.), *Current Topics in Clinical and Community Psychology*, *Vol. I*. Academic Press, New York.

Goldfried, M. R., and Kent, R. N. (1972). Traditional versus behavioral personality assessment: a comparison of methodological and theoretical assumptions. *Psychological Bulletin*, 77, 409–420.

Goldfried, M. R., and Pomeranz, D. (1968). Role of assessment in behavior modification. *Psychological Reports*, 23, 75–87.

Goldfried, M. R., and Sprafkin, J. N. (1974). *Behavioral Personality Assessment*, General Learning Press, Morristown, New Jersey.

Goldstein, S. B., and Lanyon, R. I. (1971). Parent–therapists in the language training of an autistic child. *Journal of Speech and Hearing Disorders*, 36, 552–560.

Hersen, M. (1973). Self-assessment of fear. *Behavior Therapy*, 4, 241–257.

Hilgard, E. R. (1965). *Hypnotic Susceptibility*, Harcourt, Brace and World, New York.

Homme, L., Homme, A., Baca, P. de'C., and Cottingham, L. (1968). What behavioral engineering is. *Psychological Record*, **18**, 425–434.

Jackson, D. N. (1971). The dynamics of structured personality tests. *Psychological Review*, **78**, 229–248.

Kanfer, F. H. (1972). Assessment for behavior modification. *Journal of Personality Assessment*, **36**, 418–423.

Kanfer, F. H., and Karoly, P. (1972). Self-control: a behavioristic excursion into the lion's den. *Behaviour Therapy*, **3**, 398–416.

Kanfer, F. H., and Phillips, J. S. (1970). *Learning Foundations of Behavior Therapy*, Wiley, New York.

Kanfer, F. H., and Saslow, G. (1969). Behavioral diagnosis. In C. M. Franks (Ed.), *Behavior Therapy: Appraisal and Status*, McGraw-Hill, New York.

Karst, T. O., and Most, R. (1973). A comparison of stress measures in an experimental analogue of public speaking. *Journal of Consulting and Clinical Psychology*, **41**, 342–348.

Kazdin, A. E. (1974). Self-monitoring and behavior change. In M. J. Mahoney and C. E. Thoreson (Eds.), *Self-control: Power to the Person*, Wadsworth, Belmont, California.

Kent, R. N., O'Leary, K. D., Diament, C., and Dietz, A. (1974). Expectation biases in observational evaluation of therapeutic change. *Journal of Consulting and Clinical Psychology*, **42**, 774–780.

Klopfer, B., and Kelley, D. M. (1942). *The Rorschach Technique*, World Book Company, Yonkers.

Kostlan, A. (1954). A method for the empirical study of psychodiagnosis. *Journal of Consulting Psychology*, **18**, 83–88.

Kozloff, M. (1973). *Reaching the Autistic Child: A Parent Training Program*, Research Press, Champaign, Illinois.

Krasner, L. (1971). Behavior therapy. *Annual Review of Psychology*, **22**, 483–532.

Krumboltz, J. D., and Krumboltz, H. B. (1972). *Changing Children's Behavior*, Prentice-Hall, New York.

Lang, P. J. (1968). Fear reduction and fear behavior: problems in treating a construct. In J. M. Shlien (Ed.), *Research in Psychotherapy, Vol. III*, American Psychological Association, Washington, D.C.

Lang, P. J., and Lazovik, A. D. (1963). Experimental desensitization of a phobia. *Journal of Abnormal and Social Psychology*, **66**, 519–525.

Lanyon, R. I. (1957). *Design of a Salicylic Acid Plant*. Senior thesis, Department of Chemical Engineering, University of Adelaide.

Lanyon, R. I. (1967). Measurement of social competence in college males. *Journal of Consulting and Clinical Psychology*, **31**, 495–498.

Lanyon, R. I. (1974). *Spontaneous Changes in Imagery during Systematic Desensitization*. Paper presented to the Department of Psychiatry, Massachusetts General Hospital, Boston, February 1974.

Lanyon, R. I., and Goodstein, L. D. (1971). *Personality Assessment*, Wiley, New York.

Lanyon, R. I., Manosevitz, M., and Imber, R. (1968). Systematic desensitization: distribution of practice and symptom substitution. *Behaviour Research and Therapy*, **6**, 323–329.

Lassen, C. L., and Held, M. L. (1974). Everything you always wanted to know about sex films. *Contemporary Psychology*, **19**, 481–484.

Lazarus, A. A. (1971). *Behavior Therapy and Beyond*, McGraw-Hill, New York.

Lewinsohn, P. M. (1973). Clinical and theoretical aspects of depression. In K. S. Calhoun, H. E. Adams and K. M. Mitchell (Eds.), *Innovative Treatment Methods in Psychopathology*, Wiley, New York.

Lindsley, O. R. (1968). A reliable wrist counter for recording behavior rates. *Journal of Applied Behavior Analysis*, **1**, 77–78.

Lipinski, D., and Nelson, R. (1974). Problems in the use of naturalistic observation as a means of behavioral assessment. *Behavior Therapy*, **5**, 341–351.

McCullough, J. P., and Powell, P. O. (1972). A technique for measuring clarity of imagery in therapy clients. *Behavior Therapy*, **3**, 447–448.

McFall, R. M. (1970). The effects of self-monitoring on normal smoking behavior. *Journal of Consulting and Clinical Psychology*, **35**, 135–142.

McFall, R. M., and Lillesand, D. V. (1971). Behavior rehearsal with modeling and coaching in assertive training. *Journal of Abnormal Psychology*, **77**, 313–323.

McFall, R. M., and Marston, A. (1970). An experimental investigation of behavioral rehearsal in assertive training. *Journal of Abnormal Psychology*, **76**, 295–303.

MacPhillamy, D. J., and Lewinsohn, P. M. (1971). *Pleasant Events Schedule*. University of Oregon, mimeo.

Madsen, C. H., Jr., and Madsen, C. K. (1970). *Teaching/Discipline: Behavioral Principles toward a Positive Approach*, Allyn and Bacon, Boston.

Mahoney, M. J., and Thoreson, C. E. (1974). *Self-control: Power to the Person*, Brooks/Cole, Monterey, California.

Manosevitz, M., and Lanyon, R. I. (1965). Fear survey schedule: a normative study. *Psychological Reports*, **17**, 699–703.

Masters, W. H., and Johnson, V. E. (1970). *Human Sexual Inadequacy*, Little and Brown, Boston.

Miller, N. E., Barber, T. X., DiCara, L. V., Kamiya, J., Shapiro, D., and Stoyva, J. (1973). *Biofeedback and Self-control: 1973*, Aldine, Chicago.

Mills, H. L., Agras, W. S., Barlow, D. H., and Mills, J. R. (1973). Compulsive rituals treated by response prevention. *Archives of General Psychiatry*, **28**, 524–529.

Mischel, W. (1968). *Personality and Assessment*, Wiley, New York.

Morganstern, F. S., Pearce, J. F., and Rees, W. L. (1965). Predicting the outcome of behaviour therapy by means of psychological tests. *Behaviour Research and Therapy*, **2**, 191–200.

Murray, H. A. (1938). *Explorations in Personality*, Oxford University Press, New York.

Orne, M. T. (1962). On the social psychology of the psychological experiment: with particular reference to demand characteristics and their implication. *American Psychologist*, **17**, 766–783.

Paivio, A. B. (1971). *Imagery and Verbal Processes*, Holt, Rinehart and Winston, New York.

Paul, G. L. (1966). *Insight versus Desensitization in Psychotherapy: An Experiment in Anxiety Reduction*, Stanford University Press, Stanford, California.

Peterson, D. R. (1954). The diagnosis of subclinical schizophrenia. *Journal of Consulting Psychology*, **18**, 198–200.

Peterson, D. R. (1968). *The Clinical Study of Social Behavior*, Appleton-Century-Crofts, New York.

Piotrowski, Z. (1937). The Rorschach ink blot method in organic disturbances of the central nervous system. *Journal of Nervous and Mental Disease*, **86**, 525–537.

Podell, L., and Perkins, J. C. (1957). A Guttman scale for sexual experience—a methodological note. *Journal of Abnormal and Social Psychology*, **44**, 420–422.

Rehm, L. P. (1973). Relationships among measures of visual imagery. *Behaviour Research and Therapy*, **11**, 265–270.

Rimm, D. C., and Bottrell, J. (1969). Four measures of visual imagination. *Behaviour Research and Therapy*, **7**, 63–69.

Romanczyk, R. G., Kent, R. N., Diament, C., and O'Leary, K. D. (1973). Measuring the reliability of observational data: a reactive process. *Journal of Applied Behavior Analysis*, **6**, 175–184.

Rosenthal, R. (1966). *Experimenter Effects in Behavioral Research*, Appleton-Century-Crofts, New York.

Rubin, S. E., Lawlis, G. F., Tasto, D. L., and Namenek, T. (1969). Factor analysis of the 122 item fear survey schedule. *Behaviour Research and Therapy*, **7**, 381–386.

Sarason, S. B. (1974). *The Psychological Sense of Community*, Jossey-Bass, San Francisco.

Schaefer, H. H., and Martin, P. L. (1969). *Behavioral Therapy*, McGraw-Hill, New York.

Scherer, M. W., and Nakamura, C. Y. (1968). A fear survey schedule for children (FSS–FC). *Behaviour Research and Therapy*, **6**, 173–182.

Shapiro, D., Schwartz, G. G., and Tursky, B. (1972). Control of diastolic blood pressure in man by feedback and reinforcement. *Psychophysiology*, **9**, 296–304.

Sheehan, P. W. (1967a). A shortened form of Bett's questionnaire upon mental imagery. *Journal of Clinical Psychology*, **23**, 386–389.

Sheehan, P. W. (1967b). Reliability of a short test of imagery. *Perceptual and Motor Skills*, **25**, 744.

Sines, L. K. (1959). The relative contribution of four kinds of data to accuracy in personality assessment. *Journal of Consulting Psychology*, **23**, 483–492.

Singer, J. L. (1974). *Imagery and Daydream Methods in Psychotherapy and Behavior Modification*, Academic Press, New York.

Sterman, M. B. (1973). Neurophysiologic and clinical studies of sensorimotor EEG biofeedback training: some effects on epilepsy. *Seminars in Psychiatry*, **5**, 507–524.

Stuart, R. B., and Davis, B. (1972). *Slim Chance in a Fat World: Behavioral Control of Obesity*, Research Press, Champaign, Illinois.

Symonds, P. M. (1931). *Diagnosing Personality and Conduct*, Appleton-Century, New York.

Tasto, D. L., Hickson, R., and Rubin, S. E. (1971). Scaled profile analysis of fear survey schedule scores. *Behavior Therapy*, **2**, 543–549.

Tharp, R. G., and Wetzel, R. J. (1969). *Behavior Modification in the Natural Environment*, Academic Press, New York.

Thoreson, C. E., and Mahoney, M. H. (1974). *Behavioral Self-control*, Holt, Rinehart and Winston, New York.

Ullmann, L. P., and Krasner, L. (1965). Introduction. In L. P. Ullmann and L. Krasner (Eds.), *Case Studies in Behavior Modification*, Holt, Rinehart and Winston, New York.

Underwood, B. J. (1966). *Experimental Psychology*, Appleton-Century-Crofts, New York.

Wahler, R. G., and Cormier, W. H. (1970). The ecological interview: a first step in out-patient child behavior therapy. *Journal of Behavior Therapy and Experimental Psychiatry*, **1**, 279–289.

Wallace, J. (1966). An abilities conception of personality: some implications for personality measurement. *American Psychologist*, **21**, 132–138.

Wallace, J. (1967). What units shall we employ? Allport's question revisited. *Journal of Consulting Psychology*, **31**, 56–64.

Walsh, W. B. (1967). Validity of self-report. *Journal of Counseling Psychology*, **14**, 18–23.

Walsh, W. B. (1968). Validity of self-report: another look. *Journal of Counselling Psychology*, **15**, 180–186.

Watson, D. L., and Tharp, R. G. (1972). *Self-directed Behavior: Self-modification for Personal Adjustment*, Brooks/Cole, Monterey, California.

Webb, E. J., Campbell, D. T., Schwartz, R. D., and Sechrest, L. (1966). *Unobtrusive Measures: Nonreactive Research in the Social Sciences*, Rand McNally, Chicago.

Wernimont, P. F., and Campbell, J. P. (1968). Signs, examples, and criteria. *Journal of Applied Psychology*, **52**, 372–376.

Wilkins, W. (1974). Parameters of therapeutic imagery: directions from case studies. *Psychotherapy: Theory, Research, and Practice*, **11**, 163–171.

Williams, D. E. (1957). A point of view about stuttering. *Journal of Speech and Hearing Disorders*, **22**, 390–397.

Wolff, W. T., and Merrens, M. R. (1974). Behavioral assessment: a review of clinical methods. *Journal of Personality Assessment*, **38**, 3–16.

Wolpe, J., and Lang, P. (1964). A fear survey schedule for use in behavior therapy. *Behaviour Research and Therapy*, **2**, 27–30.

SECTION IV

Theoretical, Methodological and Ethical Issues

11

BEHAVIOUR THERAPY—DOGMA OR APPLIED SCIENCE?

H. J. Eysenck

Two major claims are commonly made for behaviour therapy—one relating to its practical usefulness, the other to its scientific derivation. It is claimed, in the first place, that the methods introduced by behaviour therapists, such as desensitization, flooding, modelling, counterconditioning, aversive conditioning, token economies, shaping, and so on, are demonstrably more effective than either no treatment, placebo treatment or any form of psychotherapy, including psychoanalysis, in curing or at least improving the 'symptoms' of neurotic or even psychotic patients. This is clearly an empirical question, and the astonishing growth in the application of behaviour therapy in recent years is often quoted as partial evidence in favour of this proposition. Figure 11.1 shows the increase in the rate of publication of articles on behaviour therapy from a baseline of just a few per annum until, within the short span of less than a dozen years, the number of articles on behaviour therapy overtakes that of articles on psychoanalysis in 1972 (Hoon and Lindsley, 1974).

Direct testimony to the effectiveness of behaviour therapy comes from the investigation of a special committee set up by the American Psychiatric Association to investigate the potential and actual usefulness of these new methods; the report leaves no doubt about the practical value of behaviour therapy (A.P.A. report, 1973). Most important, of course, is the evidence presented in the literature of well-planned and well-conducted clinical and experimental studies comparing the effects of behaviour therapy with those of other methods of treatment (e.g. Birk and coworkers, 1971; Gelder, Marks and Wolff, 1967; Gillan and Rachman, 1974). While even more extensive and carefully designed experiments, embodying even longer follow-up periods, are desirable, the evidence already available solidly supports the proposition under discussion. In fact, few psychiatrists or clinical psychologists would still doubt the efficacy of the major methods of behaviour therapy, and even criticisms suggesting inevitable relapse or 'symptom substitution' attending 'purely symptomatic treatment' have ceased to be proffered, in view of the clear demonstration in follow-up studies that these negative after-effects, in fact, occur only rarely

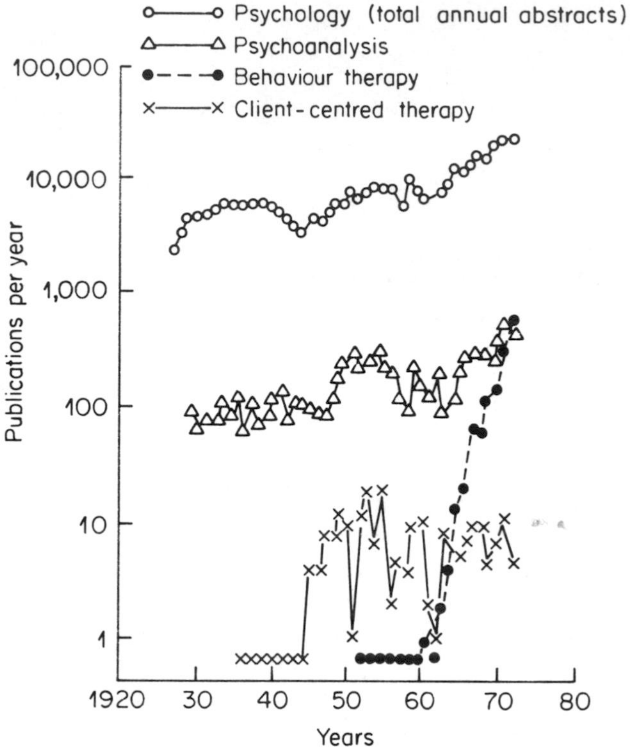

FIGURE 11.1 Comparison of psychology (total), psychoanalysis, behaviour therapy and client-centred annual
publication frequencies since 1926. (Quoted from Hoon
and Lindsley, 1974. by permission.)

(except in disorders of the 'second kind'—failure of occurrence of socializing conditioning—where, as Eysenck and Rachman, 1965, have pointed out, theory suggests that they would be expected to occur).

A rather different type of criticism has taken the place of the early views that treatment aimed directly at symptoms was futile, could not succeed in the long run and was doomed to failure. This new wave of criticism is directed at the second claim made for behaviour therapy, namely that it constitutes an applied science, deriving its procedures and methods from modern learning theory and from the conditioning laboratory. As I expressed it in my original paper introducing behaviour therapy as a general concept:

Modern learning theory, and the experimental studies of learning and conditioning carried out by psychologists in their laboratories are extremely relevant to the problems raised by the neurotic disorders. If the laws which have been formulated are, not necessarily true, but at least partially correct, then it must follow that we can make deductions from them to cover the type of behaviour represented by neurotic patients, construct a model which will duplicate the important and relevant features of the patient and suggest new and possibly helpful methods of treatment along the lines laid down by learning theory. (Eysenck, 1959).

This conception of psychiatric treatment as an applied science has been made the butt of criticism (Breger and McGaugh, 1965; Locke, 1971) and scorn (London, 1972), and it will be the main aim of this chapter in a book devoted to a consideration of the way in which my proposal has been implemented to see whether these criticisms are justified, or whether we may justifiably claim that behaviour therapy does indeed constitute an applied science, rather than a dogmatic assertion not based on fact.

Before turning to this discussion, we must first try and get rid of one particular bugbear that has befuddled discussion for far too long. It is perhaps illustrated best of all in Locke's (1971) paper entitled 'Is "behavior therapy" behavioristic?' Breger and McGaugh (1965) raise similar queries regarding the applicability of behaviouristic principles to the analysis of behaviour. Locke starts off by giving his view of what the basic premises of behaviourism are. He lists them as follows:

(1) *Determinism:* the doctrine that all of man's actions, thoughts, beliefs, etc., are ultimately determined by forces outside his control (typically, by environmental forces).

(2) *Epiphenomenalism:* the doctrine that conscious states (e.g. ideas), if they exist at all, are merely by-products of physical events in the body and/or in the external world—that they are end points in a causal chain and have no effect on either the individual's subsequent actions or his subsequent ideas.

(3) *The rejection of introspection* as a scientific method.

Locke goes on to ask whether Wolpe's methods of treatment fit in with these premises, and he concludes that they do not; *ergo*, behaviour therapy is not behaviouristic! This would be a reasonable logical conclusion if it did not contain a *petitio principii*; Locke gives us his own definition of behaviourism, but does not enquire whether this is the correct definition, or whether it would be acceptable to Wolpe or other behaviour therapists. The meaning of the term 'behaviourism' is discussed in some detail by Miles (1966), who accepts a tripartite division advocated by Mace (1948–1949). This discussion is very relevant to our purpose.

Mace distinguishes three versions of behaviourism which he labels 'metaphysical', 'methodological' and 'analytical'. The metaphysical version is a claim which purports to be in some sense a question of fact, namely whether, in addition to ordinary 'physical' objects, there exist further objects, namely 'minds'; a metaphysical behaviourist is one who says that there are not. Miles goes on to say:

> The methodological behaviourist is less ambitious; his case is rather that if there are such things as minds or mental events they cannot as a matter of methodology be regarded as proper objects for scientific study. Analytical behaviourism is the view that sentences which might appear at first glance to be about entities called 'minds' or 'mental events' turn out on examination to be sentences about behaviour (Miles, 1966, p. 33).

Mace puts this view in the following manner:

To the analytical behaviourist the existence of mind or consciousness defined as irreducibly distinct from matter and its behaviour is not even conceivable in any positive terms. It enjoys, so to speak, the status of a prime number which is more than nineteen and less than twenty-three. Statements about mind or consciousness just turn out to be, on analysis, statements about the behaviour of material things. Statements about 'perceiving' turn out to be statements about 'differential responses'. Statements about 'liking' and 'desiring' turn out to be statements about 'abient' and 'adient' responses, and so on for every kind of 'experience' or 'psychical phenomenon' (Mace, 1948–1949, p. 164).

To these major categories of 'behaviourism' must be added the whimsies, follies and idiosyncracies of individual behaviourists, which are mistaken by some writers as inherent properties of behaviourism in general. We may refer here to Watson's fanatical environmentalism, which has coloured the thinking of a whole generation of psychologists, or to Skinner's antitheoretical, antiphysiological stance, which has done equal damage to another generation of psychologists. When considering behaviourism as a working theory of behaviour therapists, we must dismiss both the philosophical speculations inherent in metaphysical behaviourism (which is simply nineteenth-century materialism ignorant of the philosophical objections to which it is subject) and the ideas peculiar to individual behaviourists such as Watson and Skinner. What is left is a methodological commitment to scientific method which does not admit introspective evidence on its own terms, but is willing to admit verbal communication when this can be shown to be firmly anchored, as Hull demanded, in antecedent and consequent conditions which are objectively measurable. Provided these conditions are fulfilled, we need not reject so-called mental events. Did not Skinner (1964) himself argue that we should not reject *a priori* the study of private events (images, sensations, etc.) simply because they were private? Behaviourism does not imply an ideological commitment to outmoded philosophical positions as Locke seems to suggest; his version of behaviourism is completely arbitrary and bears little relation to the views of active behaviourists.

It is, of course, possible that some behaviourists embrace epiphenomenalism, but some form of Spinoza's double-aspect theory is probably more acceptable, though neither is essential for modern behaviourism. Determinism, in the sense of the word given it by Laplace, is a doctrine which is not even held by physicists since the introduction of Heisenberg's principle of indeterminancy; it is not clear why psychologists should be lumbered with outworn notions of this kind. The rejection of introspection we have already discussed; provided certain precautions are observed, we need not despair of fitting verbal reports into a behaviouristic system. Marks and Gelder have used verbal reports of increasing latency in achieving mental images of negatively reinforced scenes and objects as a measure of the efficacy of aversive therapy. These were accompanied by plethysmographic recording of the changes in penis size which should theoretically follow the imagery in question. Correlation between these two methods of recording validates the introspective method, and suggests that it may be useful under conditions which make penis plethysmography impossible. These and many other methods of validating 'introspective' reports are discussed by Eysenck and Beech (1971).

Breger and McGaugh follow Locke in confining the term 'behaviourism' to a very narrow interpretation, identifying it essentially with early Hullian learning theory, and then pointing out that this particular theory is subject to certain weighty criticisms. This is true, but of course the term 'modern learning theory' does not refer to outmoded views held thirty years ago but to the most modern views, including stress on mediation (e.g. Osgood, 1953). As J. J. Thomson pointed out many years ago, theory in science is a policy, not a creed, and what Breger and McGaugh are trying to do is to confine behaviour therapists to just such a creed, namely that of early Hull. This is not the position adopted by behaviour therapists who regard their theories as signposts to better theories, more in line with the factual evidence, suggestive of policies to be adopted rather than as revealed truths. We may conclude this discussion of the question of whether behaviour therapy is behaviouristic by stating that the question is meaningless unless the term 'behaviourism' is defined unequivocally. As there are many different definitions, and as those adduced by Locke and others are quite unacceptable to behaviour therapists, the issue is a purely verbal, definitional one, rather than a factual one (Waters and McCallum, 1973). To think in these terms merely obfuscates the real issues, and it might be best to forget the term 'behaviourism' altogether in talking about behaviour therapy. We are all behaviourists now (in the methodological sense), and possible disagreements about philosophical issues is not likely to affect our theories and experiments in the fields of learning and conditioning.

Having eliminated this particular irrelevant issue from the discussion, we may now turn to the more substantive objections to the proper status of behaviour therapy as an applied science. There is one outstanding characteristic of all the many criticisms that have been made: they all assume a picture of what applied science is like which is totally unrealistic and seems to be taken wholesale from elementary primers of the philosophy of science. This is a very important point, although it does not seem to have been made before; in deciding whether or not a particular view or mode of action is 'scientific', we must first agree as to what we shall mean by 'scientific'. Critics chastise behaviour therapists because there is no unified theory of learning or conditioning from which all the observed phenomena can be deduced; they complain because in our accounts of patients' behaviour there are many anomalies which cannot easily be reconciled with the theory on which the therapist is operating; and they argue that alternative explanations have not always been ruled out in accounting for the cures observed. All this is true, but it would be quite wrong to argue in consequence that behaviour therapy is not an applied science. All these objections apply with equal force to the hard sciences in their development, and the application of physics and chemistry to practical purposes. These criticisms only seem to obliterate the claims of behaviour therapy to the status of an applied science because at the back of the critic's mind there is a simplistic, unrealistic, Platonic ideal of science which is far removed from reality, and which would rule out of court not only psychology and behaviour therapy but all the existing sciences as well. An example will make clear the difference between reality and pretence.

On March 13th, 1781, William Herschel discovered the planet Uranus. The path along which it was expected to move was calculated, but there were small deviations from that path (amounting to about twenty seconds of arc) which suggested that perhaps these were caused by another planet, even further out than Uranus. John Couch Adams, at Cambridge, and Urbain Jean Leverrier, of Paris, took up the challenge: given the deflections in the orbit of Uranus, find purely by theoretical calculation the mass and the position of the hypothetical new planet, and then, from the deduced theoretical position, actually discover the planet with a telescope (Hoyle, 1962).

J. G. Galle, of the Berlin Observatory, was shown the calculations and picked up the new planet on September 23rd, 1846; Leverrier decided to name it Neptune. The discovery of Neptune has become perhaps the most famous example of scientific prediction, the verification of a scientific theory and the triumph of the hypothetico-deductive method. It is often quoted by psychologists who feel that their science should aspire to such accuracy. A look at the facts will disabuse the reader of the notion that there is all that much difference between what goes on in psychology and what went on in the hard sciences on this particular occasion. First, note that the theory used by these astronomers, viz. Newton's theory of universal gravitation, was in fact wrong; we now know that while it makes predictions which are reasonably near the target under certain limited circumstances, nevertheless, Newton's own doubts about action-at-a-distance were only too justified. The theory was useful, but not correct; it has since been supplanted by Einstein's field theory (Berksan, 1974). Second, note that both men made very doubtful assumptions throughout their calculations; they assumed that Neptune obeyed an empirical rule (not derived or derivable from Newton's principles) called Bode's Law. This rule, which is shown in Table 11.1, is expressed by the following simple formula. For each planet first write a four, then add a number that varies from planet to planet: for Mercury, the innermost planet, the number is zero; for Venus, next nearest to the Sun, it is three. After Venus, the number is simply doubled each time—for Earth it is six, for Mars twelve, and so on. If the actual

TABLE 11.1 Planetary distances as given by Bode's Law compared with actual observation.

	Mercury	Venus	Earth	Mars	Ceres	Jupiter	Saturn	Uranus	Neptune
Arbitrary figure (a)	4	4	4	4	4	4	4	4	4
Arbitrary figure (b)	0	3	6	12	24	48	96	192	384
Bode's Law	4	7	10	16	28	52	100	196	388
Observation	3.9	7.2	10.0	15.2	27.7	52.0	95.4	191.9	300.7

mean radii of the planetary orbits are measured by a scale on which ten units represent the radius of the Earth's orbit, then the planetary orbits run in the sequence 3.9, 7.2, 10, 15.2, and so on; these figures are quite close to the series formed by Bode's Law.

Adams and Leverrier could not have made their calculations without recourse to Bode's Law, but this law is merely an empirical observation having no basis in theory. Furthermore, it requires some manipulation, such as the inclusion of the minor planet (really an asteroid) Ceres. And lastly, it does not apply to Neptune at all! Table 11.1 will show that for a predicted figure of 388, the actual observed figure is 301. This is an error sizeable even by psychological standards; few psychologists would get away with such a discrepancy. This leads us to the third observation on this miraculous event, namely that Adams and Leverrier were extremely lucky that Galle looked for the planet when he did; six months earlier or later he would have found nothing. Their calculations of Neptune's orbit and future positions turned out to be entirely wrong. Indeed, if these two had assumed that the orbit of Neptune was circular, rather than relying on Bode's Law, their calculations could have been carried through far more simply and with a far greater degree of accuracy! Thus, in the most celebrated example of scientific prediction, a wrong theory, using a purely empirical rule which normally would not apply at all, led to completely erroneous calculations about the planet's future behaviour. This is the sort of reality against which we have to measure our claims that behaviour therapy is scientific, rather than the 'no warts' picture presented by elementary histories and philosophies of science.

The importance of wrong theories in mediating advances in science is not always recognized; to criticize certain versions of learning theory as not accounting for anomalies is of course reasonable and indeed essential, but it should not be undertaken in the spirit of rejection. All scientific theories are ultimately false, as Popper (1959, 1963) has so often repeated; they cannot be proved right, but will ultimately be proved wrong. All scientific theories are full of anomalies; Newton could not even fit the movement of the moon into his system and passed sleepless nights worrying about the problem. The disturbances in the precession of the planet Mercury were never explained satisfactorily in terms of Newton's theory; the fact that Einstein could do so with great accuracy was one of the few empirical supports for his theory of relativity. Unfortunately, he assumed that the Sun was perfectly spherical; it is in fact oblate by one part in 2000, sufficient to throw out his calculations and leave Mercury's motions still unexplained. Anomalies are inevitable in scientific theories; they may find an easy explanation, they may lead to improvements in the theory or they may lead to its abandonment. Scientists only choose the latter if and when a better theory is in fact available; in its absence, they prefer to live with anomalies.

The development of quantum theory gives us a good example of the usefulness of erroneous theories (Hund, 1974). The complexity of quantum theory in its early development was partly due to the diversity of phenomena to which it had to be applied—problems of radiation, thermal properties, mechanics and spectra. The existence and consequences of electron spin had not been recognized at the time and could therefore not be distinguished from the more directly mechanical parts of quantum theory, thus making the early theory unnecessarily complicated. At the climax of the old theory, we see Bohr's impressive but wholly erroneous account of the periodicity of the elements. Yet no physicist would argue that these theories were not useful, or indeed essential; the work of Schrödinger, Heisenberg and Dirac would not have been possible without them. Erroneous theories have their uses, and should not be sent packing until something demonstrably better can be put in their place.

An example of how theories can be obviously wrong and yet extremely useful can be furnished by looking at the growth and development of the theory of the genesis of neurosis which lies at the basis of behaviour therapy. We start with the neurotic paradox, as Mowrer called it—how is it that people continue to behave in ways which are plainly contrary to their own interests and which receive negative reinforcement throughout? There are three main theories in the field. The oldest is concerned with possession by the devil; cure, exorcism. The next is concerned with possession by unconscious complexes; cure, psychoanalysis. Both of these are now of purely historical interest. The third theory, based on learning and conditioning, was first put forward by Watson; according to him, neurotic behaviour is simply caused by conditioned reflexes. His attempt to support this view, by the experiment he carried out with Miss Rayner on 'little Albert', has become very well known. But the theory itself is not only fragmentary but does not bear serious consideration. It requires some sort of traumatic conditioning, but, except for wartime neuroses, traumatic conditioning is infrequent in the genesis of neurotic disorders. The onset of neurotic disorders is usually insidious; there is a slow growth of anxiety until it becomes unbearable and there is a breakdown. Often the conditioned response (CR) is stronger than the unconditioned response (UCR)—where a proper UCR can indeed be identified. Even if we accept the existence of proper CRs as the basis of neurosis, they should quickly extinguish due to lack reinforcement; long-continued neuroses should be impossible to deduce from the theory.

A second model of the theory, put forward by Mowrer (1939), rescued it from the last of these criticisms. Mowrer's two-factor theory assumed Pavlovian conditioning as the first stage in the genesis of neurosis, but then argued that operant conditioning would protect the CR from extinction. The subject, so the argument ran, would produce abient responses when encountering the object or situation which had become the CS. In this way, avoidance would be positively reinforced (through lessening of the CR) and a secondary habit of avoidance would be conditioned.) The patient would be unable to apply reality testing to his fears and thus avoid extinction. This view clearly explains the failure of extinction to occur in many cases, and it was accepted provisionally by Eysenck and Rachman (1965) as a plausible theory of the genesis of neurotic disorder. It does not, however, account for the other departures from observation which characterize Watson's theory, and thus is still unable to account for the observational facts surrounding neurosis.

My own model (Eysenck, 1975) takes its departure from a vital change in the classical law of extinction which I have suggested elsewhere (Eysenck, 1968). The classical law states that continued presentation of a CR in the absence of its original reinforcer leads to the extinction of a classically conditioned response. This 'law' clearly does not work very well. Twenty years ago, Razran (1956), in a review of forty years of American and Russian research, remarked that 'extinction continues to be clearly a less than 100 per cent. phenomenon. Instances of difficult and even impossible extinction are constantly reported by classical CR experimenters (p. 39)'. My own suggestion is that there are two main classes of CRs and that the occurrence of extinction or incubation (paradoxical enhancement) depends on the particular class of CR involved. It has been known for a long time that CRs may act as a drive (Miller, 1948). Certain types of CRs (in particular fear/anxiety and sex) may also act as reinforcements in their own right. The CRs in a typical conditioning situation involving fear/anxiety or tumescent sexual responses are precisely identical with the UCRs, viz. fear/anxiety responses or tumescent sexual responses! If this is so, then the situation is clearly different from the one in which extinction is likely to work; there is, in fact, no absence of the 'original reinforcer', because the original reinforcer and the CR are identical. Under these conditions, we would expect the CR to perform the same function as the UCR, and act as both drive and reinforcer, causing paradoxical enhancement or incubation of the CR rather than extinction.

To illustrate our contention, consider Figure 11.2. This shows in diagram-

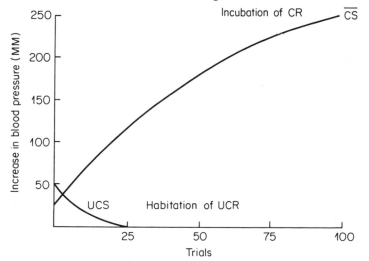

FIGURE 11.2 Habituation of the UCR and incubation (paradoxical enhancement) of the CR, as shown by rise in blood pressure in dogs. Quoted from Eysenck, 1975 by permission.

matic form the results of a series of experiments by Napalkov (see Eysenck, 1967a). The experimental animals are dogs; the UCR is a pistol shot fired behind the unsuspecting dog's ear, or some other such traumatic stimulus (Napalkov used various stimuli). The UCR is an increase in blood pressure, as shown on the ordinate. Repeated evocation of the UCR leads to quick habituation. Now consider the fate of the CR, under conditions where there is but a single CS—UCS combination; after this, only CSs are administered. It will be seen that the curve of CRs increases rather than extinguishes and there is a very marked increase in blood pressure which shows no sign of regressing, even after one hundred evocations. The CR clearly is not subject to habituation, as is the UCR, and it serves as the reinforcer for the CS–CR link. This and many other experiments are difficult to explain in terms other than some such change in the law of extinction (Eysenck, 1968; Woods, 1974). We shall here accept this emendation and see how this helps us in accounting for the facts of neurotic breakdown.

Note first that there is now no need for a traumatic event to precipitate the conditioning sequence; a sequence of relatively mild events, producing only small CRs, can add together in the manner of Figure 11.2 to produce a very strong anxiety reaction. Note also that by the same token there is now no mystery attaching to the fact that the CR can become stronger than the UCR. Last, we now have a better explanation of the failure of neuroses to extinguish; while Mowrer's two-factor theory may account for some instances, the majority are descriptively very difficult to fit into his model. We thus have a third model of neurosis, as based on conditioning theory principles; this model, while no doubt also open to criticism, appears to account for the known facts of neurosis better than do the previous models.

There are other ways in which this model is useful in clinical psychology. Consider treatment, particularly 'flooding' or extinction by response prevention. Work along these lines has shown both positive and negative effects; anxiety can either be extinguished or exacerbated. Animal work (e.g. Rohrbaugh and Riccio, 1970; Silvestri, Rohrbaugh and Riccio, 1970) has suggested that the period of exposure to the unreinforced CS is crucial; short exposure leads to incubation, long exposure to extinction. Staub (1968) has documented the same principle in human 'flooding' experiments. No doubt there are other parameters which determine the course of the extinction or enhancement of CRs; personality or strain variables are undoubtedly important, as is the strength of the original UCR. It would take us too far to enter into detailed discussion of these variables. We will merely note that the conditioning theory of neurosis is constantly advancing to account for more and more phenomena in this field and to avoid criticisms applicable to the older versions of the theory.

Objections will, of course, still be made to such a theory; e.g. it will be said that cognitive factors must play an important part in the genesis of a neurotic disorder, at least in humans, and that recourse to simple 'conditioning' leaves out many important variables. We must deal with criticisms of this kind later;

here it may be useful to ask rather whether the kind of theory put forward is in fact scientific, whether it is superior to alternative theories (such as the Freudian) and how we can decide on the answer to such questions. Clearly, without some ground rules available on which to proceed, we are unlikely to arrive at any meaningful conclusions; the difficulties attaching to the term 'behaviourism' and its use will already have made this abundantly clear. Actually, the multiplicity of views regarding the proper definition of 'science' and 'scientific' indicates the difficulty of the task. We will not consider old-fashioned and clearly erroneous views, such as inductionism. No science has ever arisen along Baconian principles of random data gathering and subsequent hypothesis formulation. In the early years of the twentieth century, inductive logicians set out to define the probabilities of different theories according to the available total evidence. If the mathematical probability of a theory was high, it qualified as scientific, while if it was low or even zero, it was not scientific. This view has some attractive features, but Popper (1959) destroyed it when he showed that the mathematical probability of all theories, scientific or pseudo-scientific, given any amount of evidence, is zero. He showed that scientific theories are not only equally unprovable but also equally improbable; in the long run, all our theories will be disproved, so that the 'truth' or even the probability criterion has no real relevance.

Popper (1959, 1963) suggested instead that we should not divide scientific theories from pseudo-scientific ones, but rather scientific *method* from pseudo-scientific *method*. Scientific method is characterized by the criterion of *falsifiability*. If our theory specifies experimental conditions which could lead to disproof of the theory, then that theory is scientific; if not, not. Thus a proposition may petrify into pseudo-scientific dogma or become genuine knowledge, depending on whether we are prepared to state observable conditions which would refute it. On this criterion, Popper decided that Marxism and Freudianism are either pseudo-sciences or else they have been refuted; he is never quite clear which of these two outcomes he believes to be the correct one. (This is due to the fact that Marxists and Freudians behave in divergent ways when confronted with 'refutations'—some trying to change the theory, others trying to argue away the evidence.)

There are difficulties connected with Popper's view which are perhaps not widely enough known. At a conference called to discuss his and Kuhn's views, it became very apparent that the falsification theory itself had serious weaknesses (Lakatos and Musgrave, 1970). Newton's theory of gravitation threw up large numbers of anomalies and contradictions, yet his followers did not give up the theory; they behaved very much like convinced Marxists and Freudians in this respect. As Lakatos once said (personal communication), 'had Popper ever asked a Newtonian scientist under what *experimental* conditions he would abandon Newtonian theory, some Newtonian scientists would have been exactly as nonplussed as are some Marxists and Freudians.' Kuhn (1970) not only argued against Popper's falsification criterion but suggested that historically the accumulation of anomalies to which any theory is subject results in a *revolution* in which new concepts and new problems take over, and in which there is little question of crucial experiments to decide between the theories. These revolutions in some way resemble religious conversions, constituting just an irrational change in commitment. This view also has found many critics; the change from one paradigm to another must have some rational foundation which ought to be identifiable.

Perhaps the most widely accepted view among philosophers of science is that of Lakatos. It may be best to present a brief version of it in his own words. It is important to get the meaning of our terms clear if we are to argue rationally about the question raised in the title of this introduction. Lakatos' view combines and transcends those of Popper and Kuhn, and while no doubt it, too, will ultimately be improved upon, it nevertheless at the moment gives us a meaningful and useful standard of scientific propriety.

This is what Lakatos says (personal communication):

In the last few years I have been advocating a methodology of scientific research programmes, which solves some of the problems which both Popper and Kuhn failed to solve. First, I claim that the typical descriptive unit of great scientific achievements is not an isolated hypothesis but rather a research programme. Science is not simply trial-and-error, a series of conjectures and refutations. 'All swans are white' may be falsified by the discovery of one black swan. But such trivial trial-and-error does not rank as science. Newtonian science, for instance, is not simply a set of four conjectures—the three laws of mechanics and the law of gravitation. These four laws constitute only the '*hard core*' of the Newtonian programme. But this hard core is tenaciously protected from refutation by a vast '*protective belt*' of auxiliary hypotheses. And, even more importantly, the research programme has also a '*heuristic*', that is, a powerful problem-solving machinery, which, with the help of sophisticated mathematical techniques, digests anomalies and even turns them into positive evidence. For instance, if a planet does not move exactly as it should, the Newtonian scientist checks his conjectures concerning atmospheric refraction, concerning propagation of light in magnetic storms, and hundreds of other conjectures which are all part of the programme. He may even invent a hitherto unknown planet and calculate its position, mass and velocity in order to explain the anomaly.

Now Newton's theory of gravitation, Einstein's relativity theory, quantum mechanics, Marxism, Freudism, are all research programmes, each with a characteristic hard core stubbornly defended, each with its more flexible protective belt and each with its elaborate problem-solving machinery. Each of them, at any stage of its development, has unsolved problems and undigested anomalies. All theories, in this sense, are born refuted and die refuted. But are they *equally* good? Until now I have been *describing* what research programmes are like. But how can one distinguish a scientific or *progressive* programme from a pseudoscientific or *degenerating* one?

Contrary to Popper, the difference cannot be that some are still unrefuted, while others are already refuted. When Newton published his *Principia*, it was common knowledge that it could not properly explain even the motion of the moon; in fact, lunar motion refuted Newton. Kaufmann, a distinguished physicist, refuted Einstein's relativity theory in the very year it was published. But all the research programmes I admire have one characteristic in common. They all predict *novel* facts, facts which had been either undreamt of, or have indeed been contradicted by previous or rival programmes. In 1686, when Newton published his theory of gravitation, there were, for instance, two current theories concerning comets. The more popular one regarded comets as a signal from an angry God warning that He will strike and bring disaster. A little known theory of Kepler's held that comets were celestial bodies moving along straight lines. Now according to Newtonian theory, some of them moved in hyperbolas or parabolas never to return; others moved in ordinary ellipses. Halley, working in Newton's programme, calculated on the basis of observing a brief stretch of a comet's path that it would return in 72 years time; he calculated to the minute when it would be seen again at a well-defined point of the sky. This was incredible. But 72 years later, when both Newton and Halley were long dead, Halley's comet returned exactly as Halley predicted. Similarly, Newtionian scientists predicted the existence and exact motion of small planets which had never been observed before. Or let us take Einstein's programme. This programme made the stunning prediction that if one measures the distance between two stars in the night and if one measures the distance between them during the day (when they are visible during an eclipse of the sun), the two measurements will be different. Nobody had thought to make such an observation before Einstein's programme. Thus in a *progressive* research programme theory leads to the discovery of hitherto unknown novel facts. In degenerating programmes, however, theories are fabricated only in order to accommodate *known* facts. Has, for instance, Marxism ever predicted a stunning novel fact successfully? NEVER. It had some famous *unsuccessful* predictions. It predicted the absolute impoverishment of the working class. It predicted that the first socialist societies would be free of revolutions. It predicted that there will be no conflict of interests between Socialist countires. Thus the early predictions of Marxism were bold and stunning but they failed. Marxists explained all their failures: they explained the rising living standards of the working class by devising a theory of imperialism; they explained even why the first Socialist revolution occurred in industrially backward Russia. They 'explained' Berlin 1953, Budapest 1956, Prague 1968. They 'explained' the Russian–Chinese conflict. But their auxiliary hypotheses were all cooked up after the event to protect Marxian theory from the facts. The Newtonian programme led to novel facts; the Marxian lagged behind the facts and has been running fast to catch up with them.

To sum up: the hallmark of empirical progress is not trivial verifications; Popper is right that there are millions of them. It is no success for Newtonian theory that stones, when dropped, fall towards the earth, no matter how often this is repeated. But so-called 'refutations' are not the hallmark of empirical failure, as Popper has preached, since all programmes grow in a permanent ocean of anomalies. What *really* counts, are dramatic, unexpected, *stunning* predictions: a few of them are enough to tilt the balance; where theory lags behind the facts, we are dealing with miserable *degenerating* research programmes.

Now how do scientific *revolutions* come about? If we have two rival research programmes, and one is progressing while the other is degenerating, scientists tend to join the progressive programme. This is the *rationale* of scientific revolutions. But while it is a matter of intellectual honesty to keep the record public, it is not dishonest to stick to a degenerating programme and try to turn it into a progressive one.

As opposed to Popper the methodology of scientific research programmes does not offer instant rationality. One must treat budding programmes leniently; programmes may take decades before they get off the ground and become empirically progressive. Criticism is not a Popperian quick kill, by refutation. Important criticism is always constructive: there is no refutation without a better theory. Kuhn is wrong in thinking that scientific revolutions are sudden, irrational changes in vision. The history of science refutes both Popper and Kuhn: on close inspection both Popperian crucial experiments and Kuhnian revolutions turn out to be myths: what normally happens is that progressive research programmes replace degenerating ones.

Lakatos, as a leading Hungarian Marxist philosopher, naturally took Marxian theory as his example of a degenerating programme shift. What he has to say there also applies, with even greater force, to Freudian theory. The claims made by Freud and his followers are certainly stunning, but there is a complete lack of empirical support for these claims. Holmes (1974) has recently reviewed the large body of experimental literature which exists in relation to the theory of repression. He concludes that 'surprisingly, it was found that none of the investigations provided support for the predictions (p. 632)'. Eysenck and Wilson (1973) have similarly looked critically at the experimental evidence for other Freudian concepts; they, too, conclude that the studies reviewed do not bear out the theory. Even in the field of psychotherapy, where the most far-reaching claims have been made, Rachman (1971), in his thorough analysis of the available literature, had to conclude that there was no acceptable evidence that psychoanalysis or psychotherapy made any contribution to the improvement or cure of neurotic patients. If we agree to define 'scientific' in terms of a progressive programme shift and 'unscientific' in terms of a degenerating programme shift, there is little doubt that Freud must join Marx in the latter category.

It is in this sense, then, that we would claim scientific status for behaviour therapy; it is part of a progressive programme shift, it replaces a degenerating one (i.e. the Freudian) and it clearly leads to new discoveries. Whether these are *stunning*, in Lakatos' phrase, it may be difficult to say; however, that they are psychiatrically important there can be no doubt. Let us just consider, as one single example, the treatment of obsessive-compulsive disorders before and after the advent of 'flooding' methods of response prevention. Prior to the discovery of these methods by Meyer, Rachman, Marks and others (e.g. Hodgson, Rachman and Marks, 1972; Rachman, Hodgson and Marks, 1971; Rachman, Marks and Hodgson, 1973) there was little hope of cure or improvement. Many hospitals were unwilling to admit patients of this kind because there was little that could be done for them by psychoanalysis or orthodox psychotherapy. With the use of the new methods, the picture has been transformed; quite short-term therapy, following a strictly prescribed course, leads to recovery in the great majority of cases, a recovery which is lasting and usually accompanied by all-round improvement in social adjustment, etc. To the layman this may be less stunning than to the professional psychiatrist or clinical psychologist; nevertheless, it does demonstrate the power of the research programme and its strong position vis-á-vis the degenerative programmes so common in psychiatry.

Our answer to those who declare that psychology in general and learning theory in particular have no generally accepted, unified theory to offer the practical worker, would be that no such theories exist anywhere in science, although at certain times there may exist an erroneous idea that the millenium has arrived and that such a final theory has been achieved. Newton's 'action-at-a-distance' theory once held such a position, but it was replaced by Faraday's and Maxwell's field theories in the field of electromagnetism, and by Einstein's field theory in the wider physical field. But does not field theory take the place of the unified theory abandoned by action-at-a-distance? Alas, no. ADE (action-at-a-distance electrodynamics) has done away with the concept of the field and has been shown to fit in with Einstein's general theory of relativity. In its predictions and consequences, ADE is indistinguishable from the conventional Maxwell field theory (Hoyle and Narlikar, 1974).

The view of electromagnetism taken by ADE is fascinating, as it deals at root with the three fundamental difficulties of Maxwell's theory: these are the concept of field itself (Maxwell puzzled for years with mechanical models of how the field propagated through space), the direction of time (which has to be imposed artificially as in Newtonian mechanics) and the infinities (which beset calculations of such things as the radiation reaction on an accelerated charge and the energy of a stationary point charge). If Maxwell and ADE are experimentally equivalent, which one is right? The answer is, of course, that both are right; the question is metaphysical.

Yet, paradoxically, it may be important to physics. There have been examples before of theories with the same experimental consequences but a very different conceptual basis—Newtonian and Lagrangian mechanics, and the Schrödinger and Heisenberg interpretations of quantum mechanics, for example. The concept of a Lagrangian (a kind of energy function) is now central to a great deal of high energy physics, whereas Newton is hardly mentioned. Heisenberg's interpretation led to the S-matrix approach to particle interactions, whereas Schrödinger's equation is much more important in theoretical chemistry. The differences in the structure of 'equivalent' theories is significant for the future of physics. Although expressing the same experimental knowledge of present physics, they suggest different kinds of development and different intuitions.

Perhaps we may interpret the discussions and arguments between conditioning theories and cognitive theories in this sort of light. These are alternative views of a particular set of facts; the whole matter is too indefinite for us to say that both explain the facts equally well (some facts appear more easily explained by one set of explanations, others by the other), but for many facts it is possible to state alternative hypotheses based on either Pavlovian conditioning or cognitive theory which predict much the same outcome. Here, too, it may not make much sense to ask which is right; in a very meaningful sense both are right, and the question is essentially metaphysical. Conditioning theory may have to reach up higher into the realm of Pavlov's second signalling system while cognitive theory may have to come down to earth a little more to embrace simple facts of contiguous association, but both may in the long run turn out to be alternative theories without discriminably different experimental consequences. There is no reason why nature should have made things easier for psychologists in this respect than for physicists!

The evidence certainly leaves no doubt that what are nowadays called 'cognitive' factors play an important part in certain types of conditioning, particularly in the genesis of conditioned electrodermal responses (GSR), where simple contiguity principles do not suffice. The work of Cook and Harris (1936), of McAllister and McAllister (1958), of Lindley and Meyer (1961), of

Bridger and Mandel (1964), of Spence (1966), of Wilson (1968), of Dawson and Grings (1968), of Zeiner and Grings (1968), of Fuhrer and Baer (1969), of Prokasy and Allen (1969), of Hallam (1971) and of Öhman (1971) leaves no doubt on this issue. But to admit this is a far cry from denying the importance of conditioning principles. It simply suggests that experimenters have unduly neglected the elaboration of theories involving Pavlov's second signalling system, which from the very beginning formed an essential part in his theorizing (Platonov, 1959).

These findings do not provide a confrontation between alternative theories; they simply provide evidence in favour of an extension of existing theories to take into account parameters previously neglected. Methodological behaviourism is not challenged by these findings and analytical behaviourism is not challenged by these findings; whether metaphysical behaviourism is so challenged would require a metaphysician to decide. It is certainly desirable that work along these lines should be extended to embrace more robust types of conditioning than GSR. The very ubiquity of these reactions makes it difficult to incorporate them within a theoretical system with any finality. Behaviour therapists should undoubtedly welcome such studies as they extend the working of conditioned reactions and of extinction paradigms, in directions that could with advantage be employed in therapy (Meichenbaum, 1972).

Even if all of this be granted, nevertheless the critics might be right in saying that behaviour therapists do not, in fact, derive practices deductively from principles of learning theory. Such a statement is difficult to prove or disprove because different people adopt different methods, and no general characterization would be at all accurate. However, a universal claim can be invalidated by a single example; we have already given one such example (the derivation of the 'flooding' type of treatment from response-prevention theories and experiments in the animal field) and another may be useful in showing in what detail treatment can, in fact, follow theory. Consider the 'bell-and-blanket' therapy for *enuresis nocturna*. The theory states that this method provides us with a conditioning paradigm which teaches the child to wake up and go to the toilet when his or her bladder is full; it also provides us with a method for producing the CR at will. Our first prediction would be that in using this method children would acquire the conditioned response more quickly than would children not so treated. Finley and coworkers (1973) have shown that this is so, using both methods with 100 per cent. reinforcement and methods with partial reinforcement. Figure 11.3 shows the result, which leaves little doubt about the efficacy of the method. Our second prediction would be that once reinforcement is omitted (i.e. after the 'cure'), extinction should set in, and we would predict numerous relapses. The authors report that this prediction also is verified. A third prediction is that partial reinforcement, which is known to reduce extinction, would lead to less relapse; this prediction also was verified. An alternative suggestion for reducing relapse by 'overlearning' (Young and Morgan, 1972) also gave positive results. It is difficult to see how practice could follow more directly upon theory and experimental paradigm than

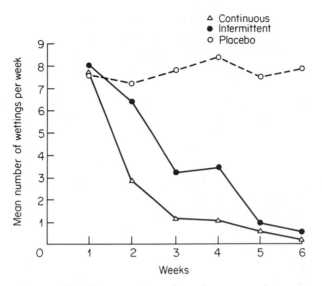

FIGURE 11.3 Mean number of wettings per week across the six-week treatment period for continuous, intermittent and placebo reinforcement groups. (Quoted with permission from Finley and coworkers, 1973.)

this. The extent to which this is typical in behaviour therapy is difficult to establish; to deny that it occurs, without detailed citation of evidence, seems to us ideological warfare, not scientific criticism. London (1972), while ostensibly attacking ideology in the therapeutic field and apparently denying the importance of learning theory in the development of behaviour therapy, never in fact comes down to discrete cases. He prefers the amusingly sarcastic denigration of this hypothesis to any detailed examination of the cases which might be quoted in its favour. This, added to a nineteenth-century-type philosophy of science, may succeed in making a 'case' against behaviour therapy. It does not shake one's conviction that it does, in fact, represent a progressive programme shift.

Critics are, of course, right when they say that many practices of behaviour therapists are lacking in detailed theoretical foundation and that sometimes the results seem to contradict the theories on which they are premised. Such cases do occur, but it is often dangerous to take published criticisms too seriously. Often what has happened is simply that the results are not in line with a particular, restricted reading of the theory and of the experimental evidence; taking into account other sets of facts and other parameters may easily show the criticism itself to have been misguided. One example must suffice in this connection. It relates to backward conditioning and its apparent appearance in connection with aversion therapy.

Franks and Wilson (1974) have argued that explanations of the effects of chemical aversion therapy in terms of conditioning are invalid because 'the unconditioned stimulus in aversion therapy (chemically induced nausea) often precedes rather than follows the conditioned stimulus'. They go on to say that 'although animal research indicates that such "backward conditioning" is relatively ineffective in the establishment of an avoidance response (Kimble, 1961), it appears to be as effective as "forward conditioning" aversive therapy. Thus, a strict classical conditioning paradigm and explanation must be considered both inadequate and misleading (p. 17)'. This, in fact, is not true, but represents a misreading of the literature on backward conditioning.

Ctibor Dostalek (1964) has shown quite conclusively that backward conditioning can indeed occur in laboratory investigations. His book should be consulted for the voluminous details without which a proper understanding of his methodology cannot be obtained. (See also Dostalek and Dostalkova, 1964; Dostalek and Figar, 1956.) Other writers who have obtained evidence in favour of Asratyan's theory concerning the existence of two-way connections between the brain areas corresponding to the UCS and the CS are Asratyan (1967) himself, Struchkov (1964) and Varga and Pressman (1963). Why is it that these experiments seem to contradict the results of well-planned and executed American work?

The answer would seem to lie in the strength of the UCS and the CS employed in these different experiments. Typically, in the U.S.A. the CS is much weaker than the UCS; under these conditions, backward conditioning either does not occur or is much weaker than forward conditioning. This may be due to a masking effect of the stronger stimulus in backward conditioning or it may be due to changes in the temporal sequence and the situational background (as suggested, for instance, by Wyrwicka, 1972). In the experiments demonstrating backward conditioning, however, both the CS and the UCS are strong (as in the work of Asratyan), or both are weak (as in the work of Dostalek.) Under these conditions, no masking (or whatever may cause the disappearance of the phenomenon when the UCS is much stronger than the CS) occurs and backward conditioning is observed.

If this analysis is correct in essence, then we should not be surprised to find that chemical aversion therapy works, even when the stimuli are applied in such a way that backward conditioning may be implied. Both the CS and the UCS are 'strong', in the sense of the word given to it by Asratyan, and these are precisely the conditions which should lead to backward conditioning. Far from counter to laboratory evidence, therefore, the clinical phenomena exemplify with great precision what can be found in the laboratory. What has failed, hitherto, has been a proper knowledge and understanding of the phenomenon of backward conditioning and a tendency to accept, as universally valid, relations in the strength of the stimuli employed which failed to sample all the available contingencies. It is to be hoped that experimentalists will take up this problem and amplify our understanding of these complex phenomena. Until this is done, we need not accept the criticism that clinical phenomena such as those here discussed cannot be understood or explained in terms of learning theory; quite the opposite is true.

In spite of the fact that this particular criticism is erroneous, there is no doubt that aversion therapy in particular has produced many anomalies which are difficult to explain in terms of the known laws of conditioning at the moment. As Rachman and Teasdale (1969) have stated, on purely theoretical grounds 'the surprising thing about aversion therapy is not that its effects are uncertain, but that it works at all (p. 65)'. There is much debate as to the precise model to adopt; some procedures best fit the classical model while others are easier to construe in terms of operant notions of negative reinforcement, or escape and avoidance. There are, of course, special difficulties in the way of proving the efficacy of treatment for 'disorders of the second kind' (Eysenck and Rachman, 1965), i.e. disorders where a deficient conditioned connection has to be elaborated in the clinic and applied in real life. Treatment for 'disorders of the first kind', where existing maladaptive connections have to be extinguished, are much easier to perform and are much less subject to relapse; this follows from theory, and while this is not much of a consolation to clinicians who have to battle with the problems presented by such patients, at least these difficulties are lawful and subject to general theory. Aversion therapy certainly presents us with a number of anomalies, suggesting that in this field our understanding is far from complete; this is freely acknowledged. One example may illustrate the sorts of difficulties which are encountered in aversion therapy.

Russell, Armstrong and Patel (1975) have reported an experiment:

> ... in which 70 heavy smokers (32 cigarettes a day) were assigned at random to one of five treatment and control procedures: (A) Electric aversion therapy, involving ten 20-trial sessions of shocks contiguous with the smoking act. (B) Simulated electric aversion, with non-contiguous shocks. (C) Non-shock smoking sessions, to control for stimulus satiation and negative practice effects. (D) Simple support and attention from therapist. (E) No treatment. Before treatment, simple 'self-monitoring' and 'self-control' reduced cigarette consumption by an average of 12% and 26% respectively. Treatment was highly effective at reducing and stopping smoking during the four-week course and for two weeks afterwards. All four treatments were equally effective, regular attendance for 15 minutes of simple support being as effective as the treatments involving additional 45-minute sessions with a second therapist. The effects of contiguous versus non-contiguous shocks did not differ. (A motor response was conditioned in 19 of the 28 subjects who received shocks but this was therapeutically irrelevant). The clinical outcome depended on the kind of subject rather than the kind of treatment.

Figure 11.4 shows the outcome quite clearly; all treatment groups succeed much better than the control group, but the treatment groups are not differentiated from each other. Clearly an explanation of the success of the treatment in terms of conditioning is quite impossible; non-conditioning treatments and what seem like placebo treatments succeed equally well. Results such as these clearly present a difficulty for conditioning theory for which, at present, there does not seem to be an answer.

But of course, again, this sort of situation is nothing new in science. Consider for a moment the redshift controversy in cosmology (Field, Arp and Bahcall, 1974.) This is one of the most passionately disputed issues in modern physics.

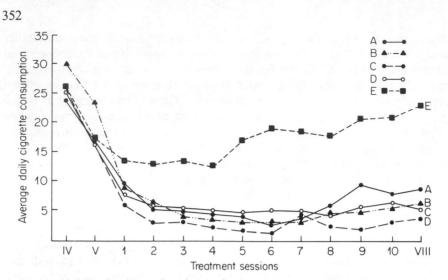

FIGURE 11.4 Session-by-session changes in cigarette consumption during treatment, expressed as average number of cigarettes smoked by subjects in each group over the first 24 hours after each session. (Quoted with permission from Russell, Armstrong and Patel, 1975.)

According to conventional astronomy, the redshifts observed in the spectra of extragalactic objects arise because galaxies are receding from us on account of the expansion of the Universe. In this picture, which forms the keystone of much current cosmological research, the redshift of a galaxy is linearly related to its distance from us. For some years a small but vociferous band of astronomers has struck a discordant note by discovering a selection of objects that seem to have redshifts which are in conflict with their apparent distances. Since our conception of the Universe depends critically on the reliability of redshifts as distance indicators, it is crucially important to weigh the evidence for and against convention in an attempt to resolve the paradox.

Alas, here too the answer simply is not known. Halton Arp has presented a formidable array of objects which he claims are physically associated with objects of different redshift. He cites, for instance, several cases where a high-redshift quasar is within a few minutes of arc of a low-redshift spiral galaxy, and argues that such juxtapositions cannot arise randomly. Bahcall, on the other hand, criticizes much of Arp's evidence on the grounds that *a posteriori* statistical arguments are used to prove that close associations of objects in the sky are physically meaningful. We need not take part in this controversy to see that anomalies of a fundamental kind may arise even in the best-conducted and most advanced areas of hard science. The fact that they also arise in psychology cannot be ground for refusing behaviour therapy and learning theory the title to be called 'scientific'.

Even granted all the arguments put forward so far, is it not true that the practice of behaviour therapy owes much to accidental discoveries, to doubtful deductions from equally doubtful principles and to sheer luck and serendipity?

And does this not rule out the possibility of calling behaviour therapy an 'applied science'? (It is often the case that scientific findings are anticipated by the combination of luck/serendipity/common sense. Thus, Plutarch tells the story of Demosthenes who suffered from a shoulder tick; he cured it by suspending a sharp sword above his shoulder, so that whenever the shoulder was thrown up, it was pierced by the point of the sword. This is a clear anticipation of aversion therapy. Similarly, and on a much larger scale, Maconochie of Norfolk Island (Barry, 1958) introduced a token economy system into the penal colony of which he was in charge, and demonstrated its successful working, one hundred years before Skinner discussed the theoretical foundations of this type of treatment. Such anticipations are nothing new in the hard sciences, nor in medicine, where they are the rule rather than the exception.) Again the answer must, of course, be that while the statement of fact is true, the argument fails because it would rule out of court all applied science, which depends just as much as does psychology on such accidental discoveries, on such doubtful deductions from equally doubtful principles, and on sheer luck and serendipity. Let us consider briefly just one example, namely cryogenic techniques as applied to superconductivity and superfluidity. The discovery that very low temperatures (within a few degrees of absolute zero) could produce a state in some metals which reduced their resistance to the passage of an electric current to vanishing point was itself accidental, and certainly not predictable on any existing theory. The same is true of the behaviour of fluids under these strange conditions, in which they seem to flow counter to gravitational pressure. Some metals show superconductivity, others do not; the reason why is not derivable from any generalized higher theory. For the most part, there is a general empirical rule that superconductivity is only observed for metallic substances for which the number of valence electrons, Z, lies between about 2 and 8, with the highest values of the transition temperature, T_c, occurring for $Z = 3, 5$ and 7.

It is also well known that superconductivity is not able to coexist with magnetism, since the magnetic state destroys the coupling between the electron pairs which leads to superconductivity. For both of these reasons, it was no great surprise that no one had discovered a transition from normal metal behaviour in palladium. The element has an almost full $4d$-band and is very nearly ferromagnetic. It is in many ways a magnetically weaker version of nickel, which of course achieves ferromagnetism and is the element directly above palladium in the periodic table. Indeed, palladium has frequently been described as a ferromagnet with a magnetic ordering temperature of -10 K and can be envisaged as having fluctuations towards magnetism that cannot quite be stabilized. The addition of just a few parts per million of iron pushes it over the brink to become magnetic.

Because it is clearly such an interesting element magnetically, palladium has been widely studied by physicists and chemists, and many other elements have been alloyed to it in order to try to modify its behaviour. It was thus a very great surprise two years ago when T. Skoskiewicz of the Polish Academy of Science, Warsaw, found that the addition of hydrogen to palladium led to superconductivity.

With hydrogen to palladium ratios larger than about 0.8, he found transition temperatures from normal to superconducting behaviour higher than 1 K, but at the highest concentration ratio of about 0.9, produced by an electrolytic process, he observed transitions at nearly 5 K. Forcing more hydrogen into the palladium, or substituting deuterium for hydrogen, raised T_c still further— a rather surprising result, as normally T_c s of superconductors vary inversely with isotopic mass, yet here the effect of deuterating rather than hydrogenating palladium raised the value of T_c from 9 K to 11 K!

Similarly surprising was the discovery that helium-3 possessed superfluid characteristics at extremely low temperatures. The superfluid behaviour of helium-4, the common isotope of this element, was of course well established, but, because of its nuclear structure, physicists believed that helium-3 could not possess similar properties. Here, too, theoretical prediction was confounded, only to lead to a better and deeper understanding of the processes involved.

These examples must suffice to illustrate the point I am making—that the hard sciences do not proceed by an easy hypothetico-deductive path towards facts involved in pure and applied research and that their theories are temporary, constantly in need of patching up and constantly being upset by empirical findings that do not fit into the existing theoretical network. So, of course, are ours; this is not a sign of weakness, but of strength. This is the way science progresses and psychology must follow the same path. To accuse learning theory and behaviour therapy of not being scientific because they act in exactly the same way as do the hard sciences seems paradoxical and slightly absurd. One suspects the motivation. No doubt any stigma is good enough to beat a dogma with, but behaviour therapy is no dogma—it is willing to change as new facts are coming in, and as new truths are uncovered and old half-truths are buried. Just as the superconductivity of palladium or the superfluidity of helium-3 do not fit into the picture of cryogenic theories, forcing a change and reevaluation in these theories, so the failure of aversion therapy in Russell's experiment and other facts noted in Rachman and Teasdale's book force upon us a reevaluation of the theories in that field. This is a long way from saying that behaviour therapy is not responsive to ascertained fact or refuses to derive its methods as far as possible from laboratory-based theories.

Is there, then, no criticism to be made of the scientific status of behaviour therapy? Curiously enough, the criticism I would make of the applied science is exactly the same I have made of the pure science (Eysenck, 1967b). Practitioners of the hard sciences know only too well that different elements behave in different ways in response to identical treatments. The Table of the Elements is the fundament on the basis of which most chemical research proceeds, although of course even much earlier the facts of differential responsiveness were well known. The ancient Greeks already speculated about the nature of these differences, and such men as Anaximander and Anaximenes put forward earth, water, air and fire as the main elements of the physical universe. More fruitful was an approach which appears to have originated with the Chinese. In chemistry we deal with a fundamental duality which is exemplified by metals and non-metals; this is, of course, due to a shortage or excess of electrons. The Chinese had already succeeded in prehistoric times in resolving red cinnabar (which they used as a magic substitute for life blood) into its elements, sulphur and mercury. To these two opposites a third element was added by Philipus Aureolus Theophrastus Bombastus von Hohenheim, who called himself Paracelsus to show his superiority to Celsus, the great doctor of antiquity. By adding the neutral *salt* he established the so-called *tria prima* as a foundation of his 'spagyric' art of chemistry.

Curious as these ancient methods of classification seem to us, yet there is good modern justification for the spagyric system of mercury, sulphur and salt. We have here a reasonable prevision of three of the four subfields into which the general field of chemistry is now subdivided: that of the rare gases, where all electrons remain attached to atoms, that of metals, where there is an excess of electrons, and that of salts, where exchanges have taken place between the metal and the non-metal ions. Even the analogy from external appearance on which the spagyric art was originally based has now found an explanation in terms of quantum theory.

Psychology, on the other hand, has consistently refused to integrate the study of general laws (experimental psychology in the narrow sense) and the investigation of individual differences (personality study) into one generalized field. It has failed to realize that experimental effects are consistently modified, and often reversed, by the properties of the organism mediating the S-R connections. There is frequent lip-service to the S-O-R formula, but little attention is in fact paid to the O element in it. For the followers of Skinner, who believe in what Boring called 'the empty organism', this is a method of choice; for most experimental psychologists, it is simply a bad habit, acquired in the days of 'Sarbondism'. The evidence is by now conclusive that experimental conditions and personality attributes interact to produce the final result, whether in conditioning, perception, verbal learning, physiological response, or what not. The criticism remains of research workers who gorge their error terms by failing to measure supremely relevant personality parameters and to introduce them into the interaction term instead.

This general line has unfortunately been followed by behaviour therapists also. It seems axiomatic to me that extraverts and introverts, high N and low N scorers, or high P and low P scorers, will usually behave differently under otherwise identical treatment conditions, and that any method which fails to take these personality differences into account must to that extent incorporate in its methodology a source of error which could easily be eliminated, and which may be as strong as the main effect in question. Evans and Nelson (1974), while cautiously favourable to this point of view, point out that while theoretically strong it lacks empirical support. They fail to add that this is precisely my complaint. No empirical support can be forthcoming until behaviour therapists take seriously the demonstrations given in the pure field (Eysenck, 1967b) and apply them to the therapeutic field. Actually, Evans is mistaken; there is at least one large-scale study which strongly supports my plea (Di Loreto, 1971) and which appears to have escaped Evans' attention.

This study compared groups of introverts and extraverts suffering from high interpersonal anxiety. They were randomly allocated to treatment methods (Wolpe's desensitization—SD, Ellis' rational-emotional therapy—RT, or Rogers' client-centred therapy—CC), to placebo treatment (NT (P) C) or to a no-contact control (NCC). Two therapists engaged in each of the treatment methods, to eliminate therapist variance. Results were assessed in relation to general anxiety, behaviour ratings and interpersonal anxiety. Predictions were made, based on the general theory of extraversion–introversion. The outcome of the study is shown in Figures 11.5, 11.6 and 11.7, where the decrements in anxiety or anxiety-related behaviour are plotted as a function of treatment, for extraverts and introverts separately. It will be clear that Rogerian therapy works much better for extraverts than for introverts, while Ellis' methods work much better for introverts than for extraverts; these differences are highly significant and in accord with prediction. Wolpe's methods work equally well with both groups. Desensitization for both groups, client-centred

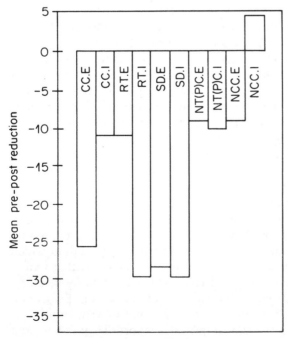

General anxiety

Legend for Figures 11.5, 11.6 and 11.7

E = extraverts
I = introverts
CC = client-centred therapy
RT = rational emotive therapy
SD = systematic desensitization
NT (P) C = no-treatment (placebo) control
NCC = no-contact control

FIGURE 11.5 Reduction in general anxiety as a function of different treatments, and of extraverted or introverted personality. (Quoted with permission from Di Loreto, 1971, Figure 3.7.)

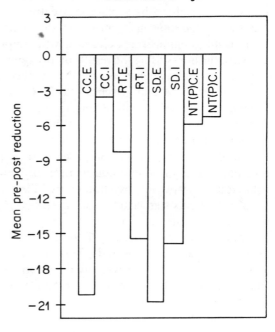

FIGURE 11.6 Reduction in anxiety-induced behaviour as a function of different treatments, and of extra-verted or introverted personality. (Quoted with permission from Di Loreto, 1971, Figure 3.4.)

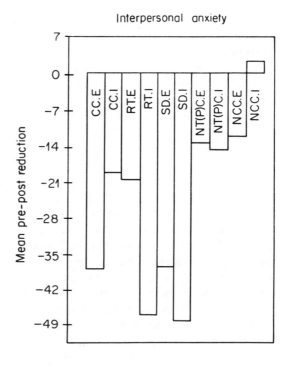

FIGURE 11.7 Reduction in interpersonal anxiety as a function of different treat-ments, and of extraverted or introverted personality. (Quoted with permission from Di Loreto, 1971, Figure 3.7.)

therapy for extraverts and rational-emotional therapy for introverts, work significantly better than placebo treatment or no treatment. No-contact extraverts (spontaneous remission) do better than no-contact introverts. These results demonstrate quite clearly the importance of including personality as a variable in assessing the results of any type of behaviour therapy treatment.

There is less evidence about the 'pathological' personality dimensions, N and P (Eysenck and Eysenck, 1975). Observation suggests that 'flooding' techniques work better with strong anxiety (high N) subjects, while desensitization may work better with low N subjects. This observation, however, needs to be established on a much stronger basis than is available at present, before it can be used for practical purposes. Rather stronger is the evidence that P predicts failure (or at least considerable difficulties) in the application of both behaviour therapy and psychotherapy. Three separate studies (unpublished) have given highly significant results in this connection. The populations studied were cigarette smokers in the Russell study already mentioned, obsessive-compulsive patients treated by 'flooding' and a routine run of neurotic patients at one of the London hospitals. This finding, that high P scorers react poorly to psychotherapy, which was predicted on theoretical grounds, may help in suggesting patients for whom the addition of pharmacological treatment (phenothiazine?) to behaviour therapy might be indicated. Again, there is some (unpublished) evidence to suggest that such addition, unusual as it is in the treatment of neurotic patients, may be of considerable help. While we must agree on the whole with Evans and Nelson that there is not enough evidence about the usefulness of personality constructs in the application of behaviour therapy, we would add that this situation should not be allowed to continue; applied science cannot afford to disregard relevant and important information.

We may now summarize this somewhat discursive discussion. There is always, among practitioners of an applied science, a distrust of laboratory investigations. It is felt that these are remote from the exigencies of practical life, that they disregard the complexities of 'real' situations and that pure science in general only touches lightly upon the concerns of practical people. As an example, consider the encounter between Preece of the Post Office and Sir Oliver Lodge in what *The Times* called 'the battle of the lightning conductors' (Jolly, 1974). This occurred at the meeting of the B.A.A.S. in Bath, in 1888. Preece, the practical man *par excellence*, had argued (in line with orthodox opinion at the time) that lightning strokes consisted of simple direct current flowing in one direction only; Lodge, in his laboratory studies using discharges from Leyden jars, concluded that the lightning flash consisted of an oscillatory current. Much calumny was heaped on Lodge's head for imagining that he could crib, cabine and confine the lightning stroke in his modest laboratory with its minute sparks, but of course he was right and Preece wrong. The battle between the practical man, impatient with the apparent futility of careful little laboratory experiments when the whole of vibrant life is beckoning outside, and the introverted experimentalist, insisting on rigour, accuracy and reliance on strict scientific method, is not confined to psychology—it has many counterparts in the hard sciences.

Application of scientific principles to practical problems always has had to go beyond simple application and has had to rely in part on intuition, guesswork and additional experimental investigation. Faraday discovered the scientific principles essential for the practical use of electricity, but it took fifty years of additional work and the genius of Edison and others to make this application a reality. It is this factor which is so often disregarded by critics who seem to feel that all application should be direct and should not require additional principles to make it work. (To say this is, of course, not to lend support to those who wish to introduce what they call 'broad spectrum therapy'. This type of therapy is simply an arbitrary mixture, an amalgam of verified and unverified, true and false, sound and speculative methods and procedures. It has no rationale, confounds contradictory premises, fails to take seriously the outcome problem and goes back to the old-fashioned and outdated doctrine that 'anything goes' in psychiatry. The application of scientific knowledge to an applied field needs insight, but does not support licence; there are rules to applied science which are no less strict than those which govern pure science. 'Broad spectrum therapy' breaks all these rules and is little more than dynamic psychotherapy garnished with a few snippets of behaviouristic semantics.) Here again they depart from what is known to work in the hard sciences, and set up arbitrary criteria in order to be able to criticize behaviour therapy for failing to reach these impossible and irrelevant idealistic concepts of what science ought to be like, but never is or was.

Behaviour therapy is an applied science, not a dogma; it is those who criticize it for being like all other applied sciences who follow a dogma of idealizing science out of existence altogether. Critics would no doubt be justified in arguing that there are many psychologists and psychiatrists who call themselves behaviour therapists but who know little of the underlying theories and experiments on which these methods are based. This is unfortuantely true, but it does not enable us to argue that the methods themselves have not been derived from general theories at least partially true, by methods at least partially rigorous. Behaviour therapy as a psychological discipline is very young, dating back only to the last years of the 1950s, and learning theory itself is not very old. To expect general, unified theories in these fields when physics and chemistry fail to possess such theories after two thousand years of study seems unreasonable. There are many deficiencies, anomalies and problems in the theories themselves and in their application; this is the fate of all progressive research programmes. It is only when the *programme* fails to predict and unearth new and important facts, when the *protective belt* safeguarding the hard core of principles becomes overburdened by fatty tissue that threatens to stifle new research and when the *heuristic* fails to integrate apparent anomalies and instead has recourse to purely verbal *post hoc* arguments trying to explain away the contradictory finding, that the programme degenerates and becomes of purely historical interest. We have witnessed the sad fate of the Freudian programme. Life for behaviour therapy has only just begun, and to date at least there are no indications that it will follow the same course. In that spirit, we ought to welcome all factual criticism and reject all purely ideological comments on the programme as irrelevant. A Kuhnian revolution has taken place in the field of behaviour modification; the final evaluation of its success must await the verdict of judges not themselves concerned with the struggle to bring about the revolution.

REFERENCES

A. P. A. (1973). *Task Force on Behavior Therapy*. Task Force Report 5: Behavior therapy in psychiatry. American Psychiatric Association, Washington.

Asratyan, E. A. (1967). Some peculiarities of formation, functioning and inhibition of conditioned reflexes with two-way connections. *Progress in Brain Research*, **22**, 8–20.

Barry, J. V. (1958). *Alexander Maconochie of Norfolk Island*, Oxford University Press, London.

Berksan, W. (1974). *Fields of Force*, Routledge and Kegan Paul, London.

Birk, L., Huddestone, W., Miller, E., and Cobler, S. (1971). Avoidance conditioning for homosexuality. *Archives of General Psychiatry*, **25**, 319–323.

Breger, L., and McGaugh, J. (1965). Critique and reformulation of 'learning theory' approaches to psychotherapy and neurosis. *Psychological Bulletin*, **63**, 338–358.

Bridger, W. H., and Mandel, I. J. (1964). A comparison of GSR fear responses produced by threat and electric shock. *Journal of Psychiatric Research*, **2**, 31–40.

Cook, S. W., and Harris, R. E. (1936). The verbal conditioning of the galvanic skin response. *Journal of Experimental Psychology*, **21**, 202–210.

Dawson, M. E., and Grings, W. W. (1968). Comparison of classical conditioning and relational learning. *Journal of Experimental Psychology*, **76**, 227–231.

Di Loreto, A. O. (1971). *Comparative Psychotherapy*, Aldine-Atherton, New York.

Dostalek, C. (1964). *Rücklaüfige Bedingte Verbindungen*, Verlag der Tchechoslowakische Akedemie der Wissenschaften, Prague.

Dostalek, C., and Dostalkova, J. (1964). On the associative character of backward conditioning. *Activitas Nervosa Superior*, **6**, 69–70.

Dostalek, C., and Figar, S. (1956). *Backward Conditioning in Man and Chimpanzee*, Proceedings of the XXth International Congress of Physiological Sciences, Brussels.

Evans, I. M., and Nelson, R. O. (1974). A curriculum for the teaching of behavior assessment. *American Psychologist*, **29**, 598–606.

Eysenck, H. J. (1959). Learning theory and behaviour therapy. *Journal of Mental Science*, **105**, 61–75.

Eysenck, H. J. (1967a). Single-trial conditioning, neurosis and the Napalkov phenomenon. *Behaviour Research and Therapy*, **5**, 63–65.

Eysenck, H. J. (1967b). *The Biological Basis of Personality*, C. C. Thomas, Springfield, Illinois.

Eysenck, H. J. (1968). A theory of the incubation of anxiety/fear responses. *Behaviour Research and Therapy*, **6**, 309–321.

Eysenck, H. J. (1975). Anxiety and the natural history of neurosis. In C. Spielberger and I. Sarason (Eds.), *Stressed Anxiety*, Hemisphere Publishing Co., Washington.

Eysenck, H. J., and Beech, H. R. (1971). Counter conditioning and related methods. In A. E. Bergin and S. L. Garfield (Eds.), *Handbook of Psychotherapy and Behavior Change*, Wiley, London.

Eysenck, H. J., and Rachman, S. (1965). *Causes and Cures of Neurosis*, Routledge and Kegan Paul, London.

Eysenck, H. J., and Wilson, G. D. (1974). *The Experimental Study of Freudian Theories*, Methuen, London.

Eysenck, S. B. G., and Eysenck, H. J. (1975). *Manual of the Eysenck Personality Questionnaire (EPQ)*, University of London Press, London.

Field, B. G., Arp, H. and Bahcall, J. N. (1974). *The Redshift Controversy*, Addison-Wesley, New York.

Finley, W. W., Besserman, R. L., Bennett, L. F., Clapp, R. K., and Finley, P. M. (1973). The effect of continuous, intermittent and 'placebo' reinforcement on the effectiveness of the conditioning treatment for *enuresis nocturna*. *Behaviour Research and Therapy*, **11**, 289–298.

Franks, C., and Wilson, G. T. (1974). *Annual Review of Behaviour Therapy*, Vo. 2. Brunner-Masel, New York.

Fuhrer, M. J., and Baer, P. E. (1969). Cognitive processes in differential GSR conditioning: effects of a masking task. *American Journal of Psychology*, **82**, 168–180.

Gelder, M. G., Marks, I. M., and Wolff, H. H. (1967). Desensitization and psychotherapy in the treatment of phobic states: a controlled enquiry. *British Journal of Psychiatry*, **113**, 53–73.

Gillan, P., and Rachman, S. (1974). An experimental investigation of desensitization in phobic patients. *British Journal of Psychiatry*, **124**, 392–401.

Hallam, R. S. (1971). *The Clinical Significance of Classical Conditioning*. Unpublished Ph.D thesis, University of London.

Hodgson, R., Rachman, S., and Marks, I. M. (1972). The treatment of chronic obsessive-compulsive neurosis: follow-up and further findings. *Behaviour Research and Therapy*, **10**, 181–189.

Holmes, D. S. (1974). Investigations of repressions. *Psychological Bulletin*, **81**, 632–653.

Hoon, P. W., and Lindsley, O. R. (1974). A comparison of behavior and traditional publication activity. *American Psychologist*, **29**, 694–697.

Hoyle, F. (1962). *Astronomy* MacDonald, London.

Hoyle, F., and Narlikar, J. V. (1974). *Action at a Distance in Physics and Cosmology*, Freeman, London.

Hund, F. (1974). *The History of Quantum Theory*, Harrap, London.

Jolly, W. P. (1974). *Sir Oliver Lodge*, Constable, London.

Kimble, G. D. (1961). *Hilgard and Marquis' Conditioning and Learning*, Appleton-Century-Crofts, New York.

Kuhn, T. S. (1970). *The Structure of Scientific Revolutions*, University of Chicago Press, Chicago.

Lakatos, I., and Musgrave, A. (1970). *Criticism and the Growth of Knowledge*, University Press, Cambridge.

Lindley, R. H., and Meyer, K. E. (1961). Effects of instructions on the extinction of a conditioned finger withdrawal response. *Journal of Experimental Psychology*, **61**, 82–88.

Locke, E. A. (1971). Is 'behavior therapy' behavioristic? *Psychological Bulletin*, **76**, 318–327.

London, P. (1972). The end of ideology in behavior modification. *American Psychologist*, **27**, 913–920.

McAllister, W. R., and McAllister, D. E. (1958). Effect of knowledge of conditioning upon eye-lid conditioning. *Journal of Experimental Psychology*, **55**, 579–583.

362

Mace, C. A. (1948–1949). Some implications of analytical behaviourism. *Proceedings of the Aristotelian Society*, **49**, 161–178.

Meichenbaum, D. (1972). *What Clients Say to Themselves*. Research Report No. 42, University of Waterloo, Department of Psychology, Ontario.

Miles, T. R. (1966). *Eliminating the Unconscious*, Pergamon Press, Oxford.

Miller, N. E. (1948). Studies of fear as an acquirable drive. *Journal of Experimental Psychology*, **38**, 89–101.

Mowrer, O. H. (1939). A stimulus-response analysis of anxiety and its role as a reinforcing agent. *Psychological Review*, **46**, 553–566.

Ohman, A. (1971). Interaction between instruction induced expectancy of strength VSS and GSR conditioning. *Journal of Experimental Psychology*, **88**, 389–390.

Osgood, C. E. (1953). *Method and Theory in Experimental Psychology*, Oxford University Press, New York.

Platonov, K. (1959). *The Word as a Physiological and Therapeutic Factor*, Foreign Languages Publishing House, Moscow.

Popper, K. R. (1959). *The Logic of Scientific Discovery*, Hutchinson, London.

Popper, K. R. (1963). *Conjectures and Refutations*, Routledge and Kegan Paul, London.

Prokasy, W. F., and Allen, C. K. (1969). Instructional sets in human eye-lid conditioning. *Journal of Experimental Psychology*, **80**, 271–278.

Rachman, S. (1971). *The Effects of Psychotherapy*, Pergamon Press, London.

Rachman, S., and Eysenck, H. J. (1966). Reply to a 'critique and reformulation' of behavior therapy. *Psychological Bulletin*, **65**, 165–169.

Rachman, S., Hodgson, R., and Marks, I. M. (1971). The treatment of chronic obsessive-compulsive neurosis. *Behaviour Research and Therapy*, **9**, 237–247.

Rachman, S., Marks, I. M., and Hodgson, R. (1973). The treatment of obsessive-compulsive neurotics by modelling and flooding *in vivo*. *Behaviour Research and Therapy*, **11**, 463–471.

Rachman, S., and Teasdale, J. (1969). *Aversion Therapy and Behaviour Disorders: An Analysis*, Routledge and Kegan Paul, London.

Razran, G. (1956). Extinction re-examined and re-analysed: a new theory. *Psychological Review*, **63**, 39–52.

Rohrbaugh, M., and Riccio, D. C. (1970). Paradoxical enhancement of learned fear. *Journal of Abnormal Psychology*, **75**, 210–216.

Russell, M. S. H., Armstrong, E., and Patel, V. S. (1975). The role of temporal contiguity in electric aversion therapy for cigarette smoking: analysis of behaviour changes. *Behaviour Research and Therapy*, to appear.

Silvestri, R., Rohrbaugh, M., and Riccio, D. C. (1970). Conditions influencing the retention of learned fear in young rats. *Developmental Psychology*, **2**, 389–395.

Skinner, B. F. (1964). Behaviorism at fifty. In T. V. Vann (Ed.), *Behaviorism and Phenomenology*, University of Chicago Press, Chicago.

Spence, K. W. (1966). Cognitive drive factors in the extinction of the conditioned eye-blink in human subjects. *Psychological Review*, **73**, 445–458.

Staub, E. (1968). Duration of stimulus-exposure as determinant of the efficacy of flooding procedures in the elimination of fear. *Behaviour Research and Therapy*, **6**, 131–132.

Struchkov, M. I. (1964). On the problems of direct and reverse conditioned connections. *Journal of Higher Nervous Activity*, **4**, 635–643.

Varga, M. E., and Pressman, J. M. (1963). Some forms of relationship between the temporarily connected motor reflexes. In E. Gutman (Ed.), *Central and Peripheral Mechanisms of Motor Functions*, Publishing House of the Czechoslovak Academy of Science, Prague.

Waters, W. F., and McCallum, R. N. (1973). The basis of behavior therapy, mentalistic or behavioristic? A reply to E. A. Locke. *Behaviour Research and Therapy*, **11**, 157–163.

Wilson, G. D. (1968). Reversal of differential GSR conditioning by instructions. *Journal of Experimental Psychology*, **76**, 491–493.

Woods, D. J. (1974). Paradoxical enhancement of learned anxiety responses. *Psychological Review*, **35**, 295–304.

Wyrwicka, W. (1972). *The Mechanisms of Conditioned Behavior*, C. C. Thomas, Springfield, Illinois.

Young, G. C., and Morgan, R. T. T. (1972). Overlearning in the conditioning treatment of *enuresis*. *Behaviour Research and Therapy*, **10**, 147–151.

Zeiner, A., and Grings, V. V. (1968). Backward conditioning: a replication with emphasis on conceptual failures by the subject. *Journal of Experimental Psychology*, **76**, 232–235.

... ...

12

MYTH AND METHODOLOGY IN BEHAVIOUR THERAPY RESEARCH

Raymond Cochrane and Michael P. Sobol

INTRODUCTION

Although we do not wish to overstate the case without having evidence of the views of large numbers of behaviour therapists, it would seem that one of the defining characteristics claimed for the discipline by its practitioners is that it is, relative to other therapies, more 'scientific'. Eysenck (1971) partly answered a critic of the use of behaviour therapy for psychological disorder by saying that the apparent oversimplification and partial nature of the theory 'is the inevitable price to be paid for attempting to approach this field scientifically'. Other claims concerning the scientific basis for behaviour therapy are not hard to find (Ullmann and Krasner, 1965; Wolpe, 1969a, 1969b).

It seems that this claim has two components. The first is that the behaviouristic approach to the modification of abnormal behaviour is consistent with the laws and findings of experimental psychology (particularly the laws of learning). Second, that specific techniques used in behaviour therapy are themselves empirically fortified on the basis of scientific research. This paper is concerned primarily with this latter claim and not at all with any other critique of behaviour therapy—be it empirical, psychological or philosophical. We set out to evaluate the claim made by Paul (1969, p. 61) that 'the stage is set for a new era in behaviour modification research, if it is not already under way—namely the experimental era'. Later in the same paper, Paul concisely defined the questions to be answered by this experimental research: 'What treatment, by whom, is most effective for this individual with that specific problem, under which set of circumstances, and how does it come about? (p. 62)'.

What we have tried to do is to examine a small portion of the experimental research that followed these claims to discover what kinds of questions *were* being asked, how they were being tackled and how closely the research followed some of the accepted criteria for scientific respectability. We did this because we believed it might be an instructive and economical way of, at one and the same time, making some possibly important methodological points and assessing the state of the field in 1973. The intention was not primarily to produce a retrospective critique but to use the analysis of some published work as a vehicle for making some suggestions, which we hope will be helpful, for the consideration of future researchers.

Each of the two authors read independently all of the specified studies and recorded on preestablished rating scales the ways in which a number of issues were handled by experimenters. Our independent ratings were then compared, and disagreements resolved by rereading the studies and forging an agreement on the basis of discussion. We make no pretence that our analysis has any objective validity or even reliability. Certainly, if someone else chooses to repeat the analysis, differences will be found. We do believe, however, that we are able to present a rather accurate overview of some of the important methodological points that concerned behaviour therapy researchers in 1973. It stands repeating that we hope the value of our analysis lies in its potential as a guide for future reference rather than only as a statement of what went on in a particular year of research.

We chose as our sample of papers to study, those appearing in four major behaviour therapy journals in 1973. Although a certain amount of relevant research appeared elsewhere, the four journals we chose must account for a high proportion of all behaviour therapy research reports. The journals were *Behavior Therapy* (BT), Vol. 4; *Behaviour Research and Therapy* (BRAT), Vol. 11; *Journal of Behaviour Therapy and Experimental Psychiatry* (JBTEP), Vol. 4; and *Journal of Applied Behavior Analysis* (JABA), Vol. 6. Only the first three parts of JBTEP, Vol. 4, were available at the time of the review.

We excluded from our analysis case reports, short articles, animal studies, technical- and equipment-oriented articles, bibliographies, book reviews, supervision transcripts and review articles. The only difficult decisions concerned multiple case studies. We excluded studies using fewer than three subjects but included all others. Some articles reported more than one investigation and these were assessed separately. Two articles were combined to form one study since the later paper reported a follow-up of the earlier (Sobell and Sobell, BT, 49; and Sobell and Sobell, BRAT, 599). This meant that there were 118 studies eventually analysed; 24 from BT, 42 from BRAT, 12 from JBTEP and 40 from JABA.

Although a total of fifty-three variables were checked for each study, it is only possible to report our findings for a few of these because of space limitation. We have grouped the results under several headings, each of which involves a number of specific points. Whenever possible, we have illustrated our findings with examples of specific studies. These were chosen not because they were particularly good or bad studies but because we hope they might make our argument clearer. We hope that the authors of the studies we have criticized will accept our comments in the spirit in which they were intended, even if they disagree with the substance of our remarks. To avoid redundancy, only a brief reference is given when papers included in the sample of studies analysed are mentioned, consisting of the journal initials and page number; these papers all appeared in 1973 in the volume numbers listed above. References to other work not included in our analysis are given in a more conventional fashion.

THE OPERATIONAL DEFINITION OF BEHAVIOUR THERAPY RESEARCH

Our first task was to define exactly of what behaviour therapy research consists. We devised broad categories into which we could slot each research report in terms of the problem area tackled and the type of therapy employed or investigated. This, in fact, turned out to be rather more difficult than it at first appeared. Several of the problem area categories ended up by containing quite a mixture of conditions. The social behaviours category included such diverse problems as marital dissatisfaction, lack of assertiveness and ward behaviour in chronic schizophrenics. Similarly, the problem-solving category included a range of educational and cognitive activities. The final category which we labelled 'non-clinical behaviour change' included all those studies which had clinical implications but which were not in any sense clinical or analogue clinical studies. This included such things as relaxation in normal subjects, conditioning of verbal operants, conditioning of heart rate in normals and social interaction in normal children.

The classification of therapeutic techniques was a little easier but a 'package' category was found necessary to accommodate studies which combined or compared aspects of several other types of treatment. The 'covert processes' category included self-reinforcement, self-instruction and self-monitoring as treatment techniques.

Table 12.1 shows a breakdown of the 118 studies by therapeutic technique and problem area. Several things emerge quite clearly. The major division in terms of therapeutic technique is between operant procedures aimed at bringing behaviour under stimulus control and all the behaviour therapy techniques which share more in common with each other than with the operant procedures. This distinction applied equally to the methodological and the theoretical aspects of the two disciplines. Operant methodology differs substantially from traditional research methods in psychology in several ways: it tends to employ relatively few subjects (down to $N = 1$); subjects act as their own control; and statistical tests of hypotheses are eschewed. It certainly appears that editors apply different methodological criteria to operant studies that to others. Which type of methodology involves a more rigorous test of hypotheses is not for us to decide, but we asked the same questions of all studies.

Turning to the analysis of problem areas researched in 1973, it is apparent that two types of problem occupied a majority of behaviour therapy researchers: analogue phobias and social-interactive behaviours. The popularity of these two areas is probably accounted for by the ease of obtaining subjects who

TABLE 12.1 Studies by problem area and therapeutic technique.

Problem area	Desensiti-zation	Modelling	Flooding	Covert processes	Operant	Aversion	Relaxation	Feedback	Package	Total
Clinical phobias	1	0	1	0	1	0	0	0	2	5
Analogue phobias	8	1	2	1	0	0	2	6	5	25
Problem-solving	0	3	0	0	14	0	0	0	0	17
Social behaviours	0	5	0	0	31	0	0	1	2	39
Alcohol/drugs/weight	0	0	0	1	2	1	0	0	3	7
Sex problems	1	0	0	0	1	1	0	0	1	4
Enuresis/Encopresis	0	0	0	0	4	0	0	0	2	6
Stuttering and tics	1	0	0	0	5	0	0	1	1	8
Non-clinical behaviour change	0	0	0	1	4	0	2	0	0	7
Total	11	9	3	3	62	2	4	8	16	118

display such behaviours. In the former case, college students can be persuaded to act as subjects in order to obtain course credit. In the latter category, school children and mental hospital inpatients represent truly captive subject pools.

The frequency with which analogue phobias were investigated is somewhat disturbing for a number of reasons. First, the foci of analogue phobias (spiders (3), snakes (10), rats (3), tests (2), mathematics, electric shock, the dark, etc.) do not seem to appear with any conspicuous frequency among real clinical phobias (Marks, 1969). Second, the nature of the fear in analogue phobias is essentially different from that encountered by clinical phobic patients. In the case of the former, mild or moderate anxiety is experienced in the close proximity of the feared object or situation whereas, in the latter, overwhelming and incapacitating anxiety may almost continuously be felt even in the absence of the phobic object or situation. The objective reasons for anxiety are also very different. Who is to say whether a feeling of anxiety when asked to handle snakes is rational or irrational? In contrast, fear of going out alone in case lethal objects fall from high places is by most objective criteria irrational. The degree to which studies of analogue phobias shed any light on the treatment of the clinical entity is a matter of some dispute (Bernstein and Paul, 1971; Cooper, Furst and Bridger, 1969; Levis, 1970). Whatever the outcome of this controversy, the impression was strongly gained that some researchers were quite desperately seeking a problem to which they could apply their undoubted skill and powerful techniques with some success.

Just as noticeable were the categories of psychological disturbance that were absent from the list of problems to which behaviour therapy research was applied. A few components of schizophrenic behaviour were included in the social behaviour category, but the major symptoms were not encountered and neither were any of the defining aspects of depression. There is a distinct bias in behaviour therapy research toward what might be considered the relatively minor aspects of psychological disturbance such as children talking in class or wetting their beds, students being afraid of exams or lacking assertiveness, delinquents not tidying the bathroom of their hostel, and so on. These problems are undoubtedly important and deserve attention in their own right, but it does appear somewhat unfortunate if more serious problems are not also to be tackled. This does not imply that there were no studies involving serious and incapacitating problems. Several of the reports published in 1973 were quite amazing in their ambitious and ingenious approaches to problems that have otherwise proved intractible. The studies which come to mind are those of Hunt and Azrin (BRAT, 91) on a community reinforcement approach to alcoholism, and Dalton, Rubino and Hislop (JABA, 251) on the use of token reinforcers and academic progress in children with Down's syndrome.

An examination of the kinds of subject typically used in behaviour therapy research is also quite revealing. The issues raised are, of course, not independent of those mentioned in the context of problem areas. Approximately 45 per cent. of all studies in 1973 were conductd on non-clinical populations—largely college students and school children. For our purposes, the clinical population

TABLE 12.2 Type of reference cited in 118 studies.

Reference	Total	Mean	Mode
Behaviour therapy	1227	10.4	9.0
Other clinical	295	2.5	0.0
Statistics	47	0.4	0.0
General experimental psychology	47	0.4	0.0
Learning	83	0.7	0.0
Social psychology	71	0.8	0.0
Developmental psychology	38	0.3	0.0
Non-psychology	59	0.5	0.0

was defined as those people who were hospitalized or had sought help either on their own initiative or in response to a press advertisement. Although many of the non-clinical subjects were involved in the studies of analogue phobias, some were also used in studies of problem-solving and social behaviour. Approximately 30 per cent. of all studies involved children (clinical and non-clinical) under the age of 12 years. Discussion of the value of non-clinical studies in behaviour therapy was conspicuous by its absence. Either the problems involved here have been resolved to the satisfaction of most investigators or, as seems possible, two separate disciplines are emerging: pure and applied research concerning behaviour therapy techniques. In terms of journal coverage, BRAT and BT are most likely to include the studies of college students while most of the studies in JBTEP were clinical. JABA gave quite equal representation to all types of study.

We then looked at the reference sections of the papers studied. If behaviour therapy is the application of the findings of experimental psychology to clinical problems (Davison, Goldfried and Krasner, 1970), then we might expect considerable reference to be made to this kind of work. As Table 12.2 shows this was not the case. Most references were to other works on behaviour therapy, with many papers making no reference to other areas of psychology at all. On average, each paper made 10.4 references to the behaviour therapy literature, 2.5 to other clinical work and 2.0 to all the rest of psychology. Thus, there is some indirect evidence for the growing belief that behaviour therapy research is becoming a self-contained discipline somewhat apart from the other areas of psychology whose laws it is ostensibly applying.

Having concluded the brief description of what constituted behaviour therapy research in 1973, the remainder of this chapter is devoted to a discussion of some selected methodological issues that arose from our analysis of the content of the 118 studies examined.

SUBJECT VARIABLES

If a research report is to be of any use to other researchers or to practitioners, they need to know certain things about the nature of the investigation as it was

TABLE 12.3 Information on subject variables.

Variable	Information		
	Given	Not given	Not appli-cable
Clinical versus non-clinical sources	117	1	44
Previous Therapy	24	50	44
Drugs	11	59	48
Social class	23	95	
Age	104	14	
Sex	93	25	

carried out. In this section we will consider what information is required concerning the subjects employed, while in the subsequent section we will look at experimenter variables. In the previous section, the types of sample studied in 1973 were discussed. Here we will merely note that practically all studies gave this information (Table 12.3). The only exception was the study of Riddick and Meyer (BT, 331) on response contingent feedback in relaxation. They merely stated: 'Eighteen subjects participated; twelve were female, six were male. Subjects ranged in age from 17 to 69 with a mean age of 30.4'. There is no indication of where or how the subjects were obtained.

Where clinical or quasi-clinical groups were used, we examined reports to find out whether information was given concerning any previous therapy the subjects might have received and whether they were currently being prescribed psychoactive drugs. Both of these variables are potentially important as they may very well interact with the experimental condition. For example, patients with some experience of token economies may react to an experimental operant procedure in a certain way whereas subjects with no therapeutic history or experience of a different kind may react in a different way. Kazdin (1973c), in an excellent methodological critique of reinforcement programmes in applied settings, makes the point that results from such studies can only be generalized to other subjects exposed to the same sequence of events within the experimental programme. By extension, it is equally improper to generalize to other patients not exposed to similar preexperimental conditions. It is therefore of great importance to be able to discover what previous therapeutic history, if any, a group of subjects has experienced. Table 12.3 shows that only 24 of 74 studies gave this information. In the other 44 studies, this question was not applicable because the subjects were students or volunteers.

Turning to the subject of drugs, the table shows that only 11 of 70 studies that should have given this information did so. In a sense this omission is even more difficult to understand because there is good empirical evidence available that drugs do systematically affect the outcome of some procedures similar to those used in therapy (Kelleher and Morse, 1968).

Where hospitalized patients are used as subjects, there is every likelihood that drugs will be involved and it may be considered incumbent on authors to report the status of their subjects in this respect. Of the 11 reports that did make mention of drugs, 7 indicated that their subjects were on medication and 4 reported that they were not. Watson, Mullett and Pillay (BRAT, 531), in their exemplary description of subject variables, include the sentence, 'Seven patients who were taking monoamineoxidase or tricyclic antidepressant drugs before treatment, and had been doing so at a constant dosage for at least three months, continued on the same medication throughout the study (p. 534)'. The authors also make some comments concerning the possible interaction between treatment outcome (prolonged exposure in agoraphobia) and drugs. Unfortunately, they do not report systematic comparisons of the responses of those patients receiving drugs and those who are not receiving drugs.

The other questions about the nature of the subjects employed concerned demographic variables. Most (108) studies stated where the subjects were obtained and most reported, or gave clues about, the age of their subjects. The breakdown by age of all subjects employed during 1973 in these studies is quite interesting. Almost 70 per cent. of all subjects were aged 20 years or less, another 8 per cent. between 20 and 30 years and under a quarter of all subjects were over 30 years of age. It certainly appears from this year's output that behaviour therapy *research* is concerned overwhelming with young people. This may have more to do with the availability and amenability of school children and students than the distribution of psychological disorders in the population.

A similar breakdown was made of the sex distribution of subjects. First, it was noted that 25 studies did not report on this variable at all. Among those that did report there was a fairly equal number of males and females used. However, they were used for different kinds of study. Analogue phobias were studied almost exclusively in women—mainly, in fact, college women afraid of spiders and rats. Studies of problems with alcohol, sex and bed wetting almost always used male subjects. Again there is no way of knowing if this reflects the sex distribution of types of psychological problems in the real world. A similar, and perhaps related, discrepancy occurred in the type of treatment used on the two sexes. *All* the flooding and relaxation experiments and most of the desensitization studies used predominantly female subjects, whereas most operant studies involved males or did not mention sex as a subject variable. Few, if any, authors commented on the reasons for using subjects of a particular sex or discussed whether generalization was possible between sexes. If the studies chosen in 1973 are anything like representative, then desensitization, flooding and relaxation as therapies have only been investigated in females and their effectiveness for males is a matter of conjecture.

Finally, we looked for information about the social class of the subjects. We were disappointed in 95 cases, although as some of these studies used college students as subjects, it might not have been unreasonable to assume a middle class background. If it is taken for granted that the therapist is himself middle class, then he will be dealing with two distinct types of patient: those like himself (middle class) in terms of education, background, expectation and language; and those not like himself on these variables (working class). It is obviously quite reasonable to anticipate different kinds of interaction in these two types of situation. Lorion (1974) made this very point in his examination of potential difficulties encountered by therapists in treating low-income patients. It appears quite possible that the expectations about participation and outcome will vary markedly with social class. Consider, for example, the contention of Hess (1970) that the frequent frustrating experiences of lower class individuals resulting from a lack of financial, social and educational resources leads to a chronic state of feelings of helplessness and, consequently, it may be assumed, to the expectation that if their problems are to be solved then someone else must solve them. This may well be in contrast with a middle class view of personal problems as something to be worked on jointly with the therapist. This is an area that warrants considerable investigation, but until this has been completed it seems reasonable to expect authors at least to report the social class of subjects even if this is not considered as a variable in every study.

The social class variable may be much more significant in some situations than others. Take, for example, the study of Goldstein and coworkers (BRAT, 31). These investigators looked at the effectiveness of modelling and social reinforcement in increasing 'independent behaviour'. Surely any psychologist would recognize the *possibility* of social class differences in both the propensity for independent behaviour and the effectiveness of observing a model and social reinforcement. These authors fail to report the social class of either the patients or the model. It may very well have been that the patients were drawn from all social classes, but there is no mention of this and no analysis is presented which takes this into account. This is an example of a study in which social class is very likely to have been a significant variable. In some other types of study (e.g. conditioning of heart rate) it may be considered somewhat less important on *a priori* grounds.

THERAPIST VARIABLES

Table 12.4 gives the results of our examination of the reporting of therapist/experimenter variables. Here we are assuming that it is valid to equate the

TABLE 12.4 Information on therapist variables.

Variable	Given	Information Not given	Not applicable
Number of therapists	55	63	
Experience	21	97	
Age	8	110	
Sex	43	75	
Interaction with subject variables	12	69	37

experimenter in what is clearly an experiment with the therapist in what is clearly therapy. The interaction between experimenters and subjects shares many of the characteristics of the interaction between therapist and patient. Therefore, when we refer to 'therapist' we also include experimenters. We always considered the person actually conducting the programme as the therapist; helpers such as models, observers, parents, ward personnel and assistants are not being considered in this section.

There is considerable evidence that therapists vary in their effectiveness and that this variation is correlated with certain therapist characteristics (see Traux 1973, Traux and Mitchell, 1971). From a behavioural viewpoint the therapist's 'style' serves two purposes: a discriminative cue function in that the therapist provides exceptations, instructions, demand characteristics and role models for appropriate therapeutic target behaviours (Kanfer and Phillips, 1970); and as a source of both explicit (direct, verbal feedback) and implicit (tone, gesture, posture) contingency management for approximations to the target behaviours (Krasner, 1962). While almost all the behavioural research on the effects of the therapist have been by analogy from the verbal conditioning situation to actual clinical practice, it is still quite likely that these variables do play an important role in the behaviour change of clinical populations.

If we accept that therapist variables can affect outcome, then the possibility of confounding treatment and therapist variables exists. If one therapist only is used, there is no way of disentangling possible interactions. We counted the number of therapists used in each study with the results shown in Table 12.4. Over one-half of the 118 studies did not specifically state the number of therapists involved. In single author studies, it might have been assumed that the author was the only therapist, but as there was no way of checking this we did not make this assumption. It seems to be totally inexcusable to fail to report who conducted the therapy or experimentation. We may take as an example the study of Rutner (BT, 338). Rat-'phobic' female undergraduates were given either feedback or therapeutically oriented instructions, or both. In all cases there was considerable interaction between therapist and subject, and yet we are not informed of the number of therapists involved (or of any other therapist characteristics).

There were 32 studies which reported the use of just one therapist, 12 used two, and 11 used three or more. We can compare the value of two studies, one of which employed only one therapist and the other employing two. Dietz and Rep (JABA, 457) conducted an experiment to determine the effectiveness of differential reinforcement of low rates of responding (DRL) schedules on classroom misbehaviour in the trainable mentally retarded. Quite clearly the introduction of contingencies was associated with a large decrease in the targeted behaviour, but this was demonstrated in one classroom with one teacher only.

Turn now to the study of Blanchard and Johnson (BT, 219) which also involved the use of operant procedures in the classroom but on this occasion for behaviour problem students. These experimenters employed two teachers as therapists and found a considerable difference in their effectiveness. This was because one of the two teachers was more successful than the other in controlling class behaviour before the experiment started. It follows that there was greater scope for the operant control procedures to be effective where the teacher had previously been relatively ineffective. It is not always possible therefore in studies, such as that of Dietz and Repp, which use only one therapist to be sure that the experimental procedure rather than the particular therapist is responsible for even a clear-cut experimental effect. What is required is a demonstation that several different therapists can employ a procedure with equal effectiveness before any power can be ascribed to the technique itself.

One very important therapist variable is experience. It might be presumed that a more experienced therapist would be more effective than a less experienced therapist. That this is not so under all conditions has also been shown (Poser, 1966), but only serves to emphasize the point that the specification of therapist experience is very important. Only 21 studies actually did so and of these 13 reported that experienced therapists were used and 8 that inexperienced therapists were used. We arbitarily defined 'experienced' as having at least one year's experience in using the kinds of technique being employed in the study.

Only one study compared therapists with different amounts of experience. Baker, Cohen and Saunders (BRAT, 79) randomly assigned acrophobic patients to one of three therapists for a desensitization-based treatment. One therapist was a Ph.D. clinical psychologist with several years' experience of behaviour therapy; one an advanced graduate student in clinical psychology; and the third an inexperienced graduate student. Although a total of only seven subjects were used, the authors state that 'treatment outcome did not correlate with therapists' prior desensitization experience (p. 85)'. Again, even if it is unreasonable to expect therapist experience to be manipulated as a variable in every study, it is quite feasible for this to be specified in every report.

We also checked for details of therapist age and sex. Only 8 studies reported age and 43 sex. In terms of given age, all 8 reports were of therapists aged less than 30. Twenty-one studies used only male therapists, 11 only female and 11 used both male and female. The potential importance for the outcome of an experiment of these variables is hard to overestimate. Consider the hypothetical case of a middle aged male patient and a young female graduate student as therapist. The social psychology of that situation would be very different from that which would obtain were the positions reversed.

An example of the need for this information in order to evaluate the procedure in question is provided by Eisler, Hersen and Agras (BT, 551) in their study of feedback and instructions on marital interaction. The subjects were middle aged couples but no information is given concerning therapist variables. The responsiveness of middle aged couples to experimental procedures *may* be in part, determined by the age and sex of the experimenter. On the other hand, it may not. The point is that we do not know. Similarly, Barlow and Agras (JABA, 355) report a study involving the treatment of male homosexuals. Again, it is not hard to imagine that the sex, age (and attractiveness) of the experimenters may interact with the experimental variables, especially as procedures for the recording of penile circumference in erection and the content of sexual fantasies were employed. Yet no mention is made of these therapist variables.

The extent to which details of therapist variables were specified in research in behaviour therapy in 1973 was very disappointing. The addition of one or two simple sentences such as, 'subjects were randomly assigned to one of four female undergraduate experimenters' (Felixbrod and O'Leary, JABA, 241), although in no way solving the problem of therapist variables interacting with treatment variables, make reports so much more valuable for other investigators because they specify the detail of the particular experiment.

CONTROL GROUPS AND EXPERIMENTAL DESIGN

Campbell and Stanley (1963) produced what is often considered to be a definitive exposition of the strengths and weaknesses of various types of control group design for psychological research. We tentatively tried to apply some of their suggestions to the 1973 studies. In behaviour therapy research, there are at least two kinds of questions that may be asked: some studies ask if a particular procedure has any effect at all on a given condition; others ask about the relative effectiveness of some form of behaviour therapy as opposed to other kinds of treatment. With this latter kind of question the researcher is aiming at exploration as well as control, in that he wants ultimately to be able to say what aspects of the technique had the desired effect. To this end he needs to introduce certain controls (e.g. for attention or placebo effect) which are unnecessary for the researcher who is concerned only to know whether his technique works, rather than with how it works or whether it works better than anything else. It all depends on the kind of statement the researcher wishes to be able to make in the end. If he wishes to say that X made people better who, without any treatment, would not otherwise have improved, then a simple no-treatment or waiting list control may be sufficient. If, on the other hand, he wishes to be able to say that X made people better because it embodied principles Y and Z and is therefore better than other treatments which did not, a more elaborate control group design is called for. We cite below examples of what are considered to be adequate and inadequate control group designs and the reasons for our decisions.

Romanczyk and coworkers (BRAT, 629) attempted to analyse the components of a behavioural treatment package for obesity. What they did was to take apart a typical multifacet programme in order to assess the component parts. Such a design provided a thorough analysis and therefore allowed them to be confident that their results meant what they appeared to mean. An outline of the treatment groups appears below:

(1) No-treatment control (waiting list).

(2) Self-monitoring control (weight only).

(3) Self-monitoring control (weight and calorie intake).

(4) Self-monitoring and symbolic aversion.

(5) Self-monitoring, symbolic aversion and relaxation.

(6) Self-monitoring, symbolic aversion, relaxation and behavioural management (stimulus control) instructions.

(7) Self-monitoring, symbolic aversion, relaxation, behavioural management and contingency contracting.

Briefly, the results showed that self-monitoring of daily caloric intake was about as effective as any of the more complex packages in producing weight loss in the short term. If this study had merely involved group 7 (behavioural package) and group 1 (no-treatment control), then it would have demonstrated the efficacy of the behavioural package. What it would not have shown is that the package works no better than the simple calorie monitoring component does. Unfortunately, such designs are expensive and employ vast numbers of subjects. However, the information gleaned from such an approach far outweights the cost.

This design could have been extended still further to determine whether any of the other components in isolation from self-monitoring might also have worked by using still other groups receiving either only a single component or permutations of all the individual components. Such a design would have also coped with any interaction effects among the various treatment components which, in the event, did not actually arise. This would require virtually unlimited supplies of subjects and experimenters, and in the absence of these Romanczyk and coworkers achieved their aim of dissecting a behavioural treatment package.

An example of a study that was considered to employ an inadequate control group design is that of Azrin, Naster and Jones (BRAT, 365). This study was designed to investigate the effectiveness of marital counselling based on reciprocated reinforcements between husband and wife. The design employed consisted of each couple receiving three weeks of a control procedure ('catharsis counselling') followed by four weeks of the experimental procedure. Measurements of marital happiness taken at many points during the seven weeks of the investigation showed that there had been no improvement during weeks 1 to 3 but great improvement during week 4, and a continuing but considerably slowed improvement for the remainder of the study period and at follow-up. The authors conclude that 'The Reciprocity Counseling procedure was effective in increasing marital happiness .... The evidence showed that the improvement during Reciprocity Counseling was caused by the specific nature of the procedure since a catharsis-type counseling of roughly similar duration did not increase happiness (p. 380)'.

The study design employed does not allow such a conclusion to be drawn (although it may very well be entirely correct) for three reasons. First, the 'catharsis counseling' of the control period was presumably conducted by the same therapists who later carried out the 'Reciprocity Counseling'. Although the report is not clear on this point (neither does it specify the age or sex of the counsellors), it seems fairly typical that control procedures are carried out by the investigator who also puts the experimental procedure into practice. It is also fair to assume that the experimenter/therapists believed in or suspected the efficacy of the 'reciprocity counseling' but did not have any faith in 'catharsis counseling'. It is quite conceivable, therefore, that they were less expert and less enthusiastic in carrying out the control period therapy than the experimental therapy. A reasonable control to use in this situation is to employ therapists to conduct the control procedure who are as dedicated to it as the researchers are to the experimental technique. Alternatively, as Paul (1966) has suggested, the behaviour modification techniques might be entrusted to an experienced psychotherapist and their relative successes compared. A third but perhaps not very practical way around the problem is for the experimenter to employ therapists who are ignorant of the hypotheses and the experimental status of the patients they are treating. Even with this device the personal hypotheses of the naïve therapists may have a contaminating effect. For a control procedure of the type used in this study to be worth employing, it should not be confounded with the expertise, experience and expectancy of the therapist.

The second design weakness in this study results from the fact that for *all* subjects the experimental therapy followed the control therapy. It is therefore impossible to rule out the possibility of a spontaneous improvement in marital happiness, a delayed effect of 'catharsis counseling', or an interaction effect, namely that 'Reciprocity Counseling' is only effective following the talking-out of problems. There are two alternative ways of handling this problem. The typical design used in studies of operant procedures looks at changes between baseline and the intervention period and then again at changes that occur when the experimental procedure is terminated (ABA design). This particular study employed only the first half of this design. The subjects were not told to stop reciprocal reinforcement during the post-experimental follow-up period. The ABA design may not be sensible if the experimenter does not subscribe to an operant orientation and hypothesizes permanent changes in his subjects' behaviour. It may also have to be ruled out on ethical grounds. The alternative which could easily have been employed in the study by Azrin and colleagues is to use a separate, matched control group. This group receives the control therapy and nothing else, while the other group receives the experimental therapy and nothing else. A differences in the behaviour of the two groups could not then be attributed to a natural improvement or an interaction effect.

The third and related difficulty with the design employed in this study concerns the timing of the comparisons between experimental and control period. The greatest increase in marital happiness occurred between the end of the last week of the control period and the first week of the experimental period (see Figure 12.1). Is it not just possible that any intervention in the existing situation produces a large improvement? There might have been an

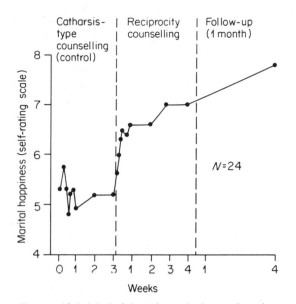

FIGURE 12.1 Marital happiness during reciprocity counselling and a control counselling procedure. Each data point is a weekly average except for the first seven days of the control counselling and the reciprocity counselling, and the one month follow-up, which are daily averages. 'Marital Happiness' was reported by each of the twenty-four clients (twelve couples) on a 1–10 rating scale of marital happiness. (From Azrin, Naster and Jones, *Behaviour Research and Therapy*, **11**, 377, Figure 2.)

equally significant improvement following the onset of 'catharsis-type counseling', but data are not provided for marital satisfaction in the pre-control period. To be sure, marital happiness is stabilized at a higher level in the second period, but we do not know the relative increases following the introduction of the two types of therapy. It may even be that the 'catharsis counseling' had a great impact following the very first session, whereas the effect of 'Reciprocity Counseling' was more delayed. The inclusion of pre-intervention data or the use of a crossover design would have confirmed or ruled out this hypothesis.

Overall we found that 33 studies (28 per cent.) used control group designs that were judged to be invalid for the purposes for which they were intended. Here, more than anywhere else, however, we are conscious of the subjective nature of our decisions.

The situation is even more complex when we consider more typical operant studies that traditionally use a within-subjects design. Here the intention is to demonstrate stimulus control over behaviour, in the simplest case, by observing the subjects in a baseline phase, introducing contingencies, and then removing contingencies and so returning to baseline. This is often described as an ABA type of design. The thorny problem of matching is avoided by using each subject as his own control. In fact, most designs encountered were far more complicated than the ABA type, often involving several different sets of contingencies and more than one return to baseline. For example, the design employed by Harris and Sherman (JABA, 405) might be described as an ABCDADADE involving four different experimental conditions (B, C, D, E) and two returns to baseline. Pomerleau, Bobrove and Smith (JABA, 383) used an ABCADEFEGHA design! The return to baseline is an essential feature of these designs because it provides the ultimate demonstration that the behaviour in question is under the control of the contingencies employed.

Although this reversal is required methodologically and theoretically, it does raise problems in practice in that it implies that operant procedures can only ever be short-term prosthetic measures. This dilemma was expressed by Hauserman, Walen and Behling (JABA, 193) at the end of their study on the reinforcement of racial integration in young children. Having successfully shown that the behaviour in question could be brought under stimulus control, they state: 'The recovery of baseline performance in the last phase of the experiment was anticipated, yet the rapidity with which it was achieved was disappointing (p. 199)'. For operant procedures to have any lasting therapeutic benefit, it is necessary to make the desired, newly learned behaviour resistant to extinction or to bring it under the control of naurally occurring contingencies. In theory, this can be achieved by gradually fading the structured reinforcement programme, while at the same time programming an increase in the salience and consistency of positive contingencies found within the natural environment. Actually, no study systematically employed such generalization procedures in 1973. Lieberman and coworkers (JABA, 57) did halve the number of reinforcements they had previously given their schizophrenic subjects for rational speech and showed that previous levels could be maintained, but they went no further. At Achievement Place, a hostel for predelinquent boys, Phillips, Wolf and Fixsen (JABA, 541) did attempt to shift the responsibility for delivering contingencies from the therapists to the peer group, but the situation and the contingencies remained very structured and could hardly be termed the natural environment.

There is an alternative design to the reversal procedure in operant studies which can have almost equal power in demonstrating the control of behaviour by contingencies. The multiple baseline design involves the collection of data on two or more bahaviours, situations or groups of subjects (Baer, Wolf and Risley, 1968). It can be achieved in a number of ways. Baseline data may be gathered for two or more groups of subjects and then contingencies introduced for one group only. At this stage it is hoped that the target behaviour will change in the contingency group but not in the others. If this is the case, then the experimental procedure can be extended to the other groups. Such a design was used by Cossairt, Hall and Hopkins (JABA, 89) in their study of teacher praise and students' attending behaviour. After ten baseline sessions for both teachers A and B in separate classes, teacher A was given instructions (to praise attention) which had a dramatic impact on students' attention. Meanwhile, teacher B remained in the baseline condition for a further ten sessions, thus providing a comparison across groups. She later was also given instructions to praise attention, by which time teacher A was moving on to a second experimental condition.

In order to demonstrate stimulus control when using a multiple baseline design, it is necessary that the behaviours displayed in the extended baseline period remain stable, i.e. they do not approach the level of frequency found in the experimental condition. However, for this to be achieved, it is necessary to consider the ecology of the experimental situation. In a study designed to examine the effects of reinforcement of one subject upon the concomitant behaviour of a second observing subject, Kazdin (1973b) found that the observer's behaviour began to approach the model's behaviour even though the observer was not receiving direct reinforcement but remained in the baseline condition. Such potential vicarious effects provide a cautionary note in the use of multiple baseline designs across subjects. An example of this potential confounding may be found in the study by Lieberman and coworkers (JABA, 57). They were interested in the effect of attention upon schizophrenic verbalizations. It was noticed that even though the control subjects remained in the extended baseline condition there was an increase in the target behaviour over successive extensions of the baseline (the slope of the baseline from first to last day being approximately -1.12, $+0.67$, $+1.67$ and $+1.07$, for each successive extension respectively). However, Lieberman and coworkers mistakenly state that irrational talk was strictly under *direct* contingency control. Given the clear vicarious effects, this datum points out the care which must be taken in using between-subject, multiple baseline procedures.

The same general design can also be used across two or more behaviours within the same individuals. Pinkston and coworkers (JABA, 115) used the multiple baseline procedure to assess the effectiveness of teacher-dispensed contingencies on children's behaviour. Two distinct behaviours were involved: aggression and peer interaction. After simultaneously recording baseline data for the frequency of occurrence of both behaviours, contingencies were applied to one of the behaviours (aggression) but not the other. The change that occurred in aggressive behaviour was not matched by a change in peer interaction. Twenty days later peer interaction was brought under contingency control. The subsequent change in this behaviour clearly showed that it was the contingencies rather than anything else which controlled the behaviours. As Kazdin (1973c) states, these designs make possible 'a powerful demonstration that the experimental condition exerts control over the behaviour. The strength of the demonstration stems from the consideration that events occurring in time other than the experimental condition cannot plausibly account for the specific changes in behavior (p. 519)'.

Two further difficulties in the design of operant studies remain to be discussed. In an evaluation of studies which employ a variant of the ABA design, one factor which must receive attention is the length of the initial baseline period and the stability of the target behaviour during this phase of the experiment

382

(Sidman, 1960, p. 153). As the operant approach, more than any other, stresses the responsiveness of the individual to changes in the environment, any large variation in target behaviour that occurs before or after the intervention period indicates spontaneous or at least unplanned changes in the environment. A relatively long baseline period is required for two reasons: First, to demonstrate that the target behaviour is relatively stable in the unmodified environment and that such fluctuations that do occur are considerably smaller and less consistent than any produced by the experimental operant procedures; and, second, that trends which may preexist in the target behaviour are unlikely to have resulted in the magnitude of any change in levels that accompanied the introduction of the operant procedures. Some results given in a study by Axelrod (BT, 83) may illustrate this point. The study revolved around the assessment of the effectiveness of individual and group contingencies for undesirable behaviour in special education classrooms. After a baseline condition lasting five days, individual contingencies (IC) were introduced into Class I and group contingencies (GC) into Class II. After five more days, the baseline was reinstated and then experimental conditions reversed for the two classes (see Figure 12.2). Finally, baseline was reintroduced for both groups.

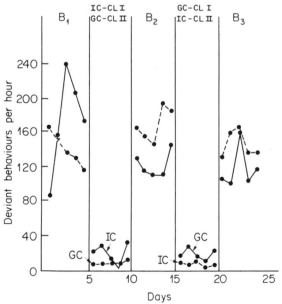

FIGURE 12.2 The number of undesirable behaviours performed by each class during the twenty-five experimental sessions. Measurements were conducted for a one hour period. The unbroken line represents Class I (Cl. 1) and the dashed line Class II (Cl. 2). B_1, B_2, and B_1 are the three baseline phases, with IC and GC denoting individual and group contingencies, respectively. (From *B.T.*, 1973, **4**, 87, Figure 1.)

As can be clearly seen from Figure 12.2, no stable baseline was achieved before the introduction of the first set of contingencies. In fact, our rough calculation reveals that the fluctuation in the deviant behaviours per hour for Class I between day 1 and day 3 was about 160 instances. The mean change from first baseline days to individual contingencies days was 154 behaviours. The author makes no mention of this important point. While not necessarily refuting Axelrods conclusion that the experimental contingencies affected behaviour, it is obvious that there were other, uncontrolled, changes in environmental contingencies as least as powerful as those instituted by the experimenter. These may have been unconnected with the experiment, or they may have been conditioned upon the presence of the investigator or changes in teacher behaviour associated with the experiment, or any number of other things. The point is that only where the target behaviour is stabilized during the baseline period can complete confidence be placed in the finding that the subsequent changes in behaviour were the result of predefined changes in contingencies.

Finally, we must turn to the problem of interaction effects. In the situation where multiple treatments are applied consecutively to a group of subjects, the effects of later treatments *may* depend upon the effects of the earlier treatment. If, as is usually the case, it is not possible to decide whether the experimental phases were or were not interacting, then it is only safe to generalize to patients exposed to a similar sequence of events. Take, for example, the study of Santogrossi and coworkers (JABA, 277), which looked at the effectiveness of several procedures on disruptive classroom behaviour. Figure 12.3 shows the design and the results of this study.

The design may be summarized as ABCDECD. It appears that the conventional token programme (teacher-determined points) was quite effective, but when it was reintroduced after a period when the students determined their own reinforcements (and a brief period of matching teacher–student evaluations which was discontinued because it led to large amounts of unruly behaviour) the teacher-determined points system was no longer so effective. This was presumably because of a carry-over effect from the previous two conditions, as the authors acknowledge. However, the authors do not mention the possibility that the relative ineffectiveness of the self-determined points system may have been because it followed the teacher-determined points system. Strictly, all that can be said is that when a self-determined points system follows a teacher-determined points system it is relatively ineffective. Nothing whatever can be said about the effectiveness of a self-determined system in its own right.

The interpolation of baseline (no-treatment) conditions between experimental conditions does not completely overcome this difficulty. As Kazdin (1973c) makes clear, reinstating the target behaviour after reversals may become easier with more and more exposures to experimental conditions. Perhaps the only solution to the problem is to use more subjects and more groups, each receiving unique treatments. This is not out of the question because the median number of subjects employed in operant studies in 1973

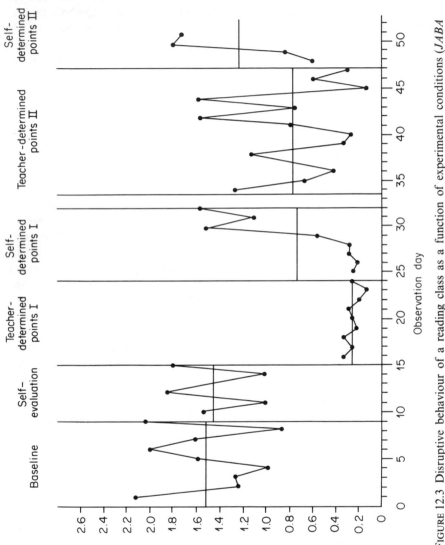

FIGURE 12.3 Disruptive behaviour of a reading class as a function of experimental conditions (*JABA* 1973, **6**, 283, Figure 1.)

was only twelve, which meant that 64 per cent. of all operant studies used ten or fewer subjects per group or condition.

OTHER DESIGN PROBLEMS

In this section, we wish to consider more briefly some further points related to the design and analysis of behaviour therapy experiments. These will be illustrated wherever possible, but space restrictions make a detailed examination impossible.

1. Follow-up

In assessing the effectiveness of an experimental therapeutic procedure, a follow-up examination is often required both because the therapeutic contact is often very short-lived (under one hour in some studies) and because the analogue with actual therapy requires some statement about the long-term outcome of a treatment. In some of the studies examined, a follow-up was not appropriate because, for example, the target behaviour was only manifested in controlled conditions (e.g. ward behaviour) or no behaviour change was involved. Of the 113 studies in which a follow-up was appropriate, only 38 were actually conducted, leaving 75 studies (65 per cent of the total) which should have employed follow-up procedures but did not.

Where follow-ups were conducted, 9 were within one month of the last experimental session, a further 19 took place between one and six months and 10 took place more than six months after the end of therapy or the experiment. That the absence of a follow-up weakens the value of a study may be seen by considering the example of the study by Walter and Gilmore (BT, 361), in which the efficacy of parent-training procedures aimed at reducing aggressive behaviour in difficult boys was assessed. The experimental programme, which lasted four weeks, produced marked improvements in behaviour compared to a placebo control group studied over the same period. As no follow-up was employed, however, it is impossible to say whether this improvement was maintained or disappeared immediately after the withdrawal of the experimental programme. Had a follow-up been included, then a great deal more could have been learned from the study with the expenditure of relatively little extra effort. Willems (1973) has presented this view most cogently (p. 100):

We know by now from other areas (e.g., the case of insecticides) that monitoring of very long sequences can be both scientifically illuminating and pragmatically critical. Somehow, the behavioural technologist must become willing to participate in such long-range concerns. The fact that the behavioural sciences cannot match the sophistication of ecological biochemistry is no excuse to wait.

[However] the most ready and reasonable response by the behaviour modifier, a function of his view of behaviour and his view of the world, will probably be: 'Whatever happens before or after my technological intervention—whether good, bad, or indifferent—is a function of chaotic or unfortunate programs of contingency or, at the least, programs of contingency that are out of my explicit control. Ergo, the occurrences are none of my business, by definition.' I would argue that he should *make* them his business, because we do not know when this response is an evasion of direct responsibility. Some behavioural interventions might unwittingly disrupt good things or set bad things in motion that become clear only over long periods of time.

2. Individual differences

In most studies more than one individual received the treatment, and responsiveness to it differed considerably. It might therefore be considered important to examine the individual differences which may explain why certain procedures are more effective for some individuals than others. Occasionally this might not be necessary if it is clear that all the subjects did react in exactly the same way (see, for example, Azrin, Sneed and Foxx, BRAT, 427, where all twelve retarded bed-wetters were successfully trained within three days). Where it was called for, however, only 20 of 113 studies performed this kind of analysis. Take as an example the study of O'Donnell and Worell (BRAT, 473) which assessed three procedures for their effectiveness in reducing racial anger. Noting that one of the procedures (desensitization and motor relaxation) worked for only half the subjects assigned to that group, the authors set about identifying the factors responsible for this differential effectiveness. They discovered that those subjects for whom the treatment worked were initially less angry, achieved greater relaxation and were more liked by the therapists. Although by no means a complete analysis, it does go some way toward explaining the differential response of subjects to the same treatment.

3. Generalization

If a therapeutic intervention is demonstrated to have an effect on a target behaviour, it is important to consider whether this effect is generalized. This may happen in two ways: either the individual will display changes in other response classes within the same situation (response generalization); or the frequency of the same response class will alter in situations other than the one in which the manipulation took place (stimulus generalization). An example of an incident reported in one study made the importance of a check on generalization clear. In the study of Azrin, Sneed and Foxx (BRAT, 427), already referred to, it was discovered that although several of the patients were prevented from wetting their beds by the experimental procedure, they were in fact getting up in the night and urinating on the floor. This might suggest that urinating (in the bed or on the floor) was maintained, for example, by staff attention. It would, therefore, have been interesting to examine other behaviours, similarly controlled by the same contingency after bed-wetting had been eliminated. Unfortuantely, this was not done.

Generalization measures were taken in 55 studies (response generalization

31 times, stimulus generalization 15 times, and both in 9 studies). The authors of the other 63 studies did not consider it necessary to measure generalization effects or were unable to devise a suitable method of doing so. We think this is somewhat disappointing.

Exactly why behaviour therapy research has yielded a dearth of generalization measures is unclear. Perhaps it relates to the general theoretical strategy of most researchers. Too often attempts at behaviour change have focused upon unitary response systems. Such an approach may be seen as a carry-over from the animal laboratory, where the concern is with single responses such as the bar-press. No consideration is given, however, to the importance of the interrelationship of response classes. Within the natural setting of human behaviour, it is very conceivable that a change in a highly functional behaviour will produce marked changes in other response classes, through a change in environmental reactions to the total response system. For example, the reduction of a phobic response might lead to improvements in self-concept, interpersonal relationships, productivity or a number of other behaviours.

Another issue involves the direction of control. Generally, we devise manipulations which invoke the therapist's or the environment's control over the subject's behaviour. However, one individual's behaviour is another individual's discriminative stimulus. To the extent that behaviour changes in one setting, it is incumbent upon the researcher to examine whether environmental agents react to the same behaviour in other situations. For example, a teacher might institute a behavioural programme for inappropriate behaviour during the morning class. Given that the behaviour of specific children is altered, would the teacher now respond to the children in a different way in the afternoon, even though the programme is not in effect at this time. This example pinpoints the need to examine generalization for both the target of change and the change agent. It is important that these issues of stimulus and response generalization receive serious attention. However, it is only when we take a more ecological perspective that answers will be forthcoming. The authors recognize that the examples presented above do not represent orthodox measures of generalization, i.e. where behaviours are measured in situations in which contingencies are held constant. However, we believe that such a static model does not correspond to the *in vivo* situation. Only by taking a wider, more dynamic view of generalization will we come to understand change within the natural setting.

'Generalization' also refers to the extent to which the results of a particular study can be applied to other people in other contexts. It is usually considered incumbent upon authors to assess the generalizability of their findings in terms of the subjects, methods, procedures and conditions they employed. It is obviously more difficult for the reader to make this kind of judgement than the author. In 1973 only 52 studies did this. The remaining 66 studies appeared to ignore completely the problem of generalization and did not even attempt to put their findings in an appropriate context.

INDEPENDENT VARIABLE MANIPULATION CHECK

The basic components of experimental research in psychology are the dependent and independent variables. The independent variable—the one controlled or manipulated by the experimenter—has received far less methodological attention than has the dependent variable. A situation has arisen in which readers and reviewers demand that experimenters take a great deal of care over the measurement and recording of dependent variables, but are willing to accept unauthenticated statements about the nature and levels of the independent variable involved. A reaction against this easy acceptance of the researcher's assumption occurred in other areas of psychology some time ago. For example, where the independent variable consists of the arousal of different levels of anxiety in different groups by using different instructions or giving different information, it is expected that some check will be made on this manipulation. In other words, it is not enough to know that different groups received different anxiety-arousing materials; it is also necessary to establish that the groups were actually made differentially anxious.

The same sort of questions can be asked of behaviour therapy research. Now, a problem arises when we look at the difficulty of deciding whether a particular behaviour therapy technology consists only of a set of instructions and procedures *or* the achievement of a certain psychological or physiological condition in the person. Take, for example, relaxation. Does the technique consist of a standard set of supposedly relaxation inducing procedures, or is it necessary to achieve *actual* relaxation in the subject in order to reduce an anxiety reaction to a phobic object or whatever? The answer to this question probably depends upon the theoretical bias of the experimenter. We decided, rather arbitrarily, that in the case of the techniques of desensitization, relaxation and aversion a check on the independent variable manipulation was not necessary so long as the stimulus that constituted the independent variable was clearly different in each group. For all other types of therapy, a check was deemed necessary. Table 12.5 indicates that of the 66 studies in which a check on the manipulation of the independent variable was appropriate, only 47 studies did, in fact, incorporate such a check.

Saxby (BT, 230) tested a hypothesis regarding the effect of cognitive dissonance on students with a fear of spiders. Those assigned to the 'high'-dis-

TABLE 12.5 Possible sources of experimental error.

	Present	Absent	Not applicable
Check on independent variable manipulation	19	47	52
Unbiased recording of dependent variable	22	49	47
Interobserver reliability checked	55	42	21
Expectancy effects controlled or checked	18	100	—
Context for subjects reported	83	35	—

sonance conditions were given a set of instructions which led them to expect an aversive encounter with a spider with minimum justification (i.e. for an 'experiment', not treatment). The 'low'-dissonance group were told that they would not be put to any discomfort and that some therapeutic benefit might accrue. No differences were observed between the groups' pre- to post-test scores on a behavioural avoidance test (BAT) or fear thermometer. The author concludes that 'it may not be possible to reduce phobic anxiety by dissonance arousal (pp. 233–234)'. In the absence of any check, however simple, that different levels of dissonance were *in fact* aroused in the two groups of subjects—especially as the instructions received by the two groups were really quite similar—it cannot really be stated that the dissonance hypothesis has ever been tested.

Operant studies were also examined for independent variable checks. We generally took for granted that the reinforcements used did have some value to the recipients, although this was rarely checked. The important issue that arose here, however, concerns the question of the dispensing of contingencies. We looked to see whether checks were incorporated, where necessary, to determine whether or not contingencies were dispensed exactly in the way specified by the research design. This really involves two checks: first, a check that the contingencies did actually follow the target behaviour and only the target behaviour at the appropriate time, level and frequency; and a check that the same class of behaviour was not being systematically influenced by other contingencies at the same time. This may be illustrated by the study of Upper (JBTEP, 137), who instituted a ticket system (resulting in a fine of tokens) to correct minor maladaptive behaviours in a hospital ward. Ward personnel dispensed the tickets twenty-four hours a day for eight weeks. Such behaviour as running, loitering, borrowing, loudness, etc., was followed by a ticket. No check was made that contingencies, in fact, followed the behaviours consistently or that ward personnel could reliably and consistently distinguish running from fast walking or loitering from slow walking. Further, no check was made that the tickets were not used for other purposes as well. Finally, no check was made that other contingencies, such as threats, rebukes and other punishments, did not also follow maladaptive behaviour. In the absence of information concerning the actual, as against intended, way the programme was run, the conclusion that 'The violation ticket system was apparently an effective means of reducing the frequency with which minor infractions of ward rules occurred (p. 139)' is hardly justified.

That this consideration also applies to the treatment of single individuals in closely controlled experimental procedures is illustrated by the study of Moore and Ritterman (BRAT, 43). Here a single experimenter had to monitor the auditory responses of stutterers, determine whether a response was stuttered or fluent, and manually dispense contingent reinforcement (money and a green light), punishment (shock and a red light), or both, depending upon the experimental condition for the duration of the stuttered or fluent response on a fixed ratio schedule! Although reliability checks were made of the experimenter's perception of stuttered responses prior to the experiment, this was presumably under more relaxed conditions. In the experimental situation itself, no such checks were reported and no observations were made of the care with which the contingencies were applied. Although the overall package of experimental procedures did reduce stuttering in the short term, the extent to which the strict application of predetermined contingencies was responsible for this is impossible to determine.

A problem of a different sort was encountered by Azrin, Naster and Jones (BRAT, 365). They employed partner-reciprocated reinforcements as a treatment for marital disharmony. With this particular package, the specification and discussion of reinforcers occurred in the presence of the therapist, but of necessity the bulk of the actual reinforcement procedures were executed in the privacy of the clients' own home. It was therefore impossible to check whether, and to what extent, reciprocal reinforcement actually occurred and was responsible for the considerable improvement in marital happiness reported. Other factors, such as exposure to new material, response cueing, increased discussion between spouses or even a conspiracy to show improvement to the therapist, could have been responsible in the complete absence of any increase in reciprocated reinforcement. In other words, even if it is accepted that the overall package worked, the active therapeutic components cannot be specified.

That some of these problems can be overcome is illustrated by several of the reports that appeared in 1973. Mathews and Shaw (BRAT, 587), in a study of flooding as a treatment for fear of spiders, exposed subjects to 'high arousal' or 'low arousal' flooding themes. They then checked reported arousal on an anxiety rating scale. In this instance, unexpactedly, they found no overall significant difference in anxiety between the high and low arousal groups. In other words, the failure of one aspect of the independent variable manipulation was revealed because the researchers were careful enough to incorporate a check.

In the operant field, several investigators checked that contingencies were applied correctly. Bennett and Maley (JABA, 609) investigated the benefit of contingent reinforcement (tokens) on interactive behaviour in chronic schizophrenics. The experimenter operated a panel of lights indicating various types of interaction which earned tokens. For two out of ten sessions the experimenter was observed through one-way mirrors by two psychologists to determine if they agreed with the experimenter's judgement that a subject's response met reinforcement criteria. Although 100 per cent. agreement was achieved, it is not reported whether the experimenter knew which sessions were being checked or whether the other non-specified behaviour of the experimenter was also checked.

Ringer (JABA, 671), Goetz and Baer (JABA, 209) and Kazdin and Klock (JABA, 643) all studied the effects of teacher response on various aspects of student behaviour. Besides providing a check on the appropriateness of designated contingency applications, all three studies also measured other potentially controlling aspects of the teacher's behaviour. Kazdin and Klock, for example, looked at non-verbal approval and student attentive behaviour. As well as checking on the manipulation of non-verbal approval, they also measured fluctuations in teacher's verbal behaviour and correlated these with changes in the dependent variable (attentive behaviour). The careful measurement and thorough analysis in this study enabled the investigators to conclude with some confidence that it was, in fact, contingent teacher non-verbal approval that accounted for changes in student attention.

MEASUREMENT OF THE DEPENDENT VARIABLE

That the precise and veridical measurement of the dependent variable in psychological investigations is of special importance has long been recognized. In behaviour therapy research, attention should be paid to two aspects of the measurement of the dependent variable: its unbiased recording and a check on the reliability of this recording. We checked on the 1973 studies with regard to both these points.

By unbiased recording of the dependent variable is meant that the measurements should be made in such a way as to avoid any contamination of the data by the hypotheses of the experimenter. Where appropriate, this applies to both the pre- and post-test measurements. If recording of the data was done by the subject himself (as in questionnaires) or mechanically (e.g. tape-recordings or galvanic skin response recordings), the question of bias does not arise. If, on the other hand, recording is done by an observer—as in the case of a behavioural avoidance test (BAT) or timing interactive or work behaviour in a hospital ward—it is important that this should be done by someone who either does not know the hypotheses being tested or who is unaware of which condition is being observed. If the experimenter himself or one of his associates who is aware of the research hypotheses does the recording, it is all too easy for minute but systematic errors in recording to be made. Rosenthal (1966, p. 158) and others have shown that the observation of simple behaviour in animals can be influenced by the set of the observer.

Table 12.5 shows that of the 71 studies where this question was appropriate, only 22 (31 per cent.) actually incorporated this fundamental precaution. In the other 49 studies, it was either not clearly reported who did the measurement (presumably the experimenter) or the measurements were made by biased observers.

The study by O'Sullivan, Gilner and Krinski (BT, 535) may be used as an example of research using a behavioural avoidance test (BAT) but not using unbiased observers to record the data. Subjects in this study of modelling and snake-avoidance were observed through a 'peep-hole' in the wall by the experimenter during the BAT. There is no information concerning the dimension of the peep-hole or its distance from the subjects or snake, so there is no way of knowing if the observer had an unobstructed view of the behaviour he was assessing. What is clear, however, is that the experimenter or his assistant was aware of the experimental condition of each subject, and were possibly aware of pre-test scores when the post-testing was carried out. In the particular BAT used, the observer had to distinguish between such behaviours as touching the snake's cage, putting a hand inside the cage, touching a snake in its cage, petting it, holding it in the cage and holding it outside the cage. Such discriminations might well be susceptible to involuntary bias in recording by an observer who is aware of the experimental hypotheses. Interestingly, the authors of this study state that they followed a procedure similar to Davison (1968) who, in fact, deliberately used naïve observers for this very test in order to avoid the possibility of bias.

Solomon and Wahler (JABA, 49), although extremely careful in all other aspects of the design and reporting of their study, neglect to state whether the three observers that they employed were aware or unaware of the purpose of the experiment. This study illustrates the difficulty of using totally naïve observers. The intention was to assess the influence of peer social reinforcement on problem behaviour in the classroom. Even a naïve observer could hardly fail to become aware of the behaviour of the nominated peer reinforcer (who was seated next to the target subject) and so become aware of the experimental hypothesis. The only way round this might be to take video-recordings of the target subject only with the peer or therapist excluded from the picture, and subject a sample of these to a truly naïve observer who could then provide validity data for the *in situ* observer.

Quilitch and Risley (JABA, 573), studying the effects of different kinds of toys on social play in a recreation centre for 7-year-olds, checked the data collected by the two regular observers against the data collected by a naïve observer who watched a sample of all the experimental sessions. They report agreements between prime and naïve observers of between 85 and 100 per cent.

Epstein and Peterson (BT, 96) used two independent experimenters in their study of conditioning by covert reinforcers. One experimenter took baseline and post-test measures and was unaware of the subject's group, while the other experimenter trained the subjects in imagining positive or aversive scenes.

Obviously, it will not always be possible to use such simple devices as those described here, but the problem of bias in recording is certainly serious enough to be considered at the design stage of an experiment. The value of studies that do not emply unbiased recording of the dependent variable is called into question.

Checking interobserver reliability presents fewer methodological problems. The need for reliability checks occurs both where data are collected by an observer and where they are recorded by a machine for later scoring. Therefore, we looked to see whether two or more observers had recorded or scored at least some part of the dependent variable data, and if information concerning reliability was presented in the report. This was independent of the use of unbiased observers. Even unbiased observers should be checked for reliability. It is a truism that unreliable observations can have no validity. Only in cases where the dependent variable data were recorded directly by the subjects themselves in their final form is a reliability check not necessary. See, for example, Koenig (BT, 193), who used rating scales to measure test anxiety before and after treatment.

Table 12.5 also shows that 55 studies did employ checks on interobserver reliability, while 42 studies where this should have been done in fact either failed to do so, or to report that it had been done. It is difficult to understand why such a large proportion of studies should have failed to take this elementary precaution which could have been taken care of with relatively little trouble or expense.

The study of O'Sullivan, Gilner and Krinski (BT, 535), already cited, employed no check on observer reliability. Another study using a BAT (this time involving dead and bloody rats) conducted by D'Zurilla, Wilson and Nelson (BT, 672) did not check observer reliability, even though it is specifically stated that two testers were available. It may appear somewhat unlikely that observation of a BAT might be unreliable. When it is remembered that the examiner had to determine the length of time a subject spent looking at the dead rat before and after treatment, and that the change scores involved in this study were relatively small, it is clear that unreliability in recording is not impossible and could make a substantial difference to the results of the study.

EXPECTANCY EFFECTS

Social psychologists have long been aware that the psychological experiment is itself a social situation in which many things are happening to affect the dependent variable apart from the conscious manipulations of the experimenter. A number of the undercurrents in the experimental situation have been analysed with sufficient thoroughness, and have been observed so often, that they deserve attention when an experiment is carried out. We have grouped these under the general heading of experimenter expectancy effects, although we have included so-called demand characteristics as well. Where an experimenter has a hypothesis concerning the efficacy of a particular type of treatment and compares the outcome of a group receiving this treatment with other groups receiving other treatments (or no treatment) and where the experimenter acts as therapist, a situation where expectancy effects may come into play is created. Although Rosenthal (1966) and others have studied expectancy effects very carefully, the way in which they operate may not be clear in any specific situation. It could be that the therapist brings more experience, expertise or enthusiasm to one therapy than another, or that one group of patients is subtly led to believe that change is likely (high demand for improvement) while the control group is not (low demand for improvement). It may be that patients receive minute clues about how the therapist expects them to behave and they comply because they wish to please him, or because they believe that it means they are getting better. The existence of the possibility of expectancy effects does not mean that results obtained can be explained in this way, but it does mean that an alternative, plausible explanation exists for any group differences that do emerge.

Interest in this problem is indicated by the reviews that have recently appeared of the possibly confounding effects of expectancies in behaviour therapy research (Agras and coworkers, 1969; Barlow and coworkers, 1972; Borkovec, 1972, 1973; Davison and Wilson, 1973; Wilkins, 1971). Although these reviewers generally conclude that the role of expectancy effects is ambiguous and varies with therapeutic technique, problem area and subject characteristics, there is sufficient substance in this area to warrant the careful attention of researcheres.

The 118 studies were examined to determine whether account had been taken of expectancy effects. Ten studies introduced deliberate controls for expectancy effects (several of these were actually concerned with expectancy as the independent variable) and 8 others checked or commented on the possibility that such effects may have influenced results. This leaves 100 studies where expectancy effects *could* have been operating but where no attempt was made to control for, or even check on, this eventuality. It is perhaps worth repeating that we have no evidence that these studies were actually not valid, but that a more or less plausible alternative hypothesis (expectancy effects) exists to account for any results that were produced.

There are several ways of dealing with expectancy effects. Borkovec (1973) suggests a design that may be used if the prime purpose of an experiment is to determine the effectiveness of a form of treatment. This calls for four groups of matched subjects. The first receives the treatment with non-therapeutic instructions; the second receives the treatment with therapeutic instructions; the third receives a placebo with therapeutic instructions; and the fourth a placebo with non-therapeutic instructions. This is called the placebo with crossed expectancy design. Although it has much to recommend it, an inherent weakness is that this design effectively equates expectancy with instructions. It is fairly obvious that there are many other possible sources of expectancy effects apart from instructions. Several studies from 1973 used variants of this design. Miller and coworkers (BRAT, 491) compared the effectiveness of treating alcoholics with electrical aversion conditioning with two high expectancy control groups. They found no differences in outcome and concluded previous work demonstrating the efficacy of electrical aversion in alcoholics may have been related to such extraexperimental factors as expectancy effects.

Barlow and Agras (JABA, 355) attempted to induce the same 'therapeutic set' (high expectancy) in their homosexual subjects during both the treatment (fading) and the control phases of the study. In this case the treatment was relatively successful and the control procedure unsuccessful in increasing heterosexual responsiveness ($N = 3$).

Although both of these studies attempted to equate expectancies resulting from instruction, neither checked to determine whether their attempts were successful. This criticism is perhaps irrelevant in the case of the Miller and coworkers paper because no differences were actually found between groups, but the authors could not have known that this would be the outcome when the experiment was designed. A simple check on the expectations of the subjects would reveal the impact of the instructions and whether other factors were operating to influence expectancy.

In a careful study, Kazdin (JBTEP, 213) both manipulated demand character-istics and measured subject expectancy and found that they were important variables determining post-test avoidance behaviour in analogue snake phobics. Kazdin makes the important point that although expectancy effects altered avoidance behaviour, attitudes, anxiety and fear-arousal in snake-avoidant college students, this does not mean that they would exert the same influence in clinical phobic populations.

In many respects the ideal way to rule out any possible contaminating expectancy effects, when the absolute or relative effectiveness of a treatment is being examined, is to employ a qualified and committed therapist of a different persuasion to give both experimental and control treatments. The most elaborate (and expensive) design of this nature would involve behaviour therapists and (for example) psychotherapists, each giving both behaviour therapy and psychotherapy to matched groups of patients in whom expectancies were measured and equated (see, for example, Paul, 1966). In this way, it might be possible to make a definitive statement about the therapeutic tech-nique, ruling out the possible influences of therapist variables, demand characteristics and expectancies.

None of the studies examined employed this design in its entirety, probably because of the large numbers of subjects required and the difficulty of obtaining the services of a non-behaviourist clinician. The closest attempt was a very enterprising study by Obler (JBTEP, 93) which looked at the effectiveness of desensitization for sexual disorders. He employed an experienced and qualified psychotherapist to treat a control group with the same problems while he himself conducted the experimental procedure. It is unlikely that his finding that desensitization was more effective could be attributed to expectancy effects. However, the use of only one therapist in each condition without a crossover of therapist and therapy means that a possible explanation on the basis of therapist variables may exist.

One study got around the problem of expectancy effects by doing away with a therapist altogether! Wilson and Hopkins (JABA, 269) constructed an apparatus which automatically switched on reinforcing pop music when the noise levels in seventh and eighth grade home economics classrooms fell below a predetermined threshold level for 20 seconds. The apparatus also recorded the duration of the music being on and off. This type of procedure is only possible in very limited circumstances.

Where it is impossible to employ any of the designs so far suggested, one other procedure could be adopted which might at least reveal the possible extent of expectancy effects. If some check is made on the actual behaviour of the therapists who operate the experimental and control conditions, it would be possible to decide whether the treatments, in fact, varied in ways other than those prescribed by the independent variable manipulation. The desirability of introducing checks on therapist behaviour has been mentioned elsewhere. O'Donnell and Worell (BRAT, 473) equated instructions regarding expectancy for improvement for three groups of subjects, but subsequently found that the four therapists involved had a strong bias regarding the relative efficacy of the treatments used. They acknowledge that this may have influenced their results.

None of the studies we examined used observers deliberately to check for the possible communication of expectancy effects from therapists to subjects. A video-recording of a sample of the treatment and control interaction between therapist and patient subjected to independent scrutiny might go some way towards determining the presence or absence of expectancy effects. Although this is second best to the use of a design to counteract expectancy effects, it might reassure those not involved that serious biases had not influenced group differences apparently attributable to independent variable manipulations.

One further factor requires consideration—the context of the investigation as it is presented to the subject. There could be a crucial difference in what a subject expects to happen if he believes he is receiving an effective therapy compared to his expectations if he is informed that he is part of a research project. The exact effects on the subject of the two types of context can only be conjectured, but they are likely to be considerably different. We presume that the subjects in most studies were capable of being aware of their surroundings and were required to participate actively, and therefore must have been told something about what was happening. What we actually checked, therefore,was whether or not authors reported the context as described to subjects. Referring to Table 12.5, it can be seen that while 83 studies did report what was said, 35 did not. Of the 83 studies that reported a context, 41 told the subjects that the programme was experimental, 17 told the subjects they were undergoing therapy and in 25 cases no information was given to subjects, either because they were unaware of their surroundings or because their consent was not required—as with, for example, children in the classroom. Attention to the variable of the subjects' perception of the context of an investigation may be very worthwhile (Borkovec, 1973).

THE STRENGTH OF RELATIONSHIPS

Many authorities have pointed out that reporting a significance level associated with a statistical test of a hypothesis is of limited use unless it is accompanied by some statement concerning the strength of relationship between dependent and independent variables. Hays (1963), for example, charges (p. 326) that psychologists:

> ... pay too much attention to the significance test and too little to the degree of statistical association the finding represents. This clutters up the literature with findings that are often not worth pursuing, and which serve to obscure the really important predictive relations that occasionally appear. The serious scientist owes it to himself and his readers to ask not only, 'Is there any relationship between X and Y?' but also

'How much does my finding suggest about the power to predict Y from X?' Much too much emphasis is paid to the former, at the expense of the latter, question.

The basis for this assertion is that very weak and possibly inconsequential relationships may be statistically significant if large enough groups of subjects are used. In fact, Hays makes the point that the only reason for failing to reject the null hypothesis in psychological studies is because N was too small. Any two groups will eventually show a significant difference on any variable if their size is increased sufficiently. A measure of the strength of a relationship, and therefore its *psychological* significance, must take into account not only group differences but group sizes.

We checked to see how many of the 118 reports paid the courtesy to readers that Hays suggested. Table 12.6 contains the result. In 50 cases it was not appropriate to estimate the strength of a relationship, either because no statistical comparisons were made or because no statistically significant differences emerged. Of the remaining 68 studies only two authors reported the strength of their findings. Actually, the calculation of the strength of relationships is quite simple. All that is necessary is the conversion of a t, F_1 or χ^2 value into a correlation coefficient. Friedman (1968) published a

TABLE 12.6 Reporting the strength of relationship.

	Number	Percentage
Not applicable	50	42.3
Applicable		
Presented*	2	1.7
Not calculable from data	18	15.3
Calculable from data	48	40.7
		100
of which, strength calculated as [†]		
0–10	3	6.3
11–20	16	33.3
21–30	7	14.5
31–40	3	6.3
41–50	6	12.5
51–60	3	6.3
61–70	3	6.3
71–80	4	8.2
81–90	3	6.3
91 +	0	0.0

*Rutner (BT, 338) strength = 79%.
 Kazdin and Klock (JABA, 643) strength = 71%.

[†]Percentage of variance in dependent variable accounted for by independent variable.

table for the rapid estimation of a statistic (r_m) which is the general form of the conversions required for different tests of statistical significance. When r_m is squared and multiplied by 100, it yields a rough estimate of the percentage of the variance in the dependent variable that is accounted for by the manipulation of the independent variable. The only information required for the use of Friedman's table is the t, F_1 or χ^2 value and the group sizes.

Eighteen studies did not even give sufficient information for the strength of a relationship to be calculated, even though this was clearly appropriate. The results of our calculations for the remaining 48 studies based on Friedman's table are also shown in Table 12.6.

The interpretation of estimates of the strength of relationship requires care for several reasons. In the first place, there is some dispute over the accuracy of Friedman's table—it may if anything overestimate the strength of relationships (Fleiss, 1970). Second, we arbitrarily chose what appeared to be the most important statistical test in any given paper if there were several to chose from. Finally, and perhaps most importantly, the meaning of the strength estimate in terms of the psychological or clinical importance of the relationship must depend upon the experimental situation. The variance of the dependent variable not accounted for by the manipulations of the independent variable obviously must be produced by other, uncontrolled variables or measurement error. In some situations there will be many important variables affecting the dependent variables, in others relatively few.

Bearing these strictures in mind, if the lower half of Table 12.6 is examined, it is apparent that about half of the statistically significant relationships reported are relatively weak (less than 30 per cent. of the variance accounted for) and only a small proportion may be called strong relationships (over 50 per cent. of the variance explained). As already pointed out, the psychological importance attached to the strength of a relationship can only ultimately be decided in context. Each paper which reported a statistically significant relationship was examined to determine whether the authors commented on the psychological, as opposed to the statistical, significance of a relationship. Only two authors did so. Miller and coworkers (BRAT, 491) comment that their most clinically relevant finding was not statistically significant; Harris and Hallbauer (BRAT, 523) make the reverse point that in their study of self-directed weight control, although a statistically significant effect was observed, the absolute amount of weight lost by their subjects (average 10.7 pounds over 7 months) was not very large. Given the rapidity with which an estimate of the strength of a relationship can be obtained and the value of the extra information provided, it is surprising that so few authors bother to report or comment on both psychological as well as statistical significance.

SUMMARY

Although it may appear somewhat pretentious, we would like to summarize by presenting a set of recommendations which may be useful in the design and reporting of behaviour therapy experiments. Obviously not all experiments can conform to one pattern, but there are some problems which all investigations have to overcome. We have attempted to incorporate into our recommendations most of the points that were discussed when the 1973 studies were reviewed and some others which space made it impossible to mention. We start by suggesting some points to be borne in mind in designing studies and then go on to aspects of reporting studies.

A. Design

1. Attention should be paid to adequate sampling procedures in obtaining subjects. Problems associated with using volunteers, only one treatment agency and response rates should be borne in mind.
2. Experimental design must be related to the questions to be answered. The use of appropriate control groups, baseline measures and within-subject comparisons should be planned. An attention or placebo control is usually better than a no-treatment or waiting list control.
3. Where it is intended to demonstrate operant stimulus control, a stable baseline must be achieved; interaction of experimental phases must be considered, and the distinction between the possible effects of the contingencies as discriminative stimuli and reinforcers must be possible. The multiple baseline design offers several advantages.
4. It is essential that the manipulation of the independent variable is checked if any conclusions about its relationship with the dependent variable are to be drawn.
5. It must be presumed that expectancy effects of one kind or another are present in all experiments. Adequate steps must be taken either to eliminate or measure them so that allowances may be made.
6. It is necessary to establish that the pre- and post-test recording of the dependent variable data was achieved in an unbiased and reliable fashion.
7. Whenever possible, more than one therapist should administer each treatment or experimental condition so that treatment–therapist interactions may be considered.
8. The inclusion of follow-up data considerably enhances the value of most studies and is probably a requirement if a result is considered to be of potential therapeutic value.
9. It is important in many cases to employ measures of stimulus and response generalization.

B. Reporting

10. Information concerning subject's clinical status, age, sex, therapeutic history, drug schedule and social class should always be reported. Where subjects vary on these factors, they should be included in a *post hoc* analysis to assess their interaction with the experimental procedures.

11. Similarly, therapist or experimenter variables such as age, sex, experience and numbers should be both reported and examined.

12. The type of analysis of the dependent variable undertaken should be clearly spelled out, the way in which any assumptions involved have been met explained and the strength of relationships calculated. In addition, it may often be necessary to distinguish between statistical and psychological significance.

13. Where analogue problems or non-clinical samples are studied, the justification for these procedures should be given and the relevance to clinical situations discussed.

14. The exact way in which data were gathered should be given, including details of the relationship of the observers to the experimenter, and their familiarity with the experimental hypotheses made clear.

15. Individual differences in responsiveness to treatments within groups should be reported, along with possible reasons for these differences.

16. The results should be placed in context for generalization in terms of the populations, situations and problems to which they may be applicable.

17. Alternative explanations for results produced should be examined and, wherever possible, ruled out as reasonable hypotheses before definitive statements concerning the experimental hypotheses are made.

REFERENCES

Agras, W. S., Leitenberg, H., Barlow, D. H., and Thomson, L. E. (1969). Instructions and reinforcement in the modification of neurotic behavior. *American Journal of Psychiatry*, **125**, 1435–1439.

Axelrod, S. (1973). Comparison of individual and group contingencies in two special classes. *Behavior Therapy*, **4**, 83–90.

Azrin, N. H., Naster, B. J., and Jones, R. (1973). Reciprocity counseling: a rapid learning-based procedure for marital counseling. *Behaviour Research and Therapy*, **11**, 365–382.

Azrin, N. H., Sneed, T. J., and Foxx, R. M. (1973). Dry bed: a rapid method of eliminating bedwetting (enuresis) of the retarded. *Behaviour Research and Therapy*, **11**, 427–434.

Baer, D. M., Wolf, M. M., and Risley, T. R. (1968). Some current dimensions of applied behavior analysis. *Journal of Applied Behavior Analysis*, **1**, 91–97.

Baker, B. L., Cohen, D. C., and Saunders, J. T. (1973). Self-directed desensitization for acrophobia. *Behaviour Research and Therapy*, **11**, 79–89.

Barlow, D. H., and Agras, W. S. (1973). Fading to increase heterosexual responsiveness in homosexuals. *Journal of Applied Behavior Analysis*, **6**, 355–365.

Barlow, D. H., Agras, W. S., Leitenberg, H., Callman, E. J., and Moore, R. C. (1972). The contribution of therapeutic instruction to covert sensitization. *Behaviour Research and Therapy*, **10**, 411–415.

Bennett, P. S., and Maley, R. F. (1973). Modification of interactive behaviors in chronic mental patients. *Journal of Applied Behavior Analysis*, **6**, 609–620.

Bernstein, D. A., and Paul, G. L. (1971). Some comments on therapy analogue research with small animal 'phobias'. *Journal of Behavior Therapy and Experimental Psychiatry*, **2**, 225–237.

Blanchard, E. B., and Johnson, R. A. (1973). Generalization of operant classroom control procedures. *Behavior Therapy*, **4**, 219–229.

Borkovec, T. D. (1972). Effects of expectancy on the outcome of systematic desensitization and implosive treatment for analogue anxiety. *Behavior Therapy*, **3**, 29–40.

Borkovec, T. D. (1973). The role of expectancy and physiological feedback in fear research: a review with special reference to subject characteristics. *Behavior Therapy*, **4**, 491–505.

Campbell, D. T., and Stanley, J. C. (1963). *Experimental and Quasi-experimental Designs for Research*, Rand McNally, Chicago.

Cooper, A., Furst, J. B., and Bridger, W. (1969). A brief commentary on the usefulness of studying fears of snakes. *Journal of Abnormal Psychology*, **74**, 413–414.

Cossairt, A., Hall, R. V., and Hopkins, B. L. (1973). The effects of experimenter's instructions, feedback, and praise on teacher praise and student attending behavior. *Journal of Applied Behavior Analysis*, **6**, 89–96.

Dalton, A. J., Rubino, C. A., and Hislop, M. W. (1973). Some effects of token rewards on school achievement of children with Down's syndrome. *Journal of Applied Behavior Analysis*, **6**, 251–260.

Davison, G. C. (1968). Systematic desensitization as a counter-conditioning process. *Journal of Abnormal Psychology*, **73**, 91–99.

Davison, G. C., Goldfried, M. R., and Krasner, L. (1970). A postdoctoral program in behavior modification: theory and practice. *American Psychologist*, **25**, 767–772.

Davison, G. C., and Wilson, G. T. (1973). Process of fear-reduction in systematic desensitization: cognitive and social reinforcement factors in humans. *Behavior Therapy*, **4**, 1–21.

Dietz, S. M., and Repp, A. C. (1973). Decreasing classroom misbehavior through the use of DRL schedules of reinforcement. *Journal of Applied Behavior Analysis*, **6**, 457–464.

D'Zurilla, T. J., Wilson, G. T., and Nelson, R. (1973). A preliminary study of the effectiveness of graduated prolonged exposure in the treatment of irrational fear. *Behavior Therapy*, **4**, 672–685.

Eisler, R. M., Hersen, M., and Agras, W. S. (1973). Effects of videotape and instructional feedback on nonverbal marital interaction: an analog study. *Behavior Therapy*, **4**, 551–558.

Epstein, L. H., and Peterson, G. L. (1973). Differential conditioning using covert stimuli. *Behavior Therapy*, **4**, 96–99.

Eysenck, H. J. (1971). Behavior therapy as a scientific discipline. *Journal of Consulting and Clinical Psychology*, 1971, **36**, 314–319.

Felixbrod, J. J., and O'Leary, K. D. (1973). Effects of reinforcement on children's academic behavior as a function of self-determined and externally imposed contingencies. *Journal of Applied Behavior Analysis*, **6**, 241–250.

Fleiss, J. L. (1970). Estimating the magnitude of experimental effects. *Psychological Bulletin*, **72**, 273–276.

Friedman, H. (1968). Magnitude of experimental effect and a table for its rapid estimation. *Psychological Bulletin*, **70**, 245–251.

Goetz, E. M., and Baer, D. M. (1973). Social control of form diversity and the emergence of new forms in children's blockbuilding. *Journal of Applied Behavior Analysis*, **6**, 209–218.

Goldstein, A. P., Martens, J., Hubben, J., van Belle, H. A., Schaaf, W., Wiersma, H., and Goedhart, A. (1973). The use of modeling to increase independent behavior. *Behaviour Research and Therapy*, **11**, 31–42.

Harris, M. B., and Hallbauer, E. S. (1973). Self-directed weight control through eating and exercise. *Behaviour Research and Therapy*, **11**, 523–529.

Harris, V. W., and Sherman, J. A. (1973). Use and analysis of the 'Good Behavior Game' to reduce disruptive classroom behavior. *Journal of Applied Behavior Analysis*, **6**, 405–411.

Hauserman, N., Walen, S. R., and Behling, M. (1973). Reinforced racial integration in the first grade: a study in generalization. *Journal of Applied Behavior Analysis*, **6**, 193–200.

Hays, W. L. (1963). *Statistics*, Holt, Rinehart and Winston, New York.

Hess, R. D. (1970). The transmission of cognitive strategies in poor families. In V. L. Allen (Ed.), *Psychological Factors in Poverty*, Markhan, Chicago.

Hunt, G. M., and Azrin, N. H. (1973). A community-reinforcement approach to alcoholism. *Behaviour Research and Therapy*, **11**, 91–104.

Kanfer, F. H., and Phillips, J. S. (1970). *Learning Foundations of Behavior Therapy*, Wiley, New York.

Kazdin, A. E. (1973a). The effect of suggestion and pretesting on avoidance reduction in fearful subjects. *Journal of Behavior Therapy and Experimental Psychiatry*, **4**, 213–22.

Kazdin, A. E. (1973b). The effect of vicarious reinforcement on attentive behavior in the classroom. *Journal of Applied Behavior Analysis*, **6**, 71–77.

Kazdin, A. E. (1973c). Methodological and assessment considerations in evaluating reinforcement programs in applied settings. *Journal of Applied Behavior Analysis*, **6**, 517–531.

Kazdin, A. E., and Klock, J. (1973). The effect of nonverbal teacher approval on student attentive behavior. *Journal of Applied Behavior Analysis*, **6**, 643–654.

Kelleher, R. T., and Morse, W. H. (1968). Determinants of the specificity of behavioral effects of drugs. *Ergebnisse der Physiologie*, **60**, 1–56.

Koenig, K. P. (1973). False emotional feedback and the modification of anxiety. *Behavior Therapy*, **4**, 193–202.

Krasner, L. (1962). The therapist as a social reinforcement machine. In H. H. Strupp and L. Luborsky (Eds.), *Research in Psychotherapy*, Vol. II. American Psychological Association, Washington, D.C.

Levis, D. J. (1970). The case for performing research on nonpatient populations with fears of small animals: a reply to Cooper, Furst and Bridger. *Journal of Abnormal Psychology*, **76**, 36–38.

Lieberman, R. P., Tiegen, J., Patterson, R., and Baker, V. (1973). Reducing delusional speech in chronic paranoid schizophrenics. *Journal of Applied Behavior Analysis*, **6**, 57–64.

Lorion, R. P. (1974). Patient and therapist variables in the treatment of low income patients. *Psychological Bulletin*, **81**, 344–354.

Marks, I. S. (1969). *Fears and Phobias*, Academic Press, New York.

Mathews, A., and Shaw, P. (1973). Emotional arousal and persuasion effects in flooding. *Behaviour Research and Therapy*, **11**, 587–598.

Miller, P. M., Hersen, M., Eisler, R. M., and Hemphill, D. P. (1973). Electrical aversion therapy with alcoholics: an analogue study. *Behaviour Research and Therapy*, **11**, 491–497.

Moore, W. H., and Ritterman, S. I. (1973). The effects of response contingent reinforcement and response contingent punishment upon the frequency of stuttered verbal behavior. *Behaviour Research and Therapy*, **11**, 43–48.

Obler, M. (1973). Systematic desensitization in sexual disorders. *Journal of Behavior Therapy and Experimental Psychiatry*, **4**, 93–102.

O'Donnell, C. R., and Worell, L. (1973). Motor and cognitive relaxation in the desensitization of anger. *Behaviour Research and Therapy*, **11**, 473–481.

O'Sullivan, M., Gilner, F. H., and Krinski, R. (1973). The influence of sex of experimenter on modeling in the reduction of fear. *Behavior Therapy*, **4**, 535–542.

Paul, G. L. (1966). *Insight versus Desensitization in Psychotherapy: An Experiment in Anxiety Reduction*, Stanford University Press, Stanford, California.

Paul, G. L. (1969). Behavior modification research: design and tactics. In C M. Franks (Ed.), *Behavior Therapy: Appraisal and Status*, McGraw-Hill, New York.

Phillips, E. L., Wolf, M. and Fixsen, D. L. (1973). Achievement Place: development of the elected manager system. *Journal of Applied Behavior Analysis*, **6**, 541–562.

Pinkston, E. M., Reese, N. M., LeBlanc, J. M., and Baer, D. M. (1973). Independent control of a preschool child's aggression and peer interaction by contingent teacher attention. *Journal of Applied Behavior Analysis*, **6**, 115–126.

Pomerleau, O. F., Bobrove, P. H., and Smith, R. H. (1973). Rewarding psychiatric aides for the behavioral improvements of assigned patients. *Journal of Applied Behavior Analysis*, **6**, 383–390.

Poser, E. G. (1966). The effects of therapists' training on group therapeutic outcome. *Journal of Consulting Psychology*, **30**, 283–289.

Quilitch, H. R., and Risley, T. R. (1973). The effects of play materials on social play. *Journal of Applied Behavior Analysis*, **6**, 573–578.

Riddick, C., and Meyer, R. G. (1973). The efficacy of automated relaxation training with response contingent feedback. *Behavior Therapy*, **4**, 331–337.

Ringer, V. M. J. (1973). The use of a 'token helper' in the management of classroom behavior problems and in teacher training. *Journal of Applied Behavior Analysis*, **6**, 671–677.

Romanczyk, R. G., Tracey, D. A., Wilson, G. T., and Thorpe, G. L. (1973). Behavioral techniques in the treatment of obesity: a comparative analysis. *Behaviour Research and Therapy*, **11**, 629–640.

Rosenthal, R. (1966). *Experimenter Effects in Behavioral Research*, Appleton-Century-Crofts, New York.

Rutner, I. T. (1973). The effects of feedback and instructions on phobic behavior. *Behavior Therapy*, **4**, 338–348.

Santogrossi, D. A., O'Leary, K. D., Romanczyk, R. G., and Kaufman, K. F. (1973). Self-evaluation by adolescents in a psychiatric hospital school token program. *Journal of Applied Behavior Analysis*, **6**, 277–288.

Saxby, P. J. (1973). Phobic responses and cognitive dissonance arousal. *Behavior Therapy*, **4**, 230–234.

Sidman, M. (1960). *Tactics of Scientific Research*, Basic Books, New York.

Sobell, M. B., and Sobell, L. C. (1973). Individualized behavior therapy for alcoholics. *Behavior Therapy*, **4**, 49–72.

Sobell, M. B., and Sobell, L. C. (1973). Alcoholics treated by individualized behavior therapy: one year treatment outcome. *Behaviour Research and Therapy*, **11**, 599–618.

Solomon, R. W., and Wahler, R. G. (1973). Peer reinforcement of classroom problem behavior. *Journal of Applied Behavior Analysis*, **6**, 49–56.

Truax, C. B. (1963). Effective ingredients in psychotherapy: an approach to unraveling the patient–therapist interactions. *Journal of Counseling Psychology*, **10**, 256–263.

Truax, C. B., and Mitchell, K. M. (1971). Research on certain therapist interpersonal skills in relation to process and outcome. In A. E. Bergin and S. L. Garfield (Eds.), *Handbook of Psychotherapy and Behavior Change. An Empirical Analysis*, Wiley, New York.

Ullmann, L. P., and Krasner, L. (1965). *Case Studies in Behavior Modification*, Holt, Rinehart and Winston, New York.

Upper, D. (1973). A 'ticket' system for reducing ward rules violations on a token economy program. *Journal of Behavior Therapy and Experimental Psychiatry*, **4**, 737–140.

Walter, H. I., and Gilmore, S. K. (1973). Placebo versus social learning effects in parent training procedures designed to alter the behavior of aggressive boys. *Behavior Therapy*, **4**, 361–377.

Watson, J. P., Mullett, G. E., and Pillay, H. (1973). The effects of prolonged exposure to phobic situations upon agorophobic patients treated in groups. *Behaviour Research and Therapy*, **11**, 531–545.

Wilkins, W. (1971). Desensitization: social and cognitive factors underlying the effectiveness of Wolpe's procedure. *Psychological Bulletin*, **76**, 311–317.

Willems, E. P. (1973). Go ye into all the world and modify behavior: an ecologist's view. *Representative Research in Social Psychology*, **4**, 93–105.

Wilson, C. W., and Hopkins, B. L. (1973). The effects of contingent music on the intensity of noise in junior high home economic classes. *Journal of Applied Behavior Analysis*, **6**, 269–276.

Wolpe, J. (1969a). *The Practice of Behavior Therapy*, Pergamon Press, New York.

Wolpe, J. (1969b). Foreword. In C. M. Franks, (Ed.), *Behavior Therapy: Appraisal and Status*, McGraw-Hill, New York.

13

THE BEHAVIOUR THERAPIES AND SOCIETY

M. Philip Feldman

INTRODUCTION

The behaviour therapies have evoked considerable public interest—sometimes favourable, frequently hostile. The latter response has invariably involved charges of 'manipulation', 'dehumanization', and the like. As pointed out elsewhere (Bandura, 1969) and in a previous chapter, *all* the psychological therapies include the influence of one person on another. It is perhaps the explicit manner in which behaviour therapists set out both the goals and the methods of their therapies that is responsible in part for the hostility which has been expressed, particularly by those raised in the tradition of liberal humanism and so outraged in the twentieth century by the totalitarian cruelties of Right and Left. In contrast, the psychotherapies appear to be trying to 'bring out' what is 'potential' within the person, rather than to train him in new behaviours or change old ones. Behaviourists would assert that the changes brought about by all psychological treatments are explicable within one set of principles, namely behavioural principles. Bandura (1969) has argued this case very forcefully. It follows that *all* therapeutic approaches raise the ethical, legal and social questions to be considered in this chapter. We shall discuss them as they apply to the behaviour therapies; a client-centred therapist or a Freudian psychotherapist could do so with equal appositeness within the context of their own approaches.

The crucial questions for this chapter concern not what is *true* about the methods and the goals of therapies and the problems of behaviour to which they are applied, but what is thought *desirable* by therapists, by clients and by others in society. We shall consider questions both of ethics and of law, as well as of the increasingly important role played by quasi-political pressure groups.

'Ethical', as defined by *The Concise Oxford Dictionary* (Fowler and Fowler, 1951), means 'relating to morals, treating of moral questions (p. 408)'. *The American Heritage Dictionary* (Morris, 1969) is more expansive, defining ethics as 'the study of the nature of morals and of the specific moral choices to be made by the individual in relation with others ... the rules or standards governing the conduct of the profession (p. 450)'. This definition is particularly apt for a discussion concerning the desirable means and ends of behaviour therapy, as is one of the definitions of 'value' given by the same source: 'A principle, standard, or quality considered worthwhile or desirable (p. 1415)'. There are three aspects of the ethical question posed to himself by a therapist: *what* conduct does he consider desirable, *for whom* and under *what circumstances?* Krasner and Ullmann (1973) point out that terms like 'desirable' and 'good' are readily translatable into the behaviour therapist's 'positive reinforcers'. The problem, of course, is that what is 'good' to one person may be 'bad' to another, and the heart of the question, as we shall see, is: 'Who is empowered (and by whom) first to decide what is good and second to act so as to achieve it?'.

Krasner and Ullmann (1973) are optimistic both that there is wide agreement as to what are 'desirable behaviours to design into an ongoing society (p. 488)', citing as examples altruism, generosity and cooperation, and that such behaviours can be deliberately enhanced by the appropriate training procedures. The latter part of their assertion may be much more correct than the former. For example, the acquisition, maintenance and performance of altruistic (helping) behaviours have been shown to be responsive to the same environmental causes and consequences which govern behaviours in general (Feldman, 1976). However, there are obvious wide disagreements, both within and between societies, concerning which behaviours are desirable. In Western society, some support the ownership of industry by the State, others oppose it, in both cases on *ideological* (i.e. on value-laden) grounds, partially irrespective of the practical merits of the case. Citizens of the liberal democracies, exposed to one set of training experiences, tend to place the goals of the individual before those of the State; the reverse is true of the Communist countries (it is a fact—unfortunate though this may be—that Solzhenitsyn and his fellow dissidents speak for only a section of Russian ópinion). Moving from the political to the personal, abolitionists regard laws limiting access to alcohol as desirable, social drinkers as undesirable; similar differences of opinion concerning what is 'good' can be found in the areas of gambling, sexual behaviour, drug-taking, educational methods ('progressive' versus 'formal'), and in many other contexts. The present discussion can only set out the questions which comprise the debate concerning desirable ends and means as they affect therapists and others, and provide examples of treatment methods and problems in which such questions have arisen, or are likely to do so. I have interpolated a number of personal assertions, indicating them as such.

Anyone attempting to set up ethical guidelines for the practice of the psychological therapies will receive scant assistance from the methods and findings of the scientific investigation of behaviour which have been drawn on for the remainder of this book. As Krasner and Ullmann (1973) state: 'There is no way in the realm of logic or social science to define 'good' absolutely. Our concepts of good are tied to specific instances and are not abstractions (p. 491)'. It is certainly possible to determine that one treatment is more effective than another, but we will only carry out such a comparative investigation if we have already made the value decision that 'effectiveness' is an important criterion for selecting one method over another. Moreover, in order to carry out such a study we have to select as 'good' certain outcomes rather than others as satisfactory measures of 'effectiveness'. The scientific method is employed *after* value decisions have been made.

The question then arises: 'What is the source of "moral choices"?' Some people would argue that man is 'naturally' good and only needs appropriate conditions for that 'good' to flower, others that man is 'naturally' evil and can avoid evil-doing only by much suffering, self-denial and constant vigilance. The behaviourist approach to psychology states essentially that either 'good' *or* 'bad' behaviours may be acquired, maintained and performed, according to the experiences to which an individual is exposed, either directly or vicariously, and according to the consequences of those experiences. A biologically oriented psychologist would add that biologically based predispositions might interact with learning experiences, but most 'environmentalists' and 'biologists' would agree that behaviour is accountable for entirely in terms of heredity or environment, or an interaction between the two. This applies to 'ethics' and 'values' as it does to any other behaviours. Ethical and value statements are simply behaviours, albeit in the form of abstract, verbal statements. Nevertheless, they arise from the same sources as other behaviours and are responsive to the same influences for potential change. Moreover, although they are abstract, they essentially refer to concrete objective operations. As Krasner and Ullmann (1973) state: 'The descriptive and emotive meanings of words are essentially acquired reinforcing stimuli. The psychological study of good (in the philosophical usage of the word) is the study of reinforcing stimuli (p. 492).' For example, at any one point in time, some people will subscribe to the value, 'capital punishment for murder is wrong'. If there then occurs a particularly unpleasant series of murders, it is safe to assert that a proportion of those previously opposed to capital punishment will change their view, particularly those in the closest proximity to the murders. A great many other instances could be quoted to support the case that moral beliefs are relative to the persons and situations concerned, and are not absolute and unchanging. It is likely that those living in a particular place, at a particular time, with a common history of learning experiences concerning the desirability or otherwise of particular behaviours, will share a common set of values, which will differ from those held by persons living in a different setting or with a different learning history. It is for this reason that moral exhortations—for example to 'good behaviour'—will fall on deaf ears unless the audience to which they are addressed has already effectively been trained in those behaviours, in which case the exhortation will operate as a cue for their performance. As Berkowitz (1973) puts it, in the context of a review of helping behaviour: 'If we want greater helpfulness we probably have to teach people that this is desirable behaviour, have them rehearse this action, and reward them when they do assist others (p. 316).'

Two conclusions follow from the above argument. First, any ethical framework within which is discussed the relationship between behaviour therapy and society is personal to the writer. Second, it is not susceptible to one of the crucial features of the scientific method, namely falsifiability by empirical test and its appeal, therefore, is *persuasive* and *emotional*, i.e. subjective rather than objective. Those who have both a common learning history and the same current group membership as the author of the framework will be more likely to find it acceptable than those who share only one or neither. To some extent, the degree of acceptance of the ways in which the framework is applied to particular problems will depend on the vigour and logical consistency of that application, but the basic axioms of the framework, the central summary statements from which actions flow, will be accepted or rejected according to whether or not they accord with the existing beliefs of the audience. Krasner and Ullmann (1973) point out: 'The only unique conceptualisation of 'good' which we have as social scientists is the *description* and *understanding of* things as they are. The value of truth or accurate observation is accepted because it makes science possible (p. 497).' Insofar as behaviour therapy is the application of methods and findings arrived at by the use of the scientific method, it seems logical to expect behaviour therapists to accept as given 'goods' the desirability of grounding their clinical practice largely, if not entirely, on empirical evidence concerning the efficacy and efficiency of competing methods of treatment. However, as behaviour therapists are not immune from the influences of other sets of values, it would be no surprise if their clinical behaviours were not, in part, influenced by such extrascientific considerations as avoiding therapeutic failures (see Chapter 8), as well as the social and political acceptability of both methods and therapeutic objectives (goals). In the remainder of this chapter, we review the major considerations which will affect the behaviours in clinical settings of therapists and clients, both 'scientific' and otherwise, and then apply them to a number of specific problem behaviours.

A FRAMEWORK FOR THE PRACTICE OF BEHAVIOUR THERAPY

The interested parties

Decisions concerning therapeutic issues always involve at least two interested parties: the person carrying out the treatment procedure and the recipient of the procedure, usually termed the therapist and the client (or patient) respectively. In addition, other parties may be involved, including the family or legal guardian of the client, his friends and his employers, the institution employing or hiring the therapist, as well as political and other pressure groups, the law courts, and local and central government.

1. Therapists

Therapists vary widely in their training, in the extent and breadth of their professional experience and in their views concerning the nature and relative importance of the issues affecting therapeutic aims and methods, both in general and in particular instances. It is a truism that behaviour is an interaction of previous experiences and their outcome and the current situation. Consider the cases of two hypothetical therapists currently working in Britain. Therapist A is aged 27, has a very good Bachelor's degree in Psychology from a rigorously behaviourist undergraduate department, and a Master's degree from an equally behaviourist training programme in clinical psychology, entry into which was highly competititive. (At the present time, British training in clinical psychology is to the Master's level.) He has since worked in a large National Health Service (N.H.S.) department of clinical psychology, practising behavioural methods of treatment with clients for whom the department has de facto responsibility, and with little or no demand for assessment of behaviour as an end in itself. His academic and clinical training and experience have emphasized empiricism and the cost-benefit approach to decision-taking. He is also a child of his time in that his undergraduate days included exposure to the student movements of the late 1960s, which reinforced previously held socialist views originally modelled by his father, an active trade unionist. He is an atheist and wears casual, rather than formal, clothes. Therapist B is aged 45. He also obtained a (mediocre) Bachelor's degree in Psychology, but in a department which was psychodynamically oriented and mentioned behaviourist psychology only in passing and in the context of animal behaviour. His clinical training was through the in-service route, for entry into which he had little competition, and was spent entirely in a setting which stressed both psychodynamic psychology and the role of the clinical psychologist as an assessor of personality—using projective instruments—and subordinate to a psychiatrist's control. More recently, he has added therapeutic responsibilities, his preferred methods of treatment being individual and group psychotherapy. His social background was middleclass and in his political and religious values he is conservative, Christian, believing in 'free will' and accepting hierarchical structures. He is inclined to defer to medical colleagues and to believe in a set of absolute, as opposed to relative, values.

These are far from idealized and extreme examples. They illustrate, and far from exhaust, the range of influences to which therapists are exposed prior to a particular encounter with a particular client. For example, therapists differ from each other in their previous experiences of clients and in their broad attitudes to clients, which range from seeing them as the major focus of their life activities to unwelcome intrusions into research, teaching, committee work, or even golf. As argued in Chapter 8, therapists tend to hope for successful outcomes of treatment, are distressed by failure and may behave so as to minimize their own distress, possibly at the expense of clients' access to effective help.

410

2. Clients

Therapists vary widely, despite the common factors of undergraduate and postgraduate training and professional practice. It follows that clients differ even more widely—in sex, occupation, age, religious and political affiliations, and so on. Their problems range in nature over the full gamut of human behaviours and in severity from the trivial to the totally incapacitating. Attitudes to therapists will vary from total belief to near complete scepticism, depending upon previous direct or vicarious experiences with therapists and the outcome of those experiences.

3. The family and other persons significant to the client

The extent to which family, friends, etc., are interested parties depends on the age of the client, the degree to which he is 'legally responsible' and the nature of the problem. A particularly salient example is the young child whose behaviour is complained of by his parents; the therapist is then the agent of the parents in bringing about changes in the behaviour of the child—although in order to so so he may have to change the behaviour of the parents. In this case, parents are very much interested parties, as are the partners of persons complaining of sexual dysfunction, the families of those carrying out obsessional rituals in which other family members participate and the families of alcoholics. It is difficult to suggest examples of problems experienced by those living in family settings which have absolutely no effect on the other members of the family, so the family members will usually be interested parties in the cases of all those who live with other persons. At the other extreme are persons who live alone, interacting, at best, only with uncaring acquaintances.

4. The institution

The *raisons d'être* of institutions vary from custodial care of patients—at best, training them in skills relevant to the continued life within the institution—to the goal of effective preparation for a full life 'outside'. It follows that the requirements imposed on therapists and the expectations held out to inmates and their families will also vary. The reputation of institutions becomes known and partially determines which therapists will seek employment in a particular setting—those who are treatment-oriented may either avoid 'custodial' institutions or see it as a challenge to change the orientation of such an institution.

5. The legal authority

The courts and other legal agencies are interested parties in several contexts: decisions as to the disposal of an offender may be based partially on psychological evidence and on the appropriateness and availability of treatment; such a course of treatment may be made a condition of a probation order or part of a custodial sentence; and the legal machinery is involved in the commitment to institutions of persons deemed in need of such care. The courts might also be appealed to by inmates of institutions to protect their rights—e.g. not to be exposed to a particular treatment or, conversely, to be given access to a treatment which might lead to their discharge. Whether or not psychologists become parties to legal requirements for treatment of offenders and others referred by society is a key ethical question, as is that of the extent to which civil rights considerations mesh or conflict with considerations of therapeutic efficacy and efficiency. In addition, all therapists, being also citizens, are subject to the same laws of the land as any other citizen. Such laws may well place constraints both on the goals of treatment and on the methods used.

6. *Professional organizations*

It is a feature of professional organizations that they lay down rules as to which professional behaviours are acceptable and which are not. Typically, a standing committee administers the set of requirements and regulates professional behaviours by imposing sanctions, up to expulsion from the profession, on those judged to have contravened the rules of professional conduct. Thus, in addition to legal constraints on the professional behaviour of therapists, there are also professional constraints. (It is assumed that the currently notional professional restraints on British clinical psychologists will acquire 'teeth' when the profession is registered—as in the United States.)

7. *Political and other pressure groups*

A number of groups have as their major purpose the protection of the interests of patients in general; some seek to protect the civil rights of prisoners and others who have been committed to institutions for custody, treatment or care. Such groups might be opposed to certain forms of treatment—e.g. those token economies which make the receipt of basic reinforcers contingent on the performance of particular behaviours, or to the application of treatment to non-consenting clients, for example, offenders. In addition, there are political pressure groups designed to advance particular causes in society in general. For example, Gay Liberation Front and other homophile organizations seek to advance the civil and legal status of homosexual persons and the Festival of Light is concerned to promote a particular view of sexual conduct and of sexually arousing material. The former is strongly opposed to therapists offering to homosexuals the possibility of a change of sexual preference; the latter could be expected to oppose the use of surrogates in the treatment of sexual dysfunction.

The above list of interested parties is not exhaustive. For example, therapists are influenced by informal social pressures—from friends and family—as well as by formal professional and political pressures. But it serves to illustrate that it is unduly restrictive to conceive of therapeutic practice being influenced only by the reciprocal effects of the most immediate participants—therapist and client. Therapists are under the influence of their professional training and experience and their non-professional life experiences, their current 'world-view', the particular client and his problem, previous experiences of clients and problems perceived as similar and of clients in general, the general and specific (to that client) requirements of his employing authority, the views of the client's family and friends and of his professional colleagues, the possibility of publication in professional journals of the particular case or cases, his current financial status (in the case of therapists in private practice), whether or not a particular problem has attracted the attention of a pressure group and the salience of that group, the degree of legal involvement (e.g. court referral), his professional code of practice, possibly even the communicated views of his family and friends. Similarly, clients are influenced by their problem (nature and severity), their previous experience with therapists and allied professions, their expectations as to the outcome modelled by significant others, their family and friends, sometimes by legal constraints or pressure groups, and in all cases by their perception of the therapist as determined by both his verbal and non-verbal behaviour. Further, other interested parties are influenced by specific therapists and by clients and are subject to changes due to broad social movements. For example, it is difficult to envisage that in the 1930s the use of sexual surrogates could have been contemplated, let alone discussed, as a serious possibility. The key point is that the interested parties are numerous, the content of their influence shifting and their lines of influence reciprocal and interacting.

The issues

This section is written largely from the standpoint of therapists, to whom this book is mainly addressed, but it is important to note the above discussion concerning the manifold nature of interested parties and the reciprocal nature of their interests. We shall consider the issues involved in therapeutic interventions under three headings: the problem, the goal and the method.

The problem

Behaviour therapists face, as do therapists in general, three questions each time they are confronted with a client: 'What is the problem?', 'What (if anything) should I do about it?' and 'What method should I use?'. The second and third of these questions are concerned respectively with ends and with means, and enter into most human activities. The engineer building a railway line and encountering a ravine has, as his end, spanning the ravine, and then has to decide on the most effective way of doing so, consistent with the minimum possible cost. The mother, faced with a child who says that he is hungry, has as her end satisfying that hunger, and has to choose between different foods, again consistent with the minimum possible cost. But in both cases the problem is not in doubt; for the engineer it is to span the ravine, for the mother it is to feed her child. However, both engineers and mothers are faced with situations in which the problems are less clear-cut. For example, the cry of a very young baby, who has not yet acquired language, may indicate hunger, physical pain or a request for social reinforcement. In time, the mother may learn to interpret between different types of crying—so answering the question 'What is the problem?'.

In the context of psychological problems a major emphasis has been placed by the psychodynamic tradition on the assertion that the problem may be quite different from what the patient reports, possibly because the real problem is too painful and so has been 'repressed' into the unconscious. For example, a patient at a case conference complained of a fear of open spaces. She had been administered the Wechsler adult intelligence scale and failed on the Similarities subtest item concerning the similarity of an egg and a seed. This was interpreted as indicating unresolved sexual problems. A similar interpretation was placed by another psychologist on her Rorschach responses and by a psychiatrist on her answers in a clinical interview. The conclusion was that the real problem was her childhood sexual feelings for her father, which she had repressed, and would need lengthy psychotherapy to resolve effectively. Those presenting the case were very proud of the fact that the three sources of evidence were independent of each other yet led to a similar conclusion. An alternative explanation was that all three clinicians shared the same general hypothesis that a fear of open spaces masks unresolved sexual feelings for the opposite sex parent. Behaviour therapists would be likely to accept the presenting complaint at face value, at least as a starting point, and to ask detailed questions concerning the relevant situational variables associated with avoidance of open spaces, as well as carrying out actual observations. Most probably the problem would, indeed, be found to relate to open spaces.

A more complicated situation arises when one has to ask not only 'What is the problem?' but also 'Who has the problem?'. For example, a parent or teacher complains of the behaviour of a child, with the clear implication that the 'problem' resides in the child, who should be 'treated'. On careful examination, however, it might become apparent that the 'problem' is concerned with the behaviours of the adult, and it is these that require modifying to effect a change in the behaviour of the child. In this case, the question concerns the *locus* of the problem, in the individual complained of or in significant others. The choice may be between the individual and his total life situation. In severely socially deprived areas, the only behaviours available to achieve valued reinforcers may be those classified as illegal. Should a change agent tackle the individual or the situation in which he lives?

We can change the form of the question and ask: '*Is* there a problem?'. A particularly salient contemporary example is that of homosexual behaviour. Is the therapist to accept the client's statement that he is homosexual in his current sexual preference and would rather be heterosexual, and proceed to assist this change to occur? Alternatively, is he to suggest to the client that his 'problem' is of society's making, and need not be viewed as such? In the latter event, the client is encouraged to believe that if there is a problem, it is one of learning how to adapt, without anxiety, to his homosexual role. The answers to such questions as 'Is there a problem?' and 'If so, is it to do with the individual, with particular others, or with his total life situation?' will depend on who asks the question, of whom, and what weight is assigned to the sources of their answers.

The goal

Having decided that there is a problem and described its salient features, the therapist then has to make a number of decisions as to how to proceed. The first of these concerns an appraisal of the existing behavioural repertoire of the client, which behaviours are to be maintained at their present level, which enhanced, which diminished, and which are absent, but desirable, so that new behaviours have to be added. The subjective question here concerns what attributes result in the behaviour being labelled worthy of maintenance, of change or of incorporation. That is, what attributes label a current or an alternative behaviour as 'bad' or 'good'? For some problem areas, there may be only one alternative to present behaviours, or, if there are several, one that stands out as clearly preferable. An example is that of a client who avoids situations in which he has a clear view of a steep drop. Unfortunately, the client's job as a managing clerk of a London firm of lawyers takes him daily into such situations. London Law Courts contain many steep stairwells, and it is very difficult, if not impossible, to avoid looking down. His distress is such that some action has to be taken. The alternatives open are to change the nature of his work within the firm, to seek other employment or to overcome the problem of avoidance of a specific situation. As the first two alternatives involve both loss of income and the acquisition of new skills, they are clearly less attractive than the third, *provided* that the goal of substituting approach for avoidance behaviour is technically attainable, i.e. if an effective method is available. We discuss below criteria, including those of efficacy and efficiency, relevant to methods of treatment.

But the question is a good deal less straightforward when a current behaviour labelled as worthy of change might be replaced by a number of equally preferable alternatives. For a male client whose current sexual preference is for pre-adolescent boys, with whom he carries out overt sexual activities, and who is in danger of suffering legal penalties, there are a number of alternatives open:

(1) To maintain his present preference, practising overtly with the same partner, with the same degree of risk.

(2) To maintain it, but to select his partners so as to minimize the risk of legal sanctions as much as possible.

(3) To maintain it but to restrict his overt sexual activities to self-masturbation (it is assumed that some sexual outlet is necessary).

(4) To change his preference to males of legal age (currently, over 21).

(5) To change his preference to females of legal age (currently, over 16).

The remaining choice—to change his preference to females under 16—while logically conceivable, is hardly likely to be considered seriously; the legal restrictions remain, so that there are no compensatory benefits to outweigh the difficulties of changing his sexual preference. It is likely that each of the five above possibilities will be attractive to some clients and some therapists (although the first seems *a priori* not to commend itself to therapists with a preference for a mode of intervention more active than simple support).

It is unlikely that all therapists will find equally desirable or possible all goals sought by all clients. There are at least seven constraints possible on such an inclusive acceptance. First, therapists are unlikely to work for goals which may have unfavourable legal consequences, whether criminal or civil, for themselves. Second, they may be equally reluctant to pursue objectives which contravene the ethical code of their profession. Third, therapists, like people in general, are likely to have formed personal evaluations of the various possible goals of therapy and may be inclined to persuade clients of the merits of goals they themselves evaluate highly, and vice versa. It is probably impossible for therapists to be neutral, but it would be desirable for them not to clothe their partiality in false garb. For example, doctors opposed to abortion on demand might be more likely to supply those seeking abortion with 'scientific' arguments concerning the risks, than those in favour of abortion on demand. Closer to home, therapist X may find distasteful the goal of training the unmarried in sexual skills; therapist Y does not. How is X to respond to the request for help of a client who is sexually dysfunctional with his occasional partners? He can (a) refuse help of the kind involved in the direct training of sexual skills, (b) try to persuade the client of the merit of an alternative goal, (c) refer him to therapist Y, who will help the client to achieve the goal that he seeks, or, finally, (d) therapist X could carry this out himself. The first two alternatives place the therapist before the client; the last gives the therapist no 'rights'. On balance, the third is the most desirable—the client has access to the goal he seeks and the therapist avoids personal participation in what he finds distasteful.

Fourth among the influences on the therapist are those exerted by political and other pressure groups. Twenty years ago many therapists would have listed only one goal of therapy for homosexuals seeking help, namely a change to a heterosexual orientation. Legal changes and the activities of homophile organizations have resulted in the addition of an alternative many would rank equally high, if not higher, namely becoming more content with and more skilled in the homosexual role. Alcoholics Anonymous are very clear that the only desirable goal of treatment for an alcoholic is complete abstention and are vehemently opposed to a conceivable alternative, namely that of controlled 'social' drinking. Fifth, therapists employed by an institution, or other organization, are potentially under the constraint of their employing institution, for reasons either of wider (e.g. national) policy or because their activities, whether general or specific, are perceived by other (and powerful) professional groups in the same institution as threatening. Thus, it is possible to be too successful. (See Cerber, 1972, for a cautionary tale of the reaction of entrenched opinion in one institution to attempts at innovation—the replacement of therapeutic for custodial goals.) Sixth, constraint is provided by the families and friends of clients. A goal attractive to the client himself may produce consequences perceived as undesirable by significant others.

Finally, some goals may be quite simply unattainable, either in the present state of knowledge or within the constraints of the available finance. Looking over the above seven constraints, it would be reasonable to conclude that 'clinical freedom', although fought hard for by doctors, is a mirage, as those interested in treating clients of interest to external pressure groups, such as alcoholics, very quickly become aware. It would be a distortion of the situation to suggest that one or more of the above constraints will operate in every case, but they are likely to do so with sufficient frequency to make their analysis a useful part of the 'case history'.

The method

Having established whether or not there is a problem and, if so, its nature and the goals of treatment, the therapist next has to consider how to achieve these goals. Typically, several methods are conceivable. What considerations will influence the selection of the method actually used?

1. Efficacy. Eysenck (1952) uncompromisingly asserted that efficacy in achieving a stated outcome was a major criterion in the choice of a therapeutic method and that on the available evidence the psychodynamic therapies appeared to produce an outcome little different from the base rate of improvement without treatment. The notion that empirically demonstrated efficacy is of major importance in selecting the method of treatment for problems of behaviour is now accepted more widely than in the early 1950s, but there is still substantial support in favour of 'experiential' rather than empirical evidence. It is probably fair to assert that, while the majority of behaviour therapists would, in principle, favour empirical tests of efficacy, the psychodynamic camp is more evenly divided. The argument that demonstrated efficacy is a key factor in the selection of method is at first sight a scientific one, but is, in fact, an ethical consideration (i.e. relating to what is held to be 'good'). Persons seeking help are as much entitled to the most effective available help as those buying any product are entitled to honesty in the results claimed for it (e.g. that a particular baby food does, indeed, contain all the food value necessary for normal growth). An alternative view is that efficacy is not measurable and that therapeutic experiences are simply experiences, valuable in and of themselves.

2. *Efficiency.* Although it is obvious that methods of behaviour change differ in the time taken to proceed from entry into treatment to a specified outcome, the importance of this variable appears to be discussed rather rarely. Yet it is of major consequence; if, for example, method A achieves a given outcome in 10 hours of therapist time, while method B achieves it in 100 hours, it follows that ten patients can be helped by method A, and to the same extent, in the time taken by method B to help one patient. If keeping psychologists in gainful employment is the major criterion for selecting a treatment method, then method B will be preferred; if it is helping the maximum possible number of clients per unit of economic cost, then A will be preferred. There are other considerations also, principally the fact that the demands on public and on private purses typically exceed the depth of both; other personal care services, as well as many alternative forms of expenditure, are in constant competition. There is an increasing tendency for cost-benefit analyses to be applied to many areas of public and private life, from 'best-buys' in public housing to 'best-buys' in can-openers and margarines. This is surely a wholly desirable tendency.

3. *The client.* Bandura (1969) has suggested a division of priority in the primacy of therapist and client—the latter selects the goals of treatment, the former uses his greater technical expertise to select the most appropriate method for achieving that goal. Many therapists would agree with such a division, but just as there is a case, as argued earlier, for allowing therapists to decline to assist a client to achieve a goal personally distasteful to the therapist, or which is legally or professionally proscribed, so there is a case for allowing clients to reject a particular method, even if it is both more effective and efficient than an available alternative. The point, once again, is that both parties, client and therapist, should *agree* as to the problem, to the goals and to the methods. If they disagree, discussion will either continue until a mutually satisfactory resolution is reached or the client withdraws and seeks an alternative therapist. This apparently simple statement conceals considerable difficulties, as we shall see when we consider the concept of 'informed consent'.

4. *The therapist.* Just as certain goals may be evaluated unfavourably by therapists, so also may certain methods, even given that they are both the most effective and efficient available. An obvious example is the employment of an aversive stimulus, such as electrical stimulation, to alter behaviour; another is the use of surrogates to assist in the treatment of sexual dysfunction.

5. *Other interested parties.* Legal authorities, political groups, families and friends may all seek to proscribe or prescribe particular methods, or would

do so given the opportunity. As we shall see, the legal authorities in the U.S.A. have acted to impose limitations on the token economy as a method of rehabilitating institutional patients. Interested pressure groups have urged that certain penal methods, such as imprisonment, should be replaced by non-institutional approaches. Conversely, it is not unknown for families or friends to urge that a client should be treated as an inpatient because of their own inability to maintain him in the home environment.

There will be complex interactions between two or more of the above influences on the method used. Other factors being equal, when one method is both more effective and more efficient than another the more effective is preferred, if the two are equally effective the more efficient is preferred, or if both are equally efficient the more effective is the method of choice. But what is the outcome when one is more efficient, the other more effective? Perhaps most pertinent of all is to ask if therapists do indeed seek the cost-benefit information relevant to such decisions and even if it exists at all. Some would urge that not only does the information not exist but it is not obtainable and it is good that this should be so. My own contentions are (a) that the relevant information is usually measurable and (b) that to attempt such a measurement is not only desirable but mandatory on all who attempt to relieve the distress of others, irrespective of whether or not they are paid for doing so, or, if paid, are in the public or in the private sectors of the health industry.

We have noted that certain therapists may find particular goals unacceptable and have urged that they resolve their dilemma by referring the client to a therapist known to be prepared to seek those goals. A similar course of action is desirable for a therapist who finds a particular method emotionally unacceptable, whatever the evidence on effectiveness and efficiency. Similar negative evaluations affecting efficient and effective methods may be held by other interested parties. It is urged that the overriding consideration should be the right of the client to seek his preferred goal, by the most effective and efficient available method which he finds emotionally acceptable.

Therapists are likely to be deterred by legal and professional constraints which promise damage to themselves for a particular course of therapeutic action. They may be sensitive enough to be deterred by public criticism levelled from a particular pressure group. Would they also be deterred from a method which, though beneficial to the client, would be deleterious to a third party, namely family and/or friends? The issues of who benefits and who loses are central to the ethical problems surrounding therapies and therapists, and we shall discuss them in more detail later. At the moment, it is asserted that the interests of the client should be paramount over those of pressure groups opposed to a method acceptable both to the client and to the therapist. Whether or not they are in practice depends on the political weight of the pressure group, the outcomes of the therapist's previous experiences of such attempts at influence and the extent to which the particular goal is attainable by alternative methods which are reasonably near to the proscribed one in efficacy and efficiency.

What is a therapist to do if no currently available method is more effective than no treatment at all? On the efficiency criterion he ought to prefer not to offer any treatment. However, his response to the particular client will take several forms, depending upon such factors as his subjective perception of the client's distress. For example, an extremely distressed client may be given non-specific 'support' rather than be turned away. A succession of such experiences may result in the therapist carrying out research to find a method which promises to be more effective. Alternatively, he may assist in a system of custodial care which does no more than keep the problem from public attention—'out of sight, out of mind'.

Prescriptions for behaviour therapists: Goldiamond

Goldiamond (1974) has written a lengthy homily to behaviour therapists, which sets out both a general framework for therapist behaviours, in terms of goals and methods, and a detailed account of the procedures to assist their attainment. He sees the American Constitution, a contract between a government and a nation, as a paradigm for the contract between a therapist and a patient. The Constitution is an example not only of a contract but of a programme, binding on both parties, and of the steps taken to achieve it. The parallel is thus with programmed instruction. The Constitution specifies *targets*, *current repertoires*, the *steps* from the latter to the former and the *consequences* contingent on such steps. To most Americans, their Constitution is not only an object of admiration but is *the* system of social ideals, the yardstick against which specific actions are compared and found acceptable or not. Thus if Goldiamond's analogy is found persuasive by his (American) audience and if he succeeds in constructing a role for behaviour therapists which appears to accord with the objectives of the Constitution, then behaviour therapy is likely to be regarded very much more favourably by Americans than at present. According to Goldiamond, the Constitution has a constructional orientation. It seeks to build what is desirable, rather than merely to specify what is undesirable.

He seeks a similar emphasis on construction for behaviour therapy; a *constructional* orientation is one which solves problems by constructing appropriate repertoires (or reinstating or transferring them), rather than by eliminating inappropriate ones. The focus is on building; thus a constructional orientation is contrasted with a *pathological* one which stresses the elimination of repertoires. Goldiamond argues that the constructional-pathological dichotomy cuts across models of approaches to explanation and treatment (e.g. the 'medical model' is not necessarily pathological) and that all approaches may contain either orientation or both.

The constructional model includes the following: contracts with patients concerning outcomes and procedures judged mutually worthwhile (termed 'goals' and 'methods', respectively, above) and areas of concern (termed 'problems' above) and their limits. The contract is between therapist and client; the latter is a directly interested participant, not a third party. Goldiamond views the therapist 'not as a reinforcement machine, but as a programme consultant, namely as a teacher or guide who tries to be explicit (p. 24)'. It helps the therapist to serve as a teacher if he can find out 'what the patient is after. ... In most cases this is readily evident—if one asks the right question or observes appropriately (p. 30)'. Goldiamond gives detailed instructions for clinical procedures, particularly emphasizing the contract, which is based on the 'write-up' (the detailed descriptive data concerning the client, his problem, etc.). The write-up 'suggests to the therapist the goals he can offer'. However, 'The patient may have other ideas ... negotiation ensues ... eventually a contract will be developed (p. 33).' The contract lists goals and such issues as renegotiations. As discussed, the therapist's conception of what is illegal or objectively undesirable affects the goals and methods he will offer. Goldiamond agrees with this. But the matter is more complex still. *Both* client and therapist must be consenting parties. A great deal turns on the term 'consenting'. A critical comment, which will be developed further below, is that the behaviours involved in 'contracting' and 'consenting' are as responsive to external sources of influence as are behaviours in general. Moreover, there will be many therapist–client pairings in which the two are not equally powerful. Who will then 'give way'? We must expect it to be the less powerful one—in most cases, the client. Thus, 'negotiation' is likely to result in a contract closer to the original position of the therapist than to that of the client. Goldiamond relates an anecdote which throws some light on how he might construe and resolve the situation in which the goals of therapist and client are at some odds. The case was that of a spider-phobic female undergraduate who for two years had had weekly meetings with successively more senior university staff until she was finally referred to Goldiamond himself. He regarded her 'problem' as an operant shaped by male attention. So effective was this as to 'preclude the shaping of other ways of a maid with a man—her own peers (p. 34)', a goal Goldiamond states as preferable. 'After discussion, this outcome was agreed upon, and she was assigned a graduate student therapist—female (p. 34).' This resolution is characterized by Goldiamond as 'successful negotiation'. A politically oriented and perhaps unkind observer might draw a comparison with 'negotiation' between a major power and a minor one, which ends with the latter ceding territory.

Goldiamond then moves to another key issue, namely 'who is the client of the change agent?'; cast into another form, 'who are the contracting parties?' He asserts that they are the change agent and the party subject to change. For example, if parents are concerned about their child, 'the contract is with them to change *their* repertoires so they can improve relations with their child (p. 44)'. Goldiamond continues: 'I do not contract with them to change their child's behaviour. If we do see the child, we contract with him separately

(p. 44).' Similarly, 'if an institution is concerned about its inmates, the contract should concern change in *institutional* behaviour (p. 44)' (Goldiamond's italics in each case). In both instances, a change agent contracts in addition with the child or with inmates. Two points are left unanswered. The first arises when it is not necessary to see the child/inmate for the change in parental/ institutional repertoire to occur. No 'consent' is needed, so none is sought! Nevertheless, there may be consequences for the child/inmate. Surely the consent of the person affected by a change in the behaviour of another is relevant, whether or not his presence is actually required in order to bring about that effect. The second arises if it *is* necessary to see the child/inmate; the changes in their behaviour which would result from a change in the repertoire of parents/institution are unwelcome, and consent is withheld. Should the change agent then decline to act? Goldiamond (see above) glosses over the problem by the phrase 'so they can improve their relations with their child'. The perceptions of parents/institutions about what is 'good' for children/ inmates may well not be contiguous with those of children/inmates. We are back with the problem of potential consent and its converse—coercion, a problem which arises with particular force in institutional or parent–child contexts but which exists in all situations involving a therapist and a client. Goldiamond's summary statement is as follows: 'I believe that the same rules which apply outside institutions also apply within their walls: consent obtained under duress, or in the absence of relevant information, is not consent (p. 58).' He then refers the reader to a quotation, given earlier in his paper, which bears very strongly on the terms 'duress' and 'relevant'. According to Stahlman, a professor of paediatrics: 'I can persuade 99 per cent. of my patients to my way of thinking if I really work at it, even if I am 100 per cent. wrong. ... I think informed consent is an absolute farce legalistically, morally, ethically— any point of view you want to talk about. The information is what I want it to be (Stahlman, 1973, p. 66, cited by Goldiamond, 1974, p. 13).' The last sentence in the above quotation is crucial. It highlights the key issue. Decisions as to goals and methods are based on the sum total of available factual information, and on the components of persuasive communication reviewed in Chapter 8. The greater the proportion of information conveyed by the particular clinician and the more effectively he manipulates the relevant components of persuasion, the more he is likely to move a patient to the position he, the clinician, holds. There has been no obvious violation of 'informed consent', simply the presentation of information by a skilled communicator. Manifestly, not only is consent manipulable but the manipulation may be accompanied by a statement by the patient that he has arrived at the decision voluntarily and without coercion. What counts is who is empowered to present the information, what information is presented and how it is presented. It is concluded that Goldiamond's statement of ethical principles concerning consent, given above, is no solution to the problem of ensuring freedom from manipulation of the client by other interested parties—by the clinician or others working through the clinician—whose goals may be different from those of the client.

The same criticism applies to Goldiamond's extension of his 'consent' principle to the actual content of treatment and the contingencies which control treatment. Referring to treatment programmes within institutional contexts he asserts that it is coercive to deprive the patients of what is available in order to use it as a reinforcer (a frequent feature of token economies in institutions—see below). Instead, he advocates the delivery or non-delivery of consequences which arise from the particular programme, rather than from the overall life of the institution, and for which the patient has contracted. But, as we have seen, 'contracting behaviour' is based on the information which led to 'consent', so that we return again to the issues of persuasive content and persuasive method, and the relative social powers of the source and the recipient. Goldiamond admits that there are indeed problems in presenting information, e.g. there are often several alternative outcomes, each of which is associated with a matrix of differentially weighted gains and losses. Hence, he states, it is desirable to present all the evidence. But one person's presentation of 'all' may not be another's, particularly when the source is an interested party. Perhaps this is the nub of the problem—how to protect clients' own preferred view of their problem, of the goals and of the methods of treatment from being overweighted by the views of other interested parties.

Prescriptions for therapists: an alternative view

Goldiamond's (1974) prescription for therapists, valuable though it is in setting out how to improve the efficacy and efficiency of therapeutic practice, fails to pay sufficient attention to one major basic problem and virtually ignores another which is even more fundamental. The former concerns the problem of bias in the presentation to clients and others of information relevant to the key issues of problems, goals and methods; the latter how to order the primacy of decision-taking by the interested parties about the key issues. In order to solve these two problems, we require some general statement as to what is 'desirable', i.e. what are the 'goods' and what the 'ills' in the social context in which therapy occurs. It has to be said immediately that total agreement is unlikely within any one society, let alone between societies. Instead of specifying the content of 'goods' and 'ills', we might restrict ourselves to the following statement which allows individuals and groups to supply their own content. Therapists should act so as (a) to increase the access of their clients to those consequences defined as positive by the client and (b) to remove consequences defined by clients as aversive. Ideally, *both* (a) and (b) should be goals for therapists, but if one is not possible, the other should still be sought. This statement means that it is the *client* who usually has the primacy of place in decisions concerning key issues. It is he who requires accurate and unbiased information relevant to the issues and it is 'goods' and 'ills' as *he* conceives them which represent the behavioural repertoires to be added, maintained or removed, respectively.

The key question then emerges: '*Who* is the client?'. One way to answer this is to seek the answer to another question: 'Who is currently suffering directly through the receipt of aversive consequences or (at least indirectly) through the absence of positive ones?'. The answer to the question names the potential client, who becomes the actual client when he approaches the therapist for assistance. The next questions are: 'What has to happen in order to deliver positive consequences to the client or remove negative ones from him?' and 'Who else is affected by what has to happen?'. If any other person is involved, he automatically becomes an interested party, with the same right to unbiased information as the complaining client. We can call the latter the initial and the former the consequential client. The 'other person' may be involved to the extent that the initial client's 'goods' can be met only by a change in the behaviour of the 'other person'. In this case he is *actively* involved; if the change in behaviour has to occur in the repertoire of the initial client but this has an effect on the life of the 'other person', then the latter is *passively* involved. The point that he *is* involved is more important than whether the involvement is active or passive. Then we have to ask: 'Are the same consequences considered positive and aversive, respectively, by both clients?'. In a more homely form: 'Do they agree on what is meat and what is poison?'. If they do, then the therapist should be in little doubt as to what is desired (its achievement in practice depends on the availability of effective methods, etc.). But suppose the clients differ. Who then has primacy? This is probably the most difficult question of all to answer. Let us take a concrete example, that of a person found guilty of sexual assault on a minor. The initial client is the court, acting on behalf of the victim, the parents of the victim and of society in general. The consequential client is the offender himself, whose behaviour might be the target of change procedures—hence he is positively involved. It is assumed that a therapist is prepared to make an attempt to change the behaviour of the offender concerned and it is known that a custodial sentence will leave the behaviour unchanged. Is it desirable that a custodial sentence remain among the choices open to the offender? It is possible that he will consider the prospect of no longer finding juveniles sexually arousing as more aversive than a spell in prison. The choice for him then would be between treatment and prison. (In the present state of the law and of public opinion a third possibility, i.e. no action, legally defined as 'unconditional discharge', is rarely open to him.) Is it desirable that he has a choice of treatment or prison, or should he be required to submit himself to treatment? In practice both may happen, i.e. treatment is given, but in a custodial setting, with custody for an indefinite period. However, following through the logic of the argument thus far, it would be desirable for there to be an independent agency ('court') to whom the offender could appeal, so that he could be allowed to serve a term in custody, but *without* any treatment. Essentially the court would be arbitrating between initial and consequential clients. It would also be desirable for it to monitor treatment and the conditions in which it is given, should treatment be directed. In a sense, such machinery already exists—the job of judging between competing plaintiffs in many areas of life is that of the civil courts—and the beginnings of an extension of this function to disagreements concerning psychological treatment have been made (see below in the discussion on long-stay patients in institutions), but a special, separate 'court of appeal' for questions relating to treatment is desirable. Who should have the status of plaintiff—i.e. who should have access to the courts in such instances? Plainly they should include therapists and initial and consequential clients, as well as victims or their representatives. Should political and other pressure groups, claiming to speak for particular groups of potential clients, also have access? The answer has to be in the positive, but the court will have to be very careful to ensure that it is the client's actual interests, not those of the pressure group, which are presented.

As a final look at the issue of primacy, we may ask: What should be the criteria by which the court should decide in cases of dispute between the interested parties?'. I consider that the court, like therapists, should adopt the principles set out earlier, which might be characterized as 'maximum benefit' and 'least harm', with pride of place going to those interested parties whose lives are most negatively affected by the problem behaviour concerned and who would most benefit from the absence of the problem. As a secondary criterion, both courts and therapists might set up the criterion of 'least consequential harm'. For example, if there are two competing therapeutic strategies, equal in every way in their effects on the recipients of therapy but with different consequential *negative* effects for other persons, then select the one which has the least negative effect.

A second kind of agency is also needed which would supply those affected (i.e. initial and consequential clients, etc.) with accurate factual information concerning such variables as efficacy, efficiency, the nature of the events which constitute treatment, and so on. Essentially, what is proposed is an extension to the context of psychological problems of 'consumerism', the movement which has led in Britain (there are parallel developments in the U.S.A.) to such organizations as the Consumers' Association, the publishers of *Which?*, and the Advisory Centre on Education (ACE), the publishers of *Where?*. Both advise on 'best-buys' in terms of *explicit criteria*. It is of interest that ACE is disinterested enough to advise on the private as well as on the public sector of education. The overriding criterion in 'consumerism' is the consumer's 'right to know' and to know with *accuracy*. Such accurate information is more likely to come from *disinterested* than from *interested* parties. Thus the particular therapist may well be biased; so may his professional organization. At the present time, such an independent agency does not exist. It is desirable that it be set up and staffed by those whose statutory responsibility is accuracy of information. Experts in therapy must obviously be involved, but they should disqualify themselves in particular instances involving their own work.

Two problems remain. The first is: 'How do we decide when an interested party can "speak for himself" and when his interests need to be represented by others?'. In extreme cases there is no problem: it is obvious that a university-educated adult, suffering neither from organic brain disease nor a functional psychosis and who is sexually aroused by minors can represent his own interests, whereas a deaf, blind, intellectually impaired child who mutilates himself, unless restrained, cannot do so. But what of the cases of an intelligent child of 11, who is described by parents or teachers as 'behaving badly', and of a long-stay inmate of an institution, whose 'florid symptoms' have long since disappeared but who is the mainstay of the institution's kitchen? Clearly, one of the functions of our 'court of appeal' will be to ensure that such 'in-between' persons are properly represented. Moreover, it is essential that court membership should include persons whose life experiences are close to those of the current plaintiff, or to which he could reasonably aspire given the means to do so. That is, persons who can ask themselves realistically: 'How would I feel if this were to happen to me, or if that were to be denied to me?'. What I have in mind is well illustrated by a quotation from Goldiamond (1974): 'In one English hospital I visited, involuntary commitments had dropped rapidly when they had to be justified before a board which included trades people, trade unionists, clergy and others in addition to professional staff (p. 64).' Our appeal court, then, should not consist solely of professional clinicians, or legally-qualified people, or of the 'great and good' from whose ranks major public committees are usually drawn, but should include the ordinary citizens who serve on juries.

The second remaining problem concerns the therapist, and was answered earlier: 'Does he go along with whatever decisions are taken by other interested parties as to problems, goals and methods, or does he have some right of refusal or limitation?'. Above, we indicated the constraints on the therapist to be legal, professional and emotional. The first two constraints are likely to apply to most, if not all, therapists for all goals and methods; the last, by definition, will apply only to some therapists for any one goal or method. If a therapist feels unable to assist a client to achieve a particular goal by a particular method, for reasons that are peculiar to himself, the onus is on him to say so clearly and suggest that another therapist be sought. It is surely undesirable for a therapist to put his own 'needs' before those of the client. Three more responsibilities lie on the therapist; the first is to ensure that clients (both initial and consequential) have access to full information (which may mean referring them for advice to our "consumer organisation"); that they are agreed as to the nature of the problem, the goals and the method; and that either the consequential client is fully aware of what is to happen and agrees or that if he cannot 'speak for himself' that his interests are adequately represented. In general, both therapists and courts should see themselves as the protectors of those who are most helpless, those suffering most from the behaviours in question, or both.

Having set out what will *inevitably* be an imperfect set of guiding principles, but which is intended to assist a developing discussion, how might they operate in a number of particularly contentious areas: parent/teacher–child problems; the problems of those not legally 'responsible' by virtue of mental handicap, brain damage or psychosis, and housed in institutions; sexual problems; and the control of offenders?

CONTENTIOUS AREAS

Parent/teacher–child problems

The interested parties in parent/teacher–child problems are the therapist, the initial client (parents/teachers) and the consequential clients (children, both those actively involved—the 'problem 'child—and those passively involved—siblings/classmates). Behaviour therapists have been very active in modifying the behaviours of children both at home and in school. Winett and Winkler (1972) characterized many of their activities as inducing children to 'be still, be quiet, be docile', i.e. to produce child behaviours beneficial to parents and teachers, and possibly to other children, but which may or may not be desired by the particular child concerned. This conclusion has been criticized by O'Leary (1972) who questions the desirability of 'informal' (i.e. 'progressive') methods for children with social or academic problems. The nub of the question however is: 'who decides what is 'good' for a child, the child himself or his parents/teachers?'. The answer depends on what are the agreed goals of parenthood/teaching. While people will disagree as to their precise content, they are likely to agree that the goals are to produce positive consequences for children and to avoid aversive ones for them. Note, the locus of consequences is the *child*, not the *parent/teacher*. The therapist then (or our appeal court if it exists) should ask himself if the objective of the parent/teacher is to make life better for themselves, for the child, or both. In the latter two instances, the therapist's involvement is desirable, in the former less so, and not at all if the consequence would be better for the parent, but might actually be worse for the child. However, the rights of other children must also be taken into account. For example, even if a particular child would gain little or nothing from a change procedure, if his behaviour produces consequences for his siblings/classmates, then treatment may be desirable. This may sound harsh, but the utilitarian principle 'the greatest good of the greatest number' is well established in our society. If behaviours are to be changed for the 'good of others', then the recipient of treatment should be provided, *if possible*, with alternative behaviours which produce for him consequences as positively reinforcing as those produced by his socially injurious behaviours. The significance of 'if possible' will be seen when we consider the problem of the control of offenders.

Inmates of institutions

In an extremely well-informed article Wexler (1973), himself a lawyer, points out that much criticism has been evoked by the use of aversive procedures to modify the behaviour of confined offenders; much less attention has been paid to positive control programmes, such as token economies, to modify the behaviour of long-stay institutional patients. The key feature of token economies is that they involve the receipt of reinforcers for designated approved behaviours. However, the judgement handed down in the American legal case of *Wyatt* versus *Stickney* has made it clear that American law will not tolerate the use of forced patient labour devoid of demonstrable therapeutic purpose. The decision in *Wyatt* versus *Stickney*, widely used in America as a precedent, barred privileges or release from hospital being conditional on the performance of labour involving hospital maintenance. This means that the receipt of basic reinforcers cannot be made contingent on appropriate behaviours. The consequence from the viewpoint of behaviour modification '. . . is that the items and activities that are emerging as absolute rights are the very same items and activities that behavioural psychologists would employ as reinforcers—that is as "contingent rights" (Wexler, 1973, pp. 11–12)'. The force of the above statement derives from the *Wyatt* definition of minimum rights in terms of specific physical and recreational facilities. Thus, 'the major problem faced by the token economy is the current trend towards an *expansion* of the category of protected inmate interests (Wexler, 1973, p. 17)'. According to Wexler, one possible answer to the problem is to seek individualized behaviour modification programmes which would utilize as reinforcers items and activities over and above those defined by *Wyatt* as minimum absolute rights. Such items and activities would be peculiar to individuals; examples include perusing mail order catalogues, being served soft instead of hard-boiled eggs and feeding kittens.

However, Wexler misses the real force of the *Wyatt* decision. *Any* reinforcer, however idiosyncratic, may be argued to be a basic right for that particular individual and thus debarred from use in a programme of behaviour modification. It seems preferable to use, as reinforcers, tokens exchangeable for monies which can then be used to purchase any desired reinforcer. Wexler goes on to point out that token economy programmes, while effective in promoting socially desired behaviours within hospitals, have been less effective in transferring generalized coping behaviours to the outside world after discharge. Treatment programmes are desirable which not only stress positive training and involve no deprivation of basic rights but, in addition, successfully overcome the transfer problem. As an example of such a programme, Wexler cites work by Fairweather and coworkers (1969), which was based on the reasonable assumption that long-stay psychotic patients would benefit on discharge if they could exercise problem-solving and decision-making skills. To achieve this, prior to discharge, small cohesive groups of patients were established, which effectively controlled the activities of their members. A step-wise progression in the achievement of relevant skills was rewarded by money and pass privileges for individuals; the group as a whole was also rewarded or demoted for general progress. The results, which were very good as indicated by post-discharge employment and community adjustment, were achieved without the deprivation of basic reinforcers. We might note also that Fairweather and coworkers sought to identify the relevant broad classes of behaviours which patients would require and then systematically trained them in their acquisition. The onus is on the interested parties first to define the goals of therapy. We can characterize these as building repertoires beneficial to clients because they are both relevant to life outside the institution and transferable to that external life; next, to consider how best to achieve this end, without deprivation of those reinforcers reasonably deemed by the courts to be minimal and not to be made contingent on particular behaviours. Once again, the issue turns on what is good for the client (the inmate) and not what is good for the institution. *After* this has been done, Goldiamond's (1974) procedural prescriptions may usefully be applied: first, ascertain the current relevant repertoires and reinforcers of the inmates; next, deploy reinforcers so as to shape the behaviours in accordance with the contract.

The control of offenders

A preamble is necessary before discussing the ethical issues involved in the control of offenders. The evidence is clear (Feldman, 1976) that most offending is carried out neither by severely socially deprived nor markedly (psychologically) disturbed individuals. The rate of crime has increased as living standards have risen, and the majority even of those apprehended (those not caught seem likely on average to be less disturbed) do not fit conventional psychiatric labels. It cannot be said that 'clearing up poverty' or solving all psychological problems would have a marked effect on the crime rate. Instead, criminal behaviour appears to be acquired, performed and maintained according to the principles which hold good for behaviours in general. For example, a theft of money which is undetected is more likely to be repeated than one which is detected before the fruits of crime can be enjoyed. Positive consequences may be more important in maintaining criminal behaviour than negative ones in reducing it, perhaps because the latter are typically interspersed with positive outcomes. It may be comforting to those who are law-abiding and who have a tender 'conscience' to think of criminals as being, first, a class apart and, second, actually suffering, otherwise they would not offend. The truth appears to be that criminal behaviour does not arise from suffering in the usual sense of that word, and is likely to be performed by any member of the population given the appropriate prior learning experiences and an instigating current situation.

Turning from the 'causes' of crime to 'cures', conventional penal methods (prison, fines, probation, etc.) have had no detectable effect in reducing criminal behaviour. No one method seems superior to any other, and none seems superior to the absence of a penal sentence. (Some first offenders, possibly those actually detected for their first offence, may be deterred by appearing in court, but even this is in doubt.) Even worse, exposure to penal methods, particularly to prison or other institution of sentence, may actually *increase* the possibility of further offending. Increasingly, experiments are being made with alternative methods, both those under the general rubric of psychotherapy and those which fit within the behaviour therapies. The former do not seem to be more effective than the conventional penal methods. This is hardly surprising in view of the general lack of effectiveness of the psychotherapies in changing the behaviours of those who suffer from problems. This being the case, it is hardly likely that they will succeed with those problems in which the victim (the 'sufferer') is another person and the performer is the beneficiary. The behaviour therapies have been applied to offenders only in the past few years, and there is as yet little or no firm evidence as to the outcome.

Our discussion will concentrate on the view of offending which appears to inform behaviour therapists working with offenders, particularly as to the target behaviours which are most frequently tackled. Two criticisms may be made. First, they frequently make the same (usually unspoken) assumption as does the psychodynamic approach, namely that criminal behaviour relates to some personal deficit in the offender, the typical emphasis being on a lack of educational skill. The implication is that if only the offender was fluent at reading, arithmetic or had a command of some job skill, he would not 'need' to offend. Hence, the behaviour being manipulated by behaviour therapists working with offenders tends to be reading or some other educational skill. Alternatively, attention is paid to deficits in the behaviour of the offender *within* his institutional setting, the emphasis being on improving the day-to-day conduct of the offender. What rarely has happened is a direct attempt to change the behaviour which led to the conviction, whether this was theft, violence or some other criminal behaviour. This indirect approach is in very sharp contrast to the behavioural approach in the clinical field, in which the emphasis has been on the problem behaviour itself, rather than on some correlate or supposed 'cause'. For example, a person who is afraid of heights would be trained to feel relaxed and calm in high places and thus not to avoid them. The second major criticism, which is related to the first, is that behaviour therapy treatments of offenders have rarely used as outcome measures such conventional indices as reconviction (let alone the much preferable self-reported or observed rate of offending). Instead, they have been more concerned with demonstrating progress, frequently spectacular, in the non-criminal areas of behaviour which have been the focus of the behavioural intervention, such as reading skills, or unsatisfactory conduct within the institution. Again, this contrasts with the situation in the clinical field in which an improvement in the problem, as defined by the client, has been the typical measure of outcome.

As will be argued later, in more detail, in the criminological field the intervention agent is *inevitably* the agent of an offended-against society (the client). Hence, outcome measures have to be in terms of reoffending, an argument implicitly recognized by the typical use of the reconviction measure by students of the efficacy of penal systems. Psychotherapists have avoided such a bald version of their true role by casting the offender in the role of patient—he offends because he is suffering; hence treat him by relieving his 'underlying' problems. If this lowers recidivism, so much the better, but the major test of outcome for the psychotherapist is a reduction of the offender/patient's psychic distress. Not sharing the psychodynamicists' belief in 'underlying' causes, behaviour therapists substitute the notion of 'behavioural deficit', improvements in which constitute a successful outcome. Like the psychotherapist, the behaviour therapist is then able to maintain his traditional role as an 'agent of the patient', rather than that of an agent of society. This is of fundamental importance in understanding why behaviour therapists typically have not behaved in the criminal field as they do in the clinic, in which they deal directly with the problem of which the patient complains. If they were to do so in the case of offenders, their services would rarely be sought. It is possible that some offenders would like their offending behaviour altered; it is more likely that the majority would not, but would prefer to retain the responses associated with their criminal behaviours. This is not to say that offenders would not welcome the opportunity to improve their skills in reading, arithmetic or in some occupational area. It is probably preferable to be a literate rather than an illiterate offender.

Instead, it is necessary to face the issue squarely, and then to decide whether or not to become involved. The interested parties are the police and the courts, the victim (and potential victims if the behaviour remains unchanged), the offender and the therapist. Writing of criminological research, Becker (1967) asks the question: 'Whose side are we on?'. He argues that criminological researchers are inevitably contaminated by sympathy for one side or the other. Traditionally, research workers have been implicitly on the side of the official power structure, but increasingly the causes of such 'deviant' groups as drug-takers and homosexuals are being taken up by sociologists. Certain prisoners, particularly those who are both black and literate, are also attracting active sympathy.

It is true that criminological research is inevitably 'action research' in the sense that its results may influence practical social policy. It is also true that the sympathies of criminological researchers will be engaged. But it is not necessarily an either–or situation, with the choice of 'sympathy' one between offenders and officialdom. There is a third party, namely the victims of offences. Moreover, the world is not divisible into *permanent* offenders and *permanent* victims. It is possible that the same research worker may at one and the same time feel a sympathy for the offender confined in an unpleasant setting and for the suffering of that offender's victims. In addition, it is possible for the research worker to perceive the current offender as someone who may previously have been a victim and may be one again. Similarly, the current victim may have offended and may do so again. The researcher himself is likely to have been both offender (particularly if he is a motorist) and victim. The third choice thus open to him is to support the view that, other things being equal, actions which reduce offending *behaviour* are more desirable than actions which increase it or leave it unchanged. 'Other things being equal' includes agreeing with the designation of any particular behaviour as being illegal (i.e. socially undesirable), as well as that it is not the more or less inevitable consequence of an intolerable social setting.

For 'researcher' in the above discussion we can substitute 'behaviour therapist'. The point is made clearer if we analyse the rights of interested parties in terms of a set of general principles. Assuming that the behavioural means to do so exist, changing the criminal behaviour of an offender may be aversive for him. It is likely to have positive consequences for potential victims. Whose claim shall have primacy? So far as the police and the courts are concerned, it should be those of the victim. Civil liberties groups, if pressed, might favour those of the offender, but they might also evade the issue by claiming that crime is only a 'symptom' of social deprivation or personal distress. As we have seen, this is not true of the majority of offenders. What is the behaviour therapist to do? First, he might simply decline to involve himself in work with offenders of any kind. Second, he might restrict himself to activities with offenders which are clearly beneficial to them, such as training in social and/or educational skills, which might provide appropriate alternative behaviours to achieve personal goals previously attained by criminal behaviours. However, it is essential to be aware that the outcome measure used by the major social agencies concerned with crime and by most, if not all, victims is that of reconviction. The benefit is to victims, not to offenders. Thus it is difficult to escape the conclusion that if psychologists involved in work with offenders do indeed benefit those offenders, such benefit is going to be judged by society as a *secondary* contribution to the major goal of intervention, the benefit of future potential victims. It is true that *both* offenders and potential victims may benefit, so that the demands of the traditional role of therapists and of society's requirements are satisfied equally. But what if the most effective means to secure society's ends involves no gain to the offender? Indeed, if he is deprived, through treatment, of those responses in his total repertoire which are relevant solely or largely to criminal ends, he may actually *lose*. In the long run, all those concerned in correctional work with offenders will have to face the question of *cui bono*—to whom good? If both offenders and society gain, then the cognitive struggle is easier than if only society gains. This ethical dilemma is of major importance. How it is resolved will determine the questions asked and the ways in which they are answered in a major area of applied psychology, namely the explanation and control of criminal behaviour. Perhaps the most haunting implication of continued research in the control of criminal behaviour is this. Even granted that it is socially desirable to reduce the distress of those assaulted or robbed by controlling such behaviours, what do we feel about the possibility of applying techniques developed for that purpose to persons whose only offence is to question the established political system and who cast their questions in verbal form only? Some psychologists might feel comfortable about applying behavioural methods to those convicted of theft or assault. But most, if not all, would be very much opposed to applying them to a British or American equivalent of Solzhenitsyn. Such opposition might be so great as to restrict sharply the application to offenders of behavioural methods of control and of research into such methods. It is not only psychologists and psychiatrists who must ask themselves such questions; the debate must involve all the professions involved in the legal process, the political representatives of the public and the public themselves.

Certainly, it is to be hoped that psychologists will avoid such public statements as those by McConnell (1970): 'I foresee the day when we could convert the criminal into a decent respectable citizen in the matter of a few months. . . . We'd send him to a rehabilitation center where he'd undergo positive brainwashing until we were quite sure he had become a law-abiding citizen who would not again commit an anti-social act (p. 74).' This is not only crass but scientifically inaccurate. First, he makes the typological error by talking about 'the' criminal. Second, because criminal behaviours, like behaviours in general, are determined by the current situation as well as by past experiences, it is impossible to be certain that criminal behaviours will not recur in situations different from that which evoked the current behaviour, unless the consequential training experiences include considerable planning for wide generalization. Otherwise, the only way to ensure the non-recurrence of any criminal behaviour is a system of social control so extensive as to train all citizens in generalized good behaviours. But the cost might be a reduction of civil liberties so severe as to be quite unacceptable.

Sexual problems

One of the most contentious problems is that of homosexual behaviour, which has attracted a great deal of attention from pressure groups. Homosexual clients stem from several sources: direct referral under a court order; self-referral associated with an actual or possible court appearance; pressure from wife/family/friends; the hope of being able to marry or to have a happier marriage (no pressure from significant others); or unsatisfactory experiences in the homosexual subculture. The interested parties may include the homosexual himself, the courts, his family/friends, his employers (particularly if he is a teacher), the therapist and homophile organizations. It is almost always the case (Feldman, 1973) that homosexual individuals' preference is either for post-pubertal adults or for pre-pubertal children—rarely both. In the latter case, the homosexual is termed a paedophile. This is still illegal behaviour and seems likely to remain so, although the age of homosexual consent may be lowered to 16, now the heterosexual age of consent. Common equity argues that this change is desirable. We can best divide homosexual referrals into two groups, those referred by the courts (currently almost entirely paedophiles) and those self-referred (albeit in many instances in response to 'pressures'). The former fits essentially into the category of offenders, discussed above, and the views expressed in that section apply to paedophiles as they do to offenders in general.

The following discussion refers only to the self-referred group. What should be the order of primacy of the interested parties? In practice this question becomes: 'To what extent should the therapist present information relevant to different treatment options, refer the client to a direct source of such information, or attempt to persuade him of one or other of the several alternatives?'. The alternative goals of treatment are a change to heterosexual preference and overt activities; continuing his homosexual preference and overt activities, but without the distress which has led to his self-referral for help; or continuing his homosexual preference, but without overt sexual activity. In practice, the last of the three is opted for much less frequently than the first two. The view of the homophile organizations is that it is desirable for homosexuals to 'accept what they are' and to select the second alternative. Following the arguments of this chapter, we assert that primacy must be taken by the client (and, if he is married, shared by his wife and family). He is the best judge of whether or not *he* is currently distressed and of what is a desirable goal of therapy. It is true that a determinist view of Man must accept that goals labelled 'desirable' are determined by the individual's experiences, but at least they are *his* experiences and not someone else's. The counterassertion of the Gay Liberation Front is that it is 'our society' which is responsible for the client's unhappiness with his behaviour and that the roles of therapists should be two-fold: to assist the client to 'accept himself' (with the aid of Gay Lib., etc.) and to campaign for changes in formal and informal social attitudes and conventions. There are two major answers to the first part of the assertion. The first can be stated as: 'Gay Lib. agrees that social attitude changes will take many years, and Mr. Smith is coming to see me again at 4.30 today, is very distressed, seeks help and wants it now'. Second, and more important, is the general desirability that it should be open to all to remain members of the particular sexual, religious, cultural or other subgroup concerned, including the homosexual subgroup, or to join other groups, and, if the latter, to be allowed to leave their old groups (by their previous associates) and be accepted and welcomed to the new group. This approach places the current assertions of Gay Lib. alongside those of other minority groups—Jews, blacks, etc.—who similarly resent one of their number 'marrying out', 'mixing with whitey', etc. The reasons for this resentment are beyond the scope of our discussion, but it is important to recognize its reality.

It is desirable that therapists do not serve as agents for competing ideologies—neither 'gay is good' nor 'straight is good'—but as agents of what the client currently seeks. In order to ascertain this with confidence, the therapist should refer to Gay Lib. those homosexual clients stating a wish for a heterosexual preference, and who are not yet well-acquainted with the homosexual subculture. (It is, of course, the client's privilege to accept the opportunity or reject it.) The therapist should then assist the client to seek *whichever* of the goals he finally asserts to be his preference. It is definitely desirable for therapists to attach an equal parity of esteem to the two alternatives, but we have to acknowledge that some therapists may find one or other of them emotionally aversive. As before, the remedy is to refer the client to a therapist who does not. What is crucial, as in therapy in general, is the consequence for the client; he is the arbiter and must have primacy of decision—in the definition of the problem and of the selection of goals and of methods. The therapist is a *guide*; he should not be a preacher (Goldiamond, 1974). In the words of Samuel Goldwyn: 'If you've got a message, give it to Western Union!'

REFERENCES

Bandura, A. (1969). *Principles of Behavior Modification*, Holt, Rinehart and Winston, New York.

Becker, H. S. (1967). Whose side are we on? *Social Problems*, **14**, 239–247.

Berkowitz, L. (1973). Reactions and the unwillingness to help others. *Psychological Bulletin*, **19**, 310–317.

Cerber, M. (1972). A word of warning to behaviour modifiers working in a restrictive social setting. *Behaviour Therapy*, **3**, 517–519.

Eysenck, H. J. (1952). The effects of psychotherapy: an evaluation. *Journal of Consulting Psychology*, **16**, 319–324.

Fairweather, G. W., Sanders, D. N., Maynard, H., and Cressler, D. L. (1969). *Community Life for the Mentally Ill: An Alternative to Institutional Care*, Aldine, Chicago.

Feldman, M. P. (1973). Abnormal sexual behaviour—males. In H. J. Eysenck (Ed.), *Handbook of Abnormal Psychology*, 2nd ed. Pitman Medical, London.

Feldman, M. P. (1976). *Criminal Behaviour: A Psychological Analysis*, Wiley, London.

Fowler, H. W., and Fowler, F. G. (1951). *The Concise Oxford Dictionary*, 4th ed., revised by E. McIntosh. The Clarendon Press, Oxford.

Goldiamond, I. (1974). Towards a constructional approach to social problems. *Behaviorism*, **2**, 1–85.

Krasner, L., and Ullmann, L. P. (1973). *Behavior Influence and Personality: The Social Matrix of Human Action*, Holt, Rinehart and Winston, New York.

McConnell, J. V. (1970). Stimulus/response. Criminals can be brainwashed—now. *Psychology Today*, **3**, 14–18.

Morris, W. (Ed.) (1969). *The American Heritage Dictionary*, American Heritage Publishing Co., New York.

O'Leary, K. D. (1972). Behaviour modification in the classroom: a rejoinder to Winett. *Journal of Applied Behavior Analysis*, **5**, 505–511.

Stahlman, M. (1973). Ethical dilemmas in current obstetric and newborn care. In T. D. Moore (Ed.), *Report of the 65th Ross Conference on Paediatric Research*, Ross Laboratories, Columbus, Ohio.

Wexler, D. B. (1973). Token and taboo: behavior modification, token economies and the law. *California Law Review*, **61**, 81–109.

Winett, R. A., and Winkler, R. C. (1972). Current behavior modification in the classroom: be still, be quiet, be docile. *Journal of Applied Behavior Analysis*, **5**, 499–506.

Wyatt versus Stickney (1972). 34.4 F. Suppl. 373 (M.D. Ala. 1972) (Bryce and Searcy Hospitals).

NAME INDEX

446

448

Tharp, R. G., 143, 302, 306, 311, 318
Thibaut, T. W., 235
Thomas, D. R., 168, 172
Thomas, E., 86
Thomas, G. V., 133, 135
Thomas, P. E., 47
Thompson, R. F., 67
Thompson, T., 130, 142, 147, 158
Thomson, L. E., 400
Thomson, J. J., 337
Thor, D. H., 161, 163, 171
Thoreson, C. E., 296, 305, 306, 316,
    317, 327
Thorndike, E. L., 101, 124, 125
Thorne, P. R., 52
Thornton, D. R., 320
Thorpe, G. L., 75, 403
Thurber, J., 234
Tiegen, J., 402
Tizard, J., 184
Tolman, E. C., 142, 272
Toomey, M., 279
Touchette, P. E., 169, 170
Tracey, D. A., 403
Trimbach, C., 34
Truax, C. B., 141, 232, 374
Trumbull, R., 68
Truscott, F. W., 286
Tsujimoto, R. N., 231
Turner, L. H., 104
Tursky, B., 307
Turtletaub, G., 200, 214
Tversky, A., 270
Twentyman, C., 206, 210, 221

Ulbrich, K. J., 69
Ullmann, L. P., 133, 135, 137, 139,
    258, 294, 329, 365, 406—408
Ulrich, R., 137, 139, 143
Underwood, B. J., 303
Ungerstedt, U., 31
Upper, D., 389
Uranus, 338
Usdin, E., 38, 41

Valins, S., 231
Valleala, P., 51
Van Belle, H. A., 401
Vanderwolf, C. H., 22
Van Lehn, R., 57
Vann, T. V., 362
Varga, M. E., 350
Veasey, H. E., 235

Venables, P. H., 43, 45, 47—49, 51,
    52, 54, 62, 63, 67—70, 83
Venus, 338
Vereczkey, L., 67
Vernon, P. E., 252
Vinokur, A., 273, 284
Viswanathan, R., 130
Vroom, V. H., 271

Wagner, A. R., 19, 86, 100, 101
Wahler, R. G., 305, 392
Wahlsten, D., 90
Walen, S. R., 380
Wallace, J., 294
Wallsten, T. S., 271, 272
Walsh, W. B., 309
Walster, E., 235, 251, 252
Walter, H. I., 385
Walters, R. H., 160, 196, 213
Wang, G. H., 50, 51
Wang, M. C., 177
Warburton, D. M., 29
Warren, A. B., 160
Waters, W. F., 337
Watson, D. L., 301, 306, 311
Watson, J. B., 101, 126, 336, 340
    341
Watson, J. P., 120, 372
Watson, L. S., Jr., 133, 174
Watts, F., 76, 212
Watts, J. C., 276
Webb, E. J., 235, 302
Webb, R. A., 82
Weber, S. J., 244
Weiner, J. S., 47
Weinman, J., 53
Weisberg, P., 160, 165, 166, 168
Weiss, A. R., 98
Weiss, L., 90, 91
Weissman, A., 29
Weldon, E., 34
Weller, M. B., 173
Werboff, J., 119
Wernimont, P. F., 294
Wesemann, A. F., 125
Westcott, M. R., 80
Wetzel, R. J., 143, 318
Wexler, D. B., 146, 151, 175, 426, 427
Whalen, C., 225
Wheeler, A. J., 180
Wheller, H., 141
Wheeler, L., 64
Whitebrook, J. S., 215
Whitehurst, G. J., 179, 181

SUBJECT INDEX